Managing
Public Relations

Managing Public Relations

JAMES E. GRUNIG

College of Journalism
University of Maryland, College Park

TODD HUNT

Department of Communication
Rutgers: The State University of New Jersey

HOLT, RINEHART AND WINSTON

New York • Chicago • San Francisco • Philadelphia • Montreal • Toronto
London • Sydney • Tokyo • Mexico City • Rio de Janeiro • Madrid

Library of Congress Cataloging in Publication Data

Grunig, James E.
   Managing public relations.

   Includes bibliographical references.
   1. Public relations. 2. Public relations—Management.
I. Hunt, Todd T. (Todd Terrance), 1938– • II. Title.
HM263.G75 1983   659.2   83–283

ISBN 0-03-058337-3

CBS COLLEGE PUBLISHING
Holt, Rinehart and Winston
The Dryden Press
Saunders College

Acknowledgments

Cover and frontispiece photo by Francene Fallick
Photo, p. xxvi, Wide World
Photo, p. 86, reproduced with permission of AT&T
Photo, p. 220, courtesy TRW Inc.
Photo, p. 372, reproduced with permission of AT&T

PREFACE

In January 1982, the International Public Relations Association issued a ''Gold Paper'' prepared by public relations professionals from around the world that proposed a model for public relations education. The Gold Paper stated that public relations should:

Be taught as a social science with both an academic and a professional emphasis.

Be drawn from both professional practice and scholarly theory.

Help public relations to become more analytical.

The report added that ''there is no all-embracing theory to tie the field together.''

We believe *Managing Public Relations* will help educators, students, and practitioners meet the goals set by the IPRA for public relations education.

First, the book provides a comprehensive conceptual framework—drawn from systems theory—that demonstrates what public relations does for an organization and how that contribution can be measured and evaluated. We analyze public relations through four historical models that are still in use today. We show why each model can be functional for different kinds of organizations in different kinds of environments.

Throughout the book, however, we argue for the superiority of what we call the two-way symmetric model of public relations—a model based on negotiation, compromise, and understanding. We see this model as a replacement for the persuasion model that has dominated thinking about public relations almost since its birth.

With the IPRA, we believe the body of knowledge that is relevant to the public relations profession can be found in the social sciences. But we believe that few practitioners have command of this body of knowledge and that no textbooks adequately interpret it for practical use in public relations.

That is why we chose the title *Managing Public Relations*. This text is a practical, how-to book in every sense of the word. Yet it is probably the most theoretical book that has ever been written about public relations. Social psychologist Kurt Lewin once said, ''There is nothing so practical as a good theory,'' and we hope this book reflects the wisdom of his words.

We demonstrate how relevant social science theories can explain common public relations problems and how they can be used to plan, coordinate, and evaluate public relations programs. We show how these theories can be used to understand the effects of different public relations techniques and to determine when these techniques should be used. In this way, we hope to bring about the integration of theory and practice called for by the IPRA.

The book deliberately includes many more notes and references than the typical public relations text. We want you to know where we got our ideas and where the relevant body of social science theory lies. Eventually, you should trace the notes to obtain firsthand exposure to that body of knowledge. Part III, in particular, summarizes much of James Grunig's research on public relations publics because it represents the product of a long-term research program to determine systematically the nature of publics.

In the last few years, a number of surveys of top managers have revealed strong dissatisfaction with the public relations people in their organizations. At the same time, organizations have passed over people trained in public relations for the top public relations positions in favor of persons with backgrounds in law, business management, or government.

This dissatisfaction has occurred because most public relations practitioners lack management skills. In the past, public relations practitioners have been trained to be communication technicians—skilled at writing, editing, and producing publications. In addition, most have been satisfied with practicing their relatively low-level skills—content to take orders and to execute public relations programs without being involved in the formulation and management of those programs.

Today, organizations face increasing conflict with publics in their environment, and technical communication skills alone will not enable public relations people to deal with that conflict. Technicians will still be needed to implement public relations programs, but someone must supervise those technicians, and the technicians themselves must understand what they are doing and why they are doing it.

At the 1981 convention of the Association for Education in Journalism, Syracuse University public relations educator William Ehling, in a paper on public relations management, stated that public relations practitioners typically have no central concept of what they are doing and why they are doing it. As a result, their work degenerates into meaningless busy work. ''They shoot arrows into the air and whatever they hit becomes by hindsight the 'target' at which the arrows were aimed,'' Ehling said.

We hope *Managing Public Relations* will fill the void in the training of public relations practitioners that has been identified by both top managers and public relations educators. At the same time, we do not neglect the traditional techniques of public relations. Most entry-level public relations practitioners begin as communication technicians and cannot get their first job without mastering those techniques. But they will never rise above the entry level to become true professionals without integrating technical skills into a management framework.

In *Managing Public Relations*, we portray public relations as a positive force in society, a force that benefits publics at least as much as the organizations that employ public relations professionals. We see public relations professionals as in-house activists—people who constantly strive to make their organizations responsible to the publics they affect. Most people who do not understand public relations see the practitioner as an apologist for an organization. We see the role in exactly the opposite way.

Managing Public Relations contains four major parts that proceed systematically from the general to the specific. Part I defines public relations, describes its history and present structure, shows how it benefits an organization and its publics, and evaluates whether it is a profession. Part II develops the central concepts of public relations management. Part III applies those concepts to the most common public relations programs. Part IV introduces the most common public relations techniques, shows how they fit into public relations management, and provides essential technical knowledge on how to apply these techniques.

James Grunig would like to thank three people who have been instrumental in shaping the ideas in this book, but whose names appear relatively infrequently in it. Bruce Westley, formerly of the University of Wisconsin and now retired from the University of Kentucky, introduced him to systems theory that now shapes this book. Richard Carter, now of the University of Washington and formerly of the University of Wisconsin, influenced Grunig's thinking in so many ways that he can no longer tell which ideas are his and which are Carter's. In particular, something resembling Carter's behavioral molecule now serves as a central integrating concept throughout the book. Finally, the late James Tirone of the American Telephone & Telegraph Company introduced Grunig to "practical" public relations research and contributed immeasurably to the integration of theory and practice found here.

Todd Hunt owes a debt of gratitude to many colleagues at Rutgers University, particularly Richard Budd and Brent Ruben, who created a climate for learning in which even a former journalist could learn to look at the world from a general systems perspective. Scores of students at Rutgers helped explore and develop many of the applied concepts in Part IV. Among the many practitioners who provided examples and illustrations, the most helpful were David Davidson of AT&T, Rob-

ert Andrews of Johnson & Johnson, Kevin Kelly of Warner-Lambert, and Brian Salisbury of Grumman Corporation.

Managing Public Relations has benefited from the helpful suggestions of reviewers: John Bowes, University of Washington; Glenn Butler, University of Florida; Hugh Culbertson, Ohio University; John Detweiler, University of Florida; William Ehling, Syracuse University; Derry Eynon, Colorado State University; William Faith, University of Southern California; Sam Feldman, California State University; Dennis Jeffers, Central Michigan University; Donald MacDonald, Southern Illinois University; Rebecca Quarles, Cleveland State University; Albert Walker, Northern Illinois University; and Donald Wright, University of Georgia.

We also thank those people at Holt, Rinehart and Winston who contributed their expertise to this project. They are Roth Wilkofsky, formerly of Holt, and Peter Sandman, Communication Adviser, for suggesting that we write this book. We also thank Thomas W. Gornick, Senior Acquisitions Editor, for taking over the project and pushing us steadily toward its completion. We are also grateful to Françoise Bartlett, Senior Project Editor, who assisted us in numerous critical tasks; Gloria Gentile, who brought creativity to the design and art program; and Annette Mayeski for her watchful shepherding of the book through composition, printing, and binding.

Finally, authors generally end their acknowledgments by thanking the typist who diligently prepared the many drafts of the manuscript. We would like to thank two TRS-80 microcomputers that typed several versions of the manuscript and set the final copy with seldom a fuss and only occasionally destroying our marvelous prose electronically.

August 1983   J. E. G.
                                               T. H.

CONTENTS

4 PROFESSIONALISM IN PUBLIC RELATIONS 62

PART II

Principles of Public Relations Management 87

5 ELEMENTS OF PUBLIC RELATIONS MANAGEMENT 89

6 DEFINING AND CHOOSING GOALS AND OBJECTIVES 114

7 IDENTIFYING ORGANIZATIONAL LINKAGES TO PUBLICS 138

8 BUDGETING AND DECISION MAKING 163

9 EVALUATION RESEARCH 179

10 LEGAL CONSTRAINTS 204

PART III
Managing Public Relations Programs 221

13 COMMUNITY RELATIONS 265

14 PUBLIC AFFAIRS AND GOVERNMENT RELATIONS 284

15 RELATIONS WITH ACTIVE PUBLICS: CONSUMERS, ENVIRONMENTALISTS, AND MINORITIES 309

16 EDUCATIONAL RELATIONS AND ECONOMIC EDUCATION 332

Contents

PART IV
Managing Public Relations Techniques

19 PUBLIC RELATIONS WRITING

20 PRESS RELEASES

21 CATERING TO THE PRESS 394

22 USING RADIO 404

25 BROCHURES, FACT SHEETS, AND DIRECT MAIL 443

26 NEWSLETTERS, NEWSPAPERS, AND MAGAZINES 454

27 PHOTOGRAPHS AND ILLUSTRATIONS 470

28 SLIDES AND MULTIMEDIA PRESENTATIONS 481

I

The Nature
of Public Relations

Part I introduces you to public relations, its nature, history, and present status. Chapter 1 examines several definitions of public relations and concludes with a definition used throughout this book. Chapter 2 uses four "models" to describe the history of public relations and to explain how public relations is practiced today. Chapters 3 and 4 look at "professional" public relations. They argue that public relations serves as an ombudsman for the public in an organization. They then examine whether public relations practitioners today qualify for the professional status needed to perform the role of advocating public responsibility.

1

THE CONCEPT OF PUBLIC RELATIONS

In 1922, Edward L. Bernays wrote a book entitled *Crystallizing Public Opinion* in which he described the "new profession of the public relations counsel."[1] Public relations counselors were to be different from the press agents and publicists of the day. The public relations counselors were to be ethical, professional, and socially responsible. They were to use the knowledge generated by social science to understand public opinion, public motivation, public relations techniques, and methods for modifying group points of view. The objective of the public relations counsel was to interpret the organization to the public and the public to the organization.

Twenty-five years later, in the late 1940s, British scholar J. A. R. Pimlott spent nearly a year studying public relations activities in the United States under a British Home Civil Service Fellowship provided by the Commonwealth Fund of New York. In a book that resulted from that year of study, *Public Relations and American Democracy*, Pimlott described the public relations professional as essential to American democracy.[2] "Public

relations is one of the methods by which society adjusts to changing circumstances and resolves clashes between conflicting attitudes, ideas, institutions, and personalities," he said.[3] Pimlott believed public relations practitioners could help to bridge "the gulf which, despite advances in education and communication, exists between 'we'—the millions of plain men and women—and 'they'—the thousands in business, government, the churches, organized labor, the universities, and elsewhere, who constitute the effective ruling class."[4] Public relations was especially important in government, Pimlott added: "Modern administration would come to a standstill if government could not constantly speak to the people as individuals and in and through the different groups to which they belong."[5]

Public relations professionals, according to Pimlott:

. . . disseminate that minimum of information without which the individual will be unable to play his part as a citizen, an economic unit, a neighbor. They tell him how and when to pay his taxes, what he must do to avoid fires, how he can feed his family to the best advantage, how to conduct himself on the roads, what a labor union stands for, the elementary economics of business, the facilities at the local university, the books he can get from the public library. In this respect, public relations is a valuable ancillary to the educational system.[6]

Seeking Professional Status

If practiced in the way described by Bernays and Pimlott, the public relations profession can provide a challenging, exciting, and socially useful career for the person choosing his or her life's work. But public relations is a young profession, which in the 1980s has only begun to approach true professional status. The profession has its roots in press agentry and propaganda, activities that society generally holds in low esteem. Most of its practitioners have little training in the social sciences. Few have been trained in public relations. According to Robinson:

> . . . an exceedingly high proportion of present-day public relations practitioners came from a variety of other fields. Predominant among these fields are journalism, advertising, and publicity. In this sense, most public relations practitioners today have one thing in common: they really didn't intend to get into the field—at least when they were young and obtaining their formal education. They couldn't. For most of them the option of planning and preparing for a career in public relations—in the sense that one would plan and prepare for a career in law or medicine—was not possible.
>
> For this reason, the practitioners in the field, along with the whole discipline of public relations itself, just "grew like Topsy," without a common body of knowledge or without evolving any theory to guide their problem-solving efforts.[7]

Thus, the average person today seldom understands public relations. Mention to a friend that you are in public relations or preparing for a career in public relations, and generally a smile will cross his or her face.

"Aha," the friend will often say, "you're in the image-making business." Or, "It must be fun putting things over on people." Some people are critical: "How can you justify taking advantage of people?" People you will meet in the news media often have their slogans: "On the one hand there is truth and on the other hand there is public relations." Many media people will call you a "flack," someone who peppers the media with promotional material in the hope that some of it will hit home.

What PR Is . . . and Isn't

Nearly every public relations textbook now on the market starts negatively, by defining what public relations is not. Nearly all agree that public relations is more than "being a pleasant fellow and glad-handing," simple publicity, lobbying or legislative representation, advertising, or propaganda.[8] Public relations instructors typically spend their first hour or two of class clarifying public relations for their students, who too often want to get into the profession because they "like people" (so do cannibals!).

In this book, we will make no apologies for public relations. We believe it is an important profession that, during the twentieth century, has made great strides in its sophistication, ethics, responsibility, and contribution to society. We do not hide the fact that the ancestors of modern-day public relations—press agentry and publicity—often were unethical and irresponsible. We must admit that many people today who call themselves public relations practitioners still do not measure up to professional standards.

In the 1979 Foundation Lecture to the Foundation for Public Relations Research and Education, Scott M. Cutlip, of the University of Georgia School of Journalism and a pioneer public relations educator, assessed "public relations in American Society."[9] He described three "minuses" of public relations. It has:

1. Cluttered choked channels of communication with the debris of pseudo-events which serve the interest of neither the sponsor nor the public.
2. Beclouded or concealed the facts of a public issue.
3. Resulted in cynicism and distrust of churches, corporations, colleges, the Presidency, and Congress by people more than twice fooled.

But he also listed three "pluses":

1. Public relations has made organizations more responsive to their publics by channeling feedback from publics to management.
2. Practitioners serve the public interest by providing an articulate, clear voice in the public forum for every idea, individual, or institution.
3. Practitioners increase the public's knowledge by providing information through the media that the media themselves do not have the manpower nor budget to provide.

Like the law or medicine, the profession of public relations provides knowledge and tools that, when used by antisocial groups, can be dangerous and damaging to society. For example, public relations helped the Ku Klux Klan increase its membership from 4,000 to 100,000 in the early 1920s.[10] The solution to antisocial use of public relations is not, however, to ban or restrict the practice of public relations, but to professionalize it. True professionals possess a body of knowledge and have mastered communication techniques that are not known by the average citizen. But they also have a set of values and a code of ethics that discourage the use of their knowledge and technical skills for antisocial purposes.

This book will attempt to teach you not only the knowledge and technical skills now available to the practitioner, but also social responsibility and professional ethics. You will be one of the next generation of public relations practitioners, a generation that could fulfill the promise of public relations first envisioned by Bernays in 1923.

Using Social Science Concepts

Bernays believed public relations should be based on knowledge from the social sciences, and many other public relations writers have reiterated that belief.[11] Robinson, for example, defined the public relations practitioner as an applied social and behavioral scientist.[12] The social sciences, however, encompass communication science, psychology, economics, sociology, social anthropology, political science, geography, and others. Each of those disciplines, in turn, contains many subdisciplines, such as cognitive psychology, social psychology, collective behavior, and organizational behavior.

Future public relations practitioners must have more than a broad exposure to the social sciences. Too much exposure to too many social science concepts can lead to "information overload." We believe students need a focused exposure to social science concepts that are relevant to public relations problems. In this book, therefore, we will build a conceptual framework for public relations that is drawn from the social and behavioral sciences. We will, however, focus that framework on the practical problems of managing public relations—research, planning, and evaluation of public relation programs, activities, and techniques.

In 1951, Pimlott wrote that public relations practitioners "will be closely affected by the progress of communication research."[13] At that time, communication research was just beginning to make its way into schools of journalism and mass communication, the academic units in which public relations is most frequently taught. Communication research originated earlier as the study of propaganda in political science, persuasion and attitude change in social psychology, and the effects of the mass media in sociology. Today, thirty years after Pimlott wrote that communication research will closely affect the practice of public relations, communication research has progressed greatly, building from the basis of the other social sciences. Public relations practitioners, however, have either not paid much attention to communication research—what we will call communication science—or they have not kept up with the new ideas in communication science.

Integrating Theory and Practice

In this book, we will introduce you to some of the newest ideas in communication science and other social and behavioral sciences. But, importantly, we will show how these ideas can solve some of the most important and long-standing problems of public relations. Often, we will show that the theoretical ideas from the social sciences confirm what public relations professionals have been doing for years.

But *Managing Public Relations* is not merely a book about theory. A true professional possesses both a body of knowledge and technical expertise. Ideally, the two should be integrated. After finishing this book, you should possess a conceptual framework for the practice of public relations and a set of technical communication skills needed to practice public relations. Most importantly, the conceptual framework should help you to know when and how to use the technical skills and how to solve public relations problems.

DEFINING PUBLIC RELATIONS

Public relations may be practiced by the $200,000-a-year vice president of a major corporation who heads a department of 100 professionals or more. It may also be practiced by a part-time employee or volunteer producing a brochure or a press release for a small-town charitable organization. One public relations person may spend all of his or her time writing—press releases, stories for an employee publication, public-service announcements, or informational pamphlets. Another practitioner may seldom write at all, spending his or her time managing other practitioners, meeting with management, or dealing with the press. Public relations professionals may draw their paychecks from large or small consulting firms or from business, government, nonprofit organizations, associations, hospitals, educational systems, or churches. On the surface, therefore, it seems nearly impossible to come up with a single definition of public relations.

Focus on Management

In one way or another, however, each of these public relations activities is part of the *management of communication between an organization and its publics*, and that will be our definition of public relations throughout this book. Communication is a behavior of individuals, groups, or organizations. People communicate when they move messages to or from other people.

Public relations professionals communicate not just for themselves, however. They manage, plan, and execute communication for the organization as a whole. They manage the movement of messages into the organization, for example, when conducting research on the knowledge, attitudes, and behaviors of publics and then using that information to counsel managers on organizational policies or actions. They may manage the movement of a message out of the organization when they help management decide how to explain a policy or action to the public and then write a news story or fact sheet to explain the policy or action.

Many, many definitions of public relations have been developed, most of them much longer than the one presented here. In 1976, Harlow found 472 definitions of public relations, after examining books, journals, and magazines on public relations and asking 83 public relations leaders for their definitions of public relations. He then combined the essential elements of the definitions into the following lengthy definition:

Public relations is the distinctive management function which helps establish and maintain mutual lines of communication, acceptance and cooperation between an organization and its publics; involves the management of problems or issues; helps management to keep informed on and responsive to public opinion; defines and emphasizes the responsibility of management to serve the public interest; helps management keep abreast of and effectively utilize change, serving as an early warning system to help anticipate trends; and uses research and sound and ethical communication techniques as its principal tools.[14]

Most parts of Harlow's definition can be reduced to "the management of communication between an organization and its publics." It goes beyond that definition, however, when it also describes the desired *effects* of public relations and the *tools* of public relations. Not all public relations practitioners use all of these tools, and not all desire the same effects. It is important to define public relations in a way that includes professional and nonprofessional public relations and in a way that includes different kinds of effects. As should be clear when we discuss four different "models" of public relations in the next chapter—ways in which public relations is practiced—our definition does just that.

Many writers have made the problem of defining public relations more difficult than it really is. At the same time as they have defined what public relations is, they have tried to describe: (1) the kinds of things public relations practitioners do, (2) what effect they think public relations should have, and (3) how they believe public relations should be practiced responsibly. Let's compare our simple definition of public relations as "managing communication between an organiza-

tion and its publics" with a few others to show what we mean.

Peake emphasized persuasion as an effect in her definition of public relations:

. . . public relations is the planned persuasion to change adverse public opinion or to reinforce public opinion, and the evaluation of results for future use.[15]

Need for Mutual Understanding

The British Institute of Public Relations emphasized mutual understanding as an effect when it defined public relations as "the deliberate, planned, and sustained effort to establish and maintain mutual understanding between an organization and its public."[16] Cutlip and Center kept persuasion as an effect in their definition and added good character, responsible performance, and two-way communication:

Public relations is the planned effort to influence opinion through good character and responsible performance, based upon mutually satisfactory two-way communication.[17]

Nolte added the idea that persuasion can be a two-way street when he defined public relations as:

. . . the management function which adapts an organization to its social, political, and economic environment and which adapts that environment to the organization, for the benefit of both. This implies two types of activity. First, the public relations practitioner must persuade management to do the things to the organization that will make it worthy of public approval. Second, the public relations practitioner must convince the public that the organization deserves its approval.[18]

Finally, two other definitions emphasize that public relations should change the organization in a way that will benefit its publics. The International Public Relations Association at its 1978 meeting in Mexico adopted the following definition:

Public relations practice is the art and science of analyzing trends, predicting their consequences, counseling organization leaders, and implementing planned programs of action which will serve both the organization's and the public's interest.[19]

The widely quoted definition of the newsletter *Public Relations News* states:

Public relations is the management function which evaluates public attitudes, identifies the policies and procedures of an individual or an organization with the public interest, and plans and executes a program of action to earn public understanding and acceptance.[20]

These definitions sound fine, you may think. What's wrong with them, then?

Take the matter of what public relations practitioners *do*. They write press releases, counsel management, research publics, etc. All of the activities are communication activities, and the word communication can define all of them.

Now take the question of *effect*. Some public relations professionals strive for persuasion, others for understanding, and others simply for communication. Let's not restrict our definition to one kind of effect. Similarly, public relations is not always effective. So, let's not say that ineffective public relations practitioners do not practice public relations. Physicians don't always cure disease, but they still practice medicine.

Finally, not all public relations is done responsibly; neither is all medicine or law or journalism. The irresponsible public relations practitioners are still practicing public relations. Public relations, therefore, is the management of communication between an organization and its publics. Let's keep the matter of what kind of effect it can have and how it should be practiced for later chapters.

PUBLIC RELATIONS AS AN ORGANIZATIONAL SUBSYSTEM

We can further understand our definition of public relations if we look at *how* and *why*

organizations carry out that managed communication function.

Organizations have nearly always communicated with their publics in one way or another, but until the late nineteenth century, they did so informally. The president or another officer gave speeches or met with employees or community residents. Frequently, the organization could impose its will on the public through coercion or by simply ignoring the public.

In the twentieth century, however, both organizations and publics became larger and more specialized. Publics could no longer be ignored or coerced, so communication took a lot more of management's time. Mass media became larger and more powerful, requiring the organizational manager to have journalistic expertise to deal with them.

Organizations, too, became larger and had more consequences on the public than the managers could keep track of on their own. Many organizations became more complicated, requiring communication experts to explain them to the public. As a result, organizations began to create a specialized communication-management role called public relations to do the work organization managers no longer had time to do. In larger organizations, the role expanded into a subsystem of the larger organizational system—a public relations department.

A "System" Focus

Organizational theorists today often look at organizations as "systems." A system is an organized set of interacting parts or subsystems. Each subsystem affects the other subsystems as well as the total organization. Systems theorists have found that most organizations have similar subsystems. For example, a hypothetical organization, the Acme Corporation, probably has the following subsystems:

Some departments function to produce products or services. These *production* subsystems include the manufacturing and engineering departments.

Some departments hold the organization together and get employees to work as a single unit. They are called *maintenance* subsystems. An example would be a personnel or employee-development department.

Still other subsystems market and distribute products and services. They are called *disposal* subsystems.

Adaptive subsystems, a fourth kind of subsystem, help the organization to survive when its environment changes. Adaptive subsystems might be research and development or planning departments.

Finally, *management* subsystems control and integrate the other subsystems. They must control conflict and negotiate between the demands of the environment and the need for the organization to survive and prosper.[21]

Public relations personnel perform what organizational theorists call a "boundary" role. That means:

They function at the edge of the organization, serving as a liaison between the organization and the external groups and individuals.

They have one foot in the organization and one outside.

As boundary personnel, public relations practitioners support other organizational subsystems by helping them to communicate across the boundaries of the organization to external publics and by helping them to communicate with other subsystems within the organization.

Public relations generally is part of the management subsystem, although it may often support other subsystems (Figure 1-1). For example:

It sometimes supports the disposal subsystem by helping that subsystem promote products or services.

FIGURE **1-1**

Public Relations as an Organizational Subsystem

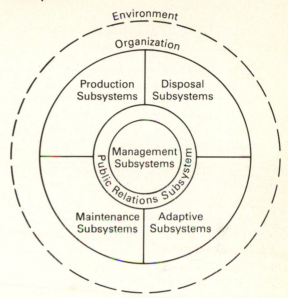

It supports the maintenance subsystem through employee communication.

It supports the adaptive subsystem by bringing in new ideas from the environment and by communicating the organization's ideas to external groups.

It functions as part of the management subsystem by helping top management plan and evaluate the organization's total communication activities

The Consequences of Behavior

We said that public relations became a formal subsystem in many large organizations at about the end of the nineteenth century and the beginning of the twentieth century because of the increased impact of organizations and publics upon one another. That historical occurrence helps us to understand why organizations need public relations departments today. Typically, organizations develop a formal communication subsystem

FIGURE **1–2**

A Model of the Public Relations Function in an Organization

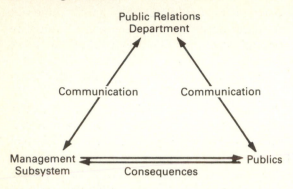

Public Relations
Department

Communication   Communication

Management   Publics
Subsystem   Consequences

when the organization or its publics behave in a way that has *consequences* upon the other. Those consequences upon one another create a *public relations problem*. Figure 1-2 describes the relationship between public relations problems and formalized communication programs in organizations.

The set of arrows at the base of the triangle in Figure 1-2 indicates that organizations and publics have reciprocal consequences upon each other. Decisions made by an organization's management subsystem may have consequences upon publics. A business firm, for example, may limit employee wages or provide poor working conditions. It may produce poor or unsafe products. It may pollute the environment, close a plant in a small community, or influence governmental decisions to serve its own vested interests. Hospitals may charge too much or provide poor care. Schools may fail to educate.

When publics learn about these consequences, they often take actions that have consequences upon the organization. They may petition government for regulation of

Organizations cannot isolate themselves from active members of their publics. Citizens speak up, often forcing organizations to make changes the citizens demand. (Wide World photo)

business. They may refuse to buy products. They may stage a taxpayers' revolt, send their children to a different school, or refuse to go to a hospital. Publics also have certain consequences that organizations seek out, such as buying their products, attending their events, using services, providing support in government.

This linkage of organization and publics through consequences explains why organizations need public relations.

The arrows that form the sides of the triangle in Figure 1-2 show how a public relations subsystem functions to solve public relations problems. In small organizations, management may handle public relations as a sideline activity, or have only one or two public relations personnel. Generally, however, organizations develop a specialized public relations department whose role, as shown in Figure 1-2, is two-way communication with both management and publics.

In communicating with publics, PR people conduct opinion surveys or talk informally with people to learn how the publics view the organization. They also explain the organization to publics through the mass media or interpersonally.

Public relations people also communicate with management by providing counsel on the publics' points of view so that management has the benefit of that knowledge when making decisions. Public relations people must also listen to management to understand its decisions and behaviors so that they can explain those decisions and behaviors to the publics.

The Utility of a Model

This simple model describes the public relations function in an organization. It should help you to put the elements of public relations that we describe in this book into an overall perspective. The elements include the definition of publics, research, counseling of management, writing for publics, and others.

At this point, however, it is important to recognize that not all organizations practice public relations as described by the full model. Some organizations don't need all parts of the model. Others simply have not thought about public relations thoroughly enough to know what they could do with the function.

Moreover, public relations has not always been practiced as described by the model. In the next chapter, we will look at how public relations has been practiced throughout history and how it is practiced today. We will describe the practice of public relations as fitting one of five categories. Many people throughout history have engaged in communication activities that resemble public relations. We will describe these communication activities as "public relations-like activities" but will separate them from formalized public relations activities in organizations.

Formalized public relations activities can be described with four models that can be identified in the history of public relations and in the practice of public relations today. Understanding these models will help you to understand the somewhat checkered past and present of public relations and will help to put the remaining chapters of this book into perspective.

NOTES

1. Edward L. Bernays, *Crystallizing Public Opinion* (New York: Boni and Liveright, 1923).
2. J. A. R. Pimlott, *Public Relations and American Democracy* (Princeton, N.J.: Princeton University Press, 1951).
3. Pimlott, p. 243.
4. Pimlott, p. 240.
5. Pimlott, p. 64.
6. Pimlott, p. 239.
7. Edward J. Robinson, *Communication and Public Relations* (Columbus, Ohio: Charles E. Merrill, 1966), p. 40.

8. John E. Marston, *Modern Public Relations* (New York: McGraw-Hill, 1979), p. 4.

9. Scott M. Cutlip, "Public Relations in American Society," *Public Relations Review* 6 (Spring 1980):3–17.

10. John M. Shotwell, "Crystallizing Public Hatred: Ku Klux Klan Public Relations in the 1920s," master's thesis, University of Wisconsin, 1974.

11. Edward L. Bernays, *Public Relations* (Norman: University of Oklahoma Press, 1952), p. 5. See also Rex F. Harlow, "Management, Public Relations, and the Social Sciences," *Public Relations Review* 1 (Summer 1975):5–13.

12. Robinson, p. 7.

13. Pimlott, p. 257.

14. Rex Harlow, "Building a Public Relations Definition," *Public Relations Review* 2 (Winter 1976):36.

15. Jacquelyn Peake, *Public Relations in Business* (New York: Harper & Row, 1980), p. 1.

16. Sam Black, *Practical Public Relations* (London: Sir Isaac Pitman & Sons, 1962), p. 3.

17. Scott M. Cutlip and Allen H. Center, *Effective Public Relations*, 5th ed. (Englewood Cliffs, N.J.: Prentice-Hall, 1978), p. 31.

18. Lawrence W. Nolte, *Fundamentals of Public Relations*, 2d ed. (New York: Pergamon, 1979), p. 10.

19. Sam Black, "Introduction," in Sam Black (ed.), *Public Relations in the 1980s: Proceedings of the Eighth Annual Public Relations World Congress* (Oxford: Pergamon, 1979), p. xi.

20. *Public Relations News*, 127 East 80th Street, New York, N.Y. 10021.

21. This discussion is based on Sue H. Bell and Eugene C. Bell, "Public Relations: Functional or Functionary?" *Public Relations Review* 2 (Summer 1976):47–57.

ADDITIONAL READING

Black, Sam (ed.), *Public Relations in the 1980's: Proceedings of the Eighth Annual Public Relations World Congress* (Oxford: Pergamon, 1979).

Cutlip, Scott M., "Public Relations in American Society," *Public Relations Review* 6 (Spring 1980):3–17.

Hammond, George, "The Hour Strikes for Public Relations," *Public Relations Review* 5 (Spring 1979):3–10.

Harlow, Rex, "Building a Public Relations Definition," *Public Relations Review* 1 (Summer 1975):5–13.

Katz, Daniel, and Robert L. Kahn, *The Social Psychology of Organizations*, 2d ed. (New York: Wiley, 1978).

Lobsenz, Amelia, "Public Relations Comes of Age," *Public Relations Journal* 37 (June 1981):36.

Pimlott, J. A. R., *Public Relations and American Democracy* (Princeton, Princeton University Press, 1951).

2

ORIGINS AND CONTEMPORARY STRUCTURE OF PUBLIC RELATIONS

Today, somewhere around 100,000 people practice public relations in the United States.[1] They work in public relations departments of organizations or in public relations counseling firms. Not all call what they do public relations. Many call their work public affairs, public information, communications, community relations, or promotion. Some call themselves press agents or publicists.

On a given day, public relations practitioners may prepare press releases, help a reporter develop a story, edit an employee publication, prepare an exhibit, interview a government official, conduct a scientific survey of public opinion, counsel management on the public relations impact of a major policy decision, write a speech, raise funds, or prepare an annual report. Practitioners do so many varied jobs that some scholars who study public relations question whether it can be conceptualized as a single activity.

In Chapter 1, we examined the role of public relations in the abstract and developed a definition that could be used to describe most kinds of public relations activities. In this chapter, we will look at different ways in which public relations has been practiced throughout history and at present. After reading the chapter, you should be able to discern some order in the apparent chaos that many scholars see in the field of public relations.

Looking for Models

We believe the history of public relations can be described in terms of four models of public relations practice and by a stage in public relations history in which communicators who did not consider themselves to be public relations practitioners practiced "public relations-like activities."

We call the four models: (1) the press agent/publicity model, (2) the public-information model, (3) the two-way asymmetric model, and (4) the two-way symmetric model. These models have different objectives, generally are found in different organizational settings, and generally require different means of evaluating their success. The models help us to understand different stages in the history of public relations, because public relations seems to have passed through stages that resemble the four models.

Our analysis of the history of the four models should also help us to understand the diversity of public relations practice today. We can compare the development of the public relations profession to the development of adult human beings. Children pass through different stages as they grow into adults. Not all adults behave like adults, however. Some do not make it through all of the developmental stages of a human being and remain in one of the stages of childhood.

Similarly, many public relations practitioners or departments today practice one of the earlier models of public relations, and have not developed fully into using a more advanced model. The history of public relations thus helps us to understand why only a minority of today's public relations practitioners practice the full concept of public relations described in Chapter 1.

Before describing each of these models, however, we turn first to some of the communication activities that preceded the formal practice of public relations. Those early activities provide some context to explain the origin of public relations.

PUBLIC RELATIONS-LIKE ACTIVITIES IN HISTORY

The term "public relations," which is common in the vocabulary of most people today, was supposedly used for the first time in 1882, when Dorman Eaton, a lawyer, addressed the Yale Law School on "The Public Relations and Duties of the Legal Profession." By public relations, he meant looking out for the welfare of the public.[2] Theodore Vail, president of the American Telephone & Telegraph Co., used the same meaning for the term when he titled the company's 1908 annual report "Public Relations." According to Bernays, Vail described public relations as follows:

Is the management honest and competent? Vail asked. What is the investment? Is the property represented by that investment maintained at a high standard? What percentage of return does it show? Is that a fair return? Is it obtained by a reasonable distribution of gross charges? If these questions are answered satisfactorily, there can be no basis for conflict between the company and the public.[3]

"Public relations" had not been used to describe the communication professional we know today, however, until Bernays coined the term "public relations counsel" in the 1920s. Before that time, the practice was known as "press agentry" (from the middle of the nineteenth century to the beginning of the twentieth century) and "publicity direction" from the late nineteenth century to the 1920s.[4]

A definitive history of public relations has yet to be written, although bits and pieces of that history are scattered throughout textbooks, journals, and biographies. Practitioners did not call themselves press agents, publicists, or public relations counselors until the mid-nineteenth and early twentieth centuries, but most public relations historians trace the origins of public relations-like roles to ancient times. Newsom and Scott, for example, have argued that:

Broadly defined, public relations is as old as civilization, because underlying all public relations activity is the effort to persuade. . . . Persuasion is still the driving force of public relations, and many of the tactics that modern PR people use to persuade have been used by the leaders of society for thousands of years.[5]

We argued in Chapter 1 that persuasion is just one possible effect of public relations. We could replace the word "persuasion" with "communication" in the above quote, and it would be an excellent explanation of why it is so easy to find public relations-like activities throughout recorded history. Most early public relations activities were done to persuade. The earliest formal public relations activities were used largely to promote something or to "spread the faith"—the original definition of propaganda.

Political, religious, and business leaders have found it necessary to communicate to publics throughout history, and many used tactics quite similar to those used by public relations professionals today. Let's begin our analysis of public relations history, then, by looking at public relations-like activities in ancient times.

Public Relations in Ancient Times

Nearly all writers of public relations textbooks cite examples of public relations-like activities used by ancient Greeks and Romans. Some find even earlier examples of public relations. Cutlip and Center, for example, found evidence of several ancient public relations activities:

> The communication of information to influence viewpoints or actions can be traced from the earliest civilizations. Archeologists found a farm bulletin in Iraq that told the farmers of 1800 B.C. how to sow their crops, how to irrigate, how to deal with field mice, and how to harvest their crops—an effort not unlike today's distribution of farm bulletins by the U. S. Department of Agriculture. What is known today of ancient Egypt, Assyria, and Persia comes largely from recorded material intended to publicize and glorify the rulers of that day. Much of the literature and art of antiquity was designed to build support for kings, priests, and other leaders. Virgil's *Georgics* was written to persuade urban dwellers to move to the farms to produce food for the growing city. The walls of Pompeii were inscribed with election appeals. Caesar carefully prepared the Romans for his crossing of the Rubicon in 49 B.C. by sending reports to Rome on his epic achievements as governor of Gaul, and histo-

rians believe he wrote his *Commentaries* as propaganda for himself. . . . Long before the complexities of communication, there was acknowledged need for a third party to facilitate communication and adjustment between the government and the people. So it was with the church, tradesmen, and craftsmen. The word *propaganda* was born in the seventeenth century, when the Catholic Church set up its *Congregatio de Propaganda*, "congregation for propagating the faith."[6]

The formal study of communication, which has provided much of the knowledge base for public relations today, probably had its origin with Aristotle, the great Greek scientist, philosopher, and social interpreter of the fourth century B.C.

Aristotle articulated the art of rhetoric in his classic book, *Rhetoric*. The *American Heritage Dictionary* defines rhetoric as the "art of oratory, especially the persuasive use of language to influence the thought and actions of listeners." The ancient Greeks considered rhetoric to be an important tool of statecraft. It was the point of contact between the statesman and the public. Thus, one could consider the *Rhetoric* to be one of the earliest books written on public relations.

It's also not stretching history too much to claim the success of the apostles in spreading Christianity throughout the known world in the first century A.D. as one of the great public relations accomplishments of history. The apostles Paul and Peter used speeches, letters, staged events, and similar public relations activities to attract attention, gain followers, and establish new churches. Similarly, the four gospels in the New Testament, which were written at least forty years after the death of Jesus, apparently were public relations documents, written more to propagate the faith than to provide a historical account of Jesus' life:

> That the gospels are from a later time than the generation of eyewitnesses of Jesus' ministry would not in itself disqualify them from serv-

ing as objective historical evidence. But it must be acknowledged further that they cannot be considered nonpartisan reports about Jesus. They are in the truest sense of the term propaganda literature. If one had to provide a single statement of purpose that would suit all four of the gospels he could probably not find a better one than the explanation given by the author of the Gospel of John:

> These are written that you may believe that Jesus is the Christ, the Son of God, and that believing you may have life in his name.
>
> —John 20:31

Both the claim that is made in behalf of Jesus as the Christ and the appeal to respond in faith to that claim are present in the intention of the Gospel writers. The gospels are, above all, documents for the propagation of the faith.[7]

The Effect of Printing

About 1,400 years later, public relations gained great power when the German Johann Gutenberg invented movable type in 1456. Gutenberg printed a Bible on his press, a printing that was quite typical of the early use of the printing press. According to Marston, religion "much concerned literate people in the fifteenth and sixteenth centuries. Since the books were widely distributed and eagerly read, their ideas proved inflammatory, and Europe was soon split by religious wars."[8]

Bernays described the Renaissance, which "changed Western society in the fifteenth and sixteenth centuries," and the Reformation, which "intensified that change in the six-

Johann Gutenberg examining the first proof from his printing press; lithograph. (The Bettmann Archive)

teenth,'' as two periods in which public opinion became important and in which communicators tried to modify it. Among other things, the Renaissance was characterized by the ''rise of the Humanists—scholars and writers who specialized in appealing to public opinion. The sixteenth century Reformation was in part a revolt of the European governments against the absolute authority of the church. It was also in part a revolt of ideas, of private opinion opposed to ecclesiastical authority.''[9]

In the seventeenth and eighteenth centuries, politicians and leaders of opposing groups used the printed word more and more to communicate their points of view to publics. Newspapers were first published in the early 1600s. They joined books, novels, and tracts—along with two places of assembly, the French salon and the English coffeehouse—as important media or tools of public communication. Slowly, publics gained power, and governments were forced to communicate with them. According to Bernays:

> In seventeenth-century England, public opinion manifested itself in a victory over Stuart absolutism and showed rulers the need for cultivating good relationships with the public. Louis XIV of France engaged in his own type of public relations. He struck medals, and sent ambassadors to various countries to enhance French prestige.[10]

The growing power of public opinion in the seventeenth and eighteenth centuries resulted in the abolition of censorship—in England in 1695, France in 1789, and the United States in 1791. That ''in turn made free public discussion possible and produced greater reliance by leaders on their public relationships.''[11]

Public Relations in the American Revolution

Many public relations historians have claimed the American Revolution to be one of the most important products of public relations-like activities in history. Schoolchildren in the United States routinely learn, and the majority of adults still believe, that the American Revolution was a popular uprising against an unpopular and oppressive absentee government. Historians tell us otherwise. The majority of influential citizens supported the British, and the majority of common citizens really didn't care that much. It took a small band of skilled propagandists to create the public support that made the revolution possible—and their job was an extremely difficult one.

No one at the time described these propagandists as ''public relations practitioners,'' and communication was not a full-time activity for them. Yet many of the things they did to push the revolution were quite similar to the techniques public relations practitioners use today. According to Cutlip and Center, ''Today's patterns of public relations practice have been shaped far more than most practitioners realize by innovations in mobilizing public opinion developed by Samuel Adams and his daring fellow revolutionaries.''[12]

In the 1976 bicentennial year, Scott M. Cutlip wrote an article in the *Public Relations Review* describing the role of public relations in the American Revolution.[13] He named several propagandists who helped bring about the war: James Otis, John Adams, Benjamin Franklin, Josiah Quincy, Thomas Paine, Thomas Jefferson, Alexander McDougall, and Christopher Gadsden. The most important, however, was Samuel Adams. ''Surely,'' Cutlip said, ''today's public relations specialists must acknowledge Adams as their progenitor.'' Adams, however, did not fit the stereotype of a public relations practitioner as a ''genial backslapper ready to buy a free drink.'' A failure as a businessman and a loner, he was suspicious of people with wealth and privilege. According to Cutlip, Adams used six techniques that practitioners still use today:

An Activist Organization • Because the revolution was not a popular uprising, it was imperative that the revolutionaries be well organized. They demonstrated that a small activitist group can win a public relations war even if they are a minority. The same is true today of the most active environmentalists, consumerists, antiabortionists, and others. Usually, a formal organization is necessary to hold the activists together, however. The revolutionaries had the Sons of Liberty and the Committees of Correspondence.

Use of Many Media • Today's PR professionals use a combination of tools to communicate to their publics. According to Cutlip, "Newspapers, pamphlets, sermons from the pulpit, town meetings, and the committees of correspondence were the primary means of carrying the attack on British rule. Other means of communication, such as broadsides, songs, plays, poems, and cartoons also were used, but in a lesser way."

Symbols and Slogans • Symbols can be remembered easily and arouse emotion. The revolutionaries, for example, had the Liberty Tree. Slogans compress complex issues into simple, easy-to-remember stereotypes. The revolutionaries had "Taxation without representation."

The Pseudo-Event • Historian Daniel Boorstin coined the term "pseudo-event" to describe a technique used today by public relations practitioners. A pseudo-event would not have occurred except to gain news coverage. The Boston Tea Party was one of the first pseudo-events: a staged dumping of tea into Boston Harbor to crystallize public opinion against what the revolutionaries considered to be unfair taxation.

Orchestrating Conflict • According to Cutlip, "Adams knew then, as public relations practitioners know today, that public attitudes are largely the result of events coupled with the way these events come to be interpreted." It is important to get your side of the story to the public first so that the public remembers your version. Actually, the Boston "massacre" occurred when a "gang of toughs" taunted British soldiers stationed near the Boston Customs House, and the soldiers fired at their tormenters. The soldiers killed five Americans and injured others. The propagandists used the event to communicate their belief that a standing army in peacetime was inherently evil. The message circulated for five years, although it had its greatest impact in Massachusetts, where fear of the British army was greatest.[14]

Need for a Sustained Saturation Campaign • Apathetic publics cannot be moved in a short period of time. The revolutionaries continued their campaign through all available media over a twenty-year period. Winning independence from England did not end the necessity for public relations in the development of the American nation, however. The loose union of states under the Articles of Confederation did not work. The next great public relations task was the ratification of the U. S. Constitution.

Public Relations in the New Land

The distinguished historian Allan Nevins, who has also been a journalist and public relations practitioner, described the use of public relations-like activities of federalist supporters of the new constitution from 1787–88 as "the greatest work ever done in America in the field of public relations."[15] The two greatest advocates of the Constitution, Alexander Hamilton and James Madison, were more than public relations specialists, Nevins said:

> We naturally think of them in a larger setting. Moreover, the powers of Hamilton and Madison transcended mere talent; they were powers of genius, especially as displayed by Hamilton, not easily defined and still less easily imitated. Nevertheless, these labors may well be studied by all workers engaged in the varied, complex, and difficult tasks of public relations.

The task of the federalists was difficult, according to Nevins. The Constitution had been passed by a Constitutional Convention in September 1787, but it had to be ratified by nine of the thirteen states. Many important leaders opposed it, including Sam Adams, the public relations hero of the Revolutionary War. "Had a popular referendum been held that autumn, unquestionably a majority of Americans would have voted against it—so at least most historians assert," Nevins added. Most loose confederations before in history had failed, as had the Articles of Confederation. "A federal government for the whole continent, uniting national strength with local liberty, would be the boldest experiment in the annals of mankind."

Hamilton and Madison had qualities that make for a successful public relations practitioner today. Nevins described Hamilton as a "born public relations man—a born master of persuasion by the spoken and written word." Hamilton possessed a "clear, original, and comprehensive mind" and could "unite mastery of statecraft and of pen." Hamilton was especially successful in speaking to large groups. Madison, "a gentleman of great modesty, sweetness of temper, and conversational charm . . . would be a power in small groups of leaders as the electric Hamilton was a power in large assemblages." Moreover, Hamilton could effectively explain the Constitution, even though it did not represent the form of government he personally favored.

The Campaign for the Constitution • Two critical elements of modern public relations were used in the campaign for the new Constitution: effective communication and "the adroit use of psychology" (although that "psychology" would not be considered behavioral science today).

The eighty-five *Federalist Papers,* written by Hamilton, Madison, and John Jay and published in leading newspapers throughout the states, provide the best example of effective communication. An expert communicator must be able to grasp complicated ideas and explain them to people unfamiliar with the ideas. According to Nevins, the *Federalist Papers* "not merely explained away misunderstandings bred by prejudice, and dispelled the nightmares of unreasoning prejudice—the fears of a king, or a military autocracy, of crushing taxes, of excessive centralization—they laid down the most expert commentary on the text of the Constitution." The papers were read widely throughout the states and bound into books even before the last had been written. Hamilton, especially, "was tactful, suave, and objective. He never attacked his opponents; he reasoned with them."

The federalists used psychology in winning the ratification by the crucial state of Massachusetts. Two leaders, Governor John Hancock and Samuel Adams, opposed the Constitution in that state. "Both were suspicious, stubborn, and negative-minded." Hancock was the "very embodiment of pompous egotism . . . open to flattery laid on with a trowel." Friends of the Constitution told Hancock the nation depended upon him. "If he accepted the Constitution that Washington and Franklin so heartily approved, Massachusetts would obey his orders, and the whole country would follow; but if he said no, confusion, dismay, and ruin would ensue." Theophilus Parsons "ghost-wrote" a speech supporting the Constitution which the governor delivered to the convention. "A friend hastily seized the manuscript lest onlookers see that it was not in Hancock's hand; and dozens of delegates crossed to the governor's side."

Adams could not be flattered, but he "fancied himself as a man of the people" who had "great confidence in the instincts of the people." Thus, supporters of the Constitution got leading mechanics of Boston to meet at a tavern, pass resolutions supporting the Constitution, and send a delegation to Adams to present the resolutions to him. Finally, advocates of the Constitution made conciliatory agreements to get the support of Adams. The supporters agreed to add a Bill of Rights after the Constitution was ratified, the first ten amendments to the Constitution. Today, compromise—as it was then—is an extremely important public relations tool.

Public relations-like activities thus played a crucial role in many great events of American history. Our final example of the early, preformal use of public relations came about forty years later as part of the rise of Jacksonian democracy.

Amos Kendall in the Jackson White House

When Andrew Jackson became President in 1829, the common person for the first time had a representative in the White House. On the day of Jackson's inauguration, masses of ordinary folk, mostly from the West, swarmed into Washington to celebrate his election. The New England Brahmins and the Virginia Dynasty no longer controlled the presidency. The new President spoke for the masses, which his enemies called "King Mob."[16] Jackson had been a member of Congress, an army general, and governor of Florida. He has been rated one of six "great" Presidents.[17] Yet, he was largely unschooled and barely literate. He needed someone to help him communicate. That person was Amos Kendall.

When Jackson assumed the presidency, Kendall, a Kentucky newspaper editor who had supported his campaign, came to Washington as fourth auditor of the Treasury, a relatively low-paying position given to reward his political support. Kendall soon became a member of Jackson's kitchen cabinet, an informal group of advisers who came to visit Jackson in the White House through the kitchen door. According to Fred Endres of Kent State University, who completed a doctoral dissertation on Kendall, "Kendall's

writing, editing, speaking and political abilities would make him one of the most valuable and versatile presidential assistants in history. By the time Jackson left office in 1837, Kendall rightly had earned the title of the first presidential public relations man." Endres elaborated:

> From 1829 to 1837, Kendall performed most, if not all public relations tasks associated with White House personnel today. He wrote stirring speeches for Jackson; authored highly important state papers and messages; penned early versions of press releases; and performed some rudimentary straw polling. He also served as a political "advance man" for presidential trips, and he was tremendously influential in establishing, implementing and publicizing political policy. Beneath all these duties was the constant attempt to build and reinforce a favorable image of Jackson as the bold, resourceful, democratic, honest, military hero-president. While many history books and public relations texts give Kendall credit for formalizing the "presidential press secretary's function," Kendall, in reality, did much more than that.[18]

Kendall did several things for Jackson that are common public relations activities today. He wrote papers and speeches that contained "words that history would record as the president's own."[19] He also wrote articles for the party newspaper, *The Globe* (in those days, each party sponsored a newspaper). He distributed articles—in effect, press releases—to Jacksonian newspapers throughout the country and served as a political adviser and advance man.

Like Hamilton, Kendall had two skills essential to a public relations person: a strong mind able to grasp and simplify complex issues, and strong communication skills. According to Endres, Kendall "possessed an active, creative mind, and he was blessed with forceful, logical, often eloquent writing and speaking skills." But Kendall also did not fit the stereotyped, smooth PR man. He was "unsocial as a bat . . . a puny, sickly-looking man, with a weak voice, a wheezing cough, narrow and stooping shoulders, a sallow complexion, silvery hair in his prime, slovenly dress, and a seedy appearance generally."[20]

These examples of noted figures in history who used public relations-like activities before practitioners began to call themselves press agents, publicists, or public relations counselors should be sufficient to show that managed communication—public relations—is as old as history itself. They show that PR techniques used today have been used for centuries. And they show that the abilities needed by a public relations person—the ability to think and to communicate—have been constant throughout history.

The examples also show, however, that in its early development, public relations generally was equated with persuasion and/or propaganda. Most people still have that concept of public relations today, explaining the common suspicion, mistrust, and even fear of it. As we will see when we turn to four models of public relations practiced by people who have managed communication for others as a full-time occupation, it took many years for a concept of public relations as something other than persuasion to develop.

FOUR PUBLIC RELATIONS MODELS IN THEORY AND PRACTICE

We've chosen the term "models" to describe the four types of public relations that we believe have evolved through history, in order to emphasize that they are abstractions. In scientific usage, a model is a representation of reality. The human mind can never grasp all of reality in total, but it can isolate and grasp parts of that reality. It then uses those parts of reality to construct ideas. Those ideas model reality, although they also simplify it by not including all of reality.

Even if you could observe the behavior of every public relations practitioner in the world, you still could not remember everything you had observed these practitioners doing. But if we construct models of public relations behavior by observing the most important components of that behavior, then we can make some sense out of the many diverse communication activities that we call public relations.

Thus, we've chosen to construct four models of public relations that we think will help you to understand the history of formal public relations and to understand how it is practiced today. But, remember, these are simplifications, and simplifications are always false in part, because they always leave something out. Not everything any single public relations person does will fit any of the models perfectly. But the models should come close enough that you can fit public relations people you meet into one of the models.

Table 2-1 summarizes four public relations models: press agentry/publicity, public information, two-way asymmetric, and two-way symmetric. The first three characteristics in Table 2-1 describe the models. The last three characteristics provide historical background and describe where the models are practiced today. Let's look at each of these characteristics in more detail, then, for each of the four models.

Purpose of Public Relations

The models first differ in purpose—the function they provide for the organization that sponsors them. Although public relations developed as a persuasive communication function, not all of these models use public relations for that purpose.

Public relations serves a propaganda function in the press agent/publicity model. Practitioners spread the faith of the organization involved, often through incomplete, distorted, or half-true information.

For the public-information model, the purpose is the dissemination of information,

TABLE 2–1   Characteristics of Four Models of Public Relations

Characteristic	Model			
	Press Agentry/ Publicity	Public Information	Two-Way Asymmetric	Two-Way Symmetric
Purpose	Propaganda	Dissemination of information	Scientific persuasion	Mutual understanding
Nature of Communication	One-way; complete truth not essential	One-way; truth important	Two-way; imbalanced effects	Two-way; balanced effects
Communication Model	Source ⟶ Rec.	Source ⟶ Rec.	Source ⟶ Rec. ⟵ Feedback	Group ⟶ Group ⟵
Nature of Research	Little; "counting house"	Little; readability, readership	Formative; evaluative of attitudes	Formative; evaluative of understanding
Leading Historical Figures	P. T. Barnum	Ivy Lee	Edward L. Bernays	Bernays, educators, professional leaders
Where Practiced Today	Sports, theatre, product promotion	Government, nonprofit associations, business	Competitive business; agencies	Regulated business; agencies
Estimated Percentage of Organizations Practicing Today	15%	50%	20%	15%

not necessarily with a persuasive intent. The public relations person functions essentially as a journalist in residence, whose job it is to report objectively information about his organization to the public.

Practitioners of two-way asymmetric public relations have a function more like that of the press agent/publicist, although their purpose can best be described as scientific persuasion. They use what is known from social science theory and research about attitudes and behavior to persuade publics to accept the organization's point of view and to behave in a way that supports the organization. The press agent/publicist's attempts at persuasion, in contrast, are more intuitive, seat-of-the-pants rather than scientific.

In the two-way symmetric model, finally, practitioners serve as mediators between organizations and their publics. Their goal is mutual understanding between organiza-

tions and their publics. These practitioners, too, may use social science theory and methods, but they usually use theories of communication rather than theories of persuasion for planning and evaluation of public relations.

If you look back at the definitions of public relations in Chapter 1, you will find that the definitions that stress *persuasion*—communicating only those characteristics of an organization that the public will accept—fit the description of the two-way asymmetric model. Those that stress *mutual understanding* fit the two-way symmetric model. There are few definitions in the public relations literature, however, that describe the first two models.

The triangular model of public relations pictured in Figure 1-2 accommodates all four descriptive models. The press agent/publicity and public-information models would not have arrows returning from publics to the public relations department or, generally, from the public relations department to management. In both two-way models, however, all of the arrows would be present.

The Nature of Communication

The four models also demonstrate the nature of the communication that the public relations person manages between organization and publics.

For the first two models, communication is always one-way, from the organization to publics. Practitioners of these two models generally view communication as telling, not listening. The first two models differ, however, in that the press agent/publicists do not always feel obligated to present a complete picture of the organization or product they represent, whereas public-information specialists do.

For the two-way asymmetric and two-way symmetric practitioners, communication flows both to and from publics. But there is a big difference in the nature of that two-way communication. The two-way asymmetric model is "asymmetric" because the effects of the public relations are imbalanced in favor of the organization. The organization does not change as a result of public relations; it attempts to change public attitudes and behavior.

Two-way asymmetric practitioners carefully plan what they communicate to publics to achieve maximum change in attitude and behavior. Communication from publics comes as "feedback." Many public relations practitioners today use feedback as a synonym for two-way communication. That was not its original meaning. In cybernetic theory, feedback is communication that helps a source control a receiver's behavior. Cybernetic theorists typically use the analogy of a thermostat to explain feedback. A thermostat monitors the effects of a furnace or air conditioner—the temperature of the air—to de-

cide whether to turn the furnace or air conditioner on or off. The feedback enables the thermostat to manipulate the furnace or air conditioner. Never does the furnace or air conditioner initiate the communication. It never gets to tell the thermostat to change the temperature setting because it is wasting fuel and that such waste is socially irresponsible. Communication in that model is truly one-sided, or asymmetric.

The two-way symmetric model, in contrast, consists more of a dialogue than a monologue. If persuasion occurs, the public should be just as likely to persuade the organization's management to change attitudes or behavior as the organization is likely to change the publics' attitudes or behavior. Ideally, both management and publics will change somewhat after a public relations effort.

Frequently, however, neither will change attitudes or behavior. The public relations staff brings the two groups together, and, as long as both communicate well enough to understand the position of the other, the public relations effort will have been successful. David Finn, chairman of the board of the Ruder & Finn public relations agency, described a public relations approach that fits the two-way symmetric model in this way:

> One of the major contributions that we can make to the process of opinion formation in a time of crisis is to help decision-makers (and often these are our clients) find new ways of thinking through problems with people who have previously not played a role in management affairs. . . . The public relations man who serves his client well will not undertake to convince everybody else that management is correct (which he probably couldn't accomplish in any case). Instead he will try to create the circumstances in which responsible people with different opinions (including his client) can put their heads together in a serious effort to find a solution that takes all relevant factors into consideration.[21]

Diagrams of Communication Models

By the time they have taken their first course in public relations, most students have been exposed to a model of communication in either an introductory mass communication or speech communication course. Generally, the model looks like this:

Source → Message → Medium → Receiver
————— Feedback —————

Many of the models are a lot fancier. They may include encoders and decoders, noise, or social context. The important point is that they presuppose a model of communication. Most of them, especially the one above, fit only the two-way asymmetric model of public relations. The fact that the arrows go from left to right, except for the returning feedback arrow, suggests that communication is something the source does to a receiver. The terms ''source'' and ''receiver'' suggest the same thing. If one of the persons, groups, or organizations communicating is a source and the other a receiver, it suggests that communication always originates with the source.

A symmetric model would not call either person or group that is communicating a source or a receiver. The individuals or groups communicating interact, changing so rapidly from source to receiver and back again that it becomes clumsy to talk about source and receiver. Instead, it's much easier to call the communicating parties Person I and Person II or Group I and Group II.

Table 2-1 thus includes a communication model for each of the public relations models. The figure leaves out embellishments of the models, such as messages, media, or noise. These are common to all of the models. The important difference is in what the two communicating groups are called and the direction of the arrows.

Research Activities in the Four Models

Research is an important component of modern public relations. Yet, one must talk to a large number of practitioners to find one actually doing or using public relations research. Generally, it's easy to identify which model a particular public relations person fits by looking at whether he or she uses research and the kind of research he or she uses. Nearly all public relations people give information to publics, although their intention in giving that information may differ. But only those practitioners whose behaviors fit the two-way asymmetric or two-way symmetric models use research as an important component of their work.

Table 2-1 shows that press agent/publicists seldom use research, unless it is informal observation of whether their publicity materials have been used in the media. At times, they may also ''count the house'' to see if they have gotten people to attend an event they have promoted or to buy products or services.

Public-information specialists also do little research. They follow a journalistic model of preparing informational materials for largely unknown publics. At times, they may do readability tests to see if the information is at the appropriate level of difficulty for their intended audience, and they may also do readership studies to see if the audience actually uses the information. But, for the most part, public-information specialists have little idea of what happens to the materials they prepare.

In contrast, research plays an important role in both two-way models—in fact, research is the very reason they are called two-way models. The research is quite different, however. There are two major types of research: formative and evaluative. Formative research helps to plan an activity and to choose objectives. Evaluative research finds out whether the objective has been met.

In the asymmetric model, the public relations person uses formative research to find out what the public will accept and tolerate. Then, the practitioner ''identifies the policies and procedures of an individual or organization with the public interest,'' to use the *Public Relations News* definition cited in Chapter 1. Tom Ford, who practiced public relations with Information Canada, the Canadian government's former communication agency, explained this definition in a way that suggests it definitely fits a two-way asymmetric model:

> First, we are supposed to ask people what they think about us. Then, I take it, we are supposed to select or identify those corporate policies or activities which the people like. And then we are supposed to flog them—hoping that this will make people feel better about us.[22]

When two-way asymmetric practitioners do evaluative research, they examine the feedback in much the same way as a thermostat monitors air temperature. The practitioner measures attitudes and behavior before and after the public relations effort to see what effect the campaign has had.

In the two-way symmetric model, practitioners use formative research to learn how the public perceives the organization and to determine what consequences the organization has for the public. This research can then be used to counsel management on public reaction to policies and on how those policies could be changed to better serve the public interest. Formative research can also be used to learn how well publics understand management and how well management understands its publics, information that helps a great deal in choosing specific communication objectives. Evaluative research in the symmetric model measures whether a public relations effort has actually improved the understanding publics have of the organization and that management has of its publics.

We will go into much greater detail about objectives and research in Chapters 8 and 11. The brief discussion here should help, however, to distinguish the four models from each other.

The Four Models in History

At the beginning of this chapter, we said the four models to be described represent developmental stages in the history of public relations.

The press agent/publicity model came first, in the period from 1850 to 1900, immediately following the historical examples that we described as public relations-like activities.

The public-information model came next, beginning about 1900 and continuing as the major model of public relations until the 1920s.

The two-way asymmetric model developed in the 1920s. The two-way symmetric model came much later, in the 1960s and 1970s, and even today practitioners are only beginning to adopt it.

Table 2–1 also names a leading historical figure who best represents each of the models. We'll use the models to further develop the history of public relations in the next section, including greater detail on the historical figures.

The Four Models in Practice Today

The last two rows in Table 2–1 provide estimates of where the four models are practiced today and of the percentages of all organizations that practice each model. These are our rough estimates, not based upon any systematic survey of public relations practitioners.

Organizations that equate public relations with publicity or promotions today generally practice the press agentry/publicity model. Those that practice it today, however, generally pay more attention to truth than did the press agents of the 1850s. Nevertheless, practitioners in these organizations concern themselves most with getting attention in the media for their organizations or clients. The best examples today include sports promotion, theater or movie press agentry, or product promotion in advertising departments.

Probably about 15 percent of today's practitioners fit this category.

The public-information model is still the most frequently practiced model today. We estimate that about 50 percent of today's public relations people use it. It is nearly always the model used in government agencies, and it is the most popular model in associations, nonprofit agencies, and educational organizations. It is also quite popular in many business firms.

These organizations carry on active press-relations programs, offering news to the media about their organization. They also produce many informational pamphlets, magazines, consumer guidebooks, fact sheets, films, and videotapes—all designed to inform publics about the organization.

The two-way asymmetric model finds most of its adherents in business firms, especially those that face considerable competition. A majority of these firms sell consumer products.

The majority of public relations consulting firms also provide two-way asymmetric services to their clients more often than services patterned after the other three models. This is especially true for public relations agencies that are associated with advertising agencies, providing complementary advertising and public relations services. We estimate that about 20 percent of all organizations follow the two-way asymmetric model.

Competition as the Catalyst • A few examples should help to clarify the two-way asymmetric model. Companies in the food industry, for example, may use research—which is often conducted by their marketing department—to determine what product features consumers like—convenience or "natural" qualities, for example. The companies then advertise the products stressing the presence of these qualities. The public relations people also prepare features and recipes for the media that emphasize the company's products and the features the public likes.

Similarly, research may tell an oil company that the public thinks oil companies should find new sources of energy. The firm then may run public relations advertisements on national television, telling little about the company other than what it is doing to find new sources of energy. Hospitals may learn from research that people want to go to a modern hospital with the newest equipment. Their public relations efforts thus stress the new heart-lung machine or a modern laboratory.

Military recruiters may prepare literature stressing positive reasons for enlisting in one of the services, reasons that may have been discovered through research. "Join the Navy and see the world" or "Join the new Army to learn a job skill" are examples. Seldom, if ever, does this literature give the recruit a full picture of what life in the military service would be like.

Regulation as the Catalyst • We estimate that about 15 percent of all organizations today use the two-way symmetric model. It is most often practiced in large firms that are regulated by government agencies—firms that must provide evidence of socially responsible behavior to their government regulators. Many public relations consulting agencies also provide two-way symmetric services to clients that ask for them—as reported, for example, by David Finn of the Ruder & Finn agency.[23]

Let's look at some examples of the two-way symmetric model in action. In press relations, many organizations have replaced the press release with invitations to reporters to come in and develop their own story about the organization. Others invite reporters to dialogue sessions with organizational officials.

Many business firms have invited educators to forums with company officials. In these forums, participants discuss controversial public issues, such as energy or environmental problems. Although the company officials may sometimes push their point of view, so do the educators attending. The result is a better understanding of each other's positions.

In community relations, some business firms have dialogue sessions with community leaders or send representatives out to interview community leaders. As a result, the company learns as much from the community leaders as the leaders learn from the company representatives.

Although there are many examples of the two-way symmetric model in action, public relations people talk about this model more than they practice it. Those who talk about it the most are leaders of professional public relations organizations and public relations educators. At the end of this chapter, we'll discuss why.

Who Fits in Which Category? • In 1980, two graduate students at the University of Maryland interviewed the head of the public relations department and the executive officer to whom the public relations head reported at fifteen varied organizations in the Washington-Baltimore area. They used the results of those interviews to place the public relations programs at those organizations into one of the four models.[24] They withheld the actual names of the organizations, but the descriptions of the kinds of organizations using each model provide some additional examples of where each of the models is practiced.

Practicing the press agentry/publicity model were a regional food store chain, a private university, and a regional bank chain. Obviously, each had something to promote.

Practicing the public information model were a national hotel and entertainment chain, a national food manufacturer, a government regulatory agency, and a local gas utility.

The two-way asymmetric model was used by an insurance company, a local communications utility, a national space and aircraft manufacturer, and a regional drugstore chain.

The two graduate students found the two-way symmetric model in a government research agency, a county school system, a local electric utility, and a metropolitan hospital.

Now that you have some idea of where these models are practiced, let's turn to their historical origins.

HISTORICAL ORIGINS OF THE FOUR MODELS

The Press Agentry/Publicity Model

When we left off our discussion of public relations history, Amos Kendall was serving Andrew Jackson as the equivalent of a modern-day presidential press secretary. It was at about that time, in the 1830s, that the first formal public relations specialists—the press agents—began to practice their trade, although journalism historian Alfred McLung Lee has claimed that there have been press agents as long as there have been newspapers.[25] Lee described Samuel Adams as a press agent, for example. He also believed that other press agents practiced in the United States in the eighteenth century and in England before that. As we have also seen, someone like a press agent had served rulers back into ancient times.

Press agents created many popular American heroes. Daniel Boone, for example, was largely the creation of a press agent representing a landowner who wanted to promote settlement in Kentucky. When Jackson grew popular with the common folk in the West, the opposition party at that time, the Whigs, used press agent Mathew St. Clair Clarke to create the legend of Davy Crockett to offset Jackson's frontier popularity.[26] Western heroes, such as Buffalo Bill Cody, Wyatt Earp, Calamity Jane, and Wild Bill Hickock, were essentially created by their promoters writing for eager readers of the Eastern press.[27] In addition, publicists passed on fantastic stories about the land, climate, and gold in California and the Oregon Territory.[28] Although press agents may have been around as long as newspapers—or any form of the written word—it was the birth of the penny press in the 1830s that allowed them to flourish. When Benjamin Day created the New York *Sun* in 1834, he sold it for a penny when most newspapers sold for six cents, a sum beyond the reach of the common man. The *Sun*, however, "shone for all." It was within the means of the common man, inviting press agents to create stories of great interest that were largely fabrications with little news value. Foremost among them was Phineas T. Barnum, the great showman who formed the Barnum & Bailey Circus.

"There's No Such Thing as Bad Publicity" • Barnum made his name promoting show attractions. Edward Bernays, for example, told the tale of Joice Heth, a Negro slave who supposedly nursed George Washington 100 years before the time.[29] "Around Joice Heth, Barnum raised a terrific editorial, popular and scientific furor. The papers gave the story space in their news and editorial columns, and Barnum kept the story boiling by writing letters to the papers under many pen names." Some of these letters claimed Barnum was a fraud, others extolled him as one who performed a great public service in bringing Heth to public attention.

Barnum said he didn't care if the newspapers attacked him as long as they spelled his name right. "There's no such thing as bad publicity," was the credo of the press agent. When Heth died, an autopsy showed her to be about 80 years old, not 160 as Barnum had claimed. According to Bernays, Barnum was—tongue in cheek—"deeply shocked" and publicly admitted he had been duped. In the meantime, however, Barnum had been collecting as much as $1,500 a week from New Yorkers eager to see the pipe-smoking old woman.

Barnum also coined the terms "jumbo," derived from his Jumbo the elephant, and "Siamese twins," the name he gave to a pair

Tom Thumb and his sponsor P. T. Barnum. (The Bettmann Archive)

of joined twins that he exhibited.[30] Among Barnum's promotions were General Tom Thumb, the midget; Jenny Lind, the "Swedish Nightingale"; Zip, the what is it?; the Cardiff Giant, "discovered in 1869, but of course a fake," and the Greatest Show on Earth, launched in 1871.[31]

Barnum even had his own press agent, Richard F. "Tody" Hamilton. Barnum was quoted as saying that Hamilton was more responsible for his success than any other man.[32]

Barnum's famous statement, "There's a sucker born every minute," lives on. As this is written, the musical Barnum is playing on Broadway and touring the country, and

T-shirts bearing the famous slogan are on sale in theater lobbies.

Barnum wasn't the only press agent. Others served numerous celebrities in the years that followed:

> Barnum was not averse to buying advertising space, he also knew the news interest of his attractions and reaped a harvest of free publicity. With Barnum, and after him, came a host of other press agents whose specialty was getting into free public print the names of actors and actresses like Lily Langtry or Anna Held, and later of a host of motion-picture, radio, and television stars. The agents' methods were not quite so important to them as the results. All manner of stunts, such as fake jewel robberies, marital spats, and love affairs were reported; and a mine of misinformation about marriages, divorces, clothes (or lack of them), opinions upon any subjects, and travels was constantly explored. Unfortunately, the public, or at least a large part of it, loved it![33]

Most press agents generally sought press exposure for the private interest of clients, but many other publicists sought exposure for social causes.[34] These included the American Peace Society, formed in 1828; the temperance movement, beginning in 1825; and, importantly, the abolitionists who sought the end of slavery. Similarly, techniques of press agentry and publicity began to assume importance in political campaigning, especially in the last decade of the nineteenth century.[35]

Eric Goldman, in a little book on the emergence of the public relations counsel written in 1948, called the era of press agentry the era of "The Public be Fooled."[36] In business circles, this was followed, or accompanied by the era of "The Public be Damned." Public relations techniques were similar in both eras, however.

In the period from 1875 to 1900, business in the United States became Big Business. Its leaders were public heroes, the "Captains of Industry." Railroads and telegraph lines crossed the continent, and a great industrial expansion took place. These captains of industry had little respect for the public, however, and communicated little with it: "Shouldering aside agriculture, large-scale commerce and industry became dominant over the life of the nation, and big business was committed to the doctrine that the less the public knew of its operations, the more efficient and profitable—even the more socially useful—the operations would be."[37]

"The Public Be Damned" • The phrase "the public be damned" supposedly originated with William Vanderbilt, son of Commodore Cornelius Vanderbilt and president of the New York Central Railroad, in an interview with a newspaper reporter. Although there is great doubt Vanderbilt ever made the statement, there were two versions of the story:

> One version is that a reporter, interviewing Vanderbilt, asked him why he was eliminating the fast extra-fare mail train between New York and Chicago. The magnate replied that the train wasn't paying. But the public found it useful and convenient, the reporter said; shouldn't Mr. Vanderbilt accommodate the public? "The public be damned!" Mr. Vanderbilt is said to have exclaimed. "I am working for my stockholders; if the public wants the train, why don't they pay for it?" Another version, related by Roger Butterfield in his book, *American Past*, is that two reporters asked Vanderbilt about the new fast train he had just put on to cut the New York-Chicago running time. Did it pay? "No, not a bit of it," snapped the railroad king. "We only run the limited because we are forced to by the action of the Pennsylvania Railroad." "But don't you run it for the public benefit?" one reporter insisted. "The public be damned!" Vanderbilt exploded.[38]

Although the quote may not have been a true one, it did accurately describe the public relations philosophy of big business in the late nineteenth century. As the twentieth century approached, however, government and labor groups began to attack business, and business responded with publicity. At the same time, business used the techniques of press agentry to promote its products.

Railroads used publicity stunts as early as 1870. In 1889, George Westinghouse formed the first corporate public relations department in his newly formed corporation. Westinghouse then entered the famous ''battle of the currents,'' promoting the Westinghouse alternating current against the direct current of the Edison General Electric Company.[39]

Advertising was growing at the same time, and the distinction between the two was not always clear. Advertisers used publicity techniques to get free space to accompany their paid advertisements. Editors, however, reacted unfavorably to the blatant efforts of press agents/publicists to get that free space.

''Flacking for Space'' • The one thing that most press agents/publicists had—and have—in common is their constant effort to get free space in the media for their clients, using every possible trick to take advantage of the newspapers and other media. Although they frequently got the publicity they sought, the media and the public have never forgotten the press agentry origins of public relations. That is why they call public relations people ''flacks''—publicists who shoot all their weapons at the press in the hope that some of the flak will hit home.

The philosophy of the press agent can be seen from statements of press agents at the turn of the century. Goldman cited the ''Confessions'' of an anonymous press agent in 1905, who said, ''Ordinarily the business of the press agent is not the decimation of truth, but the avoidance of its inopportune discovery.''[40] In his autobiography, Bernays told a similar story about a press agent who promoted Obesitea, a tea that supposedly helped people lose weight. ''Why do you continue to hoax people?'' Bernays asked:

> ''I can't see the harm a good fake does anybody,'' he answered. ''If I dealt with organizations that kept to the truth, I would tell them the truth too. But look, Ed, do the newspapers

tell the truth? Don't they have sacred cows? . . . Do they attack corporations their owners hold stock in? . . . I'm going to keep on fooling them. That's the way I make my living; that's the way they make theirs.''[41]

Fortunately, a new era in public relations was about to begin, the advent of the public-information model of the profession.

The Public-Information Model

In the twentieth century, the United States had just passed through the age of big business. Big business had increased the wealth of the country, ''stretching railroads across the land, erecting urban centers, building manufacturing facilities, providing electricity for better power and light, oil for better heating and energy,'' according to Hiebert in his biography of Ivy Lee.[42] But wealth was concentrated: ''In 1900 . . . one-half of the people owned practically nothing, and one-eighth of the people owned seven-eighths of the wealth. In fact, one percent of the population owned fifty-four percent of the wealth.''

Big business also effectively controlled government, and the vote of the common person was ''frequently sold away or manipulated into the hands of political bosses who were themselves tools of the men who owned the factories.'' Big businessmen cared more about profits than about health and safety. ''One journalist estimated that 500,000 workers were killed or maimed each year. Railroads killed thousands each year at grade crossings, but little money was spent changing the crossings or putting up necessary warning devices.''

Hiebert then explained the role of publicists/press agents for businesses in this period:

> Much of the business world in America, of course, was not guilty of such extreme excesses, but all eventually suffered because of those businesses which were. At first the press

was banned from most industrial endeavors, because public knowledge of the facts would have been fatal to many operations. At times press agents were hired to serve as buffers between business and the public to prevent the truth from getting out.[43]

Business did not, however, escape criticism and calls for reform. Laws were passed to limit the excesses of business. Workers organized into unions. Opponents of business learned that publicity could be an effective weapon against the excesses of big business.

"Raking the Muck" • Foremost in using publicity to fight big business and other large organizations was a group of journalists Theodore Roosevelt dubbed the muckrakers when he was police commissioner of New York City. When journalists exposed corruption in the police department, Roosevelt claimed that they "raked the muck wherever it might be." Roosevelt intended "muckraker" to be a derogatory term.

Although no one journalist or magazine created muckraking, *McClure's* magazine and its writers were the most influential. In 1902, publisher S. S. McClure told one of his best writers, Lincoln Steffens, to get out of the magazine's New York office building, get on the train, and go wherever it took him in search of a story.

Steffens headed west and in St. Louis found a district attorney who was being told by a political boss whom to prosecute and whom to leave alone.[44] Steffens wrote an article entitled "Tweed Days in St. Louis" for the October 1902 issue of *McClure's*. In the January 1903 issue, there were three exposés: one of Steffens' continuing exposés of city governments, "The Shame of Minneapolis"; a chapter of Ida Tarbell's devastating history of the Standard Oil Company; and an article by Ray Stannard Baker on abuses by a labor union.[45]

The work of the muckrakers also appeared as books. Examples include Steffens' *The Shame of the Cities* and Tarbell's *The His-*

tory of the Standard Oil Company, which began as articles in *McClure's*, and Upton Sinclair's novel *The Jungle*, which exposed the filth in the meat-packing industry. The exposés brought results:

> Steffens' exposés of municipal and political corruption brought about city reform movements and weakened the power of political bosses and machines. Baker's and Tarbell's disclosures of big business excesses—especially in railroad, coal, and oil trusts—stirred new legislation that put teeth into antimonopoly measures. Sinclair's revelation of meat packing industry frauds and [Samuel Hopkins] Adams' attack on patent medicines brought into being the Pure Food and Drug Act.[46]

Even more importantly, according to Eric Goldman, the muckrakers "seized hold of the general Progressive awareness of publicity and discovered conscious, controlled publicity as a major instrument of modern America."[47] Established institutions needed a new kind of public relations to respond to the publicity war against them, something more than the whitewash of press agentry or the silence of the-public-be-damned approach.

Ivy Lee: "Tell the Truth" • Ivy Ledbetter Lee, a journalist writing about business for a New York newspaper, recognized that need. He was one of the first—and probably the best-known—public relations practitioners of the public-information model of public relations. The idea was simple: Tell the truth about an organization's actions; if that truth was damaging to the organization, then change the behavior of the organization so the truth could be told without fear.

Lee, the son of a Georgia minister, graduated from Princeton and enrolled in the Harvard Law School. After one semester, he ran out of money and, early in 1899, went to New York to look for a job as a journalist. He began on Hearst's *Journal*, then worked for *The New York Times* and the *New York World*. Like many old-time journalists, he did not consider himself a true professional until he had worked for three newspapers.[48]

Lee covered many routine assignments as a reporter, but did his best work writing about banking and business. In 1902, he also sold several articles about Wall Street and business to magazines. That success encouraged him to free-lance as a publicity writer. His first publicity job was as a press representative for the New York Citizen's Union, a political reform group that was bucking the political machine, Tammany Hall, in the New York mayoral campaign.

These experiences gave Lee an idea for a new type of public relations. According to Hiebert:

> He knew he could never be either a loud-mouthed press agent or a crusading journalist. His successful articles about banking, law, investments, and Wall Street led him to feel that he had some talent for explaining complicated and misunderstood facts to a popular audience.[49]

Goldman explained Lee's brainstorm in this way:

> . . . the beginnings of muckraking sent an exciting idea through Lee's head. Was business' policy of secrecy really a wise one? If publicity was being used so effectively to smear business, could it not be used with equal effectiveness to explain and defend business?[50]

Lee met George Parker, who had been working as a publicist for the Democratic party, during his work in the New York political campaign. In 1904, the two opened Parker & Lee, the nation's third public relations agency.[51] The first agency had been the Publicity Bureau, formed in Boston in 1900, which largely provided press agentry to businesses anxious to fight off the criticism of the muckrakers. It died sometime after 1911.[52]

The second agency, formed in Washington by journalist William Wolff Smith in 1902, also lasted only about ten years.[53] Parker &

Lee lasted only four years, as Parker still had the ideas of a nineteenth-century press agent, and Lee wanted to be more.[54] Lee continued on his own, however, and in 1916, he opened a firm called Lee, Harris, and Lee.

Lee's Leading Clients • Ivy Lee represented many prominent interests during his career. The most famous were the anthracite coal operators during a strike in 1902, the Pennsylvania Railroad, and the Rockefeller family. More important than a chronicle of his services to his clients, however, is a summary of his ideas. He articulated those ideas first in his handling of the account of the Anthracite Coal Roads and Mine Company in 1906.

In 1902, the United Mine Workers union had become strong enough to lead 150,000 miners on strike in Pennsylvania. The strike began in May. In October, when winter threatened, President Theodore Roosevelt intervened to force a settlement on behalf of a country that depended on coal for heat. The union won a substantial victory in that settlement.

During this strike, the union had been open with the press, the coal operators secretive. The operators were controlled by the eight railroads that served the coal-mining regions. They, in turn, were controlled by J. P. Morgan and other powerful capitalists. Leading the operators was George F. Baer of the Philadelphia and Reading Railway. The only statement Baer made to the press during the strike was that ''The rights and interests of the laboring man will be protected and cared for not by the labor agitators, but by the Christian men to whom God in his infinite wisdom has given the control of the property interests of the country.''[55]

''The Public Be Informed'' • Four years later, in 1906, another strike loomed. By this time, Baer and the other operators had learned their lesson. They hired Ivy Lee to provide publicity on the position of the coal operators.

On their behalf, Lee developed a publicity policy of "the public be informed" to replace the policy of "the public be damned."[56] Lee sent an announcement to the press stating that he would supply it with all possible information, "realizing the general public interest in conditions in the mining region."[57] When he sent statements to the press, he included a copy of his Declaration of Principles, a statement that could still serve admirably as a description of the public-information model:

> This is not a secret press bureau. All our work is done in the open. We aim to supply news. This is not an advertising agency; if you think any of our matter properly ought to go to your business office, do not use it. Our matter is accurate. Further details on any subject treated will be supplied promptly, and any editor will be assisted most cheerfully in verifying directly any statement of fact. Upon inquiry, full information will be given to any editor concerning those on whose behalf an article is sent out. In brief, our plan is, frankly and openly, on behalf of the business concerns and public institutions, to supply to the press and public of the United States prompt and accurate information concerning subjects which it is of value and interest to the public to know about. Corporations and public institutions give out much information in which the news point is lost to view. Nevertheless, it is quite as important to the public to have this news as it is to the establishments themselves to give it currency. I send out only matter every detail of which I am willing to assist any editor in verifying for himself. I am always at your service for the purpose of enabling you to obtain more complete information concerning any of the subjects brought forward in my copy.[58]

A definition of the term "publicity" is "to make public," which is exactly what Lee did for his clients. Working for the Pennsylvania Railroad, Lee bucked the corporate hierarchy when a Pennsylvania train had an accident near Gap, Pennsylvania. Management wanted to suppress all news of the accident, as was traditional policy. Lee reversed that policy, inviting reporters to the accident scene and helping them to cover the story:

> To Lee a good press, fundamental to good public relations, was obtained not by bribing reporters with passes but by providing them with the information they needed to write their stories and perform their jobs. Also fundamental was that the organization should tell its side of the story. Then, with a good press, both sides might be told and the public might have a fairer picture from which to form a better judgement.[59]

Lee's policy of press relations also can be seen in his use of the handout, or press release as we call it today. Lee made more extensive use of the handout than anyone before him, and frequently suffered the wrath of the press for doing so. But Lee made the press release respectable. His handouts were always clearly marked to indicate who wrote them, and on whose behalf. Before, handouts had been "planted" without naming the source, or information was leaked by anonymous tips.[60]

Rehabilitating the Rockefellers • The most dramatic results of Lee's policy of openness came from his work for the Rockefeller family. His service began in 1914 when John D. Rockefeller, Jr., asked for advice on how to handle the adverse publicity that had been heaped upon him for the so-called Ludlow Massacre in Colorado.

Nine thousand coal miners went on strike in southern Colorado in September 1913. The Rockefellers were the principal stockholders in the largest company involved, the Colorado Fuel and Iron Company. In April 1914, an accidental shot resulted in a battle in which several miners, two women, and eleven children were killed. The Rockefellers were blamed, and "the Rockefeller name was being denounced from one end of the country to another."[61] Lee advised the younger Rockefeller to practice a policy of openness. After the strike, Lee advised Rockefeller to visit the mining camps to observe conditions first-

Ivy Lee, public relations executive for John D. Rockefeller. (The Bettmann Archive)

no exception. His job, he said, "was interpreting the Pennsylvania Railroad to the public and interpreting the public to the Pennsylvania Railroad. The public was his prime concern."[63] He also had a role in the development of management policy when it was still in the discussion stage, pointing out when it might be in conflict with public opinion.[64]

Yet, Lee never conducted an opinion survey. His advice to management came from an intuitive sense of public opinion. Edward L. Bernays, in comparison, once said his work was based on science, whereas Lee's was based on art.[65] In this way, Lee's work was typical of contemporary practitioners of the public-information model. They advise management on public opinion—and often understand public opinion quite well—but they rarely do any scientific research to measure that opinion.

Public, Practitioner, and Client • Lee viewed the public as made up of rational human beings who, if they are given complete and accurate information, would make the right decisions. He viewed the public relations practitioner as equivalent to a lawyer in the court of public opinion. Lee believed, however, that a lawyer does not always examine the correctness of his client's motivations. Instead, he represents his client's interests as far as possible within the limits of the law. Likewise, the publicist does not always question his client's motivation, but promotes the client's interest as far as public opinion will permit.[66]

That view seems to differ from Lee's commitment to the public interest, and perhaps explains why much criticism was heaped upon Lee during his lifetime—for he represented many clients despised by the public. In his book about the press, *The Brass Check*, for example, Upton Sinclair called Lee "Poison Ivy."

Bernays claimed that Lee sometimes "lapsed from his declared policy to the extent

hand, which Hiebert described as "a landmark in public relations."

Lee later advised John D. Rockefeller, Sr., exposed by the muckrakers as a capitalist without ethics who "would stop at nothing, not even the ruin of his friends, to create an oil monopoly." Newspapers called him the "Robber Baron" and "The Great Octopus."[62] Rockefeller also was generous in giving money to charities, but he had never told the public about it. Lee convinced Rockefeller to change his policy of "silence and aloofness." The public began to see the family differently, and today the Rockefeller family benefits from an outstanding public reputation.

Although practitioners of the public-information model devote most of their efforts to publicizing their organizations, most do so with the idea of making the organization more responsible to the public. Ivy Lee was of whitewashing his clients." Bernays added, however, that Lee's statement to the press on behalf of the mine owners in 1906 and his Declaration of Principles were "milestones in the development of business publicity."[67] Similarly, the prominent public relations practitioner Earl Newsom told the Public Relations Society of America in 1963:

> This whole activity of which you and I are a part can probably be said to have had its beginning when Ivy Lee persuaded the directors of the Pennsylvania Railroad that the press should be given all the facts on all railway accidents even though the facts might place the blame on the railroad itself.[68]

Lee died in disgrace in 1934 at the age of fifty-four. In a sense, he was a victim of his own public relations policies. Lee had long been interested in problems of international communication, believing that openness and frankness between countries could bring international understanding. In the 1920s, he carried on a personal crusade to gain understanding of the Soviet Union in the United States that was, at least in part, responsible for the official recognition of the Soviet Union by the United States in 1933.

In the early 1930s, Lee advised the Interessen Gemeinschaft Farben Industrie, more commonly know as I. G. Farben, or the German Dye Trust.[69] Eventually, the Nazis took control of the trust, and the company asked Lee for advice on how to improve German-American relations. He gave the Germans the same advice as he gave the Rockefellers: be open and honest, and change the German policies if they are unacceptable to the people. The Germans did not take his advice, however, and shortly before his death, Lee's connections with the Germans were investigated by the House Special Committee on Unamerican Activities. Headlines screamed that "Lee Exposed as Hitler Press Agent," and his name was blackened throughout the United States.[70] According to Hiebert, Lee viewed the German experiment as a way of testing his principles of public relations. It failed because "the Germans made only a superficial pretense of adopting them."[71]

Journalists in Residence • We have spent a good deal of time on Ivy Lee because he was the best known of the early twentieth-century publicists. But Lee was not alone in offering services that fit the public-information model.

Many imitators soon followed. One of these was Pendleton Dudley, who opened a publicity firm on Wall Street in 1909 that he headed for fifty-seven years until he died at the age of ninety. The firm now is called Dudley, Anderson, & Yutzy.[72] Dudley himself described most of the imitators as newspapermen who had worked on first-rate metropolitan dailies and knew what was newsworthy and what would catch the interest of the average newspaper reader.[73] Even today, the majority of practitioners of the public-information model started as reporters; as stated earlier, they perform essentially as journalists in residence in an organization.

Many large business firms also followed the public-information model in forming their own public relations departments. Foremost among these was the American Telephone & Telegraph Co. (AT&T), which has long been a leader in the practice of public relations. As we have already seen, Theodore Vail had pioneered the use of the term "public relations" in his annual reports in the early 1900s. Vail had been forced out as president in 1887, but he returned in 1907. In a history of the Bell System, John Brooks pointed out that "Public relations was totally ignored until the turn of the century, with deleterious results—specifically until 1903, when AT&T's public image had sunk so low that it finally retained the services of the Boston-based Publicity Bureau, the nation's first public relations firm."[74]

Vail hired James D. Ellsworth to handle advertising and publicity when he became president in 1907. Ellsworth had previously worked on the AT&T account at the Publicity Bureau. By 1922–23, the public relations function had been institutionalized at AT&T. Among other activities, AT&T used that department to try requests for rate increases "in the court of public opinion before presenting them to regulatory commissions."[75]

AT&T public relations reached the full embodiment of the public-information model in 1927, when Arthur Page was hired to replace Ellsworth, and to emphasize "candid disclosure rather than parochial propaganda."[76] Page stated his public relations philosophy in terms that clearly fit the public-information model:

> All business in a democratic country begins with public permission and exists by public approval. If that be true, it follows that business should be cheerfully willing to tell the public what its policies are, what it is doing, and what it hopes to do. That seems practically a duty.[77]

Already in 1925, however, the Bell system had begun to use public opinion polls, moving the company toward a two-way model of public relations.

Enter the Nonprofits and Government • Other companies also set up public relations departments at this time. Henry Ford publicized his Model T in the early 1900s and began to publish the house organ *Ford Times* in 1908. General Motors advertised the company as an institution in 1923, but did not start its first public relations department until 1931, under the direction of Paul Garrett. At the same time, many universities, the YMCA, the Red Cross, churches, associations, and other nonprofit agencies began to publicize themselves. Presidents, in particular Theodore Roosevelt and Woodrow Wilson, also made adept use of publicity.[78]

In the early 1900s, government agencies also began to use publicists to inform citizens and to influence legislation that affected them in Congress. Angered by publicity efforts that often followed the press agentry model, Congress passed the Gillett Amendment in 1913, which prohibits government agencies from

AT&T President Theodore N. Vail, surrounded by company executives, makes one of the first calls on the transcontinental telephone equipment introduced in 1915. In the months to follow, AT&T gleaned much publicity from "inaugural" calls made from dignitaries in various East Coast cities to their West Coast counterparts. (Reproduced with permission of AT&T)

George Creel. (Culver Pictures, Inc.)

hiring ''publicity experts'' unless money is specifically appropriated by Congress. That amendment has never been repealed. It has not kept public relations out of government, but it has restricted government to providing ''information'' rather than ''publicity'' and to avoid practicing ''public relations.'' Thus, even today, government agencies are essentially limited to practicing the public-information model.[79]

By 1920, then, the public-information model had replaced the press agent as the major form of public relations. But a major propaganda effort at the time of World War I was to establish a new model that relied on scientific knowledge to help efforts to persuade.

The Two-Way Asymmetric Model

During World War I, propaganda played an important role in getting the United States into the war and then in convincing the people to support the war effort.

The United States entered the war on the side of the Allies after a major propaganda effort by the British to convince Americans of the rightness of their side and the evil of the Germans. Later, when much of this propaganda was found to be distorted, Americans developed a great fear of the power of propaganda. Only a week after the United States entered the war, President Wilson appointed a former newsman, George Creel, to head the Committee on Public Information, the U. S. propaganda agency. That organization had unmatched success in mass persuasion:

Tobin and Bidwell [in the book *Mobilizing Civilian America*] ascribe to the work of the ''group of zealous, amateur propagandists'' organized by Mr. Creel ''the revolutionary change in the sentiment of the nation.'' He carried out, they say, what was ''perhaps the most effective job of large-scale war propaganda which the world had ever witnessed.'' Intellectual and emotional bombardment aroused Americans to a pitch of enthusiasm. The bombardment came at people from all sides—advertisements, news, volunteer speakers, posters, schools, theaters; millions of homes displayed service flags. The war aims and ideals were continually projected to the eyes and ears of the populace. These high-pressure methods were new at the time, but have become usual since then.[80]

Although the methods used by Creel's committee were fairly standard tools of the public-information model, the committee achieved great success because it made use, without knowing it, of psychological principles of mass persuasion. Essentially, what they and other propagandists did was to construct messages that appeal to what people believe and want to hear. The Creel Committee "was no inner clique imposing unwanted views on the general public." The committee promoted ideas that most Americans held before war was declared. "What the committee did was to codify and standardize ideas already current, and to bring the powerful force of the emotions behind them."[81]

Bernays Leads the New Generation • The Creel Committee suggested to a new generation of public relations practitioners that mass persuasion was possible and that it could have its base in social science. In addition to an idea, the Creel Committee also contributed a new generation of public relations practitioners who left the committee after the war to go into practice for themselves. Foremost among this generation was Carl Byoir, founder of the public relations agency that still bears his name, and Edward L. Bernays, the practitioner whose work best illustrates the two-way asymmetric model.

Bernays joined the Committee on Public Information as a way of providing patriotic service to the United States. He had been rejected when he volunteered for military service, and later for the draft, because of "flat feet and defective reading vision in one eye."[82] On the committee, he worked for the Foreign Press Bureau, supplying interpretive and background information to overseas media to emphasize America's contribution to the war effort.[83]

Edward L. Bernays. (The Bettmann Archive)

Bernays was born in 1891 in Vienna, Austria, and celebrated his first birthday on board ship as his parents were emigrating to New York. In New York, his father worked as a grain exporter on the Produce Exchange. Bernays was a nephew of the famous Vienna psychologist Sigmund Freud on both his father's and mother's side of the family (Bernays' father married Freud's sister, and Freud married Bernays' father's sister).[84] In the early 1920s, Bernays helped Freud publish English translations of his work, and the two corresponded frequently. It was this relationship with Freud that apparently stimulated Bernays' interest in the behavioral and social sciences.

Bernays' parents sent him to Cornell University's College of Agriculture in Ithaca, New York, in part because President Theodore Roosevelt had championed rural life and had convinced Bernays' father "that farming was the great future for young men."[85] Bernays reported, however, that he believed his father wanted him eventually to work in the family business on the Produce Exchange.

Bernays did not think much of the agricultural life and described his four years at Cornell in a chapter of his autobiography as "Barren Years at Cornell Agricultural College." His agricultural degree led to a journalistic job on the *National Nurseryman*, in Danville, New York, writing about apples, peaches, and pears. He next took an editing job in New York City for two monthly medical magazines, the *Medical Review of Reviews* and the *Dietetic and Hygienic Gazette*.

One day in 1913, a manuscript came to the *Medical Review* that eventually turned Bernays to public relations. A doctor had submitted an article about a play by a French playwright called *Damaged Goods* that attacked sexual prudery and the ignorance about venereal disease that resulted from it. Bernays published the article because he thought it would benefit the *Review's* readers, even thought it "was a daring editorial venture for that era."[86] Later, he helped to produce the play in New York, by raising funds through a Sociological Fund Committee associated with the *Medical Review*.

The experience of promoting the play made medical journalism seem tame compared to the glamour of press agentry, and so, after a trip to Europe and a visit to Uncle Sigmund Freud, Bernays turned to theater, music, and motion picture press agentry. Bernays promoted music with the Booking and Promotion Corporation and later formed the Metropolitan Musical Bureau. The highlight of this stage of his life was touring with and promoting Enrico Caruso, the great Italian tenor. World War I came, however, and Bernays joined the Creel Committee.[87]

After working on the Committee for Public Information, Bernays began to do freelance consulting, first to help the Lithuanian National Council gain the support of the American people for the recognition of Lithuania, and then to help the War Department develop employment opportunities for ex-servicemen. In the middle of the summer of 1919, Bernays opened his own office and "lured his young friend, the assistant Sunday editor of the New York *Tribune*, Doris E. Fleischman," to work with him.[88] In 1922, Bernays and Fleischman married and formed a lifelong partnership, she always using her maiden name. Fleischman died in 1980; Bernays still lives in Cambridge, Mass.

Intellectualizing PR Concepts • Earlier, we said that public relations was an art for Ivy Lee and a science to Edward Bernays. Bernays was the intellectual of early public relations practitioners. He wrote the first book about public relations in 1923, *Crystallizing Public Opinion*, in which he articulated the concept of the counsel on public relations. In 1928, he wrote his second book, *Propaganda*, and in 1952, his textbook *Public Relations*.

Bernays also taught the first course in public relations at a university, in 1922 at New York University, where he was a part-time lecturer in journalism and taught a course in the School of Commerce and Finance.[89] According to Goldman:

> For Bernays to write a book was as natural as Lee's affinity for business. In contrast to the background of Lee and most other contemporary public relations men, the Bernays family was traditionally intellectual, and the rising eminence of Sigmund Freud, who was Edward's uncle, could hardly fail to deepen the impress.[90]

In Table 2-1, we classified Bernays not only as the leading historical example of the two-way *asymmetric* model of PR, but also as one of the thinkers who helped to develop the two-way *symmetric* model. As did Ivy Lee, Bernays stressed the importance of communicating the public's point of view to management. In practice, however, both did much more to explain management's view to the public. Bernays entered public relations at a time when most people believed in the power of mass persuasion. Many believed publics could be persuaded in whatever direction the propagandist wished, but

Bernays knew publics could be persuaded to do only what was in their best interests. He also knew he must persuade management to do what was in the public interest before he could persuade the public to accept the organization.

Bernays constantly, and sincerely, stressed the role of public relations in protecting public and social welfare. But, like other practitioners of the two-way asymmetric model, he most often practiced this role by finding out what the public liked about the organization and then highlighting that aspect of the organization, or by determining what values and attitudes publics had and then describing the organization in a way that conformed to these values and attitudes. Bernays called these strategies the "crystallizing of public opinion" and the "engineering of consent."

The Power of Persuasion • Bernays' belief in the power of persuasive communication can be seen in the opening paragraph of *Propaganda*:

> The conscious and intelligent manipulation of the organized habits and opinions of the masses is an important element in democratic society. Those who manipulate this unseen mechanism of society constitute an invisible government which is the true ruling power of our country.[91]

Bernays also made use of social science theories of the day, most of which attempted to explain persuasion. While working for the Lithuanian National Council, he tried to appeal to the sympathy Americans had for liberty and freedom to spur them to write letters to congressmen and newspapers. He saw psychological theory in this approach: "Years afterward a Yale social psychologist, Leonard Doob, gave my approach a name, 'the segmental approach.' It identifies a major interest of the reader with a cause, intensifies his interest, and stimulates action."[92]

Bernays' approach to social science was intuitive and informal. He read social science research and used the knowledge he gained to think through public relations problems. He also did informal surveys of publics, management, and employees. As he put it, "Scientific research did not come until much later."[93]

Edward Bernays and Doris Fleischman had too many clients to describe in detail here. At the end of his autobiography, Bernays listed about 200 in many different fields: the arts, building and construction, business and industry, communications, education, expositions, finance, government, hotels, public-interest groups, retailers, trade associations, transportation, unions, and individuals.

One of these clients, although seemingly an insignificant one, provides a good example of the two-way asymmetric approach: the Venida Hairnet Company. After World War I, women began to cut their hair short and the market for hairnets declined. Bernays:

> . . . asked around why women wore a hairnet and found three possible reasons: (1) it enhanced a woman's beauty, (2) it was a sanitary safeguard that kept a woman's hair in place during cooking and serving of food, and (3) it protected women factory workers' hair from dangers and machines.[94]

Bernays developed a strategy to publicize each use of hairnets and succeeded in slowing a long-term trend away from their use. Bernays believed he had helped the organization he represented, and the public as well, by providing a useful product:

> I recognized the power of the processes I was working with: in each case an example of coincidence of interest between the public and the private interest. The individual had cooperated because of what he believed to be the public interest. Bringing together such interests accelerates change in society. Such processes could be applied to hairnets or important social problems.[95]

Bernays did indeed apply his method to causes more important than hairnets—e.g., the NAACP, many business firms, and several government agencies. He changed the concept of public relations from "the public be informed" to what he described as "the public should be understood and its needs considered."[96]

Bernays has been the most celebrated of the third generation of public relations practitioners, perhaps because he has defended and advocated the public relations profession for nearly sixty years. There are others, however, who also typify the two-way asymmetric model.

Founders of the New Order • One of these was Rex Harlow, who practiced public relations in the San Francisco area and taught public relations and social science at Stanford University. Harlow wrote a public relations textbook and a book reviewing theories and research from the social sciences that he believed could be applied in public relations.[97] Most of those theories had persuasion as an aim. Harlow also founded the American Council on Public Relations and the *Public Relations Journal* in the 1940s. The American Council merged with other organizations to become today's Public Relations Society of America (PRSA). He also developed the Social Science Seminar for public relations leaders in the 1950s.[98]

John W. Hill, who with Don Knowlton formed the Hill & Knowlton public relations agency in Cleveland in 1927, provides another example of the two-way asymmetric model. (After forming Hill & Knowlton, Hill moved to New York while Knowlton remained in Cleveland—operating essentially independent firms. Hill died in 1977, but his firm today ranks with Burson-Marsteller as one of the two largest public relations firms in the world.)

In his autobiography, Hill provided a two-way asymmetric definition of public relations:

It functions in the dissemination of information and facts when non-controversial matters are involved. But when controversy exists, public relations may become the advocate before the bar of public opinion, seeking to win support through interpretation of facts and the power of persuasion.[99]

Most of the historical examples we've provided of the two-way asymmetric model come from public relations counselors, but the model has also been practiced widely in business. Business practitioners simply have not written as much about themselves as have independent counselors.

As we saw above, AT&T began to move toward the two-way asymmetric model in the late 1920s, when it began public opinion polling. It was the development of the scientific opinion poll in the 1940s and 1950s, however, that made the two-way asymmetric model what it is today. Polling gives an organization the ability to learn what the public wants and will accept, thus indicating the direction a public relations program should take.

Although most practitioners of this model stress serving the public interest, in practice, the model has been an effective tool used by established groups to retain their positions in society, "by business to increase its profits . . . and by entrenched pressure groups, whether labor or engineering societies to further their special interests."[100]

Although practitioners of this model claim to advocate the public's view inside the organization, generally the only way they do that is by telling management what the public will accept. They do not tell management how to change to please the public. For public relations to fully represent publics to the management of an organization, the two-way symmetric model must be used.

The Two-Way Symmetric Model

The historical origins of the two-way symmetric model are much more difficult to trace to any individual practitioners than are the origins of the other models. In large part this is because practitioners only now are beginning to practice the model.

As we have already stated, most of the historical public relations figures from the twentieth century have defined public relations in symmetric terms, although they have practiced another model. Ivy Lee, for example, told the Rockefellers to tell the truth, "because sooner or later the public will find it out anyway. And if the public doesn't like what you are doing, change your policies and bring them into line with what the people want."[101] In *Crystallizing Public Opinion*, Bernays wrote that the public relations counsel serves "as a consultant both in interpreting the public to his client and helping to interpret his client to the public. He helps to mould the action of his client as well as to mould public opinion."[102] John Hill stated, "It is just as important for company management to understand the problems and viewpoints of its employees, neighbors, and others as it is for these groups to understand the problems and viewpoints of management. . . . It is an essential function of the public relations counsel to serve as a listening post for management."[103]

Although public relations practitioners have spoken eloquently about a two-way symmetric model, public relations educators seem to have done the most to define how the model should truly be practiced. As we will see in Chapter 4, professional fields such as public relations generally pass through several stages in their development. At the beginning, practitioners teach in colleges and universities on a part-time basis, largely using case studies and "how-I-did-it" examples. Eventually, full-time educators enter the field, and spend less time practicing and more time thinking about the field. Thus, in public relations, full-time educators who took the practitioners at their word about the need for a two-way symmetric model began thinking, beginning in the late 1950s, about how a true symmetric model of public relations would be practiced.

Advocating the New Approach
Perhaps the first educator to seriously conceptualize a symmetric model of public relations was Scott M. Cutlip, then of the University of Wisconsin and now of the University of Georgia. Together with Allen Center, then a practitioner with the Motorola Corporation, Cutlip wrote the first of five editions of a textbook that advocated a two-way symmetric model. Most of that textbook, however, described how practitioners practice the other models. In their first edition, published in 1952, Cutlip and Center used the term "public relations" to describe "the principles and practice of communications employed to build good relationships with the public."[104] They defined it, in clear two-way symmetric terms, as follows:

> Public relations is the communication and interpretation of ideas and information to the publics of an institution; the communication and interpretation of information, ideas, and opinions from those publics to the institution in an effort to bring the two into harmonious adjustment."[105]

Not all educators teach a two-way symmetric model, however. The majority of the textbooks stress the techniques necessary for the public-information model. Many educators with a background in behavioral and social sciences teach a two-way asymmetric model. Two examples of textbooks stressing such an approach are Edward J. Robinson's *Communication and Public Relations* and Otto Lerbinger's *Designs for Persuasive Communication*.[106]

Educators now are just beginning to develop the theories and techniques for a symmetric model. They have done so, in part, because recent communication research has cast serious doubt on the power of mass persuasion—the sine qua non of the two-way asymmetric model. This research has replaced persuasion with understanding as the major goal of communication.

Educators have not developed the two-way symmetric model alone, however. Many professional public relations leaders also have articulated the model. Earlier we quoted David Finn, of Ruder & Finn, as an example of a counselor who has provided symmetric PR services to clients. We also cited current examples of how some organizations practice the symmetric model. One quote should drive home the point that top professionals believe in the two-way model. According to Harold Burson, one of the founders of Burson-Marsteller:

> The public relations executive provides a qualitative evaluation of social trends. He helps formulate policies that will enable a corporation to adapt to these trends. And he communicates—both internally and externally—the reasons for those policies. . . One obvious objective for the public relations practitioner in the corporate environment is to make sure that business institutions perform as servants of the people.[107]

Those, then, are the historical roots of the four public relations models. Most of the rest of this book will present the theories and techniques needed to practice them. Before moving on, however, we will take a few more paragraphs to discuss which of the models is "right" or "best."

A CONTINGENCY VIEW OF THE FOUR MODELS

For many years, management theorists advocated "all-or-none" theories of management. Each had his best way to manage, and each advocated that approach.

Beginning in the 1950s, however, organizational researchers began to discover that traditional management principles worked only some of the time. Whether they worked or not depended on the nature of the firm, the nature of its technology, and the nature of its environment. That research led to what organizational theorists now call a contingency view of management.[108] In this view, no one approach is appropriate all of the time and for all conditions. What is the best approach depends upon the nature of the organization and the nature of the environment in which it must survive.

The contingency view represents the best way to answer which of the four models we have outlined is "right." It all depends. . . . Although it will become obvious that we prefer the two-way symmetric model and will stress that model throughout this book, we recognize that there are organizations facing problems for which the other models provide the best solutions.

If you want to sell tickets to a baseball game, for example, you should use the press agentry/publicity model.

If a government agency is charged by Congress to disseminate health information, the public-information model will work best.

If a business firm wants to use public relations to help market a product or to influence legislation, the two-way asymmetric model will work best.

A large, regulated business firm will want to use the two-way symmetric model to help maintain the social responsibility its government regulators require. At times, one organization will find that a different model works best for different problems or for different public relations activities.

Research has only begun on the various conditions that favor the four models.[109] While we wait for more research-based advice, keep in mind that the same principles will not work all of the time. Throughout this book, we will discuss theories and techniques for managing public relations. In doing so, we will also point out which model they fit and the conditions under which they are most appropriate.

NOTES

1. Scott M. Cutlip and Allen H. Center, *Effective Public Relations*, 5th ed. (Englewood Cliffs, N. J.: Prentice-Hall, 1978), p. 19.
2. Ray Eldon Hiebert, *Courtier to the Crowd* (Ames: Iowa State University Press, 1966), p. 87; Doug Newsom and Alan Scott, *This is PR: The Realities of Public Relations*, 2d ed. (Belmont, Calif.: Wadsworth, 1981), p. 20.
3. Edward L. Bernays, *Public Relations* (Norman: University of Oklahoma Press, 1952), p. 70.
4. Bernays, p. 70.
5. Newsom and Scott, p. 23
6. Cutlip and Center, pp. 66–67.
7. Howard Clark Kee, Franklin W. Young, and Karlfried Froehlich, *Understanding the New Testament*, 2d ed. (Englewood Cliffs, N. J.: Prentice-Hall, 1965), p. 55
8. John E. Marston, *Modern Public Relations* (New York: McGraw-Hill, 1979), p. 19.
9. Bernays, p. 19.
10. Bernays, p. 21.
11. Bernays, p. 22.
12. Cutlip and Center, p. 68.
13. Scott M. Cutlip, "Public Relations and the American Revolution," *Public Relations Review* 2 (Winter 1976):11–24.
14. Robert W. Smith, "The Boston Massacre: A Study in Public Relations," *Public Relations Review* 2 (Winter 1976):25–33.
15. Allan Nevins, "The Constitution Makers and the Public: 1785–1970," *Public Relations Review* 4 (Fall 1978):5–16.
16. Peter H. Odegard and Hans H. Baerwald, *American Government: Structure, Problems, and Policies* (Evanston, Ill.: Row, Peterson, 1962), p. 29.
17. Odegard and Baerwald, p. 2.
18. Fred F. Endres, "Public Relations in the Jackson White House," *Public Relations Review* 2 (Fall 1976):5–12.
19. Endres, p. 7.
20. As quoted from historian James Schouler in an 1894 book on American history in Endres.
21. David Finn, "Modifying Opinions in the New Human Climate," *Public Relations Quarterly* 17 (1972):12–15, 26.
22. Tom Ford, "The Future: Salesmanship or Dialogue?" *Public Relations Review* 2 (Spring 1976):6.
23. David Finn, "The Future of Specialized Media in Public Relations," in James E. Grunig (ed.), *Decline of the Global Village* (Bayside, N. Y.: General Hall, 1976), p. 101. Finn describes how a public relations executive of a major firm asked him to evaluate his department; described in the article cited in note 21.
24. Christopher Hardwick, "Public Relations and Organizational Effectiveness: An Open Systems Approach," master's thesis, University of Maryland, College Park, 1980; Elizabeth Nanni, "Case Studies of Organizational Management and Public Relations Practices," master's thesis, University of Maryland, College Park, 1980.
25. Alfred McLung Lee, *The Daily Newspaper in America* (New York: Macmillan, 1937), p. 40.
26. Cutlip and Center, p. 70.
27. Newsom and Scott, p. 32.
28. Ray Allen Billington, "Words That Won the West: 1830–1850," *Public Relations Review* 4 (Fall 1978):17–27.
29. Bernays, pp. 38–39.
30. Marston, p. 21.
31. Bernays, p. 39.
32. Cutlip and Center, p. 71.
33. Marston, p. 21.
34. Bernays, pp. 39–49.
35. Cutlip and Center, pp. 71–72.
36. Eric F. Goldman, *Two-Way Street: The Emergence of the Public Relations Counsel* (Boston: Bellman Publishing Co., 1948), p. 1.
37. Goldman, p. 3.
38. Bernays, pp. 51–52.
39. Cutlip and Center, pp. 73–74.
40. Goldman, p. 2.
41. Edward L. Bernays, *Biography of an Idea: Memoirs of Public Relations Counsel Edward L. Bernays* (New York: Simon and Schuster, 1965), p. 203.
42. Ray Eldon Hiebert, *Courtier to the Crowd* (Ames: Iowa State University Press, 1966), p. 35.
43. Hiebert, p. 36.
44. Eric F. Goldman, "Public Relations and the Progressive Surge: 1898–1917," *Public Relations Review* 4 (Fall 1978):52–62.
45. Goldman, "Public Relations and the Progressive Surge," p. 57.

46. Hiebert, p. 37.
47. Goldman, ''Public Relations and the Progressive Surge,'' p. 58.
48. Hiebert, p. 34.
49. Hiebert, p. 39.
50. Goldman, *Two-Way Street*, p. 6.
51. Cutlip and Center, p. 77.
52. Scott M. Cutlip, ''The Nation's First Public Relations Firm,'' *Journalism Quarterly* 43 (1966):269–280.
53. Cutlip and Center, p. 77.
54. Hiebert, p. 46.
55. Hiebert, pp. 40–41.
56. Goldman, *Two-Way Street*, p. 8.
57. Hiebert, p. 47.
58. Hiebert, p. 48.
59. Hiebert, pp. 57–58.
60. Hiebert, p. 300.
61. Hiebert, pp. 97–108.
62. Hiebert, p. 111.
63. Hiebert, p. 59.
64. Hiebert, p. 79.
65. Hiebert, p. 92.
66. Hiebert, p. 317.
67. Bernays, *Public Relations*, p. 70.
68. Hiebert, p. 61.
69. Hiebert, p. 286.
70. Hiebert, p. 310.
71. Hiebert, p. 292.
72. Cutlip and Center, p. 78.
73. Pendleton Dudley, ''Current Beginnings of Public Relations,'' *Public Relations Journal* 8 (April 1952):9.
74. John Brooks, *Telephone: The First Hundred Years* (New York: Harper & Row, 1976), p. 3.
75. Noel L. Griese, ''James D. Ellsworth, 1863–1940: PR Pioneer,'' *Public Relations Review* 4 (Summer 1978):22–31.
76. Brooks, p. 269.
77. Griese, p. 29.
78. Cutlip and Center, pp. 80–84.
79. David H. Brown, ''Government Public Affairs—Its Own Worst Enemy,'' *Public Relations Quarterly* 26 (Spring 1981):4–5.
80. Bernays, *Public Relations*, p. 74.
81. Curtis D. MacDougall, *Understanding Public Opinion* (New York: Macmillan, 1952), p. 108.
82. Bernays, *Biography of an Idea*, p. 146.
83. Bernays, *Biography of an Idea*, p. 155.
84. Bernays, *Biography of an Idea*, p. 4.
85. Bernays, *Biography of an Idea*, p. 30.
86. Bernays, *Biography of an Idea*, pp. 53–62.
87. Bernays, *Biography of an Idea*, pp. 62–152.
88. Bernays, *Biography of an Idea*, p. 93.
89. Bernays, *Biography of an Idea*, p. 292.
90. Goldman, *Two-Way Street*, p. 14.
91. Edward L. Bernays, *Propaganda* (New York: Liveright, 1928), p. 9.
92. Bernays, *Biography of an Idea*, p. 189.
93. Bernays, *Biography of an Idea*, p. 239.
94. Bernays, *Biography of an Idea*, p. 206.
95. Bernays, *Biography of an Idea*, p. 208.
96. Bernays, *Biography of an Idea*, p. 804.
97. Rex Harlow and Marvin M. Black, *Practical Public Relations* (New York: Harper & Brothers, 1947); Rex F. Harlow, *Social Science in Public Relations* (New York: Harper & Brothers, 1957).
98. Rex Harlow, ''A Timeline of Public Relations,'' *Public Relations Review* 6 (Fall 1980):3–13.
99. John W. Hill, *The Making of a Public Relations Man* (New York: David McKay, 1963), p. 6.
100. Goldman, *Two-Way Street*, p. 22.
101. Hiebert, p. 5.
102. Bernays, *Biography of an Idea*, p. 292.
103. Hill, p. 136.
104. Scott M. Cutlip and Allen H. Center, *Effective Public Relations* (Englewood Cliffs, N.J.: Prentice-Hall, 1952), p. 5.
105. Cutlip and Center, pp. 15–16.
106. Edward J. Robinson, *Communication and Public Relations* (Columbus, Ohio: Merrill, 1966); Otto Lerbinger, *Designs for Persuasive Communication* (Englewood Cliffs, N.J.: Prentice-Hall, 1972).
107. Harold Burson, ''The Public Relations Function in the Socially Responsible Corporation,'' in Melvin Anshen (ed.), *Managing the Socially Responsible Corporation* (New York: Macmillan, 1974), pp. 224, 227.
108. For an overview of the contingency view, see W. Jack Duncan, *Essentials of Management*, 2d ed. (Hinsdale, Ill.: Dryden, 1978), pp. 373–400.
109. For an example of such research, see James E. Grunig, ''Organizations and Public Relations: Testing a Communication Theory,''

Journalism Monographs No. 46 & November 1976.)

ADDITIONAL READING

Bernays, Edward L., *Biography of an Idea: Memoirs of Public Relations Counsel Edward L. Bernays* (New York: Simon and Schuster, 1965).

Harlow, Rex, ''Public Relations Definitions Through the Years,'' *Public Relations Review* 3 (Spring 1977):49–63.

Harlow, Rex, ''A Timeline of Public Relations,'' *Public Relations Review* 6 (Fall 1980):3–13.

Harris, Neil, *Humbug: The Art of P. T. Barnum* (Chicago: University of Chicago Press, 1981).

Hiebert, Ray Eldon, *Courtier to the Crowd* (Ames: Iowa State University Press, 1966).

Hill, John W. *The Making of a Public Relations Man* (New York: David McKay, 1963).

Hill and Knowlton Executives, *Critical Issues in Public Relations* (Englewood Cliffs, N.J.: Prentice-Hall, 1975).

Public Relations Review, Special Issue on Public Relations in American History, Vol. 4 (Fall 1978).

3

PUBLIC RELATIONS
AND PUBLIC RESPONSIBILITY

"Public relations is the practice of social responsibility. It holds the key to America's future."

So said Edward L. Bernays when he spoke to the public relations division of the Association for Education in Journalism, meeting at Boston University in August 1980.

To the average person, that statement may seem like a contradiction in terms. For, as we saw in the last chapter, today's public relations profession evolved from the work of nineteenth-century practitioners who believed "there's a sucker born every minute" or "the public be damned." Every major practitioner since Ivy Lee, however, has claimed responsibility to publics to be an important premise of public relations.

Stepping Up the Pressure

Until recently, organizations have generally believed they were being responsible when they convinced the public to do something they thought was to the public's benefit— such as buying a good product.

Today, powerful interest groups have made it clear that they believe organizations frequently have not been responsible to their publics. Harold Burson, of Burson-Marsteller, put it this way in an acceptance address when he was named Public Relations Professional-of-the-Year in 1977:

Answers were easier to come by 30 years ago. . . . Life was much simpler. Public relations was largely marketing oriented. Product publicity was very much the name of the game. A good public relations practitioner understood his company, understood its products and understood the marketplace where those products were sold. . . . It was obvious that the purpose of public relations was *to make the cash register ring*.

In the intervening years, the corporation has ceased to be solely an economic entity and has become a social entity as well. And that was really the making of public relations. Suddenly we broke through the old product-marketing syndrome. All at once we had to deal with the myriad social problems that beset the corporation. Consumerists and environmentalists. Women's lib and minority employment. One day we were harassed by NOW, the next by the Sierra Club. Pressure groups began to rally public support to their broader purposes, for better or for worse.[1]

Activist publics may have created headaches for organizations, but, as Burson so clearly stated, they have also created the conditions for public relations to become an important profession that works to better society. Public, or social, responsibility has become a major reason for an organization to have a public relations function. The modern public relations person frequently serves as an ombudsman for the public inside the corporation. John C. Tuffy, director of communications at McGraw-Edison Co., has stated that his staff serves "as a 'watchdog' for corporate transgressions." Tuffy said, for example, that his department "heightened the awareness of corporate management by inducing the company to abandon use of the chemical PCB in electrical capacitors and by encouraging the development of a safer substitute fluid."[2]

Achieving Balanced Communication

The pressure for public responsibility also created the conditions needed for the two-way symmetric model of public relations to replace the other three models. Balanced, two-way communication provides the most effective mechanism for an organization to evaluate its social responsibility.

Nevertheless, practitioners of the other models can also promote organizational public responsibility. The press agent/publicist or the two-way asymmetric practitioner should not attempt to persuade members of publics to do something that could harm them. The public-information specialist should report to the public what the organization has done to be responsible and should explain lapses into irresponsibility.

In none of the models does the practitioner have a license for irresponsibility. As we will see in the next chapter, public responsibility is one of the articles in the codes of ethics of professional public relations organizations.

The literature on public responsibility most often applies the concept to business corporations. Most business schools have courses in business and society or business policy. The Academy of Management has a social issues in management division. And there is a healthy and growing segment of social science research on corporate social responsibility. Thus, much of the social science research we will apply to defining the role of public relations in public responsibility in this chapter will be derived from literature on business.

It is as important for governmental and nonprofit organizations to be socially responsible as for business firms. Later in the chapter, we will discuss how. We prefer to use the term "public responsibility" rather than the more common "social responsibility" used in the business literature. We believe organizations can identify consequences on *publics* more easily than on *society*. We will elaborate the difference later in the chapter.

Let us first look at some issues of corporate responsibility, or irresponsibility, to understand what is involved. Second, we will suggest why an organization should be responsible to its publics. Then we will look at definitions of public responsibility taken from the literature on corporate social responsibility. Finally, we will describe what public relations people have done, and can do, to promote public responsibility in the organizations for which they work.

SOME ISSUES OF PUBLIC RESPONSIBILITY

It sounds exciting, and fairly simple, for an organization to be socially responsible. Advocates of social responsibility generally define it as making a contribution to, and not having adverse consequences on, the larger society of which an organization is a part.

Some issues in which social responsibility is in question are fairly clear-cut. Consider the following cases in which the organization changed when it found publics did not want what it wanted:

The Salt Institute hired the Carl Byoir public relations agency to attack environmentalists who wanted to ban the use of salt on roads. Byoir's research, however, supported the environmentalists' claims. Thus, the agency helped the institute develop proposals for laws that would provide for realistic use of salt.

The Road Information Program wanted to convince the public to build a second interstate highway system. Research by the Byoir agency showed the public didn't want a second system. It wanted improvements in existing highways. Thus, the agency worked out a public relations program to promote improvements.

In other cases, the organization—at least in the public eye—clearly was irresponsible. In three highly publicized cases—Firestone Tire and Rubber and its Model 500 radials, Ford Motor and its Pinto gas tanks, and Allied Chemical and its Kepone insecticide in the James River—companies did not provide full information on the dangers of their products and suffered serious damage in credibility with their publics.

There are many other situations in which the line between responsibility and irresponsibility is less clear. Let's consider three highly publicized cases.

Three-Mile Island

When the Metropolitan Edison Company built a nuclear power plant at Three-Mile Island near Harrisburg, Pennsylvania, it developed an extensive community-relations and educational program to explain the benefits of nuclear power. Metropolitan Edison no doubt sincerely believed that the public would benefit from nuclear power and that the nuclear plant could do little harm. Thus, it actively promoted nuclear power.

The company opened an observation center near the plant with displays on energy sources, the atom, uranium, and economic benefits of nuclear power. An average of 15,000 people visited the center each year, saw slide shows, and took home booklets. Metropolitan Edison also gave courses to teachers on nuclear power and made presentations to schoolchildren. Members of the community heard nothing but good about the plant. Metropolitan Edison told people nearby that even during the worst possible accident they could remain within a half-mile of the plant without danger.

Then, in March 1979, the impossible accident occurred. People in the community had not been informed before the accident of the dangers of a nuclear accident. The public relations people at Metropolitan Edison were not prepared to give members of publics information they needed about the danger from the plant. The public was poorly informed during a major crisis.

Most neutral observers would agree that nuclear power has public benefits and that accidents rarely occur. But it also has some dangers. Other power companies have promoted nuclear power in the same way as Metropolitan Edison. They believe nuclear power will help to resolve the energy shortage. Had the Three-Mile Island accident not occurred, few people would have considered Metropolitan Edison to be irresponsible.[3]

Love Canal

From 1942 to 1953, the Hooker Chemical Co., now a subsidiary of Occidental Petroleum, used an abandoned canal near Niagara Falls, New York—the Love Canal, named after its builder William T. Love—as a dumping site for chemical waste. The canal had been built with an impermeable clay bottom and sides that prevented the chemicals from seeping out. Hooker covered the waste materials with a similar clay seal. Hooker disposed of the wastes at the time in a way that would have met the federal standards for chemical disposal in force today.

Before the accident at the Three-Mile Island nuclear plant near Harrisburg, Pennsylvania, the Metropolitan Edison Company carried on an intensive program to educate people about nuclear power. The visitor center at the plant was an important part of this educational program. (GPU Nuclear Corporation photo)

By 1953, houses had been built in the area surrounding Love Canal, and the Niagara Falls Board of Education wanted the site for a school. Under the threat that the school board planned to take the property by eminent domain, Hooker deeded the land to the board for $1. Although no restriction was written in the deed, Hooker and the board had an understanding that only surface construction would be allowed on the site so as not to disturb the chemicals.

The school board removed soil in building the school, however, and later sold part of the land to private developers. The city built streets, and the state of New York put an expressway over the property, also disturbing the chemicals. As a result, the clay seal was broken, water entered the then buried canal, and chemicals overflowed into the soil. Eventually, chemicals entered nearby basements, sewers, drainage ditches, and the air.

Although there was much debate over the scientific credibility of the claims, the Environmental Protection Agency and state agencies claimed residents of the area suffered greater "risk of cancer, congenital malformations in their offspring, and an increased incidence of miscarriages and abortions."

Eleven of thirty-six residents tested by the EPA supposedly had suffered chromosome damage.

School board and newspaper records show that Hooker Chemical repeatedly had warned against disturbing the dumping site. The school board, state, and city did so anyway. In 1979, however, the EPA filed a complaint in U. S. District Court in Buffalo, N. Y., charging that "Hooker neither warned residents and developers in the vicinity that contact with materials at the Canal could be injurious, nor did it take any action to prevent future injuries due to exposure of the wastes." Did Hooker do enough to warn residents? Did it have a responsibility after it gave up the property? Hooker probably met its legal obligations, but should it have assumed greater responsibility in cleaning up the site?[4]

The Infant-Formula Controversy

The Nestlé Co., a Swiss company with an American subsidiary, has manufactured infant formula for over 100 years and has sold it in underdeveloped countries for over sixty years. Activist groups, most notably the Infant Formula Action Coalition (INFACT) and the Interfaith Center on Corporate Responsibility of the National Council of Churches, charged that Nestlé has actively promoted use of formula by poor mothers to the detriment of their children. The groups initiated a boycott of Nestlé products in the United States.

To promote the formula to poor mothers, Nestlé distributed free samples, sent out sales representatives dressed in white and called them "milk" nurses, sponsored "healthy baby" contests, and provided promotional materials in health centers and to health professionals. The activist groups claimed that poor mothers often mix the formula with contaminated water, causing increased disease and death in infants. They also claimed that poor mothers cannot afford to buy enough formula to feed their babies adequately. Thus,

they claimed, the babies suffer from malnutrition when breast feeding could have provided a more adequate supply of milk.

Nestlé claimed malnutrition in underdeveloped countries would be a problem even with breast feeding. In addition, Nestlé believes formula provides an important supplement to a mother's milk, which would be inadequate after the child reaches three months of age. Nestlé also claimed that formula provides mothers an alternative to breast feeding, which women throughout the world increasingly desire.

The Pan American Health Organization, the U.N. Food and Agriculture Organization, the World Health Organization, the International Pediatric Association, and other world health groups have argued for restrictions on the promotion of infant formula in underdeveloped countries. Nestlé made some superficial changes in marketing, such as changing the color of the "nurses' " uniforms to blue and restricting advertising. It also called for global solutions to malnutrition, rather than placing the responsibility on one company.

In 1981, all members of the World Health Organization except the United States voted for an international code regulating the marketing of infant formula. Is Nestlé responsible when it provides a product that it believes benefits users? Or should it give in to the pressure of activists who believe just the opposite?[5]

Were These Organizations Irresponsible?

In each of these cases, the organization did not perceive itself as a villain blindly pursuing its self-interest in spite of adverse consequences on its publics. And a fair judge who has heard both points of view might even agree that the three companies had not been irresponsible. Yet, the public mind probably pictures Metropolitan Edison, Hooker, and Nestlé as corporate criminals.

These cases are typical. Determining what

is public responsibility can never be an exact decision. Ultimately, however, publics decide whether organizations have been responsible. Thus, public relations professionals must help the organization to realize when publics believe it is behaving irresponsibly. They then should suggest how the organization can be *responsive* to its publics. At the same time, public relations professionals must also help publics understand organizational behavior, so that they can make judgments about the responsibility of that behavior based on knowledge, not on hearsay and innuendo.

WHY BE RESPONSIBLE TO PUBLICS?

Eventually, nearly every public relations professional who advocates public responsibility in an organization has to face this question: Why should we be socially responsible? What's in it for us?

The question also helps to explain why an organization needs a public relations department. Public responsibility is a basic tenet of public relations. If the organization does not need to be responsible to its publics, it also does not need a public relations function.

The question has been answered in two ways. One approach is to stress altruism. Organizations have an obligation to be responsible—even if it is not in their self-interest. In a landmark statement on corporate social responsibility in 1971, for example, the Committee for Economic Development stated, "Business functions by public consent, and its basic purpose is to serve constructively the needs of society—to the benefit of society."[6]

Altruism often makes an effective argument, until it begins to cost money. Then there is a much more effective argument. Publics that perceive organizations to be irresponsible frequently turn to government for help. Government usually helps by formulating regulations and restrictions. It costs an organization a great deal to comply. Randall

Meyer, president of Exxon, stated this premise well in a lecture at the University of Chicago in 1977:

> What should trouble us most about this pervasive public concern with the performance and responsiveness of leading private institutions is that it leads inevitably to an increasingly restrictive environment. . . . Increasingly, the public has turned to government for legislation or controls which are designed to force private institutions to be responsive to societal demands. . . . A multiplicity of these laws and regulations today hamstring industry and commerce. . . . And there are, of course, similar inequities and problems that have been created by the growing government involvement in the activities and planning of privately supported colleges and universities.[7]

Meyer added that the trend toward a restrictive environment can be reversed only if the pressure for government involvement in the private sector is relieved. That means making certain that organizations are in "harmony with society." In addition, he said, "An institution that expects to survive must maintain a strong communications link with other members of the private sector, with the government, and with the public."

Meyer has, therefore, answered our question. The organization must be responsible to maintain the freedom to behave in the way it wants, which it must do in order to be profitable or to achieve other goals. And it needs a communication link—a public relations function—to show what it has done to be responsible.

We can also use the concept of *systems* to express this idea theoretically. In Chapter 1, we said that an organization is a system composed of several subsystems. Now we can look at the organization as a subsystem of a larger "suprasystem," or a system in an environment that consists of other systems. Those systems include the government, publics, and other organizations. Because the organization is part of a larger suprasystem, all the other systems affect its behavior.

Some systems theorists argue that systems cannot survive unless they adapt to their environment—i.e., the environment controls the organization. Therefore, the organization could not survive if it did not respond to the larger society. Other systems theorists argue that the organization controls its environment. By implication, it would not have to be socially responsible.

"Interpenetrating Systems"

Preston and Post have developed a theory midway between these two positions that helps us to understand organizational responsibility.[8] They perceive organizations and systems in their environment as "interpenetrating systems," neither "completely controlling nor controlled by the social environment":

> Society may take into account and seek to influence the goals of the managerial units; and they, in turn, may take into account and seek to influence those of society at large. Neither are the two systems completely separate and independent nor does either control the other; their relationship is better described in terms of interpenetration.

Organizations, therefore, can seldom completely control other interpenetrating systems, nor do they always have to behave in the ways those other systems desire. Public responsibility results from communication, negotiation, and compromise between interpenetrating systems. It does not result from complete subservience to outside systems or from complete control of those other systems.

This theory of interpenetrating systems suggests that the press agentry and two-way asymmetric models of public relations will be practiced by organizations that attempt to control interpenetrating systems in the environment.[9] The two-way symmetric and, to a lesser extent, the public-information models will be practiced by organizations that could

simply adapt to other systems but, more often, negotiate with other systems.

HOW TO BE RESPONSIBLE TO PUBLICS

The public relations practitioner wanting some help on how to define the social responsibilities of business will have no difficulty finding suggestions in the literature on corporate social responsibility.

Students in a graduate seminar at the University of Maryland reviewed twelve representative books on corporate social responsibility and constructed a list of sixty-four business social responsibilities.[10] They grouped these responsibilities into the categories of ecology and environmental quality, consumerism, community needs, governmental relations, business contributions, economic activities, minorities and disadvantaged persons, labor relations, stockholder relations, communication, and research and development for national needs.

Categorizing Responsibilities

Johnston, in a chapter in a U. S. Department of Commerce task force report on corporate social performance, described thirteen categories of responsibilities that corporations could measure.[11] He listed ninety-two specific measures of responsibility under those thirteen categories. These categories, with one sample measure of each, are:

1. Economic Impact: number of new jobs created by type and location.
2. Quality of Products: number and type of product liability complaints.
3. Consumer Relations: number of complaints, by type; turnaround time.
4. Environmental Impacts: level of emissions, by type of pollutant.
5. Energy Conservation: amounts of energy conserved, by major type.
6. Employee Relations: Equal employment: number of minorities and women em-

ployed in nine categories defined by the U. S. Equal Employment Opportunity Commission.

7. Employee Relations: Job satisfaction: number of employees involved in career-advancement programs, or provision of day care.

8. Employee Relations: Occupational safety and health: number of accidents, by type.

9. Investments (primarily for banks and insurance companies): investments that have social impact and that may be risky and have below-normal rates of return.

10. Community Relations: Voluntary contributions: assessment of impact of charitable contributions.

11. Community Relations: Minority economic development: dollar amounts of goods and services purchased from minority-owned firms.

12. Other Community Relations Activities: number and type of community activities held on company property.

13. Government Relations: number and occupation of employees who have direct contact with government officials.

FIGURE **3–1**   **A Widening Circle of Business Social Responsibilities**

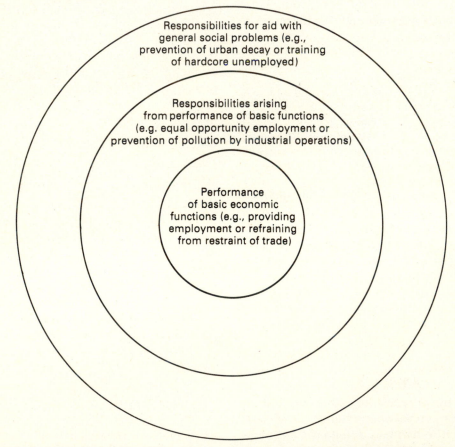

Responsibilities for aid with general social problems (e.g., prevention of urban decay or training of hardcore unemployed)

Responsibilities arising from performance of basic functions (e.g. equal opportunity employment or prevention of pollution by industrial operations)

Performance of basic economic functions (e.g., providing employment or refraining from restraint of trade)

From *Business and Society: Environment and Responsibility*, 3d ed., by Keith Davis and Robert L. Blomstrom. Copyright © 1975 by McGraw-Hill Book Company. Redrawn with the permission of McGraw-Hill Book Company.

This list gives a good idea of what many people expect of corporations today. The question, then, is which should the organization emphasize? Can it do them all? Which responsibilities should the public relations manager advocate to management?

We can get a better grip on the problem if we place these organizational responsibilities into three categories (Figure 3–1):

1. The performance of the organization's basic tasks.
2. The organization's concern with the consequences of those activities on other groups outside the organization.
3. The organization's concern with helping to solve general social problems not connected to the organization.

The conservative economist Milton Friedman has argued that a corporation has only the first responsibility. Business will be socially responsible when it increases its profits, he argues, and it has no business spending the consumer's and the stockholder's money on social problems.[12]

Preston and Post extend the responsibility to the second category, arguing that the corporation should have responsibility for what they call primary and secondary involvements.[13] They believe the firm should produce quality products and services and make a profit. They also believe the firm should clean up the fallout from those primary activities, such as pollution, product hazards, or discrimination in employment. But, they argue, the corporation should not involve itself with such social problems as the public education system, housing standards, general health issues, or voting rights.

"Public" versus "Social" Responsibility

Preston and Post use the term "public responsibility" to describe the primary and secondary involvements. They say the term "social responsibility" includes the third category of general social problems. Social responsibility, they add, has no boundary. The organization can never define where its responsibilities begin and end. Public responsibility provides the manager a better criterion of the organization's responsibility, because it suggests that the organization will be responsible if it deals with the consequences of its primary and secondary involvements and no more.

If you look back to Figure 1–2, you will discover that this definition of public responsibility fits squarely with our definition of a public relations problem. We said that an organization faces a public relations problem when it has consequences on publics or when publics have consequences upon the organization. An organization, therefore, will exercise public responsibility if it deals with its public relations problems. And, as the statement by Bernays at the beginning of this chapter suggested, public relations and public responsibility become synonymous.

The Preston and Post argument received strong support in a study of public opinion about corporate social responsibility conducted at the University of Maryland.[14] A random sample of 200 Maryland residents was asked how much responsibility business, government, individuals, and interest groups should have for eleven representative issues of corporate responsibility. Two issues represented primary responsibilities: quality of products and services, and profits. Five represented consequences of the primary activities, or secondary involvements: pollution, inflation, monopoly, human relations on the job, and employment of minorities. Finally, respondents were asked about four general social issues: decay of the cities, quality of education, support of charities, and general unemployment.

The researchers grouped respondents into three different publics (using methods to be described in Chapter 7). All three publics agreed that corporations should have responsibility for the things business was designed to do—produce products and services and make profits—and for the consequences of that activity—pollution, human relations, monopoly, etc. They believed, for example, that government and individuals should have responsibility for education, and individuals for charitable contributions. One activist public believed business should share some responsibility for the social problems, but still assigned primary responsibility to organizations other than business. For governmental and charitable organizations, solution of the social problems is a primary activity.

In contrast to this study, a study of 192 *Fortune* 500 companies in 1977 showed that investment in two of the broad social areas (charities and education) represented by far the largest areas of corporate social investment.[15] But the same survey showed that these companies had begun to move toward "specialized social interests"—those areas in which business has public consequences.

What, then, should organizations do to exercise public responsibility? Clearly, it seems, they should practice public relations and use communication to help solve their public relations problems. Let's look next at how that can be done.

HOW PR CONTRIBUTES TO ORGANIZATIONAL RESPONSIBILITY

Public relations, as we have said several times, is a communication function. Therefore, public relations managers seldom have the power to make an organization publicly responsible. What they can do is communicate to organizational subsystems what publics believe to be irresponsible organizational behaviors. They can also report to publics what the organization has done that is responsible or irresponsible, and what it is doing to rectify the areas of irresponsibility. Let's look at each public relations contribution in turn.

Internal Reporting

Preston and Post point out that organizations that put the principle of public responsibility into action must make fundamental changes in structure and policy when they realize they have been irresponsible.[16] They add that public responsibility must also be a criterion applied to management decisions and to the rewards given for individual performance by employees.

Changes in structure, policy, and rewards require decisions by top management. Public relations administrators may participate in top-management decisions, but they cannot make them alone. Thus, many public relations people perceive themselves to be a failure when top management does not do exactly what the public's ombudsman, the PR person, wants.

Never, however, should public relations managers expect to have their advice followed at all times. The important thing is that the PR manager *communicate* public perceptions of the organization's responsibility to top managers and to other subsystems that may behave in a way the public considers irresponsible.

Melvin Anshen, a Columbia University business professor and consultant to the Burson-Marsteller public relations agency, stated in a book on the socially responsible corporation that the public relations person must be "inside the door" when management decisions are made, not waiting "outside the door" to announce that decision once other managers had made it.[17] You may recall the short-lived tenure of Jerald terHorst as press secretary to President Gerald Ford. TerHorst resigned after President Ford pardoned former President Nixon, not so much because he disagreed with the decision, but because he had not been included in the making of the decision.

Many major corporations have formalized the internal reporting of perceived public responsibility into a process called "issues management." Some practitioners quibble about the term "management" because it suggests that organizations can control issues. What the public relations manager does in fact do is alert the organization to issues of responsibility, so that those issues are included in management decisions. According to Jones and Chase, issues management has four stages:

1. Issue identification.
2. Issue analysis.
3. Issue change strategy options.
4. Issue action programs.[18]

Anshen has argued that the public relations manager in the responsible organization must go beyond the traditional public relations function of product and corporate publicity.[19] He said the new public relations manager must provide an early-warning system to alert the organization of public concern about organizational behavior before publics go to government, try to elect consumer members to boards of directors, or petition the courts or regulatory agencies. Remember that those actions cost the organization money.

Secondly, Anshen said the PR manager must be brought "in from the cold" to participate in organizational decision making. In the decision-making arena, the public relations manager must ask such questions as: Has the company implemented personnel policies so that it will not be fined, given hiring quotas, or subjected to adverse publicity? Is the company vulnerable to attacks from interest groups? Should the company support or oppose a government policy?

Finally, Anshen said managers of employee communication must do more than inform employees about management policy—their traditional role. They must also sensitize employees to public responsibility so that all members of the organization practice it.

External Reporting

Organizations that report what they have done to be publicly responsible usually do so through a "social report" or "social audit."[20] The social audit was a hot topic of discussion among public relations professionals in the early 1970s, but most organizations that now evaluate and report their social responsibility do so through a report rather than through an audit.

Social audits, at least in theory, quantify public responsibility and balance the dollar value of the social "goods" against the social "bads" produced by an organization. One of the most advanced social audits was that produced by Clark Abt on his own consulting firm, Abt Associates of Cambridge, Massachusetts.[21] The ideal social audit would be constructed by an outside accounting firm and would meet the same standards as a financial audit.[22] Few organizations produce quantified social audits today, however, as the cost and value of organizational consequences on publics cannot easily be measured.

Many organizations, on the other hand, produce social reports on what they have done to contribute to the public good. Figure 3–2, for example, shows the cover of General Motors' "Public Interest Report" for 1982. In its public interest reports, General Motors has discussed such issues as the Clean Air Act, small-car safety, General Motors in South Africa, equal employment opportunity, programs for minorities and women, plant closings and relocations, philanthropic activities, the cost of government regulations, and tax revenues generated by GM activities.

One of the most extensive social reports is produced by the Clearinghouse on Corporate Social Responsibility, an organization sponsored by the American Council of Life Insurance and the Health Insurance Association of America. The clearinghouse prepares a single social report for over 200 insurance

FIGURE 3–2

General Motors' 1982 "Public Interest Report"

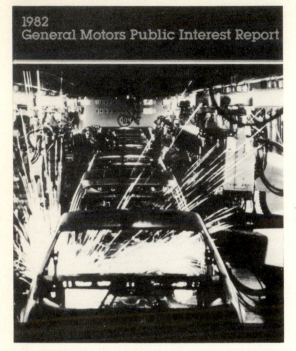

1982
General Motors Public Interest Report

Courtesy General Motors Corporation

companies. It distributes a reporting form to participating companies and reports the results in a monthly newsletter called "Response" and an annual "Social Report of the Life and Health Insurance Business." In the reporting form, each company lists its community projects, company contributions, environment and energy conservation, equal employment opportunity for women and minorities, individual involvement of employees in community projects, and social investments.

In October 1978, then Secretary of Commerce Juanita Kreps suggested in a speech at Duke University that the Commerce Department produce a "social index" to measure corporate involvement in social issues.[23] The proposal upset many business leaders, who

feared intrusion of government into business and eventual government regulations forcing social involvement. Her proposal was never implemented. The Commerce Department had been interested in business social involvement since 1961, however, when Secretary Luther Hodges organized a Business Ethics Advisory Council. The Commerce Department did establish a task force on corporate social performance that published a report in 1979.[24]

The task force presented a dismal picture of the status of corporate social reporting. It reported that 89 percent of *Fortune* 500 firms reported on their social performance in 1977 and that almost 50 percent had done so consistently over the previous five-year period. However, the task force added that the average social report was .56 pages long (about half a page). Generally, corporations include their social report in their annual financial report. The task force also found most social reports to be self-serving:

> Features that distinguish good social reporting include consistency, objectivity, comparability, and relevance to appropriate social concerns. A great deal of current social reporting lacks these qualities. Consistent reporting from year to year is the exception. Reports seldom advise readers of shortcomings in company social performance. Candid statements concerning the adverse social impacts of company operations are rarely found.[25]

The task force cited nine companies that did candidly discuss their social performance, including the General Motors Public Interest Report that we have already discussed. Two other examples will show how an organization can be forthright in discussing its problems and what it has done about them. Eastern Gas and Fuel Associates of Boston stated:

> Our industrial accident record in recent years has not been good. One standard measurement is the accident frequency rate (number of accidents versus hours worked), and our

rate has almost doubled in the last three years, going up most dramatically in gas operations. It is clear that our safety performance has been slipping. In addition, it seems that our record is poorer than that of a number of firms with whom we have compared specific records.[26]

Atlantic Richfield (ARCO) stated:

It's easy to find women and minorities for our clerical and trade positions but it's not easy in professional areas. . . . We established guidelines for our managers. Now we're trying to put some teeth into them by making our vice presidents accountable for equal employment opportunity performance. The size of their paychecks will depend in part on how well they provide opportunities for women and minorities.[27]

Organizations, it seems, can report their public performance. And they can do it in a balanced and candid way. It is the task of the public relations manager to stress the need for public responsibility, and to ask management to prepare regular social reports. If management agrees, it is then the job of the PR department to research and write the social report.

FROM BUSINESS TO ORGANIZATIONAL PUBLIC RESPONSIBILITY

Throughout the discussion of public responsibility in this chapter, we have talked about *organizational* responsibility, even though most of the research and theory we have drawn upon has been based on *business* social responsibility. We must ask, however, whether the concept of public responsibility applies equally to organizations other than large business corporations. Our answer is a clear yes.

All organizations have secondary involvements as well as primary involvements. And secondary involvements nearly always produce the need to monitor public responsibility. For business firms, economic concerns represent primary involvements, and the social spillover from them produces secondary involvements. For nonbusiness organizations, in contrast, social concerns represent primary involvements, which can produce secondary economic and social consequences on publics.

Let's look at a few examples to clarify the basic idea:

The primary task of the Environmental Protection Agency (EPA) is to protect the environment. But in applying environmental regulations to, let us say, the steel industry, the EPA might unduly damage the financial health of the industry, cost some employees their jobs, and damage the balance of payments position of the United States.

A hospital may build what it hopes will be the finest shock trauma unit in the city to save the lives of accident victims. But if other nearby hospitals already have such a unit, the new unit may unduly raise the cost of hospital care for all patients in the city.

A church may consider a campaign against abortion to be its moral obligation, but should it not also consider the social costs of laws that prohibit abortion—such as abortions performed by semicompetent physicans, emotional suffering, marital distress, etc.?

The National Rifle Association may campaign for what it believes is the constitutional right to bear arms, but should it not also consider the lives lost because of guns?

Public relations managers should be "inside the door" of management in all kinds of organizations where they can provide internal social reports on the organization's public performance.

We must pause for a moment, however, to think whether nonbusiness organizations should also produce external social reports as well. The need seems strong for economic organizations—business firms—to report their social consequences. But there seems to be an equal need for social organizations to report their secondary economic and social consequences. Should not the EPA report the economic costs of environmental regulations and what it has done to minimize those costs? Should a hospital not report what it has done to control costs as well as to save lives? Should not the NRA regularly report the number of lives taken by guns, what it has done to reduce that number, and how effective it has been?

Anshen points out that public relations practitioners trained only to be "communication technicians" seldom will have the skills needed to "participate effectively in the decision process at the level of corporate policy."[28] He added that "sophisticated communication skills will continue to be important elements in the enlarged public relations function," but that the communication technician "will lack the technical knowledge and skills of the public relations professional."

The key word is "professional." It is the role of public relations managers in monitoring and communicating about public responsibility that makes them more than press agents for whatever self-serving organization chooses to hire them. That role makes them professionals. In the next chapter, then, we will examine what it means to be a public relations professional.

NOTES

1. "The 'Bottom Line' in Public Relations," Burson-Marsteller Report No. 46, November 1977.
2. "The Corporate Image: PR to the Rescue," *Business Week*, January 22, 1979, p. 54.
3. Sharon M. Friedman, "Blueprint for Breakdown: TMI and the Media Before the Accident," paper presented to the Association for Education in Journalism, Boston, August 10, 1980. Friedman was a consultant to the President's Commission on the accident at Three-Mile Island from June to October 1979.
4. See "Notoriety Makes Love Canal a Symbol, Which Hooker Treats as a Local Issue; Classic Case of Legal Facts vs. Public Feeling," *PR Reporter*, Sept. 8, 1980. See also three Hooker FactLine booklets, "What the *Wall Street Journal* said about Love Canal," "Love Canal: The Facts (1892–1980)," and "No Demonstrated Health Effects from Love Canal Chemicals, Says Medical Review Study," Hooker Chemical Co., Public Affairs Dept., Houston, Texas.
5. Based on statements provided by the Infant Formula Action Coalition, Minneapolis; the Interfaith Center on Corporate Responsibility, National Council of Churches, New York; and "The Infant Formula Controversy: A Nestlé View," The Nestlé Company, White Plains, New York.
6. Committee for Economic Development, "Social Responsibilities of Business Corporations," New York, 1971.
7. Randall Meyer, "Responding to Public Expectations of Private Institutions: A Matter of Survival," Invitation Lecture Series, University of Chicago, April 20, 1977. Reprinted by the Public Affairs Department, Exxon Company, U.S.A., Houston, Texas.
8. Lee E. Preston and James E. Post, *Private Management and Public Policy: The Principle of Public Responsibility* (Englewood Cliffs, N. J.: Prentice-Hall, 1975), pp. 24–27.
9. For systems theories that show how organizations use asymmetric communication to attempt to control their environment, see George A. Donohue, Phillip J. Tichenor, and Clarice Olien, "Mass Media Functions, Knowledge, and Social Control," *Journalism Quarterly* 50 (1973):652–659; and Oscar H. Gandy, Jr., "The Economics of Image Building: The Information Subsidy in Health," in Emile G. McAnany, Jorge Schnitman, and Noreene Janus (eds.), *Communication and Social Structure* (New York: Praeger, 1981), pp. 204–239. Gandy argues that public relations people in health organizations only provide information that supports the organization. Thus, the "subsidized information" they provide will not always tell publics all they need to know about health issues.
10. Reported in James E. Grunig, "A New Measure of Public Opinions on Corporate Social Responsibility," *Academy of Management Journal* 22 (1979):738–764.

11. David C. H. Johnston, ''The Management and Measurement of Corporate Social Performance,'' in U. S. Department of Commerce Task Force on Corporate Social Performance, *Corporate Social Reporting in the United States and Western Europe*, (Washington: Dept. of Commerce, July 1979), pp. 110–142.
12. Milton Friedman, ''The Social Responsibility of Business Is to Increase Its Profits,'' *New York Times Magazine*, September 13, 1970.
13. Preston and Post, pp. 52–53, 95–98.
14. Grunig, note 10.
15. S. L. Holmes, ''Corporate Social Performance: Past and Present Areas of Commitment,'' *Academy of Management Journal* 20 (1977):433–438.
16. Preston and Post, pp. 129–135.
17. Melvin Anshen (ed.), *Managing the Socially Responsible Corporation* (New York: Macmillan, 1974), p. 237.
18. Barrie L. Jones and W. Howard Chase, ''Managing Public Policy Issues,'' *Public Relations Review* 5 (Summer 1979):3–23.
19. Melvin Anshen, *Corporate Strategies for Social Performance* (New York: Columbia University Press, 1980), pp. 210–229. (A chapter entitled ''Relations with Publics.'')
20. Otto Lerbinger, ''How Far Toward the Social Audit?'' *Public Relations Review* 1 (Summer 1975):38–52.
21. Clark C. Abt, ''The Social Audit Technique for Measuring Socially Responsible Performance.'' In Melvin Anshen (ed.), *Managing the Socially Responsible Corporation* (New York: Macmillan, 1974), pp. 92–122.
22. American Institute of Certified Accountants, *The Measurement of Corporate Social Performance* (New York: 1977).
23. The speech is reprinted in abridged form in the *Public Relations Journal* 34 (June 1978):10–11. See also Carlton E. Spitzer, ''Does Business Need a Social Responsiveness Index?'' *Public Relations Journal* 34 (June 1978):8–10.
24. U. S. Department of Commerce Task Force on Corporate Social Performance.
25. U. S. Department of Commerce Task Force, p. 12.
26. U. S. Department of Commerce Task Force, p. 13.
27. U. S. Department of Commerce Task Force, p. 16.
28. Anshen, *Corporate Strategies for Social Performance*, p. 220.

ADDITIONAL READING

American Institute of Certified Public Accountants, *The Measurement of Corporate Social Performance* (New York: 1977).

Anshen, Melvin, *Corporate Strategies for Social Performance* (New York: Columbia University Press, 1980).

Buchholz, Rogene A., *Business Environment and Public Policy* (Englewood Cliffs, N. J.: Prentice-Hall, 1982).

Carroll, Archie B., ''A Three-Dimensional Conceptual Model of Corporate Social Performance,'' *Academy of Management Review* 4 (1979):393–404.

Carroll, Archie B., *Business and Society* (Boston: Little, Brown, 1981).

Friedman, Milton, *Capitalism and Freedom* (Chicago: University of Chicago Press, 1962).

Grunig, James E., ''A New Measure of Public Opinions on Corporate Social Responsibility,'' *Academy of Management Journal* 22 (1979):738–764.

Jones, Barrie L., and W. Howard Chase, ''Managing Public Policy Issues,'' *Public Relations Review* 5 (Summer 1979):3–23.

Molander, Earl A., *Responsive Capitalism: Case Studies in Corporate Social Conduct* (New York: McGraw-Hill, 1980).

Preston, Lee E., and James E. Post, *Private Management and Public Policy: The Principle of Public Responsibility* (Englewood Cliffs, N. J.: Prentice-Hall, 1975).

Sawyer, George C., *Business and Society: Managing Corporate Social Impact* (Boston: Houghton Mifflin, 1979).

Sethi, S. Prakash, and Carl L. Swanson, *Private Enterprise and Public Purpose* (New York: Wiley, 1981).

Task Force on Corporate Social Performance, *Corporate Social Reporting in the United States and Western Europe* (Washington: U. S. Department of Commerce, 1979).

Yang, Y. N., *Business Policy and Strategy: Text and Cases* (Santa Monica, Calif.: Goodyear, 1981).

4

PROFESSIONALISM IN PUBLIC RELATIONS

In 1981, the Washington *Post* described a public relations conference in an article that easily could have appeared in 1920—when public relations was just emerging out of press agentry. The writer, who seemed totally unaware that public relations had changed since the nineteenth century, began:

> What happened to the backslapping, what happened to the big men's grill laughs coming out of those cigar-smoking types in stingy-brim hats, guys who were always coming into the newspaper to feed jokes to the columnists in order to publicize their clients? Like, dija hear about the new drink at the KitKat Klub? It's called the Louis XVI—after one of them you lose your head. And hey, howbouta coupla hockey tickets?[1]

The writer then reported meeting James Little, the 1981 president of the Public Relations Society of America, "who puts 'APR' after his name, meaning Accredited Public Relations. . . . He does not call himself a flack, a press agent, or a publicist, N-O no. He is a 'counselor.' "

Little told the skeptical reporter that public relations is a profession:

"We have an identifiable body of knowledge," he (Little) says. "We have an enforceable code of ethics." These are two of the defining characteristics of a profession.

A profession. Okay, if it's a profession, who are the all-time great PR men? What are the great PR cases? Who's the PR version of Dr. De Bakey, what's the PR equivalent of the Scopes trial?

After reading the history of public relations in Chapter 2, you should be able to tell this reporter about the great public relations practitioners and the great public relations cases. He may not pay much attention, however, for many journalists stubbornly refuse to believe public relations is a profession.

Journalists are not the only skeptics. Harold Wilensky, a sociologist who has researched professionalism, lumped public relations with funeral directing only a few years ago:

> Many occupations will assert claims to professional status and find that the claims are honored by no one but themselves. I am inclined to place here occupations in which a market

orientation is overwhelming—public relations, advertising, and funeral directing.[2]

Wanted: Smooth-Talkers

Many people snicker when told public relations is a profession because they have formed an impression of PR work from people in other occupations who incorrectly describe their work as public relations. A recent FBI wanted poster, for example, described the suspect's occupation as "used car salesman and public relations consultant." An article in the July 12, 1981, issue of the Fort Lauderdale *News/Sun-Sentinel* reported the arrest of "notorious" Outlaws motorcycle gang member "Big Jim" Nolan in Arizona for "allegedly pumping six bullets into a man at a bar." The arrest report described Nolan's occupation as "public relations man, Dream Enterprises," an organization promoting a Country-and-Western singer who was a former member of the Outlaws. If you read the classified advertisements for public relations positions in your Sunday newspaper, you will find more employers looking for telephone solicitors or receptionists than employers looking for true public relations practitioners.

Some public relations practitioners believe professional guidelines can separate true public relations professionals from publicists and press agents.[3] But many other public relations practitioners question whether public relations is or can be a profession. Mike Ranney, a public relations manager for International Multifoods in Minneapolis, argued in the *Public Relations Journal* that public relations cannot become a profession.[4] Unlike members of established professional groups, he said, public relations people work for "companies or organizations whose goals are relatively self serving . . . most of us must of necessity home in on objectives somewhat narrower than the health of man or the total vitality of our economic system." Ranney added, in essence, that professionalism may be only a security blanket that public rela-

tions people grab to overcome the "frustration of being unable to directly influence the events of organizations and their operations."

The majority of public relations practitioners since Ivy Lee and Edward Bernays changed the field in the early 1900s have argued, however, that public relations must become a profession. On the one hand, public relations practitioners will have much more respect for themselves and their careers if they meet professional standards. Eventually, professional status will also gain respect for public relations from journalists and the rest of society.

Even more importantly, however, professionalism may also be required for you to make it as a public relations practitioner in the future. In the previous chapter, we discussed the role of public relations in promoting organizational responsibility. We said that role would distinguish the new public relations professional from the traditional communication technician who has called himself a public relations person. In that chapter, we also discussed what Anshen said the new public relations manager must be able to do in the socially responsible corporation. What we did not report was his claim that traditional communication specialists seldom have the required skills for the new public relations role. In many major corporations, Anshen said, the public relations function will "probably be headed by executives whose prior experience has been in other functional areas."[5]

How PR Specialists Rate

A *Wall Street Journal*/Gallup survey taken in 1980 supported Anshen's claim.[6] The poll showed that only 15 percent of 282 heads of big business firms rated the performance of public relations specialists as "very good"—compared to 45 percent for accountants and 39 percent for lawyers. *Business Week* also reported that "lawyers, financial specialists, economists, and operating executives'' now hold many high-level public relations jobs because ''CEO's are saying in effect that PR has become too important to be left in the hands of old-line PR men.''[7]

If professionalism holds the key to the future of public relations, then we must look at the nature of a profession to determine whether the skeptics are right or wrong. Can public relations become a true profession? We must also look at the characteristics of a professional to determine how aspiring public relations practitioners can gain the requisites of professionalism. This chapter, therefore, will first define the nature of a profession. Then we will examine the extent to which public relations meets each of the criteria that distinguish a profession from a nonprofessional occupation: values, associations, norms, body of knowledge, and education.

THE NATURE OF A PROFESSION

In the United States today, baseball players, truck drivers, secretaries, letter carriers, and insurance agents all call themselves ''professionals.'' To most people, a professional is someone who gets paid for doing a job for which he or she has special expertise.

Social science research and theory, however, define professionalism more narrowly. According to sociologists, there traditionally have been three learned professions: law, medicine, and the clergy. In recent years, many new professions have been added to the list: education, engineering, architecture, business management, social work, pharmacy, dentistry, and others. A glance at the list of professional schools in a university catalog will tell you what they are.

Many occupations today strive for professional status. Professions have greater status than other occupations, in part because professionals supposedly care about the good of others and of society as well as about their self-interest. Doctors deliver babies in the middle of the night. Lawyers help indigents defend themselves from false charges. Clergy work for low wages to help others. According to the definition of professionalism, professionals also have high ethical standards and greater autonomy from the control of the large, self-serving organizations and interest groups that control society.

To understand the nature of professionalism, let's look first at why professions benefit society. Then we will examine the characteristics of a professional.

Impact of Professionals on Organizations

John Gardner, a secretary of Health, Education, and Welfare under John F. Kennedy and founder of the public interest group Common Cause, has argued that professionalism of occupations holds the promise of changing organizations and renewing them to the betterment of society.[8]

Traditional professionals, such as lawyers and doctors, worked independently of formal organizations. In that way, they had the autonomy necessary for professional behavior. Many of the new professionals, however, work in formal organizations—such as engineers and business managers in business firms, social workers in government agencies, educators in school systems.

Serving Two Masters • In formal organizations, professionals experience the tug of two allegiances: allegiance to the organization for which they work, and allegiance to the profession from which they gain their values and expertise. Nonprofessional workers, in contrast, judge whether they are doing a good job solely from the feedback they get from their supervisors. Professionals, however, also get feedback about how well they are doing their job from other professionals who do not work for the same organization.

A professional also may often report to a supervisor who knows little about the work the professional does and cannot evaluate it properly. Public relations professionals, for example, often work for managers who know little about public relations. Thus, professionals frequently go outside the organization to find out how well they are doing.

As a result, professionals have more autonomy to perform as they wish, rather than as the organization they work for wishes. That autonomy benefits society, because professionals force the organization to innovate and to be more responsible.[9] The organization that employs large numbers of professionals cannot ''stick its head in the sand,'' because the professionals have continuous contact with other professionals outside the organization. Those outside contacts bring new ideas into the organization, ideas that lead to innovative behavior by the organization.

Organizational research, however, also shows that organizations—especially the rigid, formalized ones—avoid hiring professionals unless they have little choice.[10] New ideas create conflict with old ideas, and many organizations prefer to avoid conflict and change.

In public relations, for example, Grunig found that the practitioners in a sample from the Baltimore-Washington area who scored high on measures of professionalism worked in relatively new and small organizations that had not set up a rigid description of what a public relations person should do.[11] Large, older, and formalized organizations—the ''Archie Bunkers'' of the organizational world—hired nonprofessional public relations people who would not upset the way the organization performs.

Research on the kinds of organizations that most often employ professionals suggests why some organizations practice one of the four models of public relations and others practice a different model. With the press agentry and two-way asymmetric models, the public relations person promotes the organization's interest and does not question it.

Most professionals would feel quite uncomfortable practicing one of these two models, as the quote from Ranney at the beginning of this chapter suggests.[12]

On the other hand, the practitioner following the two-way symmetric model of public relations attempts to change the organization as well as its publics. Only a professional could practice that model. Without professional ties, a practitioner would have difficulty getting outside the organization's ''mindset'' to be able to understand the ideas of outside publics. He or she also would have difficulty resisting organizational pressures not to upset the organization.

Practitioners of the public-information model could be professionals, but most often their professional ties are to journalism rather than public relations. Thus, they often feel like ''prostitutes,'' who must sacrifice journalistic values and report only the positive things about the organizations that employ them.

Consultants: A Fresh Outlook • Although we've talked mostly about professionals working ''in'' organizations, many professionals also work ''for'' organizations as consultants. Public relations practitioners in public relations firms, for example, serve several client organizations. Gardner argued that outside professional consultants offer organizations potential sources of innovation and renewal.[13] An organization can use its own staff of professionals, which could become rigid and out-of-touch with new ideas, or it could bring in outside professionals with fresh ideas.

Gardner added, however, that an organization can select from a large group of outside consultants. If, for example, an organization wants a nonprofessional public relations person, there are agencies that will provide that service. In fact, the pressure on agencies to provide press agentry or two-way asymmetric public relations can be enormous, because an agency needs to provide clients the services they want if the agency is to have enough clients to make a profit.

Thus, professionals in agencies generally have the same sort of relationship with organizations as professionals in organizations. But a single agency professional may be asked to provide a different model of public relations to different organizations. That can put tremendous strain on the truly professional public relations person.

Characteristics of a Professional

A substantial body of knowledge on professionals developed in sociology in the 1950s and 1960s.[14] Beginning in the 1960s, journalism researchers used that literature to develop measures of the professionalism of journalists.[15] In recent years, researchers have applied those same measures to studies of public relations practitioners.[16] The research on professionals helps us to understand what a professional is and suggests criteria to evaluate the professional status of public relations.

Social scientists have defined professionalism as a characteristic of individual practitioners more than as a characteristic of an occupation. There may be professional lawyers, doctors, journalists, or public relations practitioners. There may also be nonprofessional practitioners in each group. However, we could say that an occupation becomes a profession when a majority of its practitioners qualify as professionals.

The research, therefore, generally shows that professionals have five major characteristics:

1. *A set of professional values.* In particular, professionals believe that serving others is more important than their own economic gain. Professionals also strongly value autonomy. That is, they prefer the freedom to perform in the way they think is right to the rewards they may get for conforming to what others want.

2. *Membership in strong professional organizations.* Professional organizations provide professionals with the contact with other professionals that they need to maintain an allegiance to the profession. Professional organizations also accredit practitioners, socialize practitioners to the values of the profession, develop a professional culture, and discipline practitioners who violate the values and ethics of the profession.

3. *Adherence to professional norms.* True professions have a code of ethics and a procedure for enforcing it. Practitioners who violate the code of ethics should be excluded from the professional organization that enforces the code.

4. *An intellectual tradition and an established body of knowledge.* A profession must have a unique and well-established body of knowledge. Professionals understand that body of knowledge and apply it to their work. Nonprofessionals, therefore, cannot provide the same service or expertise as professionals because they do not possess the same knowledge. Several definitions of the ''body of knowledge'' stress that the knowledge consists of systematic theory. Nearly every definition of a profession also stresses that professionals take an intellectual approach to their work.

5. *Technical skills acquired through professional training.* Definitions stress that professionals have the technical skills needed to provide a unique and essential service. The definitions also stress that they acquire these skills during a long period of prescribed professional education. Because professionals develop specialized skills, the profession is usually a ''terminal occupation.'' That is, professionals stay in the occupation their entire lives. They do not begin in the mail room, go to sales when the opportunity arises, then to public relations, and finally to the presidency. Professionals gain satisfaction from improving the services they offer, not from moving into positions with increasing status.[17]

Given these five characteristics of a professional, let's now use each of them in turn to evaluate the professional status of public relations practitioners.

VALUES OF PUBLIC RELATIONS PRACTITIONERS

A number of social scientists have developed scales to measure professional values that can be administered to members of an occupational group to determine their level of professionalism. (See Exhibit 4–1 to take one of these tests yourself.) Some researchers have applied these scales to public relations practitioners. Although the results have been mixed, the total picture emerging from the studies is that only a minority of public relations practitioners hold professional values.

EXHIBIT 4–1   A Self-Test of Professional Values

Answer the following questions, to see if you hold professional values:

1. Different people want different things from their jobs. Check any of the following that you feel are *very* important in a job.

   ( ) Freedom from continual close supervision of your work.
   ( ) Security of the job in its being fairly permanent.
   ( ) Having a job that is valuable and essential to society.
   ( ) Salary: earning enough money for a good living.
   ( ) An opportunity to apply specialized skills and knowledge.
   ( ) Having a prestigious job in your organization.
   ( ) Recognition from other public relations practitioners.
   ( ) Recognition from superiors in your organization.

(The first, third, fifth, and seventh items represent professional values. The other four are careerist values. Did you check more professional than careerist values?)

2. Here are some groups that inevitably judge the quality of professional performance. Check the group whose judgment you believe should count the most when your overall professional performance is assessed.

   ( ) Members of the public.
   ( ) Immediate superiors in your organization.
   ( ) Fellow public relations practitioners.
   ( ) Community leaders.
   ( ) Leaders of public relations associations.

(If you checked fellow public relations practitioners or leaders of public relations associations, you would score highly as a professional. If you checked immediate superiors in your organization, you would score highly as a careerist. It's nice to please members of the public and community leaders, but they do not have the expertise to judge your professional performance. They were included as filler responses.)

Source: James E. Grunig, "Organizations and Public Relations: Testing a Communication Theory," *Journalism Monographs* No. 46, November 1976.

In a study of 216 practitioners in the Baltimore-Washington area, Grunig used four scales to separate the professional from the nonprofessional practitioners.[18] One of these scales measured four professional values:

1. Desire to apply specialized skills and knowledge.
2. Desire for autonomy.
3. Provision of a valuable and essential service to society.
4. Recognition from other public relations practitioners.

A second scale measured preference for four "careerist" values: income, security, status, and recognition from superiors (non-professionals) in the organization. Both of these scales had a possible range of scores from 0 to 3. The average score for the 216 practitioners on the professionalism scale was 1.56. The average on the careerism scale was 2.03. There was not much difference, but the scale showed more careerist than professional values.

Grunig also asked the 216 practitioners the kind of person who could best evaluate their work. Professionals would look to fellow public relations practitioners or to leaders of public relations associations. Careerists would look to immediate superiors in the organization for which they work. Again, these scales had a range of 0 to 3. The average professionalism score was .58, the average careerist score 2.07.

Grunig also measured activity in professional organizations and education in public relations. The "index of professional activity" again could go from 0 to 3. The practitioners got one point for belonging to the Public Relations Society of America, one point for attending four of the previous six meetings, and one point for having ever held an office or presented a program in PRSA. On this index, the average was .70, meaning the average practitioner did not even belong to the major professional organization and thus did not attend meetings, hold office, or present programs.

Fourthly, Grunig asked the practitioners how much training they had in public relations. They got one point for having training in public relations at the bachelor's degree level, one point for having a master's degree, and a third point if the master's degree was in public relations. On a 0 to 3 scale again, the average score was .93, meaning that the average practitioner had some training in public relations but that few had training beyond the bachelor's level.

Wright conducted three similar studies of the professionalism of public relations practitioners in Texas. His first study consisted of intensive interviews with twenty-two practitioners. These practitioners said public relations should strive for professional status, but they also objected to the idea that professional PR people must have a prescribed program of training and be accredited by a professional group, both criteria of a profession.[19]

His second study compared the values of practitioners accredited by the Public Relations Society of America with nonaccredited practitioners.[20] He found the accredited practitioners to have more professional values. But he also found the overall level of professionalism to be quite low. The practitioners, for example, ranked two key professional values—peer recognition and autonomy—much lower than other values.

In a third study, Wright hypothesized that practitioners with high scores on questions measuring professionalism would also have high scores on questions measuring social responsibility.[21] He found that only 10 percent of the 143 Texas practitioners he sampled scored high on both professionalism and social responsibility. Many with strong professional values did not score high on social responsibility, and many who did not have professional values did score high on social responsibility.

McKee, Nayman, and Lattimore found more encouraging results in a study of ninety-three Colorado public relations practitioners.[22] An average of 87 percent of the practitioners they surveyed thought each of ten professional values were extremely or quite important. But an average of 78 percent also rated ten nonprofessional items as extremely or quite important.

Although these results showed more professionalism than those of Grunig, they were quite similar in showing that practitioners scoring highly on professional values still clung to nonprofessional values. Research on the professional values of journalists by Windahl and Rosengren, however, shows that professionals may simultaneously hold both professional and careerist values.[23] In particular, they found that professionals may hold professional values and still value income and "security and promotion" in their company. Professionalism of public relations practitioners, therefore, seems to require not so much the elimination of careerist values as the adding of professional values to the careerist values.

Public Relations and Journalism

There have also been several studies comparing the professional and news values of public relations practitioners and journalists.[24] These studies consistently show that public relations practitioners and journalists have similar professional values and that they make similar news judgments. But the studies also show that journalists strongly believe that the public relations practitioners do not have professional values, do not have news values similar to journalists, and do not have equal occupational status.

Yet the journalists, when asked to rate public relations people *they know* and public relations people in general, consistently believe the practitioners they know are more ethical and professional than practitioners in general. This would suggest that journalists

do regularly work with ethical PR people, but that they continue to hold the traditional biased view of public relations as a profession.

Finally, several studies show that many public relations practitioners would like to be a lot more professional than their employers want them to be. In Wright's intensive interviews, practitioners frequently complained about restrictions management placed on their professionalism. Grunig found that professionals most often worked in small, less formalized organizations that did not have a set—and nonprofessional—definition of public relations.

In the second Wright study and the Nayman, McKee, and Lattimore study, practitioners rated professional values first as to how important they thought the values were and then as to how satisfied they were with their ability to practice the values. Generally, the practitioners rated the importance of the values higher than they rated their satisfaction with actually being able to practice the values.

Nanni attempted to determine why practitioners in fifteen Washington organizations practiced one of the four different models of public relations.[25] She found that heads of public relations departments following the two-way symmetric model almost always reported to an executive officer who had some training in public relations. The top manager's public relations training predicted which organizations would practice the symmetric model better than did the public relations person's training.

Generally, then, research shows that few public relations practitioners hold professional values, but that many aspire to more professionalism. It also shows that public relations people still do not seem to be able to innovate and improve their organizations as much as do other professionals. Only the open and innovative organizations allow public relations people to behave as professionals.

Thus, we must conclude that there are not yet enough practitioners with professional values for public relations to be called a profession. But let's look next at the professional associations and the educational system in public relations to see if they offer the possibility for increasing the number of professionals.

PROFESSIONAL ASSOCIATIONS

The ideal professional organization for public relations perhaps would be something that resembles the American Medical Association or the American Bar Association. These associations license practitioners, publish strong research journals, and serve nearly all practitioners of the profession.

Although public relations does not have a professional association with that kind of power or membership, it does have two general associations and several specialized associations. These associations allow members to learn from one another at local and national meetings. They also accredit members, support research, publish professional trade journals, and have codes of ethics.

PRSA • The largest and best-known association is the Public Relations Society of America (PRSA). PRSA was founded in 1947 when the American Council on Public Relations merged with the National Association of Public Relations Counsel. In 1961, the American Public Relations Association also merged with the PRSA.

The PRSA has its headquarters in New York. It publishes the monthly *Public Relations Journal* and a national newsletter. In 1981, it had 9,749 members. The PRSA now accredits all new members, who must pass a series of written and oral tests before they can become full-fledged members of the association and put the designated APR (Accredited Public Relations) after their name. The association has a code of ethics, which we will examine in the next section of this chapter.

The PRSA also sponsors the Public Relations Student Society of America (PRSSA), which has its own national publication and chapters at most universities that teach public relations.

Members of the PRSA established the Foundation for Public Relations Research and Education in 1956, although the foundation is independent of PRSA. The foundation awards scholarships to students, grants money for public relations research, sponsors an annual lecture, and publishes the research journal *Public Relations Review*.

IABC • The second general public relations association is the International Association of Business Communicators (IABC), which has its headquarters in San Francisco. It had 8,600 members in 1981 in chapters in the United States, Canada, and Great Britain. It also has affiliates in Australia, Belgium, Denmark, France, India, Japan, Mexico, the Netherlands, Norway, the Philippines, South Africa, and Sweden.

The IABC was founded in 1970, when the American Association of Industrial Editors and the International Council of Industrial Editors merged. Four years later, the Canadian Corporate Communicators also joined the new IABC. The IABC, therefore, had its roots among editors of employee publications and other business publications.

Since the merger, however, it has become a general association. IABC now has members in corporations, public relations agencies, associations, utilities, banks, hospitals, government, and educational organizations. The association has experienced phenomenal growth, as it had only 3,520 members in 1976. It now competes with PRSA, although many practitioners belong to both organizations.

The IABC, like the PRSA, accredits its members (ABC, standing for Accredited Business Communicator). It publishes the quarterly *Journal of Communication Management* (formerly the *Journal of Organizational Communication*) and the monthly "magapa-

Three of the major public relations journals and publications. Two of these contain mostly case studies, experiences, and advice of practitioners: *Public Relations Journal*, published by the Public Relations Society of America; and *Journal of Communication Management*, published by the International Association of Business Communicators. The third, *Public Relations Review*, published by the Foundation for Public Relations Research and Education, publishes original research on public relations and commentary related to research. (*Public Relations Journal* reprinted with permission of Public Relations Journal; copyright 1982. *Journal of Communication Management* courtesy International Association of Business Communicators. *Public Relations Review* reprinted with permission of Public Relations Review)

per'' *Communication World*, (formerly *IABC News*). It has also conducted several major research projects and holds a number of professional development seminars for members.

Specialized Associations • In addition to the PRSA and IABC, there are many specialized public relations associations whose members work for only one kind of organization. Among these associations are the National Association of Government Communicators (NAGC), the Council for the Advancement and Support of Education (CASE), the National School Public Relations Association, the Academy of Hospital Public Relations, and Agricultural Communicators in Education. The American Society of Association Executives has many public relations members and produces materials for them, although the ASAE is not exclusively a public relations association. There are also many local public relations and ''publicity'' organizations that are not affiliated with national organizations.

Public relations, therefore, certainly seems to have the professional associations needed to make it a true profession. Members of those associations do not have the exclusive right to call themselves public relations professionals, however. Thus, probably no more than a fourth to a third of the 100,000 or so public relations practitioners in the United States belongs to a professional organization. These members should be the most professional public relations people.

Again, though, we would have to conclude that public relations falls short of being a true profession, because the majority of its practitioners do not affiliate with a strong professional organization. Certainly, however, the organizational infrastructure is there to make public relations a strong profession.

CODES OF PROFESSIONAL ETHICS

Professional public relations people today are extremely sensitive about ethics—and rightly so. Many people automatically assume that unethical behavior is part of being a public relations practitioner. Thus, the true professionals go out of their way to prove they are ethical.

Few, if any, scholars have looked at what it means for a public relations person to be ethical. Public relations professionals have been especially concerned about issues such as corruption of the news media, PR agencies pirating accounts from one another, misleading of consumers, and the release of false or misleading financial information. For example, professionals frequently discuss the ethics of giving free tickets or trips to members of the news media that are not related to a news event sponsored by the PR person. They are also concerned about practitioners who threaten to place or withhold advertising in a medium in exchange for favorable publicity.

Two Basic Principles of Ethics

One can go on and on looking at specific ethical cases. What ethical practitioners need is a general principle of what it means to be ethical that they can apply as special cases come up. We would suggest two principles of ethics:

1. Ethical practitioners have a ''will to be ethical.''[26] Ethical practitioners do not do what they can get away with. They intend to be honest and trustworthy and do not willingly injure others.
2. The actions of ethical practitioners also should not have adverse consequences upon others when it is at all possible.[27]

The idea of ''adverse consequences'' gives meaning to ''not willingly injure others.'' It also brings us full circle to our definition of a public relations problem and our definition of public responsibility. When the organization the public relations professional serves adversely affects (has negative consequences on) members of a public, the ethical practitioner has the obligation to make the organization aware of those consequences. He or she also should not do anything that would injure members of publics, such as consumers or the news media. A public relations *professional*, by definition, not only exercises public responsibility but also is ethical.

To Quit . . . or, Blow the Whistle?

An extremely important question in modern organizational America is what the ethical practitioner should do if the organization refuses to exercise public responsibility. The Code of Ethics of the PRSA (Exhibit 4–2) says he or she should quit. But he may do more good staying on to argue the public's case. Also, few practitioners can afford to quit. Another option is ''whistle-blowing''—secretly informing the media about an irresponsibility in order to bring it to public attention. Whistle-blowing sometimes stops the irresponsible activity, but it usually costs the practitioner his or her job.

Generally, then, we believe ethical practitioners should stay on the job and argue for ethical organizational behavior, even if they are not always successful. If an ethical practitioner quits, he or she probably will be replaced by an unethical practitioner. In that case, no one will be left to advocate ethical behavior. Only when practitioners have no chance to change an organization, or when they are forced into unethical behavior themselves, in our view, should they resign.

True professions, we have said in this chapter, have strong professional organizations with codes of ethics and a procedure to prohibit practitioners who violate the code from practicing the profession. Public Relations has professional organizations, and both general organizations have codes of ethics. The IABC's is quite brief and basically states that the professional should have the ''will to be ethical'':

As a communicator concerned with maintaining the highest ideals of ethical performance among the members of IABC and others in this field, I agree to practice and promote the following professional objectives:

To achieve maximum credibility by communicating honestly—conveying information candidly.

To respect the individual's rights to privacy as well as protect confidential information and its sources. By the practice and promotion of these basic objectives, I hope to foster improved ethical awareness and importance to business and other organizational communication.

The PRSA has a longer and more detailed code (Exhibit 4–2). The PRSA adopted the code first in 1954 and revised it in 1959, 1963, and 1977. The code does seem to assert that professionals should have the ''will to be ethical'' and that they should exercise responsibility to the public. Thus, it meets both of our criteria for ethics.

The code is most explicit in dealing with consequences on the news media and government. It calls strongly for practitioners to present truthful information and to divulge the names of individuals or organizations for whom or for which they release information. It also defines the proper competitive relationship between practitioners seeking the same accounts or working for competing organizations. Article 13 of the code also prohibits a PRSA member from guaranteeing specific results—such as an article placed in a major national publication—that he knows he cannot guarantee. (See Chapter 6, on goals and objectives, to see what you can achieve.)

Enforcing the Code

The PRSA has a set procedure for dealing with members who violate its code. A member may bring a complaint to a grievance board. If the board rules that the member has violated the code, it presents the case to a judicial panel. The panel may find the member not guilty; give him a warning; or censure, suspend, or expel him.

Declaration of Principles

Members of the Public Relations Society of America base their professional principles on the fundamental value and dignity of the individual, holding that the free exercise of human rights, especially freedom of speech, freedom of assembly and freedom of the press, is essential to the practice of public relations.

In serving the interests of clients and employers, we dedicate ourselves to the goals of better communication, understanding and cooperation among the diverse individuals, groups, and institutions of society.

We pledge:

To conduct ourselves professionally, with truth, accuracy, fairness and responsibility to the public;

To improve our individual competence and advance the knowledge and proficiency of the profession through continuing research and education;

And to adhere to the articles of the Code of Professional Standards for the Practice of Public Relations as adopted by the governing Assembly of the Society.

Articles of the Code

These articles have been adopted by the Public Relations Society of America to promote and maintain high standards of public service and ethical conduct among its members.

1. A member shall deal fairly with clients or employers, past and present, with fellow practitioners and the general public.
2. A member shall conduct his or her professional life in accord with the public interest.
3. A member shall adhere to truth and accuracy and to generally accepted standards of good taste.
4. A member shall not represent conflicting or competing interests without the express consent of those involved, given after a full disclosure of the facts; nor place himself or herself in a position where the member's interest is or may be in conflict with a duty to a client, or others, without a full disclosure of such interests to all involved.
5. A member shall safeguard the confidence of both present and former clients or employers and shall not accept retainers or employment which may involve the disclosure or use of these confidences to the disadvantage or prejudice of such clients or employers.
6. A member shall not engage in any practice which tends to corrupt the integrity of channels of communication or the processes of government.
7. A member shall not intentionally communicate false or misleading information and is obligated to use care to avoid communication of false or misleading information.
8. A member shall be prepared to identify publicly the name of the client or employer on whose behalf any public communication is made.

9. A member shall not make use of any individual or organization purporting to serve or represent an unannounced cause, or purporting to be independent or unbiased, but actually serving an undisclosed special or private interest of a member, client or employer.

10. A member shall not intentionally injure the professional reputation or practice of another practitioner. However, if a member has evidence that another member has been guilty of unethical, illegal or unfair practices, including those in violation of the Code, the member shall present the information promptly to the proper authorities of the Society for action in accordance with the procedure set forth in Article XIII of the Bylaws.

11. A member called as a witness in a proceeding for the enforcement of this Code shall be bound to appear, unless excused for sufficient reason by the Judicial Panel.

12. A member, in performing services for a client or employers, shall not accept fees, commissions or any other valuable consideration from anyone other than the client or employer in connection with those services without the express consent of the client or employers, given after a full disclosure of the facts.

13. A member shall not guarantee the achievement of specified results beyond the member's direct control.

14. A member shall, as soon as possible, sever relations with any organization or individual if such relationship requires conduct contrary to the articles of this Code.

[a]Adopted April 29, 1977.

Source: Courtesy Public Relations Society of America.

This procedure has been used a number of times, and penalties have been meted out. However, the majority of practitioners do not belong to PRSA. In addition, many PRSA members do not file complaints when they see unethical behavior. At times, practitioners against whom complaints have been filed have simply resigned from the organization. Thus, the basic limitation that ethics holds for professional status for public relations stems not from the lack of a code of ethics, but from the inability of professional organizations to prohibit nonmembers—who are not subject to the code of ethics—from practicing unethical public relations.

Many public relations people—most notably Edward L. Bernays—have called for licensing of public relations practitioners as a means of keeping out the nonprofessionals. Most practitioners, however, do not believe licensing will work. First, the Constitution guarantees freedom of speech and of the press—the right to communicate. It does not, in contrast, guarantee doctors the right to practice medicine. Thus, the only thing licensing could guarantee is the ability to call oneself a "certified public relations counsel" or to use some similar title. It would also require the states to set up licensing boards, and that would result in much red tape for practitioners.

Again, the infrastructure for professionalism—codes of ethics—seems to exist for public relations. Public relations, however, is only in the early stages of professionalism, according to this criterion, because of the difficulty of requiring ethical behavior of all practitioners. Progress has been made, and more progress will come. Only when the majority of practitioners behave ethically will it be clear when some are unethical. Only then will nonpractitioners recognize that public relations is an ethical profession.

Thus, the solution seems to be training of

future public relations practitioners—and continuing education for current practitioners—in skills and knowledge that will help them be an ethical force in the organizations for which they work.

BODY OF KNOWLEDGE

Depending upon how one defines "knowledge," there is either an abundant body of knowledge underlying public relations or practically none at all. We learned from public relations history that Edward L. Bernays wrote two books about public relations in the 1920s and that Rex Harlow wrote two others in the 1940s. Those books borrowed concepts from the social sciences and applied them to public relations.

Today, there are also numerous textbooks on public relations. There are four major trade journals: *Public Relations Journal*, *Public Relations Quarterly*, *Journal of Communication Management*, and the *IPRA* (International Public Relations Association) *Review*. There are several newsletters: *Public Relations News*, *PR Reporter*, *Practical Public Relations*, *Jack O'Dwyer's Newsletter*, the *Ragan Report*, and the *Publicist*. There is one research journal: *Public Relations Review*. Several academic journals publish articles on or related to public relations research: *Journalism Quarterly*, *Public Opinion Quarterly*, *Communication Research*, *Academy of Management Journal*, *Human Communication Research*, and the *Journal of Communication*.

On the surface, therefore, it appears that public relations has a substantial body of knowledge.

Research or "Anecdotes"

In 1976, however, Grunig and Hickson received a grant from the Foundation for Public Relations Research and Education to examine the quality of that body of knowledge.[28] In particular, they wanted to know how much of the "knowledge" came from scholarly or scientific research and how much came from what scientists call "anecdotal evidence"—

personal "how-I-did-it" reports that have little scientific validity. Grunig and Hickson reviewed 4,141 articles or books listed in the second edition of the *Public Relations Bibliography* published by the Foundation. They reported that only sixty-three of the items actually reported scholarly research; the rest reported "anecdotal evidence." The few articles reporting research designed to build and test theory had been written by communication scientists or other behavioral scientists who were not really concerned with public relations. These few true research articles, therefore, could be applied to public relations problems but did not really address those problems.

Shortly before the time of the Grunig-Hickson report, in 1975, the first public relations research journal, *Public Relations Review*, was published. In a 1979 article in the *IPRA Review*, Grunig again evaluated the status of public relations research. He reported that *Public Relations Review* alone had published enough true research articles to have tripled or quadrupled the number of such articles he and Hickson had found in their 1976 study.[29] Yet, he added, the *Review* had received few quality research articles compared with other scholarly journals.

In August 1978, the Public Relations and the Communication Theory and Methodology divisions of the Association for Education in Journalism invited two prominent public relations researchers from business and an agency to critique academic research in public relations. AT&T's James Tirone said he believed public relations research frequently was done poorly and that, especially, it did not solve the practical problems that concerned practitioners.[30] Walter Lindenmann, head of Hill & Knowlton's research arm, Group Attitudes Corporation, said he found little valuable research in either academic or professional public relations.[31] But he expressed optimism that the famine was coming to an end, citing several examples of productive new research by public relations scholars.

Marks of "Immaturity" • Judy Van Slyke, a Syracuse University public relations educator, compared public relations to Jerome Ravetz's model of an "immature and ineffective" science and concluded that that phrase did indeed describe the body of knowledge in public relations.[32] An immature and undeveloped science can be recognized by:

1. Absence of facts achieved through results of research.
2. Reliance more on "folk science" than on verified scientific principles.
3. Emphasis on exchange of personal impressions in educational programs rather than on a body of widely accepted standard theory and concepts.
4. Inconclusive research and scholarly activity.

In the next chapter, we will discuss whether public relations is indeed a science. We will argue that practitioners themselves are not scientists, but that they should rely on scientific theories developed by communication scientists. Public relations educators, on the other hand, should be both scientists and professionals who do research and apply that research to professional problems.

At the time of the Grunig-Hickson report, J. Carroll Bateman, a former PRSA president, head of a commission on public relations education, and a leader in accreditation of public relations educational programs, claimed the report seriously underestimated the size of the body of knowledge in public relations. He particularly argued that case studies and what we have called "anecdotal" information make an important contribution to that knowledge.

In Search of a Theory

Personal experiences do provide valuable knowledge, but eventually, we believe, those experiences must be organized into a coherent theory of public relations. That theory then should be tested, in order to determine its ability to solve public relations problems.

The consensus among those who have examined the body of knowledge in public relations is that all of the pieces for a comprehensive and practical theory of public relations exist. There are many personal experiences of practitioners that can be used to develop and test a theory. There are many concepts and ideas in related behavioral and social sciences that can be used to start a theory of public relations. And, communication scholars have now begun to study public relations systematically and to build theories to solve its problems.

We also believe this book provides at least the beginnings of a comprehensive theory of public relations. Like so many elements of public relations professionalism, however, work is only beginning, and much needs to be done before public relations has the body of knowledge needed for full maturity.

When we defined the criteria for a profession, however, we said that not only must there be a body of knowledge for a profession to exist but also that practitioners must take an intellectual approach when they use that knowledge. Edward Bernays was perhaps the first "intellectual" in public relations, and there have been many intellectually oriented practitioners since. The majority of practitioners, however, still prefer to "fly by the seat of the pants" and use intuition rather than intellectual procedures to solve public relations problems.

Public relations probably will not become a full-fledged profession until its practitioners approach their work as intellectuals. Whether they do depends almost entirely upon the intellectual tradition they learn as students.

PUBLIC RELATIONS EDUCATION

Edward L. Bernays taught the first course in public relations at New York University in

1923, but even today, many, if not the majority, of practitioners have not had a formal education in public relations. Some current surveys of practitioners, however, have begun to show that more than half the practitioners surveyed have had PR education.[33]

In the 1980s, public relations education seems to have "taken off" to the extent that many schools of journalism and mass communication now have more public relations than news-editorial journalism majors. Let's look first at the usual public relations curriculum. Then, we will evaluate public relations education. Finally, we will look at continuing education for practitioners.

Public Relations Curricula

Public relations practitioners frequently criticize public relations education. Some critical practitioners have learned the trade by experience and believe public relations cannot be taught. They believe it is an art that can only be learned by experience. Instead, they advocate a general liberal arts training that will help students understand the world around them.

Other critical practitioners see public relations essentially as a journalistic skill and argue that students need mostly training in news writing, editing, and publication design.[34]

Still others argue that public relations suffers from an affiliation with schools of journalism.[35] They believe public relations students need to study social science rather than communication skills so that they can serve as public relations counselors rather than communication technicians.

Actually, all three arguments have merit, and modern public relations education incorporates all three approaches.

A Commission on Public Relations Education studied public relations education in 1975, and a second reexamined the results in 1981. In addition, an International Public Relations Association commission published a "Gold Paper" on public relations education in 1982. The recommendations of these commissions have served as a model for programs in different kinds of university units.[36] The majority of public relations courses and programs today are taught in schools and departments of journalism and mass communication.[37] Some PR courses and programs are offered in business schools, schools of education, departments of speech communication, and similar university units. Some departments of public relations exist in schools or colleges of communication. Public relations programs in journalism schools also are accredited by the Accrediting Council on Education in Journalism and Mass Communication, which has representatives from public relations education and the PRSA.

Generally, there is agreement among educators and practitioners that public relations students should have courses that provide the following:

1. A broad liberal education • The Accrediting Council requires that 75 percent of a student's courses be outside the communications unit. Most of the first two years should be outside public relations and communications. This requirement confirms the wisdom of those who believe liberal arts education is important to public relations.

2. Communication skills • Almost all entry-level jobs in public relations require journalistic skills—writing, editing, design, etc. In addition, students need courses that target these skills to public relations problems—courses that use the techniques described in Part IV of this book. Even higher-level public relations people must have mastered the communication skills before they move into management positions. Most public relations programs developed in journalism schools because those schools provide training in basic communication skills. This requirement satisfies those who stress the necessity of journalistic skills in public relations.

3. Knowledge needed for public relations management • As those who criticize journalism schools for putting too much emphasis on communication skills point out, public relations practitioners manage communication programs and counsel management—especially when they move out of entry-level skills positions. To handle these advanced aspects of public relations, students need to learn how theories of communication can be used to plan and manage public relations programs. They also need to learn theories of the behavior of publics and techniques of research and evaluation. Parts I through III of this book cover this type of knowledge.

4. Knowledge of the organization for which the PR person works • Public relations programs often are taught in university departments related to the organizations that employ public relations people: e.g., schools of business, education, or public administration. Again, there is good reason for placing a public relations program outside a communication unit. Not only must PR professionals understand communication and the behavior of publics, they must also understand the organizations for which they work. A PR person who does not can hardly serve as the ''boundary person,'' who interprets the organization to its publics and the publics to the organization. Public relations professionals must understand business and how a firm is managed if they work for a business firm or for a consulting firm as account executives for business firms. Similarly, they must understand government and the mission of the agency for which they work if they are to do governmental public relations work.

5. Practical experience • Students who have actually practiced public relations before they graduate usually get the best jobs. Thus, most work on a supervised internship and in their senior year take a ''campaigns'' course, in which they examine case studies and develop public relations programs for actual organizations.

It should be quite obvious that public relations is a multidisciplinary field—it makes use of theories and skills from many disciplines. That's why it can be located in so many places in an educational institution. Public relations entered the university through journalism schools because of the dominance of the public-information model at the time public relations was first taught and the need for journalistic skills by practitioners of that model.

As public relations evolved into the two-way asymmetric and two-way symmetric models, however, the traditional offerings of a journalism program were not sufficient. Thus, many journalism schools have developed public relations sequences that include specialized courses in the principles of public relations, the behavior of publics, public relations skills, and public relations research. Some journalism schools send their public relations students to other departments to learn those skills. In addition, public relations students generally take minors in, for example, business, sociology, health, education, public administration, or psychology, in order to develop the expertise they need about the organizations for which they will someday work.

In our view, public relations can be taught successfully in different university departments, as long as the educational program contains the above five elements. Public relations education probably will be most at home in a school of journalism—which is, most accurately, a ''school of professional communication.'' Public relations can also be taught through a separate department in a larger communication college. As we have stressed throughout this book, public relations is a communication profession that belongs with the communication professions of journalism, broadcasting, and advertising as naturally as social psychology belongs with psychology or accounting and management belong with business.

Other Academic "Homes"

There is no reason why public relations cannot be taught in a school of business or public administration—or other unit reflecting the type of organization for which a student hopes to work. The danger, however, is that students will become organization people, identifying so closely with the organization for which they work that they lose the professional's ability to see that organization as an outsider. Corporate lawyers, by analogy, are taught in law schools, not in business schools.

There also has been extensive discussion of whether public relations should be taught strictly at the graduate level, as are law and medicine. Actually, public relations has been taught more on the model provided by a program in engineering, education, or business, in which the first professional education comes at the undergraduate level. Today, PR students generally learn the communication skills needed for entry-level jobs at the undergraduate level. Undergraduates also learn enough about communication theory and research methods to put those skills into the context of public relations management. At the master's-degree level, students specialize in the concepts and skills needed for public relations management. Eventually, most professionals and educators believe, the master's degree will be required for management positions.

Finally, a small number of students may complete a Ph.D. to learn the research skills needed to work as applied public relations researchers in organizations or agencies or to develop the basic scholarly skills needed to become public relations educators.

Evaluation of PR Education

In our discussion of public relations education, we have presented an ideal or model program for public relations education. If it were adopted by universities throughout the United States—and, indeed, the world—public relations students could gain the specialized skills and theoretical knowledge they need to be true professionals.

Public relations education, like education for other professions, has, however, progressed through three stages. The model we have presented represents the third, and most advanced, stage. In the first stage, students essentially work as apprentices for skilled practitioners, usually outside the formal educational system. In the second stage, this apprentice system moves inside the formal educational system, where the skilled practitioner can teach several students at once.

In the third stage, the academic scholar and teacher replaces or supplements the skilled practitioner. The scholar-teacher begins to research, analyze, and criticize the profession rather than simply pass on existing practices.

The majority of working public relations professionals today have learned public relations on the job, through the Stage I apprenticeship system. Gradually, they are being replaced by practitioners trained in colleges and universities through the Stage II method. Both Stage I and Stage II give way eventually to Stage III, however, when a profession reaches full maturity.

A profession cannot advance simply by passing on what practitioners have done in the past, as is the case when experienced practitioners pass on their "anecdotal" experiences. Someone must stand back and analyze the profession, conduct research related to the profession, and feed new ideas to working professionals who can test them for their practical utility.

James W. Carey, dean of the College of Communication at the University of Illinois, pleaded for preservation of what he called the university tradition in professional training in his presidential address to the Association for Education in Journalism in 1978.[38] He argued that modern professional schools too often become prisoners of the professions they serve. Professional schools not only pass on the skills of the profession, Carey said, they also pass on the profession's narrow ideology and ethics:

> . . . what is troublesome . . . is that the professions as a set of social practices have become thoroughly anti-intellectual and anti-ethical. . . . There is little reward in the professions for systematically re-examining the intellectual basis of professional practice. The lawyer is rewarded for winning a case, not thinking about the law, the journalist for getting a story in print, not meditating on the nature of truth, the doctor for treating the patient, not thinking about the nature of health. . . . For this reason, universities have generally come to the conclusion that professional schools have nothing to contribute to a genuinely liberal education.

Public relations practitioners frequently have complained about the low status of public relations programs in universities. The reasons follow logically from Carey's argument. Because so many public relations programs have not passed from Stage II, many universities have concluded, with Carey, that public relations programs contribute little to a genuine university education. Often, university administrators see programs in public relations, and the other communication professions, as necessary evils that provide liberal arts students with job skills. The administrators believe professional programs deserve only marginal support, however, because the programs fail to meet the university's intellectual tradition.

Birkhead, following Carey's argument, wrote in the *Public Relations Quarterly* that public relations programs will not gain a strong foothold in colleges and universities until they do what other university departments do.[39] They must conduct research, criticize the profession, and carry on the intellectual tradition of the university. In our terms, public relations education must pass into Stage III before it can provide students the intellectual tradition needed for a true profession. Public relations education is moving in this direction, but the movement must continue for several years before public relations can qualify as a true profession.

Continuing Education

It is almost a truism that what you learn now will be out of date in five or ten years. In addition, many current public relations practitioners never benefited from a professional education.

To solve these problems, the PRSA has developed a career guide for the continuing education of practitioners.[40] It lays out four levels of professional competence, provides a checklist for practitioners to evaluate their skills, and suggests books and courses that can be used to build the skills for each level. The four levels include:

LEVEL I.   **Beginning Professional.** Introductory training, junior staff, basic skills application.

LEVEL II. **Staff Professional.** Junior management. Initial supervisory role. Basic craftsman, specialist. Eighteen to twenty-four months' experience at Level I.

LEVEL III. **Professional Manager.** Middle management. Directs staff and departmental operations, research, planning, budgeting, personnel, communications, and evaluation programs. At least five years' experience at Level II.

LEVEL IV. **Senior Professional.** Top management. Runs public relations operation. Adviser, policy-maker. Has superior knowledge of public affairs, public opinion, issues management. Up to ten years' experience at Level III.

Use these levels of professionalism now as a guide to begin the planning of your career in public relations. Consider the continuing education you will need to reach the level you desire.

IS PUBLIC RELATIONS A PROFESSION?

We have looked at the values, professional associations, codes of ethics, body of knowledge, and educational system in public relations. In each case, we concluded that public relations has the necessary infrastructure to be a true profession. We also concluded, however, that the majority of practitioners have not been exposed to that infrastructure and thus have not become professionals.

The future professionalism of the field thus lies with you. If you choose to use the professional structure of public relations to become a professional yourself, you can add one more professional to the field. When the majority of practitioners reach professional status, public relations will qualify as a true profession.

NOTES

1. Henry Allen, "PR: Swapping Hype and Sizzle for Pin Stripes and Prestige," *Washington Post*, June 24, 1981.
2. Harold L. Wilensky, "The Professionalization of Everyone?" *American Journal of Sociology* 70 (1964):142, 146.
3. Mary Fenton, "More on Professionalism," *Public Relations Journal* 33 (August 1977):16.
4. Mike Ranney, "Save Us From Professionalism," *Public Relations Journal* 33 (June 1977): 27–28.
5. Melvin Anshen, *Corporate Strategies for Social Performance* (New York: Columbia University Press, 1980), p. 220.
6. Frank Allen, "How Executives Rate Accountants, Lawyers, PR Specialists and Others," *Wall Street Journal*, Dec. 2, 1980.
7. *Business Week*, "The Corporate Image: PR to the Rescue," January 22, 1979, p. 60.
8. John Gardner, *Self-Renewal: The Individual and the Innovative Society* (Harper & Row, 1964), p. 83.
9. Richard H. Hall, *Occupations and the Social Structure* (Englewood Cliffs, N. J.: Prentice-Hall, 1975), pp. 70–71.
10. Charles Perrow, *Complex Organizations: A Critical Essay* (Glenview, Ill.: Scott, Foresman, 1972), p. 27; Warren G. Bennis, "Leadership Theory and Administrative Behavior: The Problem of Authority," *Administrative Science Quarterly* 4:259–301; Gerald D. Bell, "Formality Versus Flexibility in Complex Organizations," in Gerald D. Bell (ed.), *Organizations and Human Behavior* (Englewood Cliffs, N. J.: Prentice-Hall, 1967), pp. 98–106.
11. James E. Grunig, "Organizations and Public Relations: Testing a Communication Theory," *Journalism Monographs* No. 46 (November 1976).
12. Wright also reported that public relations practitioners say their employers frequently do not want them to be socially responsible. Donald K. Wright, "Social Responsibility in Public Relations: A Multi-Step Theory," *Public Relations Review* 2 (Fall 1976):24–36.
13. Gardner, p. 84.
14. For example, Wilensky; Hall; Howard M. Vollmer and Donald L. Mills (eds.), *Professionalization* (Englewood Cliffs, N. J.: Prentice-Hall, 1966); Oscar Grusky and George A. Miller (eds.), *The Sociology of Organizations: Basic Studies* (New York: Free Press, 1970).
15. Most notably, Jack M. McLeod and Searle E. Hawley, Jr., "Professionalism Among Newsmen," *Journalism Quarterly* 41 (1964):529–539.
16. Grunig; Blaine K. McKee, Oguz B. Nayman, and Dan L. Lattimore, "How PR People See Themselves," *Public Relations Journal* 31 (November 1975):47–52; Donald K. Wright, "Differential Effects of Professionalism and Social Responsibility in Public Relations." Paper presented to the Public Relations Division, Association for Education in Journalism, Seattle, August 1978.
17. These characteristics come from the following sources: Wilensky; McLeod and Hawley; McKee, Nayman, and Lattimore; Wright; Hall, p. 73; Ernest Greenwood, "The Elements of Professionalism," in Vollmer and Mills, p. 10;

Fred H. Gouldner and R. R. Ritti, "Professionalization as Career Immobility," in Grusky and Miller, p. 466; Jerald Hage and Michael Aiken, "Relationship of Centralization to Other Organizational Properties," *Administrative Science Quarterly* 12 (1967):72–92.

18. Grunig.

19. Wright, "Social Responsibility in Public Relations: A Multi-Step Theory," *Public Relations Review* 2 (Fall 1976):24–36.

20. Donald K. Wright, "Premises for Professionalism: Testing the Contributions of PRSA Accreditation." Paper presented to the Public Relations Division, Association for Education in Journalism, Houston, August 1979.

21. Wright, "Differential Effects of Professionalism and Social Responsibility in Public Relations."

22. McKee, Nayman, and Lattimore.

23. Swen Windahl and Karl Erik Rosengren, "Newsmen's Professionalization: Some Methodological Problems," *Journalism Quarterly* 55 (1978):466–473.

24. Craig Aronoff, "Credibility of Public Relations for Journalists," *Public Relations Review* 1 (Fall 1975):43–54; Dennis W. Jeffers, "Performance Expectations as a Measure of Relative Status of News and PR People," *Journalism Quarterly* 54 (1977):299–306; Oguz Nayman, Blaine K. McKee, and Dan L. Lattimore, "PR Personnel and Print Journalists: A Comparison of Professionalism," *Journalism Quarterly* 54 (1977):492–497.

25. Elizabeth Nanni, "Case Studies of Organizational Management and Public Relations Practices," master's thesis, University of Maryland, College Park, 1980.

26. Journalism researcher John Merrill, for example, takes this position. See John C. Merrill, *Existential Journalism* (New York: Hastings House, 1977).

27. A position that can be taken from John Dewey, *Theory of Valuation* (Chicago: University of Chicago Press, 1939). See also James W. Carey's review of Merrill's book *Existential Journalism* in *Journalism Quarterly* 54 (1977):627–629.

28. James E. Grunig and Ronald H. Hickson, "An Evaluation of Academic Research in Public Relations," *Public Relations Review* 2 (Spring 1976):31–43.

29. James E. Grunig, "The Status of Public Relations Research," *IPRA Review* 3 (April 1979):9–16.

30. James F. Tirone, "Education, Theory, and Research in Public Relations," *Public Relations Review* 5 (Spring 1979):15–25.

31. Walter K. Lindenmann, "The Missing Link in Public Relations Research," *Public Relations Review* 5 (Spring 1979):26–36.

32. Judy Van Slyke, "Defining Public Relations: Toward a Theory of Science." Paper presented to the Public Relations Division, Association for Education in Journalism, Boston, August 1980. The Ravetz model comes from Jerome Ravetz, *Scientific Knowledge and Its Social Problems* (New York: Oxford University Press, 1971).

33. For example, Wright, "Differential Effects of Professionalism and Social Responsibility in Public Relations."

34. This is a frequent finding from surveys that ask practitioners what their most valuable college course was. See, for example, David E. Clavier, "Southeastern Public Relations Practitioners Make Suggestions for PR Education." Paper presented to the Educators' Section of the Public Relations Society of America, Atlanta, November 1980; and Dennis L. Wilcox, "Preparing Today's Students for Tomorrow's Careers," *Public Relations Review* 1 (Winter 1975):47–55.

35. Most notably Denny Griswold, editor of *Public Relations News*, and Edward L. Bernays. See, for example, Edward L. Bernays, "Do Our Educational Facilities Meet Our Needs?" *Public Relations Quarterly* 25 (Winter 1980–81):18.

36. Commission on Public Relations Education, "A Design for Public Relations Education," Public Relations Division of the Association for Education in Journalism and the Public Relations Society of America, 1975; Kenneth Owler Smith, "Report of the 1981 Commission on Public Relations Education," *Public Relations Review* 8 (Summer 1982):61–70; The Education and Research Committee of the International Public Relations Association, "A Model for Public Relations Education for Professional Practice," Gold Paper No. 4, London, January 1982.

37. For an overview of public relations courses and

programs, see Albert Walker, "Status and Trends in Public Relations Education in U. S. Senior Colleges and Universities, 1981" (New York: Foundation for Public Relations Research and Education).

38. James W. Carey, "AEJ Presidential Address: A Plea for the University Tradition," *Journalism Quarterly* 55 (Winter 1978):846–855.
39. Douglas Birkhead, "Avoiding an Academic Fall: A Hard Look at PR's Prospects on Campus," *Public Relations Quarterly* 26 (Spring 1981):17–19.
40. Kalman B. Druck and Ray E. Hiebert, "Your Personal Guidebook To Help You Chart a More Successful Career in Public Relations" (New York: Public Relations Society of America, 1979).

ADDITIONAL READING

Aronoff, Craig, "Credibility of Public Relations for Journalists," *Public Relations Review* 1 (Fall 1975):43–54.

Birkhead, Douglas, "Avoiding an Academic Fall: A Hard Look at PR's Prospects on Campus," *Public Relations Quarterly* 26 (Spring 1981): 17–19.

Carey, James W., "AEJ Presidential Address: A Plea for the University Tradition," *Journalism Quarterly* 55 (Winter 1978):846–855.

Commission on Public Relations Education, "A Design for Public Relations Education," *Public Relations Review* 1 (Winter 1975):56–66.

Druck, Kalman B., and Ray E. Hiebert, "Your Personal Guidebook To Help You Chart a More Successful Career in Public Relations" (New York: Public Relations Society of America, 1979).

Grunig, James E., "The Status of Public Relations Research," *IPRA Review* 3 (April 1979):9–16.

Grunig, James E., and Ronald H. Hickson, "An Evaluation of Academic Research in Public Relations," *Public Relations Review* 2 (Spring 1976):31–43.

Hall, Richard H., *Occupations and the Social Structure* (Englewood Cliffs, N. J.: Prentice-Hall, 1975).

Jeffers, Dennis W., "Performance Expectations as a Measure of Relative Status of News and PR People," *Journalism Quarterly* 54 (1977):299–306.

Lindenmann, Walter K., "The Missing Link in Public Relations Research," *Public Relations Review* 5 (Spring 1979):26–36.

McKee, Blaine K., Oguz B. Nayman, and Dan L. Lattimore, "How PR People See Themselves," *Public Relations Journal* 31 (November 1975): 47–52.

Nayman, Oguz, Blaine K. McKee, and Dan L. Lattimore, "PR Personnel and Print Journalists: A Comparison of Professionalism," *Journalism Quarterly* 54 (1977):492–497.

Smith, Kenneth Owler, "Report of the 1981 Commission on Public Relations Education," *Public Relations Review* 8 (Summer 1982):61–70.

Tirone, James F., "Education, Theory, and Research in Public Relations," *Public Relations Review* 5 (Spring 1979):15–25.

Walker, Albert, "Status and Trends in Public Relations Education in U. S. Senior Colleges and Universities, 1981" (New York: Foundation for Public Relations Research and Education).

Wright, Donald K., "Social Responsibility in Public Relations: A Multi-Step Theory," *Public Relations Review* 2 (Fall 1976):24–36.

Vollmer, Howard M., and Donald L. Mills (eds.), *Professionalization* (Englewood Cliffs, N. J.: Prentice-Hall, 1966).

Windahl, Swen and Karl Erik Rosengren, "Newsmen's Professionalization: Some Methodological Problems," *Journalism Quarterly* 55 (1978):466–473.

II

Principles of Public Relations Management

In Part II, we move from description and evaluation of public relations to intellectual tools that can be used to manage public relations. Each chapter takes a "how-to" approach. It also takes a theoretical approach, to show you how to put social science theory to practical use. Part II begins with a chapter that presents a basic behavioral model that can be used both to manage public relations and to understand the behavior of publics. It then shows how organizations use public relations and how this behavioral model applies. The remaining chapters in Part II fill in the steps in public relations management. Chapter 6 develops relevant goals and objectives for public relations. Chapter 7 shows how a public relations manager can identify the organization's most important publics. Chapter 8 discusses how budgeting and decision making can help the PR manager spend the money allocated to him or her on the most important publics and most important objectives. Chapter 9 then presents the essential tools needed to measure public relations objectives and to evaluate programs. Finally, Chapter 10 discusses the legal context in which every public relations manager must operate.

5

ELEMENTS OF
PUBLIC RELATIONS
MANAGEMENT

When new parents bring their first baby home from the hospital, they have spent at least nine months thinking about the baby, what it means to be a parent, the baby's education and future, and how their lives will be affected.

Even while the baby is still in the hospital, things are pretty easy. The parents can admire the baby while they watch the experts feed, change, and comfort him.

Then they bring the baby home. They're on their own. The experts are gone. The diapers fall off. The baby burps up his dinner. He wakes up when he is supposed to sleep.

Actually doing something, it turns out, is a lot more difficult than thinking about it. Most parents turn, in despair, to Dr. Spock's famous baby book. Fortunately, Dr. Spock tells them how to resolve each problem that occurs.

"Now It's Your Baby!"

Why are we talking about babies in a book about public relations? The answer is quite simple. We thought it would provide a good analogy to help you make the transition from the four chapters in Part I to the rest of the book.

Part I has been *descriptive*. It has told you the nature of public relations, its history, its status, and its promise. We hope those four chapters have excited you about the profession—your new baby. You're looking forward to being a professional who contributes to the welfare of society.

Sooner or later, however, you will have to change and feed the baby. Knowing *about* public relations will not be enough. You will have to *do* public relations. Now it's time we gave you some *prescriptive* advice on how to do public relations.

We chose the title *Managing Public Relations* for this book for good reason. To manage means to direct or control the *doing* of some activity. In this chapter, we begin to tell you how to do public relations. We start at the most abstract level in Part II, to develop practical concepts that apply to the doing of all public relations functions. Then, in Part III, we apply the concepts to specific public relations programs. In Part IV, we get down to the communication techniques you need to put a public relations program into effect.

This chapter is one of the most important chapters of the book—if not the most important—because it explains some basic management ideas that we will apply throughout the rest of the book. The chapter discusses some "elements of public relations management"—basic concepts that are "fundamental or essential" components of the management process.

We start by looking at roles of individual public relations practitioners. Our discussion of these roles should make it clear that public relations departments assign management and writing/editing duties to different people. And it should help you understand why your first job might not include all of the management functions we describe.

Next, we describe a "systems" approach to management. In doing so, we will describe four essential concepts of systems management: functions, structures, processes, and feedback.

Understanding public relations functions will later help you to choose appropriate objectives for your public relations work and to evaluate whether those objectives have been met.

The discussion of structures will help you to understand why some organizations do public relations differently than do others, and why some public relations departments are organized differently than others.

We will then help you to conceptualize public relations processes and feedback by presenting a "behavioral molecule." The behavioral molecule should help you to plan and control your behavior as a public relations practitioner so that what you do is systematic and rational. We will also use this "molecule" in Chapter 6 to explain why publics behave as they do.

After reading the chapter, you should have the intellectual tools you need to plan and manage the public relations function for an organization. In the remaining chapters of Part II, we will provide additional concepts that will help you to carry out the public relations management model presented in this chapter.

PUBLIC RELATIONS ROLES

Let's start with a basic premise that escapes the majority of public relations students. Public relations departments or agencies consist of specialists who do quite different things. Only in the one- or two-person PR department of a small hospital or charitable organization, or in the one- or two-person PR firm, does a single person fill all or most public relations roles. Even in those smaller departments, many practitioners choose to fill only one of the roles.

You may like some of these roles and dislike others. You should explore different roles as you train for a career in public relations and then target your training on the roles you prefer. As you think about these roles, however, remember a second premise: roles must change if a public relations person is to advance through his or her career. If you limit yourself to some roles, you may also limit your ability to advance.

What, then, are these roles?

Research on PR Roles

Public relations researchers at the University of Wisconsin and San Diego State University have done a number of studies to identify the roles public relations practitioners fill in their jobs.[1] They began by reviewing the social science literature on professional consulting to determine the kinds of roles consultants play in all fields. Then they used this literature to construct questions to measure roles and asked these questions in a survey of 458 members of the PRSA.

The researchers used different kinds of statistical analyses to make sense of their results, and, as a result, there were some differences in the exact kinds of roles they found. Throughout these studies, however, the researchers found two dominant public relations roles.

1. Communication technician • These practitioners provide the communication and journalistic skills—writing, editing, audiovisual production, graphics, and production of messages—needed to carry out public relations programs. Communication technicians do not make organizational decisions. They implement the decisions of others, and do not do research to plan or evaluate their work.

2. Communication manager • These practitioners systematically plan and manage an organization's public relations program, counsel management, and make communication policy decisions. They are involved in all segments of public relations decision making. They frequently use research to plan or evaluate their work.

The literature on professional consulting had suggested three different kinds of communication management roles, and the Wisconsin-San Diego State research showed public relations managers frequently fill all three subroles.

2a. Expert prescriber • The public relations manager sometimes functions as the "expert" public relations person who researches and defines public relations problems, develops programs, and takes responsibility for implementing programs.

2b. Communication facilitator • In this subrole, the public relations practitioner serves as a sensitive "go-between" to keep continuous two-way communication flowing between the organization and its publics. He or she is a liaison, interpreter, and mediator.

2c. Problem-solving process facilitator • In this subrole, the public relations manager helps others in the organization solve their public relations problems. The problem-solving facilitator involves members of other organizational subsystems, or client

organizations if the facilitator works for a public relations agency, and helps them to rationally plan and implement their own public relations programs.

In addition to the communication manager and communication technician, two middle-level public relations management roles showed up in research by David Dozier:[2]

3. The media-relations role • A practitioner who maintains contact with the media and keeps others in the organization informed about what the media are doing. Media-relations people, therefore, play a two-way symmetric role with the media—they do not just produce and disseminate messages.

4. The communication liaison role • In this role, the public relations person serves higher-level public relations managers by representing the organization at events and meetings and creating opportunities for management to communicate with internal and external publics.

The two broad public relations roles include several more narrow roles. The communication technician, for example, may write press releases, prepare audiovisual materials, write and edit an employee newspaper, or write speeches. The larger the organization, the more likely the person would be to do only one of these jobs.

At middle levels of management, communication managers may manage a press relations program—as Dozier found—or an employee relations program. They could specialize in research, budgeting, or planning, or be an account executive in an agency. At higher levels of public relations management, communication managers would plan the entire public relations program, supervise middle-level managers, and counsel top managers on communication policy.

Does the PRSA Schema Really Work?

The roles that we have described as those of the communication technician and the communication manager are quite similar to the four levels of professional development developed by the PRSA and described in our chapter on professionalism in public relations.[3] The beginning professional, in the PRSA schema, is a communication technician. The PRSA's staff professional still functions as a communication technician, but he or she also supervises other communication technicians and thus begins to learn the communication manager role. The PRSA's professional manager and senior professional function solely as communication managers.

Research by Dozier showed, however, that many current practitioners—especially the technicians—do not follow the PRSA schema.[4] People who occupy technician roles have a literary-artistic bent and do not believe that public relations can be scientifically managed or evaluated. They seem content to be technicians with no aspirations to be managers.

The managers, on the other hand, have a more scientific mind, and believe in planning and evaluation. They aspire to move up the PRSA professional-development ladder. Communication managers also make more money and hold higher positions in the organization's hierarchy.

Many public relations departments may choose to fill the technician role with journalist/humanists who prefer to stay in that role throughout their careers, and to fill management roles with people trained in social science and management.

As a person trained in public relations— probably in a journalism school—your first job, and early jobs, nearly always will be as a communication technician, so don't neglect those skills. You may be content to stay in that role—especially if you consider yourself an artist or humanist rather than a scientist. If you choose nothing more than the technician role, however, be ready to accept low pay and prestige. And be prepared to accept

the fact that your organization some day may no longer need your technical skills.

If you want to advance as a professional— as the PRSA suggests—you must think beyond the technician role to the three levels of communication management. Pay attention to Parts II and III of this book and take management courses in business or public administration. Eventually, you will need them if you want to advance in public relations.

THE SYSTEMS CONCEPT OF MANAGEMENT

You may occupy only one public relations role at a time, but whether you are the senior public relations professional in an organization or the most junior communication technician, you will perform that role more effectively if you understand how it contributes to meeting both public relations department objectives and overall organizational goals.

The systems concept of management, which we introduced in Chapter 1 to explain how public relations contributes to the total organization, helps greatly to understand how your role contributes to both the public relations department and the organization as a whole.

The Closed-System Approach

For many years, management theorists used a closed-system concept to understand effective management and to teach students how to manage. Closed-system theories concentrated on how to manage a single organization or unit of an organization without thinking of how the organization or department should adjust to "interpenetrating systems" in the organization or its environment. Closed-system theories showed how to organize, motivate, and control employees. These theories paid only minor attention to "environmental matters such as technology, political influences, and social expectations."[5]

Public relations managers typically use the closed-system concept in a department that practices the press agentry/publicity or public-information models. Although all public relations people must by definition deal with the organization's environment, practitioners following these two models have typically concentrated on efficiently producing publicity or information—regardless of whether those public relations products help either the organization or environmental systems. The closed-system public relations manager concentrates on motivating a group of communication technicians to turn out a good journalistic product and on controlling the quality of their work without worrying about the need for, or the impact of the product.

The Open-System Approach

The systems concept of management has come into vogue in management in recent years because it incorporates organizational and environmental subsystems into the manager's thinking. Systems theory helps us to understand the total context of management. Systems theory seems especially useful for managing either a two-way asymmetric or two-way symmetric public relations department, both of which are designed to help the organization deal with its environment.

In contrast to closed-system management thinking, systems theory assumes that the organization is an open system. In an open system, organizational subsystems affect one another and affect and are affected by environmental systems.

Assumptions of Systems Management

Four major assumptions underlie systems theory. Let's look at each in turn.[6] Then we will look at their application to both two-way models of public relations.

1. Systems management is holistic • Holistic thinking means the manager cannot think of an organization or a department of an organization by itself. Systems managers

consider the relationship of the organization to environmental systems. They also realize that units of the organization depend upon each other to solve organizational problems. Public relations managers realize that they cannot solve public relations problems without working with other organizational subsystems. They also realize that public relations problems come from the environment and must be solved by adapting to, or controlling, systems in the environment.

2. Systems management challenges established practice • The goal of systems managers is not just to keep the organization or subsystem running. Their goal is to work with organizational and environmental subsystems to develop innovative solutions to organizational problems. Systems managers emphasize what systems theorists call a "moving equilibrium." The organization seeks equilibrium—solution of problems—but the nature of that equilibrium changes as the organization solves its problems. In public relations, practitioners do more than master communication technician roles and practice them routinely. They change their roles and develop new roles to deal with new and changing public relations problems. As we saw in the chapter on public responsibility, public relations managers also would advocate changes in the organization's structure and policy when they detect what environmental systems perceive to be organizational irresponsibility.

3. Systems management is mission-oriented • Systems managers know what they want to accomplish and systematically set out to accomplish it. They constantly monitor their progress toward meeting goals and objectives. Systems managers use such devices as management by objectives (MBO), the planning-programming-budgeting system (PPBS), or the program evaluation and research technique (PERT) to focus on progress toward objectives. You may or may not have heard of these management acronyms. Public

relations managers have only begun to use these techniques, but they will use them more and more in the future. Thus, we will discuss them and their application to public relations in the chapters on goals and objectives and on budgeting and decision making.

4. Systems managers use quantitative methods and computers • Systems managers view management as a management information system (MIS). The manager gathers and processes information and then uses computers and quantitative methods to help make decisions. MIS methods only now are being introduced to public relations, but PR managers will have to use them more and more in the future to demonstrate their ability to manage a public relations department in the same way that other organizational departments are managed.[7]

We said before that systems management would work well for both the two-way asymmetric and two-way symmetric models of public relations. There is nothing in these four assumptions, however, that suggests differences in the way these two models of public relations should be managed. Thus, we can add one more assumption about systems management that clarifies the difference.

5. Systems managers may attempt to control other systems, adapt to other systems, or do both • In systems management, there is never one right way to do anything. It all depends on the organization's environment. The public relations manager must decide when it is best to try to change publics—other systems—that affect it, when it is best to adapt to publics, and when it is best to do both.

In the chapter on public responsibility in public relations, we discussed Preston and Post's concept of interpenetrating systems.[8] They pointed out that some systems theorists believe an organization can control other systems in its environment. Other systems theorists believe an organization cannot survive unless it changes with its environment. Pres-

ton and Post argued that systems "interpenetrate," that systems both control and adapt to each other. Two-way asymmetric PR managers attempt to control systems in their environment. Two-way symmetric PR managers may attempt to adapt their organization to the environment rather than control the environment. More often, however, they think of the environment and their organization as interpenetrating systems and choose both adaptation and control as public relations goals.

Concepts of Systems Management

Systems theorists use the concepts of *input*, *output*, *throughput*, and *feedback* to describe the behavior of a system (Figure 5–1). Systems receive *input* from the environment, either as information or as matter-energy. For public relations management, we need only worry about information as an input. Informational inputs into the system identify problems that have put the system out of equilibrium with interpenetrating systems in its environment.

FIGURE 5–1

Major Systems Concepts

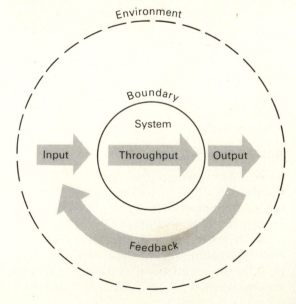

Systems process the inputs from the environment through an activity known in systems language as *throughput*. In more common terms, systems organize the information inputs they receive and formulate solutions to the problems that generated the inputs.

Systems then release *outputs* into the environment in an attempt to restore equilibrium with interpenetrating systems.

After those outputs affect the environment, the system seeks *feedback* from the environment to determine if it has solved the problem it had identified. The process continues until the system gets back into equilibrium with its interpenetrating systems.

Reactive or Proactive • These concepts may seem to describe the behavior of a system that is more *reactive* to its environment than proactive. A reactive system will change only when the environment forces it to change. If it were *proactive*, the system would try to change other systems in its environment even if the equilibrium with those interpenetrating systems had not been disturbed first.

Proactive behavior can be fit to the systems model we have described. In contrast to reactive behavior, proactive behavior begins with throughput rather than inputs. The proactive organization decides to release outputs that will affect interpenetrating systems. Those outputs put the interpenetrating systems out of equilibrium, and their reaction creates a problem for the organization that initiated the outputs. It must then deal with the new inputs that come from interpenetrating systems that want to restore equilibrium.

In other words, organizations may deliberately do things that affect their environment. They do so when they intend to develop a new moving equilibrium they consider more satisfactory. To get to a new equilibrium, however, they must anticipate problems with their environment and then deal with them.

In the two-way models of public relations, managers must work with other professionals to produce innovative ideas that will help the organization cope with its environment. (Editorial Photocolor Archives photo)

For example, an energy company may decide to strip-mine coal in a wilderness area because it needs new resources. When it mines the coal, however, it must realize that its actions will conflict with environmental groups trying to protect the pristine quality of the land or preserve the land for recreational use. When the environmental groups object to the consequences of the strip-mining, they create a public relations problem for the organization. The organization then must deal with that problem in order to restore equilibrium with interpenetrating systems.

This example should show, therefore, that the model of public relations introduced in Chapter 1 is very much a systems model of public relations.

Public relations managers must understand four specific concepts when they manage the public relations subsystem of the organization or a component subsystem of the public relations department. These concepts further elaborate the ideas of inputs, throughput, outputs, and feedback.[9]

1. *Functions* • Functions are the output or performance variables of a system. A "function" is a concept that describes what the system or subsystem does to affect the equilibrium of the larger system of which it is a part. The public relations department functions, for example, to gain understanding with interpenetrating systems or to persuade those systems to change their evaluations or behaviors. Each of the four public relations models, therefore, has a different function for the organization. The PR manager, working with other organizational subsystems, must decide what that function will be.

2. *Structures* • Members of an organization or a department of an organization occupy different positions and ranks. Each of those positions or ranks has a different role. How those roles are organized—structured—determines how the organization or department performs—how it carries out its functions. The structure integrates the subsystems of an organization or unit of an organization so that they can jointly meet objectives. Some structures work best for some functions but not for others. The public relations manager must choose a structure that will continue to provide the chosen function in the most effective way. The manager frequently describes the chosen structure in an organization chart.

3. *Processes* • Throughput is a broad term that includes many possible ways of processing inputs. The public relations manager must work out formal decision-making rules and procedures—defining who does what and how—to deal with inputs and to produce outputs.

4. *Feedback* • Without feedback, the system could not react to the impact of its outputs upon the environment. It is important to recognize, however, that a system can receive inputs from the environment other than feedback. In the chapter on models of public relations, we said that two-way asym-

metric public relations practitioners rely solely on feedback as an input from the environment. They produce an output and then seek feedback—a reaction to the effort—to see if the output had the desired effect on interpenetrating systems in the organization's environment. Two-way symmetric practitioners, in contrast, seek informational inputs other than feedback—such as research on how publics will react to something the organization plans to do—before developing a public relations program. They then seek feedback to evaluate the program.

In the last two sections of this chapter, we will look at these four concepts of systems management in detail.

In the next section we will examine the structures that a public relations manager can use to implement the communication functions each of the four public relations models provides for an organization.

In the last section, we will describe a "behavioral molecule" that can be used to manage the processes of public relations and to evaluate the feedback that results.

STRUCTURES AND FUNCTIONS OF SYSTEMS

Effective public relations managers develop and maintain a structure for the system or subsystem they manage. That means that managers organize a department or work unit, develop job descriptions, and assign people to those jobs.

Managers choose a structure by first asking what functions—outputs—the public relations department can provide that will help the total organization adapt to and control its environment.

Table 2–1 showed that the purpose of the press agentry/publicity model of public relations was to provide propaganda. The public information model disseminates information. The two-way asymmetric model provides scientific persuasion, and the two-way symmetric model provides mutual understanding. These "purposes" of public relations represent four major communication functions a public relations subsystem can provide for an organization.

In the next chapter, on goals and objectives, we will conceptualize these public relations functions more explicitly. The discussion of these functions in Chapter 2 is sufficient at this point for you to understand the organizational functions of public relations. Each model of public relations functions in a slightly different way for an organization.

Public relations managers must decide first what function will be best for the organization. This they do by examining the organization's environment. Then public relations managers must choose the appropriate public relations structure to provide that function.

They must choose both a *vertical* and a *horizontal* structure for the public relations program. The vertical structure sets up relationships between superiors and subordinates in a public relations department. The horizontal structure breaks down the work of the department into smaller units—for example, by assigning some technical work, such as the writing of press releases, to one work group and assigning other technical work, such as the annual report, to another.

Let's look, then, at the nature of environments, vertical structures, and horizontal structures.

How Organizational Environments Differ

At the end of Chapter 2, we discussed the contingency theory of management and said that the choice of a public relations model should be contingent upon the nature of the organization's environment. Now we can add to that discussion by describing how environments differ.

The choices organizations have may be limited if they face environments that are static and offer few opportunities. Aggressive

interpenetrating systems may also force change upon organizations that otherwise are reluctant to change.[10]

Environments, therefore, range from being static to dynamic. The more dynamic, or changing, an environment is, the more the organization should use the functions provided by the two-way asymmetric or symmetric models of public relations. The asymmetric model, if it works, helps the organization control the changes in its environment. The symmetric model also helps the organization change the environment, but it can help the organization change, too, when the environment changes.

In a static environment, the organization can behave routinely and can get by using the press agentry and public-information models of public relations. Those two models simply provide publicity or information about the organization as it is, without providing the feedback necessary to change the organization or the systems in the environment.

The concepts of static and dynamic environments are still pretty abstract, so let's narrow them down.

Hage says that dynamic environments are more complex than static environments.[11] He defines a complex environment as one with:

1. High levels of knowledge and technological sophistication.
2. Greater demand for the organization's services.

For example, a computer firm today has a complex environment on both criteria. On the other hand, the Board of Tea Tasters in the federal government would have a static environment on both criteria.

Grunig, similarly, found six characteristics in research on organizations that separate static from dynamic environments. They include, with some examples:

1. Changes in technology—technology in the computer and steel industries has changed dramatically.

2. Extent of mechanization—mechanized firms, such as automobile companies based on the assembly line—have a static environment.
3. Stability of demand for the organization's products or services—the demand for large as against small cars has changed drastically, making the environment dynamic.
4. Amount of competition to produce the same products or services—there is a great deal of competition to sell television sets; very little, until recently, to sell telephone service.
5. Degree of social and political support for the organization—until recently, most people supported schools and fought welfare departments.
6. Growth in the knowledge that the organization uses—knowledge in electronics has exploded, but has stayed relatively static in teaching.[12]

Levels of Complexity • In a book on the environments of organizations, Aldrich described similar characteristics of complex and less complex environments of organizations. Here is his list of characteristics, with some examples:[13]

1. Richness/leanness of resources • The richer the resources in an organization's environment, the more opportunities an organization has. Rich environments also attract more organizations and, therefore, more competition. In the early 1900s, for example, industry had rich energy resources. In the 1980s, those resources have become lean.

2. Homogeneity/heterogeneity • The greater the differences in organizations, individuals, and social forces in an organization's environment, the more flexible and innovative it must be to adapt to and control them. The National Institutes of Health have a heterogeneous environment, for example, whereas a paper mill in a small town has a homogeneous environment.

3. Stability/instability • The more frequently the environment changes, the more the organization must give up routine ways of doing things to cope with that environment. Energy companies, for example, have an unstable environment; a small-town bank has a stable environment.

4. Concentration/dispersion • The organization that has its resources or key interpenetrating systems such as consumers or suppliers widely spread to several locations cannot easily establish routine ways of exploiting resources and of dealing with consumers and suppliers. A dairy company that buys milk and manufactures and sells all its products locally has a more concentrated environment than the Kraft company, which produces and sells similar products nationally.

5. Consensus/dissensus • The greater the disagreement between an organization and groups such as consumers, publics, or government, the more flexible the organization must be to cope with these environmental systems. Until the Vietnam War, the Department of Defense generally had a consensus about the value of national defense with its interpenetrating publics. Today, that consensus no longer exists.

6. Turbulence • The organization that is connected to interpenetrating systems that change unpredictably must change, too, in order to cope with the chaos in its environment. Energy companies and automobile companies today face turbulent environments.

It is not the public relations department's responsibility to deal with all of these elements of a complex, dynamic environment. Other subsystems must also remain open to information inputs from the environment. Scientists and engineers, for example, must be continually alert to what scientists and engineers are doing in competing organizations. the same is true for CCs.

Nevertheless, the public relations department must deal with key interpenetrating publics and organizations and help other subsystems improve their communication.

The more complex, diverse, changeable, and antagonistic interpenetrating publics and organizations are, the more necessary it will be to have a two-way model of public relations.

Vertical Structures

Organizations usually develop vertical structures—structures that distribute decision-making power throughout an organization or department of an organization—that are appropriate for the kind of environment they face. Public relations managers, therefore, should assess the nature of their organization's environment and then set up appropriate working relationships between superiors and subordinates in the department.

Complex environments require flexible vertical structures. Rigid, vertical structures work best in a static environment.

The more power is concentrated with a few members of an organization's "dominant coalition" of key managers, the more *structured* the vertical hierarchy is.[14] The more power is dispersed to managers and their subordinates throughout the organization, the more *unstructured* the vertical hierarchy is.[15]

A structured vertical hierarchy practices closed-system management. An unstructured vertical hierarchy practices open-system management.

It follows, therefore, that public relations departments using the press agentry/publicity or public-information models can be managed with a structured vertical hierarchy. Departments using the two-way asymmetric or symmetric models require an unstructured hierarchy.

These are broad generalizations that require some elaboration. First, we must explain the difference between a structured and an unstructured hierarchy. Then we must explain why the structured hierarchy works best with a simple, static environment and why the unstructured hierarchy works best with a complex environment. We must also discuss the difference between the structure of the entire organization and the structure of a departmental subsystem such as public relations.

Before we address that difference, however, assume that the concepts of vertical structure can apply to both the entire organization and to its departments.

Characteristics of Vertical Structure • A vertical structure, again, is a rather abstract concept. To understand how to recognize the difference between an organization with a relatively structured hierarchy as opposed to one with a relatively unstructured hierarchy, we must define some more specific attributes of an organization's hierarchy. These attributes represent variables that managers can change to obtain the kind of structure most effective for carrying out the functions they choose. Organizational theorists have defined several such attributes. Four attributes are mentioned consistently.[16]

1. Centralization • Centralization represents the extent to which power to make decisions is concentrated at the top of the organization. The more power is centralized, the more constraints people lower in the organization have on their ability to behave as they choose. The less power is centralized, the more *autonomy* employees have throughout the organization. A structured hierarchy is more centralized than an unstructured hierarchy. To determine whether an organization is centralized, ask people how many decisions they can make on their own and how many require approval from top management.

2. Formalization • Formalized organizations have more rules and regulations. They discourage innovation. They follow a strict organization chart. Everyone has a job description and is penalized for performing a role not included in that description. Structured hierarchies are formalized. Look for published rules, charts, and procedures to determine if an organization is formalized.

3. Stratification • Structured hierarchies also are more stratified than unstructured hierarchies. Stratification means that some roles are more important than others. Employees filling the most important roles get paid more and have greater prestige. Structured organizations also make it clear which employees are most important. Those employees get corner offices, wooden desks, executive washrooms, and executive dining rooms. Important employees seldom communicate with less-important employees, except when the less-important employees make formal reports.

4. Complexity • Organizations with complex environments usually must become complex themselves in order to deal with the environment. Complex organizations have more specialized roles, more educated employees, and—most importantly—more professionalized employees. They also have more specialized departments and operate in more dispersed locations.

Vertical Structure and the Environment • Think for a moment, and it should be clear why a structured hierarchy and closed-system management work best with a simple, static environment. The environment does not change, so the organization does not have to change with the environment. It tries to do what it has always done better and better. Routine is good, because employees become more efficient when they do things over and over in the same way. The organization does not have to innovate, because change is not necessary. Innovation can hurt, because it disrupts routine. Employees should not think of new things to do; there is no need.

Thus, managers concentrate power at the top through centralization. They formalize rules and procedures to assure routine. They stratify the organization to make clear who has power. They do not need a complex organization, because there is no need to generate new ideas.

That kind of vertical structure would fail,

however, for an organization in a complex environment. When the environment constantly changes, the organization must innovate to adapt to or control that environment. Generally, the more new ideas an organization can generate, the more likely it will be to adjust successfully to its environment.

Thus, it should decentralize to give more people the power to generate new ideas and innovative behaviors. It should deformalize and thus eliminate rules and allow more flexibility. It should destratify to encourage communication between ranks. And it should increase complexity to add educated, specialized, professionals who are most likely to innovate. Because professionals demand autonomy, centralization and complexity are related. To be complex, the organization must decentralize.

The logic of these relationships helps us to understand why a structured vertical hierarchy works best for the two one-way models of public relations. Those models work in a simple, static environment. They emphasize the routine, efficient production of journalistic products.

The majority of employees in departments emphasizing those models will be communication technicians managed by only a few communication managers. The press agentry and public-information models do not require professionalized public relations practitioners. Most communication technicians happily perform their routine tasks and do not become unhappy with the structured hierarchy that constrains most of their decisions and behaviors.

Just the opposite conclusions apply to both two-way PR models. Those models must produce innovative ideas from throughout the department, if the department is to cope with the organization's environment. Communication managers must be spread throughout the public relations department, and those managers must be professional-

status quo

ized. Professionals are best managed through an open-system, unstructured hierarchy.

Differences Among Departments of an Organization • Organizational theorists have not, until recently, realized that organizations often structure some departments differently from others. They may structure some subsystems differently because some interact with more static components of the environment than others.

For example, a newspaper has both professional reporters and hourly workers in the printing plant. Business firms have researchers and assembly-line workers. A structured hierarchy would work best for the hourly workers, an unstructured hierarchy for the professionals.

Organizations also may decentralize power from top executives to middle-level executives in some departments but not in others. At other times, power may be decentralized to heads of departments, but the department heads may in turn set up a very structured hierarchy in their departments.[17]

These departmental differences are especially important for public relations. As we saw in the chapter on professionalism in public relations, public relations practitioners often do not have the training to be communication managers rather than communication technicians. Thus, top executives in the organization's dominant coalition frequently do not delegate autonomy to the public relations department.

As a result, many public relations departments are forced to provide press agentry or public-information functions, even though the organization would benefit most from one of the two-way models of public relations. The public relations department, therefore, continues to function with a structured hierarchy, under which managers merely oversee the work of communication technicians low in professionalism.

The public relations department, as a result, suffers in prestige and power in the or-

ganization. And, because the PR functions provided are not the most appropriate for the organization's environment, the PR department suffers budget and personnel cuts when funds are scarce.

Such low prestige and power seem especially evident in government public relations. Rabin, for example, concluded, after interviewing government public relations officials, that "government public information work is no more socially acceptable as a legitimate function of government than it was 40 years ago."[18] He argued, essentially, that government public relations will not be accepted until practitioners adopt what we have called the two-way symmetric model of public relations.

Horizontal Structures

Whereas vertical structures define who holds the power and authority within a system, horizontal structures define the division of labor on a single level of authority. Horizontal structures, in other words, define the roles and tasks of the subunits of a department. To our knowledge, no has done a systematic study of horizontal structures in public relations. Our experience with different kinds of organizations suggests, however, that there are seven common horizontal structures.

Some kinds of organizations appear more likely to use one structure than another. And, some of the horizontal structures are more appropriate for some public relations models than for the others. The seven horizontal structures include:

1. Structure by publics • The public relations department has components and middle-level managers for major groups of publics. These components frequently include media relations, employee relations, community relations, government relations, public affairs, financial relations, educational relations, and relations with special or activist publics. This horizontal structure is most common in business firms, especially those using the two-way asymmetric or symmetric models of public relations. It works best with an unstructured vertical hierarchy because it concentrates on key interpenetrating systems in the organization's environment.

2. *Structure by management process* • The public relations department has components corresponding to such management processes as planning, evaluation, communication, or research. This horizontal structure works best when the vertical structure has been decentralized to involve more people in key components of decision making. Thus, it works best with the two-way models of communication that are appropriate for organizations with complex environments. The process structure seems to appear most often in business firms.

3. *Structure by communication technique* • The PR department has units corresponding to major communication techniques such as press services, audiovisual productions, or publications. The technique structure appears most often in organizations practicing the press agentry/publicity and public-information models of public relations. These tend to be organizations with structured vertical hierarchies that operate in static environments. However, the technique structure also appears frequently in organizations with complex environments but in which the dominant coalition delegates little power to public relations and views PR only as a journalistic function. These organizations most often include government agencies, associations, educational institutions, and nonprofit organizations.

4. *Structure by geographic region* • Organizations dispersed throughout a region, state, or country frequently set up public relations components to serve each location. This structure seldom appears alone, however. PR departments generally combine it with one of the other structures. Thus, it can appear in all of the PR models and in most kinds of organizations. It would be most advantageous, however, for an unstructured organization that faces an environment that is complex as a result of geographic dispersion.

5. *Account executive system* • Public relations consulting firms use this system when they assign different employees to serve each client. Its advantage is that a different public relations function can be provided to fit the environments and structures of client organizations. Thus, this structure can vary tremendously. It can provide technical help. It can provide other public relations functions. It can serve one or more publics. It can also vary in vertical structure to fit the client organization.

6. *Structure by organizational subsystem* • The subsystem structure is a variation of the account executive system when that system is used by in-house public relations departments. Different practitioners serve as "account executives" for different subsystems of the organization, just as agency account executives serve different organizations. However, when the account executive system is used inside an organization, it is usually to provide press agentry/publicity or public-information models of public relations. Practitioners receive different journalistic "beats" within the organization that correspond to subsystems. Their job, then, is to publicize or provide information about the subsystems they serve. This system appears most often in governmental and educational organizations.

7. *Combination of methods* • Actually, few organizations have horizontal structures that utilize only one of these methods. They may combine, for example, the publics, management process, or geographic models. Figure 5–2 shows the organization chart for the Department of Public Relations and Employee Information of the American Telephone and Telegraph Company. It incorporates elements of the publics' and management processes' horizontal structures.

FIGURE 5-2 **AT&T Organizational Chart for the Public Relations and Employee Information Department**

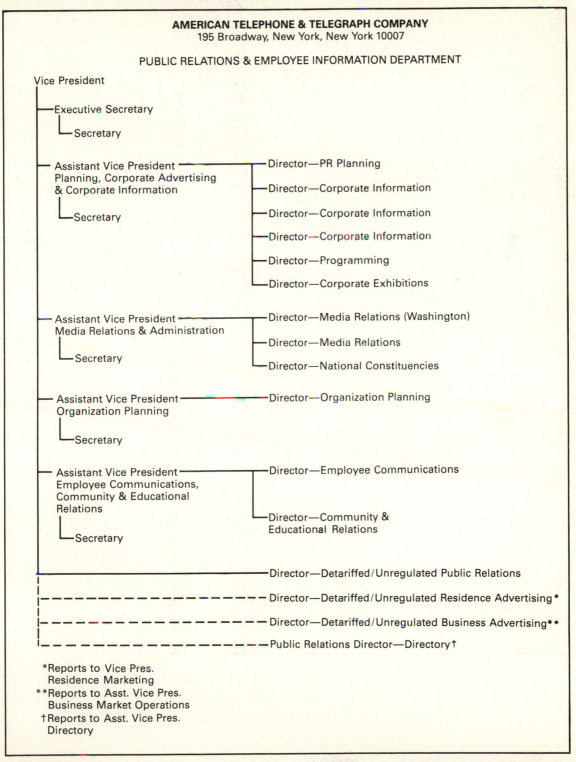

AMERICAN TELEPHONE & TELEGRAPH COMPANY
195 Broadway, New York, New York 10007

PUBLIC RELATIONS & EMPLOYEE INFORMATION DEPARTMENT

Vice President

— Executive Secretary
  └─ Secretary

— Assistant Vice President ─────── Director—PR Planning
  Planning, Corporate Advertising
  & Corporate Information ─────── Director—Corporate Information
                          ─────── Director—Corporate Information
  └─ Secretary   ─────── Director—Corporate Information
                          ─────── Director—Programming
                          ─────── Director—Corporate Exhibitions

— Assistant Vice President ─────── Director—Media Relations (Washington)
  Media Relations & Administration
                          ─────── Director—Media Relations
  └─ Secretary   ─────── Director—National Constituencies

— Assistant Vice President ─────── Director—Organization Planning
  Organization Planning
  └─ Secretary

— Assistant Vice President ─────── Director—Employee Communications
  Employee Communications,
  Community & Educational
  Relations   ─────── Director—Community &
  └─ Secretary   Educational Relations

──────────────────────────────── Director—Detariffed/Unregulated Public Relations
─ ─ ─ ─ ─ ─ ─ ─ ─ ─ ─ ─ ─ ─ ─ ─ Director—Detariffed/Unregulated Residence Advertising*
─ ─ ─ ─ ─ ─ ─ ─ ─ ─ ─ ─ ─ ─ ─ ─ Director—Detariffed/Unregulated Business Advertising**
─ ─ ─ ─ ─ ─ ─ ─ ─ ─ ─ ─ ─ ─ ─ ─ Public Relations Director—Directory†

*Reports to Vice Pres.
 Residence Marketing
**Reports to Asst. Vice Pres.
 Business Market Operations
†Reports to Asst. Vice Pres.
 Directory

Courtesy AT&T

We now have presented a taxonomy of management structures for public relations departments that are appropriate for providing communication functions for different kinds of organizations in different kinds of environments. Next we will present a theoretical model that suggests how public relations departments and individuals should plan and execute public relations functions.

SYSTEM PROCESSES AND FEEDBACK

We turn now to details of the throughput concept of systems management. "Throughput" is a broad term that describes all of the processes organizations use to analyze inputs, plan alternatives, make decisions, and put decisions into action. Throughput, in other words, includes all of the things you actually do as a public relations practitioner.

We have included feedback in this section with processes because it is one kind of input that the organization must process.

In this section, we will look first at some typical models of management processes. Then we will present a behavioral molecule that we think subsumes these other models. It should provide a planning model that you can use to organize most of your public relations work. It will also be useful later in understanding the behaviors of publics.

Some Models of Management Processes

Most management textbooks define a series of stages in the decision-making process. You could use these models as an individual public relations practitioner to structure your thinking, or you could use them as a guide for delegating responsibility for the different stages of decision making to different members of a public relations department.

Haner and Ford, for example, present five stages of management decision making:

1. Definition of the objective.
2. Formulation of measures of effectiveness.
3. Generation of alternatives.

4. Evaluation of alternatives.
5. Selection of preferred alternatives.[19]

Haynes, Massie, and Wallace include five slightly different stages in their model of decision making:

1. Consciousness of the problem-provoking situation.
2. Diagnosis, recognition of the critical problem, and problem definition.
3. Search for, and analysis of, available alternatives and their probable consequences.
4. Evaluation of alternatives and selection of course of action.
5. Securing acceptance.[20]

Public relations textbooks also provide similar models. Cutlip and Center, for example, included four stages in their public relations model:

1. Fact-finding and feedback.
2. Planning and programming.
3. Action and communication.
4. Evaluation.[21]

Marston provided the well-known RACE formula for public relations, which includes the stages of *research, action, communication,* and *evaluation.*[22] Figure 5–3, also, shows a planning and evaluation matrix developed by the Group Attitudes Corporation, a subsidiary of the Hill and Knowlton consulting firm, that is quite similar to these other decision models.

All of these decision models describe similar processes, but in our opinion they lack a strong theoretical base. Thus, we next will provide a behavioral molecule that is well-grounded in systems theory and that brings all of these decision models together into a single and powerful theory.

A Behavioral Molecule

The behavioral molecule may seem abstract at first, but if we take it apart carefully, you should be able to see its value for organizing both your thinking and your doing of things.

FIGURE 5-3 PR Research Planning and Evaluation Matrix

Group Attitudes Corporation
633 Third Avenue
New York, NY 10017

PR RESEARCH PLANNING AND EVALUATION MATRIX

	PLANNING		MONITORING				EVALUATION		
	Developing a Communications Strategy		Tracking Communications Efforts				Measuring Communications Effects		
	Research to Identify PR Problems and to Develop PR Programs						INTERMEDIATE OUTCOMES		ULTIMATE OUTCOMES
KEY AUDIENCES	EXPLORATORY RESEARCH (Qualitative)	DESCRIPTIVE RESEARCH (Quantitative)	Research to Pinpoint Communications Sources	Research to Analyze Communications Messages	Research to Assess Communications Process or Flow	Research to Measure Communications Receptivity	Research to Measure Awareness or Knowledge Change	Research to Measure Opinion or Attitude Change	Research to Measure Actions or Behavior Change

Courtesy Group Attitudes Corporation

There are two terms to understand: "behavior" and "molecule." We define behavior as doing or performing something. It can be a movement, an action, or an activity. Behaviors are the outputs produced by systems. Thus, both individuals, who are also systems, and organizations "behave." As a public relations person you may write a press release, design a brochure, conduct a survey, counsel a manager. The public relations department may conduct a campaign to change the Clean Air Act. It may carry on a community relations program. It may lobby in Congress. Each is a behavior.

A molecule is the simplest structural unit that has the characteristics of the larger units it makes up. We use the term "behavioral molecule" to name a simple model that describes how people make decisions about what to do—how to behave—and how managers organize larger systems to produce single behaviors for those systems.

Communication theorist Richard Carter coined the term "behavioral molecule."[23] In describing the molecule, Carter distinguished between the terms "behavior" and "behaviors." Behaviors are the movements, actions, or activities we described above. Behavior is the process the person or system to select behaviors. In systems language, behaviors are outputs, while behavior is throughput or system processes. To avoid confusion, we will use the terms "processes" and "behaviors" to represent what Carter meant by "behavior" and "behaviors."

Segments of the Molecule • Our behavioral molecule is similar to Carter's. It also uses some of the language from Alfred Kuhn's systems theory of behavior.[24] Our molecule draws from both Carter and Kuhn, but differs from both. Both parent models are systems theories of behavior, which connects our molecule directly to the systems theory of management.

The behavioral molecule contains several segments that describe the processes individuals and systems go through to plan and select behaviors. Thus, it subsumes most of the decision-making models we described above. Not all systems—or individual parts of systems—follow the behavioral molecule for all of their behaviors. However, those that do carry out each of its segments generally will be the most successful in adapting to and controlling their environments.

The segments of the behavioral molecule continue endlessly. Ideally, they should come in the order presented, although that order often differs in real life. The segments are:

> Detect . . . Construct . . . Define . . . Select . . .
> Confirm . . . Behave . . . Detect . . .

At this point, we ask that you think through the model as it would apply to a manager making an individual decision. Later, we will think of it as a device for delegating responsibilities to members of a public relations department. In the chapter on linkages and publics, we will also use it to understand the behavior of publics.

We played with the idea of creating a mnemonic (memory assistance) device such as an acronym (word formed from initial letters) to help implant the behavioral molecule in your mind. The task proved difficult and was abandoned. It's probably just as well. The concepts presented here are critical to understanding ideas you will encounter later in the book. So, it is best to slow down and learn them "internally" instead of merely committing the labels to memory.

Let's take each segment in turn:

1. Detect • Managers begin to think about a behavior when they detect a problem in the environment. They may detect that problem when a public protests or when other information inputs coming into the system suggest that a public relations problem exists. Managers may also conduct formal research to find problems in the environment that they would otherwise not know about.

2. Construct • Managers begin to formulate a solution to the problem they have detected. In this segment of the molecule, they try to be totally objective and do not yet make a judgment about what to do. Thus, the *construct* segment of the molecule represents thinking about the situation. It describes cognitive processes, in psychological language. In this segment, public relations managers: (1) define the problem, (2) choose an objective that suggests what it will take to solve the problem, and (3) formulate alternative solutions to the problem. The *construct* segment ends when the manager has constructed a single picture—a single idea—that makes sense of the situation. The term "construct" is an important one. Ideas do not pop into a person's head. They must be constructed through deliberate and careful planning.

3. Define • After managers formulate alternatives, they must ''define''—specify distinctly—how each alternative can be put into operation. Here public relations managers begin to think how they or others in the department would do each alternative, how long it would take, how much it would cost, and what effects it would have. Take, for example, the public relations problem of a public that resists the building of a nuclear power plant. Two alternative solutions to the problem might be an educational campaign to explain nuclear power or a proposal to management to build a nonnuclear plant. To define the first alternative, the PR manager would have to think through what information materials would be necessary, how they would be produced and delivered, what they would cost, and which of the effects discussed in the previous chapter they would have. For the second alternative, the manager would have to think of how to communicate to management—such as interpersonally, in a slide-tape show, or in a report— how the public reacts to a nuclear plant and what the consequences of building a nuclear plant will be on public opinion of the company. Thus, managers must also determine what effects they expect to have on management's ideas, evaluations, and behavior toward nuclear power. The *define* segment ends when a single plan of action has been developed for each alternative.

4. Select • Now, managers make a decision. They select one of the alternatives to implement as a behavior. Generally, they select the alternative that appears to have the best chance of solving the problem at hand. In this segment, managers may apply decision rules from previous experience, which we call *referent criteria*, to eliminate some alternatives. A referent criterion functions as a rule of thumb. It saves managers time because it tells them that certain alternatives have worked better in the past than others. Values or attitudes may also become referent

criteria. If they do, managers may reject an alternative because it conflicts with evaluative criteria they carry from situation to situation. Some public relations managers, for example, could reject manipulating the press as an alternative if it conflicts with their professional values. The *select* segment ends when the manager chooses an alternative. A manager who cannot settle on an alternative returns to the *construct* segment in order to develop a better idea of the situation.

5. Confirm • This segment seldom appears in models of management decision making. Yet, it has great importance for assuring good decisions. After managers select a behavior, they stop to confirm that the selected behavior will work and is the best alternative. In the *confirm* segment, managers should apply Murphy's famous law: ''If anything can go wrong, it will, and at the worst possible time.'' Managers think through everything that could possibly go wrong and what damage could be done if it does go wrong. If they conclude the risk is small, they go on to the *behave* segment. If they conclude the risk is too great, they return to the *construct* or *select* segments.

6. Behave • Managers do something. They write a news story, hold an open house, contact community leaders, set up a community-relations program. Communication technicians execute the program.

7. Detect • Managers now find themselves back at the beginning of the molecule. They examine the feedback from the behavioral outputs to *detect* if their objectives have been met. Managers who have met the objectives continue to *behave*. Those who have not been successful go to the *construct* segment and start the process again.

We have described how managers should use the behavioral molecule to plan professional behaviors. The molecule can also be used to develop roles for the public relations department. Researchers gather information for the *detect* and *construct* segments. Planners take the responsibility for the rest of the *construct* segment and work with communication technicians to *define* the alternatives. Top managers make the final decisions in the *select* and *confirm* segments. Communication technicians take over in the *behave* segment.

The Role of Research in the Molecule • The behavioral molecule can be described as an example of a Management Information System (MIS) discussed above. When viewed as an MIS, it suggests that managers need different information at each segment of the molecule.

Think of managers as communicators who constantly seek information.

In the *detect* segment, they seek information about the existence of public relations problems.

In the *construct* segment, they research the problem further and seek information in order to formulate alternative programs. They should do research to identify and understand their publics. And, they may look at case studies of similar public relations programs for ideas.

In the *define* segment, they gather information on costs and methods to implement alternative programs. They also seek information to identify the consequences of each alternative.

In the *select* segment, they may seek information to form a referent criterion. Information has the least value in the *select* segment, however. The manager must stop communicating and make a decision. Too much communication here merely prolongs the decision.

In the *confirm* segment, managers need further information on consequences— new information to confirm the validity of the information gathered in the *construct* segment.

In the *behave* segment, managers need information to determine if the program is underway and whether technicians need assistance in implementing it.

Finally, back in the *detect* segment, managers do evaluative research by seeking feedback inputs from the environment.

If we say that public relations managers need different kinds of information in each segment of the behavioral molecule, we say that they should do different kinds of research in each segment. Viewing public relations management through the behavioral molecule confirms the value of research in public relations. Without research, a public relations manager's behavioral molecule would consist of little more than the *behave* segment. If managers did use the other segments but did no research, they would have to rely on intuition rather than informational inputs to get through the segments.

What Are Audits? • Public relations practitioners have, in recent years, used the terms "public relations audit," "communication audit," and "social audit" to describe public relations research. They have not used the terms consistently, however. The difference in these kinds of research can be understood easily in terms of the behavioral molecule.

First, there is a difference between formative and evaluative research. Formative research takes place before a program, or behavior, begins. It takes place in the first *detect* segment and in the *construct*, *define*, *select*, and *confirm* segments of the molecule. Evaluative research takes place after a behavior—in the second *detect* segment.

Second, there are special terms for public relations research of which you should be aware. We use Lerbinger's definition of these terms and translate them into the behavioral molecule:[25]

1. *Environmental monitoring* is research to detect trends in public opinion and in the social-political climate of the organization. It takes place in the *detect* segment.

2. *Social auditing* is research similar to environmental monitoring. Social audits deter-

mine the consequences the organization has had on its publics and the extent to which the organization must correct those consequences. It takes place in the *detect* segment.

3. *Public relations auditing* is research to define publics and to determine how these publics perceive and evaluate the organization. Such research determines who the relevant publics are, how the organization stands with these publics, what issues concern these publics, and the power of the publics. The public relations audit begins in the *detect* segment, but provides most of the information the manager needs in the *construct* segment.

4. *Communication auditing* is research to evaluate whether messages have actually gotten through to receivers of the messages. Typical communication audits include readership surveys, content analysis of messages, and measurement of the readability of messages. These are evaluative methods that can be done in the *define* and *confirm* segments of the molecule as a way of pretesting messages. They can also be used in the second *detect* segment to measure some public relations objectives.

Three chapters of this book provide more detail on these methods. The chapter on public responsibility described social audits. The chapter on linkages and publics will provide detail on environmental monitoring and public relations audits. The chapter on evaluation research will describe communication audits along with other ways of measuring public relations objectives.

Communication as Behavior • Public relations models such as the RACE formula, or the Cutlip-Center factfinding-planning-communication-evaluation model, all include communication at a place in the model equivalent to the *behave* segment of the behavioral molecule. Communication fits into the *behave* segment of the behavioral molecule because communication is a behavior. It is the behavior that public relations practitioners plan, control, and evaluate.

We defined a behavior as a movement, action, or activity. Communication is a movement. A person or a system that communicates moves words or symbols to another person or system. People communicate when they take an idea, use words or other symbols to represent pieces of that idea, and then move the words or symbols to another person. People communicate ''successfully'' when other people have used the communicated words and symbols to construct an idea that reasonably reproduces the communicator's idea. Similarly, two people may not have yet constructed an idea and can use symmetric communication to construct an idea jointly. They will have communicated successfully when both have developed similar ideas. (We will discuss the nature of effective communication in more detail in the next chapter on goals and objectives.)

Do not confuse the communication that is the product of the public relations—i.e., the *behave* segment—with the practitioner's communication during the other segments of the molecule. Public relations managers communicate to help plan and evaluate the organization's public relations behavior. Because the practitioner's communication during the early segments of the molecule is also a behavior, remember that he or she can use the molecule to plan that communication also. PR people who do research in the *detect* stage, for example, should use the full molecule to plan that research. Then they should return to the segment of the molecule where they decided to do the research and use the information that resulted from the research to finish that segment of the molecule.

Management Mistakes • The behavioral molecule represents an ideal way to manage individual or organizational behaviors. It does not describe how a person or other system always behaves in practice. When Carter developed the original behavioral molecule, he stated that systems that include each segment in their processes will be the systems that survive. Systems that use all segments of the molecule will adapt to and control their environments most successfully. We believe, therefore, that a public relations manager who follows the steps of each segment will be successful more often than not.

It is also interesting to describe some of the mistakes managers make in terms of the behavioral molecule. Managers frequently do not use all of the segments of the molecule, nor do they always put the segments in the same order as we have described. As a result, they often make mistakes. We can model some of these management mistakes as follows. Perhaps you can think of other mistakes and model them.

Dogmatism: *. . . Detect . . . Select . . . Behave . . .*

Rationalization: *. . . Detect . . . Select . . . Behave . . . Construct . . .*

Habit: *. . . Detect . . . Behave . . . Detect . . .*

Procrastination: *. . . Detect . . . Construct . . . Construct . . . Construct . . .*

Indecision: *. . . Detect . . . Construct . . . Define . . . Select . . . Construct . . . Define . . . Select . . . Construct . . .*

Perfectionism: *. . . Detect . . . Construct . . . Define . . . Select. . . Confirm . . . Construct . . . Define . . . Select . . . Confirm . . . Construct . . . Define . . . Select . . . Confirm . . . Construct . . .*

Detect . . . Behave . . . Detect . . .

Rushing to the typewriter and banging out a news release every time one's company is criticized is a good example of the way *habit* can short-circuit the thinking and planning process.

PUBLIC RELATIONS AS APPLIED SOCIAL SCIENCE

Public relations educators and professionals frequently claim that public relations is an applied social science, just as medicine is an applied biological science. Lewis, for example, argued that as applied social scientists, public relations practitioners should use a Management Information System like the behavioral molecule.[26]

Scientists follow procedures like those outlined in the behavioral molecule when they do research. Thus, public relations practitioners who use the molecule follow procedures that are much like the scientific method. But does that make them scientists?

We think public relations practitioners should apply social science theories, but that does not necessarily make them applied social scientists. Two activities describe scientists. They try to systematically solve problems, and they continually use the solutions to those problems to build theories.[27]

Basic scientists have their greatest interest in building theory. They will test their theories on whatever problem provides a good test. Applied scientists take more interest in problems. They will use any theory available to solve those problems.

Public relations practitioners solve problems and use research to help them to solve problems. A few even use social science theories to help them solve the problems. Those who use theories do indeed apply social science.

To be scientists, however, public relations practitioners would have to continuously build and test theories. Few, if any, do so. Public relations scientists, who constitute a subdiscipline of communication science, should build and test theories. The practitioners apply them. Most public relations scientists will be found in universities.

In other professions, applied organizations also hire scientists. Hospitals, for example, have medical researchers; law firms have legal researchers. Some day, perhaps, public relations agencies and major organizations may have basic research units attached to their public relations departments to develop public relations theories. Several now have applied research units that do evaluative research. None that we know have basic research units.

Public relations managers should use the scientific method. Systems management and the behavioral molecule will help them do so. They should also use social science theories to help solve public relations problems. In particular, they should use the public relations theories we will describe later in this book to identify publics, choose alternatives, and evaluate results. Managers should not feel inadequate if they do not develop theories themselves. That is the job of public relations scientists.

NOTES

1. Glen M. Broom, "A Comparison of Sex Roles in Public Relations," *Public Relations Review* 8 (Fall 1982):17–22; Glen M. Broom and George D. Smith, "Testing the Practitioner's Impact on Clients," *Public Relations Review* 5 (Fall 1979):47–59; David M. Dozier, "The Diffusion of Evaluation Methods Among Public Relations Practitioners." Paper presented to the Public Relations Division, Association for Education in Journalism, East Lansing, Michigan, August 1981; Donald J. Johnson and Lalit Acharya, "Organizational Decision Making and Public Relations Roles." Paper presented to the Public Relations Division, Association for Education in Journalism, Athens, Ohio, July 1982.
2. Dozier.
3. Kalman B. Druck and Ray E. Hiebert, "Your Personal Guidebook to Help You Chart a More Successful Career in Public Relations" (New York: Public Relations Society of America, 1979).
4. David Dozier and Michael Gottesman, "Subjective Dimensions of Organizational Roles Among Public Relations Practitioners." Paper

presented to the Public Relations Division, Association for Education in Journalism, Athens, Ohio, July 1982.

5. W. Jack Duncan, *Essentials of Management*, 2d ed. (Hinsdale, Ill.: The Dryden Press, 1978), p. 80.

6. The following discussion is based on Robert B. Buchele, *The Management of Business and Public Organizations* (New York: McGraw-Hill, 1977), pp. 41–45; Duncan, pp. 79–85; F. T. Haner and James C. Ford, *Contemporary Management* (Columbus, Ohio: Charles E. Merrill, 1973), pp. 26–31; and Nicholas Henry, *Public Administration and Public Affairs* (Englewood Cliffs, N. J.: Prentice-Hall, 1975), pp. 127–133.

7. Paul M. Lewis, "Public Relations—An Applied Social Science," *Public Relations Journal* 30 (March 1974):22–24.

8. Lee E. Preston and James E. Post, *Private Management and Public Policy: The Principle of Public Responsibility* (Englewood Cliffs, N. J.: Prentice-Hall, 1975).

9. Jerald Hage, *Techniques and Problems of Theory Construction in Sociology* (New York: Wiley-Interscience, 1972), pp. 198–208; Jerald Hage, *Communication and Organizational Control* (New York: Wiley-Interscience, 1974), pp. 17–20.

10. John Maniha and Charles Perrow, "The Reluctant Organization and the Aggressive Environment," *Administrative Science Quarterly* 10 (1965):238–257.

11. Jerald Hage, *Theories of Organizations: Form, Process, and Transformation* (New York: Wiley-Interscience, 1980), pp. 437–442.

12. James E. Grunig, "Organizations and Public Relations: Testing a Communication Theory," *Journalism Monographs* No. 46 (November 1976).

13. Howard E. Aldrich, *Organizations & Environments* (Englewood Cliffs, N. J.: Prentice-Hall, 1979), pp. 63–70.

14. James D. Thompson introduced the concept of a "dominant coalition" to explain who holds power in an organization in James D. Thompson, *Organizations in Action* (New York: McGraw-Hill, 1967). For recent thinking about the concept, see Hage, *Theories of Organiza-*

tions. We also discuss the concept in Chapter 6, "Goals and Objectives."

15. Burns and Stalker say that what we call structured and unstructured vertical structures characterize what they call "mechanistic" and "organic" organizations. These structures also typify what Hage and Aiken call static and dynamic organizations. Tom Burns and G. M. Stalker, *The Management of Innovation* (London: Tavistock, 1961). Jerald Hage and Michael Aiken, *Social Change in Complex Organizations* (New York: Random House, 1970).

16. For a review of the literature, see Grunig. See also Hage and Aiken, and Hage, *Theories of Organizations*, pp. 57–83.

17. Hage, *Theories of Organizations*, pp. 83–87. See also James E. Grunig, "Evaluating Employee Communication in a Research Operation," *Public Relations Review* 3 (Winter 1977):61–82.

18. Kenneth H. Rabin, "The Government PIO in the '80s," *Public Relations Journal* 35 (December 1979):21–23.

19. Haner and Ford, p. 29.

20. W. Warren Haynes, Joseph L. Massie, and Marc J. Wallace, Jr., *Management: Analysis, Concepts, and Cases*, 3d ed. (Englewood Cliffs, N. J.: Prentice-Hall, 1975), p. 15.

21. Scott M. Cutlip and Allen H. Center, *Effective Public Relations*, 5th ed. (Englewood Cliffs, N. J.: Prentice-Hall, 1978), pp. 139–140.

22. John E. Marston, *Modern Public Relations* (New York: McGraw-Hill, 1979), pp. 185–203.

23. Richard F. Carter, "Communication as Behavior." Paper presented to the Theory and Methodology Division, Association for Education in Journalism, Fort Collins, Colorado, August 1973.

24. Richard F. Carter, "A Journalistic Cybernetic," in Klaus Krippendorff (ed.), *Communication and Control in Society* (New York: Gordon and Breach, 1979); Alfred Kuhn, *Unified Social Science* (Homewood, Ill.: Dorsey, 1975).

25. Otto Lerbinger, "Corporate Use of Research in Public Relations," *Public Relations Review* 3 (Winter 1977):11–19.

26. Lewis.

27. James E. Grunig, "The Status of Public Relations Research," *IPRA Review* 3 (November

1979):8–16. See also Larry Laudan, *Progress and Its Problems* (Berkeley: University of California Press, 1977).

ADDITIONAL READING

Aldrich, Howard E., *Organizations & Environments* (Englewood Cliffs, N. J.: Prentice-Hall, 1979), pp. 63–70.

Broom, Glen M., and George D. Smith, "Testing the Practitioner's Impact on Clients," *Public Relations Review* 5 (Fall 1979):47–59.

Buchele, Robert B., *The Management of Business and Public Organizations* (New York: McGraw-Hill, 1977), pp. 41–45.

Ehling, William P., "PR Administration, Management Science, and Purposive Systems," *Public Relations Review* 1 (Fall 1975):15–42.

Gannon, Martin J., *Management: An Organizational Perspective* (Boston: Little, Brown, 1977).

Grunig, James E., "A Multi-Systems Theory of Organizational Communication," *Communication Research* 2 (1975):99–136.

Grunig, James E., "Organizations and Public Relations: Testing a Communication Theory," *Journalism Monographs* No. 46 (November 1976).

Grunig, James E., "The Two Worlds of Public Relations Research," *Public Relations Review* 5 (Spring 1979):11–14.

Hage, Jerald, *Theories of Organizations: Form, Process, and Transformation* (New York: Wiley-Interscience, 1980).

Katz, Daniel, and Robert Kahn, *The Social Psychology of Organizations*, 2d ed. (New York: Wiley, 1978).

Killen, Kenneth H., *Management: A Middle-Management Approach* (Boston: Houghton Mifflin, 1977).

Kuhn, Alfred, *Unified Social Science* (Homewood, Ill.: Dorsey, 1975).

Lerbinger, Otto, "Corporate Use of Research in Public Relations," *Public Relations Review* 3 (Winter 1977):11–19.

McElreath, Mark P., "Planning Programs for Special Events," *Public Relations Review* 5 (Fall 1979):34–46.

6

DEFINING AND CHOOSING GOALS AND OBJECTIVES

A social welfare program (or for that matter any program) which does not have clearly specified goals cannot be evaluated without specifying some measurable goals.[1]

It is a common experience for an evaluator to be called in to study the effects of a program and not be told its purpose. . . . When he pursues the question, "What is the program trying to accomplish?" many program people give fuzzy replies, often global and unrealistic in scope. . . . Thus begins the long, often painful, process of getting people to state goals in terms that are *clear, specific,* and *measurable*.[2]

These two evaluational researchers were not referring to public relations managers when they made these statements, but they easily could have had PR people in mind. Ask the average PR person what his or her objectives are, and you will probably get responses similar to the following:

I'm trying to project a favorable image for my company.

I'm trying to sell my organization to the public.

I'm trying to get exposure in the mass media.

I want to make an impact upon attitudes in the human brain.

I want to distribute 2,500 (or some other number of) publications to the public this year.

I want to fill the football stadium on Saturday afternoons.

I want to improve employee morale and productivity.

I want to make this community a better place for our employees to live.

I want to reduce the number of patient complaints.

I want to help other departments of the organization solve their communication problems.

These statements of objectives probably sound reasonable to you, as they would to the public relations people who frequently make them. But suppose you were the vice president of public relations for an organization, and your budget next year depended on being able to prove your department had met all of these objectives. Or suppose your salary increases as a press-relations specialist were to be based on your performance, measured by how well you improved your company's "image" in the mass media. Or what if your performance rating as a community relations manager depended on how much better a place to live you had made your community?

Would you still think these objectives are reasonable? What activities, specifically, would you plan to accomplish them? How would you measure them to show you had met the objectives?

What's the Bottom Line?

Public relations people have only recently begun to pay much attention to objectives. Top managers just assumed their organizations needed a public relations department. Seldom did they ask why. When the top managers did ask, the public relations people specified vague goals and made strong promises. Had management asked for proof, the effects would have been weak.[3]

Now, more and more managers are asking their public relations staff to add up the bottom line—the equivalent of profit or loss. What has public relations done to make the organization more effective? Of what value is the beautiful company magazine? Was that brochure really necessary?

Public relations practitioners must do some kind of evaluative research before they can answer those questions. Although evaluation research will be the topic of Chapter 9, we have introduced the topic here, because evaluation must start before a public relations project begins.

The first step in evaluation is to think through what the project should accomplish, whether it is reasonable to expect the project to accomplish that objective, and whether you can show you have accomplished the objective after you have finished the project. It's also important to think about objectives when you are trying to define your public relations problem. A problem represents the absence of something you want. A public relations problem is the absence of communication or a communication effect that your organization feels is necessary.

Think in Terms of Effect

In Chapter 5, we discussed a behavioral molecule to help you develop a systematic way of thinking through the planning and management of public relations' programs and techniques. Objectives appeared three times in the behavioral molecule:

> Defining the problem and alternatives to solve it in the *construct* segment.
>
> Evaluating the alternatives in the *select* segment.
>
> Evaluating results in the *detect* segment.

Objectives thus play an extremely important role in public relations management. Without them, one cannot truly be said to be managing. But public relations people often ignore them. They think in terms of process—how many press releases must they get out, when must the annual report be done, how can the latest media crisis be handled?—and not in terms of effect—why was the press release needed, what should the annual report communicate, how should the media ideally behave in the crisis?

In this chapter, then, we will develop a clear set of public relations goals and objectives that can be used in diverse organizations facing many different public relations problems. Before presenting a list of objectives, we will first establish a theoretical rationale for them.

In Chapter 1, we promised to show where social science theory and research can be used in public relations management. Research on communication effects and organizational effectiveness can help a great deal in defining public relations goals and objectives. Therefore, we will first distinguish between goals (at the PR department level) and objectives (at the PR program and individual practitioner level). Then we will review research on organizational effectiveness to develop a set of overall public relations goals.

Finally, we will review early and recent research on communication effects and then use the knowledge gained from that review to develop a taxonomy of public relations objectives. You should be able to put these concepts to practical use in managing a public relations program or your individual public relations work.

THE NATURE OF PUBLIC RELATIONS GOALS AND OBJECTIVES

Most people use the terms goals and objectives interchangeably, and the dictionary lists them as synonyms. Both are defined as "ends toward which an action is directed." We would like to change that meaning a little, to define goals as broader and more general than objectives (Figure 6–1).

Goals are generalized ends—ends that provide a framework for decision making and behavior but that are too broad to help much in making day-to-day decisions.

Objectives, on the other hand, are ends in view—expected solutions to day-to-day problems that we can use to deal with that

problem and to evaluate whether we have solved it.[4]

Let's take an example that should be familiar to you. "Getting a degree" may be your goal in going to college. That goal won't help much in studying for a test or writing a term paper. What you need is an objective: writing ten pages by 10 p.m., understanding the professor's lectures next week, or reviewing 10 chapters of the text by Thursday morning. Meeting each of those objectives will move you toward your goal of getting a degree, but without the objectives to shoot for in the short run, that goal would be pie in the sky.

The same distinction applies to public relations. PR departments as a whole usually have goals: two-way communication, mutual understanding between the organization and its publics, public acceptance of the organization. Practitioners working in those departments, however, must specify more specific objectives to plan and evaluate individual PR programs and to plan and evaluate their day-to-day activities.

For example, the objective of the Mobil Corporation's advocacy advertising program might be to get 30 percent of the people who read the Washington *Post* to understand the company's position on the deregulation of natural gas. The objective of the person writing the ad might be to write it clearly enough

FIGURE 6–1 Goals and Objectives

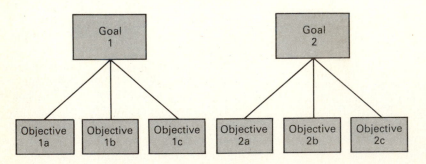

Goals are broad and abstract and cannot be tested directly.

Objectives are derived from goals. They are specific and measurable. Meeting an objective contributes to attaining a goal.

so that people who read it comprehend what the writer is trying to say. Both of these objectives, if accomplished, should move the department toward its public relations goal. Success with objectives can be measured, but progress toward the goal cannot—except by measuring the objectives that logically contribute to reaching the goal.

Who Makes Which Decisions?

Public relations people must choose both their goals and objectives carefully. The top public relations manager—usually with the title of vice president or director—has responsibility for choosing goals for the entire PR department. Middle-level managers and their subordinates—writers, researchers, program directors, et al.—usually have responsibility for choosing objectives that contribute to the overall goal.

The top manager makes large, all-encompassing *macro* decisions. The lower managers and technicians make smaller, more specific *micro* decisions. The microdecisions about objectives are most important, because objectives can be measured and evaluated. But the top PR executives often may have to defend their programs and their budgets by stating what the public relations goals contribute to meeting the overall goals of the organization. That's a tough question to answer, and as a result, chief executive officers frequently kill off public relations programs when the budget gets tight because the public relations executives cannot argue effectively that their program helps the organization in some way.

You may think it will be a long time until you head up a public relations program and make macrodecisions. Remember, though, that your first public relations job and, indeed, your later jobs may be in a small organization, where you and perhaps a few other people *are* the entire public relations program. You may have to make macrolevel decisions sooner than you think.

Thus, we will first discuss public relations goals and the contribution they make to the effectiveness of the total organization. Then we will turn to the specific objectives that contribute to public relations goals—objectives that you as a public relations person can use to manage your professional work each day.

PR GOALS AND ORGANIZATIONAL EFFECTIVENESS

Recently, the chief of the public information division of a large government research agency near Washington, D. C., made his annual budget presentation to the top administrators of the agency. His division had done extensive evaluation research, something most public relations departments don't do. He could tell how many press releases the media had used. He had surveyed the trade press and knew how the editors evaluated the materials sent them. He knew how many employees had read the employee publications and why they read them. He seemed to be able to demonstrate that the information division had met its objectives and deserved an increased budget.

The tough budget analysts were not easily persuaded, however. What good had all of these public relations activities done for the agency? they asked. Unless he could show what public relations did to help the agency, he was told, the information division would suffer ''negative budget adjustments.''

Were that question put to other departments of an organization, they might also have a difficult time responding. How, for example, would a personnel department justify itself?

In this research agency, a research department could answer quite simply that it does research and that research is the mission of the agency. Public relations people could not answer in that way, however. They had to show how the public relations department helps the rest of the organization perform better—to help the research departments do better research, for example, or to get public support for their research.

In Chapter 1, we described the parts of organizations as subsystems of the larger organizational system. The names of those subsystems suggest what they contribute to the organization: production, maintenance, disposal, adaptive, and management subsystems. Public relations, we said, supports each of these subsystems. That's the problem when it comes time to defend public relations goals to top management. Public relations helps the other subsystems communicate among themselves and with external publics. But what is the value of communication to an organization?

Defining "Effectiveness"

Let's turn to social science research and theory for some help. Organizational researchers in departments of sociology or management have studied the problem of organizational effectiveness. They have tried to solve three problems:

1. Defining what an "effective" organization is.
2. Determining why some organizations are effective and others are not.
3. Determining what individual departments contribute to the overall effectiveness of the organization.

Solving the third problem would help us to understand if and how public relations contributes to organizational effectiveness. That third problem can't be solved, however, unless we can solve the first one, and organizational theorists haven't come to much agreement on a definition of organizational effectiveness. Two general ideas, however, run through their definitions of effectiveness: (1) organizations are effective if they attain their goals, and (2) organizations are natural systems that are successful if they survive within their environment and acquire re-

sources from their environment for themselves.[5]

The goal approach seems simple at first glance. All one would have to do is determine the most important goal or set of goals for an organization and then determine if the organization has met that goal or goals.

However, organizations have many goals, and those goals change frequently.[6] For a business firm, you might think that profit is the obvious goal. But not even economists believe that profit is the only goal of a business firm. Some firms want to increase sales. Some want to get larger. Some firms, as we saw in Chapter 3, even want to be socially responsible. Obviously, profit is not an important goal to nonprofit and service organizations.

One organizational scholar listed thirty goals that researchers have used to define organizational effectiveness—such as productivity, efficiency, profit, quality, control of the environment, adaptation/flexibility to the environment, growth, job satisfaction, stability, and even *information management and communication*.[7] It seems clear, then, that scholars will never find a single goal (or set of goals) that represents the ultimate definition of effectiveness for all organizations. That means also that we cannot come up with a simple answer, for all organizations, of how public relations contributes to organizational effectiveness.

The natural-systems approach also has its limitations for defining organizational effectiveness. The early versions of this approach argued that an organization is effective when it acquires valuable resources from its environment. Most organizational scholars agreed that early systems approach was too limited. Organizations do much more than acquire resources. They also produce outputs and, as we saw in Chapter 1, have consequences on the environment.

Thus, Katz and Kahn, in an extremely influential book on organizational theory, expanded the system definition to include "political" relationships with the environment.[8] Organizations must do more than acquire resources, Katz and Kahn said. They must also be able to control their environment and adapt to the environment in order to survive.

Controlling or Adapting

We can look at *control* and *adaptability* as the most important, and the most abstract, of organizational goals. They are too broad to help decision makers in planning, but they do help us to get a broad definition of organizational effectiveness. They also suggest what public relations contributes to an organization.

Communication can be used both to attempt to control other people and groups—when persuasion is the objective—and to adapt to other people and groups—when understanding is the objective. Thus, logically, public relations can help the organization to survive and to adapt to the environment.

Hardwick, in a study of fifteen organizations in the Washington, D.C., area, found support for this idea.[9] The chief executive officers and public relations heads of the fifteen organizations defined their public relations goal as environmental control when they used the press agentry/publicity or two-way asymmetric models of public relations. They described their public relations objective as adaptation to the environment when they used the public-information or two-way symmetric models. And, as we saw in Chapter 2, the organizations that used the press agentry/publicity and two-way asymmetric models generally were in highly competitive environments.

The organizations that used the public-information and two-way symmetric models generally were in less competitive environments. This study showed not only that the different models of public relations contribute to organizational effectiveness in different ways, but also that the contingency model described in Chapter 2 really works. Orga-

nizations use the model of public relations and choose public relations goals that contribute the most to organizational effectiveness for the kind of environment they face.

To say that public relations contributes to organizational effectiveness by helping the organization control and adapt to its environment seems like a neat theoretical solution to a practical problem facing most public relations practitioners. But it is too theoretical to satisfy most of the chief executives to whom PR people must justify the need for a public relations program. A theory of organizational effectiveness developed by two professors of industrial administration at Carnegie-Mellon University in Pittsburgh, Johannes Pennings and Paul Goodman, seems to shed light on the practical problem of proving the value of the public relations function in an organization.[10]

Who Sets the Goals?

Pennings and Goodman begin with the general conclusion we have already discussed, that organizations have many goals and that goals change as the environment changes. They also assume that no one goal is always more important than another. It's important to know, then, *who* determines the organization's goals.

Pennings and Goodman argue that organizations have several constituencies, both inside and outside the organization. The internal constituencies are the individuals and departments that make up the organization. The external constituencies may be other organizations that buy, sell, or use the organization's products or services; the government; consumers; or publics.

Each of these constituencies has a say in determining what the organization's goals should be, but some constituencies have more power than others in making that decision. It all depends on how central and indispensable the constituency is to the organization. The constituencies with the most power both inside and outside the organization make up the *dominant coalition* of the organization. That coalition determines what the organization's goals should be, and the organizations use those goals to determine how much individual departments have contributed to the success.[11]

The Pennings and Goodman theory suggests that organizations will include public relations goals in their definition of effectiveness when the public relations department and key external publics—such as the government, consumers, or pressure groups—become part of the organization's dominant coalition (Figure 6–2). Our discussion of professionalism in Chapter 3 now would lead to the conclusion that public relations people generally do not have the freedom to behave as professionals unless they are part of the dominant coalition.

Thus, when the external publics or the public relations department become part of

the dominant coalition, they have the power to include such goals as social responsibility, public understanding, or two-way communication among the organization's goals. When the organization has such goals, it is easy to see the value of public relations and to develop communication objectives that the public relations department can show it has met.

Two-Way Symmetric Goal-Setting

Social responsibility, public understanding, and two-way communication are adaptive organizational goals that are best achieved with the two-way symmetric model. Organizations accept them as goals most often when government or pressure groups are key constituencies that are part of the dominant coalition, or when the public relations executive is a professional and part of the dominant coalition so that he or she can argue effectively for such goals.

FIGURE 6–2   **The Public Relations Department and Interpenetrating Publics Inside and Outside the Organization's Dominant Coalition**

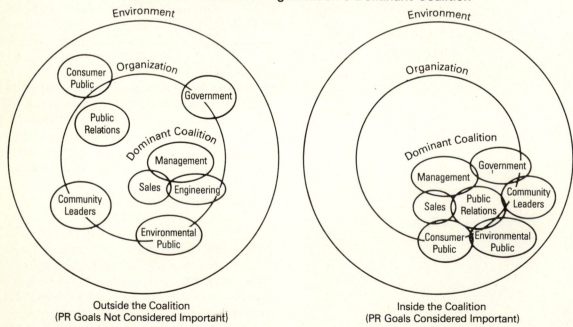

Outside the Coalition
(PR Goals Not Considered Important)

Inside the Coalition
(PR Goals Considered Important)

When neither pressure groups nor government representatives are in the dominant coalition, public relations executives frequently will not be in the dominant coalition. Then they may accept environmental control as the justification for public relations.

At times, public relations executives who are part of the dominant coalition may accept environmental control rather than adaptation as the proper function of public relations. Perhaps they have not been trained in the two-way symmetric model, and do not realize that adaptation is a legitimate public relations goal.

Environmental control, translated into a public relations goal, means persuasive public relations practiced through the press agentry/publicity or two-way asymmetric public relations models.

From this discussion, we can reach three conclusions about the relationship between public relations goals and organizational effectiveness.

First, public relations goals become organizational goals when the public relations executive or key external publics become part of the organization's dominant coalition. When the public relations goals become organizational goals, it will be possible to show that public relations contributes to organizational effectiveness.

Second, the organization's public relations goals are more likely to be adaptive than control goals when key publics are in the dominant coalition and when the public relations executive is in the dominant coalition and understands the two-way symmetric model of public relations.

Finally, if neither the key publics nor the public relations executive are part of the dominant coalition it will be difficult to justify the public relations function to the dominant coalition no matter how well the PR people meet their communication objectives. Let's turn, then, to the more specific objectives that can be used to plan and evaluate day-to-day public relations activities.

SETTING PUBLIC RELATIONS OBJECTIVES

The public relations department as a unit has selected a broad goal such as mutual understanding (adaptation to the environment) or public persuasion (control of the environment). The top executives of the department duly state the goal in a public relations plan, and—ideally—top management accepts the public relations goal as an organizational goal. Now it's time to translate that goal into concrete objectives that can be used to "manage by objectives."

Duncan describes management by objectives, or MBO, as "... an attempt to *involve* managers and subordinates in *defining* areas of individual responsibility in terms of the *results* expected. The organization's goals are identified and used to *reformulate* unit and individual goals and as a *measurable standard* against which actual performance will be evaluated."[12]

Making MBO Work

To put MBO into practice, top PR managers must work with middle-level PR managers to define goals for such programs as press relations, employee relations, government relations, or community relations. The middle managers must, in turn, work with subordinates to develop individual objectives for carrying out the program objectives.

Your first reaction probably will be that each public relations program is so different that each requires different objectives. To some extent that reaction is accurate. Keep in mind, however, that nearly all public relations programs are communication programs. Therefore, the effect that should be measured will be a communication effect.

Our purpose in this section of the chapter

will be to develop a set of communication effects that can be used to translate overall organizational goals into specific, measurable public relations objectives.

There are numerous theories and ample research available in the field of communication science to help us develop a typology of communication effects. Unfortunately, however, many of those theories come to different and often to conflicting conclusions. Add to that the common ideas that the average person and public relations practitioner have about communication effects, and the result is the typical set of ill-defined, unreasonable, and unmeasurable communication effects that public relations people generally state as their objectives.

One of the striking differences that one notices between academic communication scholars and public relations professionals is in their perception of the power of communication—particularly of the power of the mass media. Mass communication is only one form of communication, but let's use it as an example of communication effects for the moment.

Typical public relations practitioners believe the mass media have great power to change attitudes and behavior. They live in fear of their organization being ''exposed'' on CBS's *60 Minutes* or even in the local newspaper. At the same time, they believe that getting the organization's chief executive officer on a popular talk show or getting the right publicity will have a profound effect on the public.

Often, practitioners promise strong effects when they define their objectives. The communication scholar, on the other hand, learns in graduate school that the media have a limited effect. Largely, they reinforce what people already believe.[13]

Actually, current research suggests that both are wrong, but there seems to be more truth on the academic's side than on the practitioner's. To understand this gulf between academics and practitioners, let's look at some early communication theories before examining the more recent ones.

EARLY THEORIES OF COMMUNICATION EFFECTS

When we looked at the history of public relations in Chapter 2, we saw that propaganda efforts during World War I and after created both a great expectation and a great fear about the power of public relations. At first, most of the scholarly writing about propaganda and persuasion was humanistic and qualitative. At the time of World War II, however, both the U. S. military and commercial marketing interests began to provide funds for behavioral science studies of communication effects.[14]

The most famous of these studies were those done by Carl Hovland and his colleagues at Yale University, with support from the U. S. Army.[15] The Army wanted to learn how to persuade soldiers to support the war effort. The Yale studies searched for methods of persuasion and studied the effects on persuasion of such concepts as source credibility, fear appeals, and one-sided and two-sided messages. Those concepts remain part of the communication scientist's vocabulary today.

It is important to recognize that communication science has never been a pure, basic science like physics or chemistry. Scientists in those fields often get research money from ''neutral'' funding agencies such as the National Science Foundation or the National Institutes of Health.

Communication science has always been mostly an applied science. Its research funds have come from government agencies wishing to promote the military, to encourage people to stop smoking, to study the effects of television violence. Funds also have come from the media themselves, advertising and public relations agencies, corporations, and citizen interest groups. These granting organizations have almost uniformly believed that communication could persuade, and they have provided research money to find out how. So, for many years, communication scientists looked only for persuasive effects of communication, and that is all they found. (A simple, but powerful, rule of human nature is that people seldom find that for which they do not look.)

Can We Really Be "Persuaded"?

In the late 1940s and 1950s, however, evidence began to mount that communication, especially through the mass media, rarely has a persuasive effect. Most of this evidence came from voting studies and studies of the flow of information from the media to individuals.[16]

The researchers started out to find how the media affected voting decisions. Instead, they "discovered people." They found that most people made voting decisions after talking with other people who shared similar views, and that most made up their minds before the campaign began. During the campaign, voters read mostly about the candidate they preferred and ignored the other candidate.

Researchers developed the concepts of selective exposure and retention to explain why the media have such limited effects. People selectively exposed themselves to the messages they wanted to hear and selectively retained only the messages they wanted to retain.

In the late 1950s, social psychologist Leon Festinger developed one of the best-known theories of social psychology, the theory of cognitive dissonance.[17] It was mostly an attitude theory, but it also seemed to explain the limited effects of communication.

Dissonance theory stated that an attitude could be changed if it were juxtaposed with a "dissonant" attitude, an attitude that was logically inconsistent with the first. For ex-

ample, you might have a negative attitude toward General Motors because your Chevrolet breaks down frequently. If General Motors gives a $10,000 grant to your child's school, you probably would develop a positive attitude toward GM. The positive attitude juxtaposed with the negative could change the negative one for the better.

What Information Do We Seek?

More important than its explanation of attitude change, however, was the explanation of communication behavior provided by dissonance theory. Previous communication theories had been source ⟶ message ⟶ receiver theories. That is, they assumed that communication began with a source who presented a message to a receiver. The message, then, had some effect on the receiver—and most communication scientists assumed this to be a persuasive effect.

Dissonance theory turned this cause-effect relationship around: communication begins when a receiver *seeks* a message from a source. A message obviously could have no effect on a receiver unless the receiver first sought it out. Dissonance theory stated that receivers seek only messages that are "consonant" with their attitudes. They do not seek out "dissonant" messages. For example, people who do not smoke read anti-smoking literature much more than people who smoke. Dissonance theory seems to explain why.

In the 1950s and 1960s, dissonance theory appeared to provide a perfect explanation of the limited effects of communication that resulted from selective exposure and attention. More recent research has uncovered many problems with the theory.

In particular, it now seems clear that people select information more often because it is relevant to them than because it reinforces their attitudes. For example, before people buy an automobile, they seek information about several kinds of autos they could buy.

After buying the auto, they generally seek information about the auto they purchased. Dissonance theory would state that they are reducing dissonance by not learning about how the rejected choice could have been better than the chosen auto. A better explanation seems to be that information about a rejected alternative no longer has any relevance when the choice has been made. What a person then needs is information about how to use the auto he has purchased.

Nevertheless, dissonance theory has been extremely important in communication science because it has put the power of communication into a realistic perspective.

A great many academic communication scholars and public relations practitioners still hold these two opposite and extreme views of communication effects. The academics hold to the limited-effects view. The practitioners are attracted to the all-powerful view.

Leading communication scientists have now moved away from the limited-effects view to theories that lie somewhere in between. That "in-between" view offers a great deal of promise for conceptualizing public relations objectives. Before looking at it, how-ever, let's describe the dominant public relations view of communication effects and discuss what's wrong with that view.

It is easy to remember how many public relations people view communication effects if we call that view the domino theory.

The Domino Theory of Public Relations Effects

Remember the domino theory of the Vietnam War days. Some foreign policy experts believed that if Vietnam fell to the Communists, Laos, Cambodia, and Thailand would fall also. One domino would topple the others in an inevitable progression.

Public relations people seem to look at communication effects in a similar way. They have four dominos: message, knowledge, attitude, and behavior (Figure 6-3).

For example, a public relations practitioner working on an economic education program—a program designed to educate people about business, economics, and the free-enterprise system—stated in a public relations class that the objective of his program was to increase knowledge about business and economics, because that knowledge

FIGURE 6-3   A Domino Model of Communication Effects

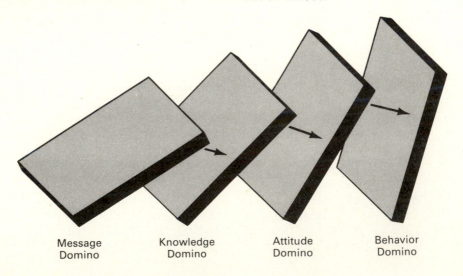

| Message Domino | Knowledge Domino | Attitude Domino | Behavior Domino |

would eventually lead to attitudes and behaviors that would support the free enterprise system.

Some studies show that economic knowledge does at times lead to favorable attitudes toward business.[18] Other studies, particularly on environmental and business topics, show that the most knowledgeable people often have the most negative attitudes—when negative means those people oppose the organization's point of view.[19] Evidence from these studies shows that the most knowledgeable people generally have *some* attitude about an issue and are most likely to do *something* about the issue (to engage in a behavior).

There is little evidence that the knowledgeable person's attitude or behavior will consistently be that advocated by the organization communicating a particular message. Once publics communicate about your organization and understand it, they may like what it is doing and support it. But it is equally likely that they will not like what the organization is doing and oppose it. It may be true that you can't love someone unless you understand him, but it is equally true that you can't hate someone unless you understand him. What's more, there is no assurance that everyone to whom you direct a message will choose to expose himself to it. And, not everyone who is exposed to a message will remember that message.

The dominos may fall, but only rarely do they fall in a line and topple each other.

The Hierarchy of Effects

There has also been a theory in marketing and advertising that, in its early stages, made pretty much the same assumptions as the domino theory. It was called the hierarchy of effects model.[20]

The hierarchy of effects can be envisioned as a stairstep. Before you can get to the top step, you have to start at the bottom. These stairs have been labeled awareness, compre-

hension, conviction, and action. They have also been called awareness, interest, desire, and action. You should be able to see that these stairs are nearly identical to the dominos. The names differ only slightly.

In psychological terms, either the stairs or the dominos can be labeled as cognitive, affective, and conative effects:

Cognitive means thinking: people become aware of your message.

Affective means evaluation or attitude: people evaluate your message favorably.

Conative means movement or behavior: people move or behave in the way you want them to.

According to marketing researcher Michael Ray, the hierarchy theories assumed the stairstep notion: cognitive effects precede affective effects, and, similarly, affective effects precede conative effects. Ray concluded, "Both empirical evidence and theory indicate that the stairstep hierarchy notion is, at the very least, too simple."[21] The effects may not be connected, and they do not always occur in the order assumed by the model.

Recent communication research has identified communication effects that are more realistic than those of the domino theory and more powerful than those defined by the 1950s' limited effects theory. They have great utility in managing public relations by objectives.

RECENT THEORIES OF COMMUNICATION EFFECTS

On the television program "That's Incredible," a man set a record for the number of dominos set up that subsequently toppled one another. He had spent hours placing the dominos on the floor of a gymnasium: in circles, over bridges, and in other intricate patterns. Finally, with a national television audience watching, he pushed the first domino.

It toppled the next domino, and within minutes all the dominos had fallen.

Imagine, however, what his reaction would have been had the dominos not fallen and toppled one another. Everyone *knows* that dominos always topple one another if they are set up at an appropriate distance from one another. But what if they didn't do what everyone knows they must do?

The reaction you would expect was about the reaction that most communication scientists had in the 1950s when research showed the knowledge, attitude, and behavior dominos were not toppling each other. Everyone at that time "knew"—as do the majority of public relations practitioners today—that communication changed attitudes and behaviors. They researched all kinds of communication strategies—all kinds of ways of setting up the dominos. But . . . the dominos only rarely toppled the way they were supposed to.

Many of the researchers gave up. Sociologist Bernard Berelson wrote in the *Public Opinion Quarterly* in 1959, for example, that communication yielded few effects and therefore was not worth the effort for a sociologist to study any longer.[22]

The "Golden Egg" Parable

At an annual convention of the Association for Education in Journalism in the early 1970s, Richard Carter, of the University of Washington School of Journalism, poked fun at Berelson's pessimism and illustrated recent research on communication effects by telling the parable of "the chicken who couldn't lay the golden egg." Poultry scientists, according to Carter's story, *believed* chickens could lay golden eggs, if only they had the proper conditions. So the poultry scientists put the hens in different housing, with different temperatures and humidities. They fed them different rations. They tried different breeds of chickens. In desperation, they even dissected the chickens to see if there were any golden eggs inside. There were none.

In frustration, one of the leading poultry scientists wrote an article in a leading poultry journal, in which he stated that research showed chickens could not lay golden eggs, that they were worthless creatures, and that they no longer were worth researching. That was the state of the discipline until a few years later when a group of young poultry scientists discovered that chickens could lay plain eggs, that those eggs were good to eat, and that research could show how and when chickens would lay more eggs.

Carter's analogy illustrated what was then happening in communication research, particularly in schools of journalism and mass communication. A new group of researchers had realized that communication had effects other than attitude and behavior change. It could create awareness and increase understanding. It might not tell people "what to think," but it could tell them "what to think about."[23]

Multiple Effects of the Media

According to one of this new breed of researchers, Steven Chaffee, there are at least eighteen kinds of media effects, whereas attitude researchers had looked for only one. Chaffee came to the number eighteen by constructing a matrix of three kinds of effects.

Media could have an effect because of their content or simply because of the time people spend with them. Either of those two effects could be cognitive (on knowledge), affective (on attitudes), or conative (on behavior). And, those six effects (2×3) could have an effect on individuals, on interpersonal relations, or on larger social systems such as communities or societies ($6 \times 3 = 18$ kinds of effects).

The majority of communication researchers, Chaffee added, have studied only one of the effects: the effect of content on the attitudes of individuals.[24]

McLeod and Reeves developed a similar typology of media effects and came to the same conclusion. They conceptualized five two-way distinctions of effects:

1. Micro vs. macro (individual vs. social).
2. Direct vs. conditional (depending on the presence of other conditions).
3. Content specific vs. diffuse effect of media content in general.
4. Attitudinal or behavioral vs. cognitive.
5. Altering attitudes, knowledge, or behavior vs. stabilizing them.

A matrix of these combinations would provide thirty-two possible communication effects. But researchers have mostly studied one of the thirty-two: the combination of specific microeffects on altering the attitudes of individuals.[25]

Chaffee and McLeod and Reeves were thinking about the effects of the mass media, but their types of effects apply to most other forms of communication used by public relations practitioners as well. We don't have to worry about all sixteen or thirty-two effects in public relations, but their matrices of effects should drive home the point that the domino theory describes only one of many possible communication effects—and an infrequent effect at that.

Especially important in conceptualizing public relations objectives are the differences between the effects that communication has on a single person or group and its effect on the *relationship* between two or more people or groups. For example, public relations may help an organization affect a public, or it could change the relationship between an organization and that public. Also of great importance are the differences among knowledge, attitudinal, and behavioral effects. Three recent theories help us to understand these effects.

Coorientation

As you may already have realized, the domino theory of communication effects fits especially well with the two-way asymmetric model of public relations. It also has the same presuppositions as the press agentry model, although few users of that model ever think theoretically about the effects of what they are doing. (The shortcomings of the domino theory should also help to show why the press agentry and two-way asymmetric models usually do not work as effectively as their adherents believe and promise.)

Attitudinal effects of communication can also be called *orientational* effects, as the term attitude literally means orientation. An attitude describes how people orient themselves to objects in their environment, such as organizations, governments, basketball teams, automobiles, or other people. The press agentry and two-way asymmetric models of public relations try to change that orientation so that people who make up publics will move in the direction the public relations person wants.

In the two-way symmetric model, however, public relations people do not change only the orientation of publics. They try to change the way the organization and its publics jointly orient to each other and the common parts of their environments. Communication scientists have coined the term "coorientation" to define that joint orientation. Figure 6–4 shows a model of coorientation, which is similar to one originally developed by McLeod and Chaffee.[26] The model depicts the possible relationships between two persons (or groups) that communication could affect. In public relations, these two "persons" would be the organization and a public.

In Figure 6–2, both the organization and a public have an idea—a *cognition*, or what each thinks the organization, an issue, or a problem is like. Each also has an *evaluation* of

FIGURE **6–4** A Coorientation Model

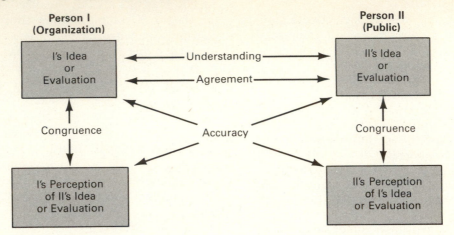

that cognition—an attitude, or whether the organization or public thinks the idea is good or bad.

The organization and the public each have a perception of the other's idea and evaluation—what one thinks the other thinks or how one thinks the other evaluates the organization, issue, or problem.

For example, the organization may think putting a new automobile plant in a city where it wants to put the plant will increase employment, enlarge the tax base, and stimulate further industrialization. A community public, however, thinks the plant will increase traffic congestion, air pollution, and racial discrimination. (As you may be able to see, ideas usually consist of attributes of the perceived object—here, the new plant.) The organization evaluates the plant favorably, but the public evaluates it unfavorably.

Do the Perceptions Coincide? • The parts of the coorientation model that help us to define symmetric communication effects are the relationships between the ideas and evaluations and the perceived ideas and evaluations:

Congruence is the extent to which each person thinks the other person's idea or evaluation is similar to his own.

Accuracy is the extent to which one person's perception of the other person's idea or evaluation approximates the other person's actual idea or evaluation.

Understanding represents the extent to which the two ideas are the same.

Agreement represents the extent to which the evaluations are the same.

Let's say the organization's "idea" is that the new plant will create employment in the community, and it perceives that the community public also thinks the new plant will create employment. The organization perceives congruency between itself and the public.

The public, however, thinks the plant will create more pollution than jobs. At the same time, it perceives that the organization thinks the plant will create jobs. The public perceives low congruency with the organization. We can also see that there is little understanding (the two have different ideas about the plant).

Accuracy is low between the organization and the public (the organization thinks the public sees employment as an attribute of the plant, but the public sees pollution). Accuracy is high between the public and the organization (the public knows what the organization thinks).

Suppose, next, that the public has a negative evaluation of the way it perceives the plant, while the organization has a positive evaluation. Then, we would say that agreement as well as understanding is low.

Research using this model has shown that communication between the two persons or groups frequently improves accuracy, less often increases understanding, and least often increases agreement.[27] (Congruency is an effect that occurs within each of the two persons, so it has less relevance as a communication objective.)

In our example, the organization could hold a community meeting to discuss the plant, thus communicating with the public. After members of the public discuss the pollution the plant will create, the organization should know better what the public's idea about the plant is and how the public evaluates the plant (accuracy in knowing both the public's idea and evaluation should increase). The same should happen to the public.

The meeting may also change the organization's and public's ideas (both may see that the plant will create employment and pollution). Thus, understanding will increase. Agreement could also increase, but it is quite likely that the organization will still think the plant is more desirable than will the public.

Adapting Coorientation to the Four Models • Accuracy, understanding, and agreement are important symmetric communication effects that should be major public relations objectives in the two-way symmetric model. They can also be adapted for the other three public relations models. Although the coorientation model depicts communication as symmetric, one can also use it to envision the effects of the other public relations models.

For the other models, communication would flow only from Person I to Person II. In the two-way asymmetric model, feedback could flow from Person II to Person I, but Person II would not communicate first. Thus, the only changes in accuracy, understanding, and agreement in the model would be those that occur when Person II, the public, changes its idea or evaluation.

We will come back to the coorientation model at the end of the chapter, when we present a list of public relations objectives. First, however, we need to look at recent attitude and behavioral research to understand how effective a persuasive public relations program can be.

The Attitude-Behavior Relationship

To attitude researchers over the years, finding that attitudes do not predict behaviors very well has been almost as upsetting as finding that communication often doesn't change attitudes. Attitude theorists previously assumed that attitudes were the mental orientations that direct a person's behavior. Attitudes were "predispositions to respond," part of an underlying, "latent process" that caused behavior.[28]

Already in 1934, LaPiere found evidence that attitudes do not predict behavior. He sent Chinese couples to 251 restaurants on the West Coast to see if restaurant owners would serve them. At that time there was prejudice against Chinese. Only once was a couple refused service. Six months later, LaPiere sent questionnaires to the restaurant owners asking if they would serve Chinese people. All but one said they would not.[29]

In 1964, Festinger expressed surprise that everyone assumed attitudes caused behavior but that few researchers had searched for evidence that the relationship actually existed. He searched the literature for such studies and found only three—one, he said, "of dubious relevance and one of which required reanalysis of data."[30] He concluded that there was little research evidence of a link between attitudes and behavior.

Thirteen years later, in 1977, Seibold found sixteen additional studies published since Festinger published his conclusion.[31] About half the studies found that attitudes predicted behavior, and half found that they did not. Only one of the studies found that the attitude-behavior relationship was a strong one.

The difficulty of finding a relationship between attitudes and behavior, therefore, has turned into one of the greatest controversies in recent social science.[32] After much argument about the problem, researchers now seem to have solved the problem of why attitudes do not cause behaviors, but they have had to change the way they conceptualize "attitude" to be able to do so. As a result, we now have a better idea of why the attitude domino does not topple the behavior domino.[33]

"Situational" Attitudes • First, researchers have learned that attitudes are not some underlying mechanism in the brain that causes people to behave in a consistent way in different situations. Instead, attitudes are much more specific. They are evaluations or conclusions that people make about specific problems or issues. The specific conclusions are not connected to some broad attitude.

For example, public relations people have frequently assumed that people have a broad attitude that predisposes them for or against business in many different situations. If a person has a negative attitude toward business, a public relations person viewing an attitude as an underlying predisposition to respond would logically expect the person with the negative attitude to oppose business consistently—on such issues as the environment, taxes, health, and safety.

In contrast, recent research has shown that the same person frequently opposes business on one issue and supports it on another.[34] How can that be? The answer is sim-

ple. Attitudes do not "cause" behavior. They are simply mental conclusions that people make when thinking about specific issues. When attitudes are defined in this more narrow way, they turn out to be much more consistent with behavior. In other words, attitudes are part of conscious thinking; they are not hidden predispositions that cause people to do things.

In addition to finding that attitudes are specific, attitude theorists have learned that both attitudes and behaviors are *situational* (a word we will use a lot in this text, especially in the next chapter). To say that attitudes and behaviors are situational means that people do not think and act in relation to broad values that they apply to all situations, but they change their attitudes and behaviors to fit the situation.

In one situation, buying stock, say, a person may be probusiness and support it by purchasing shares. In another, say his TV set breaks down, the same person may turn antibusiness and complain to the Better Business Bureau.

Constraints on Consistency • There are also logical reasons why in many situations attitudes and behavior are not consistent with each other. Sometimes, people may behave in a way that is inconsistent with their attitudes (what they want to do) because of *constraints* in the situation. Put simply, that means they may not always be able to do what they want.

You may think your instructor is a poor teacher, but you wouldn't tell any instructor that if you believe he or she would give you a poor grade. You could, similarly, decide to buy a sports car, but not have enough money to put your attitude into action.

At other times, you simply may not care enough about your attitude to put it into action. Most people frequently get angry about an automobile or a TV set that does not work. Seldom, however, do they write the manufacturer, regulatory agencies, or legislators to demand that something be done about the company.

Viewing attitudes and behaviors as specific and situational thus seems to explain why researchers have not always found attitudes and behaviors to be consistent in previous research. Attitudes and behaviors generally are consistent when it is logical for them to be consistent. But attitudes do not "program" behavior, and communication cannot "reprogram" people's minds so that they will consistently do what we want them to do.

Recent attitude-behavior research thus leads to the conclusion that the mass persuasion believed possible by those who practice the two-way asymmetric model of public relations seldom occurs—at least not on a long-term general basis.

Public relations can provide people the information they need to form and change attitudes, but those attitudes are specific and situational and therefore won't last long. You may be able to persuade someone on one issue, but you will have to start over on the next issue. And, then, you may not be so successful on the next issue.

"Hedging and Wedging"

Two of the most widely accepted new theories of attitude—theories that conceive of attitudes as specific and situational—have been proposed by Fishbein and Ajzen[35] and by Triandis.[36] Both theories separate out the cognitive (thinking) and affective (evaluational) components of attitude.

In the coorientation model in Figure 6–4, we called these two components ideas and evaluations. We also equated attitudes and evaluations, whereas some—Fishbein and Ajzen, for example—consider ideas and evaluations to be components of attitude. They also call ideas "beliefs." Beliefs are a person's concept of the attributes an object has.

The distinction between beliefs and evaluations (attitudes) is an important one in defining your public relations objectives. What people believe your organization is like and how they evaluate it are different things that may not always be consistent.

For example, the Du Pont Company learned that it could use corporate "image" advertising to change people's beliefs about the company, but not how they evaluate those beliefs.[37] After a Du Pont corporate advertising campaign, people who saw the ads were more likely to believe Du Pont was a socially responsible company than people who had not seen them. Not every one who viewed the ads, however, evaluated the attribute "social responsibility" as highly, and the advertising campaign did not change their evaluation.

For those viewers who evaluated social responsibility highly, however, the change in belief did increase their overall evaluation of the company. You can see this effect in the Fishbein-Ajzen formula that reads:

Evaluation of Company =
(Belief) × (Evaluation of Belief)

An increased belief that a company has a positively evaluated attribute—even though the evaluation of the attribute does not change—leads to a more positive evaluation of the company.

The Du Pont results show that if you can successfully implant ideas—beliefs—about your organization in people's minds that they evaluate favorably, you should be able to affect how favorably they view the organization as a whole. That, of course, is the heart of the two-way asymmetric model of public relations. Tell people only the good things and ignore the bad. Unfortunately, only rarely will you be the sole source of information people have about your organization.

A newspaper may report that a Du Pont factory, for example, pollutes the air. People believe the negative as well as the positive things they hear. What should you do? Practitioners of the press agentry model would try to keep unfavorable information away from publics, no matter what devious, non-professional means they must use. You would be better advised to deal with both positive and negative beliefs. The concepts of hedging and wedging help to understand what effects you can have.

Two Compatible Strategies • Hedging and wedging are two *cognitive strategies* that Stamm and several coresearchers developed to explain why environmental publics often seemed to hold two incompatible beliefs and frequently changed their beliefs from situation to situation.[38]

Their findings simply could not square with the conventional wisdom that had come from attitude theory. Someone could not hold a proenvironment attitude and hold conflicting beliefs. How could people believe that the environment should be cleaned up in one situation and that nothing needed to be done in another? The research showed that they could, and Stamm defined his cognitive strategies as a way of explaining how. People *hedge* when they hold two conflicting beliefs; they *wedge* when they hold one belief and reject the other.

These two cognitive strategies poke holes in the thinking of public relations practitioners who expect to change a public's "attitude" completely from being unfavorable to favorable. Translated into cognitive strategies, that means they want people to change from wedging unfavorable beliefs about the organization to wedging favorable beliefs.

An example is what we call the "Little League Baseball Syndrome." People may believe an organization is doing something they consider bad, such as polluting the air. To change that belief, the organization sponsors a Little League baseball team. It expects the favorable belief about the good done by helping youth to wedge out the unfavorable belief about the pollution. Realistically, the best that could be expected is replacing the wedged unfavorable belief with hedged favorable-unfavorable beliefs. That is, people will like the baseball team, but they won't forget the pollution.

Organizations also frequently communicate their position on a policy issue, such as the need for tax reform, and expect to develop a belief that will wedge out beliefs in opposing views. Research on the beliefs publics hold on business policies suggests, however, that most people believe the antibusiness point of view. If business communicates well, it can get publics to hedge a probusiness belief with the antibusiness belief. People do not give up the antibusiness view, however.

We have now looked at all of the pieces of theory about communication effects that we need to put together a realistic and measurable set of public relations objectives. To that task we now turn.

A TAXONOMY OF PUBLIC RELATIONS OBJECTIVES

Earlier in this chapter, we discussed two taxonomies of communication effects, one by Chaffee that included eighteen categories, and the other by McLeod and Reeves that contained thirty-two categories. In contrast, most of the research on communication effects has examined only one of the effects. These two taxonomies were developed as a way of understanding the effects of the mass media, and not all of the effects in them will be important to public relations. For example, media affect how people use their time, an effect not terribly important to public relations.

Public relations objectives should state what effects communication content will have on publics and organizational subsystems. Publics and organizational subsystems may react to communication differently than the individuals that make them up, but we will save a discussion of that difference until the next chapter.

The effects may be cognitive, attitudinal, or behavioral. We should not ignore communication alone as an objective. Frequently, a public relations person simply wants to communicate with a public or with management, regardless of the effect. Most of the effects will be conditional, depending on the nature of the public. We also will wait with that distinction until we develop the concept of public in the next chapter.

Finally, the objective may be an asymmetric or a symmetric effect.

Our taxonomy of public relations objectives, therefore, has three dimensions:

1. Target of the objective.
2. Direction of the effect.
3. Nature of the effect.

Each of the objectives may be chosen for a public relations program, such as press or community relations, or for a public relations technique, such as a press release or an open house. The objectives may also be chosen to evaluate the performance of an individual practitioner as part of a management-by-objectives program. The taxonomy is outlined in Exhibit 6–1.

In choosing one of the objectives for a program—from communication to affecting behavior—you might first jump to the conclusion that you want to achieve all of them. Or, you may believe that your program will not be successful without changing attitudes or behavior.

Remember, though, that each effect is less and less likely to occur as you move from communication to behavior. You might realistically expect to communicate with about half of your target group. About half of the people you communicate with will retain the message. But most of the members of the target group—70 to 85 percent—will have some kind of cognition and attitude.[39]

Generally, however, the majority will not have thought out these cognitions and attitudes thoroughly (we'll explain which publics do think them through thoroughly in the next chapter). Those cognitions also can just as easily be negative as positive.

You generally will find no more than 20 percent of a target group engaging in any kind of behavior—and those behaviors also can be both positive and negative.[40]

So be realistic about objectives. Most frequently, your objective will be communication, accuracy, or understanding—especially if you practice the public-information or two-way symmetric models of public relations. Save attitudes and behaviors for PR problems where those objectives are absolutely necessary: such as fundraising, promotion, or lobbying. Or use them if you work for an organization that needs press agentry/publicity or two-way asymmetric public relations.

If you do choose attitudes and behaviors as your objectives, be realistic. Don't expect to affect more than 20 percent of the target group.

Finally, when you choose an objective, remember the following rules gleaned from the communication effects literature we've just reviewed:

Communication effects are specific. Even though you're successful with one public relations problem, expect to start over with the next problem.

Communication effects are situational. Talk about the problem at hand, not about broad generalizations about the free enterprise system or how wonderful your organization is.

Communication effects are not always connected. Communicating doesn't always leave a message with someone. People may not always believe you when they do get the message. They may dislike your message as well as like it; oppose you as easily as support you.

Be flexible in choosing effects as objectives. Different PR problems call for different effects.

Communication effects differ greatly when conditions are different. In particular, you must choose different objectives when you communicate with different publics.

EXHIBIT 6–1 A Taxonomy of Public Relations Objectives

I. Target
   A. External Publics
      Any particular public relations problem will generate a number of publics. Different objectives may be necessary for each.
   B. Organizational Subsystem
      These subsystems may be employee "publics," which are targets for communication from management, or subsystems that receive communication from external publics.
II. Direction of the Effect
   A. Asymmetric
      The effect is unbalanced. Generally, the organization attempts to affect publics.
   B. Symmetric
      The effect is balanced. The relationship between publics and the organization will be affected.
III. Nature of the Effect
   A. Communication
      The target public or subsystem receives a message. Stories are placed in the mass media and publics read them; publics see an advertisement, attend a special event, read a brochure; management meets with public leaders, reads the results of a public opinion poll.
   B. Retention of Messages
      "Accuracy" in the coorientation model. The public or organizational subsystem should not only be exposed to the message, it should also retain the message. Thus, this objective essentially is one of comprehension. The recipients of the message do not necessarily agree with the message or plan to do anything about it. They simply remember what you said. Targets know the other's beliefs and evaluations. They do not necessarily hold the same beliefs and evaluations, however.
   C. Acceptance of Cognitions
      Understanding in the coorientation model. The target not only retains the message explaining the other's beliefs, but accepts the message as its beliefs about reality. The target may "hedge" or "wedge" cognitions.
   D. Formation or Change of an Attitude (Evaluation or Behavioral Intent)
      Agreement in the coorientation model. The target should not only believe the message, but should evaluate its implications favorably and intend to change its behavior.
   E. Overt Behavior
      Targets actually change or begin a new or repeated behavior. Publics may write to a government official, avoid a product, buy a product, attend an event, give money to a cause. Management may change a policy, or not build a plant, or give customers a refund.

The last rule will make much more sense when you understand the nature of publics. That is the subject of the next chapter.

NOTES

1. Peter H. Rossi, "Testing for Success and Failure in Social Action," in Peter H. Rossi and Walter Williams (eds.), *Evaluating Social Programs: Theory, Practices, and Politics* (New York: Seminar Press, 1972), p. 18.
2. Carol H. Weiss, *Evaluation Research* (Englewood Cliffs, N. J.: Prentice-Hall, 1972), p. 26.
3. A paraphrase of what evaluation researcher Peter Rossi said has been typical in the management and evaluation of most social programs. Rossi, p. 16.
4. This distinction is derived from John Dewey, *The Theory of Valuation* (Chicago: University of Chicago Press, 1939).
5. Robert L. Kahn, "Organizational Effectiveness: An Overview," in Paul S. Goodman and Johannes M. Pennings (eds.), *New Perspectives on Organizational Effectiveness* (San Francisco: Jossey-Bass, 1977), pp. 235–248.
6. Bruce A. Kirchhoff, "Organization Effectiveness Measurement and Policy Research," *Academy of Management Review* 2 (1977):348–355.
7. John P. Campbell, "On the Nature of Organizational Effectiveness, in Goodman and Pennings, pp. 13–55.
8. Daniel Katz and Robert Kahn, *The Social Psychology of Organizations*, 2d ed. (New York: Wiley, 1978), p. 251.
9. Christopher J. Hardwick, "Public Relations and Organizational Effectiveness: An Open Systems Approach," master's thesis, University of Maryland, College Park, 1980.
10. Johannes M. Pennings and Paul S. Goodman, "Toward a Workable Framework," in Goodman and Pennings, pp. 146–184.
11. The concept of dominant coalition was first developed by Thompson in James D. Thompson, *Organizations in Action* (New York: McGraw-Hill, 1967).
12. W. Jack Duncan, *Essentials of Management*, 2d ed. (Hinsdale, Ill.: Dryden Press, 1978), pp. 316–317.
13. The concept of limited effect was defined by Klapper in Joseph T. Klapper, *The Effects of Mass Communication* (New York: The Free Press, 1960).
14. F. Gerald Kline, "Theory in Mass Communication Research," in F. Gerald Kline and Phillip J. Tichenor (eds.), *Current Perspectives in Mass Communication Research* (Beverly Hills: Sage Publications, 1972), pp. 17–40.
15. For one of the books resulting from the Yale research, see Carl I. Hovland, Irving L. Janis, and Harold H. Kelley, *Communication and Persuasion* (New Haven, Conn.: Yale University Press, 1953.
16. Two of the most important books reporting this research were Paul F. Lazarsfeld, Bernard Berelson, and Hazel Gaudet, *The People's Choice* (New York: Columbia University Press, 1948), and Elihu Katz and Paul F. Lazarsfeld, *Personal Influence* (Glencoe, Ill.: Free Press, 1955).
17. Leon Festinger, *The Theory of Cognitive Dissonance* (Stanford, Calif.: Stanford University Press, 1957).
18. Walter Barlow and Carl Kaufmann, "Public Relations and Economic Literacy," *Public Relations Review* 1 (Summer 1975):14–22; Byron Reeves and Mary Ann Ferguson-DeThorne, "Measuring the Effects of Messages about Social Responsibility," *Public Relations Review* 6 (Fall 1980):40–55.
19. James E. Grunig, "Developing Economic Education Programs for the Press," *Public Relations Review* 8 (Fall 1982):43–62; Phillip J. Tichenor, G. A. Donohue, C. N. Olien, and J. K. Bowers, "Environment and Public Opinion," *Journal of Environmental Education* 2 (Summer 1971):38–42; James E. Grunig, "Review of Research on Environmental Public Relations," *Public Relations Review* 3 (Fall 1977):36–58.
20. Michael L. Ray, "Marketing Communication and the Hierarchy of Effects," in Peter Clarke (ed.), *New Models for Communication Research* (Beverly Hills: Sage Annual Reviews of Communication Research, vol. 2, 1973), pp. 147–176.
21. Ray, p. 150.
22. Bernard Berelson, "The State of Communication Research," *Public Opinion Quarterly* 23 (1959):1–15.

23. An explanation of the "agenda-setting" effect of the mass media. See Maxwell McCombs, "Agenda Setting Function of Mass Media," *Public Relations Review* 3 (1977):89–95.

24. Steven H. Chaffee, "Mass Media Effects: New Research Perspectives," in G. Cleveland Wilhoit and Harold de Bock (eds.), *Mass Communication Review Yearbook*, vol. 1 (Beverly Hills: Sage, 1980), pp. 77–108.

25. Jack M. McLeod and Byron Reeves, "On the Nature of Mass Media Effects," in G. Cleveland Wilhoit and Harold de Bock (eds.), *Mass Communication Review Yearbook*, vol. 2 (Beverly Hills: Sage, 1981), pp. 245–282.

26. Jack M. McLeod and Steven H. Chaffee, "Interpersonal Approaches to Communication Research," *American Behavioral Scientist* 16 (1973):469–500. The model is also described in Glen M. Broom, "Coorientational Measurement of Public Issues," *Public Relations Review* 3 (Winter 1977):110–119.

27. For example, Daniel Wackman, "Interpersonal Communication and Coorientation," *American Behavioral Scientist* 16 (1973):537–550.

28. Melvin L. DeFleur and Frank R. Westie, "Attitude as a Scientific Concept," *Social Forces* 42 (1963):17–31.

29. Richard T. LaPiere, "Attitudes vs. Actions," *Social Forces* 13 (1934):230–237.

30. Leon Festinger, "Behavioral Support for Opinion Change," *Public Opinion Quarterly* 28 (1964):227–236.

31. David R. Seibold, "Communication Research and the Attitude-Verbal Report-Overt Behavior Relationship: A Critique and Theoretic Reformulation," *Human Communication Research* 2 (1975):3–32.

32. Allen E. Liska, "Introduction," in Allen E. Liska (ed.), *The Consistency Controversy* (Cambridge, Mass.: Schenkman, 1975), pp. 1–20.

33. See Alice H. Eagly and Samuel Himmelfarb, "Attitudes and Opinions," *Annual Review of Psychology* 29 (1978):517–554; Howard Schuman and Michael P. Johnson, "Attitudes and Behavior," *Annual Review of Sociology* 2 (1976):161–207; James E. Grunig, "Communication Behaviors and Attitudes of Environmental Publics: Two Studies," *Journalism Monographs* No. 81 (March 1983).

34. James E. Grunig, "A New Measure of Public Opinions on Corporate Social Responsibility," *Academy of Management Journal* 22 (1979):738–764.

35. Martin Fishbein and Icek Ajzen, *Belief, Attitude, Intention, and Behavior* (Reading, Mass.: Addison-Wesley, 1975).

36. Harry C. Triandis, *Interpersonal Behavior* (Monterey, Calif.: Brooks/Cole, 1977).

37. Robert C. Grass, "Measuring the Effects of Corporate Advertising," *Public Relations Review* 3 (Winter 1977):39–50.

38. Keith R. Stamm and John E. Bowes, "Environmental Attitudes and Reaction," *Journal of Environmental Education* 3 (Spring 1972):56–60; Keith R. Stamm and James E. Grunig, "Communication Situations and Cognitive Strategies in Resolving Environmental Issues," *Journalism Quarterly* 54 (1977):713–720; James E. Grunig and Keith R. Stamm, "Cognitive Strategies and the Resolution of Environmental Issues: A Second Study," *Journalism Quarterly* 56 (1979):715–726.

39. James E. Grunig, "The Message-Attitude-Behavior Relationship: Communication Behaviors of Organizations," *Communication Research* 9 (1982):163–200.

40. These estimated frequencies are based on actual probabilities of the communication effects reported in Grunig, "The Message-Attitude-Behavior Relationship."

ADDITIONAL READING

Broom, Glen M., "Coorientational Measurement of Public Issues," *Public Relations Review* 3 (Winter 1977):110–119.

Chaffee, Steven H., "Mass Media Effects: New Research Perspectives," in G. Cleveland Wilhoit and Harold de Bock (eds.), *Mass Communication Review Yearbook*, vol. 1 (Beverly Hills: Sage, 1980), pp. 77–108.

Eagly, Alice H., and Samuel Himmelfarb, "Attitudes and Opinions," *Annual Review of Psychology* 29 (1978):517–554.

Fishbein, Martin, and Icek Ajzen, *Belief, Attitude, Intention, and Behavior* (Reading, Mass.: Addison-Wesley, 1975).

Goodman, Paul S., and Johannes M. Pennings (eds.), *New Perspectives on Organizational Effectiveness* (San Francisco: Jossey-Bass, 1977), pp. 235–248.

Grunig, James E., "The Message-Attitude-Behavior Relationship: Communication Behaviors of Organizations," *Communication Research* 9 (1982):163–200.

Grunig, James E., "Communication Behaviors and Attitudes of Environmental Publics: Two Studies," *Journalism Monographs* No. 81 (March 1983).

Katz, Daniel, and Robert Kahn, *The Social Psychology of Organizations*, 2d ed. (New York: Wiley, 1978), p. 251.

Liska, Allen E. (ed.), *The Consistency Controversy* (Cambridge, Mass.: Schenkman, 1975).

McLeod, Jack M., and Byron Reeves, "On the Nature of Mass Media Effects," in G. Cleveland Wilhoit and Harold de Bock (eds.), *Mass Communication Review Yearbook*, vol. 2 (Beverly Hills: Sage, 1981), pp. 245–282.

Oskamp, Stuart, *Attitudes and Opinions* (Englewood Cliffs, N. J.: Prentice-Hall, 1977).

Petty, Richard E., Thomas M. Ostrom, and Timothy C. Brock (eds.), *Cognitive Responses in Persuasion* (Hillsdale, N. J.: Lawrence Erlbaum Associates, 1981).

Ray, Michael L., "Marketing Communication and the Hierarchy of Effects," in Peter Clarke (ed.), *New Models for Communication Research* (Beverly Hills: Sage Annual Reviews of Communication Research, vol. 2, 1973), pp. 147–176.

Schuman, Howard, and Michael P. Johnson, "Attitudes and Behavior," *Annual Review of Sociology* 2 (1976):161–207.

Seibold, David R., "Communication Research and the Attitude-Verbal Report-Overt Behavior Relationship: A Critique and Theoretic Reformulation," *Human Communication Research* 2 (1975):3–32.

7

IDENTIFYING ORGANIZATIONAL LINKAGES TO PUBLICS

Although "public" is one of two words in the term "public relations," few public relations practitioners have a clear idea of just what a public is. Many practitioners use the term "public" to refer simply to the opposite of "private"; they do not use it to refer to a group of people.

Other practitioners equate a public with the audience of a newspaper, magazine, or television station. Still others broadly define publics as such groups as employees, communities, or consumers, without realizing that there are different kinds of employee, community, or consumer publics.

Many public relations practitioners believe publics have common demographic characteristics, such as age, sex, race, or location of residence. They think, for example, of the elderly, women, blacks, or urban dwellers as single publics, when these social categories may include many publics or may not constitute publics at all.

If really pressed about the nature of their publics, many practitioners will claim to be communicating to the general public. As you will see in this chapter, a "general public" is a logical impossibility. Publics are always specific; they always have some common problem. Thus, they cannot be general.

Although the categories that public relations people generally use to define their publics may indeed contain important publics, those categories do not by themselves define publics. Publics come and go. Today, one community public may exist; tomorrow, it may be replaced by another. It all depends on what an organization does and how people and organizations in the environment react to that organizational behavior.

The Key to the Dilemma

The key to determining an organization's publics can be found in the definition of a public relations problem, which we introduced in Chapter 1—consequences that an organization and its publics have on one another. For the publics of an organization, the common problem that creates and identifies a public will usually be some consequence that an organization has on a public or that a public has on an organization.

If the organization has no consequences upon other systems in its environment, and if those systems have no consequences upon the organization, there is no need for public relations. If there are no consequences outside the organization, there is no need for the organization to think about its public responsibility. Without consequences, systems would not interpenetrate, and organizations could limit themselves to a closed-system approach to management.

Similarly, it is the *detection* of consequences outside the organization that sets off the management process described by the behavioral molecule. Determining how consequences link an organization to other systems in its environment, therefore, represents the most central question that public relations practitioners must face.

In the public relations management process, PR managers should begin by determining how organizational consequences "link" their organization to other systems—publics and other organizations—in the environment. Then, managers should research those publics and organizations to define the exact nature of the public relations problem and to choose a realistic public relations objective.

In this chapter, we will explain two concepts that are essential for implementing this stage of the process:

Organizational "linkages" to the environment.
The nature of publics.

We will begin by defining the most frequent linkages organizations have with other systems. These linkages identify likely groups of publics that have mutual consequences with the organization. Then we will discuss the difference between active and less active publics and explain why those different kinds of publics require different public relations objectives and strategies. Next, we will present a theory that can be used to identify publics and to determine how active those publics are. Finally, we will show how to determine which objective defined in the previous chapter is most appropriate for each public.

THE CONCEPT OF LINKAGES

In the previous chapter, we said that public relations goals become organizational goals when key external constituencies become part of the organization's dominant coalition. These external systems, to use terms we have used frequently, then interpenetrate the subsystems of the organization.

In Chapter 5, Elements of Public Relations Management, we also said that systems should strive for a moving equilibrium. Each time an interpenetrating system upsets the equilibrium, the systems manager tries to restore it. Sociologist Peter Blau described these relationships with interpenetrating systems:

> In complex social structures with many interdependent, and often interpenetrating, substructures, particularly, every movement toward equilibrium precipitates disturbances and disequilibrium and thus new dynamic processes. The perennial adjustments and counteradjustments find expression in a dialectical pattern of social change.[1]

A "dialectical pattern of social change" means, simply, that an interpenetrating system may do something that creates conflict with the organization. To resolve the conflict, the organization generally will have to negotiate and compromise with the interpenetrating system, and frequently change its behavior.

Managers of a public relations program help the organization plan for disruptions of its equilibrium with the environment in three ways:

1. Identifying interpenetrating systems.
2. Determining which interpenetrating systems are most likely to upset the equilibrium.
3. Planning communication programs with the systems likely to upset the equilibrium, so that the movements in the "moving equilibrium" can be smooth ones.

We will use the concept of linkages to determine the interpenetrating systems most likely to upset an organization's equilibrium. Organizations are "linked" to other systems through consequences—either when the organization has consequences on another system, or when another system has consequences on the organization. The linked, or interpenetrating, systems may be other organizations, such as a government agency that regulates a business firm, or they may be "publics," groups of people with common interests who are not always organized into a formal organization. Publics may, however, be found among the members of other formal organizations that interpenetrate an organization.

Looking for Linkages

Several sociologists have described types of linkages that the public relations manager can use to identify an organization's most important interpenetrating systems. Evan, for example, used the term "organizational set" to define linked organizations.[2] He then used systems terminology to define two kinds of organizational sets: *input sets* and *output sets*.

In its input set, an organization is linked with organizations that supply inputs. Those organizations may be suppliers of materials the organization needs to produce products; or organizations that supply workers, such as labor unions; or governmental agencies that input regulations.

The output organizational set may include, for example, dealers franchised by an automobile company, advertising agencies helping to sell products, trade associations helping to influence governmental legislation, or community charitable organizations.

Parsons identified three types of linkages that an organization has with "the institutional structure and agencies of the community."[3] His linkages include publics as well as formal organizations. The first kind of link occurs when the organization violates laws or standards of good practice. Then "public opinion" or law-enforcement agencies intervene to stop that organizational consequence. This would represent a linkage to a public. The second link is with a formal organization such as a board of directors of a business firm or the governing board of a university. The third link is with government agencies, which link the organization to "public authority."

Four Key Linkages

Esman listed four types of linkages that he believed to be critical for an organization to survive.[4] He developed his concepts of linkages working with the Agency for International Development to help found new organizations in underdeveloped countries that would survive and bring changes in those countries.

Esman's concepts seem equally useful for understanding the key linkages of established organizations in developed countries. His linkages subsume those of Evan and Parsons and seem to explain why so many organizations have public relations programs aimed at such groups as government, employees, or consumers. Let's examine Esman's concepts and then see how they apply to public relations management. The four kinds of linkages, depicted in Figure 7-1, are:

1. **Enabling Linkages** • These are linkages with organizations and social groups that provide the authority and control the resources that enable the organization to exist.

FIGURE **7–1**   **External Linkages of Organizations**

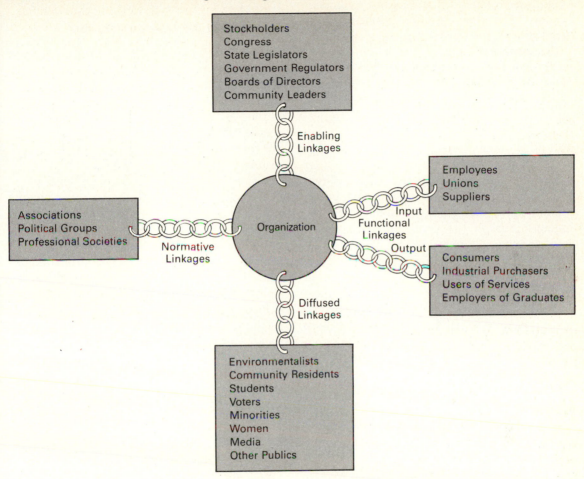

Government regulatory agencies, boards of directors, stockholders, Congress, and state legislatures are examples. Evan would call these members of the input organizational set. Parsons would call them linkages to public authority or to governing boards. Public relations departments plan programs in government relations, public affairs, stockholder relations, and community relations to communicate with these linked organizations and groups.

2. Functional   Linkages • These   are linkages with organizations or publics that provide inputs and take outputs. Thus, functional linkages can be further divided into Evan's:

a. Input linkages • These linkages include relations with employees and unions and with suppliers of raw materials. Public relations programs for these linkages are called employee relations, labor relations, and supplier relations;

b. Output linkages • These linkages may be with other organizations that use the organization's products, such as automobile companies that use steel, or organizations

Identifying Organizational Linkages to Publics   **141**

that use government services. They may also be with individual consumers of products or services. The most common public relations program to serve these linkages is called consumer relations.

3. Normative Linkages • These linkages are with organizations that face similar problems or share similar values. Universities have joint programs with other universities. Business firms join in the National Association of Manufacturers or the U. S. Chamber of Commerce. Political groups join with other political groups with the same values. Organizations generally do not have formal public relations programs for these linkages, but the linkages explain the need for associations. Associations exist to facilitate communication between member organizations so that the members can jointly attack common problems. Normative linkages, therefore, also explain why association public relations people must spend most of their time dealing with member relations.

4. Diffused Linkages • Esman described diffused linkages as linkages with "elements in society which cannot clearly be identified by membership in formal organizations." Thus, he seemed to have in mind "publics" that arise when the organization has consequences on people outside the organization. Diffused linkages also seem to include what Parsons called linkages with "public opinion" that occur when the organization violates laws or "standards of good practice." Organizations have developed such public relations programs as environmental relations and minority relations to deal with diffused linkages. Although consumer relations and community relations also can be explained by other categories of linkages, the publics served through these two programs also can be described as diffused. In addition, organizations have media relations programs because the media inform diffused publics about consequences that the organization has

on them and thus help to bring those diffused publics into existence in the first place.[5]

How to Use the Linkage Concepts

This listing of common organizational linkages has two uses for the student of public relations. First, it should help you to understand why organizations have such public relations programs as consumer relations or media relations. Second, you can use linkage concepts to plan what public relations programs an organization needs and then to justify the programs to top management.

Try working through the linkage concepts for your college or university as an example to see what organizations and publics it should communicate with. Every state university, for example, has enabling linkages with the legislature, the governor's office, the Board of Regents, the state Board of Higher Education, and the U. S. Department of Education. It has input functional linkages with faculty, staff, students, and parents. It has output linkages with employers of students and users of research. It has normative linkages with other universities. Finally, it has diffuse linkages with the community, sports fans, the area news media, and residents of the state. It's also not surprising that most state universities have public relations programs designed to service each of these linkages.

There are two other things you should remember about these linkages. First, enabling and functional linkages generally have consequences on organizations. Thus, they represent organizations and publics that the organization seeks out in its public relations programs. On the other hand, the organization usually has the consequences on diffuse publics—rather than the other way around.

Too often, the organization does not design a public relations program for a diffuse public until that public organizes, puts pressure on the organization, or seeks regulation of the organization from government—that is, when the diffuse linkage seeks out the organization. The socially responsible organization, however, thinks through its consequences on publics and tries to alleviate those consequences before the public threatens consequences on the organization. We will expand on this idea in the next section of this chapter.

Second, remember that organizations with more complex and changing environments will have more linkages with the environment and that those linkages will change frequently.[6] That idea takes us back to the discussion of environments in Chapter 5: The more complex the environment, the more numerous and changing will be the organization's linkages. The more numerous and changing the linkages, the greater the organization's need for a two-way model of public relations—particularly the two-way symmetric model.

The Role of Boundary Personnel • Organizational theorists point out that organizations make contact with linked organizations and publics through boundary personnel. In Chapter 1, we defined a boundary person as an organizational employee who has as much contact outside the organization as inside. Public relations people are boundary personnel. So are salesmen, service representatives, and social workers.

Public relations people do not always serve all of the linkages we have discussed. They are more likely to deal with linked publics than with linked organizations, although they may help other boundary personnel communicate with linked organizations. For example, the president and vice president of a state university communicate most with the governor and state legislature, but they are backed up and assisted by public relations people.

Because public relations programs primarily serve linkages with publics, we will

next conceptualize the nature of publics to help you understand what publics are, how they originate, and how they differ.

PUBLICS

In the 1940s, sociologist Herbert Blumer and philosopher John Dewey defined publics in ways that still provide two of the clearest and most useful definitions in use today. Unfortunately, social scientists and public relations practitioners today often have not learned of those definitions or have forgotten them.

For example, social scientists, commercial research firms, and public relations people today measure ''public opinion'' with public opinion polls. Blumer's and Dewey's definitions of ''public'' make it clear that these polls may measure opinions, but that they do not measure opinions of publics. Instead, they measure mass opinion.

Blumer distinguished between publics and the mass. He argued that pollsters measure mass opinion rather than public opinion.[7] The mass is heterogeneous, a public is homogeneous. Individuals make up a mass not because they have something in common, but because they are all tuned in to the same mass medium or just happen to live in the same city or country. Members of a public, in contrast, have something in common—they are affected by the same problem or issue.

According to Blumer, a public is a group of people who:

1. Are confronted by an issue.
2. Are divided in their ideas as to how to meet the issue.
3. Engage in discussion over the issue.

Dewey defined a public in much the same way.[8] He said a public is a group of people who:

1. Face a similar problem.
2. Recognize that the problem exists.

3. Organize to do something about the problem.

Recall the behavioral molecule, and you should see similarity to the Blumer-Dewey definitions of publics:

Detect . . . Construct . . . Define . . . Select . . . Confirm . . . Behave . . . Detect . . .

The definitions of both Dewey and Blumer begin by stating that members of a public *detect* a problem or an issue. Next, the definitions state that members of a public discuss the issue and organize to do something about it. In the terms of the behavioral molecule, the members of the public pass through the *construct*, *define*, *select*, and *confirm* segments of the behavioral molecule when they discuss the problem. When they organize for action, they enter the *behave* segment of the behavioral molecule.

"Behavior" Is the Key • Dewey's and Blumer's definitions of publics, when translated into the terms of the behavioral molecule, suggest that publics consist of individuals who detect the same problems and plan similar behaviors to deal with those problems. Members of publics may behave in a similar way without ever seeing one another face to face.

For example, environmentalists throughout the United States may react in a similar way to a proposal to strip-mine on the borders of a national park, even though they do not formally meet. They may have learned of the proposal through the mass media or through information disseminated to them by environmental organizations. Other publics might meet face to face and organize strikes, demonstrations, or picket lines.

In either case, members of a public function as a single system because they input and process the same information and output similar behaviors. Thus, we can define a public as a loosely structured system whose members detect the same problem or issue, interact either face to face or through mediated channels, and behave as though they were one body.

Masses, in contrast to publics, do not behave as though they were a single body. In fact, they usually do not behave at all; they are inactive.

If you now think back to our definitions of public relations problems and of linkages, you should be able to see how this definition of publics fits the concept of public relations we have been building throughout this book. The concept of consequences ties public relations problems, linkages, and publics together.

"Consequences" Create Publics • When organizations have consequences on people outside the organization, those consequences create problems for the people affected. Some people *detect* the consequences—recognize a problem. They become members of a public. Thus, consequences create the conditions needed for publics to form. The presence of the publics, in turn, creates a public relations problem for the organization.

For example, a steel mill that pollutes the air has consequences on people who must breathe the air. The people who *detect* the pollution develop into an air-pollution public. That public may then discuss the problem and even organize into an activist environmental group to confront the steel mill. Without the pollution, there would have been no public. The presence of the public, in turn, created the public relations problem.

The linkage concept fits into this picture because the people for whom the organization most often has consequences are those linked to the organization in one of the four ways we described in the previous section.

Public relations managers can identify their publics by defining the linkages of their organization in their mind or through discussion with other members of the organization.

Then, they must research the people identified through the linkage concepts to determine if the linkages have created any publics. (We'll discuss how to do that research later in this chapter.)

For example, the air-pollution consequence would create a diffused linkage with people affected by the pollution who may or may not form into a public. The enabling linkage of a state university to state legislators may or may not result in legislator ''publics'' who *detect* the university's financial needs as a problem deserving their attention and action.

In our discussion of linkages, we said several times that organizations may be linked either to other organizations or to publics. The concept of a public can help us to understand both kinds of linkages, for, as we said before, publics may be found in organizations.

When an organization has a linkage to another organization, such as a university to the state legislature, it does not try to communicate with the entire linked organization. It tries to communicate with those members of the organization whose formal role or informal interest causes them to *detect* the consequences described by the linkage. Those members of the organization can be described as publics, just as can people who make up diffused organizational linkages.

For example, the legislators interested in the state university problem will probably be found on the education committee or will have constituents who ask for more funds for the university. Various members of a formal organization—the legislature—can constitute publics, just as can those diffused individuals concerned with the air pollution caused by the steel mill.

Not all people affected by the consequences of an organization's behavior recognize the consequences. And not all of those who recognize the consequences discuss them with other people and organize with others to do something about the consequences. As a result, there are several different kinds of publics. Those publics differ, primarily, in the extent to which they become active in doing something about the organizational consequences.

Types of Publics

Dewey's definition of a public contains three conditions he considered necessary for a public to exist. To repeat that definition, a public is a group of people who:

1. Face a similar problem.
2. Recognize that the problem exists.
3. Organize to do something about the problem.

If we recognize that some groups of people meet the first or second of these conditions, but not the second or third, then we can use Dewey's definition to identify three types of publics.

First, we would define a group for whom none of these conditions apply as a *nonpublic*. For a nonpublic, the organization would have no consequences on the group or the group would have no consequences on the organization.

When the members of a group face a similar problem created by organizational consequences but do not detect the problem, they would constitute a *latent* public. When the group recognizes the problem, it becomes an *aware* public.

When the public organizes to discuss and do something about the problem it becomes an *active* public.

These four categories of groups and publics differ in the extent to which they participate in active behavior to do something about organizational consequences. That is, they differ in the extent to which they have passed from the *detect* to the *behave* segment of the behavioral molecule.

Common PR Errors Regarding Publics

If public relations managers can determine the category into which each of their publics falls, they can develop an appropriate public relations strategy for each public. If the practitioner has a nonpublic, his or her organization has no public relations problem and need not concern itself with that group. Many public relations practitioners miss that point, however, and plan public relations programs for groups of people who are not part of a public relations problem.

Other practitioners wait for publics to become active before addressing the public relations problem. That, too, is a mistake. The organization may choose not to communicate with a latent public, but it runs the risk that the public may become aware or active before the organization has a chance to communicate with the latent public about the consequences that affect it.

When a public becomes aware of the consequences, the organization must actively communicate with that public before the public actively opposes the organization or seeks redress by way of government or other enabling linkages.

If the organization does not communicate with an aware public, that public will actively seek the information from other sources, which may distort the nature or severity of the organization's consequences. Certainly, the other information sources will not explain the organization's point of view about those consequences as well as the organization could itself.

When a public becomes active, the public relations practitioner will have great difficulty communicating with it. An active public has made a decision and has entered the *behave* segment of the behavioral molecule. In that segment of the molecule, the public seeks mostly information that reinforces the decision made in the *construct, define, select,* and *confirm* segments of the behavioral molecule.

It will not be open to the same information that it would have sought in these three segments when it was still an aware but not an active public.

Thus, an active public most often communicates in the way predicted by the cognitive-dissonance theory introduced in the previous chapter. It selectively seeks and retains information that reinforces the attitudes and behaviors it has previously chosen.

Getting the Attention of a Public

The only chance public relations people have to communicate with a selective, active public is to somehow get it to *detect* that a problem still exists and that it must reconsider the decision it made before. Seldom is that easy to do unless the consequences that brought the public into existence have gotten worse or new consequences have developed that are worse than the original ones.

For example, a public affected by air pollution may have, in the absence of any information from the polluting company, managed to get government regulations to restrict the pollution. The public seldom will give up those regulations unless the organization can show that the regulations made the pollution worse or that they created economic consequences—a plant shut down or employee layoffs—that represent a more severe problem than the original pollution consequence.

It is also important that as a public relations practitioner you remember that it is the active publics who define what it means for an organization to be socially responsible.[9] They take their position to the mass media or to government and other enabling linkages. The problems active publics articulate will relate to the behaviors of your organization that others will use to judge its public responsibility.

The best way to influence the definition of public responsibility, therefore, is to communicate with aware publics to try to reach an accommodation with them before they become active. Such an accommodation could make a great deal of difference in how your organization is evaluated by other linkages.

The Effects of Size and Situation

There are two other characteristics of publics with which you should be familiar. First, remember that, as we stated in the previous chapter, recent social science research has shown that attitudes generally are *situational*. To say that attitudes are situational means that people may evaluate your organization favorably in some situations, such as its performance in producing a quality product, but unfavorably in other situations, such as its record on air pollution. They will not have one broad attitude toward your organization on all issues. In this chapter, it is also important to point out that publics are situational. Each consequence may bring about a public with different people in it.

The air-pollution problem may create one public. The quality of your organization's product or service may create another. Your publics will constantly change. Each consequence will bring about new and, frequently, different publics. Public relations managers, therefore, must constantly review organizational consequences and research how publics react to those consequences so that their public relations programs do not aim at publics that no longer exist.

Secondly, remember that size and cohesion affect how active a public becomes. If publics become too large and diffused, they seldom move from the aware stage to the active stage. Thus, a small group of local activists, such as a local group organized to stop the building of a plant, may do your organization more damage than a large environmental group that is not organized at the local level.

Economist Mancur Olson has explained this phenomenon using the economic theory of monopolistic competition, which you probably studied in a basic economics course.[10] This theory states that when there are many producers of essentially the same product, such as aspirin or mouthwash, they seldom compete by lowering their price, because no one seller affects the market enough to gain a sales advantage. Instead, price-cutters just lower their own revenues.

According to Olson, a similar principle holds for publics. When there are many members of a public, no one member has a strong incentive to become active to secure benefits from large organizations or from government. Each member thinks someone else will do the necessary work.

In a small, cohesive public, however, each member knows that without him or her the group may fail because no one else will do the work. Thus, every member of a small, cohesive public works hard to solve the problem that brought the public about. That effort makes such publics more effective organizational adversaries than large, diffuse publics.

At this point, you should understand publics and recognize different kinds of publics. Now we need to follow up our statement that public relations managers should do research on potential members of publics to determine the nature of the publics with which their organization must deal. We turn, therefore, to a theory that can be used to identify publics and to determine their nature.

A SITUATIONAL THEORY TO IDENTIFY PUBLICS

The publics that develop around problems or issues differ in the extent to which they are aware of the problem and the extent to which they do something about the problem. Public relations managers must have an elaborate theory of publics to help them do research to identify and classify their organization's publics.

Publics arise when organizations do things that have consequences on people. The publics become active when they recognize those consequences and organize to try to eliminate them. (Editorial Photocolor Archives)

Grunig has developed such a theory to explain when and how people communicate and when communications aimed at people are most likely to be effective.[11] The concepts in the theory parallel those we have taken from Dewey and Blumer to define publics. Therefore, the theory provides a well-developed set of variables that public relations managers can measure through survey research to identify and classify their publics.

Variables in the Theory

Like the definitions of publics and attitudes we have developed, the Grunig theory is a situational theory. The theory states that communication behaviors of publics can be best understood by measuring how members of publics perceive situations in which they are affected by such organizational consequences as pollution, quality of products, hiring practices, or plant closings.

There are three major independent variables in the Grunig theory. In research terms, an independent variable explains one or more dependent variables. The independent variables in the Grunig theory can separate people who are part of publics from those who do not belong to a public. They can also indicate when people will communicate actively or passively about an issue and, in doing so, identify which publics are latent and which are aware or active.

The independent and dependent variables we shall examine in the following pages are:

Independent Variable #1—PROBLEM RECOGNITION

Dependent Variable A—Information Seeking
Dependent Variable B—Information Processing

Independent Variable #2—CONSTRAINT RECOGNITION

Independent Variable #3—LEVEL OF INVOLVEMENT

Independent Variable #1—Problem Recognition • Grunig calls the first of the three independent variables *problem recognition*. He takes the concept from John Dewey's theory of human behavior, which is much like Dewey's explanation of the conditions necessary for a public to develop.[12]

Problem recognition represents the *detect* segment of the behavioral molecule. The basic idea behind the concept is that people do not stop to think about a situation unless they perceive that something needs to be done to improve the situation. When they detect such a problem, they enter the *construct, define, select*, and *confirm* segments of the behavioral molecule. It is in those segments that they do most of their communicating, because it is in those segments that they need information to help solve the problem they have detected.

Thus, measuring whether people who you think might be members of a public detect an organizational consequence is a reliable way of determining whether they will communicate about that consequence with the organization and whether they will be members of a public. (To learn how to measure problem recognition and the other variables of this theory, see Exhibit 7–1.)

Before looking at the other two independent variables of the theory, let's look at the dependent variables of the theory. Doing that should help you to understand the importance of problem recognition and the other variables in identifying publics. It should also help you to put the pieces of the theory together into one coherent theory of publics.

Each of the three independent variables explains when people will communicate in two ways—that is, it explains two dependent variables. Each also explains when these two types of communication behavior will have one of the communication effects defined in the taxonomy of communication effects in the previous chapter—that is, communication effects are a third dependent variable. Grunig calls the two types of communication behavior *information seeking* and *information processing*.

Dependent Variable "A"—Information Seeking • *Information seeking* can also be called "active communication behavior." Actively communicating members of publics look for information and try to understand it when they obtain the information. Thus, publics whose members seek information become aware publics more often than publics whose members do not communicate or who only process information.

Because actively communicating publics try to understand the information they receive and then use the information to plan their behavior, the messages they receive usually are more effective in one of the ways described in the previous chapter than are messages aimed at publics who do not communicate or who process rather than seek information.

Dependent Variable "B"—Information Processing • *Information processing* can be defined as "passive communication behavior." Passively communicating members of a public will not look for information, but they will often process information that comes to them randomly—that is, without any effort on their part.[13]

Because the Grunig theory is a "situational theory," problem recognition, constraint recognition, and level of involvement must be measured for each of several organizational consequences. In a study of policy issues important to several large business corporations, people interviewed over the telephone were asked one question to measure each variable for four different issues. In some studies, as many as sixteen issues were included. That many issues can be included, however, only when a mail questionnaire, rather than a telephone interview, is used. Here is the way each variable is measured.

Problem Recognition

Remember that the theory says people do not think or communicate about an issue unless they detect a problem. Thus, whether they "stop to think" about an issue would be a logical consequence of problem recognition and an indicator of its presence. The question:

1. First, I would like you to consider how often you *stop to think about* each of four issues. After I name each of these issues, please tell me whether you stop to think about the situation often, sometimes, rarely, or never. The first issue is:

	Often	Sometimes	Rarely	Never
Deregulation of natural gas	4	3	2	1
Breaking up the Bell telephone system	4	3	2	1
Chemical disposal sites	4	3	2	1
Acid rain from air pollution	4	3	2	1

Constraint Recognition

Remember that a person feels constrained when he, as an individual, cannot do anything about an issue. The following question, therefore, represents a simple measure of that concept:

2. Now, would you think of whether you could do anything personally that would make a difference in the way these issues are handled. If you wanted to do something, would your efforts make a great deal of difference, some difference, very little difference, or no difference?

	Great Deal	Some	Very Little	None
Deregulation of natural gas	4	3	2	1
Breaking up the Bell telephone system	4	3	2	1
Chemical disposal sites	4	3	2	1
Acid rain from air pollution	4	3	2	1

Level of Involvement

The key term used to measure level of involvement, as specified by the theory, is "connections." Thus, the question asks:

3. Now, I have a third question about the same issues. For each situation, tell me to what extent you *see a connection* between yourself, personally, and each of these situations. There

would be a connection if you believe the issue has affected or could affect you. Tell me if the connection is strong, moderate, weak, or if you see no connection. The first issue is:

	Strong	Moderate	Weak	None
Deregulation of natural gas	4	3	2	1
Breaking up the Bell telephone system	4	3	2	1
Chemical disposal sites	4	3	2	1
Acid rain from air pollution	4	3	2	1

For example, few people seek out television commercials, but they take in information from commercials that are sandwiched into the content of a program they are watching. Similarly, people take in information they encounter while skimming through a newspaper or magazine or listening to television news. Students process much of the information provided by their professors or textbooks in required courses that they would not seek if the course were not required. (We hope you are seeking the information in this textbook, rather than merely processing it.)

The members of a public exert less effort to understand information they process than information they seek. Thus, processed information has fewer communication effects than information that is sought. Studies have shown, for example, that many viewers of television news do not remember anything they heard fifteen minutes after the program. Professors will also tell you that students who process information learn less than students who seek it. Publics whose members process information often remain latent publics. Sometimes, they become aware publics, but seldom will they become active publics.

Problem recognition, to return to the theory's first independent variable, increases the likelihood that a member of a public will both seek and process information. People who recognize a problem will seek information because they need it in each of the stages of the behavioral molecule to plan a behavior to ad-

dress the problem. For example, a newly graduated college student, for whom the lack of a job is a problem, will write letters and seek out a placement manual from the library to help find a job.

The person who recognizes a problem, likewise, will also be more likely to process information that comes randomly than will the person who does not recognize a problem.

For example, some television commercials talk about career opportunities. Both the new graduate seeking a job and an employed person will hear such commercials, but the new graduate will be most likely to pay attention to them and to remember them—that is, to process the information to which he or she is exposed. Thus, problem recognition not only increases the likelihood of information seeking and processing, it also increases the likelihood that both will have an effect.

Independent Variable #2—Constraint Recognition • Now that we've discussed how problem recognition increases information seeking, information processing, and communication effects, let's go to the other two independent variables of the theory.

The second variable in the theory, *constraint recognition*, represents the extent to which people perceive that there are constraints—or obstacles—in a situation that limit their freedom to plan their own behavior. If people realize that they have little choice of behavior in a situation, information that helps them *construct, define, select,* and *confirm* a behavior has little value to them.

Thus, a high level of constraint recognition lessens the likelihood that people will *seek information* about an organizational consequence or that they will pay attention to and *process information* about the consequence that comes to them randomly.

For example, many members of organizational publics believe there is little they can do to help solve the problem of air pollution. As a result, these people seldom communicate about the issue. Similarly, poor people face many constraints in their lives. Those who have little education have much difficulty getting a job. As a result of the education constraint, poor people seldom look for information about jobs that require more education than they have. Similarly, few professors communicate about Cadillacs, because most professors are constrained by a modest salary.

Independent Variable #3—Level of Involvement • Whereas *problem recognition* and *constraint recognition* increase the likelihood of both information seeking and processing, the third independent variable, *level of involvement,* helps to distinguish whether the person's communication behavior will be active or passive.

People's level of involvement represents the extent to which they connect themselves with the situation. For example, we might ask a man whether he thinks air pollution or a plant closing has a personal effect upon him. When a person perceives himself as involved in a situation, he will be likely to *seek information* actively because his own behavior is involved—he is going through the behavioral molecule—and he needs information to help plan and control that behavior. A man involved in a plant closing, for example, probably calls his supervisor for information, attends special meetings, and eagerly reads news accounts of the closing to find out what is happening.

A member of a public who perceives a strong involvement in an issue generally also has high problem recognition and low constraint recognition for that issue.[14] As a result, an involved public usually will be the most active public. It will seek and process information and use that information to develop ideas, attitudes, and behaviors.

High involvement usually leads to problem recognition because it is difficult to be affected by an organizational consequence without seeing that consequence as a problem. High involvement decreases constraint recognition because involved people generally try to remove constraints that otherwise would discourage them from communicating and doing something about the problem.

The involved person most frequently gets rid of constraints by organizing with others facing the same constraints—that is, by becoming a member of an active public. For example, an individual citizen may not be able to do much about air pollution from a nearby steel mill, but a citizen's organization can pressure the government to regulate the polluting plant.

Publics can still be aware and, at times, active even if their members do not perceive an involvement with the issue. The reason is that people will randomly *process information* about issues that do not involve them directly.

For example, few Americans have a direct involvement in the infant-formula controversy we discussed in Chapter 3, on public responsibility. Most Americans probably know about the issue because they have processed information about it from the news media or their churches. Many, then, are members of an aware public on the formula controversy. Low-involved publics, however, will seldom pay much attention to information they process, and they will not become active unless their members also recognize the issue as a problem and do not feel constrained from doing something about it.

Using the Independent Variables to Define Publics

Thus far, we have described each of the three independent variables separately, although we referred to the different effects that result from combinations of the variables when we discussed the effect of level of involvement. We can summarize the individual effects of each variable by saying that high problem recognition, low constraint recognition, and high level of involvement increase information seeking. High problem recognition and low constraint recognition also increase information processing. Level of involvement, however, has a limited effect on information processing.

The theory can be used most effectively to identify publics when we develop different combinations of the three independent variables. First, let's simplify things by assuming that a measure of each variable taken through a survey of potential members of a public will yield either a high or a low score (see Exhibit 7-1). Three variables with two possible scores yield eight combinations of variables (2×2

$\times 2 = 8$). People whose scores on the measures of the three variables fit into each one of these combinations of variables for any issue—air pollution, for example—can be called a public. The behavior of each of these publics closely approximates the behavior of nonpublics and latent, active, and aware publics as we defined them above.

Table 7-1 shows these eight kinds of publics and shows how they relate to the kinds of publics we described above. Start looking at the first column of the table. You will notice four kinds of behavior described by combinations of problem recognition and constraint recognition.

These are further broken down by level of involvement in the headings of the next two columns. Each of the combinations is labeled by initials to give a shorthand way of referring to each public. For example, HIPF stands for a high-involvement, problem-facing public.

Problem facing describes the behavior of a public that results when members of that public recognize the problem caused by a

TABLE 7-1   Eight Kinds of Publics Defined by the Three Independent Variables of the Grunig Theory of Communication Behavior

	High Involvement (HI)		Low Involvement (LI)	
	Behavior Type	Type of Public	Behavior Type	Type of Public
Problem-facing behavior (PF): High Problem Recognition, Low Constraint Recognition	HIPF	Active	LIPF	Aware/Active
Constrained behavior (CB): High Problem Recognition, High Constraint Recognition	HICB	Aware/Active	LICB	Latent/Aware
Routine behavior (RB): Low Problem Recognition, Low Constraint Recognition	HIRB	Active (Reinforcing)	LIRB	None/Latent
Fatalistic behavior (FB): Low Problem Recognition, High Constraint Recognition	HIFB	Latent	LIFB	None

particular organizational consequence and face no constraints. Members of a public who fit this type of behavior will be highly likely to seek and to process information and to be affected by the information.

High involvement will increase the likelihood of each of those effects, although the effects will occur frequently even when involvement is low. Generally, this will be an active public, although it may remain as only an aware public when involvement is low.

Constrained behavior occurs when members of a public recognize a problem but feel constrained from doing anything about it. The constraints discourage communication, but problem recognition encourages it. This public will seek and process information in spite of the constraints, however, when involvement is high.

When involvement is high, therefore, the public engaging in constrained behavior will be either an aware or active public. When involvement is low, this public will have less motivation to communicate in spite of the constraints and will be either a latent or an aware public.

When members of a public have freedom from constraints—when they can do something about a problem—but still do not recognize the problem, their behavior can be described as *routine behavior*. They have made up their minds. They think the problem has been solved.

When they have a high level of involvement, members of publics engaging in routine behavior seek information to support their solution to the problem. They selectively seek reinforcing information in the way predicted by cognitive-dissonance theory. Then they are active publics who try to preserve their solution. In that sense, they are conservative publics.

When involvement is low, routine behavior publics do not care about the problem and usually fit the category of nonpublics or latent publics.

Fatalistic behavior describes the behavior of a public that would seldom if ever actively communicate about an issue and that would be the public least likely to process information that comes to it randomly. The term "fatalistic" suggests that, for the organizational consequence that creates the potential for a public, these people don't care and make no effort to plan a behavior for that issue.

When the public is involved and still fatalistic—which is rare—it constitutes a latent public that could become aware or involved if something happens to make it recognize the problem. If a fatalistic group of people has a low level of involvement, it is not really a public and does not deserve the attention of the public relations manager.

Although all eight kinds of publics described by these combinations can occur, some occur more often than others. This is because the three independent variables affect each other. For example, as we stated above, level of involvement generally increases problem recognition and decreases constraint recognition. Thus, HIPF (high-involvement problem facing) and LIFB (low-involvement, fatalistic behavior) occur often, but HIFB (high-involvement, fatalistic behavior) seldom occurs.

Public relations managers can measure the three variables of the Grunig theory to place people who might be members of their organization's publics into one of these eight types for each of the consequences the organization has on the potential members of publics. Having placed these people into one of the types, a manager would know what communication strategy would be best for each.

To understand these strategies, we will next look at some research evidence that gives more exact information about the communication behavior of each of the eight types of publics and the likelihood that public relations messages directed at the publics will be effective.

Probabilities of Communication Behavior and Effects for the Eight Kinds of Publics

In the previous section, we discussed the effects of the three independent variables of the Grunig theory in terms of the "likelihood" that a member of each of the eight kinds of publics would seek or process information or that they would be affected by messages directed at them by public relations people. Statisticians have a more precise word than "likelihood." They talk about the "probability" of something occurring.

A probability is simply the relative frequency with which something occurs. For example, a weather forecaster who says the probability of rain today is 50 percent simply means that on 100 days in which the meteorological conditions are the way they are today, it would rain on fifty of those days. Rather than saying that members of a high-involvement, problem-facing public are "highly likely" to seek information, we could be more precise and say that the probability of information seeking is 75 percent for that public. That would mean that seventy-five out of 100 members of that public would actually seek information on an organizational consequence that could bring about a public.

The Grunig theory of publics would be especially useful to public relations managers if reasonably accurate probabilities could be computed for information seeking and processing, and communication effects, for each of the eight kinds of publics. Then, managers could estimate whether they have a reasonable chance of communicating with each public that arises from the consequences their organization has on potential members of publics.

As we will see in the next chapter, the probabilities can help PR managers estimate whether the probability of communication is high enough to justify the cost of communicating with a public.

Grunig has calculated probabilities of information seeking and processing in several studies, and of communication effects in a recent study of corporate-government policy issues. Table 7–2 presents probabilities calculated in the study of corporate policy issues. In that study, Grunig took four issues that had generated controversy about corporate behavior. These issues included the question of the safety of the gas tanks on Ford Pintos, the question of nuclear power, the infant-formula controversy, and the question of whether steel imports should be restricted. Each of those issues could generate different kinds of publics.

For each issue, Grunig asked a sample of people questions to measure problem recognition, constraint recognition, and level of involvement. (You can examine these questions in Exhibit 7–1.) He then placed each person interviewed, for each of four issues measured, into one of the eight types of publics listed in the first column of Table 7–2.

For example, a person interviewed would be placed into the high-involvement, problem-facing public if he said he often or sometimes stops to think about an issue (problem recognition), could make a great deal or some difference in the way the issues are handled (constraint recognition), and that he perceives a strong or moderate connection to the issue (level of involvement).

The column labeled *Proportion of Total Publics* shows how many of the people interviewed actually fit into each category. For example, 15 percent fit in the high-involvement, problem-facing public. The largest public was the low-involvement, fatalistic public—the category into which 34 percent of the people interviewed fell. (If you still don't understand how Grunig placed the survey respondents into these eight publics, go back and read through Exhibit 7–1 once more.)

Now, let's discuss where the probabilities of information seeking, information processing, and the five communication effects came from.

TABLE 7-2   Probabilities of Communication Behaviors and Effects in Eight Behavioral Situations

	Proportion of Total Publics	Info. Seek.	Info. Proc.	Message Retention	Pro-Bus. Cognit.	Anti-Bus. Cognit.	Attitude	Behavior
				(percentages)				
High Involvement								
Problem-Facing Behavior	15	74	96	47	94	97	97	48
Constrained Behavior	19	58	92	29	88	91	90	25
Routine Behavior	5	33	77	55	73	90	93	28
Fatalistic Behavior	12	33	76	54	84	84	90	13
Low Involvement								
Problem-Facing Behavior	3	55	93	37	74	82	92	11
Constrained Behavior	7	52	85	35	80	93	90	26
Routine Behavior	5	30	84	54	57	73	81	9
Fatalistic Behavior	34	18	62	39	62	70	76	7
Total Probability	100	40	79	41	76	83	86	20

Source: James E. Grunig, ''The Message-Attitude-Behavior Relationship: Communication Behaviors of Organizations,'' *Communication Research* 9 (1982):163–200.

Grunig measured information seeking by giving a sample of people a title of a hypothetical free brochure—one title for each of the four issues—that could be available from a ''government agency, corporation, or association.'' He then asked each person interviewed how likely he or she would be to send for the brochure.

Grunig measured information processing by reading a hypothetical opening line for a television news program—again, one for each issue—and asking how much attention they would pay to the rest of the story.

For each of the eight kinds of publics, he then estimated the percentage that had high scores on these measures of information seeking and processing. These percentages are the probabilities in Table 7–2.

As we explained above, the first column of Table 7–2 shows how many potential members of publics in Grunig's sample of 200

residents of Maryland fell into each of the eight publics for the four issues. Because each person could be in a different public for each of the four issues, there were four times as many members of publics as there were people interviewed. For example, one person might have fit the problem-facing category for all four issues or for one, two, or three of the issues. A person might be in a problem-facing public on the nuclear-power issue and in a fatalistic public for steel imports. Thus, when Table 7–2 says that 15 percent of the members of the total publics were members of a problem-facing public, it means that 120 members of publics (0.15 × 800) fit that category.

This first column of Table 7–2 shows that some publics will be found more often than others, as the above discussion of combinations of the three independent variables suggested. For these business policy issues, high-involvement, constrained behavior; high-involvement, problem-facing behavior; and low-involvement, fatalistic behavior characterized the three most common publics. In fact, the low-involvement, fatalistic behavior category accounted for fully a third of the participants.

Confirming the Theory

The probabilities of information seeking and processing in the second and third columns of Table 7–2 also turn out to be generally what the theory predicts they should be. The bottom row, "total probability," shows that members of all publics process information about twice as frequently as they seek it—79 percent vs. 40 percent. This is to be expected, as information processing occurs randomly, which requires little effort, while a person must exert more effort to actively seek information.

For the same reason, there are also smaller differences among the eight publics in information processing than in information seeking. You can also compare the differences in the probabilities among the eight kinds of publics to confirm that they do support the theory as we have explained it in this chapter.

The last five columns of Table 7–2 show the probabilities of the communication effects discussed in the previous chapter. The probability of "message retention" shows how many members of each of the eight publics correctly answered a multiple-choice question that measured whether they could identify the stand that a large corporation had taken on each issue—for example, Bethlehem Steel on steel imports.

The pro- and antibusiness cognition columns show how many members of publics had developed some cognition, as opposed to no cognition, on what are the positive or negative consequences of nuclear power, the Ford Pinto, infant formula in underdeveloped countries, or steel imports. As you will remember from the previous chapter, these two cognition questions, when put together, measure whether members of publics hedge or wedge on such issues.

The Grunig theory does not predict what *kinds* of cognitions members of publics will have or whether their attitudes will be positive or negative. Instead, it shows which publics are most likely to have *some* cognition or attitude. The theory shows which publics will communicate most about organizational consequences and which publics will be most likely to develop ideas and evaluate those ideas.

Thus, the theory shows which publics will be *aware* publics—those that have cognitions and attitudes. The last column of Table 7–2 also helps to identify the *active* publics. It shows how many members of each public said they had actually done something about the issue, such as writing a letter to a congressman, boycotting Ford products, or attending an antinuclear rally.

Because the theory predicts when people will have some cognition, the probabilities in the pro- and antibusiness cognitions columns do not indicate whether the persons interviewed agreed or disagreed with the companies involved in the four issues. A high probability in the probusiness column means that members of that public agreed *or* disagreed with a probusiness statement on one of the issues. A low probability means that members of a public chose to say they had "no opinion" on the issue.

The same is true for the "attitude" column. A high probability means members of a public have made an evaluation about what they think should be done about an issue. For example, they would agree *or* disagree with the statement, "Nuclear power plants should no longer be built." A low probability would mean members of the public responded that they have "no opinion" on that statement.

(In the next chapter, we will have more to say about how to measure cognitions and attitudes.)

What the Probabilities Imply

Look now at the implications of the probabilities of these four kinds of effects. You will notice first that the probabilities of message retention in Table 7–2 are relatively low for all eight kinds of publics and relatively high for cognitions and attitudes. The probability that a public will engage in some kinds of behavior is relatively low, but differs substantially among the publics.

Message retention probably was low because people in the survey were asked about only one factual item for each issue, and even the actively communicating publics might not have sought out *that particular fact*. The probability of having cognitions was relatively high for all publics, but it was highest for the aware and active publics, such as the high-involvement, problem-facing public, and low for the nonpublics, such as the low-involvement, fatalistic-behavior group.

The study also could not measure how well thought out the cognition was. Members of the latent and nonpublics could have had a cognition that was not logical and thoroughly reasoned out. The study did not measure that aspect of cognition.

The probability of having an attitude also was high for all of the publics, although it was lowest for the latent and nonpublics. The relatively high overall probability of having an attitude, however, shows that many people do make evaluations that are not based upon complete information. Again, however, the members of latent and nonpublics probably do not hold their attitudes as strongly as do members of active and aware publics, and the study did not measure that aspect of attitude.

Finally, the probabilities of behavior support our contention of the previous chapter that change in behavior is an infrequent effect

of public relations. Only one in five people in this study said they had done anything about these issues. Table 7–2 shows, however, that the Grunig theory does an excellent job of identifying who will be the members of the actively behaving publics.

Table 7–2, then, provides research evidence that generally confirms the Grunig theory of publics. In the next chapter, we will use these probabilities further and show how public relations managers can use them to make decisions about public relations programs.

Communication Strategies Based on the Theory

Let's suppose that you, as a public relations manager, have done the research necessary to place potential members of your publics into one of these categories. Then, you would probably ask, "So what? How does knowing what my publics are like help me?" The beauty of a theory is that it not only *explains* what your publics are like, it also *predicts* what you should do once you understand them.

Here are five implications of the Grunig theory that you can apply after you have identified your publics.

1. When you have a public with a low probability of information seeking and processing and a low probability that messages directed at it will be effective, seldom should you waste time and money on a public relations program to reach that public. No one will be listening or acting.

2. If the low-probability public is important because it can have a severe consequence for your organization, such as publics that are linked to the organization through an enabling linkage, you can possibly reach that public through information processing. You cannot expect such a public to seek information, nor can you expect your messages to have much of an effect other than partial message retention. In other words, members

of such a public may remember part of what you said. But that might be enough to stimulate problem recognition, which would then make that public more likely to seek and process information and thus become an aware or active public.

3. When you communicate with a public that will process rather than seek information, you need a different communication strategy. Actively communicating publics help communicators get their message across. They look for information and try to understand it when they obtain the information. A passively communicating audience, on the other hand, does not look for information and generally will do little to understand the information that comes to it randomly. Thus, a message must have style and creativity to get the attention of the information-processing public. Passive publics must be lured into processing information with such devices as photos, illustrations, clever writing style, catchy phrases, or slogans. Remember, for example, what Sam Adams did to gain attention for the American Revolution.

4. When you must deal with active publics—those with high probabilities of information seeking and of behavior—you cannot let your organization maintain "a low public profile." If your organization does not communicate with these publics, they will seek information elsewhere and base their cognitions, attitudes, and behaviors on that information. Seldom will other sources of information present your organization's point of view as well as you could. In addition, those sources frequently will put your organization in a bad light.

5. As we argued in the last chapter on communication effects, don't expect changes in cognition, attitude, and behavior from many members of your publics. Only the aware and active publics, such as the high-involvement, problem-facing publics, go through the behavioral molecule far enough to develop reasoned cognitions and attitudes

and to engage in a behavior. And, no more than 40 percent of those publics go that far. If your objective must be a change in attitude or behavior, then concentrate on those publics with the highest probability of having an attitude and engaging in a behavior. If, for example, you are in fund-raising, concentrate on the people who fit the high-involvement, problem-facing category. Otherwise, you have a low probability of success. Remember, however, that the public could develop a negative attitude and behavior toward your organization as well as a positive one. Active publics seek information from many sources, they make reasoned decisions, and they are difficult to persuade.

Common Groupings of Publics Found by Research

Grunig has used this theory to identify publics for a number of public relations programs, including employee relations, community relations, environmental relations, consumer relations, economic education, and public affairs. We will discuss the results of these studies in more detail in the chapters in Part III that deal with the management of these programs. Here, however, we mention some general conclusions from these studies that should help you to understand the theory better.

As explained in Exhibit 7–1, Grunig measures the variables of the study for each of several organizational consequences or issues that fit under one of these programs. For example, he used the Ford Pinto, infant-formula, steel-imports, and nuclear-power issues in the public-affairs study we just discussed.

For employee relations, he measured sixteen consequences a scientific organization had on its employees, including benefits, management decisions, and recreational opportunities. Although it is possible that each consequence could bring about totally different publics, generally some issues will bring about the same publics. For example, the publics for the nuclear-power and steel-import issues were largely the same. In addition, some people will be in the same publics for all of the issues. On environmental issues, some people will be active on environmental issues ranging from urban air pollution to the runoff of fertilizer from farmland into lakes.

Grunig's studies show a regular pattern of publics. For most of the major programs of public relations, these types of publics emerge:

1. Publics That Are Active on All of the Issues • In the public-affairs study, for example, one group of people surveyed fit into the high-involvement, problem-facing (HIPF) category for the Ford Pinto, nuclear-power, steel-import, and infant-formula issues. Such people fit into what can truly be called activist publics that challenge organizations on many different issues.

2. Publics That Are Apathetic on All Issues • These are nonpublics (low-involvement, fatalistic behavior) on all the issues to which the theory is applied. Organizations need pay no attention to them.

3. Publics That Are Active Only on Issues That Involve Nearly Everyone in the Population • In an environmental study, for example, members of this public were apathetic about every issue but the shortage of gasoline. On that issue, every person sampled could be considered the member of an active public. Similarly, some employees in an employee relations study were active only about the issue of their own salaries, for which all employees were members of active publics.

4. Single-Issue Publics • These publics crusade for one issue and pursue it doggedly while ignoring other issues. The infant-formula controversy brought about such a public in the public-affairs study, as did the controversy over Russian and Japanese killing of whales in an environmental study.

We now have conceptualized the nature

of publics and have shown how they can be measured. Public relations practitioners can use these concepts to do their own research on publics, or they can use studies of publics such as those we have just discussed and will discuss more thoroughly in Part III, to plan public relations programs.

Before leaving the topic of publics, however, let's look briefly at one additional kind of research needed on publics.

DETERMINING OBJECTIVES FOR EACH PUBLIC

In Chapter 5, Elements of Public Relations Management, we discussed formative and evaluative research. Formative research helps the manager plan a public relations program. Evaluative research determines how successful that program has been. Research on publics is formative research.

At the same time that public relations managers do research to identify their publics, they should also ask questions of members of these potential publics to determine the extent to which the organization's communication objectives have already been met before the public relations program begins. Managers should determine how much each public knows of their organization, what ideas and attitudes that public has about the organization, and what kinds of behaviors that public has been practicing. Chapter 9, Evaluation Research, will show how to measure those objectives.

Knowing the extent to which public relations objectives have been met before a program has been implemented will suggest whether new information must be given to publics or whether misinformation must be corrected. It will also show whether attitudes and behaviors already exist and whether they should be changed or reinforced.

In the next chapter, we show how the public relations manager can organize and evaluate the information gained in formative research on publics to make decisions about public relations programs. Then, in Chapter 9, we will return to the question of how to measure objectives both for formative and for evaluative research.

NOTES

1. Peter M. Blau, "Social Exchange Among Collectivities," in William M. Evan (ed.), *Interorganizational Relations* (New York: Penguin, 1976), p. 56.
2. William H. Evan, "An Organizational-Set Model of Interorganizational Relations," in William M. Evan (ed.), *Interorganizational Relations*, pp. 78–90. See also William H. Evan, "The Organization-Set: Toward a Theory of Interorganizational Relations," in James D. Thompson (ed.), *Approaches to Organizational Design* (Pittsburgh: University of Pittsburgh Press, 1966), pp. 175–191; and Rolf T. Wigand, "A Model of Interorganizational Communication Among Complex Organizations," in Klaus Krippendorff (ed.), *Communication and Control in Society* (New York: Gordon and Breach, 1979), pp. 367–387.
3. Talcott Parsons, "Three Levels in the Hierarchical Structure of Organization," in William M. Evan (ed.), *Interorganizational Relations*, pp. 69–90.
4. Milton J. Esman, "The Elements of Institution Building," in Joseph W. Eaton (ed.), *Institution Building and Development* (Beverly Hills: Sage, 1972), pp. 19–40.
5. For support of this conclusion, see Paul M. Hirsch, "Processing Fads and Fashions: An Organization-Set Analysis of Cultural Industry Systems," *American Journal of Sociology* 77 (1972):639–659.
6. Michael Aiken and Jerald Hage, "Organizational Interdependence and Intra-Organizational Structure," *American Sociological Review* 33 (1968):912–929.
7. Herbert Blumer, "The Mass, the Public, and Public Opinion," in Bernard Berelson and Morris Janowitz (eds.), *Reader in Public Opinion and Communication*, 2d ed. (New York: Free Press, 1966), pp. 43–50 (originally published in 1946); Herbert Blumer, "Public Opinion and Public Opinion Polling," *American Sociological Review* 13 (1948):542–554.
8. John Dewey, *The Public and Its Problems* (Chicago: Swallow, 1927).
9. Lee E. Preston and James E. Post, "Private Management and Public Policy," *California Management Review* 23 (Spring 1981):56–62.
10. Mancur Olson, *The Logic of Collective Action* (Cambridge, Mass.: Harvard University Press, 1971).
11. The theory has been described and applied in several articles. See, for example, James E. Grunig, "A New Measure of Public Opinions on Corporate Social Responsibility," *Academy of Management Journal* 22 (1979):738–764 and James E. Grunig, "Describing Publics in Public Relations: The Case of a Suburban Hospital," *Journalism Quarterly* 55 (1978):109–118. For a complete explanation of the theory and its uses, see James E. Grunig, *Communication Behavior: Theories and Theory Building in Communication Science* (New York: Holt, Rinehart and Winston, in process).
12. John Dewey, *Logic: The Theory of Inquiry* (New York: Holt, Rinehart and Winston, 1938); John Dewey, *Human Nature and Conduct* (New York: Modern Library, 1922).
13. The concept of passive information processing originated with Krugman. See Herbert E. Krugman, "The Impact of Television Advertising: Learning Without Involvement," *Public Opinion Quarterly* 29 (1965):349–356 and Herbert E. Krugman and Eugene L. Hartley, "Passive Learning from Television," *Public Opinion Quarterly* 34 (1970):184–190.
14. James E. Grunig, "A Simultaneous Equation Model for Intervention in Communication Behavior." Paper presented to the Communication Theory and Methodology Division, Association for Education in Journalism, Houston, August 1979.

ADDITIONAL READING

Dewey, John, *The Public and Its Problems* (Chicago: Swallow, 1927).

Evan, William M. (ed.), *Interorganizational Relations* (New York: Penguin, 1976).

Grunig, James E., and James B. Disbrow, "Developing a Probabilistic Model for Communications Decision Making," *Communication Research* 4 (1977):145–168.

Grunig, James E., "Evaluating Employee Communication in a Research Operation," *Public Relations Review* 3 (Winter 1977):61–82.

Grunig, James E., "Describing Publics in Public Relations: The Case of a Suburban Hospital," *Journalism Quarterly* 55 (1978): 109–118.

Grunig, James E., "Describing Publics in Public Relations: The Case of a Suburban Hospital," *Journalism Quarterly* 55 (1978):109–118. 764.

Grunig, James E., "Communication Behaviors and Attitudes of Environmental Publics: Two Studies," *Journalism Monographs* 81 (March 1983).

Olson, Mancur, *The Logic of Collective Action* (Cambridge, Mass.: Harvard University Press, 1971).

Perry, Joseph B., and M. D. Pugh, *Collective Behavior: Response to Social Stress* (Minneapolis: West, 1978).

Wigand, Rolf T., "A Model of Interorganizational Communication Among Complex Organizations," in Klaus Krippendorff (ed.), *Communication and Control in Society* (New York: Gordon and Breach, 1979), pp. 367–387.

8

BUDGETING
AND DECISION MAKING

"Ideas are a dime a dozen!"

That old saw means that it is much cheaper to come up with ideas than it is to implement them. The last two chapters should have helped you to generate ideas for public relations programs. But many "good" ideas simply aren't technically or financially feasible.

In this chapter, therefore, we will discuss some management techniques that public relations professionals can use to weigh the costs and benefits of their ideas before implementing them.

In the last two chapters, we discussed concepts and techniques that the public relations manager can use in the *construct* segment of the behavioral molecule. That segment, you will recall, comes after the public relations manager has *detect*ed a public relations problem. In the *construct* segment, PR managers define the problem, formulate objectives, and develop alternative solutions to the problem. When they finish that segment of the molecule, they should have *construct*ed

a single picture of the alternatives for dealing with the problem.

But PR managers should not put the idea into motion—i.e., go to the *behave* segment of the molecule—before carefully weighing whether the cost of each alternative and the practical problems involved in implementing it are greater than the possible benefits. Managers, that is, should not forget the *define*, *select*, and *confirm* segments of the molecule.

In this chapter, we will discuss three techniques that PR managers can use in the *define*, *select*, and *confirm* segments. First, we will discuss budgeting, an important part of defining ideas into financial terms and then in *confirm*ing that sufficient resources are available to implement the ideas. Second, we will discuss the technique of network analysis, which can be used to *define* and *confirm* the time needed to implement an idea. Finally, we will look at techniques for comparing costs and benefits, which can be used to *select* the alternatives to be implemented.

BUDGETING: DEFINING COSTS

A budget can be defined as the "price tag" of a public relations program or as the financial plan for the program.[1] Public relations managers prepare two kinds of budgets, the *administrative* budget and the *program* budget.

Administrative and Program Budgets

The administrative budget is the budget for the entire public relations department. It shows how much money has been allocated for different programs or other budget categories for a fixed period of time, which is usually a year.

The head of the public relations department must develop an administrative budget and have it approved by an organizational budget committee or by a higher-ranking manager in the organization. When seeking approval of an administrative budget, top public relations managers must show how the department's programs, as reflected in the budget, support organizational goals. They can best do that by building the administrative budget from budgets developed for public relations programs that are designed to solve public relations problems that threaten organizational goals.

The administrative budget, therefore, should be built from program budgets constructed by middle-level public relations managers. Each middle-level manager generally will have responsibility for groups of potential publics, such as media, government, community, or employee publics. Program budgets flow directly from the public relations planning process described by the behavioral molecule.

In the *define* segment of the molecule, middle-level public relations managers prepare preliminary budgets for each alternative program constructed to communicate with the publics identified in the *construct* stage of the molecule.

In the *select* stage, managers choose one or more of the alternative programs, and then the budgets for the chosen programs become part of the department's administrative budget.

Program budgeting has been described with the acronym of PPBS: the planning-programming-budgeting-system. PPBS begins from the ground up. Managers develop programs to meet objectives and prepare budgets for each program. Those program budgets then are aggregated into the departmental budget request.[2]

Other budgeting systems, in contrast, work from the top down. In other systems, managers seek a budget allocation and then distribute it to existing programs.

You should be able to get a clearer picture of the nature of the PPBS by looking at its three parts. Henry defined these three parts as follows:

Planning. Defining and choosing operational goals and methods to achieve those goals over a specified time period.

Programming. Scheduling and implementation of projects to fulfill the goals as effectively as possible.

Budgeting. Attaching price estimates to each goal, plan, program, and project.[3]

Try Zero-Based Budgeting • One variation of PPBS, zero-based budgeting, can also help public relations managers clarify whether existing programs still are needed.[4]

Most public relations departments continue programs year after year without considering new and different programs or considering whether the existing programs are even necessary any longer. That is, they continue in the *behave* segment of the behavioral molecule without continuously going through the other segments. Zero-based budgeting means literally "starting from zero." Department or program managers must plan all of their programs and budgets as though they had no previous budget or programs.

Zero-based budgeting forces managers out of the *behave* segment and into the other segments, making them justify budgets and programs in terms of current organizational goals and public relations problems rather than of goals and problems that existed when the programs first were formulated.

The public relations manager who uses zero-based budgeting every year, however, may unduly disrupt ongoing programs. Although zero-based budgeting probably should not be used every year, it can be used regularly, such as every three or five years, to identify programs that should be eliminated.

What Should Go into a Public Relations Budget?

Different kinds of public relations programs will seldom have exactly the same categories of expenses. An employee-relations program will require typesetting and printing of a newspaper, magazine, or magapaper. A community-relations program may require open houses, contributions to community projects, and the cost of sponsoring memberships for employees in community organizations. An educational relations program will require printed or audiovisual materials for distribution to schools. Some programs may require only employee salaries.

Although it's impossible to give you a sample budget that will work for all public relations programs, you should be able to use the following categories of expenses for most programs.

1. *Salaries and benefits*. Determine what proportion of their time full-time employees spend on each program. Allocate that proportion of their salary and benefits to the program. Add in the costs of necessary part-time employees and consultants.
2. *Production*. Determine the costs of printing, typesetting, art and design, photographs, audiovisual materials, purchase of media time and space, reproduction of press releases, etc.
3. *Equipment*. Determine the costs of new equipment needed for a program, or for maintenance and depreciation of equipment already on hand.
4. *Overhead*. Determine what percentage of rent, postage, telephone, utilities, etc. should be allocated to each program.
5. *Special project costs*. Determine costs such as those of renting a hotel room for a press conference, renting exhibit space at a conference, providing meals or snacks at an open house, buying memberships for employees in community organizations, or contributing to community programs.
6. *Travel*. Determine the costs of the local and out-of-town travel that will be necessary for each program.
7. *Other costs*. Each kind of public relations program will have unique expenses. Determine what they are, and include them in this category.

Budgets in the Confirm and Behave Segments of the Behavioral Molecule

Most of the work in developing a budget comes in the *define* segment of the behavioral molecule. In that segment, public relations managers define the cost of alternative programs so that they can then choose the most effective and efficient program in the *select* segment of the molecule. Budgets, however, also have great practical value in the *confirm* and *behave* segments of the management process.

In the *confirm* segment, final budget approval gives a manager the authority to proceed with a program. He or she can then proceed to implement the program and spend the money allocated. In the *behave* segment, then, managers can use the approved budget to monitor the progress of the program. They then continually ask if more money is being spent than was budgeted. A manager who *detects* any excessive expenditures should stop the program and reevaluate whether it can meet its objectives for the amounts budgeted.

NETWORK ANALYSIS: DEFINING TIME

It is usually easier for public relations managers to avoid budgeting the time needed for a project than it is to avoid budgeting the money needed. Superiors seldom will approve a program without a cost estimate or allow a project to continue if it costs much more than estimated, but they generally allow public relations professionals to plan their own time.

Many people budget their time poorly. As a result, they must work overtime to complete projects that were scheduled over an unrealistic time span. Or they find that projects cannot be finished by deadline.

Snoopy, that profound beagle philosopher of the "Peanuts" comic strip, expresses the need for budgeting time. Sitting atop his doghouse, Snoopy looks at the calendar and goes into shock: "Good Grief! Is it November already?" Drooping over the edge of the house, he laments, "My life is going by too fast! . . . I think someone pushed the 'fast forward' button!"

All of us occasionally would like to hit the reverse button of the tape recorder to have more time to complete projects. In November, students would like more than a month to complete the fall semester's work. Quite frankly, we would have liked more time to finish writing this book. Unfortunately, it's not possible to push the reverse button. With some advance planning, however, it is possible to push the play button and to keep the recorder running smoothly without running out of tape.

In the *define* segment of the behavioral molecule, public relations managers should, in addition to budgeting financial requirements of each alternative program, estimate the time needed to implement each program and then schedule the sequence of events leading to the conclusion of the program. These time estimates can then be used to *confirm* that the program can be carried out in the time allotted and to keep track of its progress in the *behave* segment of the molecule.

Management scientists have developed several methods of network analysis that public relations managers can use to plan and monitor the time sequence of a program. Management scientists call these methods network analysis because they define the network of interrelated events that must be completed in sequence before the total project can be completed. We will look at three methods of network analysis: the Gantt chart, the program evaluation and review technique (PERT), and the critical path method (CPM).

Gantt Charts

The Gantt chart, developed in the early 1900s by the "scientific management" theorist Henry L. Gantt, is the simplest of the network methods and the forerunner of the PERT and CPM methods.[5]

Figure 8–1 provides an example of a Gantt chart for a typical public relations effort, preparing for a press conference. A Gantt chart shows the activities to be completed on the vertical axis and the total time required on the horizontal axis. The activities are sequenced from top to bottom, so that the activities at the top must come first and those at the bottom must come last. Horizontal lines show how much time each activity requires.

When a Gantt chart is used for a longer and more complicated project than the press conference example shown in Figure 8-1, a second line may be drawn under each horizontal line in the chart. That second line is filled in to show the actual amount of time taken to complete each activity. The second set of lines provides managers with an on-

FIGURE 8–1   A Gantt Chart for a Press Conference

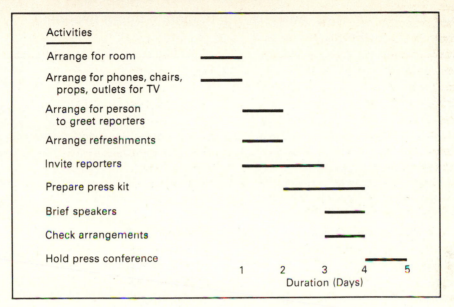

going record of progress and thus helps them to know whether the project can be completed on schedule or whether adjustments must be made to get the project back on schedule.

PERT: Program Evaluation and Review Technique

The U. S. Navy developed PERT in 1958 to improve the planning and evaluation of the Polaris submarine program.[6] The technique helped the developers of the submarine reduce the time needed to complete the program. That success led to its adoption by many large business firms, especially to plan large and complicated projects for which the organization had no previous experience. PERT has been used to plan activities as diverse as house construction and Broadway plays.[7]

Network models such as PERT can be used for most public relations programs, although they are less necessary for ongoing programs than for new, uncharted programs. PERT can be used as a "zero-based" time budgeting technique for all programs, however, to help determine whether program managers are using their time efficiently in current programs.

The Network Diagram • The heart of the PERT process is a network diagram that illustrates the relationships between two fundamental concepts, *activities* and *events*.[8] An event marks the start or completion of a task. It does not consume time, personnel, or resources. An activity represents the effort needed to complete a task. Events consume time, personnel, or resources.

In the PERT diagram, a circle represents an event, and an arrow represents an activity (Figure 8–2). The diagram thus shows which activities and events must precede other activities and events to complete a project.

In Figure 8–2, for example, Event 1 must be completed before Event 2 and Event 3. But Event 2, as well as Event 1, must precede

EXHIBIT 8-1   A PERT Analysis of a Corporate Social Reporting Program

The following network diagram illustrates how PERT could be used to plan a corporate social-reporting program.

The program begins when the public relations manager communicates with management about the consequences of an organization's plans. It moves through the research and reporting phases of the program. The time estimates are expected times (with 50 percent probability of occurrence) and represent the number of working days needed for each activity. The total program should be completed within a year.

Double arrows show the critical path. The total number of days on the top of the circles, which depict events, is the running total of days along the critical path.

Numbers in circles = event number.
Numbers under each arrow = time needed to complete the activity.
Numbers over circles = cumulated time for critical path.

Event Description

1. Social report assignments made.
2. Management interviewed on decisions or plans that affect publics.
3. PR discussion of consequences on publics of decisions and plans.
4. Presentation of expected consequences to management.
5. Agreement on consequences with management.
6. Assignments made for survey research on publics.
7. Sample procedure developed.
8. Sample selected.
9. Questionnaire developed.
10. Pretest completed.
11. Questionnaire revised.
12. Data collected.
13. Survey results analyzed.
14. Internal report communicated to management.
15. Management sends report to departments for response.
16. Departments respond to management.
17. Management decision on changes in plans and decisions and response to be reported in external social report.
18. External report assignments made.
19. Articles for report written.
20. Copy for report edited.
21. Management approves copy.

22. Type set for report.
23. Galley proofs read.
24. Illustrations prepared.
25. Photos taken.
26. Photos and illustrations selected for report.
27. Layout completed.
28. Page proofs completed.
29. Page proofs corrected.
30. Final management approval of social report.
31. Printing completed.
32. Report distributed.

FIGURE 8–2

A Blank PERT Diagram

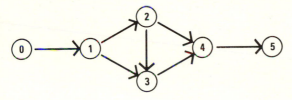

Event 3. Finally, both Events 2 and 3 must precede Event 4, and Event 4 must precede Event 5. (See Exhibit 8-1 for a complete example of PERT for a public relations program.)

Time Estimates • The manager who uses PERT first determines the events needed to complete a program and their interrelationships and depicts them in a network diagram similar to the one in Figure 8-2. Most managers find it easiest to construct the diagram working backward. That is, they determine which events must precede the completion of the program, which events must precede those events, and so on. At times, however, you may find it easier to work forward, determining which events must come first, which must come second, and so on.

Secondly, the manager estimates the time required to complete each activity. That time may be estimated in hours, days, or months, depending on the total time needed for the program. These time estimates should be placed on the arrows that represent the activities. Figure 8-3, for example, shows the same network diagram as Figure 8-2, with time estimates added.

Although you may want to make only one time estimate for each activity path, most users of PERT make three time estimates: optimistic (O), pessimistic (P), and most likely (M). The optimistic estimate represents the minimum time necessary to complete a project if everything goes well. The pessimistic estimate expresses the time needed if many things go wrong (think of Murphy's law again).

These three estimates can be combined, using the following formula, to develop the "expected time" (Te) for each activity:

$$Te = \frac{(O + 4M + P)}{6}$$

The formula assumes that the optimistic and pessimistic estimates have an equal chance of

FIGURE 8–3

A Blank PERT Diagram, with Activity Time Estimates Added

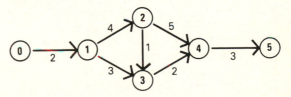

occurring and that the mostly likely estimate has twice the chance of occurring as the other two together. The expected time estimate, in other words, is a weighted average of these three estimates. The statistical distribution of *Te* is such that you can expect to complete the project on schedule 50 percent of the time (for proof of this statement, see the additional references suggested at the end of this chapter).

Suppose that your optimistic estimate of the time needed for an activity is three days, your pessimistic estimate ten days, and your most likely estimate seven days. Then you would complete the equation as follows:

$$Te = \frac{3 + (4 \times 7) + 10}{6} = \frac{41}{6} = 6.83 \text{ days}$$

Should you want an expected time that will occur more or less often than 50 percent of the time, you can compute another statistic, the variance, and, with the help of another formula and some tables, you can determine the number of days in which you could expect to complete an event, say, 80 percent or 30 percent of the time. We'll leave those statistics to your further reading should you want to become more sophisticated in your use of PERT.[9]

The Critical Path • After making an estimate of the time needed for each activity in the network diagram, add the times needed to complete each of the paths in the diagram. The path that takes the longest is known as the critical path, as it defines the shortest possible time in which a project can be completed. In Figures 8–2 and 8–3, there are three paths: 0-1-2-3-4-5, 0-1-3-4-5, and 0-1-2-4-5. The first path takes twelve days, the second ten, and the third fourteen. Thus, the third path is the critical path.

As a manager, you should pay particular attention to the critical path, because you cannot shorten the time of a project without cutting the time needed for one or more of the activities along the critical path. Similarly, exceeding the estimated time of completing an activity on the critical path will lengthen the time of a project. If you should cut the time of the critical path, however, make certain another path does not become longer, and, therefore, become the critical path.

Slack • Paths in the network that are not critical can be completed in less than the total time needed to complete the project. The excess time on these noncritical paths is called slack. When slack is available, the manager can use people or resources that are not fully utilized on the noncritical path to speed up the activities on the critical path. The manager can also delay the start of activities on the noncritical path. Slack, in other words, gives the manager flexibility in completing noncritical paths.

CPM: The Critical Path Method

The Critical Path Method works much like PERT, although its purpose is slightly different.[10] As a public relations manager, you could use CPM to help cut minimum project completion time, and to cut it as cheaply as possible. CPM makes explicit how much it will cost you to cut project time.

The manager using CPM makes two estimates of project completion time rather than the three in PERT. The two estimates are known as the "normal time" and the "crash time." You can complete an activity in the normal time if you use normal operating procedures. The crash time represents the time in which a project can be completed when no resources are spared.

To use CPM, construct a network chart, as in PERT, first using the crash time estimates. Determine the critical path in this crash network. The sum of the crash times needed to complete each of the activities on the critical path is the minimum possible time it will take to complete the project. Your objective then is to determine the minimum cost at which the project can be completed within the minimum time without incurring the full crash costs.

To meet that objective, construct a second network diagram using the normal times rather than the crash times. Determine the critical path in this second diagram, which may be different from the critical path in the crash time diagram.

Then, estimate the cost of crashing each activity along the critical path. Select one activity on the critical path that has the lowest crash cost. Change the time for that activity to the crash time. Determine if the critical path has now changed with the change in time of that activity.

Then repeat the same process. Look for each successive activity with the least crash cost on the new critical path. Keep going through this process until the time along the critical path equals the minimum project time that you calculated from the first crash diagram. The total amount spent to crash activities up to this point represents the minimum crash cost of reaching the shortest project time.

DECISION MAKING: SELECTING AN ALTERNATIVE

Let's assume that you have traced the linkages of your organization and have used the Grunig situational theory described in the chapter on publics to determine whether the potential publics identified by the linkage concepts are nonpublics or latent, aware, or active publics. Then let's assume you have *defined* alternative public relations programs to reach each of the publics and that you have budgeted the money and time that would be needed for each program.

Now, you should be ready for the *select* segment of the behavioral molecule. You have two kinds of decisions to make:

1. Which is the best alternative to reach each public?
2. Which publics are the most important—and, given limited resources, which deserve first priority when you decide on the possible public relations programs you will implement?

You can use fairly straightforward thinking to answer the first question—choosing the best alternative public relations program to reach each public. The situational theory of publics tells you what kind of technique and medium are most appropriate. Remember that actively communicating publics seek out information on their own. You can use written information and print media, and you can provide in-depth information for publics that *seek* information.

In contrast, you must gain the attention of *passively* communicating publics if you want them to *process* and retain even part of your message. Thus, you will have to use such techniques as visual media, simple and short messages, or pictures and illustrations to reach the information-processing publics.

There may be several alternative strategies to reach each public, but you will usually want to choose the alternative that costs the least and that can be implemented most easily within the time constraints you face.

Once you've developed a communication strategy for each public, however, you will face the second, more complicated, decision. Nearly always you will have found more publics and devised more programs to reach those publics than your public relations department has the money and time to implement. You will want to choose public relations programs that maximize the use of resources and contribute most toward organizational goals.

As our last step in this chapter, therefore, we will discuss three methods that you can use to help maximize the return per dollar and day spent on public relations programs.

Cost-Benefit Analysis

There is nothing complicated about the idea behind cost-benefit analysis. You simply add up the costs of a program and then determine the monetary value of the benefits from that program. Unless the benefits that result from a program exceed their cost, the manager should not implement the program.

Many business leaders, for example, have argued that cost-benefit analysis should be applied to environmental regulations, because they believe the costs of the regulations exceed the value of the benefits the regulations bring. A public relations manager, similarly, would want to be certain that the monetary value of the benefits that a public relations program brings to the organization exceeds the cost of the program.

Although the idea behind cost-benefit analysis is simple, the implementation of the idea is not. It's quite difficult to determine the value of the benefits of a program.

For example, an environmental decision maker would have to determine how much clean air or water is worth in dollar terms. That's extremely difficult to do. The public relations manager would have to determine how much such public relations objectives as understanding or attitude change are worth to the organization in dollar terms. That's even more difficult.

If you could estimate the value of the benefits that your public relations programs bring, you could choose to implement only those programs for which the benefits exceed the costs. You will find it extremely difficult, and probably impossible, however, to make reasonably accurate monetary estimates of benefits. You'll be on more solid ground if you use the idea of cost-benefit analysis to choose the programs that maximize the benefits for the resources spent without trying to estimate the exact dollar value of the benefits. Two additional techniques, expected value analysis and simplified programming, can help you make such estimates.

Expected-Value Analysis

The expected value of a program can be calculated by multiplying the "payoff value" of the program by the probability that the payoff will occur.[11]

For example, I might invest $10 in a lottery ticket that pays $500 if my number is drawn. However, only one in 100 people who buy a $10 ticket win $500. Thus, the probability of winning the payoff value is 1 percent, and the expected value (0.01 × $500) is only $5.

Although the payoff values of public relations programs usually cannot be measured in dollar values, they can be estimated in other terms. You could use a ten-point scale, for example, to estimate the value of communicating with each of the publics you have identified by using the linkage concepts and the Grunig situational theory of publics. You might assign a value of ten to an enabling linkage, for example, that is extremely important to your organization's efforts to achieve necessary funding. Other publics may have few consequences on your organization and rate a value of only one or two.

To estimate the importance of a public, think of the severity of the consequences a linked public might have on your organization. If a public or other organization is linked to another organization through an enabling linkage—to a funding or regulatory agency, for example—you would assign a high value, for that public can threaten the survival of your organization.

If the public is linked through an input or output functional linkage, as are employee or consumer publics, it would deserve a high value if those publics have ever refused to work or to buy, or if your organization faces strong competition for the services or purchasing dollar of those publics.

If you are considering a normative-linkage public, give it a high value if your organization can gain from the information or support the other organization could provide.

Finally, assign a high value to diffused-linkage publics that might organize to pressure or embarrass your organization, restrict its freedom, or secure government regulation.

After you have assigned payoff values to each public, you might think, at first, that the public relations department's resources should go to programs aimed at the publics with the highest payoff values. That could be a mistake, because the probability of actually communicating with some high-payoff publics may be low. That is why you multiply the payoff value by the probability that communication could occur in order to get the expected value of a public relations program.

Calculating the Payoff • You looked previously at probabilities of information seeking and processing in Table 7–2, page 156, that can be used to calculate the expected value of communicating with each public.

Before using these probabilities, however, you should make a correction that will allow you to compare the probability of information seeking with that of information processing. For some publics, especially low-involvement publics, you would use message techniques and media designed for information processing. For other publics, your chosen program might aim at information seeking. Because the probability of information seeking will always be lower than for information processing, you cannot use the probabilities interchangeably in calculating expected values.

We suggest you multiply the probabilities of information processing by one-half to make them comparable to the probabilities of information seeking. That's because we think that passively processed messages will usually be about half as effective as messages that

are sought out. Thus, you can calculate the expected value of each public relations program by using the appropriate one of the two following formulas:

Expected Value
= ProbInfoSeek × EstPayoffValue

Expected Value
= 1/2 × ProbInfoProcess × EstPayoffValue

ProbInfoSeek represents the appropriate probability of information seeking; ProbInfoProcess represents the appropriate probability of information processing; and EstPayoffValue represents your estimation of the payoff value of communicating with each public.

Let's take a simple example, so you can see how to estimate expected values.

Suppose you work for a university public relations department and have *defined* programs for four publics: members of the state legislature who fit the high-involvement, problem-facing (HIPF) public defined in the chapter on publics; other members of the legislature who fit the low-involvement, routine behavior (LIRB) public; students who fit the high-involvement, constrained behavior (HICB) public; and students who fit the low-involvement, fatalistic behavior (LIFB) public.

Members of the state legislature are critical for your organization, so you assign both of the legislative publics a payoff value of ten. Students also are important, but not as important as the legislators, so you assign both student publics a payoff value of six. You design a program based on information seeking for the high-involvement legislative and student publics and information processing for the two low-involvement publics.

You would calculate the expected values of the programs defined for the four publics as follows, using probabilities from Table 7–2:

Expected Value (HIPF Legislators)
= .74 × 10 = 7.4

Expected Value (LIRB Legislators)
= 1/2 × .84 × 10 = 4.2

Expected Value (HICB Students)
= .58 × 6 = 3.48

Expected Value (LIFB Students)
= 1/2 × .62 × 6 = 1.86

These results suggest that the university's public relations department should first have programs for the two legislative publics, then have programs for the two student publics only if resources permit.

Note that priority should be given to the LIRB legislators rather than the HICB students, even though the probability of successfully communicating with this legislative public is lower than the probability of communicating with the student public. The reason, you will note, is the higher payoff value of communicating with the legislators (which may explain why your university frequently seems to care little about communicating with students).

Why Not Calculate "Effects"? • During this discussion of expected values, you probably realized that we have been using probabilities of communication behavior to estimate the expected values of public relations programs for different publics rather than probabilities of communication effects such as message retention, holding of cognitions, holding of attitudes, and behavior. There are several reasons for this choice.

First, comparing the expected value of communication with publics fits well with the two-way symmetric model of public relations.

Second, we know that, generally, the greater the amount of communication behavior, the more often the effects occur, especially behavior, and that information seeking results in communication effects more frequently than does information processing

(that is why we multiplied information processing by one-half). Thus, you would not gain a great deal of accuracy in decision making by using probabilities of communication effects rather than of communication behaviors.

Third, we don't know whether cognitions, attitudes, and behavior will be favorable or unfavorable to the organizaton, making it difficult to compare their probabilities.

Finally, we have not yet done enough research on the probabilities of communication effects shown in Table 7–2 to use them with the same confidence as the probabilities of the two communication behaviors.

Expected value analysis should help you to make most decisions about which public relations programs to implement first and which to drop when you have used up your resources. One question remains, however. What if a program with a high expected value costs more to implement than a program with a lower expected value? Should you go with the high-priced or the low-priced program? One last technique, simplified programming, should help you to make that decision.

Simplified Programming

Public relations managers are rarely able to develop and implement communication programs for each public they identify. Most managers have limited money and limited people-hours available. In management science language, we would say these managers are constrained by resources.

When alternative programs require combinations of money and time that differ substantially, you will not find it easy to decide which programs to implement strictly on the basis of their expected value. You will need a decision-making procedure that allows you to maximize the expected value of your public relations programs within the constraints of your resources.

Management scientists use a powerful, and relatively simple, method called linear programming to solve these kinds of problems. Linear programming was developed in 1947—like PERT, for military use.[12]

To use linear programming, the manager must meet four criteria:

1. You must have a goal that you would like to maximize. Business managers, for example, most frequently use profits as such a quantitative goal. (Linear programming may also be used to minimize a goal, such as minimizing the distance from warehouses to retailers, but that use of the technique is not relevant to us here.) Public relations managers cannot attribute profits or monetary returns to public relations programs, but they can attempt to maximize the quantitative expected values from public relations programs, as explained in the previous section.

2. You must have alternative means of accomplishing your goal. Public relations meets that criterion. Designing several alternative communication programs to reach different publics translates into having alternative means for maximizing the value of public relations to the organization.

3. The resources you need to meet the goal must be in short supply. Again, public relations qualifies. The public relations manager has at least two scarce resources—money and time.

4. You must be able to exchange units of each alternative and to express the relationships between the alternatives in a mathematical formula.

An example of the fourth requirement would be an electronics company that produces both hand calculators and computer games. It might take six minutes to produce a calculator (C) and eight minutes to produce a computer game (G). If the company had 420 minutes a day to produce both products, we could express the relationship between the alternatives and the time constraint as:

$$6C + 8G \leq 420$$

That is, the product of six minutes times the number of calculators produced in a day and eight minutes times the number of computer games produced in a day must be less than, or equal to (not exceed), the number of minutes in a workday. A manager who knows the profit per calculator and per computer game could determine which combination of the two products would maximize the profit produced within the 420 minute constraint.

This fourth criterion presents a problem for the use of linear programming in public relations, because public relations programs usually are not divisible. It's not possible to think of producing a public relations program—such as the programs for legislators or students discussed in the previous section—more or less than once within a time span such as a year. Thus, we can't think of six units of a legislative relations program being substituted for eight units of a student relations program.

A Useful Variation for PR Use • Fortunately, however, an agricultural economist at North Carolina State University has developed a variation of linear programming, called simplified programming, that allows us to overcome the problem of indivisibility of public relations programs and to still use the logical power of linear programming to make public relations decisions.[13] Although most linear programming problems cannot be solved without a computer, simplified programming can be done without a computer.

Let's proceed with our previous example of four alternative programs for your university's public relations program to see how the technique works.

Table 8–1 displays all of the data you need to decide how to allocate scarce resources to the four publics we discussed in the previous section on expected values. The first column of the table shows the total amount of money and time available to your university's public relations department. The next four columns show the amount of money and time needed

TABLE 8–1 **Step 1 in Simplified Programming of PR Programs for Four University Publics**

Resources	Total Available	HIPF Legislators	LIRB Legislators	HICB Students	LIFB Students
Money	$50,000	$30,000	$30,000	$10,000	$10,000
People Days	520	250	200	100	100
Expected Value		7.4	4.2	3.48	1.86

to complete each of the four alternative programs. The last row shows the expected value of each of the four programs, as calculated in the previous section.

To make the decision about how to allocate your resources to the four programs, you would enter the table at the Expected Value row and choose the program with the highest expected value. Thus, your first choice would be the program for the HIPF legislators. Before making the final decision, however, check to make certain that the resources required for this program do not exceed the constraints of the total resources available.

The resources required for the program for the HIPF legislators do not exceed the constraints. Thus, you would allocate $30,000 and 250 people-days to the program for the HIPF legislators.

Your next step would be to reconstruct Table 8–1. The reconstructed Table 8–1 (Table 8–2) should show the three remaining programs and new resource constraints that are calculated by subtracting the resources re-

quired for the first program chosen from the previous total amount of each resource available.

Now, you would use Table 8–2 to repeat the same process. Choose the public relations program with the next highest expected value. That would be the program for the LIRB legislators, which has an expected value of 4.2. You will notice, however, that this program requires more resources than are available. Since it does not fit within the resource constraints, it cannot be used.

Go, therefore, to the program with the next highest expected value, the program for the HICB students. It does not require more resources than are available, so you would choose it as your second program and allocate $10,000 and 100 people-days to it.

Now you would reconstruct Table 8–2 once again to show the remaining resources and possible programs (Table 8–3).

In Table 8–3, you should be able to see that you have only one feasible alternative left, the program for the LIFB students. It ex-

TABLE 8–2 **Step 2 in Simplified Programming of PR Programs for Four University Publics**

Resources	Total Available	HIPF Legislators	LIRB Legislators	HICB Students	LIFB Students
Money	$20,000	Chosen	$30,000	$10,000	$10,000
People Days	270	Chosen	200	100	100
Expected Value		Chosen	4.2	3.48	1.86

TABLE 8-3 Step 3 in Simplified Programming of PR Programs
for Four University Publics

Resources	Total Available	HIPF Legislators	LIRB Legislators	HICB Students	LIFB Students
Money	$10,000	Chosen	$30,000	Chosen	$10,000
People Days	170	Chosen	200	Chosen	100
Expected Value		Chosen	4.2	Chosen	1.86

actly exhausts your dollar resources and leaves only seventy days of people-time. Those seventy days of people-time represent slack that can be used to fill gaps in other programs or, perhaps, for additional projects that require no money.

You have finished your simplified program and have allocated resources to three of the four possible programs. In doing so, you have done what linear programming sets out to accomplish. You have maximized the expected value attained from your resources. You have eliminated one program with the second highest expected value, however. It cost too much to be feasible.

MOVING TOWARD IMPLEMENTATION

In this chapter, we have looked at several budgeting and decision-making techniques that can help the public relations manager in the *define, select,* and *construct* segments of the behavioral molecule. Other kinds of organizational managers regularly use these techniques. Public relations managers will use these techniques, too, as public relations becomes more and more sophisticated and is managed in the same way as other organizational processes.

In the public relations process, you should now be ready to implement your programs— i.e., to *behave.* Part IV of this book details the techniques generally used in the *behave* part of the public relations process. It is in the *behave* segment that the communication tech-

nicians take over and the manager becomes an observer.

There is one important management step left, however. That is the second *detect* segment of the behavioral molecule, the evaluation of the effectiveness of the programs you have chosen to implement.

NOTES

1. Kenneth H. Killen, *Management: A Middle-Management Approach* (Boston: Houghton Mifflin, 1977), p. 271.
2. W. Warren Haynes, Joseph L. Massie, and Marc J. Wallace, Jr., *Management: Analysis, Concepts, and Cases,* 3d ed. (Englewood Cliffs, N.J.: Prentice-Hall, 1975), p. 349.
3. Nicholas Henry, *Public Administration and Public Affairs* (Englewood Cliffs, N. J.: Prentice-Hall, 1975), p. 164.
4. Henry, p. 171.
5. W. Jack Duncan, *Essentials of Management,* 2d ed. (Hinsdale, Ill.: Dryden Press, 1978), p. 434; Robert B. Buchele, *The Management of Business and Public Organizations* (New York: McGraw-Hill, 1977), pp. 132–133.
6. T. Harrell Allen, ''PERT: A Technique for Public Relations Management,'' *Public Relations Review* 6 (Summer 1980):38–49.
7. Desmond L. Cook, *Program Evaluation and Review Technique: Applications in Education* (Washington, D.C.: University Press of America, 1979), p. 2.
8. F. T. Haner and James C. Ford, *Contemporary Management* (Columbus, Ohio: Merrill, 1973), pp. 242–250.

9. Allen and Cook both provide further explanations that can be understood with relatively little difficulty.
10. Haner and Ford, pp. 250–257.
11. For discussions of expected value analysis, see Haner and Ford, pp. 108–115, and Haynes, Massie, and Wallace, pp. 400–401.
12. Haner and Ford, pp. 219–240; Duncan, pp. 442–453.
13. C. R. Weathers, ''Simplified Programming— A Tool in Farm Planning,'' North Carolina Agricultural Extension Service Bulletin, January 1964.

ADDITIONAL READING

Allen, T. Harrell, ''PERT: A Technique for Public Relations Management,'' *Public Relations Review* 6 (Summer 1980):38–49.

Cook, Desmond L., *Program Evaluation and Review Technique: Applications in Education* (Washington, D.C.: University Press of America, 1979).

Duncan, W. Jack, *Essentials of Management*, 2d ed. (Hinsdale, Ill.: Dryden Press, 1978), Chapter 15, on operations management.

Gannon, Martin J., *Management: An Organizational Perspective* (Boston: Little, Brown, 1977), Chapter 13, on decision-making techniques.

Haner F. T., and James C. Ford, *Contemporary Management* (Columbus, Ohio: Merrill, 1973), Chapter 5, on probability concepts and applications; Chapter 9, on linear programming; and Chapter 10, on introduction to network models.

Haynes, W. Warren, Joseph L. Massie, and Marc J. Wallace, Jr., *Management: Analysis, Concepts, and Cases*, 3d ed. (Englewood Cliffs, N.J.: Prentice-Hall, 1975), Chapter 15, on accounting in managerial decisions, and Chapter 17, on quantitative methods in business decisions.

9

EVALUATION RESEARCH

At a meeting of the Public Relations Division of the Association for Education in Journalism in 1977, the director of public relations for a major meat-packing company was asked what kind of evaluation research his department did. "We've been lucky," he replied. "Management has always accepted the need for public relations. We haven't had to prove our value."

That was the standard in public relations until only a few years ago. Public relations was accepted without proving its value to the organization or without showing that something had happened as a result of spending the money allocated to the department. Directors of public relations who were asked to prove their department's worth could serve up a snowjob—in fact, a snowstorm of press clippings.

Robert Marker, manager of press services in the advertising and marketing services department of Armstrong Cork Co., described how all of this changed for him one day. An executive asked Marker to describe just what the company was getting for the money it spent on public relations. Marker came

loaded with "a considerable volume of newspaper clippings, magazine features, and case histories. I pointed out," Marker said, "that all this publicity—if strung end to end—would reach from his office located in the west wing of the building, clear across the center wing to the east wing, down the stairs, and out into the main lobby—and there'd still be enough left over to paper one and a half walls of his office. I leaned back in my chair thinking the day had been won," Marker added. But then the executive asked a question no one had asked before: "What's all this worth to us?"[1]

EVALUATION NOW ESSENTIAL TO PR MANAGEMENT

The days of nonexistent and sloppy evaluation in public relations have ended. Public relations managers, as evidenced by the following quotes from James Tirone of AT&T and Richard Franzen of the National Bureau of Standards, must prove with hard evidence that they have met their objectives. Tirone said:

We now all perceive that public relations is not only a creative act. . . . in the management of public relations we are ill-advised to assert that we in PR are "different." The corporation is better served, and I think so is the profession, when public relations deliberately attempts to fit itself into the standard procedures of the corporation, by meeting the same tests of performance as other functions and managers.[2]

According to Franzen:

Of more consequence, in this highly scientific organization, are the benefits resulting from the careful approach to data gathering which this study [of an employee communication program] represents. As is true with any information office, our ability to function depends upon the degree of credibility with which we are perceived by top management and the extent to which our efforts are seen as contributing to the achievement of management goals.[3]

AT&T set up an extensive measurement program when state regulatory commissions and the Federal Communications Commission repeatedly asked the company why, as a regulated monopoly, it should spend the consumer's money on public relations. As a result, AT&T developed the most thorough program of public relations evaluation in the United States.

Newspaper writers regularly ask why government agencies should spend taxpayers money to "sell them something they have already purchased." Administrators of the National Bureau of Standards didn't have enough money to support the agency's function of doing scientific research, so they asked why the Bureau should spend part of its scarce resources on public relations. Armstrong Cork executives wanted to know how much favorable product publicity was worth to the company.

None of those questions can be answered without evaluation research. Public relations managers who do no evaluation research frequently have their programs cut or eliminated. Even if there were no threat of cutting the budget or eliminating the public relations program, a manager could not administer individual public relations programs or personnel without evaluation research. There simply would be no way of judging success or failure.

Ma Bell Keeps Careful Tabs

AT&T responded to the challenge for evaluation by developing ongoing measures for five programs run by the public relations departments in its semiautonomous operating telephone companies and in Western Electric, Bell Laboratories, and AT&T Long Lines (the long-distance subsidiary). Those programs included overall administration of the department, press relations, employee communication, community relations, and educational relations.

To evaluate administration of public relations, AT&T calculated the average budgets of the public relations departments and the range of those budgets, so that managers of each unit could compare their expenditures with those of similar units.

For press relations, AT&T essentially measured whether communication had taken place—as that objective was described in Chapter 6. Remember that we defined communication as a behavior—the movement of symbols from one person to another or, in public relations, from an organization to a public. Thus, AT&T wanted to know what kind of information about the company appeared in the mass media and how much company press representatives had done to affect the nature of press coverage. Actually, AT&T measured only whether it had communicated with the media, not whether its messages had actually moved on to—been read by—a public.

AT&T hired an outside firm to analyze the content of press clippings about the company and to tabulate the results on a computer. AT&T wanted to know how many clippings originated from the efforts of company press representatives. It also wanted to know what messages the press relations people actually communicated and the extent to which the messages appearing in the media reflected themes the press relations people were supposed to stress.

Finally, the press evaluation determined how many of the articles were favorable, neutral, or unfavorable to the company. The computer tabulation also could trace how each of these measures changed from month to month and year to year. Armstrong Cork used the same system to quantify the extent to which its hallway full of press clippings actually communicated the themes the company wanted to communicate.

For employee communication, AT&T conducted a yearly survey of employees to determine how many actually received publications (a measure of the communication objective), how many remembered what certain articles said, and how understandable they perceived the articles in the publications to be (both measures of "accuracy," or message retention). AT&T also measured the readability of the employee publications, a means of evaluating messages that we will discuss later in this chapter.

For community relations, AT&T first determined how often community relations teams used such techniques as open houses, interviews with community leaders, or talks to community groups to communicate with community leaders and residents of each community served by the Bell System. Later, the community relations evaluation measured the effect of each community relations activity on message retention, acceptance of cognitions, and overt behaviors of community leaders.

Finally, for educational relations, AT&T measured the extent to which schoolchildren learned themes relevant to the company that were presented in materials provided to schools by the company.

Evaluation at the Bureau of Standards

The National Bureau of Standards responded to its challenge for evaluation by conducting readership studies of its major publications and by surveying editors to determine whether the press materials supplied were useful. It also did an extensive study of employee publics using the techniques discussed in Chapter 12. In each of these studies, the Bureau simply measured whether it was meeting the objective of communicating relevant information to its publics.

These examples demonstrate three points. First, public relations people can evaluate their programs. Second, the objectives can be communication, message retention, and acceptance of cognitions. Public relations does not have to change attitudes and behaviors to be successful. But, third, the examples show that evaluation must be specific to individual programs. Broad polls of public attitudes may help the company in "environmental scanning," as described in the typology of public relations research discussed in Chapter 5. But evaluation and environmental scanning require different techniques and measures.

In Chapter 5, we distinguished between formative and evaluative research. Formative research helps to define the public relations problem and communication objective. Evaluative research determines whether the objective has been met. In Chapter 7, we showed you some measures that can be used to determine the nature of your publics and the best communication objective for each of those publics. These are examples of formative research. Then, in Chapter 8, we showed you some planning techniques that can be used to decide which publics should receive your attention.

We now assume you have actually begun a public relations program for those publics and are ready to evaluate the results. We turn, therefore, to the concepts, methods, and measures needed to evaluate a public relations program. This chapter will not provide you with all of the skills and techniques needed to do public relations research. It should, however, help you to understand research and the purpose it serves in a public relations program. To learn research skills you should read additional books or take courses on social science research.

STAGES OF EVALUATION

On the surface, at least, an evaluation is quite simple. It has five stages.[4]

Specify Objectives • Although the organization you work for may define its public relations objectives differently, we recommend that you choose an objective or objectives from the taxonomy developed in Chapter 6. They represent realistic, measurable, objectives with known probabilities of success.

Measure the Objectives • Each objective specifies what effect you expect your public relations program to have. To evaluate whether these effects have occurred, you must measure—or observe in some organized way—whether each objective has been accomplished. Later in this chapter, we will provide sample measures for each objective outlined in Chapter 6.

Collect and Analyze the Data • Administer the measure or observe the effect for a sample of your target public. Compare the results with the effects expected for each public. Determine if the objectives have been met. Think through why they have or have not been met, so that you can make recommendations for changing and improving programs.

Report the Results to Decision Makers • Write a report in clear, understandable language. For public relations executives, stress the extent to which public relations objectives have been met and what changes will be made to better meet objectives. For top organizational managers, report the same objectives, but explain how accomplishing public relations objectives helps to meet organizational goals and justifies the need for a public relations program.

Apply the Results to Decisions • An evaluation is worthless unless the results are put to use. Evaluations should change programs. Don't use them to support your program when the results show the program worked and ignore them when the results show the program did not work.

Stage 1, specifying objectives, was discussed in detail in Chapter 6, and Stages 4 and 5 need little further explanation. Stages 2 and 3 will be discussed next in this chapter. First, though, there are four aspects of the relationship between evaluation research and decision making that require our attention.

EVALUATION AND THE MANAGEMENT PROCESS

Stamm has defined four ''strategic questions'' that a public relations manager should ask before doing evaluative research.[5] He argues, essentially, that evaluation should be done at all stages of decision making and be done continuously, not just in one shot at the completion of a program.

When? • Evaluative questions and research should be asked during planning—the *construct* and *select* segments of Chapter 5's behavioral molecule. If not, you may not correctly identify the public relations problem. A program designed to solve the wrong problem will have no chance of success. Combine evaluation questions with studies to define publics, as described in Chapter 7.

Where? • Too often, evaluations are conducted from the organization's point of view rather than the audience's. Public relations should affect both the organization and the public.

How? • Too many practitioners do large, one-shot studies. Programs must be continuously evaluated, reconsidered, and changed. It's better to do several smaller evaluations over the course of a program.

What? • Measure something other than attitudes or the demographic characteristics of publics—age, sex, income, etc. Demographics by themselves do not define publics. Measure concepts such as those used to define publics in Chapter 7. Attitudes represent only one kind of communication effect. Measure cognitive objectives such as those discussed in Chapter 6.

APPLYING EVALUATION RESULTS TO DECISIONS

Many public relations practitioners fear evaluation, especially those in nonmanagerial positions. They assume that the only decision that can be made is a go/no-go decision. They fear that an unfavorable evaluation could cost them their jobs or pet projects. To reduce your fear of an evaluation, reach an understanding with your supervisor that you will evaluate to improve programs or to replace programs with better programs—not to find out which programs to kill or which people to fire.

Weiss described six decisions that may result from an evaluation, only one of which leads to a go/no-go decision:

To continue or discontinue the program.

To improve its practices or procedures.

To add or drop specific program strategies or techniques.

To institute similar programs elsewhere.

To allocate resources among competing programs.

To accept or reject a program approach or theory.[6]

PROCESS EVALUATIONS

Evaluations may either be "process" or "outcome" evaluations.[7] So far, we have discussed mostly outcome evaluations, the effects of public relations programs.

Process evaluations also are important. They ask whether a program is being administered effectively. Process evaluations follow Stamm's logic of continual evaluation rather than one-shot studies. Evaluation should not tell simply whether a program works once but should continue to show how well it is working.

AT&T's evaluation program, for example, first determined whether its public relations programs have had an effect—an outcome evaluation. But the company has also developed continuing measures of the performance of a program. AT&T public relations managers want performance data on a monthly or yearly basis that indicate, for example, trends in press relations or employee relations. Data on press clippings show trends in numbers of favorable, unfavorable, or neutral stories. The employee survey shows trends in exposure, comprehension, and readability.

Such process evaluations provide both managers and subordinates with continual measures of the effectiveness of a program and the performance of the people working in the program.

WHO SHOULD EVALUATE?

At some time, you will face the question of whether evaluation should be done by an insider or outsider. Outsiders may be consulting firms eager to get your business or researchers available at universities. Outsiders are generally more objective evaluators, as they have no vested interest in preserving a program or a job. But they also know less about the programs they evaluate. Outside evaluators tend to find more serious and frequent problems than insiders, because, psychologically, they would not feel they are doing their job unless they find something to correct.

Eventually, we hope, most public relations departments will have their own personnel to do evaluations. Today, few have trained researchers on their staffs, or managers with enough research courses in their background, to do their own research. If a public relations department has the personnel to do its own evaluation, it probably will do more evaluation, do it continuously, and do process evaluation. It is simply easier to keep evaluation going when it is a daily component of a public relations manager's job.

On the negative side, insiders may not be as objective as outsiders. And they may not be able to overcome the personal infighting that often occurs over decisions to keep or alter programs. Senior public relations managers frequently think the "experts" in outside research firms know more than people with research background in the department, and thus they devalue the results of internal research.

Which is best? We suggest that public relations managers hire personnel capable of doing research, so that they can make evaluation internal, continuous, and part of the management process. But we suggest they call in consultants when new and detached ideas become important, and when the objectivity of an outsider is needed to satisfy top management, rate commissions, or Congress that your program is meeting its objectives.

EVALUATION METHODS

Evaluation methods are techniques of data gathering that you can use to administer measures of public relations objectives to members of the publics or organizational subsystems that you intend to affect. You will have to make a basic choice between quantitative methods and qualitative observations.

Quantitative methods are more objective, and the data they produce can be analyzed more easily. Qualitative methods, however, produce more detail and context on your targets. Qualitative methods cost less, but they may take more time, and they are not always easier to administer. Here, then, are some of your choices.

Surveys

Public relations practitioners use surveys more than any other research method. With a survey, you write questions to measure the objectives or other concepts included in your study, gather those questions into a questionnaire, and administer the questionnaire to a sample of your publics.

With a survey, as opposed to an experiment, you cannot always control who is exposed to the public relations program you want to evaluate, and you cannot usually control conditions other than your program that might influence the effects of the program. By measuring the presence of some of these additional conditions, however, you can generally use a survey to trace the effects of your efforts.

Survey data can be collected through a personal interview, a telephone interview, or a mail questionnaire. Keep the following points in mind when you choose one of the three methods:

Personal Interviews • Personal interviews generally have the highest response rate of the three methods. Responses also are the most accurate, because the interviewer can establish rapport with the respondent and can observe when the respondent does not answer questions with care or thought. Personal interviews also can be longer than telephone interviews. Fewer personal interviews can be completed per day, however, making this method the most costly.

Sampling for personal interviews is also more difficult because people must be interviewed in their homes or offices, which generally are spread throughout a city or rural area. In addition, many people in urban areas will not let a stranger into their homes for an interview.

In contemporary public relations research, personal interviews are used most often for community leaders or other "name" people. These leaders would be offended by the informality of a telephone interview. They

Group Attitudes Corporation
633 Third Avenue
New York, NY 10017
212-697-5638

Confidential Survey

A questionnaire developed for a study of a college's alumni by Hill and Knowlton's research subsidiary, the Group Attitudes Corporation. Question 9 essentially measures the behavior objective, questions 10 and 11 the communication (exposure) objective. (Courtesy Group Attitudes Corporation)

TO: *ALMA MATER ALUMNUS*

Please answer all of the questions in this form and return it at your earliest convenience.

Mail the form in the enclosed postage-paid business reply envelope to Group Attitudes Corporation. Do not sign this form. All responses will be kept completely confidential.

Thank you for your valuable help.

Walter K. Lindenmann,
President

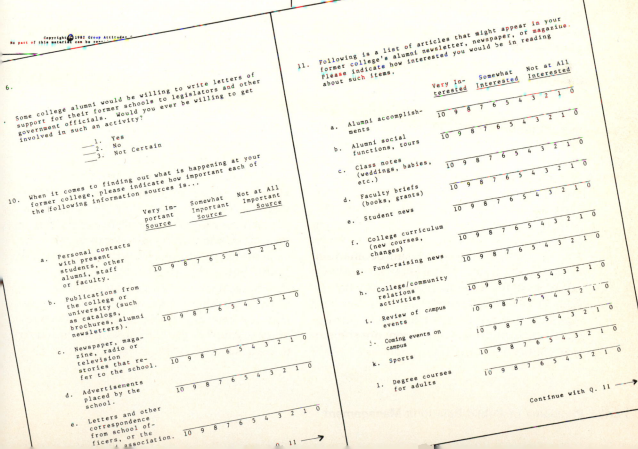

6.
Some college alumni would be willing to write letters of support for their former schools to legislators and other government officials. Would you ever be willing to get involved in such an activity?

___ 1. Yes
___ 2. No
___ 3. Not Certain

10. When it comes to finding out what is happening at your former college, please indicate how important each of the following information sources is...

	Very Important Source	Somewhat Important Source	Not at All Important Source
a. Personal contacts with present students, other alumni, staff or faculty.	10 9 8 7 6 5 4 3 2 1 0		
b. Publications from the college or university (such as catalogs, brochures, alumni newsletters).	10 9 8 7 6 5 4 3 2 1 0		
c. Newspaper, magazine, radio or television stories that refer to the school.	10 9 8 7 6 5 4 3 2 1 0		
d. Advertisements placed by the school.	10 9 8 7 6 5 4 3 2 1 0		
e. Letters and other correspondence from school officers, or the ... association.	10 9 8 7 6 5 4 3 2 1 0		

Q. 11 →

7.

11. Following is a list of articles that might appear in your former college's alumni newsletter, newspaper, or magazine. Please indicate how interested you would be in reading about such items.

	Very Interested	Somewhat Interested	Not at All Interested
a. Alumni accomplishments	10 9 8 7 6 5 4 3 2 1 0		
b. Alumni social functions, tours	10 9 8 7 6 5 4 3 2 1 0		
c. Class notes (weddings, babies, etc.)	10 9 8 7 6 5 4 3 2 1 0		
d. Faculty briefs (books, grants)	10 9 8 7 6 5 4 3 2 1 0		
e. Student news	10 9 8 7 6 5 4 3 2 1 0		
f. College curriculum (new courses, changes)	10 9 8 7 6 5 4 3 2 1 0		
g. Fund-raising news	10 9 8 7 6 5 4 3 2 1 0		
h. College/community relations activities	10 9 8 7 6 5 4 3 2 1 0		
i. Review of campus events	10 9 8 7 6 5 4 3 2 1 0		
j. Coming events on campus	10 9 8 7 6 5 4 3 2 1 0		
k. Sports	10 9 8 7 6 5 4 3 2 1 0		
l. Degree courses for adults	10 9 8 7 6 5 4 3 2 1 0		

Continue with Q. 11 →

may also be hard to reach by phone and too busy to complete a mail questionnaire.

Telephone Interviews • Telephone interviews have recently become the most popular survey technique. They are less expensive than personal inteviews, because the interviewer need not travel from one location to another to interview people. National random samples can be constructed using long distance or a WATS line. Sampling is easier because names of respondents can be taken from the telephone directory or chosen using a technique called random digit dialing.[8]

Many survey research books state that telephone interviews must be short (no more than ten minutes in length). Recent studies have shown, however, that telephone interviews can run as long as personal interviews.[9] On the other hand, rapport may be more difficult with telephone interviews. And the interviewers cannot judge the quality of answers as well as they can with personal interviews.

All things considered, however, the telephone provides a fast and inexpensive way of conducting a survey. It is suited for most public relations studies.

Mail Questionnaires • Mail surveys also provide an inexpensive way of developing a large sample.[10] Increases in postage costs have rapidly decreased this advantage, however. Mail questionnaires can also be longer than personal interviews and telephone interviews. People who answer mail questionnaires also answer them more thoroughly than they do personal or telephone interviews. They have more time and can complete the questionnaire when it is convenient for them.

The disadvantage is the response rate. People generally do not return questionnaires that do not relate to a topic that involves or interests them. Busy executives and community leaders get far more questionnaires than they have time to answer. Thus, you should use a mail questionnaire only if the respondents have a great deal of interest in the topic or if you do extensive mail and telephone follow-ups to increase the response rate.

Public relations researchers use mail questionnaires most for surveys of publics and subsystems that have a higher level of involvement with an organization, such as employees or members of associations. For studies of external publics, public relations researchers most often use mail questionnaires in ''panel'' studies—studies in which a group of people is selected and paid to complete questionnaires on a continuing basis. One organization may send the same questionnaire to the same panel at different times to see how responses change. Other organizations may also use the same panel for a different study, especially when the research is done by a commercial research firm that maintains panels for several clients.

Experiments

The controlled experiment is, when carried out properly, probably the most powerful method of seeking answers to research questions available to the behavioral scientist . . . the controlled experiment is our best—and very nearly only—way of finding out what causes what.[11]

Surveys measure several concepts and objectives at one point in time. They may *suggest* whether your program caused the effect, but they cannot *prove* that the effect would not have occurred without the program. Generally, you cannot establish time order— whether the program preceded the effect— with survey data, unless you use some complicated new statistical procedures that have been developed by social scientists.

An experiment may not provide absolute proof, but it can establish time order. With the experiment, you can make certain the effect was not there before the program began, and you can usually control for most of the other conditions that might cause the effect to occur.

Figure 9-1 shows an experimental model. You randomly choose one group of people to participate in a program and another group of people as a control group that does not participate. You measure your objective on both groups before and after the experimental group participates in the program. If you find a greater difference in the experimental group on the measures taken before and after the program than you find in the control group, you can conclude that your program has been a success.

Experiments may be conducted either in the laboratory or in the field. In the laboratory, you bring subjects onto your turf. You may, for example, bring a group of students into your office to view a film or have them read pamphlets on new sources of energy. You also bring in a control group and give them a program on something else—say, on careers in education. You administer a knowledge test on energy to both groups before the program and administer another test after. If your program worked, people in the experimental group should have increased their knowlege of energy more than those in the control group.

For a field experiment, on the other hand, you go onto the turf of the subjects. You could have a schoolteacher administer the program in the classroom. The control group would be a similar class studying what they normally would be studying. Public relations re-searchers use field experiments much more than laboratory experiments, although there are many possibilities for laboratory experiments, especially for employees and other "captive" publics.

In practice, it is almost impossible to conduct a perfect controlled experiment, especially in action programs such as public relations. You often cannot randomly assign people to experimental and control groups, because your program is designed to reach key publics, and you do not want to ignore some people just for the sake of evaluation. Often, you can't find a comparable control group for a field experiment. At other times, members of the control group interact with members of the experimental group, and it's difficult to sort out effects.

Usually, you will have to resort to a "quasi-experimental" design or even a non-experimental design based on the logic of the controlled experiment.[12] There are four experimental designs that can be used in public relations evaluation.

Pretest Posttest • You have only an experimental group and measure your objective before and after a program. You know for certain if a program had no effect, but can never be certain whether a positive effect resulted from your program or from some other factor that you did not control.

Posttest Only • You compare an experimental group with a control group after ran-

FIGURE **9-1**   **The Experimental Model**

	Before	After
Experimental	A	B
Control	C	D

If the difference between A and B is greater than the difference between C and D, you have reason to conclude that your program is a success.

From Carol H. Weiss, *Evaluation Research: Methods of Assessing Program Effectiveness*, © 1972, p. 61. Re-drawn by permission of Prentice-Hall, Inc., Englewood Cliffs, N.J.

domly assigning subjects to both groups. Randomization should assure that differences between the experimental and control group occurred because of your program. Nevertheless, you can never be certain that your program caused the desired effect.

Multiple Pretest Posttest • You administer a pre- and a posttest of your objective to both experimental and control groups. Then you know that your effect did not occur by chance.

Nonequivalent Control Group • Use this design when you cannot randomly assign subjects to either an experimental or control group. Look instead for a reasonable control group for your experimental group. If you want the employees in a plant in Buffalo to improve their knowledge about the economic system, for example, apply the same test — after the same amount of time has elapsed— to a similar group of employees in a plant in Syracuse. It's not a perfect random design, but it's usually the best you can do. In public relations research, the first three types of experiments nearly always will be done on nonequivalent control groups.

Secondary Data

You may be in an organization that cannot afford original research. If you are, you may at times find data available from other sources that suggest whether your program has worked or will work.

Commercial research firms collect survey research data that they make available to several clients at less cost than an original poll. Academic research reported in such journals as *Public Relations Review, Public Opinion Quarterly, Journalism Quarterly, Communication Research*, or *Human Communication Research* may suggest whether your program works. National survey organizations, such as the Survey Research Center at the University of Michigan or the National Opinion Research Center at the University of Chicago, make data from their interviews available. Fre-

quently, you can reanalyze such data to answer your research questions.

Secondary data, however, seldom tell whether *your* program worked. They can only suggest, unless the data were collected on members of your target public after your program began. Rarely is that the case.

At other times, you may be able to piggyback your research questions, for example, onto a survey of employees done by the personnel department, or a survey of consumers done by the marketing department. Make certain you know who is doing research in your organization, and on whom.

Qualitative Analysis

Many behavioral scientists mistakenly equate qualitative methods with loose, unstructured methods of gathering data. Researchers who use qualitative methods, instead, use all of the faculties of the mind to observe a situation or the outcome of a program. They do not limit themselves to what can be counted or measured quantitatively. According to Christians and Carey, qualitative research has four characteristics.[13]

Naturalistic Observation • Researchers get as close to the situation and the participants as possible. They attempt to "re-create in imagination and experience the thought and sentiments of the observed."

Contextualization • Researchers do not restrict themselves to a few statistical measures of variables. They look at the total context in which an effect occurs.

Maximized Comparisons • Researchers look at the total public, the total community, or the total organization and compare them with similar units. They do not limit themselves to a few hypotheses for a few people.

Sensitized Concepts • The language of the qualitative researcher must make sense to the people observed as well as to the observer. It describes the actual responses of target groups to a program in words they would use.

You can use three types of qualitative research in evaluating a public relations program.

1. Qualitative Observation[14] • The researcher goes into the field either as a "participant observer" or as an "onlooker." Participant observers experience a program and share those experiences with the others around them. Onlookers simply watch participants; they do not participate themselves. Sometimes, qualitative researchers do overt observation: participants know they are being observed by a researcher. At other times, the researchers are covert observers: participants do not recognize them as evaluators. Qualitative researchers use theory to guide their observations, such as our taxonomy of effects, but they do not limit their observations to the concepts of the theory. They use them as "sensitizing concepts," guiding what they observe but not limiting their observations.

2. Qualitative Interviews[15] • Qualitative researchers can use three types of interviews: (1) the informal conversational interview, (2) a general interview guide, or (3) a standardized open-end interview. With the informal conversational interview, researchers talk to program participants without any preconceived notions of what will happen. With the general interview guide, they look for certain effects but do not ask structured questions. With the open-end questionnaire, they ask the same questions of everyone they interview but proceed flexibly to learn of effects that they may not have anticipated. For example, they may ask a general question about communication, beliefs, or behavior, opening the way for the people being interviewed to elaborate on how they communicate with the organization, what they believe, or what specifically they have done.

3. Focus Groups • Focus group interviews are an offshoot of the structured interview approach. To conduct them, a researcher invites a small group of people who are typical of the public or subsystem that is the target of a PR program to a neutral meeting place—usually a hotel conference room. The researcher then asks the group prepared questions related to the effects he or she hopes to observe. The members of the group respond and may react to one another's ideas. Such groups allow the researcher to observe people's ideas and evaluations in a group setting, which is the natural place they occur. The disadvantage is that members of the group may influence each other more than would happen in the outside world.

A Sense of "What's Happening"

Too often, researchers choose sides over qualitative or quantitative methods and use one to the exclusion of the other. Both have a role in public relations evaluation. Qualitative methods work best in formative evaluations, when the researcher wants to evaluate what will work. An example of such use is the community case study approach originated by Group Attitudes Corp., the research arm of the Hill & Knowlton public relations agency.[16] With this approach, a team of researchers spends only a few days in a community, intensively interviewing community residents and leaders. After even that short time, they can come away with a sense of what is happening in the community and what kind of public relations program the sponsoring organization should develop there.

PR people who do not have the money to do a quantitative study can do a reasonably adequate qualitative study if they go out and talk with the targets of their programs or observe people experiencing the program.

Not everyone can immediately become a qualitative researcher, however. It takes training and skill to observe people and situations objectively. Remember the theory of cognitive dissonance, which states that people hear only what they want to hear. That tendency can be overcome, but it takes practice.

If the public relations researcher conducts qualitative research objectively and skillfully, the results may be as useful—in fact, even more useful—than those of a quantitative study. One caution, however: hard-nosed managers often aren't as impressed with qualitative data as they are with numbers.

Time Budgets

A time budget is a record of how people spend their time during a day, week, or other time period. Mass-communication researchers have used time budgets to determine how much time people spend with different mass media.[17]

Time budgets could be used in public relations to determine how much time employees spend with company media. They could also be used to determine how managerial and public relations people use their time, especially to isolate the amount of time they spend communicating and with whom. And, time budgets can be used as an internal management control technique to examine how people on a public relations staff allocate their time in different forms of communication.

Public relations agencies, for example, have long had their employees keep time records so that they can bill clients for time spent on their accounts. The Office of Personnel Management, in the federal government, has set up time budgets for personnel departments and has offered to do the same for public relations departments. Georgetown University has used time budgets to demonstrate to administrators what the public relations department does for the organization.

There are three ways to calculate time budgets:

First, each person can maintain a diary on an hourly basis during a specified period. This method provides the most extensive budgets, but people may behave differently when they have to report their time than they would when they know their behavior is not being recorded.

Second, interviewers can question people the day after about the previous day's activity and enter results on an interview schedule.

With the third method, the people being observed are told to record what they are doing at randomly selected times. One person is given a list of the randomly selected times, and he or she announces to the people being observed when each set time arrives. No one other than the one person knows, however, what the set times will be. Over a week or longer periods, the random times give an accurate picture of what groups of individuals do with their time.

These, then, are most of the evaluation-research methods you may want to use in public relations. Next, we turn to measures of public relations objectives. We will first introduce the kinds of questions used to measure concepts in social science research. Then we will provide examples of how these kinds of questions have been used to measure the objectives discussed in Chapter 6.

MEASURES USED IN SOCIAL SCIENCE RESEARCH

You will first have to choose between open- and closed-end questions. Closed-end questions specify the responses available to the person answering the question. Open-end questions allow the respondents to answer in their own words.

Try to use closed-end questions whenever you can. They are easier for respondents to answer and easier for you to analyze. Use open-end questions for qualitative research and in exploratory, formative evaluations. You can also use them for probe questions, when you want more detail about a person's opinion that has been measured on a closed-end question. Let's look, then, at the most common types of closed-end questions.[18]

Fact Questions

These generally are demographic questions about the respondent: sex, age, income, number of television sets owned, or newspapers read. Give the respondent multiple choices. Generally, you should provide five response choices, although some social scientists prefer more or less. An example:

In which age group are you?

( ) under 20   ( ) 50–64
( ) 21–34   ( ) 65 or over
( ) 35–49

Evaluative Questions

These measure beliefs and attitudes. Evaluative questions place respondents at some point on a numerical scale that starts with a low number and ends with a high number. Ideally, you should use several measures of the same attitude or belief and then sum them into a single scale. You have four major choices:

A multiple choice item, such as:

How would you rate the Jiffy Widget Company as a place to work?

( ) Excellent   ( ) Poor
( ) Good   ( ) Very poor
( ) Average

Agreement or disagreement with a statement that represents an extreme position (these are generally called "Likert-type" questions, after psychologist Rensis Likert, who developed the technique). Use five response choices; one should be a neutral point:

The Semantic Differential Technique: A set of adjectives with opposite meaning ("polar adjectives") placed at opposite ends of a seven-point scale. Respondents choose one of the seven points between the two adjectives to show where their evaluation lies:

How would you describe the Jiffy Widget Company?

Bad _____ _____ _____ _____

_____ _____ _____ Good

Old _____ _____ _____

_____ _____ _____ Young

Responsible _____ _____ _____ _____

_____ _____ _____ Irresponsible

Rankings:

How would you rank the social responsibility of the Jiffy Widget Company in comparison with other business firms in this community? Give a 1 for the company you rank the highest, a 2 for the company you rank next, and so on.

( ) New England Telephone Company
( ) Jiffy Widget Company
( ) Dexter Shoe Company
( ) Procter & Gamble
( ) Levi Strauss.

To what extent do you agree or disagree with each of the following statements? Do you strongly agree, agree, neither agree nor disagree, disagree, or strongly disagree?

	SA	A	N	D	SD
The Jiffy Widget Company should be forced to pay higher wages	5	4	3	2	1
The Jiffy Widget Company treats its employees well	5	4	3	2	1

Information Questions

Information questions ask respondents how much they know, what they know, how they learned about something, or when they heard about something. In the next section, we will use these questions to measure retention of messages. Frequently, they also are used in readership studies in public relations.

Information questions generally should be written as multiple choice questions. For example:

An article in the Jiffy *Widgetarian* (the employee newspaper) last week discussed the company's safety program. Which statement do you think best describes what that article said?

( ) The work done by Jiffy employees is relatively safe. Therefore, the company has an excellent safety record and does not need a safety program.

( ) The Jiffy company has an active program to promote employee safety that has resulted in an excellent company safety record.

( ) Although much of the work done by Jiffy employees is relatively dangerous, the company prefers to encourage safety informally without having an active safety program that employees think is a nuisance.

( ) Don't know.

Self-perception Questions

Self-perception questions ask people's opinions about the facts or about their own behavior. Respondents provide their own perceptions, which may or may not be accurate. The questions used to measure problem recognition, level of involvement, constraint recognition, referent criterion, and information processing in Chapter 7, for example, were self-perception questions:

How often do you stop to think about the problem of air pollution caused by the Jiffy Widget plant in Jiffyville?

( ) Often   ( ) Rarely
( ) Sometimes ( ) Never

Now let's look at how these questions can be used to measure public relations objectives.

SAMPLE MEASURES OF PUBLIC RELATIONS OBJECTIVES

In Chapter 6, we said that public relations objectives must be clear, specific, and *measurable*. In that chapter, we reviewed the literature on communication effects to isolate clear and specific public relations objectives.

Now we will provide some examples of measures of these objectives, using the methods and measures discussed thus far in this chapter. You will recall that these five objectives include communication, retention of messages, acceptance of cognitions, formation or change of an attitude (evaluation), and overt behavior. The effects can be asymmetric or symmetric. If you don't remember these objectives, you might review them in Exhibit 6–1 on page 134 before proceeding.

Communication

When you define your objective as communication, you measure it by looking for some evidence that your message has moved to, and been received by, either target publics or by target members of the management subsystem. You can measure it by counting how frequently different kinds of communication take place between organizational subsystems and publics.

At times, you may have to take short cuts in measuring communication in order to reduce the cost of your measurements. For example, most organizations measure the effectiveness of press relations by counting how many clippings appear in the media. That does not always provide a measure of communication, as it is entirely possible that few people, if anyone, read the articles. To learn if anyone read the story, you would have to conduct a readership survey of members of the public.

Here are some examples of these indirect measures of communication:

Numbers of press clippings appearing in the media.

Number of contacts made with journalists.

TV or radio ratings provided by rating companies.

Attendance counts at exhibits, open houses, or special events.

Number of speeches given by employees.

Number of people exposed to educational materials.

Number of publications distributed to each public.

Number of organizational managers briefed on public opinion by the public relations staff.

Number of dialogue sessions between managers and members of publics (an example of symmetric communication).

Readership studies (see Exhibit 9–1).

Content analysis of clippings or publications (see Exhibit 9–2).

Retention of Messages

There are four ways you can measure whether members of publics or organizational subsystems have retained a message:

Readability Formulas • Readability formulas do not measure message retention directly; they measure how difficult it is for someone to read and understand a piece of writing.[19] The easier it is for people to comprehend a message, however, the more likely

they will be to retain the message. Nevertheless, many publics will not retain a message that does not interest them even if it is readable, as we saw in Chapter 7. Readability formulas can provide a useful indicator of the potential for message retention. However, they measure only a part of the difficulty of the material, and they should be used only as general indicators of difficulty and the appropriateness of the written materials for your audiences. (See Exhibit 9–3.)

The Signaled Stopping Technique (SST) • Richard Carter of the University of Washington, who developed this technique, has called it a psychlotron.[20] Its analogue, the cyclotron, allows the physicist to see inside the atom. The SST allows the public relations evaluator to see what goes on in the readers' minds as they read a piece of writing or hear or view a message or picture, and to determine if the reader processes the information. (See Exhibit 9–4.)

Multiple-Choice Comprehension Questions • In these, the organization's or public's correct message is one of several reasonable sounding alternatives. For example, the following question measured retention of a Mobil Oil public relations advertisement on nuclear energy in a study done at the University of Maryland:

Which of the following statements represents the Mobil Oil Company's position on nuclear energy?

( ) Nuclear power is far safer than coal or hydroelectric power in meeting our energy needs in the future.

( ) Scientists know more about controlling the pollution from burning coal than they do about controlling radiation.

( ) Solar power is the safest and most viable source of energy for the future if it can be researched and developed.

( ) I don't know.

(The correct answer was the first alternative.)

EXHIBIT 9—1   Readership Survey Questions

Readership surveys document whether anyone read the clippings that appeared in the mass media, whether employees read a publication, or, if a viewership study, whether anyone saw a television advertisement or news program. Readership studies may be done by personal interview, telephone, or mail questionnaire. If done in person, the interviewer shows the respondent the publication in which an article appeared and asks two self-perception questions:

1. Do you recall having seen this article on air pollution created by the Bethlehem Steel Co. in Baltimore?
   ( ) No (GO TO NEXT QUESTION)
   ( ) Yes↓

       2. How much of that article would you say you read. Did you:
          ( ) Read all
          ( ) Read most
          ( ) Read some
          ( ) Not read it at all.

In a telephone or mail questionnaire, you would have to tell the reader a little about the story, or read the title: "Do you happen to remember a story that appeared in the *Baltimore Sun* discussing air pollution caused by the Bethlehem Steel Co.?" Then you would proceed with the same second question as above.

Sometimes, researchers ask readership questions about entire publications. For example, a study of employees at the National Bureau of Standards asked:

How Often Do You Read?	Always	Most of the Time	About Half of the Time	Hardly Ever	Never
NBS Standard	5	4	3	2	1
Technical Calendar	5	4	3	2	1
Dimensions Magazine	5	4	3	2	1
Bulletin Boards	5	4	3	2	1

Readership questions can also be asked about general types of content in publications. The same National Bureau of Standards study asked:

Next, would you indicate about how often you would read each of the following types of articles if it appeared in an NBS publication? Would you read it:

	Always	Most of the Time	About Half of the Time	Hardly Ever	Never
News of appointments or awards	5	4	3	2	1
News about pay and benefit plans	5	4	3	2	1
Messages from the director	5	4	3	2	1

EXHIBIT 9–2   Content Analysis

Content analysis is a systematic, quantitative method of determining the content of the mass media, clippings about your organization, publications produced by the public relations department, speeches given by organization members, or other messages. It is a way of quantifying what we read and observe in these publications.

Content analysis goes one step beyond other indirect measures of the communication objective, in that it determines what the communication was about. It can be used to determine the themes discussed in press clippings about the company; to evaluate whether the clippings were positive, negative, or neutral; or to trace different content categories through time. It can be used as a check on editors of organizational publications to determine what they are including in their publications and to suggest that certain topics are being used too little or too much. Content analysis has many similar uses in public relations.

Content analysis has five major stages:*

1. Select a unit of analysis. Will you examine entire articles, paragraphs, or sentences?
2. Construct categories. What themes, evaluational dimensions, or other units do you want to measure? The categories should be defined by what the PR program was designed to communicate.
3. Sample content. Not all clippings or articles need be examined. You may, for example, select articles randomly, take one entire week, or reconstruct a hypothetical week or month from a year-long period.
4. Code the units of analysis. You either do the coding yourself or train coders. Coders classify articles or number of column inches into the categories chosen. It is also important to check on coder reliability by having more than one coder code the same units and then comparing the results. If the two coders place the units into different categories more than 10–20 percent of the time, reconstruct the categories.
5. Analyze the results by computer or hand tabulation.

* Guido H. Stempel, III. "Content Analysis," in Guido H. Stempel, III, and Bruce H. Westley (eds.), *Research Methods in Mass Communication* (Englewood Cliffs, N. J.: Prentice-Hall, 1981), pp. 119–131.

EXHIBIT 9-3   Readability Formulas

Readability research originated with education researchers as early as 1888. Readability research-ers have attempted to develop a quantitative formula that indicates whether written materials are appropriate for audiences with different educational backgrounds. Researchers have also tested the ability of readability formulas to predict ''listenability'' of broadcast writing—writing read aloud.* This research shows that readability formulas predict listenability as well as read-ability.

All of the most widely used readability formulas today have two components: the difficulty of the words, and the length of the sentences. Three of the frequently used formulas—the Flesch Reading Ease Formula, the Gunning Fog Index, and the Farr-Jenkins-Patterson formula—use the number of syllables in a word as a measure of word difficulty.

With the Flesch formula, researchers must count the average number of syllables in a 100-word sample of the writing. With the Gunning Fog index, they count the number of words with polysyllables (three or more syllables). With the Farr-Jenkins-Patterson formula, they count the number of monosyllables (one-syllable words). For the fourth formula, the Dale-Chall formula, the researcher measures word difficulty by counting the number of words in a 100-word sample that do not appear on a list of the 3,000 most common English words.

Let's take the Flesch formula as an example. As reconstructed by Powers, Sumner, and Kearl—to reduce its prediction error—the formula is:

$$R = (.0778)(ASL) + (.0455)(\text{syllables}/100 \text{ words}) - 2.209$$

where R = readability and ASL = average sentence length.†

To use the formula, take any continuous sample of 100 words, preferably not at the beginning of an article. Count the number of sentences and divide that into 100 to find average sentence length. (A sentence is considered to end with semicolons and dashes as well as periods.) Then count the number of syllables in the 100 words. Plug the two numbers into the formula to get a readability score. Interpret the scores as follows:

4.0–4.5—Very easy, like pulp fiction, drugstore novels
4.5–5.5—Fairly easy, like slick fiction, movie magazines
5.5–6.5—Standard, like newspapers or *Reader's Digest*
6.5–7.5—Quality, like intellectual magazines, *Harper's*
7.5–above—Academic, like learned journals.

To calculate the Gunning Fog Index, take a sample of 100 words, find the average sentence length and the number of words of three syllables or more.** In counting polysyllables, however, do not include: (1) capitalized words, (2) combinations of short easy words (such as bookkeeper), (3) verbs that have three syllables because of ''ed'' or ''es'' at the end (such as created). Total the average sentence length and number of polysyllables and multiply by 0.4. The score approx-imates the number of years of education required to read a passage easily and to understand it. A score of 16 suggests writing for a college graduate. Most best-selling books test at 7–8. A score of 13 is the danger line for most readers. Try to keep your writing below that.

* Carl Jon Denbow, ''Listenability and Readability: An Experimental Investigation,'' *Journalism Quarterly* 52 (1975):285–290.

† Richard D. Powers, W. A. Sumner, and B. E. Kearl, ''A Recalculation of Four Adult Readability Formulas,'' *Journal of Applied Psychology* 49 (1958):104.

** Robert Gunning, *New Guide to More Effective Writing in Business and Industry* (Boston: Industrial Edu-cation Institute, 1963), pp. 2–15. Also Robert Gunning, *The Technique of Clear Writing* (New York: McGraw-Hill, 1952), p. 36.

EXHIBIT **9—4** **The Signaled Stopping Technique**

When people read or listen to words, they put them together to construct ideas, or what Carter calls "pictures." These people stop, however, when they cannot process the information into a single idea, when they get the idea and want to think about it, or when they agree or disagree with it.

To use the SST, give people who represent your publics the message you have written. Ask them to put a slash mark anywhere in the written passage where they feel like stopping. Then ask them to indicate their reason for stopping, using the following notation:

C—Because of confusion: You stop or pause in reading because you feel you have lost the idea the writer is trying to communicate

R—To reread: You stop because you have lost track of the idea but you can get back on track by reading a passage again

?—To ask a question: You stop because you feel that if you could just ask the writer a question it would help you to understand the idea he or she is trying to communicate

T—To think about the idea: You stop to mull over what you have read and try to put it all together

U—Because you understand: You stop because you do understand the writer's main idea and want to "let it sink in"

A—To agree: You agree with what the writer said

D—To disagree: You disagree with what the writer said.

Write in any other reason.

A subject might, for example, make the following notations while reading the first two sentences in this exhibit.

When people read or listen/ ^C to words, they put them together to construct ideas, or what

Carter calls "pictures."/ ^D These people stop/, [?] however, when they cannot process/the [?]

information into a single idea, when they get the idea/ ^R and want to think about it, or when

"I'm bored!"
they agree or disagree with it./

As you should be able to see from this example, the SST provides a detailed look at how readers construct the idea you want them to retain. It also shows whether they believe the idea and evaluate it favorably (two other PR objectives). Studying the various readers' reasons for stopping will suggest how you can improve the writing so that readers can grasp your idea.

If you go through the SST yourself on your own writing—especially the day after you write something—you'll be surprised at what goes through your own mind when you process the message you wrote. You can then use the codes you write to improve your writing, and that will spare the reader a lot of grief. The SST also can be used for spoken messages (speeches, radio, TV), if you have the subjects write down the codes as they listen. It is difficult to trace their reactions to specific parts of the message, however, for the spoken material.

A similar question could be constructed for management after a survey had been taken to determine what percentage of the public agreed with each statement. The question would read: "Which of the following statements do you think would be the most frequent position given by members of the public if asked which statement they most agreed with?"

Open-end Questions or Any Informal Method That Can Determine What the Public or Organizational Subsystem Thinks Is the Other's Position on an Issue •

Acceptance of Cognitions

The "acceptance of cognitions" objective can be measured with questions that follow up the multiple-choice comprehension questions that we suggested for the "retention of a message" effect. To measure acceptance, however, you should ask survey respondents whether they agree with the company position, ask managers whether they agree with the public's position. Then, you can use the responses to measure hedging and wedging, concepts that we discussed in Chapter 6.

The follow-up question would be an eval-uative—or Likert-type—question. A measure of cognitions is a measure of a respondent's beliefs. Thus, you write statements that either management, organizational critics, or members of publics believe to be fact. The extent to which respondents agree with the statement is a measure of their beliefs.

Believing Conflicting Statements • From Chapter 6, you will recall that a respondent may hedge (believe that conflicting points of view are both factual) as well as wedge (believe only one point of view is true). Thus, when you measure cognitive beliefs, you should prepare at least two statements—one to represent what your organization believes about the issue, the other to represent an antiorganization belief. However, the statements should not be exact opposites of each other. The respondent should be able to agree with both.

For example, the question on nuclear power that we used as an example of how to measure message retention was followed in the questionnaire by two questions. (They were mixed with other belief questions, however, so that the two did not follow one another in the interview.):

Now, I would like to ask your opinion on these issues. For each statement that I read, please tell me if you strongly agree with the statement, agree with it, are neutral, disagree, or strongly disagree. If you have no opinion on the statement, please tell me that.

	SA	A	N	D	SD	No Opinion
Nuclear power is far safer than coal or hydroelectric power in meeting our energy needs in the future	5	4	3	2	1	0
We know very little about the health and environmental risks of nuclear power	5	4	3	2	1	0

As you might have guessed, the first statement represented the position taken by Mobil Oil, the second the position taken by critics of nuclear power. Both are alleged statements of fact. A reasonable person could agree with both.

Converting the Questions to "Hedging and Wedging" Scores • You can develop a quantitative measure of wedging by subtracting a respondent's scores on the two measures and ignoring the sign: i.e., by using the absolute value (ABS) of the difference. (An absolute value is a value that ignores whether the score is positive or negative.) The wedging formula:

Wedge = ABS (Question 1 − Question 2)

It's a little more complicated to measure hedging. Remember that a person who wedges on an issue believes both statements to be true. The simplest way to measure hedging would seem to be adding a person's scores on the two measures of conflicting beliefs.

But there's a problem. A score of 1 and 5 would give a hedging score of 6, as would scores of 3 and 3. The score of 6 that resulted from adding two 3 scores does indeed represent moderate hedging—the respondent was midscale on both statements. The score of 6 that resulted from adding 1 and 5, however, is a high score that falsely suggests the person is hedging. Clearly, a person who has the highest score on one question and the lowest on another would be wedging and not hedging.

You can eliminate the false hedging scores that result when a person is at the extreme scale point on one of the two questions if you add the two scores together and then subtract the absolute value (ABS) of their difference to give the hedging score:

Hedge = Question 1 + Question 2
− ABS (Question 1 − Question 2)

With this formula, the 1 and 6 scores would result in a hedging score of 2: (1 + 5) − ABS (5 − 1) = 6 − 4 = 2. The 3 and 3 scores would give a hedging score of 6. Clearly, the hedging score now provides an accurate measure of the concept.

One further caution. If you use a "no opinion" response, as we did in this example, you cannot calculate hedging and wedging for the people who respond in that way for either question. They have no beliefs. As you will recall from Chapter 6, having no belief is a viable response and must be accounted for in any measurement.

Qualitative Measures of Cognitions • In addition to closed-end questions, you can use open-end questions or informal methods to ask people whether they believe the company's position, the position of critics, or both. The same can be done for managers. With these methods, you get respondents to talk about the issue or problem and to introduce as many supposed factual statements as possible. Ask people what they think of those statements.

A Coorientational Measure of Understanding

You may recall the coorientation model we discussed in Chapter 6. It provided a symmetric concept of overlapping cognitions—"understanding"—that you can use to measure the extent to which a public relations program has brought the cognitions of your organization and a public closer together. "Understanding" is a symmetric counterpart to the asymmetric "acceptance of cognitions" objective we discussed in the last section.

To quantify understanding, you would calculate a "difference score," which expresses the distance in cognitions among people in your organization and in a public. The more people in your organization have the same cognitive beliefs as people in the public, the more they "understand" each other. A difference score, therefore, indicates how far apart their beliefs are. The higher the difference score, the lower the level of understanding.

Calculating a Difference Score • To calculate a difference score, subtract the average score of management (or another group that you are measuring) from the average score of the public that management is supposed to understand. The absolute value of the difference measures understanding. (You use the absolute value because it matters little which is higher than the other; it is the difference alone that matters.)

For example, if the average score of management on the first question on nuclear power was 4.5, and the average score for the public was 2.2, the difference score would be 2.3. On the 1 to 5 scale we have used, the largest possible difference score would be 4, the smallest 0. On this question, therefore, the two groups would have a medium level of understanding.

Attitude (Evaluation/Behavioral Intent)

You can measure attitude using the same evaluative, Likert-type questions that we suggested as measures of cognitions. Evaluative questions that measure this objective, however, ask respondents how strongly they agree that stated solutions to problems or possible behaviors should be chosen. In contrast, the evaluative questions used to measure cognitions ask respondents the extent to which they believe each of the supposedly factual statements are true.

In the study of nuclear power, respondents evaluated the following statement:

	SA	A	N	D	SD	No Opinion
The United States should build nuclear power plants in the future	5	4	3	2	1	0

Other Measures Related to Attitudes • In addition to this quantitative measure of attitude, you can also use open-end questions or informal methods to ask people what they think *should be done* about the problems or issues you are measuring. You would use methods we have already discussed.

You may also want a symmetric—coorientational—measure of overlapping attitudes, which we called agreement in the coorientation model presented in Chapter 6.

Agreement, you will recall, represents the extent to which two people or groups have the same evaluations. You can measure agreement using the same difference scores that we suggested for understanding. In this case, you would calculate the differences between the average scores on the above evaluative question.

Overt Behavior

To measure actual behaviors, you can ask respondents what they have actually done in an attempt to influence or resolve the issue you are studying. Here are four ways to get information on behaviors:

Closed-end questions are those in which you ask respondents whether they have engaged in behaviors you specify, plus an open-end final option in which they can report other behaviors. For nuclear power, for example, we asked:

On the issue of nuclear power, have you:

( ) Put a bumper sticker on your car?
( ) Attended an antinuclear rally?
( ) Written a letter to the Nuclear Regulatory Commission?
( ) Written a letter to a U.S. senator or congressman?
( ) Refused to travel near a nuclear power plant?
( ) Done anything else related to the issue? If so, what?

Open-end or informal questions ask respondents what they have actually done about an issue.

Informal or formal observation may be made of the behaviors of members of publics or organizational subsystems.

Actual counts of behaviors may be made of such factors as the number of long-distance telephone calls, numbers of letters, funds raised, attendance at the theatre or football game.

Combination of Methods

There are times when you can combine open- and closed-end questions and measure several objectives in sequence.

For example, the following set of questions was designed to evaluate the effect of one community relations activity—paying the dues for employees and giving them time to attend meetings of local civic organizations. Community leaders in four communities were asked:

Are you a member of any clubs or organizations in which there are XYZ company employees who are also members and whose names you can remember?

( ) Yes ⟶ How many clubs or organizations? (   )
( ) No   (Go to question 17)
( ) Don't Know (Go to question 17)

Would you think back to any discussions you might have had in the last three years with members of those organizations who are XYZ company employees and tell me if you have learned anything about the company from them that you didn't know before.

( ) No ⟶ Go to question 14
( ) Yes ⟶ What did you learn? _____
_____
_____
_____

Do you believe the XYZ company activity that you heard about in this conversation is a good thing for this community, a bad thing, or that it has no effect either way?

( ) Good thing
( ) Bad thing
( ) No effect

Did you do anything personally either to support or to oppose the XYZ company activity that you heard about during that conversation?

( ) No ⟶ Go to question 14
( ) Yes ⟶ What did you do? _____
_____
_____
_____

Was that to support (   )
or to oppose (   )
the XYZ company?

SOME FINAL ADVICE

We have provided you with the basic concepts, methods, and measures needed to do evaluation research in public relations. The chapter should have taught you enough to be able to work with researchers in your organization or in outside consulting agencies.

If you want to do your own research or become a full-time researcher, you will need to know much more than what is in this chapter. You must learn sampling theory, more about questionnaire construction, and some basic statistics.

Many public relations degree programs require that students take courses in research methods and in statistics. We think that is a good idea. As research becomes more and more a day-to-day component of public relations, you will need research and statistical skills. Public relations no longer is purely an art. It can and must be measured and evaluated.

NOTES

1. Robert K. Marker, "The Armstrong/PR Data Measurement System," *Public Relations Review* 3 (Winter 1977):51–52.
2. James F. Tirone, "Measuring the Bell System's Public Relations," *Public Relations Review* 3 (Winter 1977):38.
3. Richard S. Franzen, "An NBS Internal Communications Study: A Comment," *Public Relations Review* 3 (Winter 1977):88.
4. Carol H. Weiss, *Evaluation Research: Methods for Assessing Program Effectiveness* (Englewood Cliffs, N. J.: Prentice-Hall, 1972), pp. 24–25; Harvey K. Jacobson, "The Role of Evaluation and Research in Management," in A. Westley Rowland (ed.), *Handbook for Institutional Advancement: Programs for the Understanding and Support of Higher Education* (San Francisco: Jossey-Bass, 1977).
5. Keith R. Stamm, "Strategies for Evaluating Public Relations," *Public Relations Review* 3 (Winter 1977):120–128.
6. Weiss, pp. 16–17.
7. Glen C. Cain and Robinson G. Hollister, "The Methodology of Evaluating Social Action Programs," in Peter H. Rossi and Walter Williams (eds.), *Evaluating Social Programs* (New York: Seminar Press, 1972), pp. 110–111.
8. In random digit dialing, you choose the last four numbers of a telephone number from a table of random numbers. The first three are chosen either from a listing of telephone exchanges or from listed numbers in the telephone book. Random digit dialing works better than sampling complete numbers from the telephone book because it reaches unlisted numbers. See, for example, K. Michael Cummings, "Random Digit Dialing: A Sampling Technique for Telephone Surveys," *Public Opinion Quarterly* 43 (1979):233–244.
9. For example, Theresa F. Rogers, "Interviews by Telephone and in Person: Quality of Responses and Field Performance," *Public Opinion Quarterly* 40 (1976):51–65.
10. The "bible" on mail surveys is Paul L. Erdos, *Professional Mail Surveys* (New York: McGraw-Hill, 1970).
11. Bruce H. Westley, "The Controlled Experiment," in Guido H. Stempel, III, and Bruce H. Westley (eds.), *Research Methods in Mass Communication* (Englewood Cliffs, N. J.: Prentice-Hall, 1981), p. 196.
12. Weiss, pp. 67–78; Westley, pp. 203–207.
13. Clifford G. Christians and James W. Carey, "The Logic and Aims of Qualitative Research," in Stempel and Westley, pp. 342–362.
14. Michael Quinn Patton, *Qualitative Evaluation Methods* (Beverly Hills: Sage, 1980), pp. 121–194.
15. Patton, pp. 195–263.
16. Walter K. Lindenmann, "Use of Community Case Studies in Opinion Research," *Public Relations Review* 6 (Spring 1980):40–50.
17. James E. Grunig, "Time Budgets, Level of Involvement, and Use of the Mass Media," *Journalism Quarterly* 56 (1979):248–261; John P. Robinson, *How Americans Use Time: A Socio-Psychological Analysis of Everyday Behavior* (New York: Praeger, 1977).
18. Charles H. Backstrom and Gerald D. Hursh, *Survey Research* (Evanston, Ill.: Northwestern University Press, 1963), pp. 70–72.
19. An excellent review of readability research can

be found in Werner J. Severin and James W. Tankard, Jr., *Communication Theories: Origins, Methods, Uses* (New York: Hastings House, 1979), Chapter 6.

20. Richard F. Carter, W. Lee Ruggels, Kenneth M. Jackson, and M. Beth Heffner, "Application of Signaled Stopping Technique to Communication Research," in Peter Clarke (ed.), *New Models for Communication Research* (Beverly Hills, Calif.: Sage, 1973), pp. 15–44.

ADDITIONAL READING

Babbie, Earl R., *The Practice of Social Research* (Belmont, Calif.: Wadsworth, 1979).

Dillman, Don A., *Mail and Telephone Surveys: The Total Design Method* (New York: Wiley, 1978).

Erdos, Paul L., *Professional Mail Surveys* (New York: McGraw-Hill, 1970).

Flay, Brian R., and Thomas D. Cook, "Evaluation of Mass Media Prevention Campaigns," in Ronald E. Rice and William J. Paisley (eds.), *Public Communication Campaigns* (Beverly Hills, Calif.: Sage, 1981), pp. 239–264.

Guttentag, Marcia and Elmer Struening, *Handbook of Evaluation Research* (Beverly Hills, Calif.: Sage, 1975).

Jacobson, Harvey K., "The Role of Evaluation and Research in Management," in A. Westley Rowland (ed.), *Handbook for Institutional Advancement: Programs for the Understanding and Support of Higher Education* (San Francisco: Jossey-Bass, 1977).

Morris, Lynn, Carol Fitz-Gibbon, and Marlene Henerson, *Program Evaluation Kit* (Beverly Hills, Calif.: Sage, 1978).

Patton, Michael Quinn, *Qualitative Evaluation Methods* (Beverly Hills, Calif.: Sage, 1980).

Stempel, Guido H. III, and Bruce H. Westley (eds.), *Research Methods in Mass Communication* (Englewood Cliffs, N.J.: Prentice-Hall, 1981).

Weiss, Carol H., *Evaluation Research: Methods for Assessing Program Effectiveness* (Englewood Cliffs, N.J.: Prentice-Hall, 1972).

10

LEGAL CONSTRAINTS

The First Amendment to the U. S. Constitution assures freedom of speech—for organizations as well as individuals. Public relations managers obviously depend on that right in order to facilitate maximum communication between their organization and its publics.

Nevertheless, a large, growing, and constantly changing body of public law places many constraints on the free flow of information in our society. In the past decade, government regulatory bodies in particular have promulgated regulations and rulings that have implications for what public relations practitioners may or may not say or print on behalf of an organization. Moreover, changing interpretations of laws covering libel, copyright, and privacy make it imperative that public relations managers keep abreast of important legal decisions.

In Chapter 1, we noted that "adaptive subsystems" help the organization survive when the environment changes, and management subsystems negotiate between the demands of the environment and the need for the organization to survive. Lawyers are not the only professionals charged with steering the organization on a legal course; it is also the role of public relations professionals to fit the goals of the organization to the demands and regulations of society.

First we shall explore the legal articulation of the right to communicate of various parties in public policy issues. Then we shall turn to restrictions that have been put on those rights for the public good.

THE RIGHT TO COMMUNICATE

Historically, organizations, including corporations, have enjoyed many of the same human rights as individuals. The courts have held that an organization, even if it lists profit as its main motive, is entitled to participate in our society's free exchange of ideas.[1] Judicial decisions have asserted that along with the organization's right to speak goes the even more vital right of the individual to hear. The public debate must be extensive, even antagonistic, in order for the citizen to make an informed decision.[2]

Of course, regulation of advertising by government agencies such as the Federal Communication Commission and the Federal Trade Commission places some limits on communication by organizations that would not affect individuals. But some decisions extending First Amendment protection to commercial speech have suggested that the courts recognize the need for free flow of information. States have struck down statutes that prohibited pharmacists from advertising prices of prescription drugs or lawyers from advertising services and rates.[3]

Corporations May Be Partisan

The Federal Election Campaign Act and its various amendments passed in the 1970s place limitations on communication between an organization and its employees, stockholders, and the general public. But Federal Election Commission regulations also spell out many ways that an organization can become involved in public debate over political issues.

For example, a corporation may make partisan statements to its stockholders and administrative personnel in connection with a federal election, and it may sponsor appearances by candidates of its choice (although it may not directly solicit funds for those candidates). Voter registration and get-out-the-vote drives are permissible, as long as the effort is jointly sponsored by a nonprofit civic organization.[4] One Supreme Court justice pointed out that, were states allowed to decide what issues were legitimate for corporate communications, "corporate activities that are widely viewed as educational and socially constructive could be prohibited."[5]

The "right of reply" to attacks or charges that have been made in the print media is not really a "right" in this country, but it has become a well-accepted feature of most newspapers and magazines.[6] Newspapers, especially, have instituted mechanisms for permitting groups or individuals who feel their viewpoints have not been expressed, or believe they have been wrongly represented, to have more-or-less equal space and display in the news columns.

The letters-to-the-editor column has long provided such an outlet, and in the past decade the op-ed page (opposite the editorial page) essay or opinion piece has been offered to representatives of groups or of viewpoints differing from those stated by the newspaper's regular editorial writers and columnists. A handful of newspapers have named an ombudsman, a member of the editorial staff designated to review complaints from readers or news sources, and empowered to use the news columns to correct or balance biased or incomplete reporting.

Getting Access to the Broadcast Media

An organization's right of access to the public's attention is much more specifically spelled out in the case of the broadcast media. Owing to the limited number of channels, and the "privilege" enjoyed by those licensed to broadcast over them, the Federal Communications Commission in 1949 promulgated its Fairness Doctrine, which calls for an "affirmative obligation" to devote a reasonable percentage of air time to the coverage of public issues, and a "balancing obligation" to present opposing viewpoints.[7]

The FCC's personal-attack rule further stipulates that, when an attack upon the honesty, character, or integrity of a person is broadcast during the discussion of a controversial issue of public importance, the broadcaster must notify the person—or group—attacked and afford the person or group a reasonable opportunity to respond.[8]

The FCC does not suggest that exact "equal" time must be given, but it does insist that, generally, the reply must be run at the same time of day and reach the same general audience. The reply need not be provided free of charge if the original broadcast was a paid announcement.[9]

Reviewing the Fairness Doctrine upon its twenty-fifth anniversary, the FCC reiterated that its purpose is to foster "uninhibited, robust, and wide open debate" on controversial public issues.[10] Familiarity with FCC regulations and recent interpretations can afford the public relations department many opportunities to get its organization's viewpoints heard. Throughout its early years, the Reagan administration was seeking changes that would lessen regulation of the broadcast media.

Getting Access to Information

In order to mount an effective information campaign, it is imperative that the public relations department have access to the necessary raw material: information! It is difficult to affect public policy discussion when the opponent, especially if that opponent is a government agency, is privy to data not available to your organization.

The U. S. Freedom of Information Act, enacted in 1966 and amended in 1974 and 1976, stipulates that "any person"—including corporations and associations—has a right, enforceable in court, to access to all "agency records." Generally, that means any record in the possession of a federal agency, except to the extent that the records are covered by the FOI Act's nine exemptions, which include national security, trade secrets, and matters of personal privacy.[11] All government and executive branch departments are covered by the act, along with regulatory agencies, military departments, and government corporations.[12]

Because some agencies have tried to use severely limited hours of access and exorbitant photocopying fees to circumvent the intentions of the FOI Act, it has been amended to prohibit such practices and to assure that fees are limited to "reasonable standard charges for document search and duplication."[13] Any FOI request must "reasonably describe" the records desired. The requester need not explain the reason for access to the records, although to do so may aid agency personnel in making a faster search.[14] Again, PR practitioners must keep up with constantly changing interpretations of FOI laws.

RESTRICTIONS ON THE RIGHT TO COMMUNICATE

We have seen a number of ways in which the organization's participation in free and open communication is aided by the law and by custom. Balancing those protections are several familiar legal restraints, including:

Libel and slander laws.

Copyright laws.

Privacy laws.

Financial reporting requirements.

Regulation of advertising.

Consumer-protection measures.

Laws protecting the rights of employees.

Laws affecting lobbyists and foreign agents.

We shall look at the basic principles in each of these areas, concentrating on the ways they affect the public relations manager.

LIBEL AND SLANDER

"What, me libel someone? Why should I even worry about it? My job consists of saying nice things about people."

The newcomer to public relations may feel that the chances of getting involved in a libel or slander suit are remote. But consider this example: the editor of the employee magazine runs a picture depicting the festivities at the annual office holiday party. The cutline mentions that "everybody had plenty of 'bubbly' and got right into the spirit of things." One of the workers pictured turns out to be a lay minister in a denomination that frowns on drinking. The employee sues the company and names the editor as corespondent. A minor public relations item that seemed merely frivolous has led to a libel suit.

Whenever an organization fires someone and the press requests an official statement, the danger of libel or slander is present. The organization must weigh its need to justify the personnel action publicly against the possibility of defaming the former employee with the explanation. A company that is sued by a researcher who was dismissed may wish to counter her claims that the firm tried to force her to overlook deficiencies in a new product. But in defending its ethical conduct, it may have to brand the former employee a liar.

The corporate lawyers, always conservative, will counsel "no comment." But the public relations department will want to prepare a release that, at the very least, quotes an officer of the company about "standing on its reputation of some fifty years" and having "every confidence that litigation will absolve the company of the claim of wrongdoing." Even then, the lawyers will fret over every word in the release. What was that about the job consisting only of saying "nice things about people"?!

Libel is written defamation, and slander is spoken defamation. Defamation has been defined generally by the U. S. Supreme Court as "an utterance tending to impugn the honesty, virtue or reputation, or publish the alleged or natural defects of a person and thereby expose him to public hatred, contempt, or ridicule." Public relations law specialist Morton J. Simon points out that while various courts have different understandings of the concept of defamation, the key word appears to be "reputation."[15] False derogatory statements that injure a person's or an organization's professional standing, trade, business, or office will surely lead to a suit, although retraction and/or apology can reduce the amount of the damages.[16]

Avoid "Punitive" Damages

Besides actual damages—the amount the plaintiff stands to lose because of diminished reputation—the courts may award punitive damages in cases where malice, "calculated falsehoods," or "reckless disregard for the truth" can be established.[17] While it is difficult for an organization to avoid occasional lawsuits, care on the part of those who speak or write on behalf of the organization can prevent huge punitive damages. Simon warns that when there is antagonism toward a company because of its high-handed ways, the jury may decide to "teach the defendant a lesson" not only with a guilty verdict, but with whopping punitive damages as well.[18]

It is important to understand that the jury decides guilt, and thus words that were not construed as libelous or slanderous at another time or in another place may be found defamatory in the present situation. Thus, the public relations manager, in addition to exercising care, must have a feeling for the values and standards of the community in which information is disseminated. A chief executive officer might deliver a stinging attack on a competitor before a professional meeting in a large city and get away with it. The same words, spoken to a gathering of the general public in a rural area, might constitute slander in the minds of the local citizens.[19]

Public relations specialists must also be concerned with advertising, which is covered by libel laws just like other printed material. If, for example, a libelous advertisement was created or placed by a public relations firm on behalf of a client, the PR firm can be held responsible.[20]

In fact, an advertisement led to the most important libel decision in recent decades: *New York Times v. Sullivan*, in 1964. An advertisement placed in the newspaper in defense of Dr. Martin Luther King, Jr., libeled a public affairs commissioner in Montgomery, Alabama. The U. S. Supreme Court, reversing lower courts, said:

[The First Amendment] prohibits a public official from recovering damages for a defamatory falsehood relating to his official conduct unless he proves that the statement was made

```
          PHOTOGRAPHIC RELEASE FORM
          ──────────────────────────────


                                    Date _____


          I hereby consent to the use of the photograph described
     below for publicity and promotional purposes by (XYZ Corp.),
     and I waive all claims for compensation for such use, or for
     damages.

          Description of photograph:



          Signature _____

          Name (printed) _____

          Signature of parent or
          guardian if signing
          for minor child.        _____


          Address _____


                  _____


          Photographer _____
```

This simple form, which can be typewritten and reproduced by mimeograph, should be carried on assignment by every photographer who obtains publicity and promotional pictures. Otherwise, it is the responsibility of the public relations department to obtain releases from all identifiable persons in a photo. If payment is to be made, the statement should begin: ''In return for consideration ($1.00) I hereby . . . etc.''

with ''actual malice''—that is, with knowledge that it was false or with reckless disregard of whether it was false or not.[21]

Subsequent court decisions have somewhat narrowed the landmark Sullivan precedent. However, the protection of commentary about ''public'' persons, whether elected officials or not, is generally quite wide in this country, as long as the writer does not show total disregard for the facts. Again we can see that current interpretations of the law favor wide and robust discussion of public issues.

COPYRIGHT

The public relations specialist is an assimilator who weaves the thoughts, ideas, deeds, and pronouncements of others into a new fabric. Often, in writing or creating visual images, there is a need and desire to incorporate material that, in the eyes of the law, is the property of others. One must make arrangements, and sometimes pay a price, in order to appropriate what belongs to another.

The public relations writer or designer cannot make the assumption that broad usage of a piece of information means that it has passed into the "public domain"—that it can be used by anybody without securing the permission of the originator. A number of people assumed that Martin Luther King's "I have a dream" speech—because it was made to such a large group at a civil rights march in Washington in 1963, and because copies of it had been disseminated to the press beforehand—was in the public domain. Some newspapers offered reprints of the speech, and a record company brought out an unauthorized version of it. But King had filed for copyright, and he successfully got injunctions against its unauthorized use by others.[22]

Copyright law in the United States dates from 1790, and is intended to promote creative expression by securing the rights of authors. The law of 1909 established a once-renewable 28-year term of copyright for authors and their heirs. One of the major changes introduced by the general revision of the copyright law that took effect in 1978 is the provision that the term of copyright is the life of the author plus fifty years. One important exception affects the public relations writer who is employed by an organization to prepare articles and other materials. Protection of a "work made for hire" runs seventy-five years from publication (or a maximum of 100 years from the date of the creation of the work, in cases where the work is not published).[23] Writers who sometimes publish on their own for profit should have a firm understanding with the public relations department concerning who owns a work, the writer or the company.

The new copyright law also provides for statutory protection of unpublished works, which previously could be protected only by "common law"—the concept that "what is mine is mine, if I can prove it is mine." Other important provisions of the extensive copyright law revision affect sound recording, cable television, photocopying, and U. S. government works.[24]

Always Obtain Permission

The public relations department should always ascertain who owns the rights to a literary or artistic property, and should arrange to obtain permission before using the material. Even such a "tiny" excerpt as two lines from a popular song is protected, inasmuch as those two lines constitute a considerable portion of the artistic work. The copyright law does provide for "fair use" of material, depending upon (1) the purpose and character of the use, (2) the nature of the copyrighted work, (3) the amount used in relation to the work as a whole, and (4) the effect of the use upon the potential market for the copyrighted work.[25] (As an example, the previous sentence was adapted nearly verbatim from a duly cited technical volume, for use in a textbook, and represents but a minuscule fraction of a percent of the original work; thus it can be assumed to fall under the doctrine of fair use. Besides, the author cited drew his terminology from a U. S. government document, which, according to the law, cannot be copyrighted and is thus in the public domain!)

Even where copyright is not an issue, it is a basic tenet of "good PR" that an organization that decides to quote, cite, or appropriate ideas from another person or organization should show the professional courtesy of informing the original author in advance.

Applying for copyright is simple. Forms are available from The Copyright Office, Library of Congress, Washington, DC 20559, for each of the various categories: books, periodicals, works of art, photographs, commercial prints or labels, or motion pictures.

The completed form, with claim of authorship and the requisite number of copies of the work to be protected, is submitted along with the required payment ($10 in 1983). The form is officially registered with time stamp and government seal, copies of the work are filed, and a copy of the document is returned to the author. Registration of copyright does not "prove" originality of a work. It merely certifies that a copy of the work was duly registered by the government. It is up to the courts, when provided with competing claims, to ascertain which is the original, and thus entitled to protection.

PRIVACY

A report prepared for the Public Relations Society of America points out that "it is precarious, at best, for a society to maintain that delicate balance between the need for individual privacy and the need for information gathering."[26] Commercial organizations and government agencies tend to gather voluminous data about their publics and to guard that information jealously, preventing those reported upon from knowing what the organization knows about them. Although we may consider personal privacy one of the basic American rights, it was only in 1961 that the Fourth Amendment to the United States Constitution was considered applicable to a state government's unlawful attempts to intrude into the privacy of the individual.[27]

An individual has "the right to be let alone; to live one's life as one chooses, free from assault, intrusion or invasion except as they can be justified by the clear needs of community living under a government of law."[28] The individual is protected from (1) intrusion, (2) misappropriation of his or her name, (3) publicity that places him or her in false light, and (4) publicity that discloses private and embarrassing facts.[29]

The Privacy Act of 1974, which is aimed at controlling the federal government's data-collection activities, requires annual publication in the *Federal Register* of the nature and function of files maintained by government agencies. It also permits individual access to federal records and authorizes challenging and correcting of personal information.[30]

Two items are of special concern to public relations people: When is a person a "public figure" who has given up some of the right to privacy? And when must permission be obtained to use the image or description of a person in promotional material?

We saw in the case of libel laws that "public figures" give up much of their protection. The notoriety that comes from being a sports figure, an entertainment star, or a political name means that such individuals must expect to hear and see "casual" use of their names in promotional materials. However, when extensive use is made, or when endorsement is implied, the permission of the celebrity must be obtained.[31] If an advertising agency, a public relations agency, or a news medium has previously paid for promotional material involving a celebrity, or if it has made use of the material in a "legitimate news" capacity, it may use replications of the same material in advertisements promoting a publication or an event.[32]

Is It "News" or "Promotional"?

When groups of people visit a plant on a tour, the facility takes on a "semipublic" character. Thus, if a photograph of a large group of Boy Scouts is published in the employee newspaper, the privacy of the children and their parents probably has not been invaded. However, if the photographer takes an appealing close-up of a particular young person examining a machine or sampling a product, and if the picture is to be used in a "promotional" rather than a "news" context, it will be necessary to obtain a release from the parents of the minor child. ("Promotional" use obviously includes any advertisement, and probably would include the annual report and any news release that focused on the product rather than the visit of the youth group to the plant.)

In return for a small consideration, perhaps only one dollar, the parents must sign a form stipulating for what purposes the photograph may be used, and for what duration. The waiver of rights to privacy is complex, and any public relations department that makes frequent use of endorsements or "real people" situations would do well to review the excellent section on privacy and publicity in Morton J. Simon's *Public Relations Law*.[33]

Care must be taken when using photographs of employees, even if the shots were taken on the job or in a work-related situation. While employment may imply a waiver to be photographed on the job, the limits of "normal reporting" and "good taste" must be observed, and distribution of information about the employee beyond the "corporate family" may raise questions of exploitation.[34]

FINANCIAL REPORTING REQUIREMENTS

When the press agent for a movie star issues a news release loaded with conjecture and inflated rhetoric ("Miss Darling wants to do the life story of Eleanor Roosevelt, but only if she is paid $5 million and given full artistic control") the public merely smiles . . . or groans. But the area of financial public relations is light years away from press agentry in terms of the proprieties required by law. The sound you hear if you release speculative information about a stock offering is not merely a groan, but the Securities and Exchange Commission (SEC) enforcement people knocking at your door.

Following the abuses that culminated in the stock market crash of 1929, Congress passed the Securities Acts of 1933 and 1934. The basic purpose of these two measures, along with the Investment Company Act of 1940, was "to require the dissemination of adequate and accurate information concerning the issuers and their securities in connection with the offer and sale of securities to the public."[35] The SEC, in its Special Study of the Securities Market, issued in 1963, acknowledged the importance of informal corporate publicity "in order to keep shareholders, the investment community and the general public continuously informed of corporate developments."[36] However, it bans many promotional activities, including:

> Optimistic sales and earnings reports and projections that "seem to be based primarily on wishful thinking."
>
> Glowing descriptions of new products still in the experimental stages.
>
> Announcements of mergers and acquisitions that are only "vague possibilities."
>
> Undue stress in publicity on favorable news and developments.
>
> "Leaking" and creation of rumors of impending stock splits, mergers, etc.
>
> Favoring certain analysts with otherwise undisclosed but material news (news affecting stock price or sales) without making such developments public generally.[37]

Avoid "Issuance of Prospectus"

If your privately owned company decides to "go public" and offer shares of stock on a major exchange, your intuition as a public relations person tells you to put out a news release, or perhaps even a fancy brochure extolling the virtues of the company and recommending that people buy shares in it. But if you do, you have broken the law. Your publicity constitutes issuance of a "prospectus," but it is not in the proper form and does not contain all of the required information.[38] The SEC specifically prohibits the issuance of certain types of information during the period immediately prior to registration of a security, the "quiet period" when the registration is being accomplished, and the immediate postregistration period.

The cover of Johnson & Johnson's Form 10-K carries all of the basic information required by the SEC. Inside pages of the 28-page presentation provide information about property, plants, equipment, subsidiaries, products manufactured, reserve assets, short-term borrowing, and the makeup of the board of directors. (Courtesy Johnson & Johnson)

Perhaps you have noticed a phrase such as "This is not an offering; offering may be made only by prospectus . . . " in advertisements or other publicity about a company. That's just one of the ways that the public relations department attempts to comply with SEC requirements while engaging in promotions necessary to keep the company in the public's attention. The SEC recognizes the need to maintain normal visibility during the period when a new stock offering is being registered. Thus, it does not prohibit product advertising, the publication of service brochures, quarterly or annual reports to stockholders, proxy statements, press releases about business developments, responses to inquiries from the public, and other generally accepted publicity practices.[39]

The "Annual Report" Requirement

Of particular concern to the public relations department is the requirement that an annual report be prepared, using SEC Form 10–K, no later than ninety days after the close of the company's fiscal year, for delivery to shareholders.[40] The SEC also has a complex set of rules for interim quarterly reports to stockholders.[41] Most companies manage to package the required information in the stipulated format as part of a glossy annual report that resembles a slick magazine, replete with color photographs designed to enhance the public's image of the company.

The SEC is taking a hard look at reporting procedures, and in the future the annual report's public relations value may be greatly diminished. The 10–K may be expanded to include requirements for discussing unfavorable trends, explaining how sales predictions were arrived at, and discussions of each individual department or section of the operation in order to bring adequate focus on divisions or products that may be unprofitable.[42] The SEC's aim is to foster "continuous disclosure" of information about every company's financial operations in a manner that is as comprehensive and detailed as that required in the original prospectus.[43] Obviously, the role of the financial public relations practitioner is growing more complex, and more important to the business community.

"Timely Disclosure"

The SEC specifically prohibits manipulation of information through timing or routing of releases in such a way as to favor some potential investors over others. Disclosure must be timely, which means that a release must be disseminated as soon as information is known, not when the company feels it will have the most desirable effect. The New York Stock Exchange, for example, includes a "Procedure Insuring Immediate Publicity of News Releases" in its company manual, and stipulates that releases should be phoned or delivered immediately to the major wire services and Dow, Jones & Company.[44] The manual also makes it clear that "hold for release" announcements are not to be used.[45] One of the reasons for timely disclosure is to prevent "insiders"—including public relations people—from profiting on the basis of information not available to the general public. In the landmark Texas Gulf Sulphur case, the lawyer who was the company's manager of public relations was said by the court to have used "material undisclosed information to his advantage" and thus violated the Securities Exchange Act.[46]

One more caveat for the financial public relations specialist: it is unethical for the PR practitioner to be compensated for services in connection with a new stock offering in shares instead of money. The code of professional standards of the Public Relations Society of America holds that such compensation would place the PR practitioner in a position of conflict of duty to client, employer, or the investing public.[47]

REGULATION OF ADVERTISING

Advertising—especially in the areas of corporate identity, public policy discussion, and consumer information—is an important tool of public relations. The Federal Trade Commission is one arm of the federal government charged with controlling advertising practices:

> The specific authority of the Federal Trade Commission rests in Section 5 of the Federal Trade Commission Act, which, very broadly, outlaws "unfair or deceptive acts in commerce." . . . In the eyes of the FTC "deceptive advertising" can be a statement, claim, or pictorial demonstration which may have the capacity or the tendency to deceive the average man on the street. It should be noted that the Commission does not have to prove that anyone was deceived, it must prove only that there was a capacity to deceive. Deceptive advertising can take in any number of things—misrepresentation of the product or its efficacy; misrepresentation of the product's size, shape, weight, origin, or whatever; the use of an unauthorized or untrue "testimonial"; false disparagement of a competitor's product; or an ambiguous statement.[48]

While the FTC does not actually have the power to censor an advertisement before it appears, it does publish guidelines that have the effect of warning advertisers in advance of trouble areas, and it will offer "advisory opinions" if a company requests guidance. The agency uses public hearings and special investigations to focus attention on areas where it feels there may be abuses, and its capacity to dispatch investigators to company plants has a chilling effect on questionable advertising practices.[49]

The FTC is particularly alert to false claims about products or services, and it looks at news releases as well as advertisements for violations, such as false claims that a product is original or first in its field, approved by a government agency, patented, developed in a nonexistent research laboratory, has nonexistent nutritional content, or has proven effectiveness beyond its bona fide lifetime.[50]

Of course, any company can fight an FTC finding in the courts, but the process is expensive, and often it results in a protracted battle, during which the company name is dirtied and the reputation of the product is doubtful in the minds of the consumer. As a result, public relations counsel may be called in to help the company decide whether to sign a "consent decree" with the FTC. A consent order agreement permits the company to change its advertising or promotional practices in line with the FTC's suggestions in order to have the matter over with and to resume favorable promotion of the product.[51] Even if a company takes the "easy out" route, the public relations department may find itself battling intense adverse publicity simply because various activists and consumer groups depend on flailing at a well-known adversary in order to keep themselves and their causes in the attention of the media and the public.[52]

The FTC is just one of more than three dozen federal agencies that oversee or control various aspects of advertising.

CONSUMER PROTECTION

President John F. Kennedy pressed Congress for four basic consumer rights: the right to safety, to be informed, to be able to choose, and to be heard. By the end of the l960s, Congress had enacted measures regulating packaging and labeling, child protection, automobile and highway safety, cigarette advertising, comprehensive health planning, and truth in lending.[53]

All of these consumer protection laws affect the public relations department. Let's look at just one example. In l968, the Consumer Credit Protection Act (CCPA) was passed. Among other things, the act includes the following:

Requires disclosures in consumer credit transactions.

Provides mechanisms for resolving billing errors.

Restricts certain debt-collection activities.

Prohibits credit discrimination on the basis of sex, marital status, race, etc.[54]

A set of guidelines drawn up by the American Bankers Association suggests that a fundamental step for lending institutions is to designate one person as a "consumer compliance officer" to train company personnel and oversee a "compliance task force" of management people. Procedures must be established by each company to handle consumer complaints and to disseminate notices about company policies that comply with the Consumer Act.[55] Public relations personnel usually are instrumental in drawing up such procedures.

RIGHTS OF EMPLOYEES

The Wagner Act, also known as the National Labor Relations Act of 1935, set up the National Labor Relations Board (NLRB), provided for free choice of representation for employees, and spelled out what constituted unfair labor practices. It subsequently was amended by the Taft-Hartley (1947) and Landrum-Griffin (1959) acts.[56] Public relations departments dealing with employees and their labor unions must be familiar with this formidable body of legislation, its interpretations, and the guidelines issued by the NLRB.

Specifically, a company must not interfere with the workings of the labor union or the rights of employees to bargain. A speech, written in the PR department for an executive to deliver to employees, that contains threats of reprisals or promises of benefits is unlawful, although company employees may give noncoercive talks to their fellow employees on company time and company property.[57]

One of the basic rights of employees is the right to clear and complete information. Failure to provide full and adequate explanation of retirement or insurance benefits, for example, may result in a judgment against the company.[58]

Since 1978, rights of federal employees who "blow the whistle" on their superiors have been protected by the Civil Service Reform Act.[59] IBM has published a "bill of rights" for employee privacy, and companies such as Xerox and General Electric have ombudsmen to hear employee grievances.[60]

Another headache for PR departments is caused by orders issued by the Occupational Safety and Health Administration (OSHA). The agency, which was set up in 1970, is intended to protect employees from danger while on the job.[61] The public relations practitioner must attempt to avoid adverse publicity by anticipating violations and working to ensure that the company avoids being fined or put on notice by OSHA. When unexpected violations do occur, the PR department must minimize the negative effect by pushing management to correct the problem.

Equal Employment Opportunity Commission (EEOC) guidelines issued in 1980 suggest that firms with government contracts should draw up a company policy on the issue of sexual harassment on the job—yet another example of a government agency creating work for the public relations department.[62]

LOBBYISTS AND FOREIGN AGENTS

The First Amendment to the Constitution gives citizens the right to "petition the government." When the petitioning is done in the halls of Congress or a state legislature, the activity is referred to as "lobbying," which is defined as "frequenting the lobby of a legislature in order to influence the members." At its purest, lobbying means providing sufficient data to a legislature so that all of the facts can be known before a vote is cast. At a less lofty plane, lobbying may mean taking a legislator to lunch or inviting congressional leaders to a party where business and pleasure can be mixed. At its most corrupt, lobbying has meant buying votes with money or favors, as was made painfully evident in the Abscam revelations of 1980–81.

Usually, a lobbyist is not known to the general public. Indeed, those whose identities become front page news usually have compromised their effectiveness, as happened when it became known that Marion Javits, wife of the New York senator, was handling the Iran National Airlines account for the Ruder & Finn agency,[63] or when columnist Jack Anderson revealed that ITT lobbyist Dita Beard wrote indiscreet memos to her superiors describing negotiations at the highest level of the White House on behalf of the firm's merger negotiations.[64]

The Federal Regulation of Lobbying Act of 1946 requires those representing the interests of others in Washington, whether lawyers, public relations practitioners, or others, to register and to file quarterly reports of significant sources of income as well as expenditures. The law also is meant to include organizations outside Washington that initiate letter-writing and telegram-sending campaigns from around the country aimed at Washington. However, it excludes the news media, elected officials, and persons testifying before congressional committees on legislative matters.[65]

Over half of the individual states control lobbying by various types of registration, so an organization that hopes to influence legislation in various statehouses should begin by contacting the secretary of state in each jurisdiction in order to find out who must register and how.[66]

Representing Foreign Governments

The lobbyist representing domestic organizations is, of course, exercising a constitutional right. But one who is representing a foreign organization or government obtains the privilege only through the ''grace'' of the U. S. government.[67] The Foreign Agents Act of 1938 was amended in 1966 to provide disclosure by agents who are engaged in politics, public relations, financial negotiations, consultancies, or other activities on behalf of foreign governments.[68]

Registration places no limitations on the activities in which an agent may engage, and it is not intended to stigmatize the agent. In addition to providing a full account of their activities and finances, agents for foreign governments must properly identify themselves when dealing with legislators or government officials, and they must open their books to government inspection. In general, these requirements do not inhibit legitimate agents.[69] In fact, enforcement of both the domestic and foreign lobbying acts has been conspicuous by its absence, except in cases where the news media expose an outright scandal. At the beginning of the 1980s, the only agency expressing an interest in tightening lobby legislation and its enforcement was, not surprisingly, the Internal Revenue Service, which would like to eliminate tax deductions for many types of lobbying activities.[70]

LIVING WITH THE LAW

Although this chapter has been condensed to fit the scope and purpose of our discussion, it now should be obvious to the student of public relations that those who endeavor to inform the public are affected by a myriad of regulations, decisions, and precedents. Inevitably, we must depend upon counsel to guide us through this ever-thickening forest of legal constraints.

Public relations law expert Morton J. Simon has been cited frequently here, and it is useful to conclude the discussion with his observations concerning the necessary interrelationship of public relations and the law:

Public relations and law both deal with human behavior, the former supplementing the latter, which deals essentially with the restraints upon conduct that are necessary to provide an orderly and balanced human and corporate existence. . . . The public relations practitioner and the lawyer have so much in common that they must approach their relationship constructively. Their points of departure and their vehicles may differ, but the destination is the same: to serve the client and the public interest.[71]

And finally:

The public relations function should—from the very first indications of legal trouble—prepare for and initiate a long and continuing aggressive campaign, forehanded, educational and flexible enough to adjust eventually to the court's decision.[72]

NOTES

1. John Henry Brebbia, "First Amendment Rights and the Corporation," *Public Relations Journal* (December 1979):18.
2. Brebbia, p. 19.
3. Brebbia, p. 20.
4. Frank Walsh, "Election Laws and the Corporation," *Public Relations Journal* (October 1980): 14–16.
5. Leo J. Northart, "The Corporation's Right of Free Speech," *Public Relations Journal* (November 1978):8.
6. Morton J. Simon, *Public Relations Law* (New York: Appleton-Century-Crofts, 1969), p. 124.
7. Andrew O. Shapiro, *Media Access: Your Rights to Express Your Views on Radio and Television* (Boston: Little, Brown, 1976), p. 107.
8. Shapiro, p. 192.
9. Shapiro, pp. 157–160.
10. "In the Matter of the Handling of Public Issues Under the Fairness Doctrine and the Public Interest Standards of the Communication Act," FCC Docket No. 19260 (June 27, 1974), quoted in Eugene S. Foster, *Understanding Broadcasting* (Reading, Mass.: Addison-Wesley, 1978), p. 339.
11. Alan B. Levenson and Harvey L. Pitt (eds.), *Government Information* (New York: Practicing Law Institute, 1978), p. 69.
12. Levenson and Pitt, pp. 14–15.
13. Levenson and Pitt, p. 279.
14. Levenson and Pitt, pp. 90–91.
15. Simon, pp. 213–214.
16. Simon, p. 232.
17. Michael S. Lasky, "Guidelines Against Libel," in *Law and the Writer* (Cincinnati, Ohio: Writer's Digest Books, 1978), pp. 23–24.
18. Simon, p. 212.
19. Paul P. Ashley, *Say It Safely* (Seattle: University of Washington Press, 1966), p. 14.
20. Simon, p. 222.
21. Simon, p. 229.
22. *King v. Mister Maestro, Inc.*, 224 F. Supp. 101 (1963); see also Joseph J. Hemmer, Jr., *Communication Under Law* (Metuchen, N.J.: Scarecrow Press, 1980), pp. 146–147.
23. Frank Walsh, "The New Copyright Law: Stronger and More Specific," *Public Relations Journal* (August 1977):6.
24. Waldo Moore, "Ten Questions About the New Copyright Law," in *Law and the Writer* (Cincinnati, Ohio: Writer's Digest Books, 1978), pp. 41–43.
25. Hemmer, p. 155.
26. Gail J. Koff, "Right of Privacy vs. Society's Need to Know," *Public Relations Journal* (October 1975):26.
27. Koff, p. 27.
28. Harry M. Johnston III, "Invasion of Privacy," in *Law and the Writer* (Cincinnati, Ohio: Writer's Digest Books, 1978), p. 32.
29. Johnston.
30. Koff, p. 28.
31. Simon, p. 264.
32. Johnston, p. 35; Simon, p. 264.
33. Simon, pp. 267–281.
34. Simon, pp. 254–255; see also Felix H. Kent, "The Law of Advertising," in Russell F. Moore, editor, *Law for Executives* (New York: American Management Association, Inc., 1968), pp. 80–81.
35. Simon, p. 734.
36. Simon, p. 741.
37. Simon, pp. 741–742.
38. Robert W. Taft and Edward O. Raynolds, "Going Public," *Public Relations Journal* (April 1981):20.

39. Taft and Raynolds, p. 21.
40. "Corporate Reporting Requirements," *Public Relations Journal* (April 1974):49.
41. H. Zane Robbins, "Your New Quarterly Report," *Public Relations Journal* (April 1976):24.
42. Robert W. Taft and John C. Long, "SEC's New Proposals," *Public Relations Journal* (August 1980): 17; see also Kolman Glicksberg and Richard F. Kotz, "The Annual Report to Stockholders—More Work and Increasing Liability," *Public Relations Journal* (September 1974):6
43. John G. Gillis, "Securities Law and Corporate Disclosure," *Public Relations Journal* (April 1976):18.
44. Simon, pp. 757–758.
45. Simon, p. 765.
46. Simon, pp. 768–769.
47. Taft and Raynolds, p. 24.
48. Kent, pp. 68–69.
49. Simon, pp. 115–117.
50. Edward L. Graf, Jr., "Product Publicity and the Law," *Public Relations Journal* (July 1971): 19; see also Morton J. Simon, "You Could Get Into Legal Hot Water," *Public Relations Journal* (May 1976):11.
51. Morton J. Simon, "To Consent or Not to Consent," *Public Relations Journal* (March 1972):18–26.
52. Morton J. Simon, "The Fractured Legal Structure of Consumerism," *Public Relations Journal* (October 1971):6–10, 44–48.
53. Simon, *Public Relations Law*, pp. 640–641.
54. American Bankers Association, *A Planning Guide for Consumer Compliance* (Washington: ABA, 1979), pp. ix–x.
55. American Bankers Association, pp. 98–99, 105–108, 114–115.
56. William R. Linke, "The Complexities of Labor Relations Law," in *Law for Executives*, pp. 141–142.
57. Simon, *Public Relations Law*, p. 723.
58. Simon, p. 705.
59. Roy G. Foltz, "Due Process," *Public Relations Journal* (December 1980):6.
60. Foltz.
61. Edward J. Kehoe, "The Federal Occupational Safety and Health Act: Its Impact on Management, Safety and Public Relations," *Public Relations Journal* (August 1972):25–28.
62. Eliza G. C. Collins and Timothy B. Blodgett, "Sexual Harassment: Some See It—Some Won't," *Harvard Business Review* (March–April 1981):76–95.
63. *New York Times* (Feb. 27, 1976) 6:1.
64. Robert M. Goolrick, *Public Policy Toward Corporate Growth: The ITT Merger Cases* (Port Washington, N.Y.: Kennikat Press, 1978), p. 153.
65. Simon, *Public Relations Law*, pp. 805–812.
66. Simon, *Public Relations Law*, pp. 815–820.
67. Simon, *Public Relations Law*, p. 806.
68. Harry Kennedy, Jr., "What You Should Know About the Foreign Agents Registration Act," *Public Relations Quarterly* (Fall 1966):17–18.
69. Simon, *Public Relations Law*, pp. 827–830.
70. Wes Pedersen, "Washington Focus," *Public Relations Journal* (March 1981):2.
71. Morton J. Simon, "Developing Rapport With the Lawyer," *Public Relations Journal* (May 1969):7.
72. Morton J. Simon, "Public Relations and the New Judiciary," *Public Relations Journal* (February 1977):9.

ADDITIONAL READING

Moore, Russell F., Editor, *Law for Executives* (New York: American Management Association, Inc., 1968).

Pember, Don R., *Mass Media Law* (Dubuque, Iowa: Wm. C. Brown, 1981).

Shapiro, Andrew O., *Media Access: Your Rights to Express Your Views on Radio and Television* (Boston: Little, Brown, 1976).

Simon, Morton J., *Public Relations Law* (New York: Appleton-Century-Crofts, 1969).

Writer's Digest, *Law and the Writer* (Cincinnati: Writer's Digest Books, 1978).

Managing Public Relations Programs

Part III moves down one level of management from Part II and examines middle-range public relations programs aimed at the most frequent organizational publics. These publics include the media, communities, employees, voters and governments, consumerists, environmentalists, minorities, students, teachers, the financial community, and publics that might buy services or give money. Each chapter applies the theoretical tools developed in Part II in discussing how to manage programs for these publics and describes typical programs that organizations have developed for these publics. Each chapter then examines the communication behaviors of the publics. Whenever possible, the chapter describes publics identified in research that was based on the situational theory of publics described in Chapter 7. Each chapter then ends by describing feasible objectives and methods of evaluation for programs aimed at the publics discussed in that chapter.

11

MEDIA RELATIONS

Relations with the news media are so central to the practice of public relations that many practitioners—especially those guided by the press agent/publicity and public-information models of PR—believe that public relations *is* nothing more than media relations. Chapter 2 showed that public relations did indeed evolve out of efforts to influence press coverage of organizations and individuals. Today, however, media relations should be considered only one of several important public relations programs aimed at specialized publics.

Media relations occupies a central position in public relations because the media serve as "gatekeepers," controlling the information that flows to other publics in a social system. Media workers really aren't publics in the sense that they are affected by organizational consequences that do not affect other people.

But, in another sense, they are publics. They seek and process information just like other people, then pass on that information to their readers and viewers. The communi-

cation behavior of journalists, therefore, sets limits on the information available for other publics to seek and process.

Nearly every public relations department has a section devoted to press relations, a middle- or top-level manager to manage the section, and several communication technicians who write for the media and help the media cover the organization. We begin Part III, then, with a management analysis of this most traditional and central public relations program.

MEDIA RELATIONS PROGRAMS

An Area of Conflict

To listen to journalists and public relations practitioners talk about each other is to get the impression that the field of media relations is a battleground. Journalists feel besieged by hordes of press agents and publicists—"flacks," as they call PR people—who dump unwanted press releases on their desks and push self-serving stories that have little news value.

Public relations practitioners, on the other hand, feel they are at the mercy of reporters and editors who are biased against their organization, who would rather expose than explain, and who know little about the complexities of their organization.

The Media's Side • Newspaper editors frequently form their impressions of media relations specialists from the press releases they get in the mail. One sharp-tongued editor vented his frustration this way:

> When I moved from managing editor . . . I took my desk-height wastebasket with me. I can slide the press releases into it while talking on the phone. I don't need to crumple anything, or even aim carefully. I seldom need to read anything.[1]

In 1982, the Washington *Post* declared itself off limits to all public relations people. In an article entitled, " 'Post' Stabs PR in the Flack," *Advertising Age* reported on a memo written by editorial page editor Meg Greenfield to executive editor Benjamin Bradlee:

> Ms. Greenfield's memo to Mr. Bradlee is replete with phrases which indicate she feels she is being used. She wrote: "Why should we be in their campaign plans as something 'deliverable' by their various agents who can 'reach' us?" She insisted: "We don't want any of that damn crowd around here, and if people want to get to us they need only know two things: It's easy as pie, so long as they don't come in (or send their manuscripts in or make their request) via a flack firm. . . . We have adopted a rule of simply refusing to deal with these people—period."[2]

A study of Texas journalists and public relations practitioners in 1975 showed a wide gap between the two on the value of media relations specialists to newspapers.[3] Of the journalists surveyed:

> 59 percent thought public relations and the press are partners in the dissemination of information, contrasted to 89 percent of the PR practitioners.

48 percent thought public relations people help reporters obtain accurate, complete, and timely news, contrasted to 91 percent of the PR practitioners.

78 percent believed public relations has cluttered channels of communication with pseudo-events and phony phrases, contrasted to 42 percent of the PR practitioners.

82 percent said PR people obstruct reporters from seeing people they should be seeing, contrasted to 38 percent of the PR practitioners.

84 percent said PR material is usually publicity disguised as news, contrasted to 29 percent of the PR practitioners.

89 percent believed PR people do not understand such journalistic problems as meeting deadlines, attracting reader interest, and making the best use of space, contrasted to 39 percent of the PR practitioners.

Pointing up the fact of their negative feelings about public relations people, only 10 percent of the journalists agreed that public relations is a profession equal in status to journalism; 76 percent of the PR people surveyed agreed with that statement.

In another part of the same study, journalists and public relations practitioners ranked six news values.[4] Both journalists and practitioners ranked "accuracy" and "interest to the reader" as the two top values. When asked to predict how the other group would rank the six values, however, the journalists predicted that the PR people would put accuracy and interest among the lowest three values and that they would rank "depicting the subject in a favorable light" and "prompt publication" as the most important values. The PR people, in contrast, accurately predicted the news values of the journalists.

The PR Side • The Washington *Post's* Meg Greenfield seemed to think she had the obvious answer to her frustration with public relations representatives: Get rid of them and let organizational executives speak for themselves. That answer is oversimplified, PR people would respond. Executives fear the media and would be crucified without PR help. According to PR counselor, Carlton Spitzer:

> High-level executives, who coolly manage the affairs of multi-million-dollar international corporations, crumble at the sight of an unfavorable story in a newspaper and reach instant boiling point when confronted with a misleading headline. . . . The news media are the most powerful outside force in the life of a business executive. An uncontrollable, unpackageable force, seemingly out to get business . . .[5]

Managers of large organizations, particularly business leaders, believe the media have a definite bias against them.[6] At least one public relations director has attributed this alleged media bias to a shift from an "objective" to an "interpretive" style of reporting.[7]

In a survey of 470 members of the Public Relations Society of America, 53 percent of the respondents said they had been misquoted during the past year.[8] When asked, "What do you believe is the major cause for a lack of fairness in news reporting?" the respondents cited either individual or organizational bias as the major reason:

Personal bias by reporter	43.8 percent
Bias of paper, magazine, etc.	31.1 percent
Sloppy reporting	27.0 percent
Poorly trained reporters	22.3 percent
Haste in reporting	20.6 percent

The last three answers to this survey also suggest that reporters and editors frequently misinterpret or fail to understand the information they get from public relations sources. The Weyerhaeuser Co., for example, told *Time* magazine that the Mount St. Helens volcano had destroyed 4 percent of its St. Helens Tree Farm—a farm that made up 8 percent of the company's worldwide timber holdings. *Time* reported, however, that the volcano had destroyed 4 percent of all of Weyerhaeuser's holdings.[9]

Who Wears the "Black Hat"? • When we look at research on media representatives as publics later in this chapter, we will see that the alleged media bias against business— and other large organizations—is more imagined than real. But this brief review of media-public relations conflict should show you that both PR practitioners and the media frequently fail in their dealings with one another. There are, no doubt, many inept and unprofessional public relations practitioners. But there are also many inept and unprofessional journalists.

What the conflict between press and PR hides is the interdependence of the two upon each other—and the dependence of American publics on the two working together as part of one public information system.

When he was Secretary of Health, Education, and Welfare in the Nixon Administration, Caspar Weinberger (then called "Cap the Knife") cut the number of public-information specialists in the department. He calculated that there were 2,400 public relations people in the department, serving only two reporters covering HEW full-time. He thought a 1,200-to-1 ratio was overkill!

Weinberger ignored the fact that most of those public relations people did not work in media relations, and that many other reporters covered HEW part-time. Most importantly, however, he ignored the fact that a handful of reporters could not begin to cover a department as huge as HEW then was without the assistance of public relations practitioners.

A series of studies of news media in Milwaukee in 1963 and 1975 showed the extent to which the media depend on public relations sources.[10] Those studies showed that about 45 percent of the news items in newspapers and about 15 percent of news items on radio and television originated in one way or another with public relations sources. A somewhat lower percentage of the actual column inches and airtime came from public relations sources, because PR-originated material usually resulted in shorter stories than media-originated material.

A 1977 survey of business and financial editors by the Hill & Knowlton PR agency showed that these editors considered public relations people to be their most important source of information.[11] And, it is common knowledge that most community newspapers could not exist—and definitely could not cover their communities adequately—without the help of public relations people.

Although media relations may often be a battleground, it doesn't have to be—and it shouldn't be if the public information system is to function properly. PR practitioners can work together, and the two-way symmetric model of public relations suggests how.

What Helps and What Hurts Media Relations

It's impossible to supply much more than a cursory list of the tips that experienced media relations specialists have developed for dealing with the media. Many of these tips relate to specific techniques, for which we refer you to the chapters in Part IV.

You will probably find it easier to learn a few principles, however, from which you can derive more specific rules of press relations. Our four models of public relations provide such principles.

Press Agentry Abuses • Most of the abuses of the press that taint PR's relationship with the press stem from the press agent/publicity model.[12] Some examples:

Promises to ''deliver'' the media—decried by the Washington *Post*.

Threats to withhold advertising if editors do not use an item, or a promise to buy advertising if they do use it.

Calling an executive of a newspaper or broadcast station to pressure a reporter or editor to use a story.

Sending reams of news releases with little news value to an extensive mailing list of media that have no use for them—often done to show your superiors or clients that you are keeping busy and promoting their pet projects.

Taking the attitude that the more releases sent, the greater the chance that they will be used, in the belief that editors use them randomly when they have a space to fill.[13]

Catering to television at the expense of the print media, especially at press conferences.

Mailing releases to out-of-town media, when the information has no local relevance to those media.

Sending multiple copies of the same release to different departments or individuals in the same publication or broadcast outlet.

Offering to take reporters or editors out for a drink or meal, when the meeting does not help the reporters or editors get the information they need for a story and instead wastes valuable time.[14]

Holding press conferences or parties, which waste a journalist's time, when a simple press release or phone call will convey the necessary information.

Name-dropping; trying to set up conferences with editors on routine news releases; phone calls to see if the editor got a news release in the mail.

Failing to understand how the news media work—not being aware of deadlines, news values, and beats.

Public Information Abuses • Media relations specialists who follow the public information model, you will recall, function essentially as ''journalists in residence.'' Most worked previously as journalists and can avoid the abuses of the press agents just discussed. Two errors are common to practitioners of this model, however:

The jargon error. Often, public information specialists write in the coded language of their organization, frequently because their work must be cleared by superiors who want the information disseminated in specialized language.[15]

The Parkinson's Law error. Parkinson's famous law of bureaucracy states that "the work expands to fill the time available." We suggest the Grunig-Hunt corollary to this law: "Production of press releases expands to fill the time available." When the major skill of the practitioner is writing news articles, that is how he or she will fill his or her time. There may be no objective reason to write many of the articles, and many of them will have limited news value.

Two-Way Press Relations • Media relations practitioners of both the two-way asymmetric and two-way symmetric models of PR approach their task more systematically, make fewer errors that alienate journalists, and do more research and planning.

Asymmetric practitioners set objectives for what information they want the media to disseminate. In contrast to press agents, however, they understand news values and package that information in ways journalists will accept. They:

Stage events or write releases that have legitimate news value, in which they articulate the position of their organization.

Rebut what they consider to be erroneous or misleading information in the media, often by purchasing advertising if necessary (see Chapter 32, Public Relations Advertising).

Understand the behavior of journalists, so that they can tailor their messages to the communication habits of journalists.

Conflict may still result from the asymmetric model because media relations specialists usually try to control coverage of their organization and to limit it to organizational public relations objectives. Journalists frequently want open access to an organization,

something the asymmetric model may try to limit.

Symmetric practitioners think less about controlling the content of information that flows from their organization to the media. Their objective is to open up their organization to the media and to help journalists cover it, in the belief that such openness and assistance will result in more accurate and less biased coverage.

Public relations consultant Richard Detweiler has described the role of what we call a two-way symmetric press representative as a middleman or arbitrator between management and the press.[16] "There is much of the irresistible force/immovable object confrontation involved here. 'Torn apart' may be putting it mildly," Detweiler said:

. . . seldom does either press or management comprehend the arbitrator role of the press officer. In the executive's generally simplistic view he wants a propagandist, a docile functionary who can hawk the party line precisely the way it is given, without a lot of bother and backtalk or expenditure of his time and thought. The two-way street of public relations—the response obligation—generally eludes him.

To the press, of course, the public relations professional is a nuisance or worse. He or she is an irritating obstacle to unfettered access to the primary news source, an unwelcomed watchdog at the gate of truth.

Detweiler then added, "the key to good press relations strategy is to make the newsman's job easy. That is, give him news of substance, with facts he can rely on—all this conveniently packaged and delivered in good time."

There are many ways in which a media representative can make the journalist's job easier—the objective of symmetric press relations. Here are just a few suggestions:

Send out fewer press releases and rely more on direct contact with journalists, at both their initiative and yours. Be avail-

EXHIBIT
11–1

News & Feature Leads from Science & Industry

VOL. 6   No. 4   HILL & KNOWLTON, INC.   MAY/JUNE

1. SELF-CONVERGING PROJECTION TV TUBES. Scientists have developed a new projection TV picture tube system that eliminates the need for convergence correction circuitry or adjustments. The patented three-tube system provides the sharpest, most stable picture in big-screen projection TV sets for the home. The new tube concept eliminates distortion and convergence adjustments common in conventional projection TV systems because the faceplates on the right and left tubes have been tilted. The manufacturer has used a very simple concept: the angle of projection creates a distorted picture -- the tilted faceplate also distorts the picture. The two distortions cancel each other out providing a perfectly-converged picture every time. Registry is constant and automatic. The new tubes have shorter necks and can be housed in space-saving cabinets. (Photos, diagrams, background information.)

2. CRYOGENIC REFRIGERATION. A new cryogenic cooling system has been developed by a U.S. laboratory and NASA's Goddard Space Flight Center to provide maintenance-free operation in space for 5-years or more. Friction and wear has been eliminated by replacing life-limited bearings with magnetic fields to suspend the piston and displacer. The motor-driven reciprocating elements are guided by magnetic bearings which levitate those elements in a closely centered rectilinear path. The system is commercially applicable to computers, robotics, food processing and textile machinery, medical equipment and other mechanical devices which could operate with virtually no mechanical deterioration. (Photos, press kit, background information.)

3. TECHNOLOGY PARK SLATED FOR NEW YORK. A $210 million Metrotech Center is now being planned which would bring hi-tech industry to New York City. Plans include a technology science library, a center for telecommunications technology, office and research facilities for hi-tech businesses, and a conference and hospitality center. Among potential tenants are those specializing in the avionics, telecommunications, computers, and imaging sciences industries. (Press kit, photos, drawings.)

New York
Joel A. Strasser
Hill and Knowlton, Inc.
(212) 697-5600

Los Angeles
Dick Rosengarten
Hill and Knowlton West
(213) 937-7460

Published as a service to news media to provide ideas and information for news and feature stories. Many of the ideas may also be appropriate for radio and TV. For additional technical or background information on any of the subjects covered, or for assistance in scheduling interviews, please contact the Industrial and Scientific Communications Services coordinator or representative closest to your location.

Chicago
Al Lind
Hill and Knowlton, Inc.
(312) 565-1200

Washington
Ben Zingman
Hill and Knowlton, Inc.
(202) 638-2800

The Industrial and Scientific Communications Services of Hill and Knowlton sends a newsletter entitled ''News and Feature Leads from Science and Industry'' to 2,500 editors in the fields of science, technology, industry, medicine, health care, and general and business news. Each newsletter contains five to eight items from clients that use a ''teaser,'' or news lead, format to attract the attention and interest of editors. Editors hear about news items at a fraction of the cost of a conventional news release. Editors can send for press releases and photos, or they can have their own reporters initiate the story. (Courtesy Hill and Knowlton, Inc., Industrial and Scientific Communications Services unit, Joel A. Strasser, director [Component of the Advanced Technology Network]) able to the media: Wes Christensen, PR director at Georgetown University, for example, reports that he receives about 500 calls from the media each month. Call reporters when you think you have a story that interests them. Make sure, however, that the story has a local angle or content relevant to the reporter's publication.

Set up interviews for journalists with management or specialists in your organization. Help reporters cover your organization. Don't try to do it for them.

Instead of press releases, send the media a sheet of one-paragraph news tips that they can follow up themselves. Exhibit 11–1 shows an example of such tips provided by the Hill and Knowlton agency.

Interview people in your organization yourself and record the interview on cassette tapes. Provide these tapes to journalists so that they can integrate the interview into their own stories.

Set up an information storage and retrieval system (on a computer if possible) in which you maintain fact sheets (see Chapter 25), complete articles, interviews, and background information. Tell journalists what is in this system, and that they can have access to it whenever they wish. Update the information regularly.

If you practice two-way symmetric media relations, you must take a chance on the accuracy and responsibility of the news media. The more open you can make your organization, the greater is the likelihood of fair and accurate media coverage. Sometimes, however, you may get burned. If you do, don't be afraid to provide a rebuttal. Symmetric communication is give and take. If the media err, provide them information to clarify the error. If you have had good relations with journalists, they won't mind your rebuttal. Never, never threaten or beg, however.

Effective relations with media publics require knowledge of media behavior and effects. We turn now to theories that explain them.

MEDIA PUBLICS

In the chapter on publics, Chapter 6, we argued that public relations people could communicate with publics more often and more effectively if they understood the communication behavior of those publics. Active publics can be reached in one way, passive publics in another. If journalists behave as publics, then the concepts and techniques we outlined in Chapter 6 could be used to type and classify journalists—and to help the media relations specialist communicate with each journalist public. Let's see, then, whether the variables used to define publics apply to journalists.

Journalists Seek and Process Information • The dependent variables from our theory of publics—information seeking and processing—seem to fit the behavior of journalists well. Most of us think of journalists as communicators who disseminate information. But they also seek and process information when they cover events, interview news sources, or assign stories.

You also may think of journalists mostly as active seekers of information—enterprising reporters. But more of their behavior can be described as the passive processing of information: rewriting press releases, routinely covering events or hearings, reacting to the initiative of news sources.

Sigal, for example, classified the sources of 1,146 stories in the Washington *Post* and New York *Times* and found that about three-fourths of the stories resulted from what we would call information processing.[17] Fifty-eight percent of the stories came from such routine sources as official proceedings, press releases, or press conferences. Another 16 percent came from informal sources such as briefings, leaks, meetings, or conventions. Only 26 percent resulted from the active seeking of information, or what Sigal called enterprise reporting: from interviews or the reporter's own analysis.

Hess found that Washington reporters got 80 percent of their news from "events" that occurred within 24 hours.[18] Quite clearly, the reporters "processed" the news from those events.

And, when reporters process information more than they seek it, media relations specialists can influence their communication behavior much more than they could if reporters actively seek information.

Do Journalists Report According to Personal Interests? • To apply our theory of publics to journalists, however, we must also ask whether their information seeking and processing—like the behavior of other organizational publics—can be explained by personal perceptions that reporters have of situations created by organizational consequences.

Do journalists, for example, report about pollution from a steel mill because they personally recognize that problem, feel involved with it, or feel unconstrained about doing something about it? Or, do journalists simply report situations or events that are assigned to them by an editor, that other journalists are reporting, or that journalists perceive readers and viewers of the media have an interest in?

Theoretical Explanations of Journalists' Behavior

We can answer these questions by turning to a domain of mass communication research called "communicator analysis"—study of the behavior of professional communicators.

Researchers first tried to show that journalists seek information and write stories that reinforce their attitudinal biases, just as many media relations specialists have assumed that journalists are motivated by antiorganizational biases. These theories resembled the early attitude theories of audience behavior that we described in Chapter 6.

David Manning White conducted the first "gatekeeper" study in 1950, when he asked a newspaper wire editor he called Mr. Gates to explain why he accepted or rejected each wire story.[19] White concluded that Mr. Gates decisions were "biased and subjective."

Similarly, Janowitz classified journalists as either neutral "gatekeepers" or subjective "advocates" of a position.[20] Starck and Soloski typed journalists as either "neutrals" or "participants" in a news event.[21] You will also recall from the discussion earlier in this chapter that public relations practitioner Donald Van Deusen attributed antibusiness reporting to what he termed a switch from "objective" to "interpretive" reporting.[22]

Recently, researchers have looked for better explanations of the behaviors of journalists than bias.[23] Whitney reviewed studies of communicators and concluded that organizational and institutional variables explain communicator behavior better than individual variables. "Real news," Whitney concluded, "is an organizational product born of routines."[24]

David Manning White's "Mr. Gates," for example, did not appear to be so subjective and biased when McCombs and Shaw analyzed White's data in a different way.[25] They found Mr. Gates' selections of stories to be highly correlated with the numbers of stories that came over the wire. The more stories in a given category, the more of those stories Mr. Gates chose, regardless of his biases.

Levels of Analysis in Journalistic Behavior

Mass-communication researchers, therefore, now do not think the behavior of journalists can be explained by a concept as simple as "bias." Instead, they have developed theories that include three "levels of analysis":[26]

Individual level. The extent to which journalists' behavior results from their own interests, as well as their biases, values, or ideals.

Organizational level. Organizational factors that constrain the behavior of a reporter, such as assignments given by editors.

Institutional level. The constraints that the larger society places upon a journalist, such as the requirement that a medium be profitable, the perceptions journalists have of their readers, the traditions of journalism, and the unconscious influences that reporters have upon each other.

The institutional level may be the most difficult for you to understand, because it represents influences most reporters may not be aware of. For example, research shows that most reporters cover what other reporters cover to protect themselves from being scooped. The wire services play an especially important role, because editors use wire reports to determine whether their reporters have missed a story. Reporters, therefore, do not try to get stories their competitors don't have. They make sure they get the same stories as their competitors. The result is an institutional routine.[27]

By now, you should realize that press representatives would use a different strategy to deal with journalists for each of these levels of analysis.

At the individual level, they would try to channel stories to reporters who have either a personal interest in the story or a bias that favors the organization's position.

At the organizational level, media specialists would work with editors to get a story assigned to a reporter.

At the institutional level, they would stage events and cater to the tendency of one reporter to copy others.

Public relations people seem to stress the individual level when they deal with the media, especially when they try to counteract what they perceive to be media bias. Mass-communication research, however, suggests that organizational and institutional factors may be more important.

Let's turn next to two studies that combine these levels of analysis to develop a typology of journalistic publics.

Two Studies of Journalist Publics

Grunig has done two studies, one of student journalists and one of Washington reporters, that used the theory of publics developed in Chapter 7 to determine how many types of journalist publics exist. These two studies show that attitudes and biases explain little about journalistic behavior. They also show that some journalists are motivated by individual variables, while others are motivated by institutional and organizational variables.

Journalists Aren't Biased; They Have Different Interests • The first study was designed to examine the effect of economic-education programs designed for college and university journalism students.[28] That study will be discussed in more detail in Chapter 16, on economic education and educational relations. It is relevant here, however, because it compares the attitudes and communication behaviors of journalism students with those of business students—from which we can derive some implications about professional journalists and businesspeople.

When Grunig used two questions to measure general attitudes toward business and government, he found the business students to be slightly more probusiness than the journalism students. Both, however, were antigovernment. The business students also said they were more liberal than did the journalism students.

When Grunig measured the cognitive strategies of hedging and wedging (see Chapter 6) on three specific business issues—pollution, government regulation, and the effect of the law of supply and demand—he found little difference between the two groups. Both business and journalism students accepted an antibusiness position on pollution and wedged out a probusiness position. On the impact of government regulation on business, both groups hedged—they believed both a pro- and antibusiness position. When presented a pro- and antibusiness statement about the effect of the basic economic law of supply and demand, neither group had much of a cognition at all—the issue wasn't really relevant to them.

Thus, "bias" didn't seem to separate the journalism students from the business students. Individual communication behaviors did separate them, however. The three dependent variables of the Grunig theory described in Chapter 7 were used to identify publics in the two groups of students on three sets of issues—three basic economic issues (size of corporate profits, capitalism vs. socialism, and supply and demand), three secondary business consequences on publics (quality of goods and services, prices of goods and services, and pollution), and three governmental relationships (regulation of business, taxation of business, and government spending).

Statistical analysis isolated two publics—one made up mostly of the business students and one made up of journalism students. The business student public was an active public on all nine issues—high involvement, high problem recognition, low constraint recognition. The journalist public, however, was an active public only for the three secondary business consequences.

The study suggests, therefore, that journalists aren't really biased against business—and probably not biased against other large organizations either. More likely, they take an interest in business only when it has secondary consequences on publics— remember the primary, secondary, and tertiary effects of business described in Chapter 3 on public responsibility.

Journalists behave like most other publics. They don't worry about business unless it has an adverse consequence upon them. From the business viewpoint, however, this means that journalists concern themselves mostly with the negative side of business.

Businesspeople, however, take an interest in the general workings of business and its role in the economy. They seek that information. Journalists and most other publics do not—as other research has shown.[29] Publics, including journalist publics, just aren't interested in all aspects of business, and public relations practitioners must deal with that fact. Antibias campaigns probably will affect behavior of journalists very little.

Washington Reporters, Too • It's wise to have reservations about generalizing from students to practicing journalists. However, a similar study of practicing Washington reporters showed almost identical results. Grunig included four business policy issues in this study: breakup of the Bell telephone system, deregulation of natural gas, chemical disposal sites, and acid rain.[30] Again, he could find no consistent pattern of bias in the hedging and wedging cognitions or in attitudinal evaluations of policy prescriptions.

However, he did find, as he had in a study of nonjournalist publics,[31] that the journalists generally believed an antibusiness statement on each issue and hedged it with a probusiness statement on some issues. Most publics—journalists and nonjournalists—believe business has negative consequences outside the organization. They don't drop those beliefs when they learn positive things about business; they hold both beliefs.

A 1982 study of 240 elite journalists and broadcasters working for influential media such as as the New York *Times*, Washington *Post*, *Wall Street Journal*, *Newsweek*, and the TV networks demonstrated the same media hedging.[32] Although these journalists generally were more liberal than other people on religious and social issues, they combined liberal social views with many cognitions favored by business.

Most of the journalists surveyed supported environmental protection and women's and minority rights. But most also said they believed that free enterprise gives workers a fair shake, that deregulation of business would be good for the country, and that private enterprise is fair to working people.

Remember in Chapter 6 that we said a change from wedging against your organization to hedging is a more realistic objective than changing negative wedging to positive wedging. That advice seemed to be confirmed by these studies.

Which Levels of Analysis Explain Best? • Although attitudes or bias did not explain the behavior of Washington reporters well, Grunig still asked whether individual interests of the reporters explained their behavior or whether organizational or institutional factors did. What he found was five reporter publics, three of which were motivated by individual interests, and two by institutional forces.

After a pretest, Grunig had dropped organizational variables from the study because the reporters had few constraints upon them from their home offices—most had almost complete autonomy in what they reported. He asked the 160 Washington reporters questions to measure the three independent variables of the situational theory—problem recognition, level of involvement, and constraint recognition—for themselves and as they thought their readers would answer the questions (this measured coorientation, as discussed in Chapter 6).

Grunig also asked questions to determine whether the reporters would actively seek or passively process information about the four issues—breakup of the Bell System, acid rain, chemical disposal, and deregulation of natural gas. He also asked whether they had actually written stories about the four issues in the last year. He then correlated the scores on the independent variables for the reporters themselves and the scores they predicted for their readers with information seeking, information processing, and the number of stories the reporters had actually written.

If the self-scores were highly related to the three communication variables, the reporters would be seeking stories according to their self-interests. If the predicted scores for readers correlated with the communication variables, they would be reporting for their readers' interests—an institutional relationship. If neither the self- nor the reader scores correlated with the independent variables, the reporters probably cover stories because of journalistic convention—because events occur and other reporters cover them.

More Than One Explanation of Reporter Behavior • The results showed that no one level of analysis explained all reporter behavior. Of the five reporter publics, two appear to be motivated by individual perceptions of the situation.

One public, which Grunig called the Environmental Reporters, had levels of problem recognition, involvement, and constraint recognition that showed them to be active self publics for the two environmental issues—chemical disposal sites and acid rain. They covered the science/environment beat and actively reported these issues. They also were most likely to hold antibusiness cognitions and attitudes. This public perceived that its readers would also have levels of problem recognition, involvement, and constraint recognition that would make them active publics on these two environmental issues.

A second public also had a high self-interest in the two environmental issues but perceived that their readers would be active publics only for the Bell System issue. These reporters, whom Grunig called the Reader Bell/Self Environment Public, actively reported their own environmental interests and ignored what they believed to be their readers' interest in the Bell issue.

A third reporter public displayed a combination of self and institutional reasons for its behavior. The Self- and Reader Bell/Self Environment Public followed its personal information needs in gathering news, but only as long as it believed that news also would meet its readers' information needs. These reporters were active publics for the Bell System issue and perceived that their readers would be, too. They said they would seek information about that issue and had actually written stories about it. They also were active publics on the two environmental issues—and said they would seek information about them. But these reporters had not actually written stories about the environment, because they did not perceive their readers as active publics on those issues.

Two final publics seem clearly motivated by institutional factors:

In Chapter 7, we described four typical kinds of publics found in studies of publics. One of these became active only for issues that clearly affect nearly everyone—such as the shortage of gasoline in the late 1970s. One of the reporter publics, which Grunig called the Deregulation of Natural Gas Public, fit this type. It was likely to be moderately active—and perceived its readers in the same way—only on the deregulation issue—the issue most likely to affect people. These reporters had written stories about the issue, but they had passively processed rather than actively sought the information. Institutional factors—the prominence of the issue—apparently forced them to passively report the issue.

A final public, the Reader Environment Public, had no self-interest in any of the four issues, but wrote about the two environmental issues because they perceived their readers to be interested in them. The reporters had few cognitions or attitudes about the issues but wrote about them because they thought their readers expected them to—a clear institutional explanation.

Varied Strategies Needed • So, reporters don't all behave in the same way. Neither do other people. That doesn't make the job of the media relations specialist easy—but it doesn't make it impossible. The media relations specialist must treat different kinds of reporters differently.

Grunig's results suggest that you will usually deal with some enterprising reporters seeking out stories in areas in which they take personal interest. Most likely, they are specialized reporters—in science, the environment, business, regulatory agencies, and the like. These reporters are well informed about the issues in which they are interested. You should help them to get complete, factual information on your organization's position on the relevant issues—as you should help all active, information-seeking publics.

Other reporters process information passively. These reporters still can communicate an organization's information to other publics, as long as it is made available for them to report. They won't seek it out. The media relations specialist must "put it on the agenda" for the reporters.

That takes us to a final media concept, agenda setting, which is essential for you to understand if you are to set objectives for and evaluate media relations.

MEDIA RELATIONS OBJECTIVES AND EVALUATION

In Chapter 6, when we were searching for realistic communication effects that could be used as objectives for public relations programs, we examined some of the history of ideas about the effects of mass media. Mass-media theorists originally believed in a hypodermic-needle theory, which assumed powerful media effects on attitudes and behavior. They gave up that theory for a limited effects theory when they learned that media seldom had strong effects.

In the early 1970s, researchers realized

that the mass media may not change attitudes and behavior, but they thought the media must have some other important effects. In 1972, mass communication researchers Maxwell McCombs and Donald Shaw coined a term that is now widely accepted as the major effect of the media. They found a strong relationship between the amount of space given to different issues in the media and the importance people think those issues have. The media, McCombs and Shaw concluded, "set the agenda for public discussion."[33]

McCombs and Shaw took a phrase from Bernard Cohen's book *The Press and Foreign Policy* that distinguished the agenda-setting effect from effects on attitudes and behavior.[34] The media, according to Cohen, do not tell us what to think, but they do tell us what to think about. Without the media people would not be aware of many issues—from pollution in their hometown to an invasion in Afghanistan. After the media create awareness, however, people go on to form many different cognitions, attitudes, and behaviors from the information they get from the media.

Recall now the five effects outlined in Exhibit 6–1: communication, retention of messages, acceptance of cognitions, formation or change of an attitude, and overt behavior. The agenda-setting effect entails the first two effects. When the media choose to put certain issues on the public agenda, the public can communicate about those issues and become aware of them (retain messages about the issues).

Agenda-setting research suggests that media relations specialists can choose communication and message retention as realistic objectives for their programs. First, they should work with the press to put an organization's message about an issue or program onto the media agenda (to make communication possible). Once the message is on the media agenda, they want it to be there long enough for the public to be aware of it (retain the message).

After achieving those objectives, the media relations specialist has little control over what publics do with information on the media agenda. Publics use the information for many purposes and get many gratifications from using it. This is the domain of another contemporary approach to mass communication—the uses and gratifications approach.[35]

Ongoing Research on Agenda Setting

Research on agenda setting today occupies many researchers and has isolated many relevant theoretical variables.[36] We can't review all of that research here, but we can present a few highlights:

A story must be on the media agenda for some time—about three to five months—before people become thoroughly aware of it.

Newspapers seem to set the public agenda more than television. Television introduces issues but doesn't stay with them long enough to affix them on the public agenda; newspapers do.

Not all people pick up personal agendas from the media to the same degree as other people. In particular, the more involved people are with issues, the less the media affect how important these people think the issues are. Involved people actively seek information from many sources. They don't just process it passively from the media. Also, people with a "high need for orientation"—a great deal of uncertainty about a problem they recognize—accept the media agenda more than people with less uncertainty. When people don't have cognitions about important issues, in other words, they develop them from the most ubiquitous source of information—the media.

Sociologists Kurt and Gladys Lang think the media "build" an agenda rather than "set" it.[37] They argue that the original concept of agenda setting was that the media chose issues to report from a large list of existing issues. Instead, they say, issues "build" when organizations, politicians, or other news sources say something about a situation and journalists choose to report what the sources say. Issues never really become issues unless news sources say something, and unless journalists report what they say. News sources and journalists, in other words, interact to build media agendas—an important point for media relations specialists whose objective is to put their organization or its position on an issue on the public agenda.

How to Evaluate the Media Agenda

Most media relations specialists already use a commercial clipping service so that they can evaluate their work—but they usually monitor the clippings haphazardly. A clipping service is a specialized company that, for a fee, will clip all articles that mention an organization from media specified by the media relations specialist. Media relations people peruse these clippings and frequently mount them carefully to present to management as a demonstration of the effectiveness of their efforts.

At times, media relations people may commission a major attitude study to evaluate how well they are doing their jobs. The more frequent and favorable the media coverage, the better public attitudes will be, they reason. As Chapters 6 and 9 should have made clear, however, attitudes have little relationship to the effectiveness of media relations.

If we define the objective of press relations as "getting the proper message on the media agenda," then the clipping service isn't really such a bad idea. The clippings show how frequently and in what context the organization has appeared on the media agenda. The media relations manager must

set objectives for the kind of media coverage desired and then systematically analyze press clippings to see if those objectives have been met.

PR DATA, Inc., a commercial research firm in Connecticut, has developed a system for analyzing press clippings that has been used by several major companies, including AT&T and Armstrong Cork.[38] PR DATA asks the organization to determine what themes it wants to stress in articles that appear in the media and the media in which it would like those articles to appear. For example, AT&T might want its position on an antitrust case to appear in financial media. PR DATA researchers analyze the content of press clippings or tapes of radio and television broadcasts and use a computer to determine how frequently the desired themes actually appeared in desired media (see Chapter 9 for a discussion of content analysis).

AT&T also has the researchers classify clippings as to whether they are positive, negative, or neutral, charting the results year by year to monitor progress in media relations. When stories are unfavorable, AT&T looks for a "rebuttal ratio"—the relative proportion of times the media relations person gets a later rebuttal to an unfavorable article onto the media agenda. It also looks for the relative number of stories initiated by the company's media relations people compared to the stories initiated by the media themselves—to see if the same coverage would have resulted without media specialists.

Many organizations cannot afford a commercial firm to analyze their press clippings, but they can do it themselves with a little knowledge of content analysis. A computer makes comparisons and calculations easier, but it is not essential. Any organization, in other words, can go one step beyond what it is doing—collecting clippings—to do a much more adequate job of evaluating media relations.

At times, media relations managers may also want to determine whether target publics retain the media agenda as their own. In other words, they want to know whether publics remember the themes of articles that appeared in the media. To measure such public agendas requires a survey of the publics. The survey should measure message retention—recall of the themes stressed in the media—not attitudes or behaviors. See Chapter 9 for sample questions to measure message retention.

NOTES

1. Charles Honaker, ''News Releases Revisited,'' *Public Relations Journal* 37 (April 1981):25–27.
2. *Advertising Age* (April 26, 1982), pp. 3, 74.
3. Craig Aronoff, ''Newspapermen and Practitioners Differ Widely on PR Role,'' *Public Relations Journal* 31 (August 1975):24–25.
4. Craig Aronoff, ''Credibility of Public Relations for Journalists,'' *Public Relations Review* 1 (Fall 1975):45–56.
5. Carlton E. Spitzer, ''Fear of the Media,'' *Public Relations Journal* 37 (November 1981):58–63.
6. See, for example, S. Prakash Sethi, ''The Schism Between Business and American News Media,'' *Journalism Quarterly* 54 (1977):240–247; S. Prakash Sethi, ''Battling Antibusiness Bias: Is There a Chance of Overkill?'' *Public Relations Journal* 37 (November 1981):22–24, 64; Joseph R. Dominick, ''Business Coverage in Network Newscasts,'' *Journalism Quarterly* 58 (1981): 179–185.
7. Donald T. Van Deusen, ''The 'Shrinking News Hole' Syndrome,'' *Public Relations Journal* 31 (October 1975):16, 19.
8. Frank W. Wylie, ''Attitudes Toward the Media,'' *Public Relations Journal* 31 (January 1975):6–7.
9. W. W. Marsh, ''Public Relations and the Big Blow Up, Part II,'' *Public Relations Journal* 36 (November 1980):38–42.
10. Scott M. Cutlip, ''Public Relations in the Government,'' *Public Relations Review* 2 (Summer 1976):19–21.
11. Lucien Toney File, ''How Business Editors View Public Relations,'' *Public Relations Journal* 34 (February 1978):8–9.
12. One can find many articles in professional public relations journals that report how journalists react to the excesses of press agents. Among these are Paul Poorman, ''Public Relations—The Newsman's View,'' *Public Relations Journal* 30 (March 1974):14–16, 40; Chuck Honaker, ''Why Your Releases Aren't Working,'' *Public Relations Journal* 34 (March 1978):16–19; Honaker, ''News Releases Revisited''; Gary B. Bassford, ''The Tube vs. the Pencil Press,'' *Public Relations Journal* 35 (May 1979):16, 21–22; ''An Editor's 10 PR Commandments,'' *Public Relations Journal* 33 (1977):26.
13. An empirical study, using sophisticated statistical techniques, showed that editors do not select news releases randomly. Generally, they select articles that have a local angle. Craig Aronoff, ''Predictors of Success in Placing Releases in Newspapers,'' *Public Relations Review* 2 (Winter 1976):43–57.
14. One study showed that contact with journalists decreased the likelihood that a news release would be used. Phillip J. Tichenor, Clarice N. Olien, and George A. Donohue, ''Predicting a News Source's Success in Placing News in the Media,'' *Journalism Quarterly* 44 (1967):32–42.
15. For example, most of the information released by public relations people after the Three Mile Island nuclear accident was written in technical jargon. Sharon M. Friedman, ''Blueprint for Breakdown: Three Mile Island and the Media Before the Accident,'' *Journal of Communication* 31 (Spring 1981):116–128.
16. Richard Detweiler, ''What Every Successful Executive Should Know About His Press Officer's Terrible Secrets,'' *Public Relations Journal* 32 (August 1976):20–23.
17. Leon V. Sigal, *Reporters and Officials* (Lexington, Mass.: Heath, 1973), p. 121.
18. Stephen Hess, *The Washington Reporters* (Washington: The Brookings Institution, 1981), p. 15.

19. David Manning White, "The Gatekeeper: A Case Study in the Selection of News," *Journalism Quarterly* 27 (1950):383–390.
20. Morris Janowitz, "Professional Models in Journalism: The Gatekeeper and the Advocate," *Journalism Quarterly* 52 (1975):618–626.
21. Kenneth Starck and John Soloski, "Effect of Reporter Predisposition in Covering Controversial Story," *Journalism Quarterly* 54 (1977):120–125.
22. Van Deusen.
23. For a review of this research, see Phillip J. Tichenor, Clarice N. Olien, and George A. Donohue, "Gatekeeping: Mass Media Systems and Information Control," in F. Gerald Kline and Phillip J. Tichenor (eds.), *Current Perspectives in Mass Communication Research* (Beverly Hills, Calif.: Sage, 1972), pp. 45–79.
24. D. Charles Whitney, "Mass Communicator Studies: Similarity, Difference, and Level of Analysis," in James S. Ettema and D. Charles Whitney (eds.), *Individuals in Mass Media Organizations: Creativity and Constraint* (Beverly Hills, Calif.: Sage, 1982), pp. 241–254.
25. Maxwell E. McCombs and Donald E. Shaw, "Structuring the Unseen Environment," *Journal of Communication* 26 (Spring 1976):18–28.
26. Paul M. Hirsch, "Occupational, Organizational, and Institutional Models in Mass Media Research: Toward an Integrated Framework," in Paul M. Hirsch, Peter V. Miller, and F. Gerald Kline (eds.), *Strategies for Communication Research* (Beverly Hills, Calif.: Sage, 1977), pp. 45–79.
27. For an example, see Sharon Dunwoody, "The News-Gathering Behaviors of Specialty Reporters: A Comparison of Two Levels of Analysis in Mass Media Decision-Making." Paper presented to the Association for Education in Journalism, Houston, 1979.
28. James E. Grunig, "Developing Economic Education Programs for the Press," *Public Relations Review* 8 (Fall 1982):43–62.
29. James E. Grunig, "The Message-Attitude-Behavior Relationship: Communication Behaviors of Organizations," *Communication Research* 9 (1982):163–200.
30. James E. Grunig, "Communication Behavior of Washington Reporters on Business Policy Issues." Paper presented to the Association for Education in Journalism, Athens, Ohio, July 1982.
31. Grunig, "The Message-Attitude-Behavior Relationship."
32. "The Media Elite: White, Male, Secular, and Liberal," Washington *Post* (January 3, 1982), p. C3.
33. Maxwell E. McCombs and Donald L. Shaw, "The Agenda-Setting Function of the Mass Media," *Public Opinion Quarterly* 36 (1972): 176–187.
34. Bernard Cohen, *The Press and Foreign Policy* (Princeton, N. J.: Princeton University Press, 1963).
35. See, e.g., Jay G. Blumler and Elihu Katz (eds.), *The Uses of Mass Communications* (Beverly Hills, Calif.: Sage, 1974).
36. For reviews of research, see Maxwell E. McCombs, "The Agenda-Setting Approach," in Dan D. Nimmo and Keith R. Sanders (eds.), *Handbook of Political Communication* (Beverly Hills, Calif.: Sage, 1981), pp. 121–140 and Maxwell E. McCombs, "Agenda Setting Function of Mass Media," *Public Relations Review* 3 (Winter 1977):89–95.
37. Kurt Lang and Gladys Lang, *The Battle for Public Opinion: The President, the Press and the Polls During Watergate* (New York: Columbia University Press, 1983).
38. James F. Tirone, "Measuring The Bell System's Public Relations," *Public Relations Review* 3 (Winter 1977):21–38; Robert K. Marker, "The Armstrong/PR Data Measurement System," *Public Relations Review* 3 (Winter 1977):51–59.

ADDITIONAL READING

Cole, Robert S., *The Practical Handbook of Public Relations* (Englewood Cliffs, N. J.: Prentice-Hall, 1981).

Davis, Dennis K., and Stanley J. Baran, *Mass Communication and Everyday Life: A Perspective on Theory and Effects* (Belmont, Calif.: Wadsworth, 1981).

DeFleur, Melvin L., and Sandra Ball-Rokeach, *Theories of Mass Communication*, 4th ed. (New York: Longman, 1982).

Ettema, James S., and D. Charles Whitney (eds.), *Individuals in Mass Media Organizations: Creativity and Constraint* (Beverly Hills, Calif.: Sage, 1982).

Hess, Stephen, *The Washington Reporters* (Washington: Brookings Institution, 1981).

McCombs, Maxwell E., "Agenda Setting Function of Mass Media," *Public Relations Review* 3 (Winter 1977):89–95.

McCombs, Maxwell E., "The Agenda-Setting Approach," in Dan D. Nimmo and Keith R. Sanders (eds.), *Handbook of Political Communication* (Beverly Hills, Calif.: Sage, 1981), pp. 121–140.

McCombs, Maxwell E., and Lee B. Becker, *Using Mass Communication Theory* (Englewood Cliffs, N. J.: Prentice-Hall, 1979).

Marker, Robert K., "The Armstrong/PR Data Measurement System," *Public Relations Review* 3 (Winter 1977):51–59.

Tirone, James F., "Measuring The Bell System's Public Relations," *Public Relations Review* 3 (Winter 1977):21–38.

12

EMPLOYEE AND MEMBER RELATIONS

Remember those good old pre-whistle-blowing days when company loyalty was considered a virtue? The ideal employee was one who spent 50 years with the same employer without once uttering a word of complaint. At least not loud enough to be heard. For such durability, he received a gold watch upon retirement to mark time till the end of his days.[1]

Reading an employee publication is like going down in warm maple syrup for the third time.[2]

As one industrial relations manager put it, referring to his company's newspaper: "We don't view an employee publication as some sort of 'free press' where employees can bitch at management."[3]

Modern employee relations programs can be traced to the development of employee publications during World War I and especially during World War II. When U. S. industry expanded to support the two war efforts, it found itself with large numbers of new employees who had not developed the proper allegiance to the organization and its goals.

Organizations developed company publications to socialize employees to the organization—to "build the individual's pride in, and identification with, the organization, . . . build participation in those activities that improve the organization's efficiency and effectiveness, . . . develop loyalty to the company, . . . humanize management, . . . promote social and recreational activities, . . . [and] recognize the accomplishments of individuals and groups."[4]

Organizations, in other words, wanted their employee publication to help them develop the loyal, fifty-year employee who would work hard, never complain, and retire happy—gold watch in hand.

Employee publications frequently tried to accomplish this objective through controlled management propaganda or with "warm maple syrup"—babies, bowling scores, retirements, recipes, and high school football scores—that would "humanize" the organization.

Totalitarian Organizations

Most of these organizational media weren't too different from the media in a totalitarian state. The Burson-Marsteller report, cited in the first quote above, went on to say, for example, that, "By definition, a corporation is not a pure or even a representative democracy; its employees are not empowered to elect management or decide who their bosses will be."

An organization is a system of constraints that has been designed to control and channel the behavior of its members. Often organizations use communication to convince employees that the constraints are good for them or to compensate for the constraints by touting employee accomplishments or activities—"humanizing" the constraints. As we will see later in this chapter, therefore, the concept of constraint recognition introduced in Chapter 7 has great importance for understanding the communication behavior of employees.

Today, nearly every organization has some kind of employee relations program within its public relations department—programs that now do much more than produce an employee newspaper or magazine. Many employee relations programs continue to provide propaganda or innocuous material designed to improve employee morale. But many have found that the traditional program no longer controls or motivates employees—if it ever did.

According to the Burson-Marsteller report, the traditional program "runs counter to the nature of our society, which is based upon the right to air grievances, express opinions and voice disapproval." Enlightened companies, the report added, realize they "cannot function in a manner that goes against the grain of the broader society." Organizational researchers have also learned that constraints must be loosened if employees are to be satisfied with their jobs and to be productive workers.

Thus, according to Burson-Marsteller, enlightened companies have "built bridges between the managers and the managed so employees could speak out without fear of reprisal." Those that have not opened up

their internal communication have "found themselves beset by increasing numbers of disgruntled employees."

Large numbers of disgruntled employees have made employee relations the second most important public relations program, according to a survey of chief executive officers in California—second in priority only to government affairs.[5]

Four Eras of Employee Communication

In 1964, the well-known organizational communication consultant, C. J. Dover, described three eras of "management" communication:

> The era of entertaining employees, in the 1940s, to convince them the organization is a good place to work.
>
> The era of informing employees, in the 1950s.
>
> The era of persuasion, in the 1960s.[6]

These three eras of internal communication closely parallel our press agentry/promotion, public information, and two-way asymmetric models of public relations. The new "open" communication with employees suggests that many organizations now have moved into a fourth era, that of two-way symmetric communication.

Today, organizations practice all four models of PR in their internal relations. In this chapter, we will look at some of those programs and show the advantages of the symmetric model. Then we will examine how objectives of employee relations depend upon the structure of the organization. Next, we will look at studies of employee publics, then conclude with a discussion of how to evaluate employee communication programs.

Although this chapter will be devoted mostly to employee communication, it is also relevant to the member communication programs of associations. Most associations produce a magazine or newspaper and many other publications for their members. Often, the objectives are the same, and the publics behave similarly. The greatest difference is in the structure of the organization, a difference we will explain later in the chapter.

INTERNAL RELATIONS PROGRAMS

Today's internal relations programs have evolved substantially from the "house organ" of the past. John Bailey, the executive director of the International Association of Business Communicators, has described the change as follows:

> The "house organ," that chatty little paean to baby photos and bowling scores, has, for the most part, been scuttled. It has been replaced by bold and creative publications—newspapers and newsletters and magazines—that rank with the best in writing and design. Today's organizational publications deal with real issues and relate those issues to real people. These publications are supplemented—and, in some cases, replaced—by a wide range of media: bulletin boards and telephone hotlines, video cassettes and films, displays and group meetings, slide/tape shows, and much more.[7]

As Bailey's quote suggests, internal-communication managers use most of the techniques discussed in the chapters in Part IV. Because internal relations programs have their roots in printed newspapers or magazines, four kinds of publications highlight most programs (see Chapter 26 for more detail).[8]

Magazines use a feature style, many photos, and extensive art. Produced less frequently than other publications—monthly, bimonthly, or quarterly; magazines are most appropriate for humanizing an organization. Quality magazines give employees the impression that they work for a quality organization.

Newspapers are usually a tabloid format, similar to community newspapers. They contain more timely news than magazines and fewer photographs and illustrations. They can be produced more quickly and cheaply than magazines. Newspapers are better than magazines for symmetric programs because they can contain hard news about the organization soon after events or decisions occur.

Newsletters are simpler, faster, and less complicated than the other publications. Flexible enough to meet the needs of small organizations, they can be mimeographed or printed.

Magapapers are hybrids of newspapers and magazines, straddling the fence between news and information, and feature an in-depth treatment.

In addition, employee relations programs use many of the following media:[9]

Bulletin boards.

Daily news sheets.

Booklets and brochures.

Audiovisual presentations.

Videotapes and films.

Exhibits and displays.

Open houses.

Teletype news networks.

Dial-the-news telephone system.

Telephone hotlines.

Closed circuit television.

Annual reports distributed to employees.

Paycheck inserts.

Letters to employees from a plant or office manager.

Benefit books, films, and slide presentations.

Personalized benefit computer printouts.

Recruiting booklets.

Orientation media.

The plain and predictable "house organ" has been replaced by "bold and creative publications . . . that rank with the best in writing and design," according to IABC Executive Director John Bailey. (Courtesy CBS Inc.; PSE&G Marketing Services Department; St. Regis Paper Company, news photo by Sal Ficara; and *Sohio News,* employee publication of The Standard Oil Company [Ohio])

side

Clang, clang! Cable-car bells have been a San Francisco sound since 18/3.
Find out on page 2 how Sohioans are helping to keep the bells ringing

OHIO NEWS

VOL. 35 No. 4 MAY 1981

ama line to speed oil eastward

Old
into
coo

ne Ruttler *Staff Writer*

has signed a three-year agree-
with Petroterminal de Panama
ip 130,000 barrels a day of
sa North Slope crude oil through
nned pipeline crossing Panama
the Pacific Ocean to the Atlantic.
etroterminal is owned by the Pan-
anian government and a group of
s companies headed by Northville
ndustries of Melville, N.Y. Sohio
as no financial interest in the pipe-

oil shipments through the Panama
Canal.

The pipeline bypassing the Panama Canal is expected to cost $250
million to build. Work started in
March on clearing land for construction of the 75-mile line from Puerto
Armuelles on the Pacific Ocean to
Chiriqui Grande on the Atlantic.

The line will be nearly 100 miles
closer to Valdez, the southern terminal of the trans-Alaska pipeline. It
also, Brinkley adds, will provide a

lion barrels
Armuelles wh
Exxon USA/
ducers of Ala
— unload cr
smaller tan

The Pan
cludes the
with a s
lion ba

Bri
have
mu

☼ PSEG

Consumer News

Volume 2 No. 2
Summer 1981

New Money-Saving Air Conditioning Tips

ST REGIS NEWS

Volume 6   Number 4   St. Regis Paper Company   June 1978

---

lumbing

FALL

AND THE NEW TECHNOLOGIES

MAGIC MILL™

**remium
me storage**

heat

g wheat/triple cleaned
/certified seed wheat
s/hardy northern grown

t wt. 50 lbs.

These media contain many different types of information. Among the most common:[10]

General business information.

Industry information.

General organizational information.

Organizational policy information.

Systems and procedures.

Day-to-day operating information.

Public affairs or economic education information.

Marketing, advertising, and sales information.

General information on individual divisions and departments within the organization.

Personnel policies.

Benefits.

Employee and management activities.

Personal development.

Job and skill training.

Often, however, the content of internal media reflect inane press agentry. Many publications are filled with pictures of employees standing in a row at an award ceremony or during a plant visit. One publication we know includes pictures of every high school football team in the community, recipes for homemakers, a message from a different member of the clergy each issue, a "clip-art" woman in a bikini amidst group pictures of employees, and, of course, a motivational message from the president in each issue.

Preoccupation with Technique

Still other publications reflect the public-information model in excess. It takes journalistic expertise to produce most of these publications, and until recently, most internal communications specialists have been communication technicians rather than managers (as these roles were defined in Chapter 5).

Each year, the International Association of Business Communicators (IABC) surveys its members—among other things, it asks for job titles. In 1970, 60 percent of the members had the title of "editor." By 1977, that percentage had dropped to 26 percent; almost a third had the title of "manager."[11]

In Chapter 4, we described the IABC as one of the two major public relations associations. The IABC, you will recall, was formed in 1970 from two associations of "industrial editors"—the American Association of Industrial Editors and the International Council of Industrial Editors.

The change in title of individual practitioners of internal communication and in the name and function of the largest organization of those practitioners reflects a trend away from the press agentry/publicity and public-information models of public relations. Many employee relations specialists, however, retain their major interest in techniques rather than in management and in print media rather than communication media in general.

In an article in *Public Relations Journal*, Stanley Peterfreund, an organizational communication consultant, described an afternoon-long workshop on employee newspapers and magazines for "business communicators," which illustrates this preoccupation with technique:

> "This one is clutter," "Too many pictures on one page, not enough opposite," "The headlines aren't eye-catching." Etc. Etc. Three hours of criticism of technique. Barely a mention of content. Seldom a discussion of why the item was in the publication in the first place. Excitement ran high; the "business communicators" ate it up.[12]

Then Peterfreund added:

> And there's the problem! Often top management and editors who are responsible for formal employee communications, seem to be concerned with format, style, graphics, art work and layout, meeting deadlines, and filling space, more so than with fulfilling a publication's purpose and objectives. As a result, a great deal of money is spent achieving a de-

gree of journalistic slick which does little in communicating to employees but does much to satisfy the ego of the communications technicians.

Two-Way Programs

In many organizations, management—often in the personnel department—has looked upon employee communication as a way of persuading employees to accept management goals for the organization. While the communication technicians worry about journalistic slick, management dictates that the content reflect the management line. One house organ editor, for example, once told us that he really only had an audience of five— the top managers who run the organization.

Many of these asymmetric programs truly are two-way programs that include extensive research on employee attitudes and satisfaction. The programs use that research to design messages they hope will reinforce or change attitudes and behaviors. Increasingly, however, public relations practitioners have turned to a two-way symmetric model of internal relations—the ''open organization'' described in the Burson-Marsteller report cited at the beginning of this chapter.

''Conventional house organs,'' according to management consultants Ronald Goodman and Richard Ruch, ''simplistic preachments in company newspapers about the need to 'waste not,' and age-old supplications to use the suggestion box, are outmoded, outworn, and not working.''[13]

Goodman and Ruch added that five years of intensive research has shown them that the way in which employees perceive top management affects job satisfaction more than anything else. Employees, they found, want to work for organizations that practice public responsibility and that are managed progressively. They want top management to:

Inform employees ahead of time about changes that will affect their jobs.

Care about how employees really feel about their work, and be open and honest in dealing with employees.

Give supervisors enough authority to get the job done.

Make a strong commitment to serving the customer.

Have the ability to solve major company problems.

Run a socially responsible organization.

Provide new products and services to meet competition.

Place more emphasis on quality than quantity.

And, Goodman and Ruch reported, employees want management to communicate openly about what it is doing: ''Employees must know what's going on in the company. They want to know that management cares about them and that the caring is genuine.''

With two-way symmetric internal relations, organizations still produce printed publications. But they make those publications more employee-centered than management-centered. The publications provide information about the organization, its management, its plans, its performance, and its problems. They genuinely help employees evaluate the organization for which they work.

Symmetric programs also use many nontraditional, nonprint media and techniques. Several years ago, the IBM Corporation initiated a program called Speak-Up, which has been copied by many other organizations. A double postcard on which employees can ask questions of management is made easily available on bulletin boards and literature racks. Employee questions go to a specially designated person in the employee-communication program, who asks management people for answers to employee questions. Questions and answers with broad interest are then published in the employee newspaper or magazine. Other responses go directly to the employee asking the question. A similar two-way employee inquiry feature was instituted in 1982 by Warner-Lambert *World*, a publication we examine in greater detail in Chapter 26.

Dialogue and Interpersonal Communication

Symmetric programs also emphasize interpersonal communication and dialogue with management. They include employee briefings and seminars, closed-circuit televison, videotape, and interpersonal communication training for managers. Some examples:[14]

> Connecticut Mutual Life Insurance employees eat breakfast with executives and participate in a rap session in which no questions are barred.

> Bank of America has a program of open meetings, which are conducted separately in each department. Five to thirteen employees attend sessions with management to discuss employee opinions and complaints. A summary of the session and a plan of action to deal with the issues goes to the rest of the staff.

> Burlington Northern employees can dial-the-boss through an internal system that records their questions for the chairperson or vice chairperson of the company. Telephoners get a reply through the mail.

> The Tucson Medical Center puts on a monthly TV newsprogram that features employees and is staffed by employees. No management people can appear unless there is no other news source.[15]

> Ohio Bell runs a program called RSVP that integrates print, video, face-to-face communication, and feedback.[16] A seven-member task force drawn from all divisions decides editorial content, analyzes information from employees, meets with management, and gets responses to employee concerns. Small groups see a monthly videotape that contains news clips, an executive forum, analysis of issues, feedback from employees, progress reports, and investigations of sales and service problems. They then discuss the tape, led by a discussion leader. Viewers respond on an RSVP feedback form. In addition, the program includes a monthly newsletter that contains information employees need to perform their jobs, and special reports in either print or video format.

Internal-communication programs vary predictably among organizations with diffrent structures. We can understand those programs better if we look at the objectives of the programs and how those objectives vary in different organizations.

INTERNAL-COMMUNICATION OBJECTIVES

In Chapters 5 and 6, we described the relationship between the vertical structures of organizations, their environments, and their organizational goals and objectives. We showed that organizations with static environments generally are highly structured vertically. That is, they:

> *Centralize* decision making at the top.

> Set up *formalized* rules and regulations to ensure that everyone knows and fills his or her role.

> *Stratify* roles to clearly separate employees with more prestige from those with less prestige.

> Do not become *complex*; they do not develop specialized roles that are filled with educated and professional employees.

Organizations with dynamic environments, in contrast, are less structured. They decentralize decision making, have more formalized and stratified roles, and become more complex.

We then tied these two types of organizational structures to the two overarching organizational goals: control of, and adaptation to, the environment. We said:

Structured organizations emphasize control of the environment.

Less-structured organizations are the only type of organization likely to include adaptation among their goals. They try both to control and to adapt to their environments.

Organizations with dynamic environments, you will remember, must be open and flexible if they are to innovate enough to cope with their environments. Organizations with static environments need not innovate. The static environment continues to accept the organization's outputs, and the organization tries to produce those outputs as efficiently as possible. A rigid structure helps gain that efficiency.

Finally, we said that structured organizations generally use the press agentry/publicity or two-way asymmetric model of public relations to try to control their environments. Less-structured organizations, in contrast, interact with their environment by using the public-information or two-way symmetric model. The public-information model, however, does not work as well as the two-way symmetric model for a dynamic environment, because it does not bring information from the environment into the organization.

Now that we are dealing with the internal, rather than the external, relationships of an organization, we can expand this theory to provide a picture of the goals and objectives of internal communication.

Research on Goals and Objectives

Communication takes place inside organizations in many ways, and not all of it is the responsibility of the public relations department. In addition to the formal—or "scheduled"—communication activities that are the province of public relations, much informal—"unscheduled"—communication also takes place. Managers talk with employees. Employees talk with each other. Departments hold meetings. Supervisors evaluate subordinates. Or employees talk with people outside the organization.[17]

In the past, public relations people have not had responsibility for improving unscheduled—generally interpersonal—communication. Instead, "organizational communication" specialists, most often in the personnel department, have had that responsibility.

If you have taken a course in organizational communication in a department of speech communication, psychology, or business administration, you probably have been exposed to literature related to the interpersonal part of organizational communication. (We do not limit organizational communication to interpersonal communication inside the organization—as these courses generally do.)

Much of the research on interpersonal communication in organizations has great relevance to public relations, however. Our discussion of symmetric internal communication shows that public relations people now have more responsibility for researching and improving both scheduled and unscheduled communication. If scheduled internal media are to be effective, they must complement overall internal communication.

What, then, does the research on total internal communication tell us about goals and objectives of an employee relations program?

Control and Adaptation Goals Relevant Again • First, it shows that the two general organizational goals of control and adaptation also work well for internal relations.

> More-structured organizations try to control the behavior of their employees by setting up a rigid system of constraints.

> Less-structured organizations set up fewer constraints for their employees. They adapt to the employees as much as employees must adapt to the organization. Generally, organizational theories refer to the adaptation goal as the goal of "coor-

dination'' of behaviors inside the organization.

Second, the literature shows that researchers have paid much more attention to communication objectives that follow logically from the goal of employee control than to objectives that fit the coordination goal. These researchers have given most of their attention to two major effects of internal communication:[18]

Employee satisfaction with job, supervisor, and the total organization.

Employee performance on the job—productivity, output, absenteeism, work performance, or turnover.

These organizational ''control'' objectives also represent the effects most often desired by top management and the public relations practitioners they hire to achieve their employee relations objectives.[19] Too often, management wants an easy way to gain the loyalty of employees and to get more work out of them. And it's much easier to change methods of communication than it is to change organizational structure and role relationships—more realistic ways of affecting performance and satisfaction.

Research on whether communication actually affects satisfaction and performance shows mixed results. Daly and Korinek did a lengthy review of studies that examined that relationship and concluded that ''communication is positively related to satisfaction'' and that ''in some cases communication can affect performance.''[20] Seldom, however, will communication alone be sufficient to bring about satisfaction or improved performance.

Satisfaction and performance essentially equate to the objectives of using communication to gain positive attitudes and supportive behaviors, as we defined them in Chapter 6. Although the research on organizational communication shows that communication may affect satisfaction (attitude) and performance (behavior), these objectives are not the most appropriate if the communication goal is coordination rather than control—a symmetric rather than an asymmetric goal. In that case, the objectives of ''communication,'' ''retention of the message,'' and ''acceptance of the message'' are more relevant.

Coordination Objectives

Hage has argued that organizations should strive to maximize *collective* efforts, rather than *individual* efforts.[21] Unstructured organizations cannot maximize their collective efforts unless they can coordinate the activities of the specialists that occupy the subsystems of the organization. Coordination requires communication. And, as you will recall from Chapter 1, one role of the public relations subsystem is to facilitate communication among the other subsystems of the organization.

Subsystems do not naturally communicate with each other. The Grunig situational theory of communication described in Chapter 7 explains why people in different subsystems have little motivation to communicate with each other. People in different subsystems are *involved* in different tasks, face different *problems*, and confront different degrees of *constraint* (people high in the hierarchy face fewer constraints than people lower in the hierarchy). Thus, employees in different subsystems seek different information—and usually seek it more from inside their own subsystem than from other organizational subsystems. If they communicate with other subsystems, most often they passively process the information.

Thus, it is extremely important that internal communication managers in unstructured organizations facilitate symmetric communication between subsystems to coordinate their behavior toward a collective organizational effort. That is, their major objective should be the facilitation of communication—our first objective in Chapter 6. In Hall's words, ''More, and more accurate, communications do not lead inevitably to greater effectiveness for the organization. The key to the communication process in organizations is to ensure that the correct people get the correct information (in amount and quality) at the correct time."[22]

Research shows that more communication takes place inside unstructured organizations than in structured organizations.[23] And, it shows that employees generally are more satisfied with their jobs in unstructured organizations.[24] Thus, the correlation between the amount of communication and employee satisfaction may be a coincidental effect of changing from a structured to a less-structured organization.

Contingency Theory Again

In Chapter 2, we said that some models of public relations—with their accompanying goals and objectives—are more relevant for some organizations and some organizational subsystems than for others. The same applies for internal communication. Structured organizations require an internal-communication system different from that of unstructured organizations. Let's look at how communication systems differ.

THEORIES OF MANAGEMENT

Before internal communication managers can choose the appropriate goals and objectives for their programs, they must analyze the structure and environment of the organization. These managers must recognize the management approach used in their organization—an approach that usually fits logically with the organization's structure and environment.

We can best explain these management approaches by looking at four historical theories of management.[25] Management in structured organizations reflects the first two of these theories—machine theory and human relations theory. Management in unstructured organizations reflects the other two—human resources and systems theory.

Machine Theory

Katz and Kahn used the term "machine theory" to describe a group of theories that gained great popularity in the first half of the twentieth century, including Frederick Taylor's scientific management, Henri Fayol's classical management theory, and Max Weber's principles of bureaucracy.[26]

To Katz and Kahn, these are machine theories because they treat the organization and the people in it as a machine whose control and coordination can be engineered. Employee behavior can be "engineered" by setting up a system of constraints that leave the employee little freedom—little autonomy. Some of the major management devices advocated by machine theory include:

Subdivision of tasks into partial tasks that can be easily learned.

Standardization of roles into the "one best way" to perform each task.

Unity of command and centralization of decision making: one central command unit; no one reports to more than one superior.

Limited span of control: supervisors should not have more people reporting to them than they can control, usually about five.

Uniform treatment of all employees at the same status level.

No duplication of function: no more than one part of the organization performs the same function.

"Economic Man" • Although these devices probably seem like reasonable ways to make sure all employees do their job, few people enjoy working in a machine. Nevertheless, machine theorists believed, employees are economic creatures who gladly accept wages and decent working conditions as compensation for giving up their freedom to the organization.

Communication has little place in machine theory. What little communication there is resembles the commands a programmer gives to a computer. Communication is necessary to instruct employees on how to do a task and to tell them the penalties for not complying with orders. All communication is asymmetric—designed by management to control subordinates. Machine theorists generally recommended that messages be written (so the employees do not forget them) and supplemented by oral communication (to make sure the employees understand the message).

When you understand machine theory, it's easy to see where the management propaganda in traditional employee publications came from. In machine-managed organizations, publications provide information that reinforces management's control over employees.

Communication Flows in the "Machine" • We can understand how commu-

nication works in a machine-managed organization—and in other types of management theories later—if we look briefly at typical internal communication flows. Organizational theorists generally describe five kinds of internal communication (Figure 12–1):

Downward, from superiors to subordinates.

Upward, from subordinates to superiors.

Horizontal, between individuals in the same department or work unit.

Horizontal, between individuals in departments (subsystems) at the same level of the organization.

Crisscross, between individuals in different departments at different levels of the hierarchy not directly connected on an organization chart.[27]

Machine theory emphasizes downward communication—orders, commands, and exhortations to produce more. In addition, organizations that use machine theory would like employees to communicate upward, par-

FIGURE 12–1   **Internal Communication Flows in an Organization**

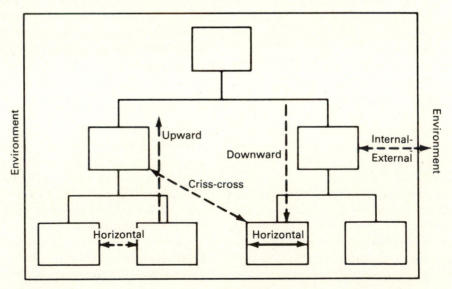

ticularly to reveal when something is going wrong. Instead, however, employees generally communicate upward only when it will make them look good, or to praise management.

Machine management discourages horizontal communication: it wants to avoid "unscheduled" communication through the grapevine that spreads rumors and inaccurate information. Machine management wants messages to flow through the vertical chain of command, so that superiors always know what subordinates are doing. Frequently, however, employees communicate horizontally with fellow employees to express dissatisfaction and frustration with their highly structured work situation.

Something More Needed • In the 1930s, managers of highly structured organizations discovered that machine theory alone could not control an organization and still keep employees satisfied and productive. The result was human relations theory, which eventually produced the warm maple syrup in employee publications and other internal communication channels.

Human Relations Theory

The human relations approach to management arose from two sources in the late 1930s and early 1940s—both connected to the Bell Telephone system.

The first was a series of studies conducted between 1927 and 1932 at the Hawthorne plant of the Western Electric Co. in Cicero, Illinois, just outside Chicago. The studies were conducted by Harvard industrial psychologists Elton Mayo, Fritz Roethlisberger, and William Dickson.[28]

These studies suggested that employees would be more productive if management paid special attention to them. They also showed the importance of social relations in organizations—instead of the economic relations of machine theory. Human relations theorists found that workers would produce

more if other members of their work group encouraged them. They also found, however, that the group would ostracize fellow employees who worked too hard and produced too much—in spite of management programs to increase productivity.

The Practicing Manager Writes a Book • The second source of human relations theory was a book written by Chester Barnard, a president of the New Jersey Bell Telephone Company.[29] Barnard put communication at the forefront of management: The first function of the executive, Barnard wrote, is to establish an effective communication system.

What Barnard had in mind, however, was "expressive" rather than "instrumental" communication—communication to make workers feel good, not to help them do their jobs. Barnard believed organizations were more rational than individuals and that informed workers would be willing to "cooperate" with management. If they did not cooperate, then Barnard believed the workers must be indoctrinated to show them the wisdom of cooperation.[30]

Human relations theorists did not advocate abandoning the constraints of machine theory. And they certainly did not want symmetric relations between management and workers. What they wanted was to exchange expressive communication and humane treatment—"human relations"—for compliance with organizational constraints, rather than exchanging money for compliance, as in machine theory.

Expressive Communication Gimmicks • Human relations management still emphasized downward communication—but now of expressive as well as instrumental messages. Thus, it produced warm maple syrup publications that tried to make employees feel like one big, happy family.

And, it stressed the importance of superficial upward communications through such gimmicks as suggestion boxes, open-door policies, visits by executives to work areas, and company picnics.

Like machine theory, human relations theory also tried to discourage unscheduled horizontal communication through the grapevine. Chester Barnard believed, for example, that the formal communication system was rational, the informal system, irrational.

Today, machine theory and human relations theory together provide the management model and internal communication system that is typical in most highly structured organizations—a centralized, constrained system in which communication is used to give orders, secure "cooperation," and express appreciation for the contributions of employees. In the terms of Chapter 6, the communication objectives are to produce cooperative attitudes and productive behaviors.

The communication system in a less structured system is quite different, however. To understand it, we must look at two newer theories of management.

Human Resources Theory

Human resources theory developed as a spin-off of human relations theory. Although human relations theorists advised managers to communicate personally with employees to make them feel part of the organization, this employee involvement was pseudo-involvement. Decision making remained highly centralized.

Human resources theory, in contrast, advocated actual involvement as a way of motivating employees—involvement that required a less structured organization and more individual autonomy.

Most human resources theories have their roots in psychologist Abraham Maslow's "hierarchy of needs."[31] According to Maslow, people first pay attention to their lower-order needs—for food, shelter, and security. These needs can be met through the economic exchange of machine theory. Once these needs

are met, however, people will not be satisfied unless their higher-order needs for self-esteem and "self-actualization" are met.

Desirable vs. Undesirable Management • Most human relations theories advocate a "desirable" approach to management—which gives employees the autonomy they need to be self-actualized and to be satisfied with their work and contrast it with an "undesirable" approach—which constrains employees and meets only their lower-order needs.

Some of the more prominent examples of human resources theories are:

Douglas McGregor's Theory X and Theory Y.[32]

Rensis Likert's four systems of management.[33]

Frederick Herzberg's motivation-hygiene theory.[34]

Robert Blake and Jane Mouton's managerial grid.[35]

In each of these theories, open communication with employees about organizational decisions that affect their jobs makes up an essential part of the desirable management theory.

Open Communication Flows • It is difficult to separate upward and downward communication in an organization managed through human resources, because the theory encourages symmetric give and take between superiors and subordinates. Human resources theory also recognizes the value of horizontal communication among specialists in one department and in different departments. And it encourages crisscross communication among employees at different levels throughout the organization.

In essence, then, human resources theory simply says that employees will work hardest and be most satisfied in a less-structured organization that has an open, symmetric communication system.

Earlier in this chapter, we said that research does show that employees tend to be satisfied when they have autonomy and open communication. But there is little evidence that this kind of communication system is best for all organizations.[36] In fact, some research shows that many employees prefer rigid, standardized work that has little uncertainty.[37] They can become quite unhappy when their routine is threatened.

Human resources theory, therefore, describes the communication system that works best in a less-structured organization—but not in a more-structured organization. In addition, many less-structured organizations have subsystems that are more structured than others, and for which an open communication system would not be best.

The last management theory shows when the other three theories are most appropriate, and when they are not.

Systems Theory

The three management theories we have discussed so far all have a common fault: each is an "all-or-none" theory.

Machine theory specifies that all organizations can be managed most effectively with the same rigid pattern of constraints.

Human relations theory adds that humanizing techniques must be used to soften the blow of machine theory.

Human resources theory, in contrast, argues that all organizations should be decentralized and that all employees should be given more autonomy.

Systems theory, with which this book should by now have made you quite familiar, maintains that no one structure—and its accompanying communication system—will be appropriate for all organizations.[38] It all depends on each organization's environment and its technology.

Likewise, no one structure and communication system will work best for all subsystems of a single organization.

A system or subsystem in a static environment generally will have a centralized, formalized, stratified, and less complex structure. Its communication system will stress downward communication from management to subordinates—and will be a mixture of orders, propaganda asking for "cooperation," and warm maple syrup.

Less-educated, less-specialized, and nonprofessional workers will be most satisfied and productive in this structure and with this communication system. It will not work for professional, specialized employees.

The system or subsystem in a dynamic environment will give employees autonomy and have an open, symmetric communication system. There will be more horizontal and crisscross communication than in the more structured organization.[39] Employee media and other communication programs will emphasize "getting the right information to the right people at the right time"—the communication objective—rather than persuading employees to have attitudes and to behave in ways that support management.

As a result, educated, specialized, and professional workers will be most satisfied in the less structured organization.

Contingency Theory Once Again • This analysis of organizational structures and communication systems shows again why many organizations persist in using press agentry or asymmetric models of public relations—even though the symmetric model may be preferred on professional grounds. These "unprofessional" models generally work well in the environment of structured organizations.

Now that we understand why organizations choose different internal-communication goals and objectives, let's look at two special cases of these objectives.

Internal-External Communication

Public relations practitioners frequently state that internal communication programs are extremely important to their overall public relations programs, because employees communicate information about the organization for which they work to external publics.

Interpersonal communication specialist Linda McCallister, for example, wrote in the *Public Relations Journal* that "many research studies," including one she conducted for a Michigan school district, "indicate that the people inside an organization are a primary source of information for external publics."[40]

External-communication objectives usually merge with internal objectives. The structured organization wants publics in the environment to feel good about the organization. It wants its employees to feel the same. The less-structured organization wants to facilitate open communication with environmental publics—the same with internal publics.

Thus, organizations must realize that failing to meet internal objectives can make it difficult to meet external objectives. Employees who dislike a structured organization will communicate that dislike to outsiders. Employees in a less-structured organization who are not well informed cannot communicate accurate information to external publics.

A Note on Member Relations in Associations

Earlier in this chapter, we said the theories and programs discussed here would be as relevant to the member relations programs of associations as they are to single organizations. We added, however, that associations have the same objectives and that their publics behave similarly. But, we added, associations differ in structure.

We can now explain that difference.

Associations are made up of organizations—such as the Chamber of Commerce—or of individuals—such as the American Chemical Society. In either case, the members are highly autonomous from the association. They can join or drop the association at will. They cannot be constrained by a centralized or formalized structure.

Members join associations to gain essential information about, for example, products, government regulations, or research. Almost always, therefore, associations will be less-structured organizations whose member-communication program must consist of two-way symmetric communication, designed to get the appropriate information to members when they need it and to facilitate communication among members.

INTERNAL PUBLICS

In Chapter 7, we described several linkages that organizations have with other organizations and publics. Of these linkages, the "functional" linkage is to publics that supply inputs and take outputs. The functional linkage to employees is critical for an organization because employees supply necessary labor and expertise, and if they are unproductive, the organization will be unproductive.

The functional linkage to employees, however, is not to a single homogeneous group. Employees fall into the different categories of publics defined by the situational theory discussed in Chapter 7, and each employee public requires a different communication strategy.

The three concepts of Grunig's situational theory of publics can easily be translated into terms appropriate to internal publics:

Employees work at different tasks in an organization—that is, they face and recognize different kinds of problems. Employees, therefore, are most likely to seek and process information relevant to the problems they face.

Employees have more or less autonomy, depending on their rank in the organization and the extent to which the organization is structured. The more autonomy employees have, the fewer constraints they will face, and the more they will communicate.

Employees who make decisions in an organization generally feel more involved with the organization. Employees higher in the hierarchy, or employees in decentralized organizations, make more decisions. The greater the involvement, the more active an employee's communication behavior will be.

Internal Publics Can Be Created

Because the management subsystem can change the tasks, constraints, and involvement of an organization's employees, it has the power to create different kinds of employee publics—something that cannot be done with external publics. For example:

Highly structured organizations will have mostly low-involvement constrained-behavior and fatalistic-behavior publics lower in the hierarchy, and a few high-involvement problem-facing or routine-behavior publics at the top. The low-involvement publics will have little reason to communicate actively, but if given time, they will passively process management propaganda and expressive communication. The management publics will actively seek internal communication.

Less-structured organizations will have high-involvement problem-facing publics dispersed throughout the organization, because authority is dispersed to individual subsystems. These publics will actively seek information related to the tasks of their subsystem: engineers will seek engineering information, accountants accounting information, and so on. However, these specialized publics will passively process information from other subsystems, including the management subsystem.

Several studies have been conducted of internal publics using the Grunig theory that illustrate the way in which organizational structure creates publics. Let's look at them briefly.

Internal Publics in Two Structured Organizations

Grunig conducted studies of management and nonmanagement employees in two public utilities—one a regional telephone company, the other an electric company.[41] Employees at lower levels of both organizations perceived them to be highly structured. Thus, the two studies show the kinds of publics that emerge in a more structured organizational setting.

Grunig asked questions to measure whether employees think about (problem recognition), feel constrained about, and perceive an involvement in, their daily organizational tasks, and whether they think about and feel constrained about taking a new job in another organization.

Statistical techniques revealed three publics in one organization and four in the other:

A management public in both organizations.

An older-employee public, of lower-level employees, in both organizations.

One or two publics of younger employees. In one company, this public was called the dissatisfied younger employees. In the other company, one was called more-educated younger employees, the other, less-educated younger employees.

The management public was an active public. Members of this public were most involved, most likely to recognize problems, and least constrained in their daily tasks (but not in considering another job). They also were most likely to use all employee publications—more than the lower-level publics for whom the publications were designed. They reported more interest in hard news about the company than in management propaganda or human relations materials.

The older-employee public did not think much about their work or taking another job (low problem recognition). But they had adapted to high constraints and perceived a moderate level of involvement in the company. Apparently, the pseudo-involvement cultivated by human relations techniques had worked. These older workers were loyal to the company, satisfied with their supervisors, and preferred information that reinforced that viewpoint. But the older employees did not use employee media much. When they did, they were most interested in soft material—in particular, stories about other employees.

The dissatisfied younger employees in one organization, and the *more-educated younger employees* in the other, fit the low-involvement constrained-behavior category. They recognized the constraints they faced in making day-to-day decisions (their positions were generally lower in the hierarchy), and they did not feel involved. But they did recognize problems in their daily work and did compare their job with a similar one in another organization.

These younger employees were not happy with their organization—something that organizational researchers Porter, Lawler, and Hackman say is typical of younger employees who have not yet been socialized into an organization.[42] As a moderately active public, these younger workers used company media, particularly for information to help them evaluate their future in the organization and to compare opportunities there with opportunities elsewhere.

These younger workers also showed up in a 1971 survey of employees of the Bank of America.[43] In that survey, younger employees were more negative about bank publications and had ''particularly strong interests in more open, candid, two-way communication.''

The less-educated younger employees fit a low-involvement fatalistic public. They, too, disliked their work and the company, but they did not use employee media and had little interest in information about the company or other employees. They were, in other words, a public that had not yet responded to human relations techniques.

Internal Publics in Three Less-Structured Organizations

Grunig and two graduate students at the University of Maryland have conducted studies of internal publics in three technical, highly professional organizations—organizations that generally fit the unstructured category we have described throughout this chapter:

> The National Bureau of Standards, a research organization located in the suburbs of Washington, D.C., whose employees are mostly scientists.[44]
>
> The Naval Surface Weapons Center, a research unit of the Department of Defense, also located in the Washington suburbs, whose employees are mainly engineers and technicians.[45]
>
> A university-based research and development center located in the Midwest, whose employees are mostly university researchers.[46]

The researchers identified four almost-identical employee publics in each of these organizations, although the fourth public did not show up in the university R&D center. The researchers again asked questions to measure problem recognition, level of involvement, and constraint recognition for about fifteen organizational situations—such as research in different units, the budget, employee recreation activities, and appointments of new administrators. Statistical techniques identified the publics and described which internal media each public used and other communication behaviors of each public.

The nature of these publics reveals the differing communication needs of professionalized specialists, administrators, and less-educated support personnel in an unstructured organization.

The studies showed that most employees in unstructured organizations passively process the information in company media, and thus spend relatively little time using those media. But the studies also showed that specialists do engage in active interpersonal communication with each other.

The Specialist Public • This public consisted mostly of scientists, engineers, and researchers—professionalized specialists. The specialist public actively communicated horizontally and in crisscross fashion inside the organization—as organizational theory would predict for an unstructured organization.

Members of this public communicated actively about research and technical organizational situations or about the few administrative/budgetary problems that affected their work. They passively processed articles about research that appeared in employee publications and spent relatively little time using formal media. More often, they communicated interpersonally with other specialists. Or they used technical publications, attended technical seminars, and sought out technical information related to their jobs.

The Administrative Public • Members of this public generally had administrative jobs that made them think about problems throughout the organization, although they did not perceive a high level of involvement with these problems. As a result, members of the administrative public communicated passively about most organizational situations—except administrative problems with which they were personally involved. They, too, generally processed, rather than sought, information from organizational media.

The Employee Context Public • Members of this public came from lower levels of the hierarchy, where they faced a more structured work situation than the specialists. They were the janitors, secretaries, doormen, and other service workers in these highly technical organizations. They faced more constraints than other employees and perceived little involvement in research and administrative situations.

These people did feel involved with "employee context" situations such as pay, benefits, sports, and social activities—much of the material in warm maple syrup publications. They actively sought information about these employee situations from organizational media and nonselectively processed much information about research from these media. They had little interest in administrative information, however—often because it is management propaganda.

These nonspecialists in a specialized organization need human relations treatment that the specialists do not need—as their organizational setting is more structured.

The Noninvolved Public • This public, also composed of more constrained lower-level employees, perceived little involvement in any organizational situations—even the employee-context situations. In one organization, the members of this public did think about—recognized—research, administrative, and employee organizational problems. But because of their low involvement and high constraints, they spent very little time with organizational media, and they only processed the information that appeared there.

Like the less-educated younger workers in the utility described above, these employees apparently cared little about their work or the organization that employed them. They did not respond to human relations techniques.

Uninvolved, unconcerned employees will, no doubt, be found in nearly every organization.

Drawing Some Conclusions

The nature of these four publics points out the difficulty of providing adequate employee media in less-structured organizations. In those organizations, employees need specialized horizontal and crisscross communication—most of it interpersonal. The employee communication manager can help to facilitate that communication by studying and improving communication flows. Lower-level employees, on the other hand, need traditional human relations communication.

Employee publications, therefore, serve two purposes:

> For specialists, they help integrate the organization by making specialists aware of what other specialists are doing and how these different activities contribute to a single organizational mission. Thus, articles about research activities and about overall organizational policy, budgets, and support are important. Specialists will process rather than seek this information, however.

> Some lower-level service workers will process some of the same information and gain a sense of pseudo-involvement in the organization from doing so. But they also need employee-related human relations information in organizational media.

These three studies suggest, therefore, that employee publications must be diversified in a nonstructured organization—as are commercial media. They should contain current organizational news up front, with research features, employee profiles, and articles about employee achievements and social activities inside.

Member Publics of an Association

In 1979, Grunig conducted a study for the American Association for Health, Physical Education, Recreation, and Dance (AAHPERD), which demonstrates the open and specialized communication necessary in an association.[47] AAHPERD is an association of professionals who teach or do research in colleges, universities, primary and secondary schools, or health and recreation departments.

When he used the situational theory and the same statistical techniques as in the three studies of specialist organizations, Grunig found four member publics. These publics, and their communication behaviors, reflected specialized work situations—similar to the publics in the three specialized organizations. Each was an active public, and each sought out association publications that provided essential work-related information.

The four publics:

> An administrator public, found in schools, universities, and health and recreation departments, which used mostly publications aimed at administrators.

> A teacher/researcher public, found mostly in universities, whose work included both teaching and research. It used technical journals and attended research conferences.

> A teacher public, whose members spent all of their time teaching in schools or non-research colleges. They used publications that contained research reports that were related to their teaching.

> An innovator public, of younger members interested in changing their programs and doing their work innovatively. This public most often used general association publications that contained profiles and case studies detailing innovations and practices of association members.

Three Studies of Internal-External Communication

Grunig also conducted three studies that improve our understanding of communication between employees of an organization and outsiders.

As a part of the study of two utilities described above, Grunig asked the employees surveyed how often they talked about the organization with outsiders.[48] The answers showed that employees who communicated the most inside the organization—the management and the more-educated younger employee publics—also communicated the most outside the organization. Employees who face the most constraints and are least involved in their work apparently have little reason to talk about their work when they leave the job.

Communication from Outsiders to Insiders • The two other studies addressed the question of whether employees of an organization will communicate information accurately from clients of the organization to decision makers inside the organization.

Organizational research has shown that lower-level employees have more contact with outsiders than higher-level employees. That research has two implications.

First, in a highly structured organization, upward communication from lower- to higher-level employees usually will be distorted in favor of what the superior wants to hear. Thus, research suggests that accurate information will not flow from outsiders to subordinates to superiors.

A study of internal-external communication in an antipoverty agency showed, however, that accurate information would go directly from outside clients to top administrators if administrators are appointed who are similar to, and interact with, the clients.[49] In most antipoverty agencies, the clients and the lower-level employees were black, and the top administrators were white. In this organization, however, the top administrator was black, and whites were dispersed throughout the organization.

Second, lower-level employees, who usually have the most contact with clients and other outsiders, face the most constraints and are less involved in the organization than upper-level employees. Thus, they are more likely to process, rather than seek, information from outsiders.

A study of the same regional telephone company described above showed the impact of processing rather than seeking information from outside.[50] Clients and other outsiders more often voice complaints to an organization than suggestions or complementary information. The study showed that lower-level employees processed the negative information and did not seek out other information. Thus, information flowing into an organization from outsiders leads employees to overestimate external dissatisfaction with the organization.

Only when the organization takes formal polls or sets up other formal communication channels with outsiders (see Chapter 13, on community relations) do top administrators get accurate information from outside.

EVALUATION OF INTERNAL RELATIONS

Many research techniques have been developed that are appropriate for evaluating the effectiveness of internal communication. Which technique should be used depends on the structure of the organization and the relevant goals and objectives of its communication system. Let's look at five evaluation methods.

Communication, Retention, and Acceptance of Messages

Internal communication, particularly downward communication, can be evaluated by determining exposure to publications or other information sources, and by asking questions such as those in Chapter 9 to measure whether employees retain and believe these messages.

Such an evaluation is appropriate for a structured organization that wants to communicate management information downward to subordinates as accurately as possible. It is also relevant to a less-structured organization in which the managers want to see if messages are flowing throughout the organization and are being retained and believed.

AT&T, for example, measured the communication objective by asking a sample of employees whether they received their company publication within forty-eight hours of distribution.[51] The company also measured retention by asking the employees sampled whether they remembered reading stories that appeared in the publication. AT&T also measured readability to see if publications were written at a level that made it possible for employees to retain the information. Finally, AT&T measured acceptance of the message by asking employees whether the publication was understandable, presented both sides of an issue, and was an "excellent" source of company information.

The Group Attitudes research subsidiary of Hill and Knowlton has conducted many employee studies that also fit this category. Most were designed to determine how well employees retain and believe messages about the organization. For example:

> A major oil company had invested considerable money in internal publications and wanted to know what kind of perceptions employees had of the company as a result.
>
> A large manufacturer had just gone through a strike and wanted to know how employees perceived the company after the strike.
>
> A large company dispersed throughout the country wanted to know how employees in its subsidiaries perceived the parent corporation.[52]

Coorientational Evaluations

The coorientation method described in Chapters 6 and 9—in which members of two groups try to predict the cognitions and attitudes of the other—can tell an evaluator how accurately superiors and subordinates perceive each other, and the extent of their understanding and agreement.

In an unstructured organization, the technique can measure how well members of different subsystems can predict the cognitions and attitudes of members of other subsystems—both are essential if the subsystems are to coordinate their behaviors.

In Grunig's study of employee publics in the two utilities, for example, a coorientation measure showed that the nonmanagement publics accurately predicted that management was concerned with increasing profits and production.[53] But they underestimated management's concern for consumers and overestimated management's concern for the environment and for employees.

At the same time, management employees believed nonmanagement employees were less concerned with profits and production than they really were; they predicted that employees would be concerned only with their own happiness and with having a safe and pleasant workplace.

Human Relations Audits

Many human relations researchers have developed measures of employee attitudes toward their job, their supervisor, and the organization. Appropriate questionnaires can usually be obtained from an organization's personnel department or from a commercial firm.

These audits tell little about the extent to which the communication, retention, and acceptance objectives have been met. But they do show whether human relations techniques have affected attitudes and behaviors. Thus, they are useful only for evaluating expressive communication in a structured organization.

Communication Satisfaction

Researchers who specialize in interpersonal communication in organizations have developed extensive questionnaires that can be used to measure employee satisfaction with communication in the organization. The best-developed of these questionnaires is the audit technique developed by members of the Organizational Communication Division of the International Communication Association (ICA).[54]

Audits of communication satisfaction fit the logic of the human resources theory of management, which stresses autonomy, self-actualization, and open communication. The ICA audit, for example, asks employees how much information they receive and whether they need more information about such topic areas as job duties, pay and benefits, and their own performance.

The audit asks similar questions about communication with superiors, subordinates, and coworkers, and about such channels as publications, media, or bulletin boards. The ICA questionnaire also asks questions about "communication outcomes" such as job satisfaction, and asks employees to describe specific experiences they have had in which communication has been effective or ineffective.

The satisfaction audit is quite popular, but it has important limitations. It asks employees for their perceptions of the effectiveness of communication. Employees may not know, and it may be necessary to employ more objective measures, such as those suggested here.

Even more important, however, is the fact that employees tend to say they are satisfied with communication when they are happy with the organization. Thus, the satisfaction audit does not adequately separate communication satisfaction from total job satisfaction. This shortcoming makes the satisfaction audit much like the human relations audit—it measures employee attitudes, not the effectiveness of communication.

Network Analysis

A network analysis measures the communication objective by using one of several methods to develop a diagram of who talks to whom in an organization and how messages flow through the organization. Some types of network analysis also measure retention of messages by asking people what they have heard and comparing what they say with an original message released into the organization.

Network analysis works especially well for evaluating the communication system of an unstructured organization, a system that consists mostly of unscheduled communication activities. It is effective because it helps the communication manager learn what is going on in the unscheduled network and to determine how effective that network is.

There are five kinds of network analyses:[55]

The duty study. Respondents record their communication behaviors and people with whom they have communicated.

Observers. Trained observers accompany respondents and record their communication behaviors and interactions with other people.

Cross-sectional interview or questionnaire. Respondents are asked who, in general, they interact with and what they talk about.

"Small-world" technique. An experimenter releases a message into the organization that is intended for a specific person and then traces the flow of the message.

Diffusion method. Messages that occur naturally are traced as they flow through the organization. This is also known as the ECCO technique (episodic communication channels in organizations).[56]

Communication researchers have developed more methods to evaluate internal communication programs than any other type of public relations program. No longer must managers of those programs rely on the beaming face of a fifty-year employee receiving a gold watch at retirement to determine the success of their programs.

NOTES

1. "Opening Doors in Closed Corporations," Burson-Marsteller Report No. 60 (Summer 1981).
2. Robert Townsend, *Up the Organization* (New York: Knopf, 1970).
3. Richard Nemec, "Internal Communications—A Scary Science," *Public Relations Journal* 29 (December 1973):6–8, 27.
4. Dennis W. Jeffers and David N. Bateman, "Redefining the Role of the Company Magazine," *Public Relations Review* 6 (Summer 1980):11–29.
5. Roy G. Foltz, "Internal Communications," in the "Public Relations At Large" section, *Public Relations Journal* 37 (February 1981):8.
6. C. J. Dover, "Three Eras of Management Communication," in W. Charles Redding and George A. Sanborn (eds.), *Business and Industrial Communication: A Source Book* (New York: Harper & Row, 1964), pp. 61–65.
7. John N. Bailey, "Preface," in Carol Reuss and Donn Silvis (eds.), *Inside Organizational Communication* (New York: Longman, 1981), pp. xi–xii.
8. Joan Kampe and Lyn Christenson, "Publications: What's in the Package," in Reuss and Silvis, pp. 110–123.
9. Douglas P. Brush, "Internal Communications and the New Technology," *Public Relations Journal* 37 (February 1981):13; Joseph A. Varilla, "Employee Relations and Communications," in Philip Lesly (ed.), *Lesly's Public Relations Handbook*, 2d ed. (Englewood Cliffs, N.J.: Prentice-Hall, 1978), pp. 162–165; William P. Dunk and Philip F. Bamforth, " 'Targeted' Media," in Reuss and Silvis, pp. 147–156.
10. Brush.
11. Jeffers and Bateman.
12. Stanley Peterfreund, "Employee Publications: Deadly But Not Dead Yet," *Public Relations Journal* 30 (January 1974):20–23.
13. Ronald Goodman and Richard S. Ruch, "In the Image of the CEO," *Public Relations Journal* 37 (February 1981):14–15, 18–19.
14. Jean L. Farinelli, "Fine Tuning Employee Communications," *Public Relations Journal* 33 (January 1977):22–23.
15. Frank L. Riggs, "Turning Employees On With TV," *Public Relations Journal* 36 (February 1980):22–24.
16. Lee Coyle, "RSVP: The Ohio Bell Approach," *Public Relations Journal* (February 1981):24–26.
17. The terms "scheduled" and "unscheduled" come from Jerald Hage, *Communication and Organizational Control: Cybernetics in Health and Welfare Settings* (New York: Wiley, 1974), pp. 163–189.
18. John A. Daly and John T. Korinek, "Organizational Communication: A Review via Operationalizations," in Howard H. Greenbaum and Raymond L. Falcione (eds.), *Organizational Communication: Abstracts, Analysis, and Overview*, Vol. 7 (Beverly Hills, Calif.: Sage Publications, 1982), pp. 11–46; Cal W. Downs and Tony Hain, "Productivity and Communication," in Michael Burgoon (ed.), *Communication Yearbook 5* (New Brunswick, N. J.: Transaction Books, 1982), pp. 435–454; Keith Brooks, James Callicoat, and Gail Siegerdt, "The ICA Communication Audit and Perceived Communication Effectiveness Changes in 16 Audited Organizations," *Human Communication Research* 5 (Winter 1979):130–137.
19. See, for example, Joyce Asher Gildea and Myron Emanuel, "Communications and Productivity," *Public Relations Journal* 36 (February 1980):8–12; and Louis C. Williams, Jr., "Trends and Issues: Challenges Ahead," in Reuss and Silvis, pp. 293–294.
20. Daly and Korinek, pp. 13, 15.
21. Jerald Hage, *Theories of Organizations: Form, Process & Transformation* (New York: Wiley, 1980), p. 298.
22. Richard H. Hall, *Organizations: Structure and Process*, 2d ed. (Englewood Cliffs, N.J.: Prentice-Hall, 1977), p. 292.
23. Hage, *Communication and Organizational Control.*
24. Everett M. Rogers and Rekha Agarwala-Rogers, *Communication in Organizations* (New York: Free Press, 1976), pp. 120–121; Daly and Korinek; Hage, *Theories of Organizations*, pp. 293–309.
25. For a more extensive discussion of these theories, see Rogers and Rogers, Chapters 2 and 3.
26. Daniel Katz and Robert L. Kahn, *The Social*

Psychology of Organizations, 2d ed. (New York: Wiley, 1978).

27. For example, Phillip V. Lewis, *Organizational Communication: The Essence of Effective Management*, 2d ed. (Columbus: Grid, 1980), pp. 59–76. The idea of criss-cross communication comes from Hage, *Communication and Organizational Control*, pp. 163–189.

28. Fritz J. Roethlisberger and William J. Dickson, *Management and the Worker* (Cambridge, Mass.: Harvard University Press, 1947).

29. Chester Barnard, *The Functions of the Executive* (Cambridge, Mass.: Harvard University Press, 1938).

30. Perrow provides an especially illuminating review of Barnard's ideas. Charles Perrow, *Complex Organizations: A Critical Essay*, 2d ed. (Glenview, Ill.: Scott, Foresman, 1979), pp. 70–86.

31. Abraham Maslow, *Motivation and Personality*, 2d ed. (New York: Harper & Row, 1970).

32. Douglas McGregor, *The Human Side of Enterprise* (New York: McGraw-Hill, 1960).

33. Rensis Likert, *The Human Organization* (New York: McGraw-Hill, 1967).

34. Frederick Herzberg, *Work and the Nature of Man* (Cleveland: World Publishing, 1966).

35. Robert R. Blake and Jane S. Mouton, *The Managerial Grid* (Houston: Gulf Publishing, 1964).

36. Perrow, pp. 114–132.

37. Michel Crozier, *The Bureaucratic Phenomenon* (Chicago: University of Chicago Press, 1964).

38. Many theorists have taken a systems approach to management theory. Katz and Kahn, however, have been the most influential systems theorists.

39. For empirical support of this statement, see Jerald Hage, Michael Aiken, and Cora B. Marrett, "Organization Structure and Communications," in Daniel Katz, Robert L. Kahn, and J. Stacy Adams (eds.), *The Study of Organizations* (San Francisco: Jossey-Bass, 1980), pp. 302–315.

40. Linda McCallister, "The Interpersonal Side of Internal Communications," *Public Relations Journal* 37 (February 1981):20–23.

41. James E. Grunig, "Some Consistent Types of Employee Publics," *Public Relations Review* 1 (Winter 1975):17–36.

42. Lyman W. Porter, Edward E. Lawler III,

and J. Richard Hackman, *Behavior in Organizations* (New York: McGraw-Hill, 1975), pp. 162–170.

43. Nemec, p. 7.

44. James E. Grunig, "Evaluating Employee Communications in a Research Operation," *Public Relations Review* 3 (Winter 1977):61–82.

45. Karen Pelham, "Internal Communication at the Naval Surface Weapons Center: An Analysis Using Grunig's Multi-Systems Theory," master's thesis, University of Maryland, College Park, 1977.

46. Larissa Schneider, "Employee Communication at a University-Based R&D Center: An Analysis Using Grunig's Theory of Communication Behavior," master's thesis, University of Maryland, College Park, 1978.

47. James E. Grunig, "Membership Survey and Communication Audit." Report to the American Alliance for Health, Physical Education, Recreation, and Dance, Washington, D. C., May 1979.

48. Grunig, "Some Consistent Types of Employee Publics," p. 34.

49. James E. Grunig, "Communication in a Community Development Agency," *Journal of Communication* 24 (Autumn 1974):40–46.

50. James E. Grunig, "Accuracy of Communication from an External Public to Employees in a Formal Organization," *Human Communication Research* 5 (1978):40–53.

51. James F. Tirone, "Measuring the Bell System's Public Relations," *Public Relations Review* 3 (Winter 1977):27–31.

52. Group Attitudes Corporation, "General Thoughts Concerning Image and Issue Research Relating to Employees," New York, undated.

53. Grunig, "Some Consistent Types of Employee Publics," pp. 27–28.

54. Gerald Goldhaber and P. Krivonos, "The ICA Communication Audit: Process, Status, and Critique," *Journal of Business Communication* 15 (1977):41–64.

55. Richard V. Farace, Peter R. Monge, and Hamish M. Russell, *Communicating and Organizing* (Reading, Mass.: Addison-Wesley), pp. 207–214.

56. Grunig used this method, for example, in the study of the National Bureau of Standards dis-

cussed earlier in this chapter. He took news items about research, employee achievements, and administrative problems and asked respondents if they had heard the item and what they had heard. The administrative public was most likely to have heard the administrative items accurately, for example. Likewise, the technical public was most likely to have heard the research items.

ADDITIONAL READING

Baird, John E., Jr., *The Dynamics of Organizational Communication* (New York: Harper & Row, 1977).

Farace, Richard V., Peter R. Monge, and Hamish M. Russell, *Communicating and Organizing* (Reading, Mass.: Addison-Wesley), pp. 207–214.

Hall, Richard H., *Organizations: Structure and Process*, 2d ed. (Englewood Cliffs, N.J.: Prentice-Hall, 1977), p. 292.

Hage, Jerald, *Communication and Organizational Control: Cybernetics in Health and Welfare Settings* (New York: Wiley, 1974), pp. 163–189.

Hage, Jerald, *Theories of Organizations: Form, Process & Transformation* (New York: Wiley, 1980), Part III on the human factor.

Jeffers, Dennis W., and David N. Bateman, ''Redefining the Role of the Company Magazine,'' *Public Relations Review* 6 (Summer 1980):11–29.

Koehler, Jerry W., Karl W. E. Anatol, and Ronald L. Applbaum, *Organizational Communication: Behavioral Perspectives*, 2d ed. (New York: Holt, Rinehart and Winston, 1981).

Lewis, Phillip V., *Organizational Communication: The Essence of Effective Management*, 2nd ed. (Columbus: Grid, 1980).

Perrow, Charles, *Complex Organizations: A Critical Essay*, 2d ed. (Glenview, Ill.: Scott, Foresman, 1979).

Reuss, Carol, and Donn Silvis, *Inside Organizational Communication* (New York: Longman, 1981).

Rogers, Everett M. and Rekha Agarwala-Rogers, *Communication in Organizations* (New York: Free Press, 1976).

13

COMMUNITY RELATIONS

Organizations do many things in the name of community relations. For example:

Members of a professional basketball team visit sick children in a hospital.

Families visit a local firehouse; children climb on the fire engines, slide down the pole, and pet the Dalmatians.

Employees of a local company enter a "crazy canoe" race on the Ohio River during a Fourth of July celebration.

Members of a community relations team provide free coffee at a rest stop on an interstate highway during Labor Day weekend.

A business firm invests in an urban renewal program to rebuild the downtown portion of a decaying city.

A hospital sponsors special lectures on health for members of the community.

A local manager gives a speech to the Rotary Club.

A government agency holds a community open house every summer.

A local company sponsors an art exhibit, community concerts, or Little League baseball team.

Members of a community relations team conduct formal interviews with community leaders once a year.

A local plant manager calls on political leaders to persuade them to make changes in zoning regulations.

"Expressive" vs. "Instrumental" Activities

This welter of community relations activities makes more sense if you realize that the activities are either "expressive" or "instrumental"—the same categories that we used to describe employee communication in the previous chapter.[1]

Organizations use "expressive" community relations activities to promote themselves and to show their goodwill to the community. They use "instrumental" activities to improve the community or to change the community to make it easier for their organization to work there.

As in employee relations programs, expressive activities typically are used in community relations programs that reflect the press agent/publicist and, at times, the public-information model of public relations. Examples include the professional basketball team visiting a hospital, the open house at the firehouse, or sponsorship of athletic teams.

More often, community relations programs based on the public-information model have instrumental goals for the program—as would the executive's speech to the Rotary Club or the hospital's seminar on health.

Programs based on the two-way symmetric and two-way asymmetric models generally stress instrumental community activities, although asymmetric programs may supplement the instrumental with expressive activities to soften attempts to persuade. For example, the community relations team that interviews community leaders could have either an asymmetric or symmetric objective—to persuade the leaders to do what the organization wants or to reach a mutual understanding. The asymmetric team might offer to sponsor a community concert or to enter the crazy canoe race at the same time.

Interdependence of Organization and Environment

Regardless of the model of public relations used, community relations programs reflect the interdependence of an organization and its environment—in this case the part of the environment occupied by the local community or communities in which organizations have offices or facilities.

The retired director of community relations for the Illinois Bell Telephone Company described this interrelationship when he defined community relations as "an institution's planned, active, and continuing participation with and within a community, to maintain and enhance its environment to the benefit of both the institution and the community."[2]

The community relations section of Champion International Corporation's *Public Affairs Guide* describes the interdependence of organization and community more explicitly (Champion International is a large forest products firm):

> We ARE important to those communities. Our payroll may be the bulwark of the area's economy. The taxes we pay support local schools and government. Our voluntary contributions, both financial and in the forms of employees' personal services, help the communities grow and prosper.
>
> And these communities are important to US. Without public acceptance, no industry can realize its full potential. The good will of the people who live in our plant communities is essential and must be earned.

Let's look more closely, then, at programs designed to facilitate the organization-community relationship.

COMMUNITY RELATIONS PROGRAMS

The term "community" is used in two major ways today in the social science and communications literature:

1. As a locality—people grouped by geographic location.
2. As a nongeographic community of interest—people with a common interest, such as the scientific community or the business community.

Nearly all community relations programs are designed for the first kind of community. The second definition of community essentially is the definition we have given to a public—a group with a common problem or interest, regardless of geographic location.

The two types of communities may overlap. There may be several publics within a single geographic community. And publics may overlap geographic communities. A community usually will not be a single public, and most communities will contain many publics.

Sociologist Jessie Bernard also has identified locale as the one characteristic that has persisted in social science definitions of community.[3] Often, these communities are defined by political units; at other times, they may be larger or smaller than the political unit.

Communities may be rural areas, small towns, urban centers, or neighborhoods or suburban areas within an urban complex. As we will see, community relations programs should differ for these different kinds of communities.

Community relations programs, therefore, are specialized public relations programs to facilitate communication between an organization and publics in its geographic locality.

Community relations programs typically stress one of two types of community activities:

Activities to help local plant or office managers or employees to communicate with community leaders and residents.

Activities that involve the organization in the community, such as supporting urban renewal, supporting schools, or making financial contributions to local organizations.

Public relations people usually have major responsibility for the communication activities and make recommendations for involvement projects to management. Let's look at some examples of both kinds of community relations programs.

Communication Activities in the Community

Before the agreement to break up the Bell Telephone system in 1982, AT&T and its member companies had what was perhaps the most extensive community relations program in the United States. (The network will probably remain after the Bell System is split into several autonomous companies.) Community relations is essential to AT&T because of its size and the fact that it does business in 10,000 communities throughout the United States. Its employees live and work in almost every large metropolitan area of the United States.[4]

In a 1975 speech, Edward M. Block, AT&T's vice president for public relations, said, in essence, that community relations provides a mechanism for local managers and employees to communicate with people in the community in which they work—to prevent them from "delegating public relations to the public relations department." The AT&T Community Relations Guide defines community relations as "public relations at the community level . . . knowing and meeting the needs and expectations of all segments of the community as they relate to the company."

In his speech, Block described the communication objectives of community relations even more explicitly—and in terms that are clearly two-way symmetric. The purpose of community relations, he said, is to:

Sense how customers perceive our service. And to give them a sense we really want to know.

Sense how customers perceive the whole of our business—our policies and our practices, our people, our rates, our character.

Stay on top of complaints and criticisms.

Involve all employees in the process of representing the company to the public—and vice versa. And by so doing, to build employee understanding—and pride—in the importance of what they do and, most especially, in the importance of their roles, individually, in giving good service.

Provide customers timely information about matters of interest and significance, always with special attention to matters of local interest.

Bell Telephone companies implement their community relations program through community relations teams in each local community. Teams consist of both managerial and nonmanagerial employees—not public relations specialists—who volunteer for the teams. A community relations specialist from the public relations department works with the teams—to train, assist, and evaluate them.

There may be only one team in a small community, and several teams in each of the urban and suburban communities of a large metropolitan area.

The activities of the teams vary somewhat from one Bell company to another, but generally their activities include:

Local media relations. Headquarters media relations specialists cannot deal with local media in all the communities served by the company. Thus, the community re-

lations team works with local media for coverage of community projects and issues.

Employee newsletters. Many teams produce internal newsletters to inform employees of their activities, what employees are doing in the community, and community problems.

Company talks. Employees give talks to local civic groups, business and professional clubs, schools, and other organizations.

Company-sponsored memberships. The company pays the dues and expenses of employees that it sponsors as members of key local organizations.

Exhibits, displays, open houses, tours, film showings. Teams sponsor these activities to disseminate information about the company to residents of the community.

Participation in community activities. Teams participate in special community

Most companies associated with the Bell System have a community relations team for each community served by the companies. Teams, composed of management and nonmanagement employees, meet regularly to plan programs for community leaders and other members of the community. (Courtesy Southwestern Bell Telephone Company Public Relations Department)

events, programs to clean up a park, or a fund-raising drive. The teams encourage all employees to volunteer for, and participate in, community activities.

Dialogue sessions with community leaders and groups. Community leaders are invited to a group session to talk about the performance of the telephone company in each community and the problems that may need to be resolved.

Community leader interviews. Teams make up a list of important community leaders. Individual team members personally interview each of these community leaders.

Depending on the community, some of these community relations activities fit each of the four models of public relations. The majority of the community participation activities are "expressive" activities that fit the press agent/publicity model. The open houses, tours, talks, and company-sponsored memberships are typical of the public-information model. The dialogue sessions and community leader interviews are two-way activities—sometimes symmetric and sometimes asymmetric.

We will come back to the AT&T program later in this chapter to discuss research on the effectiveness of these activities, research that showed the two-way symmetric activities to be the most effective in meeting community relations objectives.

Community Relations at Ford and General Motors • In a study of the community relations activities of the Ford Motor Company and General Motors in Michigan, sociologist Paul Mott found programs much like those of AT&T.[5] Both companies have local community relations teams made up of management personnel in each community in which the company has a factory. The teams are coordinated by regional community relations specialists and can call on corporate specialists for advice on unusual community problems.

According to Mott, the Ford program was the most extensive. It included expressive—"goodwill"—activities, such as donating used motors to automobile shops in local schools and donating cars for driver education. In addition, Ford loaned films to local groups, maintained a speakers' bureau, held a visitors' day at the factories, invited political leaders to lunch at the factory, and coordinated the speeches given by executives.

Ford also encouraged its employees to engage in civic activities, gave annual awards to employees for civic work, and permitted leaves of absence to employees elected to political office. Each committee also did an annual community "climate" study to identify problems in the local community.

The General Motors committees concentrated on monitoring local political activities for signs of problems that could affect the company. Any problems identified were reported to the appropriate department of the company for action.

Some Further Examples • Many other organizations engage in similar communication activities in the community:

The Pennwalt Corporation's *Community Relations Manual* describes the following community relations activities: employee communication, relations with local media, community relations during an emergency, communication with local government, special events, speakers, and charitable contributions.

The Champion International Corporation lists the following community relations activities in its *Public Affairs Guide*: tours, open houses, speeches, booklets, local advertising, participation in local events, employee participation in service organizations, sponsoring dues and memberships, and school and university relations.

Champion International also has a "white paper" program that it uses whenever it decides to move a plant and that move has considerable impact on the community. Champion prepares a white paper to explain the move, its timing, and the reasons for the move. Employees, community leaders, the media, and elected officials receive the paper. Champion International prepares a similar white paper whenever it plans to build a facility in a new community—a paper based on a "comprehensive sociological and political audit of the area."[6]

The National Institutes of Health holds an annual Medicine for the Layman lecture series in which NIH specialists give lectures on its campus to people in the Washington, D.C., community. The East Liverpool (Ohio) City Hospital holds a similar community education program.[7]

Community-Involvement Projects

In addition to these communication activities, many organizations actively participate in projects to improve the communities in which they have facilities. Organizations may encourage employees to participate in community groups or to run for political office—as described in the previous section. Or they may make financial contributions to community groups and charitable organizations.[8]

The American Paper Institute's *Public Affairs Leader's Manual*, for example, suggests that its member firms, at the local level, engage in corporate philanthropy, employee volunteer activities, and political and civic activities.

Organizations also help to rebuild urban centers, provide summer jobs for teenagers, offer job training, help the elderly, support minority businesses, plan a civic center, or support the schools. Many business firms loan their management specialists or technicians to government agencies to help solve community problems or to schools as special resource people.

Sometimes major organizations form community coalitions to rebuild a city. The Illinois Bell Telephone Company, for example, was one of twenty-five industry, labor, education, and religious groups to join a coalition to rebuild East St. Louis, Illinois.[9] Major corporations have also been notably involved in such coalitions in Minneapolis and Pittsburgh.[10]

Many organizations become involved in their local communities because of a sense of social responsibility and not because they believe their own well-being is involved. (The lists of organizational social responsibilities in Chapter 3, for example, included community relations.) When organizations participate for that reason, they recognize tertiary organizational responsibilities—responsibilities that do not result from primary organizational functions or from the secondary consequences of organizational behaviors. The American Paper Institute's *Public Affairs Manual* states, for example, that corporations must accept responsibility for the well-being of the community.

Most organizations participate in the community, however, because they realize that a strong community helps them to be a stronger organization. Employees will be more satisfied if they live in a desirable community, and better employees can be attracted to work there. Employees working in highly constrained job situations also become more satisfied with their job if the organization helps them to use their talents in the community.

In addition, an enlightened political system makes it easier for an organization to work with that system and provides better public services. Better schools produce better prospective employees. Crime and violence, a poor system of public transportation, or restrictive local regulations all make it difficult for an organization to perform its basic economic or social functions in a community.

These advantages of community participation take us into a discussion of the publics and the objectives of community relations.

OBJECTIVES AND PUBLICS

In the previous section, we quoted AT&T vice president Edward Block's description of the two-way symmetric purpose of community relations: sensing how customers perceive the company and its service; involving employees in two-way communication with community publics; and providing customers with timely local information. Quite clearly, Block is saying that the objective of community relations is the communication objective that we defined in Chapter 6.

In the same speech, Block went on to say that he would not necessarily expect changes in attitude or behavior from community relations:

> . . . you won't sell everyone. You won't convert everyone. To expect to is unrealistic. But don't be discouraged. Because making converts—and you will make many—is not the only index of success. The very process of personal, local, face-to-face communication is what's important.

Most organizations do expect long-term changes in the community that will benefit them, however. Champion International's *Public Affairs Handbook,* for example, states that community relations will have the following benefits for the company, some of which fit the communication objective and others the attitude and behavior objectives:

> Fair, nondiscriminatory taxes.
>
> An open forum in the halls of local government when it is time to present Champion's point of view or to make special requests.
>
> Local rules and ordinances that are not arbitrary or unreasonable.
>
> A ready pool of eager workers—people prefer to be employed by a good company.
>
> A sincere amount of goodwill that the company can bank on in times of adversity or economic downturn.

An early-warning source of information concerning community developments that may impact the company.

The communication objective clearly is reasonable for a community relations program. The extent to which the other objectives are reasonable depends upon the nature of the community and the publics in it.

What Are the Community Publics?

Most community relations specialists talk loosely about communicating with community leaders and community residents. That would assume that communities are a single, homogeneous public that has an identifiable group of leaders. Champion International is more specific about its community publics. Its manual lists:

> Our employees and their families.
>
> Local news media.
>
> Community opinion molders and thought leaders.
>
> Elective and other governmental officials.
>
> Local business, civic, and service organizations.
>
> Advocacy or special-interest groups.
>
> The public at large.
>
> Our customers, if any have a presence in the plant area.

This list suggests that Champion International—and most other organizations—want to communicate with community publics that fit the four organizational linkages described in Chapter 7:

> Enabling linkage—local government—especially key officials.
>
> Functional linkage—local employees and customers.
>
> Normative linkage—other local organizations with common interests, such as business, civic, and service organizations.
>
> Diffused linkage—activist publics at the local level that impact upon the organization (especially their leaders).

We can conceptualize the publics for a community relations program if we think of an organization as one subsystem of a community system. How an organization interacts with other community subsystems and what effects it can have on the other subsystems vary with the structure of the community.

Social scientists have researched community structure extensively. Let's look at the implications of that research for identifying community publics and for choosing reasonable objectives for community relations programs aimed at those publics.

Research on Community Structure

The question of what holds a community together has interested sociologists and political scientists since the early 1920s. In the 1950s and 1960s, that interest reached a peak and polarized researchers into two camps:

> Those who believed a power elite controlled communities.

> Those who believed control was decentralized to many different groups and interests.

Theories of community structure provide near mirror images to the theories of organizational management that we discussed in the previous chapter. Many researchers believed communities were highly structured; others believed them to be less structured.

Although there is by no means a consensus today, community researchers now seem to accept a contingency theory of community power. That theory states that some communities fit the centralized model and others the decentralized model—contingent upon several community characteristics.

The "Power Elite" vs. Pluralism • The earliest studies of American communities concentrated on social class as the force that organizes communities.[11] The most famous of these studies was W. Lloyd Warner's research on Yankee City (Newburyport, Massachusetts)[12] and Robert and Helen Lynd's research on Middletown (Muncie, Indiana).[13] Later, C. Wright Mills wrote *The Power Elite*, a book that tied the local ruling class into a national military-industrial complex.[14]

Social class had only limited value for explaining the organization of American communities, however, and subsequent research concentrated more upon an economic and political power structure. In 1953 and 1961, two classic studies were published that established competing models of community structure.

Floyd Hunter published his study of a southern city he called Regional City (Atlanta) in 1953.[15] Hunter identified members of the power structure using a new research technique he called the "reputational" approach. Before that time, researchers had used a "positional" approach to identify members of the power structure. With the positional approach, the researcher identified community leaders as people in positions of power—such as mayors or councilmen. The reputational approach, in contrast, did not assume that people in power occupy formal positions of power. Economic elites, for example, could control a community without ever holding a formal position. To discover these informal elites, the researcher asked a panel of knowledgeable "judges" to make a list of people they think have power in the community.

Hunter identified forty men who constituted a pyramid of power in Atlanta, many of whom were local business leaders. Although he found several pyramids for different local issues, he found one to be preeminent for many issues. One elite power structure, Hunter concluded, did indeed control Atlanta.

In 1961, Robert Dahl published a study of New Haven, Connecticut, that presented the opposite picture of an American community.[16] Dahl took issue with Hunter's reputational approach. He argued that community leaders should be identified by their participation in community decision making, not by their reputation for power.

Dahl used a "decisional" method to determine who had influenced actual community decisions. He found the community to be much more *pluralistic* than had Hunter. Different people had been influential in different decisions, and no single power structure had been involved in all of the decisions.

The Contingency Theory Emerges • In the early 1960s, there was much "sound and fury" in the debate between the elitists and the pluralists—to the extent that there were many more ad hominem remarks (attacks on the researchers) than new ideas.[17]

At that time, other researchers began to wonder whether the academic fields of the researchers or the method they used predetermined the results. John Walton, for example, examined thirty-nine studies of sixty-five communities, most of which had been conducted by followers of Hunter and Dahl.[18] He concluded that sociologists more often found an elite power structure and political scientists a pluralistic structure. However, he also found that sociologists were more likely to use the reputational method, political scientists, the decisional method. And researchers who used the reputational method generally found an elite structure; those who used the decisional method, a pluralistic structure.

However, Walton then looked at additional case studies of communities that had been studied by researchers outside this central core of advocates of one position or another—bringing his sample of communities to 166. Then he found that discipline or method made little difference in the results. Instead, he found that the extent to which power was centralized in a community depended upon structural characteristics of the community—such as population size, presence of a reform government, or absentee ownership of major business firms.

Thus, as so often occurs in scientific controversies, the solution to the argument between elitists and pluralists was that both were right. Some communities have a highly centralized power structure, others a more pluralistic structure. Like organizations, communities develop a structure that works best in their environment.

Community researchers then began to do studies of large numbers of communities rather than case studies of single communities.[19] These studies have allowed them to identify the characteristics of centralized and pluralistic communities.

Aiken found, for example, that:

Older, northern cities tend to have a decentralized power structure.

Cities with more absentee-owned business firms (such as large corporations with plants or offices in the community) have more dispersed power.

Cities with a decentralized power structure are more heterogeneous—with more ethnic groups and a larger working class.[20]

In addition, Mott found that communities have more "centers of power"—more publics—when they have:

A larger population.

Diverse ethnic groups. | Indianapolis

High in-migration.

High economic diversity.

Many self-conscious social classes.[21]

Community Relations Should Vary by Degree of Pluralism • The bottom line of over fifty years of research on community power, therefore, is that communities vary in the extent to which they are pluralistic. Community relations programs should be contingent upon the degree to which a community is more or less pluralistic—in much the same way that structured and unstructured organizations require a different kind of employee relations program.

Community Pluralism
and Community Relations

One of the most extensive programs of research on communication in communities with different degrees of pluralism has been conducted by a team of researchers at the University of Minnesota—Phillip Tichenor, Clarice Olien, and George Donohue.[22] Although their major purpose was to explain the role of the media in more and less pluralistic communities, the research tells us much about the publics in different communities and the appropriate objectives for communication with those publics. Thus, we can make the following generalizations from research of the Minnesota group and related community research.

There are more publics in a pluralistic community. As a result, there is more conflict in the community, along with a greater diversity of opinions. Thus, an organization will find it difficult to please all publics in a pluralistic community. It can communicate with all publics, but it cannot expect all publics to agree. Likewise, community participation projects will not please all publics in a pluralistic community.

Less-pluralistic communities value stability, more-pluralistic communities change. Thus, community relations programs that communicate expressive symbols of shared values, such as parades or community ceremonies, will be more effective in the less-pluralistic community—just as expressive, human relations messages are most effective in the more-structured organization.

In less-pluralistic communities, the function of political leaders is to maintain the status quo; in more-pluralistic communities, to mediate conflicts between diverse publics. Neither set of political leaders, therefore, can be expected to change the community after contact with community relations representatives.

Community leaders are more cosmopolitan than other community residents in a less-pluralistic community. They dominate the community but are not typical residents. Frequently, they are more aware of national issues than local issues. As a result, community leaders are less-accurate sources of community opinion in less-pluralistic communities than in more-pluralistic communities.

Nonpolitical community leaders—leaders of nongovernment publics—have influence across issue areas in less-pluralistic communities (more control, as in Hunter's Atlanta study). Nonpolitical leaders are specialized to issue areas in more-pluralistic communities. Thus, community relations contacts will have broader influence in less-pluralistic communities than in more-pluralistic communities.

Media are more likely to reinforce the status quo and to ignore conflict in less-pluralistic communities and are more likely to report conflict and to cover more community issues in more-pluralistic communities. Thus, more publicity and more favorable publicity can be expected from expressive community relations activities in less-pluralistic than in more-pluralistic communities. The media also will seek more access to the organization in more-pluralistic communities.

Rural vs. Urban vs. Suburban • The extent to which a community is more- or less-pluralistic varies fairly systematically with size and the degree of rural or urban character of the community. Many community relations programs that were designed for rural communities—especially those that emphasize expressive communication activities and involvement projects such as open houses, participation in parades, or sponsorship of athletic teams—fail dismally in urban and suburban communities that are more pluralistic.

Remember the general rule that press agentry/publicity and two-way asymmetric community relations work better in a less-pluralistic community, two-way symmetric community relations work better in a more-pluralistic community.

Also remember that:

Rural communities, suburbs made up primarily of one ethnic group, and suburbs whose residents work and do business in the suburb rather than in a central city tend to be low on pluralism.

Older, industrial cities with diverse ethnic groups, large numbers of blacks, and other minorities tend to be high on pluralism.

Cities or suburbs with homogeneous populations tend to be low on pluralism.

Residential suburbs (whose residents work elsewhere) have large numbers of residents with professional occupations and tend to be high on pluralism. Frequently, however, these residents do not feel involved in the residential community and perceive their profession or employer as their major community.

Absentee Ownership and Community Structure

One type of community relations program needs some attention before we move on—that of the major national corporation in communities other than its headquarters location. The early community power studies generally found that local businesspeople play an important role in the power structure or in the decisions made in a community.

In many communities, however, the key businesspeople do not have a primary connection with the local community because they are affiliated with a major national corporation—such as General Motors and Ford in Ypsilanti, Michigan.[23] These representatives of absentee owners supposedly give their primary allegiance to the national corporation and not to the local community—because the company may move them from community to community. Theoretically, these outside businesspeople should not get involved in local decision making. We know

from the discussion in this chapter, however, that major national corporations take great interest in local community relations, and several community studies show the same.

Many social scientists picture the community relations activities of large organizations as a sinister force in community affairs—generally in press agent or two-way asymmetric terms. For example, there is the study of a southern metropolitan area of 200,000 people, which the researchers called Bigtown:

> There exists in Bigtown, as elsewhere in the nation, an almost incredible preoccupation with "public relations"—i.e., a constant and vociferous campaign designed to apprise the populace of the magnanimity and generosity of the corporations. . . . In the same way, the corporations are contributing money and time to community projects as a favored means of creating and reinforcing a favorable public image of the corporation. . . . Not only does the corporation dictate the terms, but it decides what social values are to be implemented by its choice of projects and the policies followed by its agents.[24]

A National Elite Network? • G. William Domhoff analyzed the data from Dahl's New Haven study and claimed to have identified a national elite network that controls local communities through absentee ownership, social connections, and interlocking memberships of corporate boards.[25] Other researchers, however, have found that absentee corporations dilute the local power structure—make it more pluralistic—because they involve themselves only in community problems that affect the company.[26]

Absentee organizations may try to influence the community, but they do not attempt to control local politics as much as would local economic elites. Sociologist Paul Mott, for example, found that even when Ford or General Motors employees were elected to office, the company could not control their behavior.[27]

Instrumental community relations activities of large absentee corporations do, with little doubt, benefit the community. However, community researcher Terry Clark found that absentee-owned corporations "withdraw from instrumental community activities and apply their talents to more consummatory [expressive] activities," such as charity, educational, and cultural activities.[28] The more "immobile the enterprise," however, the more likely Clark found it would also participate in instrumental activities. In systems terms, the more the company is involved with other subsystems of the community, the more it will use community relations to change or improve the community for its own benefit.

Instrumental activities help communities the most, but even those organizations who use expressive community relations can benefit communities. The absentee organization makes donations, sponsors Little League teams, or sponsors art shows. These activities may not change communities much, but they don't harm them either.

A Study of Community Relations Effects

In 1979 and 1981, Grunig conducted two studies of community relations teams in the Bell System as part of AT&T's efforts to evaluate its separate public relations functions (see also Chapter 9 for an overview of this project).[29] These studies show clearly the importance of:

Two-way symmetric community relations.

The communication objective, rather than the attitude or behavior objective.

Aiming community relations programs at community-interest group publics and their leaders.

Instrumental rather than expressive community participation.

A National Study of CR Teams • As you will recall from the discussion above, Bell System companies carry out community relations through teams of nonpublic-relations employees—teams that are advised and supported by the public relations department. Thus, Grunig designed the first study to determine whether a national sample of community relations teams performed differently when they got more support from the public relations department.

The research showed that public relations support did make a difference. And it showed what activities are typical of the most effective teams.

This first study compared how often the teams with more and less PR support used each of the community relations activities typical in the Bell System. The teams with less PR support concentrated their activities into the easiest and most traditional categories. They participated in a lot of civic ceremonies, showed films, held open houses, and participated in simple community-service projects. These low-support teams also did not plan and evaluate the activities in which they participated.

The teams with more PR support, in contrast, sponsored fewer activities but planned them better. Most importantly, however, these better teams concentrated on two-way symmetric activities. They were more likely to interview community leaders, hold group dialogue sessions with community leaders, and to pass the results of those interviews and sessions on to management.

Secondly, this study showed that the teams with more public relations support concentrated their efforts on contacts with community leaders—not on disseminating information to the community-at-large. Also, when the poorer teams interviewed community leaders, they most often inter-viewed other businesspeople. The better teams interviewed more nontraditional leaders of important community-interest groups, such as consumerists, minorities, or government.

Effects of Active Community Relations Teams • After establishing what the most active community relations teams did, Grunig designed a second study to determine the effects of their efforts. The first study had shown that teams supported by the public relations department met the objective of communication with leaders of community-interest groups more than did the teams with less support. The second study measured whether communication with these community leaders also accomplished the message-retention, message-acceptance, attitude, and behavior objectives. (Some questions from this study are shown in Chapter 9.)

Grunig chose two communities that had active community relations teams and two that had less active teams. He then interviewed twenty-five community leaders in each community, asking them how often they had participated in the different community relations activities typical in the Bell System—to measure the communication objective—and asking them questions to measure the other four objectives.

The results confirmed those of the first study. Just as the more-active teams reported more contacts with community leaders in the first study, so the community leaders reported more contact with the active teams in the second study. The active teams also had more contact with the nontraditional leaders, many of whom could be expected to be negative toward the telephone company.

Just as in the first study, community leaders were more likely to report having experienced two-way symmetric communication activities with the active teams. With less-active teams, community leaders reported more contact with one-way activities designed to disseminate the company's position, such as open houses, tours, talks, or company-sponsored memberships.

When Grunig looked at the effects of community relations, he found that community relations seldom changed attitudes or pro-duced behaviors that supported the company. In fact, the community leaders who had contact with the active teams were less favorable toward the company than those who had less contact. The contact didn't make them negative, however. The leaders were found to be more negative only because the teams had been brave enough to contact community leaders who were already negative.

Quite importantly, however, Grunig found some evidence that the community-leader interviews reduced the number of negative behaviors by community leaders. The negative community leaders did not go out and support the company after hearing its position. But fewer of them went out and actively opposed the company.[30] Most community leaders understood the company's position better after the interview. Also, they directed most of their behaviors toward the company, expressing approval or disapproval to company representatives, rather than by expressing dissatisfaction to political leaders, opposing the company in policy or regulatory conflicts, or refusing to use company services.

The second study also showed that community relations activities other than interviews and dialogue sessions had little effect on the community leaders. Generally, the teams used the speeches, open houses, and similar activities to disseminate noncontroversial information on such topics as new technology or services. Most of the community leaders already had heard the information, and few disliked the message.

In one case, however, discussion of a controversial topic in company talks—a rate increase—increased retention of the company's message, but did not make the attitudes and behaviors of the community leaders more supportive. These results suggest that an organization could use many of the traditional community relations techniques to discuss controversial community topics and, as a result, increase community knowledge of its positions.

Community-Participation Projects • Finally, Grunig asked the community leaders to evaluate the two most recent community-involvement projects sponsored by each team. Generally, these projects had been expressive activities, such as visiting a home for the elderly. Few leaders interviewed criticized these projects, but neither could they get enthusiastic about them.

Other data suggested, however, that instrumental community projects would get more appreciation from community leaders. Leaders were asked to name the three most important community problems and to rate the responsibility the telephone company should have in solving them. Generally, the leaders rated the company's responsibility higher than they rated the actual contribution of the company in solving these problems.

Some Conclusions

From these two studies, Grunig reached the following conclusions about the objectives and publics of community relations:

Community relations should be a two-way symmetric communication process, a dialogue rather than a monologue.

Community relations personnel should seek out diverse community leaders who may represent constituencies that do not necessarily support the organization.[31]

Community relations personnel should communicate about controversial topics.

Community relations personnel should develop and maintain a mechanism for channeling information, especially about controversial topics, back to management.

Don't expect community relations to result in active support or even passive acceptance of organizational positions.

Use community relations as a mechanism to help the organization solve important community problems.

Formative Research Through the Community Case Method

This chapter should have made clear to you that a community relations program cannot be planned adequately unless the practitioner knows the following information:

Extent to which a community is pluralistic or centralized.

Different kinds of community leaders in the community.

Controversial issues and problems in the community.

Linkages of an organization with publics and other organizations in the community.

Community researchers have long used, and greatly improved, the case-study method to gather this information. It is a method that can be used for formative community relations research.

The Group Attitudes Corporation research subsidiary of Hill and Knowlton, for example, recently began to use the case-study method instead of standard opinion surveys for community research. Group Attitudes sends a researcher into a community for two to three days of intensive research, using methods essentially the same as those described in this chapter. Walter Lindenmann, the Hill and Knowlton senior vice president who directs Group Attitudes, has described how such research was done for an electric utility:

Our procedure was for a researcher to live in a community under study—staying in a local hotel or motel—and to utilize—as appropriate—observation, participation, role-playing, and informal field-interviewing as tools for fact- and opinion-gathering. The researchers spent their time—working around the clock—participating in community activities (such as attending civic and business group meetings); observing events (such as the disruptions in a neighborhood when a power company work crew is active); carrying out a number of totally unstructured, snowball technique depth interviews with community influentials; and doing content analyses of items appearing in the local media pertaining to the energy issues under study.[32]

Lindenmann also decribed three kinds of publics Group Attitudes researchers found in a community he called Pleasant Gardens, a community in the metropolitan area of ''Metropolis'':

The Old Guard—a circle of business influentials who manage most of the financial interests of the community.

Younger, more cosmopolitan individuals more oriented to Metropolis than to the community in which they live.

''A circle of influentials who appear to worry only about the quality of life on the neighborhood level, as well as circles of influence among the blacks and the Spanish-speaking population.''

Each group, Lindenmann concluded, required a different communication strategy by Hill and Knowlton's utility client.

Research on Community Publics Using the Situational Theory

You have learned that more-pluralistic communities have a greater number of publics and more diverse publics than less-pluralistic communities. Grunig's research for AT&T also shows the importance of symmetric communication with leaders of each of these diverse publics—although his study did not compare community relations in pluralistic and less-pluralistic communities.

Research also suggests that publics that arise around general community problems—such as urban renewal, tax changes, or flood control—will not be the same as the publics that arise from organizational consequences on some members of the community—such as layoffs, construction, or disruption of neighborhoods.[33]

Stamm and Fortini-Campbell found that community residents who most often read a community newspaper personally *identified* with the residential community (essentially the same thing as *problem recognition* in the Grunig situational model) and were involved in community activities (*level of involvement* in the situational model). Because Stamm and Fortini-Campbell's concepts were so similar to the situational model, the results of their research suggest which people are likely to be members of active publics for an organization's community-participation projects.

Research also shows that different publics will arise when an organization has consequences on some, but not all, members of a community. Stamm and Fortini-Campbell found, for example, that involvement in ''social group communities'' in a metropolitan area—as opposed to the residential community—did not correlate with readership of the community newspaper.

''Consequential'' Publics of a Community Hospital • Grunig was able to show more precisely the kinds of publics that arise from organization-community linkages. In a study of a suburban community hospital, he showed that specialized community publics will develop from the involvements, problems, and constraints people have with an organization—as the situational theory predicts is possible.

Grunig surveyed 139 residents of Prince Georges County, Maryland, to determine publics of the county's hospital, The Prince Georges Hospital and Medical Center.[34] He did so by asking questions to measure the concepts of the situational theory for seven situations related to hospital service—choosing a hospital, rising hospital costs, inability to pay for a hospital, a shortage of doctors in the county, delay in the emergency room, treatment of cancer, and dealing with an aged person needing medical care.

Statistical analysis revealed four hospital publics in the community. On two of the issues—rising hospital costs and delay in the emergency room—all four publics had a high level of involvement and problem recognition, but they felt constrained from doing anything about the situations. The results showed that the hospital had to communicate with everyone in the community about these involving linkages, because the high level of constraint could result in frustrated and angry—but active—publics.

On the other issues, however, the publics differed. The striking finding was that lower- and middle-income people, not elite members of the community, made up the most active hospital publics.

An older white-collar public—made up mostly of relatively wealthy, professional people—felt involved and recognized most of the situations as problems. But it also felt constrained about doing anything, even though it felt it knew what to do about the issues. It also was more likely to use private hospitals rather than this public hospital. As a result, this public would not actively seek information from the hospital.

A younger white-collar public did not feel involved in any of the hospital situations, except the costs and emergency room issues. It was too young to be concerned about anything but emergency hospital care, and thus it would not communicate much with the hospital.

A low-income public fit the constrained-behavior or fatalistic-behavior category on all issues, but felt involved in four of the seven issues. Those results showed that, in contrast to what might have been expected, low-income people were a potentially active public for the hospital to deal with—especially if it could remove the constraints that prevent the poor from having an impact on the hospital.

A blue-collar public was the most active public. Members of that public recognized problems and felt involved in all seven situations and felt constrained in only two.

As a public hospital, Prince Georges Hospital was involved more with the low- and middle-income publics than with the more wealthy white-collar publics. These two publics, then, were its most important community publics—not the elite of the community. It's interesting to note that three years after this study, the county executive tried to sell the hospital to private interests—a task made easier at the political level by the lack of an elite public for the hospital.

Two other significant findings came out of the hospital study.

The most important source of information about the hospital for community publics was other people—particularly people who had used the hospital—not the media or hospital publications.

In contrast to what hospital administrators expected, the hospital did not have what the administrators called a ''negative image'' among its publics. As the situational theory would predict, the elite, nonactive public had no image—held very little information—about the hospital. The active publics were about even in holding positive and negative evaluations of the hospital—it all depended on their personal experiences with the hospital.

EVALUATION OF COMMUNITY RELATIONS

A manager of a community relations program could measure each of the five objectives defined in Chapter 9 to evaluate a community relations program. The research that Grunig did on the AT&T community relations program, however, shows how to substantially narrow what the manager needs to measure.

That research showed that the communication and message retention objectives should be stressed and that a community relations programs should be aimed at leaders of diverse community interest groups. According to the research, the attitude and behavior objectives seldom can be achieved, although managers of press agentry and two-way asymmetric programs may still want to measure them—as Grunig did in the AT&T study. The research also showed that community relations can reduce negative behaviors and direct them away from government and toward the organization. Thus, the number of negative behaviors can be used to evaluate community relations.

After completing the AT&T studies, Grunig suggested that the following measures—mostly to be collected in a survey of community leaders—be used as an ongoing evaluation of a community relations program. The leaders surveyed would differ in more-pluralistic and in less-pluralist communities, and they could be identified using the positional, reputational, and decisional approaches, as well as the social network approach described in footnote 31. The nature of the local interest groups could be determined using the situational theory, as in the Prince Georges Hospital study.

To evaluate communication programs, Grunig suggested measuring:

The number of local governmental officials reporting contact with community relations representatives.

The number of members of local publics—interest groups or "constituencies"—reporting contact with community relations representatives.

The number of community leaders who report having discussed controversial or policy issues with community relations representatives—measured with open-end questions on what was discussed during contacts with representatives.

The number of community leaders who understand the organization's position on controversial or policy questions. Questions to measure message retention from Chapter 9 would be used.

The number of community leaders who report giving information to community relations representatives about service or community problems. Another open-end question would be used.

The number of organizational managers who report having received information about service or community problems from community relations representatives.

The number of managers reporting that they have made changes in policy or behavior as a result of the information received about service or community problems.

The number of negative behaviors reported by community leaders. (See questions to measure behavior in Chapter 9.)

The percentage of negative behaviors directed toward the organization rather than through outside groups or agencies.

To evaluate community involvement projects, Grunig suggested:

Ratings by community leaders of the extent to which the organization has helped to solve the three most important community problems defined by each leader—as measured in Grunig's second study.

NOTES

1. Community sociologist Terry Clark has used these same two terms to describe community relations activities of business firms. Terry N. Clark, *Community Structure and Decision-Making: Comparative Analyses* (San Francisco: Chandler, 1968), p. 102.
2. Wilbur J. Peak, "Community Relations," in Philip Lesly (ed.), *Lesly's Public Relations Handbook*, 2d ed. (Englewood Cliffs, N.J.: Prentice-Hall, 1978), pp. 64–79.
3. Jessie Bernard, *The Sociology of Community* (Glenview, Ill.: Scott, Foresman, 1973), pp. 185–188.
4. Edward M. Block, vice president for public relations, AT&T, speech to a joint conference of the Public Affairs Council and the Public Relations Society of America, May 20, 1982.

5. Paul E. Mott, "The Role of the Absentee-Owned Corporation in the Changing Community," in Michael Aiken and Paul E. Mott (eds.), *The Structure of Community Power* (New York: Random House, 1970), pp. 170–179.

6. Robert S. Colodzin, vice president for external affairs, Champion International Corporation, "Redefining the Role of the Corporation in the Community," speech to the Public Affairs Council 44th Roundtable for Public Affairs Officers, Washington, D. C., November 18, 1981.

7. Dolores A. Sutula, "Community Education as a Communications Tool," *Public Relations Journal* 37 (February 1981):27–28.

8. Examples can be found in Bryan Putman, "How to Build a Community Relations Program," *Public Relations Journal* 36 (February 1980):28–31.

9. Block.

10. For further examples, see The Conference Board, "Corporations in the Community: How Six Major Firms Conduct Community Participation Programs," Research Bulletin 103, 1981.

11. For an overview of these studies, see Bernard, pp. 51–89.

12. W. Lloyd Warner and Paul S. Lunt, *The Social Life of a Modern Community* (New Haven, Conn.: Yale University Press, 1941), the first of several volumes on the Yankee City research.

13. Robert S. Lynd and Helen Merrill Lynd, *Middletown* (New York: Harcourt, Brace, 1929) and *Middletown in Transition* (New York: Harcourt, Brace, 1937).

14. C. Wright Mills, *The Power Elite* (New York: Oxford University Press, 1956).

15. Floyd Hunter, *Community Power Structure: A Study of Decision Makers* (Chapel Hill: University of North Carolina Press, 1953).

16. Robert A. Dahl, *Who Governs?* (New Haven, Conn.: Yale University Press, 1961).

17. Terry Nichols Clark, *Community Power and Policy Outputs: A Review of Urban Research* (Beverly Hills, Calif.: Sage, 1973), p. 75.

18. John Walton, "Discipline, Method and Community Power: A Note on the Sociology of Knowledge," *American Sociological Review* 31 (1966):684–689. For summaries, see Clark, *Community Power and Policy Outputs*, pp. 75–76 or Bernard, pp. 78–79.

19. One of the most extensive comparative studies of communities was Terry N. Clark, "Community Structure, Decision-Making, Budget Expenditures, and Urban Renewal in 51 American Communities," *American Sociological Review* 33 (1968):576–593.

20. Michael Aiken, "The Distribution of Community Power: Structural Bases and Social Consequences," in Aiken and Mott, pp. 487–525.

21. Paul E. Mott, "Configurations of Power," in Aiken and Mott, pp. 85–100.

22. Phillip J. Tichenor, George A. Donohue, and Clarice N. Olien, *Community Conflict and the Press* (Beverly Hills, Calif.: Sage, 1980). For a shorter summary of the research, see Phillip J. Tichenor, George A. Donohue, and Clarice N. Olien, "Community Research and Evaluating Community Relations," *Public Relations Review* 3 (Winter 1977):96–109.

23. Mott, "The Role of the Absentee-Owned Corporation in the Changing Community."

24. Roland J. Pellegrin and Charles H. Coates, "Absentee-Owned Corporations and Community Power Structure," in Aiken and Mott, pp. 163–170.

25. G. William Domhoff, *Who Really Rules?* (New Brunswick, N. J.: Transaction Books, 1978).

26. Robert Mills French, "Economic Change and Community Power Structure: Transition in Cornucopia," in Aiken and Mott, pp. 180–189; Clark, *Community Structure and Decision Making*, p. 102.

27. Mott, "The Role of the Absentee-Owned Corporation in the Changing Community," p. 176.

28. Clark, *Community Structure and Decision Making*, p. 102.

29. Unpublished reports to the Planning Division, Public Relations and Employee Communication Department, AT&T, New York, 1979 and 1981.

30. Mott found evidence of the same result in his case study of Ford and General Motors community relations programs. ". . . the greatest value of their community relations programs rests in what does *not* happen," he concluded. Mott, "The Role of the Absentee-Owned Corporation in the Changing Community", p. 177.

31. Freeman et al. give a helpful description of three kinds of community leaders and how to locate them:

1. Institutional leaders are the heads of government, business, and other formal organizations. They can be located with the positional and reputational methods. They lend prestige to community decisions, but usually do not take an active part in the decision.

2. Effectors are the active participants in decisions. Often they are subordinates to the institutional leaders in government, business, and other organizations. They can be identified with the decisional method.

3. Activists are active in and often hold office in voluntary organizations. Activists usually represent smaller organizations in the community. They participate in decisions, although not as frequently as the Effectors. Their commitment of time and effort, however, can help to shape community affairs. They can be identified by tracing social activities of individuals in volunteer groups.

See Linton C. Freeman, Thomas J. Fararo, Warner Bloomberg, Jr., and Morris H. Sunshine, "Locating Leaders in Local Communities: A Comparison of Some Alternative Approaches," in Aiken and Mott, pp. 340–347.

32. Walter K. Lindenmann, "Use of Community Case Studies in Opinion Research," *Public Relations Review* 6 (Spring 1980):40–50.

33. Keith R. Stamm and Lisa Fortini-Campbell, "Community Ties and Newspaper Use," News Research Report No. 33, American Newspaper Publishers Association (Washington, D.C., Oct. 30, 1981).

34. James E. Grunig, "Defining Publics in Public Relations: The Case of a Suburban Hospital," *Journalism Quarterly* 55 (1978):109–118, 124.

ADDITIONAL READING

Aiken, Michael, and Paul E. Mott (eds.), *The Structure of Community Power* (New York: Random House, 1970).

Bernard, Jessie, *The Sociology of Community* (Glenview, Ill.: Scott, Foresman, 1973).

Clark, Terry N., *Community Structure and Decision-Making: Comparative Analyses* (San Francisco: Chandler, 1968).

Clark, Terry N., *Community Power and Policy Outputs: A Review of Urban Research* (Beverly Hills, Calif.: Sage, 1973).

The Conference Board, "Corporations in the Community: How Six Major Firms Conduct Community Participation Programs," Research Bulletin 103, 1981.

Domhoff, G. William, *Who Really Rules?* (New Brunswick, N. J.: Transaction Books, 1978).

Lindenmann, Walter K., "Use of Community Case Studies in Opinion Research," *Public Relations Review* 6 (Spring 1980):40–50.

Tichenor, Phillip J., George A. Donohue, and Clarice N. Olien, "Community Research and Evaluating Community Relations," *Public Relations Review* 3 (Winter 1977):96–109.

Tichenor, Phillip J., George A. Donohue, and Clarice N. Olien, *Community Conflict and the Press* (Beverly Hills, Calif.: Sage, 1980).

Warren, Roland J., *New Perspectives on the American Community: A Book of Readings*, 3d ed. (Chicago: Rand-McNally, 1976).

14

PUBLIC AFFAIRS AND GOVERNMENT RELATIONS

The 1970s saw a rapid growth in what is generally called the corporate public affairs function—*the activities of an organization to manage its response to political issues and its relationships with governments.*[1] Almost 60 percent of the public affairs programs in existence today were created in the 1970s. Nearly a third were created from 1975 to 1981. The size of staffs and budgets devoted to public affairs has also grown dramatically since 1975.[2]

It's important to establish just what we mean by "public affairs" early in this chapter, because many organizations—especially government agencies and some business firms—use the term as a euphemism for public relations. A 1976 study of "external relations" programs in 176 corporations by the Conference Board—a nonprofit business research organization—showed "public relations" and "public affairs" running dead even as a title for the program—33 percent for public relations and 32 percent for public affairs.[3] O'Dwyer's *Directory of Corporate Communication* (1981), however, showed "public affairs" running a poor third (13 percent) to "public relations" (24 percent) and "corporate communication" (22 percent) in *Fortune* 500 companies.[4]

Most of the changes in this name game have resulted from top management's dissatisfaction with traditional public relations (see also Chapter 4 on professionalism)—which has focused too narrowly on publicity and media relations. In many corporations, the change in name has signaled an expansion of the public relations function from the press agentry/publicity or public-information model to the two-way asymmetric or symmetric model.

Frequently, that expansion has included the merger of several communication units into a single public affairs department. Prudential Insurance, for example:

. . . took its Communications Department, consisting of Public Relations and Advertising as the core, and put them into a Public Affairs Department. It also moved into this department the futurist activity, community relations (consisting of urban affairs and contributions), external environmental monitoring, consumer relations, and an attitudinal research unit. Federal government relations were also moved in from the law department.[5]

Public Relations Broader Than Public Affairs

To corporate executives who have reorganized their organizations in this way, public affairs is a broader function than public relations because it involves all of an organization's contacts with its environment. These managers define public relations narrowly—generally as the dissemination of information to publics. If public relations is defined as it is in this book—as the management of communication between an organization and its publics—then public relations fulfills the broad function executives want. We prefer to reserve the term "public affairs," therefore, for a specialized public policy and government relations program that is managed by the organization's public relations subsystem.

According to the Public Affairs Council, an organization of public affairs executives of major corporations:

> From the date of the establishment of the first public affairs department, there has been continuous—and often fruitless—discussion about distinctions between public relations and public affairs, and the appropriate relationships between the two functions. Perhaps the only thing on which there has been a general consensus is that public affairs tends to be more government relations oriented, and public relations more communications oriented.[6]

A working definition of public affairs, according to the council, is "the management function responsible for interpreting the corporation's non-commercial environment and managing the company's response to those factors"—which is almost identical to our definition of public relations.

The council added that "a more practical, though too restricted, view would be that public affairs usually refers to a company's

activities in political education and government relations"—a working definition that fits our use of the term.

Evolution from Government Relations

Most major corporations—and many other organizations—have had government relations programs within their public relations departments for many years. Usually, their programs provided information to the organization about changes in government that could affect the organization, or they had a lobbyist who pushed the organization's interest in government.

The traditional government relations program was reactive—it waited for government to do something and then either adapted to the government action or tried to stop it. Today, organizations—especially major corporations—have more proactive programs that try to shape policy before government acts. And, to reflect that change, they call the programs "public affairs."

In an article on what it called the recent "public relations invasion of Washington," the *National Journal* described how Washington PR agencies provide "public affairs" counseling to help organizations influence "public policy:"

> The watchwords of the industry in Washington these days are "issues management," "government relations," "issue tracking," and "grassroots coalition building"—not PR.
> To a large extent, this difference in terminology marks some very real distinctions. These days PR techniques are more sophisticated and varied than in the past. More and more, PR firms are laboring outside of Washington to influence legislation. They help to cement alliances of diverse interest groups, contrive conferences to highlight issues, and assist clients in establishing political action committees, all in an effort to direct pressure on legislators from within their own districts.[7]

Most corporations today give top priority to public relations programs that fit into the public affairs area. And they give them top priority not from an altruistic desire to be good citizens, but because of the growing impact that government legislation and regulations have upon their company.[8]

Large business corporations have the largest and most active public affairs and government relations programs. But they are also assisted by such associations as the National Association of Manufacturers, the U. S. Chamber of Commerce, the Business Roundtable, or the American Petroleum Institute.

Nonbusiness associations also have extensive programs, such as the National Rifle Association or the National Education Association. Over 2,500 associations have their headquarters in Washington, mostly because of the importance of public affairs and government relations. Many activist groups of consumerists, minorities, or environmentalists also carry on public affairs work in Washington and throughout the country (see Chapter 15).

In addition, government agencies have "congressional relations" staffs to monitor legislation that affects the agency. State and local governments also maintain programs to communicate with Congress and federal agencies.

Symmetric Policy Debates

What all this adds up to is a large number of organizations bringing their demands to government and mobilizing support for their positions from their publics. Lowi has described the political system that results as "interest group liberalism," in which each group comes to government for help individually.[9] He argues that government responds to each request in sequence and does not think of the cumulative consequences of all requests.

Lowi would be describing the U. S. political system correctly if all organizations were applying the press agentry or two-way symmetric models to their public affairs/government relations programs, and pushing their own programs without bargaining or negotiating. But if organizations approach public affairs symmetrically, "interest-group liberalism" could result in true democracy—as each organization could state its position and then negotiate that interest with competing organizations. Organizations that cannot communicate their positions effectively will receive nothing from government and may be injured by government actions.

Paisley describes the difference between asymmetric and symmetric public affairs campaigns as reactive vs proactive strategies.[10] With reactive campaigns, the "metaphor was war, and the campaigns were conflicts. . . . The strategy of reactive campaigns was to polarize the stakeholders until a drastic solution was inescapable."

With a proactive campaign, "the metaphor was negotiation, and the campaigns are bargaining sessions. The solution can be a compromise":

> In this period of transition from reactive to proactive campaigns, we see big stakeholders—federal agencies, private associations, and corporations—learning the techniques of proactive campaigning first. Their new reasonableness ("come let us reason together") is evident in current campaigns focusing on health care, environmental protection, energy conservation, and so on.

Most organizations that have public affairs programs face dynamic rather than static environments.[11] Thus, they learn quickly that one-way programs (press agentry or public information models) do not work well. They must have a two-way model of public affairs to cope with their environment. The asymmetric model may often work well for the organization. But for the democratic political system to work well, it's clear that most organizations should have symmetric public affairs programs.

Let's look more closely, then, at the specifics of public affairs and government relations programs.

PUBLIC AFFAIRS AND GOVERNMENT RELATIONS PROGRAMS

Major national business corporations generally have the most extensive public affairs and government relations programs. And their programs have been described more often in the public relations and business-policy literature than similar programs in other organizations. Although we will concentrate on corporate programs in this section, keep in mind that most of the corporate programs and techniques have been used by, or can easily be adapted for, other kinds of organizations.

According to John Webster, manager of public affairs programs for the IBM Corporation, the 100 largest corporations generally structure their public affairs programs in one of three ways:

A Washington office interacts with the federal government, but does not carry on other public affairs functions. Usually, it is a part of the public relations department.

A public affairs program located outside Washington conducts research and analyzes issues. It reports to management and writes speeches for management on public affairs. It does not usually report to the Washington group.

Public affairs and government relations are merged, and the joint program is located in the Washington office. The unit reports to management in the same way as the second type of program.[12]

IBM has the third arrangement, as does AT&T. In the case of AT&T, the public affairs department is separate from public relations and is headed by a separate vice president.

The Boston University Study

In 1978, five researchers at Boston University's School of Management formed a Public Affairs Research Group to study corporate public affairs departments. A major project of that research team was a survey of 1,000 firms that had public affairs units, to which 401 firms responded.[13]

The results showed that public affairs centers around two activities—community relations and government relations. (As we saw in the previous chapter, community relations usually is handled by a separate unit, although it has a close relationship to public affairs.) Based on the percentages of respondents who said their unit had responsibility for them, four activities stood out as public affairs functions:

Community relations—84.9 percent.

Government relations—84.2 percent.

Corporate contributions—71.5 percent.

Media relations—70.0 percent.

Fewer than half of the respondents said public affairs had responsibility for public relations activities that normally fall into the jurisdiction of other PR programs: stockholder relations, advertising, consumer affairs, graphics, institutional investor relations, and customer relations. The high percentage naming media relations does not mean that public affairs handles all media relations. Rather, it shows that public affairs specialists frequently work with the media to complement their other activities.

Two other parts of the study provide additional detail on what public affairs units do. First, the following percentages of respondents said they engage in these activities to influence corporate planning:

Identify public issues for corporate attention (92.8 percent).

Set or help set priorities for these issues (78.5 percent).

Identify public issues for department, division, and/or subsidiary attention (74.2 percent).

Set or help set priorities for these issues (64.8 percent).

Provide forecasts of social/political trends to the corporate planning office (74.1 percent).

Provide forecasts of social/political trends to departments, divisions, and/or subsidiaries (73.0 percent).

Review corporate plans for sensitivity to emerging social/political trends (69.1 percent).

Prepare a narrative section regarding future social/political trends, which is included with directions for preparing corporate plans (57.8 percent).

Review department, division, and/or subsidiary plans for sensitivity to emerging social/political trends (55.0 percent).

Techniques Used in Public Affairs • Next, respondents said they used the following techniques to manage emerging issues (with the mean rank in parentheses—5 = most-frequently used, 1 = least frequently used):

Monitor emerging issues (4.1).

Lobby within trade associations (4.0).

Scan to detect emerging issues (3.9).

Communicate company position to managers (3.9).

Lobby at the federal level (3.9).

Lobby at the state/local levels (3.9).

Communicate company position to government agencies (3.9).

Communicate company positions to employees (3.4).

Use issue manager (3.1).

Change company information systems (3.0).

Change company policies (2.9).

Use interdepartmental public affairs issue research committees (2.9).

Communicate company positions to the general public (2.9).

Change company or subunit objectives (2.9).

Communicate company positions to stockholders (2.9).

Change company reward and penalty systems (2.3).

The relative ordering of these activities suggests that the two-way asymmetric model may characterize public affairs programs more than the two-way symmetric model. But the responses that state the company may change as a result of public affairs were near the midpoint of the 5-point scale (3.0)—suggesting that the symmetric model does exist in some of these programs.

What the Public Affairs Council Says

In its 1982 informational brochure, the Public Affairs Council said a typical public affairs department has four major functions, with several subdivisions:

Government relations
　　Federal
　　State
　　Local
Political action
　　Political-action committees
　　Political education
　　Grassroots activities
　　Communications on political issues
Community involvement/corporate responsibility
　　Community relations
　　Philanthropy
　　Social-responsibility programs
　　Volunteerism
International
　　Political risk assessment
　　Monitoring international sociopolitical developments

Educational Background Varies

Public affairs is a public relations specialty in which people trained in public relations usually are complemented by people with other specialties. The Conference Board report on corporate-federal relations showed the three most common backgrounds of public affairs specialists, in order of frequency, to be:

Law.

Public affairs (including those with background in community and social affairs, as well as communications and public relations practitioners).

Government (elected and appointed).

The report added:

The type of person employed to head government relations can provide a clue to the company's government relations philosophy. A company that is communications oriented, and that views the function as one of getting the company's message to legislators, to employees, to stockholders, and other publics, tends to hire a person with experience and training in public affairs, communications, or public relations. Companies more concerned with regulatory matters, or in which government relations grows out of the legal function, typically recruit lawyers. Those becoming more active in issues management are hiring political scientists and economists.[14]

These varied backgrounds do not necessarily suggest that students interested in public affairs work should study law or economics rather than public relations. They do suggest, however, that such students should include work in economics and political science in their public relations studies, and perhaps that they should pursue a joint degree in law and public relations.

With this overview of the public affairs function in mind, then, let's look at some of the specific activities in more detail.

Relations with the Federal Government

The power of the federal government makes it a key enabling linkage for most large corporations (and other kinds of organizations).

Most, therefore, focus their public affairs programs on federal government relations.

Corporations carry on government relations in one of several ways:[15]

Open a Washington government relations office.

Handle the entire Washington operation from the home office and commute to Washington when necessary.

Rely totally on trade associations, such as the National Association of Manufacturers or the U. S. Chamber of Commerce.

Hire Washington-based consultants—legal, public relations, or political/economics firms.

A combination of the above—such as a government relations unit both at home and in Washington, having a Washington office and working with trade associations, and hiring independent consultants to supplement the organization's own staff.

The Boston University study showed how frequently corporations use these different methods:[16]

Trade association (67.8 percent).

Frequent visits to Washington by senior executives (58.4 percent).

Company office in Washington (42.7 percent).

Washington law firm (as needed or on retainer) (38.0 percent).

Washington-based government relations counsel (11.9 percent).

Washington public relations firm (as needed or on retainer) (8.6 percent).

What the Washington Rep Does • Washington representatives work with three areas of government:[17]

Legislative branch—working with key legislators as well as congressional staffs. This is the area in which most government relations units concentrate their efforts.

EXHIBIT **14**–1

Summer 1982

Acid rain and reason

by David Litvin

Editor's note:

Acid rain. The subject generates heated controversy in Congress and in the media. Here, David Litvin, Sohio Federal Government Affairs associate director, gives a status report on the issue. Litvin was with the Kennecott government affairs office in Washington when Sohio and Kennecott merged. In January, the Sohio and Kennecott Washington offices joined forces. Environmental affairs and mining are Litvin's specialties. More commentary on environmental issues is inside this edition of Energy and You.

Emotions are running high in Washington about the little-understood but much-publicized phenomenon known as acid rain.

Few people realize that rain is naturally acidic.

Environmentalists have characterized acid rain as precipitation (rain or snow) which is more acidic than what some scientists consider normal.

Acid rain is frequently said to be related to sulfur dioxide and other emissions from power plants in the Midwest and East. In the atmosphere, these emissions are converted to acids and, some people believe, are transported hundreds of miles to the Northeast, where they fall to earth in precipitation.

Certain areas in the country, particularly in the Northeast, are sensitive to acid rain because the soil does not contain sufficient acid-buffering elements. Acid rain is blamed for reducing, over time, the ability of lakes in the Northeast to support aquatic life. It is believed that excess acidity reaches the lakes through acidic runoff from the surrounding land.

Acid rain is an important environmental issue which has received widespread press coverage. The word "acid" itself seems to signal danger.

However, scientists still disagree on the causes and effects of acid rain. Here are a few of the question marks about acid rain:

- Precipitation may, or may not, be becoming more acidic. Increases and decreases in rain acidity have been measured at the same locations in the U.S. at different times.
- It is not known how much acid rain may be caused by emissions from local sources — for example, from commercial building boilers, home heaters, and autos — and how much may come from emissions transported long distances.
- It's not clear how great a factor nature itself is in acid rain. Significant amounts of acid-forming compounds are released by volcanoes, lightning, and forest fires. Ice samples hundreds of years old taken from remote areas of the world have been found to be more acidic than "normal."

Despite these uncertainties, environmentalists and some scientists believe the effects of acid rain are potentially so serious that Congress should act now to regulate emissions suspected of causing acid rain.

Because of the lack of a clear, scientific understanding about acid rain, and because the cost of acid rain regulations would be so high — possibly without yielding results — industry and some scientists have urged Congress to study the issue further before beginning a regulatory program.

Spurred by environmentalists' concerns, Sen. George Mitchell (D., Me.) has been pushing adoption of an acid rain-control program as an amendment to the Clean Air Act, which is before the Senate environment committee for review. (See story, page 2.) The committee on July 22 adopted an acid rain-control program similar to Sen. Mitchell's.

The program would require an eight-million-ton reduction in sulfur dioxide emissions over 12 years. The amendment affects the 31 easternmost states.

(Continued on page 3)

Welcome, new readers

This *Energy and You* has a new, larger audience. Joining us are shareholders, employees, and annuitants who responded to our spring mailing which offered *Energy and You.* Thank you for taking us up on the offer. And thanks to those of you who said you'd like to continue receiving the newsletter.

Managers who joined Sohio through the Sohio-Kennecott merger last year have also been added to our mailing list. If you're one of them, you're being sent Sohio's legislative newsletter to help inform you of government issues which affect you and your business.

We hope new and continuing *Energy and You* readers will find our newsletter useful and thought provoking. We welcome your comments and suggestions for future articles. Please write to Jean Evans, editor, at 1762 Guildhall Bldg., Cleveland, Ohio 44115.

Published by the Government and Public Affairs Department of The Standard Oil Company (Ohio), 1762 Guildhall Building, Cleveland, Ohio 44115. Jean B. Evans, editor.

Standard Oil of Ohio keeps its employees and stockholders informed about energy policy issues through a newsletter called ''Energy and You.'' (Courtesy Government and Public Affairs Department, Standard Oil Company, Ohio)

Executive branch—a minority of companies maintain contact with such departments as Commerce, Labor, Transportation, or Health and Human Services.

Regulatory agencies—working with the agencies that translate legislation into regulation, such as the Environmental Protection Agency, the Federal Trade Commission, the Federal Communications Commission, or the Securities and Exchange Commission.

In carrying out these relations, Washington representatives engage in five kinds of communication activities.[18]

Fact-finding • The most basic aspect of the Washington rep's job provides the organization with advance information on what government policies or rules are in the making. Many Washington offices gather information by setting up like a news bureau, with staffers covering a regular beat such as Congress, the Department of Commerce, or the Environmental Protection Agency. The information is frequently communicated to members of the organization through a printed newsletter (Exhibit 14–1)

Liaison • The representative makes personal contacts to exchange information with government officials, reporters, members of professional societies, or scientists. He or she attends hearings, interviews officials, calls on congressional and agency staff members, and talks with trade association executives. Entertaining is an important part of this function.

Interpretation of Government Action to Management • Once representatives have gathered facts and maintained liaison, they interpret the results to management. They explain the legislation, regulation, or ruling and analyze what action might be necessary.

Information Giving • Information also flows from Washington representatives to government. They provide statistical data or market information, and explain the effect that legislation or rules being considered might have on the organization they represent.

Advocacy • If the fact-finding or liaison work shows that the organization should take action, the representative recommends what should be done—lobbying, grassroots campaigns, or communication campaigns. Washington representatives may function as lobbyists; they must register as lobbyists if they spend the majority of their time trying to influence the passage or defeat of legislation. Generally, however, government relations people coordinate the persuasive efforts of others. They bring in experts, technicians, consultants, or company executives to testify at congressional hearings or to meet personally with legislators to persuade them to vote for the company's position. (See Chapter 33 for a complete discussion of lobbying techniques.)

Non-Business Organizations, Too • When we mentioned that corporation representatives frequently work with representatives of associations in federal government relations programs, we underscored the importance of government relations for association public relations people as well—not just for business trade associations but also for associations of educational institutions, scientists, gun owners, etc. Congressional representatives of government agencies also practice most of these same government relations activities.

State Government Relations

State governments today have increased influence over business corporations—making an ongoing program to facilitate communications with this key enabling linkage essential. According to the Public Affairs Council:

> . . . there is a gradual resurgence of the power of state legislatures—partly attributable to the

reapportionment decisions of the Supreme Court in the mid-60s and the more recent implementations thereof, and partly due to the growing realization that the federal government is just too big and too remote to deal directly with the needs of local communities.[19]

The council added that states are large enough to handle such problems as pollution, transportation, education, land use and urban growth, crime, poverty, and health—most of which are important issues for corporations.

State relations differ according to whether a company operates in one state or several.

One-State Companies • The one-state company has to deal with only one state government, so it can develop a full-fledged program, like those at the federal level, including:

Professional lobbyists on staff who work in the state capital.

Managers who cultivate relationships with legislators from their districts.

Hiring of legal or public affairs consultants.

Coordination with trade assocations, especially the state Chamber of Commerce.

Seeking support of "satellite groups," such as suppliers, customers, or unions.

Direct appeals to the people to influence the legislature.

Multistate Companies • The company that has facilities in several states cannot always have a full program in each state. It generally has a professional staff member at its headquarters in charge of state relations.

Multistate companies usually concentrate on the state where the company is headquartered and on a few of the states that influence the company most. They frequently regionalize the program, with a specialist in charge of the states in a given region. To supplement their program in states where they cannot have a full program, multistate companies work with trade associations, use consultants, and involve local managers in state relations.

Many other organizations pay special attention to state governments, particularly public universities and local school systems, which get a large proportion of their money from the state.

Political-Action Committees

Business firms, associations, labor unions, and other interest groups have an obvious stake in who gets elected to office. Yet, business firms are prohibited from making contributions to candidates for federal office by the Tillman Act of 1907 and the Corrupt Practices Act of 1925. The Labor-Management Act of 1947 applied the same restrictions to unions.[20]

The Federal Election Campaign Practices Act of 1971, which became effective in 1972, and amendments to the act in 1974, 1976, and 1979, stimulated businesses and associations to form groups called political-action committees (PACs), which previously had been used mostly by unions.[21] Employees or members of an organization can give money to a PAC, which can in turn donate those funds to political candidates and parties.

PACs can also spend funds for political education, for direct and indirect lobbying, for endorsement of candidates among employees, stockholders, or members and their families, and for voter registration and get-out-the-vote drives.[22]

The law governing PACs allows organizations to use general funds to administer the committee and to solicit contributions from employees, members, or stockholders. Each individual can donate no more than $5,000 to a PAC in each election, and a PAC can give no more than $5,000 to a single candidate in a single federal election.

Rules of the Federal Election Commission prohibit organizations from coercing members or employees to give money to a PAC.[23]

A PAC must have a chairman and treasurer. Top corporate officers rarely serve as officers of the PAC, but government relations, public affairs, finance, and legal personnel usually are represented.

Companies surveyed in the 1979 Conference Board study reported using the following devices to solicit contributions from employees:[24]

Letters from the chief executive officer or PAC chairman.

Individual contacts.

Solicitation meetings.

Solicitation brochures.

Management newsletter.

The Impact of PACs • The number of PACs has grown tremendously each year since 1974, and the amount of money they donate sets a new record with each election. Yet, not all companies have PACs.[25] Companies most affected by government most often seem to have PACs:

> A clear pattern emerges when reviewing who does and who does not have a PAC—the more regulated an industry and the more obvious an industry is as a congressional target, the more likely it is to have a political-action committee within the associations or within the companies that make up that industry. As the government moves closer and closer to partnership with an industry, the result of that liaison is a PAC. . . .
>
> When looking over PAC lists, is it such a surprise that railroads, utilities, oil, timber/paper, banks, savings and loan associations, drug companies, and government contractors in the aerospace industry seem to have a higher proportion of PACs than consumer product companies or retailers?[26]

There are frequent claims that PACs are upsetting the political system, or that PAC contributions have influenced votes in Congress. Yet, as one company executive explained, "The PAC is not designed to influence elections, but to open the doors."[27]

Although labor PACs give heavily to Democratic Party candidates, business PACs generally give to members of both parties and to challengers as well as to incumbents. PACs, in other words, function best when they function as part of a two-way symmetric public affairs program.

Grassroots Lobbying Efforts

Corporations with active government relations programs frequently realize the need for support from their publics at the "grassroots" level. Many of these publics represent "constituencies" that share common interests with the organization. Corporations, therefore, have set up systems to communicate with these constituencies and to ask them to provide political support by writing letters, calling or visiting legislators, or otherwise supporting the organization's position.

According to the 1979 Conference Board study, the most common corporate grassroots constituencies, in order, are:[28]

Employees.

Stockholders.

Plant communities.

Retirees.

Labor unions.

Two Formal Network Systems • Some corporations have organized members of their grassroots constituencies into formal networks that the corporation can mobilize whenever it needs support (Exhibit 14–2). Two of these include:[29]

The government key contact program. The company selects employees to serve as communication links with government officials. The individuals chosen understand the company and the political process—and live in the district of the legislator targeted for contact.

The congressional district identification system. Key constituents are identified, and their names are entered into a com-

EXHIBIT **14–2**

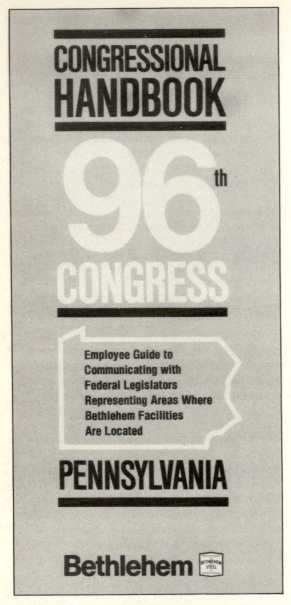

CONGRESSIONAL HANDBOOK

96th CONGRESS

Employee Guide to
Communicating with
Federal Legislators
Representing Areas Where
Bethlehem Facilities
Are Located

PENNSYLVANIA

Bethlehem

Bethlehem Steel Company does grassroots lobbying among its employees by encouraging them to communicate with federal legislators. Bethlehem's "Congressional Handbook" for employees lists names and addresses of representatives and gives advice on how to reach them. (Courtesy Bethlehem Steel Company)

puterized system for each legislative district. They can then be contacted when it is necessary to reach a particular legislator.

Communications on Political Issues

In addition to appeals targeted directly at known grassroots constituents, corporations also use media relations and advocacy advertising to communicate their positions to influential publics who use important national media and participate in the political process. Most members of these publics will not support the corporation as strongly as will its grassroots constituents.

In an article on corporate political communication, the Washington *Post* gave the following examples:

> Weyerhauser in its ads doesn't sell paper, it preaches conservation. Kellogg doesn't peddle cereal, it promotes nutrition. Bethlehem Steel argues the fine points of U.S. trade policy. American Telephone and Telegraph celebrates technology. Citibank expounds on the greatness of the capitalist system. And Mobil addresses itself to just about everything.[30]

Corporate Right of Free Speech • Corporations today have gained the right to speak out on many public issues—even those that do not directly affect the company. A landmark Supreme Court decision in 1978 (*First National Bank of Boston* vs. *Bellotti*) struck down a ruling by Francis Bellotti, the attorney general of Massachusetts, that the First National Bank could not spend money to publicize its opposition to a graduated state income tax.[31] Bellotti had argued that the bank could not spend money for a campaign because the tax measure did not directly affect the bank's operations. That ruling, the Court said, violated the corporation's First Amendment right to free speech.

That ruling also affected similar laws in thirty states that restricted corporate free expression. Although there are still efforts to restrict corporate speech, the Bellotti decision does make it easier for corporations to speak out on public policy issues—even those not directly related to the corporation.

How Corporations Speak Out • Most Washington offices or headquarters public affairs units have media relations specialists whose job it is to publicize a company's positions on policy issues. They use such techniques as stories on speeches by senior executives, stories quoting government experts, "canned" editorials, signed columns, and "economic reality" stories.[32]

Corporations have also become active in responding to national television programs such as CBS's *60 Minutes* or ABC's *20/20*, demanding access when they believe they have been portrayed wrongly. In 1980, for example, Kaiser Aluminum objected to a *20/20* segment on Kaiser's involvement in aluminum wiring. ABC granted Kaiser time to run a four-minute unedited response. Kaiser then sent materials to journalism educators throughout the United States describing the controversy and urging the educators and their students to watch the response.

Corporations who believe they have been denied access to the media—most notably Mobil Oil—and others who simply want to present their opinion unaltered by media gatekeepers have turned to paid advocacy advertising.

S. Prakash Sethi, an academic expert on advocacy advertising, says it is a "two-edged instrument:"

> When properly employed, it can contribute to a greater understanding on the part of the public of what can be reasonably expected of corporations in meeting society's expectations. When employed as a substitute for positive corporate action, it can lead to greater public hostility and a demand for further governmental control of management processes.[33]

Sethi went on to suggest that advocacy advertising works best when it is based on what we would call the two-way symmetric model: "Too often, advocacy advertising is confined to what the corporation wants the world to hear rather than what the world wants the corporation to talk about."

Some Unexpected Benefits from Advocacy Advertising • A University of Maryland study sheds some light on why corporations turn to advocacy advertising and on the effects it has for their public policy communication program. Kenneth Kalman correlated the amount of advocacy advertising done by oil companies with the amount of enterprise reporting—active information seeking—done by the media, as opposed to the passive processing of "information subsidies" presented to the media by the oil companies (see Chapter 11 for a discussion of enterprise reporting).[34]

Kalman's study turned out much like the studies of media publics discussed in Chapter 11. The media passively processed information subsidies from the oil companies, except during the gasoline shortages of 1974 and 1979. Then they did more active reporting of energy issues, and—as Chapter 11 shows frequently happens—the active reporting turned up more negative than positive information about the oil companies.

The oil companies responded by increasing their advocacy advertising. But the advocacy advertising had an unexpected benefit to the oil companies. The advertising apparently attracted so much attention that it put the oil companies on the media agenda—as a result, the media used the companies more as information sources about energy.

We will defer the topic of advocacy advertising, because Chapter 32 is devoted to public relations advertising. That chapter contains several examples of advocacy advertising campaigns. In addition, Chapter 15 is devoted entirely to communication programs related to such public affairs problems as the environment, consumer issues, and minority concerns.

Public Issues Management

Beginning in about 1975, "public issues management" became one of the key phrases in public relations circles. In 1977, public relations consultant W. Howard Chase wrote that "the management of public issues has achieved astonishing currency in less than eighteen months":

> . . . Stauffer Chemical has created the nation's first corporate Department of Public Issue Management. Companies such as Gulf, Shell, and Mobil Company, along with Ford Motor Company, the Business Round Table, General Electric, American Can, and scores of others are deeply involved in identifying and analyzing the impact of public issues on their corporate or institutional futures.[35]

Corporations turn to public issues management to make it possible to shape government policy on issues that affect them, rather than just to adapt to policy changes that already have been made. Buchholz, for example, described four possible responses to policy issues:[36]

> Reactive—fighting change.
>
> Accommodative—adapting to change.
>
> Proactive—influencing change.
>
> Interactive—adjusting to change.

Corporations use issues management to make proactive and interactive responses to policy questions. The proactive response fits the two-way asymmetric model, the interactive the two-way symmetric model. Buchholz added that the interactive—symmetric—response is where public issues management works most effectively:

> The interactive corporation tries to get a reasonably accurate agenda of public issues that it should be concerned with, analyzes the elements of those issues, and develops constructive approaches to these issues, which it attempts to implement in the public policy arena and in its own structure and behavior.

With issues management, government relations becomes more than listening to what government is doing, and public affairs becomes more than fighting changes in government policy. The corporation tries to shape or influence issues before they result in policy changes.

ALCOA and IBM • Two examples of issues-management programs show how the process works.

ALCOA began the process by interviewing representatives from interest groups such as the Chamber of Commerce, Ralph Nader's Congress Watch, and Common Cause to determine what issues they thought would be on the public agenda.[37] The interviews yielded a list of 149 issues—such as social security financing, decontrol of natural gas, and revision of the Clean Air Act.

Management in the firm then was asked to rank these issues for their importance to ALCOA. The result was that fifteen issues were given top priority. The fifteen issues then were turned over to committees of experts from throughout the organization, which ALCOA called issue centers, in such areas as the environment, energy, health and safety, and economics. These committees researched the issues and made recommendations on how to respond to them. The recommendations then went to a central group of top managers, who used the political policy information along with economic and technological informaion in making major decisions.

IBM has a similar program.[38] It centers its issues-management program in the Washington office, where staff "issues managers" have responsibility for groups of issues—such as taxation, trade, personnel, telecommunications, and marketing. Each issue manager has the "intellectual responsibility" for researching these issues, working with "client" specialists inside the organization, developing a strategy acceptable to the corporation, and implementing the strategy in Congress.

To scan and monitor issues, the issue managers use the library, read journals, read major newspapers, work with consultants and academic specialists, and analyze public opinion polls.

Figure 14–1 summarizes the typical issues-management program in the form of a flowchart.

The Payoffs from Issues Management • There are many examples of beneficial changes in corporate policy and behavior that have resulted from issues-management programs, according to the Conference Board.[39]

> Whirlpool Corporation's technological monitoring efforts recognized the significance of permanent-press fabrics early, so that Whirlpool manufactured the first washer capable of laundering the fabrics.

> A major food processor anticipated the furor over red dye # 2 and withdrew the additive from its product line before the controversy began.

> Bank of America identified credit discrimination against women as an issue and changed its policies. Independent researchers later credited the bank with making considerable progress in reducing discrimination.

Stakeholder Management

In addition to "issues management," another new term leaped into the management and public relations vocabulary in the 1970s—"stakeholders."

Stakeholders are defined as "a group whose collective behavior can directly affect the organization's future, but which is not under the organization's control."[40] Henry Schacht, president of Cummins Engine Company, elaborated during a 1976 Conference Board conference on business credibility:

From Rogene A. Buchholz, *Business Environment and Public Policy: Implications for Management,* © 1982, p. 472. Redrawn by permission of Prentice-Hall, Inc., Englewood Cliffs, N.J.

FIGURE 14–1

Flowchart of Public Issues-Management

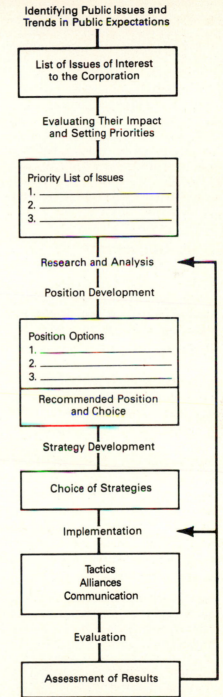

Identifying Public Issues and Trends in Public Expectations

List of Issues of Interest to the Corporation

Evaluating Their Impact and Setting Priorities

Priority List of Issues
1. _____
2. _____
3. _____

Research and Analysis

Position Development

Position Options
1. _____
2. _____
3. _____

Recommended Position and Choice

Strategy Development

Choice of Strategies

Implementation

Tactics
Alliances
Communication

Evaluation

Assessment of Results

I would offer the not new and not unique concept that business is responsible to a variety of stakeholders, and that the mix of stakeholders changes slowly and imperceptibly over time, and that legitimacy of business is derived solely from its ability to relate usefully to the variety of stakeholders. Your list would be as good as mine: It would include employees, communities, local governments, the state and national governments, foreign governments, bondholders, shareholders, certainly, customers, suppliers, creditors, people who come in contact with the results of your product, people who live near the noise and pollution caused by your production. The conflicting claims of this variety of stakeholders need to be met.[41]

The concept of a stakeholder should sound familiar to you by now, as it is almost identical to our concepts of linkages and publics defined in Chapter 7. The stakeholder concept seems less precise to us, however, and less able than our four linkages and our idea of organizational consequences to identify the key publics—the key stakeholders of an organization. The idea of stakeholder relations, however, neatly ties our notion of publics into the public affairs process.

Stakeholder management takes the public affairs manager one step beyond issues management. Issues management identifies the issues that will be important. Stakeholder management identifies the publics that also have a stake in the issue, assesses their potential for cooperation or competition in the policy process, and then works out a strategy for dealing with each stakeholder.

Two examples show how corporations have used stakeholder management:

The U. S. Brewers Association used it to plan its strategy for responding to proposed legislation that would prohibit disposable cans and bottles.

AT&T has used it to plan a national strategy for introducing local measured service—billing local calls in the same way as long-distance calls—to local regulatory agencies.

Stakeholder management can take the form either of the two-way asymmetric or two-way symmetric model. The process stresses bargaining and negotiation, however, and works best with the symmetric model.

Community Relations

The Boston University study described earlier in this chapter identified community relations as one of the most frequent activities of a public affairs program. Generally, however, the public affairs component of community relations emphasizes community participation projects, philanthropy, and contacts with local political leaders, rather than the other communication activities described in Chapter 13.[42]

In our opinion, community relations not only should include activities other than public affairs, it should also be managed as a separate program from public affairs. In Chapter 13, we described how a community relations program should be structured.

Involving Management in Public Affairs

Just as Chapter 13 showed that community relations is not just the job of the public relations department, so this chapter's description of public affairs programs should have made it clear that people throughout an organization also get involved in public affairs and government relations—it is everyone's job.[43] People throughout an organization testify before legislative bodies, meet with government officials and their staffs, discuss policy issues in speeches and with reporters, and participate in issues-management committees.

Organizations do not leave these public affairs activities to chance, however. Many have formal programs to train their executives in public affairs. A Conference Board study found that the following activities were used by corporations to give managers public affairs training and experience:[44]

Providing courses, seminars, or workshops—in-house or outside.

Bringing outside people with special public affairs knowledge to address and/or meet with company managers.

Introducing new media/methods (e.g., newsletters) for communicating public affairs ideas to management.

Rotating or assigning managers to jobs that develop public affairs competence.

Making or approving full-time or part-time assignments outside the company related to public affairs.

Assigning managers to standing committees, special committees, or task forces with public affairs missions.

Giving managers special assignments with public affairs content.

Including public affairs responsibilities in appraising performance and in the compensation and reward system.

Encouraging self-development (through reading or other means) in public affairs.

Encouraging managers to participate in public affairs or community activities on a voluntary, essentially after-hours, basis.

PUBLIC AFFAIRS PUBLICS

Public affairs and government relations programs are diverse, but they generally seem to be designed for three kinds of publics:

Active, constituent publics, which recognize the same problems as the organization and perceive an involvement with issues of concern to the organization.

Activist publics, which object to one or more consequences of organizational actions—such as pollution or unsafe products—and bring their complaints to the policy arena.

Governmental publics—legislators, regulators, and members of the executive branch who broker appeals from organizations and publics and then formulate and enforce public policy.

Let's look at research on the first two types of publics first, and then look at governmental publics.

Constituent and Activist Publics

In Chapter 7, we pointed out that research using the Grunig situational model of publics generally has identified four types of publics that result from a set of issues or organizational consequences:

Active on all issues in the set.

Apathetic on all issues.

Active only on issues that involve nearly everyone in the population.

Single-issue publics.

Both constituent and activist publics generally could be expected to fall into an all-issues public or the single issue publics.

These would be the two types of publics of most concern to the organization in a public affairs program, and, indeed, most public affairs programs seem directed at those publics. Totally apathetic publics would not be a target for a public affairs program. And the public that is active only on an all-involving issue—such as the energy crisis—would be a target only when such an issue arises.

Grunig's two studies of the publics that arise from public affairs issues confirm the presence of these publics for the programs described in this chapter.

Corporate Responsibility Publics • The first of these studies was discussed briefly in Chapter 3, on public responsibility. Researchers interviewed a random sample of 200 Maryland residents and asked questions on eleven issues that writers on corporate social responsibility had mentioned as being the responsibility of business.[45] Most of the issues also are public policy issues that can be classified according to the primary, secondary, and tertiary responsibilities of business, as described in Chapter 3. The issues studied:

Primary responsibilities (basic economic functions)—quality of products and services, corporate profits.

Secondary responsibilities (consequences of these basic functions)—pollution, inflation, monopoly, human relations on the job, employment of minorities.

Tertiary responsibilities (general social problems)—decay of the cities, quality of education, support of charitable organizations, unemployment.

Statistical analysis identified three publics resulting from these eleven issues:

A large aware public that has high involvement and problem recognition mostly for the secondary responsibilities—the consequences of corporate behavior. This public also had high constraint recognition on most of the issues—believing it could do little to resolve the problems.

This public fits somewhere between a single-issue public and a public that gets involved only when it is personally affected. It has the potential for being an activist public; it does not seem to be a constituent public. This aware public is an important public affairs public—especially for communications about how the corporation has corrected the consequences of its behavior—because constrained publics frequently turn to government for help in removing the constraints.

An activist public with a high level of involvement and problem recognition about every issue but support of charity. This public also had a high level of constraint recognition on every issue, explaining why activist publics frequently join pressure groups and work with government on social issues. This public was the only public, also, that believed business should have responsibility for dealing with general social issues. It is clearly a competing activist public, not a constituent public.

This second public, therefore, seems to represent the politically active groups that are the targets of corporate communications about policy and advocacy advertising. It is a public likely to support interest groups such as Common Cause or Congress Watch, and to demand change from business as part of policy negotiations.

A passive public, with a low level of involvement and problem recognition on all of the issues except those that involve nearly everyone—pollution, quality of products and services, inflation, education, and human relations at work. In addition, this public did not feel constrained on some of the issues for which it perceived an involvement.

This generally passive public is one of the four typical publics. Although generally passive, it will not be passive on all issues, and public affairs specialists must pay attention to it when such issues come up.

Publics from Four Policy Issues • In a second study of public affairs publics, Grunig surveyed 200 residents of Montgomery and Prince Georges County, Maryland, about four public affairs issues.[46] Both counties border Washington, D.C. Montgomery County is a wealthy, white-collar area with many residents who would be in the active and governmental publics that are the targets of public affairs programs. Prince Georges County, a middle-class area with a substantial black population, is typical of most urban areas in the United States.

This study identified publics resulting from two negative policy issues (from a corporation's standpoint) for which publics have accused corporations of being socially irresponsible: the controversy over the Nestlé Company selling infant formula to poor mothers in underdeveloped countries (see Chapter 3 for a discussion of the issue), and the controversy over the safety of the Ford Pinto because of the location of its gas tank. The study also applied the theory to two positive corporate efforts to secure active public support: Bethlehem Steel's campaign for changes in steel import policies, and Mobil Oil's issue advertising in support of nuclear power.

Nuclear Power Generates the Most Activism • First, Grunig compared the levels of problem recognition, involvement, and constraint recognition for the four issues. The results showed that nuclear power was the issue most likely to generate active publics. Nearly 75 percent of the respondents gave responses that placed them in the categories of high-involvement problem-facing or high-involvement constrained-behavior—the categories that define the most active publics (see Chapter 7).

The Ford Pinto issue brought nearly as many active publics. On the Nestlé issue, which Chapter 3 showed has generated great controversy, nearly 50 percent of the respondents fell into the low-involvement fatalistic category—a nonpublic category; the other respondents were scattered in several other categories. For steel imports, about 65 percent of the respondents were in the fatalistic-behavior category, although a third of that group still thought the issue involved them.

Statistical analysis of the responses for the four issues together identified five publics: an activist public, an apathetic public, and three single-issue publics.

The Activist Public • This public had high problem recognition and level of involvement and low constraint recognition on all four issues. It was also most likely to have retained messages, to hold cognitions and attitudes, and to have engaged in some kind of behavior related to each of the four issues. Members of this public were young and well educated. They appeared to be a public that would pressure government to force changes in business behavior. They were not, however, consistently anti- or probusiness in their cognitions and attitudes. It was also the smallest public: 6 percent of the sample. Each of the other four publics made up 21 percent to 28 percent of the sample.

The Apathetic Public • This public fit the general category of being apathetic on all issues but the most involving one—in this case, the nuclear power issue. It fit the low-involvement, fatalistic-behavior category (a nonpublic category) on the other three issues. Even on the nuclear power issue, this public had only moderate levels of problem recognition and involvement. This public processed some information on the nuclear issue, but otherwise did not communicate about, hold cognitions or attitudes, or engage in behaviors related to any of the four issues.

The Steel/Nuclear Public • This was the first of the single-issue publics. It fit the high-involvement problem-facing category, especially for the steel issue and, to a lesser extent, the nuclear issue. It would communicate only about these single issues. Many members of this public worked for business firms and thus took an interest in these issues in which business was seeking support. This public should be a constituent public of business, but it did not have either consistently pro- or antibusiness attitudes on the two issues. It hedged both pro- and antibusiness cognitions.

The Ford Pinto Public • This was a single-issue public much like the steel/nuclear public, but interested instead in the Pinto gas tank issue. Many members of this public also worked for business or owned stock in a business firm; thus, they should constitute another constituent public. Members of this public did not have strong cognitions or attitudes, but they did have a slight tendency to hold the antibusiness cognitions and to wedge out the probusiness cognition—showing that constituent publics can be critical of business.

The Nestlé Activist Public • Like the activist public, this public was young and well educated, but was more likely to be female and black. It fit into the high-involvement problem-facing category only on the Nestlé issue—an issue, you will recall, that the majority of respondents in the study did not perceive to be a problem or an issue that involves them. This public wedged out the probusiness cognition with a strong antibusiness belief on the Nestlé issue. It also had a strong antibusiness attitude and was very likely to engage in antibusiness behavior. Strangely—according to the situational theory—this public did not seek or process much information about the issue. It had strong attitudes and put them into effect, but it did not bother to seek or process information related to those attitudes.

Hedging the Most Likely Public Affairs Effect • In Chapter 11 on media relations, we discussed a study of Washington reporters that showed most of the reporters interviewed as believing antibusiness cognitions, though sometimes hedging them with probusiness beliefs. The publics in this study held similar cognitions. Most believed the antibusiness view. If they believed the probusiness view they did not drop the antibusiness view. They believed both; they hedged.

A public affairs program, therefore, could get an activist or a constituent public to hedge its antibusiness view with a probusiness view, but such a program could not get them to wedge out the antibusiness view.

Governmental Publics

No studies have been done in which the theory of publics developed in this book has been applied to government decision makers. It is possible, however, to use political science research to piece together some ideas about how and why decision makers—in particular, legislators—communicate and make decisions.

The governmental relations specialist eventually would like to influence the behavior of government officials (see also the next section on objectives). Basically, there are two ways of influencing behavior:

By forcing or constraining the official to behave as you want.

By communicating with the official to persuade him or her to vote as you want or to negotiate a mutually acceptable position.

Constraint Recognition • The first possibility takes us logically to the concept of constraint recognition. Remember that people who perceive constraints have little need to communicate; their behavior is determined for them by outside forces. The behavior of government officials also will be affected by constraints.

The government relations specialist, therefore, could determine the behavior of government officials if he or she could place constraints upon them. If the specialist is successful, the only communication necessary would be to give the officials information that lets them know the constraints are there.

Many people try to use payoffs, bribes, threats, and other illegal or unethical constraints. Obviously, we do not recommend them.

There are legal ways, however, to place constraints upon decision makers. Most stem from the decision maker's need to be reelected. To place such constraints, the government relations person must mobilize pressure on legislators to suggest to them that if they do not vote as desired, they will not be reelected.

In the book *How You Can Influence Con-*

gress, for example, Alderson and Sentman listed "ten ways you can put heat on your congressman." Among them are:

Getting help from friends in high places.

Showing public support through letter-writing campaigns, petitions, rallies, and similar activities.

Getting help from local VIPs who have special access to, or credibility with, your congressman.[47]

In the chapter "Environmental Constraints" in a book on *Congressmen in Committees*, Richard Fenno listed these constraints:

Other members of the same house.

Members of the executive branch.

Clientele groups.

Members of the major political parties.[48]

These constraints can be put in place through alliances and coalitions with these other groups (see Chapter 33).

Working Through Communication • The discussion of programs and techniques throughout this chapter, however, shows that government relations people work more through communication with government officials than through constraint. It's important, therefore, to understand what government officials communicate about and why they do it.

A study of Wisconsin state senators showed that these government officials communicated both asymmetrically and symmetrically with their constituents.[49] The senators who communicated asymmetrically concentrated on giving out information, and usually they could not predict their constituents' views accurately. They also didn't get elected as often. Those who communicated symmetrically knew their constituents' views and got reelected more often.

The government relations person can communicate best with the government officials that communicate frequently and symmetrically. The situational theory explains who they might be.

Involvement • Remember that communication behavior is situational. This means that government officials will communicate actively about some issues but not about others. Remember, too, that they communicate most actively about issues that involve them. For legislators, the most involving issues are those that involve their home districts or states. That is why grassroots lobbying programs work well. Legislators listen to people with whom they share involvements.[50]

Problem Recognition • In addition to their involvements at home, however, legislators also specialize in certain issues. Sometimes these issues match their involvements, but not always. Information overload is a problem that faces every member of Congress. It is simply impossible to keep up with information about every issue before Congress, and the overload gets greater every year. In 1965, for example, representatives spent one day a week on "legislative research and reading." By 1977, that time was down to eleven minutes per day.[51]

Legislators specialize in certain issues—in recognizing certain problems—according to the committees on which they sit. The problems in which legislators specialize, therefore, will be the ones they communicate about. Legislators in the House of Representatives can specialize more than those in the Senate, because there are more representatives in the House, and therefore each representative sits on fewer committees.[52]

There are many committees in Congress, but they can be classified into the following groups, with obvious implications for the government relations specialist picking a communication target:

Foreign relations, national defense, and science and technology.

Environment, energy, national resources, and agriculture.

Economic policy.

Domestic social policy.

Legal and judicial systems.[53]

Legislators, however, are too busy to see every government relations representative. They turn much of that work over to their personal staffs and to committee staffs. And, as many government relations specialists know, staff members may be their best publics. Staff members and representatives of corporations and interest groups make up "issue networks" that are extremely important in Washington politics.[54]

Political scientist Michael Malbin has found that the interests of staff members (the problems they recognize) limit the information that flows to members of committees.[55] Staff members have become "entrepreneurial," Malbin added, meaning they initiate policy work on their own.

For the communication aspect of government relations—as opposed to setting up constraints—legislative staffs are extremely important because their role is to gather information that the elected representatives use to make decisions. Malbin pointed out, for example, that on the issue of deregulation of natural gas, the role of the staff is to find out who *would* bear the cost of deregulation. The role of the elected representatives is to decide who *should* bear the cost.

Passive Communication Behavior • Although our discussion of the communication behavior of government officials has thus far emphasized how to identify the officials who communicate actively, there is also the possibility of getting other officials who communicate passively to process information.

All representatives can vote. So it's possible that if you can get information to representatives who do not specialize in the issue of concern to your organization, yours will be the only information they get. And their votes may be based on that limited information!

Thus, it is important to find ways to get legislators to process information. One way is to communicate with the active legislative publics, so they will pass on the information to the passive publics. Personal contact, brief reports, and letters from constituents may also be effective.

OBJECTIVES AND EVALUATION

Of our five objectives for public relations programs defined in Chapter 9—communication, message retention, message acceptance, effect on attitude, and behavior—you might think that public affairs and government relations is the specialized area of public relations where the behavior objective is the obvious objective. Indeed, public affairs specialists do frequently claim credit for behavioral changes in government. The *National Journal* provided several examples.[56]

> Hill and Knowlton did not minimize its role on behalf of the Calorie Control Council—dominated by the soft drink industry—in turning the tide against a ban on saccharin by the Food and Drug Administration.
>
> Burson-Marsteller took credit for defeating, or at least delaying, a Federal Trade Commission ban on television advertising directed at children.
>
> The Daniel Edelman firm took partial responsibility for securing landing rights for the supersonic Concorde in the United States, and on behalf of the American Seat Belt Council, for blocking a Department of Transportation requirement that air bags be installed on all new cars.

The Boston University Study

Research conducted by the Boston University public affairs research group indicated that corporate public affairs specialists evaluated their own efforts most frequently in terms of attitude and behavior objectives.[57] The three evaluation methods cited were:

Measures of audience response to communications efforts: "A key phrase used to describe this was 'acceptance of our views by the public.'" (The attitude objective.)

Results of lobbying efforts: passage, defeat, or modification of legislation or regulations. (The behavior objective.)

Financial or competitive impact of effort: reduced costs, increased profits, a line of business protected. (Objectives that Chapter 9 showed are unrealistic.)

Yet, when the same public affairs specialists were asked which of their government relations activities were most effective, their responses suggested that the communication objective worked best. On a scale from 1 to 5 (5 being the highest), the respondents rated four activities as follows:

Serving as eyes and ears (4.0).
Representing the company to regulatory agencies (3.4).
Influencing proposed legislation (3.3).
Influencing compliance with regulation (3.0).

Stress Communication, Message Retention, and Cognitive Effects.

The studies on public affairs publics discussed in the previous section on publics showed that public affairs programs may achieve message retention and acceptance (hedging but not wedging), but that they cannot control attitudes and behavior. These, then, should be your objectives for communication programs. They can be measured using the techniques discussed in Chapter 9.

Research on relations with governmental publics also shows the importance of the communication objective.[58] It is important to evaluate your performance by your ability to communicate with government officials. If you don't get to see them, you can't get your message to them. Thus, measuring communication contacts is the most important way to evaluate government relations efforts.

Message retention and acceptance also are important, but it is quite difficult to measure them with survey research on public officials. Instead use informal methods to observe whether those officials remember what you said and believe what you said is true (see Chapter 33, on lobbying, for further ideas).

NOTES

1. William H. Gruber and Raymond L. Hoewing, "The New Management in Corporate Public Affairs," *Public Affairs Review* 1 (1980):13–23.
2. Edwin A. Murray, Jr., "The Public Affairs Function: Report on a Large Scale Research Project," in Lee Preston (ed.), *Research in Corporate Social Performance and Policy*, vol. 3 (Greenwich, Conn.: JAI Press, 1982). A shorter report on this study is found in Public Affairs Research Group, School of Management, Boston University, "Public Affairs Offices and Their Functions: Highlights of a National Survey," *Public Affairs Review* 2 (1981): 88–99.
3. Phyllis McGrath, *Managing Corporate External Relations: Changing Perspectives and Responses* (New York: The Conference Board, 1976), p. 46.
4. "Special Report: Fewer Major Corporations have 'Public Relations' Departments," *Jack O'Dwyer's Newsletter* (August 1981).
5. Seymour Lusterman, *Managerial Competence: The Public Affairs Aspects* (New York: The Conference Board, 1981), p. 1.
6. "The Public Affairs Council 1982," informational brochure published by the Public Affairs Council, Washington.
7. Michael R. Gordon, "The Image Makers in Washington—PR Firms Have Found a Natural

Home," *National Review* 12 (May 31, 1980):884–890.

8. A Conference Board study showed that 71 percent of corporation executives surveyed attributed their greater involvement in public affairs to "the impact of recent government regulations and legislation." Phyllis S. McGrath, *Redefining Corporate-Federal Relations* (New York: The Conference Board, 1979), p. 1.

9. Theodore J. Lowi, *The End of Liberalism: The Second Republic of the United States,* 2d ed. (New York: W. W. Norton, 1979).

10. William J. Paisley, "Public Communication Campaigns: The American Experience," in Ronald E. Rice and William J. Paisley (eds.), *Public Communication Campaigns* (Beverly Hills, Calif.: Sage, 1981), pp. 15–40.

11. Murray.

12. John Webster, manager of public affairs programs, IBM, in a speech to a conference on public policy and the business environment, sponsored by the Center for Business and Public Policy, University of Maryland College of Business and Management and the American Assembly of Collegiate Schools of Business, June 20–25, 1982, College Park, Maryland. See also McGrath, *Redefining Corporate-Federal Relations,* p. 57.

13. Murray.

14. McGrath, *Redefining Corporate-Federal Relations,* p. 63.

15. Public Affairs Council, "Checklist for the Washington Corporate Office" (Washington: 1974); McGrath, *Redefining Corporate-Federal Relations,* p. 57.

16. Murray.

17. McGrath, *Redefining Corporate-Federal Relations,* p. 7.

18. Public Affairs Council, "Checklist for the Washington Corporate Office." See also Public Affairs Council, "The Federal Connection: Opening A Washington Public Affairs Office" (Washington: 1978), and Robert W. Miller and Jimmy D. Johnson, *Corporate Ambassadors to Washington* (Washington: Center for the Study of Private Enterprise, The American University, 1970).

19. Public Affairs Council, "The Third House: An Informal Survey of Corporate Lobbying at the State Level" (Washington: July 1973).

20. Rogene A. Buchholz, *Business Environment and Public Policy* (Englewood Cliffs, N.J.: Prentice-Hall, 1982), pp. 191–192.

21. Herbert E. Alexander, "Political Action Committees and Their Corporate Sponsors in the 1980s," *Public Affairs Review* 2 (1981):27–38. See also Thomas H. Boggs, Jr., and Douglas Stevens, "What the New Election Law Means to Association PACs," *Association Management* 32 (March 1980):69–70.

22. Alexander, p. 29.

23. McGrath, *Redefining Corporate-Federal Relations,* p. 49.

24. McGrath, *Redefining Corporate-Federal Relations,* p. 49.

25. McGrath, *Redefining Corporate-Federal Relations,* p. 49.

26. Michael J. Malbin (ed.), *Parties, Interest Groups and Campaign Finance Laws* (Washington: American Enterprise Institute for Public Policy Research, 1980), p. 11.

27. McGrath, *Redefining Corporate-Federal Relations,* p. 50.

28. McGrath, *Redefining Corporate-Federal Relations,* p. 50.

29. S. Prakash Sethi, "Corporate Political Activism," *Public Relations Journal,* 36 (November 1980):14–16.

30. "The Corporate Voice: Business Asks Wider Freedom of Speech," Washington *Post* (March 25, 1979), pp. H1–H2.

31. "The Corporate Right to Speak Out—and the Public's Right to Be Informed," *Burson-Marsteller Report* No. 54 (Fall 1979).

32. Ronald N. Levy, "Public Policy Publicity: How to Do It," *Public Relations Journal* 31 (June 1975):19–21, 35–36.

33. Sethi, "Corporate Political Activism." See also S. Prakash Sethi, *Advocacy Advertising and the Large Corporation* (Lexington, Mass.: Lexington Books, 1977).

34. Kenneth Kalman, "An Analysis of the Relationship Between Advocacy Advertising of Oil Companies and the Use of Information Subsidies by the New York Times," master's thesis, University of Maryland, College Park, 1982.

35. W. Howard Chase, "Public Issue Management: The New Science," *Public Relations Journal* 33 (October 1977):25–26. See also Barrie L. Jones and W. Howard Chase, "Managing Public Policy Issues," *Public Relations Review* 5 (Summer 1979):3–23.

36. Buchholz, p. 464.

37. John Holtzman, manager of public policy issues, ALCOA, speech to a conference on public policy and the business environment, sponsored by the Center for Business and Public Policy, University of Maryland College of Business and Management and the American Assembly of Collegiate Schools of Business, June 20–25, 1982, College Park, Maryland.

38. Webster.

39. James K. Brown, *Guidelines for Managing Corporate Issues Programs* (New York: The Conference Board, 1981), p. 33.

40. James R. Emshoff and R. Edward Freeman, "Stakeholder Management: A Case Study of the U.S. Brewers and the Container Issue," The Wharton Applied Research Center, Philadelphia, Pa., May 1979.

41. Phyllis S. McGrath (ed.), *Business Credibility: The Critical Factors* (New York: The Conference Board, 1976), p. 5.

42. See, for example, Lusterman, p. 3.

43. McGrath, *Redefining Corporate-Federal Relations*, p. 70.

44. Lusterman, p. 13.

45. James E. Grunig, "A New Measure of Public Opinions on Corporate Social Responsibility," *Academy of Management Journal* 22 (1979):738–764.

46. James E. Grunig, "The Message-Attitude-Behavior Relationship: Communication Behaviors of Organizations," *Communication Research* 9 (1982):163–200.

47. George Alderson and Everett Sentman, *How You Can Influence Congress: The Complete Handbook for the Citizen Lobbyist* (New York: E. P. Dutton, 1979), pp. 161–162.

48. Richard F. Fenno, Jr., *Congressmen in Committees* (Boston: Little, Brown: 1973), p. 15.

49. Michael B. Hesse, "A Coorientation Study of Wisconsin State Senators and Their Constituents," *Journalism Quarterly* 53 (1976):626–633, 660.

50. Richard F. Fenno, Jr., *Home Style: House Members in Their Districts* (Boston: Little, Brown, 1978).

51. Michael J. Malbin, *Unelected Representatives: Congressional Staff and the Future of Representative Government* (New York: Basic Books, 1980), p. 243.

52. Thomas P. Murphy, *The Politics of Congressional Committees: The Power of Seniority* (Woodbury, N.Y.: Barron's, 1978), p. 37.

53. Murphy, p. 67.

54. Malbin, *Unelected Representatives*, p. 244.

55. Malbin, *Unelected Representatives*, pp. 240–242.

56. Gordon.

57. Murray.

58. In addition to the references already cited, for treatment of lobbying as a communication process, see Lester W. Milbrath, *The Washington Lobbyists* (Chicago: Rand-McNally, 1963).

ADDITIONAL READING

Brown, James K. *The Business of Issues: Coping with the Company's Environment* (New York: The Conference Board, 1979).

Brown, James K., *Guidelines for Managing Corporate Issues Programs* (New York: The Conference Board, 1981).

Buchholz, Rogene A. *Business Environment and Public Policy* (Englewood Cliffs, N. J.: Prentice-Hall, 1982).

Fenno, Richard F. Jr., *Home Style: House Members in Their Districts* (Boston: Little, Brown, 1978).

Fox, J. Ronald, *Managing Business-Government Relations: Cases and Notes on Business-Government Problems* (Homewood, Ill.: Richard D. Irwin, 1982.

Jones, Barrie L., and W. Howard Chase, "Managing Public Policy Issues," *Public Relations Review* 5 (Summer 1979):3–23.

Lusterman, Seymour, *Managerial Competence: The Public Affairs Aspects* (New York: The Conference Board, 1981).

McGrath, Phyllis S., *Redefining Corporate-Federal Relations* (New York: The Conference Board, 1979).

Malbin, Michael J., *Unelected Representatives: Congressional Staff and the Future of Representative Government* (New York: Basic Books, 1980).

Malbin, Michael J. (ed.), *Parties, Interest Groups and Campaign Finance Laws* (Washington: American Enterprise Institute for Public Policy Research, 1980).

Murphy, Thomas P. *The Politics of Congressional Committees: The Power of Seniority* (Woodbury, N.Y.: Barron's, 1978).

Nagelschmidt, Joseph, *Public Affairs Handbook* (New York: American Management Association, 1982).

Nimmo, Dan D., and Keith R. Sanders (eds.), *Handbook of Political Communication* (Beverly Hills, Calif.: Sage, 1981).

15

RELATIONS WITH ACTIVE PUBLICS: CONSUMERS, ENVIRONMENTALISTS, AND MINORITIES

Until the civil rights, environmental, and consumer movements were born and gained power in the late 1950s and 1960s, large organizations could pretty much ignore most of the adverse consequences their actions had on the environment, consumers, and minorities. Now, groups such as the Sierra Club, Common Cause, Ralph Nader's Public Citizen lobby, the NAACP, and the National Organization for Women represent powerful adversaries for most organizations. These groups not only apply pressure to organizations to do something about the adverse consequences of their behavior, but they also go to government to seek regulation when organizations refuse to change.[1]

Many organizations have not developed new institutional structures to deal with the public relations problems created by activist publics. These organizations simply have turned the problems over to such existing programs as media relations or employee relations.

Other organizations relate to activist publics through their public affairs programs, as Chapter 14 showed. Indeed, it is because of active adversaries that most organizations developed public affairs programs in the 1970s. Generally, public relations programs designed for activist publics represent an extension of the organization's basic public affairs function.

Many other organizations, however, institutionalized new programs for activist publics. The most common institutionalized program is the consumer relations program, although business firms for which pollution is a particularly difficult problem—such as Bethlehem Steel—have formed special environmental relations programs. Minority relations problems generally are handled through community relations or employee relations programs, although some organizations have set up special "urban relations" programs to deal with minorities.

In addition to looking at how organizations respond to activist groups, we need to look at the public relations behaviors of the activist groups as well. It is because of their public relations skill that activist groups have become powerful adversaries of big business, big government, and other large organizations.

Let's examine in more detail, then, some of these programs.

ENVIRONMENTAL, CONSUMER, AND MINORITY RELATIONS PROGRAMS

Public relations programs aimed at activist publics would seem to be the area of public relations where the two-way symmetric model would be essential. But such has not been the case. In the early days of such programs, most organizations thought that whitewash publicity—the press agentry/publicity model—would make the problems go away. But press agentry programs have almost always antagonized the activists and made them even more irate than before. Some examples:

> Potlatch Forests, Inc. ran an advertisement with a photograph of "breathtaking natural beauty" and the headline, "It cost us a bundle but the Clearwater River still runs clear." *Newsweek* magazine, in its December 28, 1970, issue reported that the photo was snapped some fifty miles upstream from the Potlatch pulp and paper plant in Lewiston, Idaho. Downstream from the plant, the river "looked like a cesspool."[2]

> American Airlines developed a minority relations program in which female flight attendants went into inner-city schools to show young women how to properly put on makeup.[3]

> Many companies responded to consumerism by investing heavily in "ads and pronouncements that tell the public what a good job they're already doing . . . they haven't really changed their ways of doing business, only their ways of advertising."[4]

> A frequent corporate response to minority problems is to put more pictures of blacks and Hispanics in their advertising.[5]

Public Information Doesn't Work Either

Other organizations have been more honest and "informational" in their relations with active publics, although they haven't always known what information their publics wanted to hear. They have employed the public-information model.

Until the consumer movement heated up in the early 1960s, many consumer products companies provided information to consumers about how to use their products—but did little more. Food companies and associations of food producers, for example, had—and most still have—home economists on their staffs to disseminate recipes and nutritional information.[6]

At the same time that electric utilities were developing and implementing plans for nuclear power plants, they also released massive amounts of information about nuclear power and its benefits (but not its dangers). The case study of the Metropolitan Edison Company and Three Mile Island in Chapter 2 provides one such example.

One study has shown that too much positive information about environmental, consumer, or minority problems can make a public believe an organization is too myopic to see the negative consequences of its own behavior—a study of public perceptions of an Army Corps of Engineers dam and flood control project in North Dakota.[7] The Corps had provided the public plenty of accurate information about the benefits of the project, but no information about the disadvantages.

Using the coorientation method described in Chapters 6 and 9, Stamm and Bowes found that members of the public recognized both advantages and disadvantages of the project. But when interviewers asked them what they thought representatives of the Corps thought would be advantages and disadvantages, members of the public predicted the Corps would see the advantages but not the disadvantages. The public knew the disadvantages, and the Corps missed a good chance for symmetric communication by refusing to talk about these disadvantages.

Frank Shants, public relations manager of the Public Service Company of New Hampshire, who had to deal with the protest by the Clamshell Alliance against the building of the Seabrook, New Hampshire, nuclear plant, declared, in essence, that the public-information model had been a failure for the nuclear power issue:

> Efforts by the electric utility companies and their allies to reach the public on the issue of nuclear power have generally been guided by the belief that once the people are informed and educated, they will support nuclear power, adequate energy supplies, and so forth.
>
> Yet, even though Americans support nuclear power—by a solid two to one margin—the outlook is anything but bright. . . . Because silent support is no good. This is a political issue that requires action and visibility. People can't be mustered to jump on a bandwagon and support the status quo. Getting the facts to the people and hoping they will actively campaign in favor of nuclear power just isn't working.[8]

Is the Asymmetric Model the Only Resort?

Instead of the public-information model, Shants advocated the equivalent of the two-way asymmetric model, because, he said, that is what the activists have used successfully:

> Instead of trying to arouse the public for nuclear power, we should change course and try to arouse the public against the anti-nuclear groups and what they advocate. Give the people something unattractive to be against instead of something beneficial to be for.

The two-way asymmetric model can work reasonably well for an organization whose publics are passive. You find out what those publics want, couch your message in those terms, and gather feedback to see if you have been successful. As long as your organization is the only one telling these publics about an issue, you can usually control the cognitions—and sometimes the attitudes and behaviors—of these publics.

But in an environmental public relations war, there are activist groups using the same tactics to communicate with the same relatively passive publics. They are also telling the public what it wants to hear—and it usually is to put your organization in a bad light. The result is that a lot of accurate, but incomplete, information is publicized, and publics do not get enough information to make reasonable decisions about new technology such as nuclear power.

Environmental activist groups do seem to employ the two-way asymmetric model quite well. Catherine Wolff, the public relations director for the Clamshell Alliance, said her job was to gain respect for the Alliance's civil disobedience at the Seabrook nuclear plant site.[9] The Alliance had no intention of negotiating with the power company. It wanted to stop the construction of the plant. But its public relations were designed to couch the demonstration in terms that would not alienate local residents—the purpose of the asymmetric model. The Alliance took the following actions:

> Repeatedly stressed that Seabrook and eight surrounding towns had voted against nuclear power. It distributed leaflets several times, including 8,000 at crowded beaches, discussing problems of evacuating the area if a nuclear accident occurred at the plant.
>
> Informed police of evacuation plans and asked for their cooperation. A leaflet explaining nonviolent civil disobedience was distributed to National Guardsmen the week before the occupation of the plant site.
>
> Encouraged local groups to handle media relations to show the campaign had local support.
>
> Asked for a meeting with conservative Governor Meldrim Thompson when he claimed to have intelligence showing the

Alliance to be a terrorist group. The meeting helped to portray the Alliance in non-violent terms.

Peter Sandman, the media and outreach coordinator for the New Jersey Campaign for a Nuclear Weapons Freeze and a communication professor at Rutgers University, has outlined plans for an activist campaign in clear two-way asymmetric terms. Among several "notes on 'selling' the freeze," was the following, which stresses describing the movement in terms acceptable to the audience, but not of negotiating the objectives of the freeze against the objectives of groups who want more defense spending:

> Reinforce audience values. People change more, and act more, when you support their values than when you challenge them. The golden rule of persuasion is thus to look for existing audience values to which you can hook your message, values that already incline your audience toward your message. If there are existing values that incline your audience the other way, the less you mention them the better—you want to remind people why they want to agree with you, not why they want to disagree. The following are widespread (though not universal) values that are easily hooked to the freeze: taxes are high; social priorities (schools, parks, and buses as well as welfare) are unmet; children deserve a less threatened future; the world contains people, places, and activities we love; mass suicide/murder/eco-cide is the ultimate arrogance.[10]

The "Pros" Fight the "Antis" with the Same Tactics • In the quote on page 311, electric-utility PR practitioner Frank Shants argued that the organizations fighting activists should respond by describing the activists in terms of negative values the public has. The "activists" are struggling to give the public something to like about their cause; the "reactivists" are struggling to give the public something to dislike about the activists.

Bruce Harrison, who writes a regular column on energy and the environment for the *Public Relations Journal*, found cause for rejoicing in 1982 when the Sierra Club "fumbled" a claim that specific petrochemical plants were releasing suspected carcinogens into the air—only to "discover later that it was riddled with falsehoods, inaccuracies, outdated and speculative information."[11]

Harrison described an upsurge in environmental activism that had resulted from the Reagan Administration environmental policies and its controversial Secretary of the Interior James Watt. He asked, rhetorically, what industry and labor could do to balance environmental and economic values. He responded in asymmetric terms:

> Hang in there. Tides ebb and flow. Opportunities open up—for instance, following the Sierra Club debacle. Only persistence will insure that you are positioned to step in with your message.
>
> Simplify your messages. Complex technical explanations are hard to deliver and receive. Pare the message to the manageable pieces, and repeat, repeat, repeat. The message of industry and labor on the Clean Air Act, for example, is that the law needs to be streamlined to allow both clean air and jobs, and that industry and labor are responsible citizens who want to help lawmakers as they consider tough issues.

Is industry really interested in changing the Clean Air Act to protect jobs, or is it to increase profits and open up wilderness areas for exploitation? Whichever, the asymmetric message that jobs are at stake clearly goes over better with a semi-informed public than does a message about profits.

Two-Way Symmetric Communication Could Bring Peace • In the previous chapter, we quoted communication theorist William Paisley, who distinguished between what he called reactive and proactive communication campaigns.[12] As you will recall, reactive campaigns were "too desperate for a doctrine of reasonableness. The metaphor was war, and the campaigns were conflicts." With proactive—or symmetric—campaigns, Paisley said "the metaphor is negotiation, and the campaigns are bargaining sessions. The solution can be a compromise."

Generally, the arguments of both the activists and the organizations that resist them have merit—it just depends on who is suffering which consequences. Environmentalists want clean air and the beauty of pristine areas preserved. Businessmen want to mine coal, produce electricity, and make more profit. Both cannot have all of what they want.

Public relations warfare can be held in the policy arena. Or two-way symmetric communication can be used to compromise. Henry Schacht, president of the Cummins Engine Company, showed the difference nicely in an exchange with Ralph Lewis, editor and publisher of the *Harvard Business Review*, at a 1976 Conference Board conference on business credibility.[13]

Lewis first stated that the environmentalists couldn't be pleased and pressed Schacht for an answer:

> . . . I think we all know cases in which it is uneconomical to clean up plant operations to the point that the environmentalists will be pleased with us, and the alternative is to build a new plant some place else and throw all those people out of work. Are you saying that we should sit up here and say, OK, so we'll cause a little more unemployment, this is what we should do?

Schacht replied, advocating a symmetric approach:

> The solution to that problem had to come years before in the definition of how that individual company related to its constituencies. The solution is a redefinition of the relative roles in a nonadversary climate, no matter what it takes. The rule makers are not evil, capricious, unthinking people, but more likely hardwork-

ing public servants. They can, with some sense of community, engage in a dialogue with the people from whom they feel pressures to provide some external boundary conditions, so that those boundary conditions can balance the conflicting needs of employment and the environment.

Public relations programs based on the four models of public relations, therefore, differ substantially in their philosophy and tactics. Let's look next at some of the specific programs that organizations have set up to communicate with consumers, environmentalists, and minorities.

Environmental Programs

A few organizations have set up special environmental relations programs when they have continual environmental problems—especially in dirty industries such as steel, coal mining, oil, chemicals, or electric power. Exhibit 15–1, for example, shows the outline of a report on acid rain produced by the Edison Electric Institute, the association of electric companies. Exhibit 15–2 shows a brochure produced by the Atlantic Richfield oil company to promote a speakers bureau (see Chapter 24) on energy topics. Speakers are offered to speak on such topics as:

> Alaska—The Struggle for Resources.
>
> The Drive for Conservation.
>
> The Continental Shelf—A Search for Energy.

In most cases, however, organizations develop short-term environmental public relations campaigns when they have a crisis such as Seabrook or Three-Mile Island, or when they want to smooth the way for a project that has apparent environmental effects—such as an offshore drilling project.[14] Perhaps that is why so much of environmental public relations is reactive. Organizations wait to develop environmental PR programs until environmental activists challenge them or

EXHIBIT **15–1**

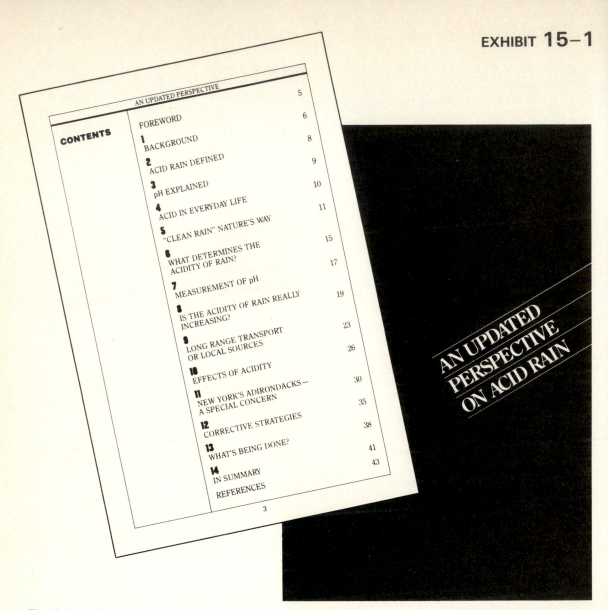

AN UPDATED PERSPECTIVE   5

CONTENTS

FOREWORD   6

1 BACKGROUND   8

2 ACID RAIN DEFINED   9

3 pH EXPLAINED   10

4 ACID IN EVERYDAY LIFE   11

5 "CLEAN RAIN" NATURE'S WAY   15

6 WHAT DETERMINES THE ACIDITY OF RAIN?   17

7 MEASUREMENT OF pH   19

8 IS THE ACIDITY OF RAIN REALLY INCREASING?   23

9 LONG RANGE TRANSPORT OR LOCAL SOURCES   26

10 EFFECTS OF ACIDITY   30

11 NEW YORK'S ADIRONDACKS— A SPECIAL CONCERN   35

12 CORRECTIVE STRATEGIES   38

13 WHAT'S BEING DONE?   41

14 IN SUMMARY   43

REFERENCES

3

AN UPDATED PERSPECTIVE ON ACID RAIN

The Edison Electric Institute, the association of electric companies, issued a detailed report on acid rain, an environmental problem that environmentalists claim results in large part from the emissions of electric generating plants. (Courtesy Edison Electric Institute)

until they fear a challenge from environmentalists over a new project that will affect the environment.

In 1977, Grunig reviewed what public relations practitioners had written about environmental programs and concluded that "most public relations professionals writing on environmental PR problems argue that public relations should advocate environmentalism within their organizations."[15]

314   Managing Public Relations Programs

EXHIBIT 15–2

energy in the 80's

This Atlantic Richfield Company brochure offers speakers on many energy topics through the company's speakers bureau. (Courtesy Atlantic Richfield Company)

Harold Burson, chairman of Burson-Marsteller, for example, argued that the PR manager should:

> . . . impress on management the need to articulate genuine concern about the environment. It's not enough to issue positive papers and press releases. The public relations man must convince his management that communication with environmental critics should be a continuing activity, with much of it on a face-to-face basis.[16]

Burson-Marsteller has provided one example of how this can be done. It produced an elaborate multimedia presentation to be shown to executives of the Gulf Oil Company to sensitize them to pollution. The presentation bombarded the viewer with pictures of birds coated with oil from an oil spill, beer cans floating in rivers, and similar examples of pollution.

Grunig summarized the literature on environmental public relations by stating:

> . . . the public relations person's role is much the same as if he were working for an organization which seeks public support for conservation programs and attempts to arouse public concern about ecology. The basic difference is that the practitioner for the polluting firm may have more difficulty dealing with the internal management public than with the external public.

As we have seen, however, organizations don't always practice such two-way symmetric public relations programs for environmental issues. The professional literature suggests they should. But managers of polluting firms frequently don't want a symmetric environmental relations program.

Consumer Relations Programs

Consumer relations programs, as we've already said, are nothing new to major corporations, especially consumer products firms. Many had modeled consumer information programs on the press agentry/promotional or the public-information model of public relations. Generally, these programs were designed to supplement the company's product advertising. Stanford University marketing

EXHIBIT
15–3

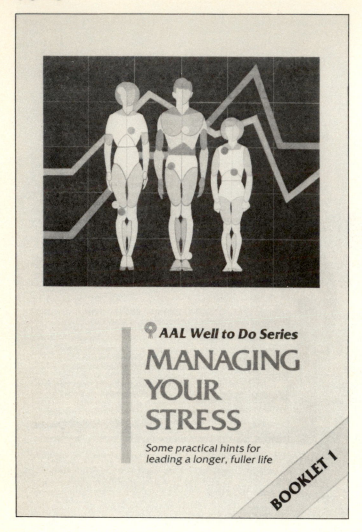

AAL Well to Do Series

MANAGING YOUR STRESS

Some practical hints for leading a longer, fuller life

BOOKLET 1

The Aid Association for Lutherans insurance company of Appleton, Wisconsin, helps its consumers live healthier lives by providing them with a series of booklets on health topics. (Courtesy Aid Association for Lutherans Fraternalife Insurance)

theorist Michael Ray described such supplementary consumer educational material in a book on advertising management:

Consumer educational material would include cookbooks and recipe materials such as those sent out by companies like General Mills, teaching materials such as the comprehensive program developed by Procter and Gamble,

recipe and service materials that are sometimes distributed through special company-controlled magazines, and materials distributed to people who can recommend the brand (such as doctors, pharmacists, auto mechanics, and home economists and their classes).[17]

In the early 1960s, however, President John F. Kennedy gave impetus to the consumer movement when, in a message to

Congress, he declared four basic consumer rights:

The right to safety.
The right to be heard.
The right to choose.
The right to be informed.[18]

Kennedy formed a ten-member Consumer Advisory Council, and his successor, Lyndon Johnson, established the office of Special Assistant to the President for Consumer Affairs (with directors such as Esther Peterson, Betty Furness, and Virginia Knauer). By 1977, there were more than 200

EXHIBIT
15-4

a guide
for
parents

children's hospital
national medical center

Directory Of Services
A Referral Manual For Physicians
And Health Professionals

Children's Hospital National Medical Center, Washington, D.C.

Children's Hospital National Medical Center in Washington, D.C., has an excellent reputation for helping its consumers—children who need medical attention and their parents—to have as pleasant an experience as possible in the hospital. It publishes "A Guide for Parents" and "A Guide for Referring Physicians." (Courtesy Children's Hospital National Medical Center) appointed consumer specialists in government who were supposed to "respond to the needs of consumers . . . and the lobbying efforts of both the activists and the business-appointed consumer officers."[19]

The consumer movement and government's response to it changed the structure of consumer relations programs in major corporations. A Conference Board study of typical corporate consumer relations programs found a number of activities to be typical of such programs.[20]

> Handling, resolution, and analysis of customer complaints and inquiries.
>
> Developing and disseminating to consumers better information on the purchase and use of products or services sold by the company.
>
> Serving as an internal consumer "ombudsman" and consultant on consumer matters within the company.
>
> Providing liaison with consumer-interest organizations outside the company.

Esther Peterson and Giant Food Company • The Giant Food Company, a regional supermarket chain with headquarters in Landover, Maryland, a suburb of Washington, D. C., formed a consumer affairs program in 1970 that attracted national attention. That program came as close as any consumer relations program to being a two-way symmetric program. Giant's program attracted attention because Joseph Danzansky, then the company's president, hired Esther Peterson, President Johnson's first Special Assistant for Consumer Affairs, to direct the program and gave her free rein to develop an activist consumer program.

Peterson developed a consumer bill of rights for Giant similar to the one she developed for the President. As Giant's consumer adviser, her operating philosophy was:

> . . . "never force a program on a particular department." She seeks instead to advise them

about difficulties shoppers may have in interpreting labels, product displays, using certain packages, etc., and to suggest appropriate solutions they should consider.[21]

Giant also developed several innovative consumer services, including:

> Unit pricing—tickets showing the price per pound, per quart, or per count as well as the price per package.
>
> Open dating—use of calendar dates rather than secret codes on packages to indicate when a package should be removed from the shelf.
>
> Nutritional labeling. Giant consulted with a well-known Harvard nutritionist to provide nutritional information on its private-label products.
>
> Percentage labeling—indicating the percentage of different ingredients in a package.

Giant also developed a consumer advertising program in which, among other things, it said, "Don't buy our hamburger this week. It's too expensive in relation to other products." Peterson left Giant to again serve in government, but her program was continued under a new consumer adviser, Odonna Mathews, who had been a member of Peterson's staff.

AT&T Launches System in 1977 • In 1977, AT&T launched its Bell System consumer affairs program at a joint conference of the consumer services and public relations vice presidents.[22] That program, which appears to be a model of symmetric communication with consumers and consumer activists, includes:

> Interdepartmental consumer affairs committees at the vice-presidential level in AT&T and the local telephone companies, with the power to review policies and change them when desirable.
>
> Consumer advisory panels made up of representatives from major consumer organizations.

Employee consumer panels, which make recommendations to top management based on the experiences that employees have with customers.

Staff support in public relations and other departments.

Complaint System Valuable • Of the typical activities of a consumer relations program, one of the most valuable is the complaint system, which can be computerized to organize and channel consumer complaints to appropriate departments or managers—thus informing organizational subsystems about adverse consequences that the company's products may have on consumers. The Conference Board study, for example, showed the importance of the complaint system in several companies.

Amoco Oil Company, to monitor the complaints that arise in its extensive service station network.

Ford Motor Company, to handle complaints from customers who cannot get satisfaction from local dealers, and a system to provide early warning of product complaints.

Motorola, Inc., to handle complaints about color TV sets, one of the most complex of consumer products and a frequent source of consumer complaints.

Many Don't Fit the Symmetric Model • In 1973, a new organization of consumer relations professionals, the Society of Consumer Affairs Professionals in Business (SOCAP) was formed, with headquarters in Washington, D. C. In 1981, SOCAP had nearly 2,000 members.[23] A 1980 membership survey of SOCAP members, however, showed that many work for one-way programs that fit a model other than the two-way symmetric model:

10 percent spend over 50 percent of their time processing and resolving complaints.

10 percent spend over 50 percent of their time on consumer education and information programs.

However:

Nearly 50 percent are not involved in external liaison work at all.

35 percent spend no time informing company personnel about consumer issues.

20 percent never consult with management on consumer issues and nearly half spend less than 10% of their time doing so.

Minority Relations Programs

If organizations discriminate against minorities in their hiring, contracts, promotions, purchases, or advertising, these activities have obvious consequences that create minority publics and public relations problems with these publics. In most cases, organizations turn minority hiring problems over to the personnel department, with assistance from the public relations department in identifying the problems.

Organizations must do more than eliminate *discrimination*, however. They are also responsible for *affirmative* action—meaning they must take positive action to increase the number of minority employees:

Affirmative action, the process of taking deliberate steps to hire females and members of minority groups, is specifically required in companies that perform government subcontracts. Other employers are not initially required to file plans of affirmative action with any government agency, but if they are found to discriminate, they will be required by the court to initiate an affirmative action program.[24]

Beyond Hiring of Minorities • D. Parke Gibson, a black management and public affairs consultant, listed four approaches that organizations use for minority relations.[25] The first of these is taking initiative for affirmative action:

Ask the personnel department (for organizations with more than twenty-two employees) to show you EEO Form 100, which details minority group employment and the affirmative action plan to increase minority employment.

He also suggested:

Determining what the organization is doing that is of particular interest to minority groups. (Keeping in mind that what is done for blacks usually will not interest other minority groups, and vice versa.)

Conducting research to determine how the organization is regarded in minority communities or among minority-group leadership in headquarters, plant, or branch cities.

Researching ethnic-oriented publications to determine what kind of public relations material is being carried, including that of competitive firms and organizations.

These recommendations follow closely our recommendations for identifying and researching publics and determining the kinds of information, cognitions, and attitudes these publics have. However, they apply that approach to organizational consequences that affect minority publics more than other publics.

Community Relations with Minorities • Writing in the *Public Relations Journal*, Frank Escobar, the director of the Office of Citizen Services in Santa Clara County, California, suggested that public relations for a minority public should include a review of advertising to make sure it does not ignore minorities or contain sexist or racist material; he said it is also important to cooperate with equal-employment and affirmative-action programs.[26]

He also suggested community participation programs with the minority community—especially joint programs with public schools that have a high minority enrollment. For example, he added, a San Jose, California, high school has a career opportunity day, during a week-long Cinco de Mayo celebration of the Mexican defeat of French troops in 1862, in which Hispanic business leaders are invited to speak to classes with a high enrollment of students with Spanish surnames.

Washington, D.C.'s Potomac Electric Power Company (PEPCO) has had a similar program for students in the city's predominantly black schools. PEPCO representatives travel to high schools in the company's Pepmobile, where they help black students to become aware of career opportunities and to make career choices.

Frequently, then, minority relations programs are part of a community relations program—following the outline of such programs in Chapter 13—but emphasizing dialogue with minority community leaders and participation in minority community projects.

Sensitization Sessions • One other technique has been used frequently to sensitize management to minority concerns. Managers come to a "training session" with trained black or other minority leaders. The managers are forced to have a dialogue with the black leaders, who play the role of black activists and accuse the managers of prejudice, discrimination, or worse. For many managers, it is their first encounter with a black activist—the first time they have been forced to listen to, and communicate with, an outspoken minority person.

Public Relations of Activist Groups

Most of the programs we have discussed have been developed by organizations that must respond to challenges by activist groups. As we mentioned earlier, however, most of these activist groups also have their own public relations programs.[27]

The environmentalists have, perhaps, done the most. Many have developed environmental awareness or information programs to make people more concerned about the environment.[28] These programs include environmental education programs and camps for schools or youth groups such as the Boy Scouts of America.

Large, relatively conservative environmental groups such as the National Audubon Society or the National Wildlife Federation publish magazines such as *Ranger Rick, National Wildlife*, or *Audubon* that promote environmental values. These organizations also publish legislative alerts to inform their members of environmentally related legislation. And, in 1981, the National Wildlife Federation led a drive to remove Secretary of the Interior James Watt from office.

More-activist groups, such as the Sierra Club or the Clamshell Alliance, use confrontational techniques to pressure organizations to change or to secure government regulation—they use techniques discussed earlier in this chapter. One of their major goals is to increase the number of their supporters who will pressure legislators and regulatory agencies, using grassroots lobbying techniques like those described in the previous chapter on public affairs programs.[29]

Environmental groups are not the only activists, however, as minority and consumer groups also use the public affairs techniques described in Chapter 14 to bring changes in organizational behavior or government policy. The power of black activist organizations to bring change in government and business organizations needs little discussion. In addition, there are now powerful consumer organizations with active public relations programs—the giant of which is the Consumer Federation of America.[30]

ENVIRONMENTAL, CONSUMER, AND MINORITY PUBLICS

Research on publics that arise from environmental, consumer, and minority issues generally shows that publics fall into one of the four kinds of publics described in Chapter 7 and reviewed in the previous chapters of Part III:

Publics active on all related issues, such as environmental or consumer issues.

Publics apathetic on all related issues.

Publics active only on an issue or a small number of issues that involve nearly everyone in the population.

Publics active only on single issues.

More research based on, or related to, the situational theory of publics has been done on environmental issues than on consumer and minority issues. Thus, we will examine environmental publics first and then look for similarities in consumer and minority publics.

Environmental Publics

A great deal of research was done in the 1970s to determine how much concern people have for the environment. This research showed concern for the environment was—to use a cliché—"a mile wide and an inch deep."[31] Many people say they care, but only a young, liberal group of activists do much about their concern.

A number of polls have shown that people believe pollution is an important national problem or that the environment receives too little financial attention from government. The number of people polled who say they are concerned about the environment has also increased over the years.

Other evidence from the polls suggests, however, that people mention the environment as a problem simply because activists repeatedly place environmental issues on the media and public agendas—not because they have a great personal concern. When polls use open-end questions to ask people to list important national problems, fewer people mention the environment than when they are asked to agree or disagree with closed-end questions about the environment.

In an Illinois poll, for example, 95 percent and 91 percent of the respondents agreed with fixed-response statements that air and water pollution, respectively, are important national problems. But only 13 percent mentioned pollution when an open-end question asked them to name the most important national problems.[32]

Young Liberals are the Activists • Research also shows that people who are the most concerned about environmental issues are:

Young.

White.

College educated.

In upper occupational classes.

Liberal in their political orientation.

More cosmopolitan.

Likely to appreciate aesthetic and rural values.

People with these demographic characteristics, therefore, would seem to fit the category of a public that is active on all environmental issues. The rest of the people seem to be part of an apathetic public that does little more than process some information about the environment.

Involvement Makes Everyone Interested • Other environmental researchers have found, however, that apathetic publics become more aware of, and active on, environmental issues that directly involve them— as our four categories suggest should happen. The University of Minnesota research team of Donohue, Tichenor, and Olien found that when an environmental issue directly affected a community, people with less education and of lower status had as much knowledge about the issue as those with the above demographic characteristics.[33]

Other researchers have shown that people who recognize environmental problems only when they are personally involved frequently do not support the environmentalist position if their self-interest is at stake. For example, the residents of an Illinois city who were most committed to solving a water pol-

lution problem caused by a local meat-packing plant were those who would not lose their jobs or business created by the plant if the plant were closed.[34]

Likewise, people in four Minnesota communities were less likely to support restrictive environmental measures that would affect employment in their community than they were to support such measures in other communities. This was especially true of people who lived in small, less-pluralistic communities (see Chapter 13 for more on pluralism).[35]

These results, then, suggest that when environmental regulation costs people their jobs, people who recognize an environmental issue as a problem will often oppose the environmentalist position—as many businesspeople have hoped.

Two Studies Using the Situational Theory • Grunig worked from this early research to develop two studies that used the situational theory to identify environmental publics.[36] The first study was based on 231 interviews in the metropolitan areas of four major cities: Washington, Baltimore, Chicago, and Cleveland. In the second study, researchers conducted 225 interviews in nine rural communities: five in Maryland, two in Missouri, and two in Washington State.

The researchers measured problem recognition, level of involvement, and constraint recognition for eight environmental issues in each study, and used a statistical procedure to identify publics. Four issues were used in both studies: air pollution, extinction of whales, the energy shortage, and strip mining. Four other issues were used only in the urban study: superhighways in urban areas, disposable cans and bottles, water pollution, and oil spills. In the rural study, the four additional issues included dam and flood-control projects, effect of pesticides on wildlife, fertilizer runoff in lakes and streams, and nuclear power plants.

A preliminary analysis of these issues

showed that most of the people interviewed, in both the urban and rural studies, perceived five of the eight issues in the same way. For example, people who recognized one of the five as a problem also recognized the others. The same was true for level of involvement and constraint recognition.

Four issues, on the other hand, stood out as being different from the others. Two of these were the issues that involved the most people—air pollution and the energy shortage. As a result, air pollution and energy created publics that fell into the third category of public found in previous research—a public that is aware or active only when an issue involves nearly everyone in the population.

The other two issues identified single-issue publics. In the urban sample, concern for the superhighway issue was limited to people affected by a highway coming through their neighborhood. In the rural sample, concern for the extinction of whales was limited to a small, single-issue public. Most other people had low problem recognition and level of involvement and high constraint recognition on the whale issue.

Environmental Publics Fit the Four Typical Categories • Further statistical analysis classified the publics into five publics in the urban study and four in the rural study. These were publics that fit one of the four categories described in Chapter 7 and at the beginning of this section.

General Environmentalists • A general environmentalist public appeared in both the urban and the rural samples. Its responses fit into the high-involvement problem-facing category (high problem recognition and level of involvement; low constraint recognition) on all eight environmental issues—both the five general issues and the three special issues. The only exception was the rural environmentalist public, which had little concern for the extinction of whales issue.

The demographic characteristics of these general environmentalist publics fit those that had previously been identified in the literature. In the urban sample, members of this public were young, white, well educated, and below average in income. They also read environmental publications and hiked, camped, bicycled, and commuted. They did not hunt and fish. In the rural sample, the general environmentalists were also likely to be female and not to be farmers. They fished but did not participate in the other environmental activities.

Involving Issues Only • One of the publics in each of the samples was a public concerned only about the most involving issue. In the rural sample, this public was concerned only about the energy issue. In the urban sample, it was also concerned about the superhighway and air pollution issues—which also have a direct consequence on most urban residents.

Members of this involving-issue public felt constrained from doing anything about the few issues that affected them, although their problem recognition and involvement were high. As a result, they did not seek or process much information about the involving issue—or any of the environmental issues. That kind of communication behavior has also appeared in a study of publics arising from the issue of drunken driving.[37]

Publics that are concerned only about the most involving issue frequently communicate little more than those who are apathetic about all of the issues. In the urban sample, this involving-issue public was likely to be white, relatively well educated, of upper income, and male. It also did not participate in environmental activities, except to hunt and fish (characteristics of businesspeople, it would appear). In the rural sample, this public was male, white, poorly educated, of above average income, and a hunter (the stereotyped "redneck," perhaps).

An Apathetic Public • In the urban sample, one public was unconcerned about all of the issues—low problem recognition and level of involvement, high constraint recognition on all of the issues. As previous polls showing "mile wide but inch deep" support for the environment had suggested, however, this apathetic public did say it would process information on several of the environmental issues.

Demographic variables showed this public to be relatively well educated, black, and female; to read some environmental publications but definitely not to join environmental organizations; and to swim and bicycle but not to hike, hunt, or fish.

Special-Issue Publics • The statistical analysis also revealed three special-issue publics: air pollution, superhighway, and whale publics.

In both the urban and rural samples, the air-pollution public was aware of this one issue but not active in doing anything about it. This public had about the same demographic characteristics as the involving-issue publics—male, white, and of above-average income.

A superhighway public was evident in the urban sample—an actively communicating public especially likely to join organizations to do something about the issue. Apparently, this is a public that moves actively to save its neighborhood. It was likely to be black, less educated, of low income, and female—apparently residents of neighborhoods through which superhighways typically pass.

A whale public was found in the rural sample. This was the only rural public that the whale issue put in the high-involvement problem-facing category. This public was also concerned about the four general environmental issues. Apparently, it is is a subpublic of the general environmental public, an environmentalist public that has a special concern for whales. Members of this public were educated, white, and male. They were likely to hunt and to camp but not to participate in other outdoor activities.

Environmental Media Publics

Environmental communication researchers have also looked extensively at how the mass media cover environmental issues and, by inference, at the nature of media publics that result from environmental issues. Grunig reviewed this research and concluded that it suggests that media coverage of environmental issues has gone hand in hand with increasing public concern for the environment.[38]

The reason why the public seems concerned with the environment—but mostly in a superficial way—is because the media have devoted more and more attention to it. But the media cover the environment superficially, and as a result, people who are most concerned and most knowledgeable about the environment use specialized environmental media rather than the mass media for environmental information.

In 1973, Rubin and Sachs found that the media were creating specialized environmental beats and increasing their coverage of governmental agencies that deal with the environment.[39] Although these findings might seem ominous for business firms and other organizations that want their public relations people to keep their environmental sins out of the news media, Rubin and Sachs also found that environmental coverage generally was so poor that the polluters have little to worry about.

They concluded that the media are prisoners of the pseudo-event system for environmental news. Unless an environmental group or government agency issues a report or stages a press conference, environmental news does not get used. As one writer told the researchers: "When the Federal Trade Commission got after Standard Oil and F-310, then I was free to get after them, too. Until then, there just wasn't enough to hang the story on."

If you recall the discussion of media publics in Chapter 11, you should be able to see that this writer's reasoning is typical of the institutional explanation of journalistic behavior. Reporters don't seek out the story, they wait for it to happen.

Activist Groups Understand the Media • Activist groups understand well that institutional forces affect journalistic behavior. This is why staged events such as the protest at the Seabrook nuclear plant or the massive Earth Day event staged in 1970 get extensive media coverage. Earth Day, for example, got more media coverage in *Time, Newsweek,* and *U.S. News and World Report* than any other piece of environmental news in the 1960s.[40]

Environmental Afghanistanism • Research evidence also shows that local media avoid exposing polluters in their circulation area. Rubin and Sachs analyzed the performance of the media after a press conference in which a report on air pollution in the San Francisco Bay area was released. Although the report named polluting companies, newspapers ignored the names in their circulation area, placed the story in an obscure place in the paper, covered "generalities and polls," and wrote nothing that "would help the public help itself."

University of Oregon researchers Steven Hungerford and James Lemert called such media avoidance of local environmental problems "environmental Afghanistanism."[41] They took the term from an editorial writer, who, in 1948, said: "You can pontificate about the situation in Afghanistan in perfect safety. You have no fanatic Afghans among your readers."

Hungerford and Lemert found that newspapers in Oregon wrote about environmental problems in "the community up the road." And they found more environmental news about places outside the circulation area of the newspaper than they found for other types of news.

National Reporters Are Different • In Chapter 11, we discussed Grunig's study of media publics in a sample of Washington reporters.[42] In that study, the one reporter public that did "enterprise reporting"—active information seeking—was the "science/environmental reporters." They also were the most antibusiness reporter public.

Reporters who are trained in environmental science apparently research environmental issues more than general assignment reporters or reporters given the environmental beat without prior training. And reporting at the national level frees them from the constraints of their newspaper's connections in the community.

Also, it appears, environmental reporters are much more likely to cover national environmental policy issues than to expose local polluters—unless a government agency or an activist group stages an event that the reporters can cover.

Consumer Publics

There has been a great deal of research and theorizing about consumer behavior, and most public relations students will, or should, take a course in that area in a school of business or department of consumer economics. Most consumer researchers, however, have attempted to learn how and why consumers use product information and buy the products they do—as opposed to explaining the behavior of publics that arise on consumerism issues.

In addition, consumer researchers have generally limited their explanations of consumer behavior to theories of attitude, personality, or other cross-situational characteristics of the buyer.[43] We have generally rejected these cross-situational theories in favor of the situational theory of publics and communication effects used throughout this book.

Marketing researchers Thomas Robertson and Scott Ward also have argued for more situational theories of consumer behavior.[44] They concluded that consumer research has stressed characteristics of the consumer—such as "private-brand usage, brand-loyalty proneness, opinion leadership, innovativeness, or whatever" and has "ignored situational variables" such as the "latitude for purchasing a new car." ("Latitude" is simply another name for constraint recognition.)

Consumer Decision Theories Fit the Behavioral Molecule • Consumer researchers have devoted a large part of their efforts to developing theories of the consumer decision process. If a marketing manager "knows the steps the consumer takes to make a decision," Stanford's Michael Ray argued, "then it will be possible to provide information for each relevant step.[45] The steps Ray found in the consumer decision process are similar to the segments of the behavioral molecule that we have used both to guide the management of public relations and to understand the behavior of publics. The molecule, you will recall, includes these segments:

. . . Detect . . . Construct . . . Define . . .

Select . . . Confirm . . . Behave . . . Detect . . .

According to Ray, there are four common steps in most models of consumer behavior:

Developing a need (*detect*).
Searching for and comparing alternatives (*construct* and *define*).
Purchasing (*behave*).
Postpurchase (the second *detect*).

As you should recall from Chapter 5, however, this consumer model leaves out several important steps from the behavioral process. It is important, though, because it shows that consumer behavior can be explained with the same situational theory that we have used for other publics. We have just conceptualized that behavior more extensively than have marketing researchers.

Using the Situational Model • Because the four types of publics described at the beginning of this chapter have appeared consistently in research on different kinds of issues, we would expect them to appear for consumer issues in much the same way as they did for environmental issues.

We would expect a general consumerist public to emerge on many national consumer-policy issues—such as the need for a consumer-advocacy agency in the federal government or regulation of consumer products by the Federal Trade Commission.

We would also expect one public to be apathetic until it had a bad experience with a product. At that point, it would be an "involving issue only" public that would complain to the offending company. In the study of "social responsibility publics" described in the previous chapter, for example, the issue of "quality of products and services" was one of the issues that made the otherwise passive public active.

Finally, we would also expect single-issue publics, such as the Ford Pinto public in the study of public affairs publics described in the previous chapter.

A Study of Giant Food's Consumer Publics • For organizations that provide consumers, or users of their services, product- or service-related information—such as the Giant Food program described earlier in this chapter—we would expect to find publics that would behave in ways that can be explained by consumer-decision models. People who recognize a problem (*detect*) and do not feel constrained are most likely to go through the full decision process described by the behavioral molecule, and thus to be the most active users of consumer information.

That was indeed what Grunig found in a study of Giant's consumer program.[46] At the time this study was conducted, Grunig had developed only two of the three concepts in the situational theory—problem recognition and constraint recognition. And he measured them for only one problem—the choice of one food store over another.

The Giant study showed that active consumer publics—those who do the most seeking of information about their purchases—also are most likely to use the consumer information and consumer services provided by a consumer relations program like Giant's.

Grunig identified three consumer publics:

A working-class public that "thinks about" (recognizes the problem of) comparing food stores. This public also was constrained from comparing stores because it did not have transportation other than to the nearest store.

A professional public that also had below-average problem recognition in choosing a supermarket (although not as low as the working-class public) and moderately high constraint recognition. The important constraint for this public was time. Both husband and wife were generally working professionals who did not have time to do more than shop the nearest supermarket.

A middle-class, blue-collar public that fell into the problem-facing category—high problem recognition and low constraint recognition.

As the situational theory predicts, the middle-class public was most likely to seek consumer information and to use the four Giant consumer programs described above—unit pricing, open dating, nutritional labeling, and percentage labeling.

The middle-class public was likely to have heard about the programs, the working-class public not to have heard about them. The professional public was almost as likely as the working-class public to have heard about the programs, but it learned about them mostly while in the store—not from the media or other people. Apparently, members of this public processed information about the programs while shopping.

The middle-class public also communicated more actively about its purchase decisions than the other publics. It was the public most likely to pay attention to food advertisements and to compare the specials advertised by different supermarkets.

The Media and Consumer Issues • Analysis of consumer reporting suggests that our conclusions about media coverage of environmental issues applies also to consumer issues: active—"enterprise"—reporting of national issues but avoidance of local issues that might offend advertisers.[47] Many major metropolitan newspapers, however, have converted their "food pages" to consumer pages and have changed this general tendency.[48]

Minority Publics

No research has been done using the situational model to identify publics arising from minority issues, so we can only speculate about the nature of these publics. Let's discuss black minority publics only, as they are the publics for which we have the most research-based information. The same conclusions should apply to Hispanic and female publics, however.

We would expect that a large proportion of blacks fall into the constrained-behavior or fatalistic-behavior categories—both categories in which constraint recognition is high—because blacks have had less power to control their environment than whites.[49]

Pulling Together Evidence from Previous Chapters • We can find some evidence about the nature of black publics from other studies of publics we have reviewed so far in Part III of this book. On environmental issues, you will recall, a larger relative number of blacks were in the apathetic—and constrained—public than whites.

In the study of the community publics of

a hospital discussed in Chapter 13, however, blacks made up a relatively large proportion of the "low-income" public—a constrained-behavior public. We did conclude that this public was relatively active in communicating with the hospital and could be more active if the hospital could remove the constraints.

The study of "corporate social responsibility publics" described in the previous chapter showed that young, black professionals made up a large part of the public that was concerned about nearly all of the issues studied—recognized problems—but also felt constrained about most of the issues. We also have evidence that blacks can be members of high-involvement problem-recognition publics. In the public affairs study described in the previous chapter, young, black women were strongly represented in the Nestlé activist public.

All of these issues represent general and not necessarily minority-specific issues. We would expect a minority person to perceive a high level of involvement in an issue such as job discrimination that affects blacks more than whites. The constraints might still be there, but the presence of both high involvement and high constraint recognition would logically make minority publics likely to seek the help of government in removing their constraints. The civil rights movement demonstrates this to be the case.

Thus, we can reasonably expect the same four kinds of publics—general activist, special-issue, apathetic, and involving-issue only publics—to arise on minority issues as they do on other issues. But we would expect a high level of constraint recognition among these publics. That would suggest that minority relations programs should place a high priority on community participation programs to help minorities remove their constraints—such as affirmative action on minority contracts. The discussion of minority

relations programs earlier in this chapter suggests that organizations do indeed stress such programs.

OBJECTIVES AND EVALUATION

Public relations managers for both activist organizations and businesses and other organizations that respond to them have concentrated almost exclusively on the attitude and behavioral objectives for their programs. They have adopted the domino theory described in Chapter 6—messages topple the knowledge domino, which topples the attitude domino, which topples the behavior domino.

Activists want to convert the masses to their cause by cultivating proenvironment or proconsumer attitudes. Corporations or other organizations want to fight back by trying to prevent the development of such attitudes or by developing a "projobs" attitude.

Stamm described the holy war—from the standpoint of an environmental activist—as similar to the quest by early scientists for a way to turn lead into gold:

> . . . environmental communicators often arrive at a purpose closely parallel to that of early alchemists who sought to transform less desirable metals into gold. The environmental communicator, too, begins with a material of lesser desirability—the unlovely human mind, in many instances wholly lacking in environmental awareness and ecological values. The communicator hopes to add something to the cognitive material that will elevate it to a state of "ecological conscience." . . . The problem is to discover the manipulations, the treatments that bring this transformation about.[50]

The attitude and behavior objectives would be the logical objectives when the two-way asymmetric model is applied to environmental, consumer, or minority issues. But we have demonstrated that that model doesn't work well for these programs—and that these objectives are difficult to achieve.

Communication Objective for the Symmetric Model

For symmetric programs developed for activist publics, then, the communication objective should have first priority. Evaluate it by counting the number of times members of your organization—whether it is an activist or antiactivist organization—make contact with members of the opposing side. Count articles telling your side that appear in environmental, consumer, or minority media. Count contacts with government officials in regulatory agencies.

You can also expect to achieve message retention and the cognitive effect of hedging from such a program. In fact, hedging is a particularly important objective to measure.

Two Studies of Hedging and Wedging

Two studies by Stamm and Grunig showed, for example, that environmentalist publics do not consistently wedge out a pro-economic development cognition with a proenvironment cognition.[51] They identified two major beliefs about environmental issues:

> The belief in "reversal of trends"—that environmental problems should be solved by reversing the trend toward using up a scarce resource. This is usually the position that environmentalists try to get government to implement through restrictive regulations on industry.

> The belief in "functional substitutes"— that once used up, scarce resources can be replaced by equivalent resources. An example is the oil industry's advocacy of seeking new sources of energy to replace oil.

Stamm and Grunig found that environmentalists generally hold the reversal-of-trends position, but on many issues they hedge it with the functional-substitutes position. In particular, they hedge when they are personally involved—as they were with the gasoline shortages in the late 1970s.

That is also what industry wants—to get environmentalists to hedge their concern for the environment with economic considerations. The Stamm and Grunig research shows that is possible. Chapter 9 shows how to measure that objective.

Research hasn't shown yet, however, whether it is possible to get industry to hedge its functional substitutes position with an environmentalist—reversal of trends—position. That should be the objective of the public relations program internally: to get management to hedge.

NOTES

1. Al Gordon, "Hill Lobbying: Same Methods, More of It," *Congressional Weekly* (June 12, 1976):1512.
2. David M. Rubin and David P. Sachs, *Mass Media and the Environment* (New York: Praeger Special Studies, 1973), p. 14. Rubin and Sachs also cite a number of similar abuses.
3. One example of a public relations program in the film, *The Opinion of the Publics,* produced by the Foundation for Public Relations Research and Education.
4. E. Patrick McGuire, *The Consumer Affairs Department: Organization and Functions* (New York: The Conference Board, 1973), p. 5.
5. Frank Escobar, "Public Relations and the Minority Community," *Public Relations Journal* 37 (July 1981):27–28.
6. For an evaluation of such programs using the coorientational method described in Chapters 6 and 9, see Joyce Elaine Knodell, "Matching Perceptions of Food Editors, Writers, and Readers," *Public Relations Review* 2 (Fall 1976):37–56.
7. Keith R. Stamm and John E. Bowes, "Communication During an Environmental Decision," *Journal of Environmental Education* 3 (Spring 1972):49–55.
8. Frank B. Shants, "Countering the Anti-Nuclear Activists," *Public Relations Journal* 34 (October 1978):10–11.
9. Catherine W. Wolff, "Activist Public Rela-

tions: Integrity and Respect," *Public Relations Journal* 33 (December 1977):19–22.

10. Peter M. Sandman, "Notes on 'Selling' the Freeze," 1982.

11. Bruce Harrison, "Environmental Activism's Resurgence," *Public Relations Journal* 38 (June 1982):34–36.

12. William J. Paisley, "Public Communication Campaigns: The American Experience," in Ronald E. Rice and William J. Paisley (eds.), *Public Communication Campaigns* (Beverly Hills, Calif.: Sage, 1981), p. 39.

13. Phyllis S. McGrath (ed.), *Business Credibility: The Critical Factors* (New York: The Conference Board, 1976), p. 7.

14. Jack J. Yovanovich, "The Controversy Over Energy," *Public Relations Journal* 30 (December 1974):20–22.

15. James E. Grunig, "Review of Research on Environmental Public Relations," *Public Relations Review* 3 (Fall 1977):36–58.

16. As quoted in "How Press Agents Handle Polluters," *Sales Management* 106 (Jan. 15, 1971):56.

17. Michael L. Ray, *Advertising and Communication Management* (Englewood Cliffs, N.J.: Prentice-Hall, 1982), p. 344.

18. Richard A. Aszling, "Consumer Relations," in Philip Lesly (ed.), *Lesly's Public Relations Handbook*, 2d ed. (Englewood Cliffs, N.J.: 1978), pp. 198–208.

19. Doug Newsom, "Communication Theory and the Consumer Movement," *Public Relations Review* 3 (Fall 1977):62.

20. McGuire, p. 5.

21. McGuire, pp. 66–69.

22. Edward M. Block, "The Public Relations Component: New Challenges and Approaches in Corporate Communications," speech to the Public Affairs Council/Public Relations Society of America Conference, Minneapolis, May 20, 1982.

23. Harland W. Warner, Consumerism column in *Public Relations Journal* 31 (February 1981): 7–8.

24. Phyllis G. Krasner and Margaret V. Turano, "Affirmative Action: The Employer's Responsibility," *Public Relations Journal* 33 (January 1977):20–22.

25. D. Parke Gibson, "Working and Communicating with Minority Groups," in Lesly, pp. 88–95.

26. Escobar, pp. 27–28.

27. John Paluszek, "The Eco Organizations: They are Legion," *Public Relations Journal* 29 (May 1973):25–27.

28. For a description of such PR programs, see John E. Ross, "Azimuths in Conservation Communications Research," *Journal of Environmental Education* 1 (Spring 1970):88–92.

29. For a discussion of how to get supporters to join the environmental cause, see Peter M. Sandman, "Motivating Change: Psychological Jujitsu and the Environmental Movement," *Not Man Apart* (May 1982):19, 22.

30. Aszling, p. 208.

31. This research is reviewed in Grunig, "Review of Research on Environmental Public Relations," and in James E. Grunig, "Communication Behavior and Attitudes of Environmental Publics: Two Studies," *Journalism Monographs* No. 81 (March 1983).

32. Rita James Simon, "Public Attitudes Toward Population and Pollution," *Public Opinion Quarterly* 35 (1971):93–99.

33. George A. Donohue, Phillip J. Tichenor, and Clarice N. Olien, "Mass Media and the Knowledge Gap: A Hypothesis Reconsidered," *Communication Research* 2 (1975):3–23.

34. Navin C. Sharma, Joseph E. Kivlin, and Frederick C. Fliegel, "Environmental Pollution: Is There Enough Public Concern to Lead to Action?" *Environment and Behavior* 7 (1975): 455–471.

35. Phillip J. Tichenor, George A. Donohue, Clarice N. Olien, and J. K. Bowers, "Environment and Public Opinion," *Journal of Environmental Education* 2 (Summer 1971):38–42; and George A. Donohue, Clarice N. Olien, and Phillip J. Tichenor, "Communities, Pollution, and the Fight for Survival," *Journal of Environmental Education* 6 (Fall 1974):29–37.

36. Grunig, "Communication Behavior and Attitudes of Environmental Publics: Two Studies."

37. James E. Grunig and Daniel A. Ipes, "A Theoretical Anatomy of a Public Communication Campaign." Paper presented to a session sponsored by the Foundation for Public Re-

lations Research and Education and the Educators' Section of the Public Relations Society of America at the 1982 PRSA convention, San Francisco, November 1982.

38. Grunig, "Review of Research on Environmental Public Relations," pp. 43–46.

39. Rubin and Sachs, Chapter 2.

40. G. Ray Funkhouser, "Trends in Media Coverage of the Issues of the 60's," *Journalism Quarterly* 50 (1973):533–538.

41. Steven E. Hungerford and James B. Lemert, "Covering the Environment: a New Afghanistanism," *Journalism Quarterly* 50 (1973): 475–481, 508.

42. James E. Grunig, "Communication Behavior of Washington Reporters on Business Policy Issues." Paper presented to the Association for Education in Journalism, Athens, Ohio, July 1982.

43. Ray, Chapter 5.

44. Thomas S. Robertson and Scott Ward, "Consumer Behavior Research: Promises and Prospects," in Scott Ward and Thomas S. Robertson (eds.), *Consumer Behavior: Theoretical Sources* (Englewood Cliffs, N.J.: Prentice-Hall, 1973), pp. 5–42.

45. Ray, p. 131.

46. A study described in James E. Grunig, "A Multi-Systems Theory of Organizational Communication," *Communication Research* 2 (1975): 99–136.

47. Francis Pollack, "Consumer Reporting: Towards Protecting Consumers," in James E. Grunig (ed.), *Decline of the Global Village: How Specialization is Changing the Mass Media* (Bayside, N.Y.: General Hall, 1976), pp. 279–286.

48. Knodell.

49. See, for example, Jessie Bernard, *The Sociology of Community* (Glenview, Ill.: Scott, Foresman, 1973), pp. 123–148.

50. Keith R. Stamm, "Conservation Communication Frontiers: Reports of Behavioral Research," in Clay Schoenfeld (ed.), *Interpreting Environmental Issues* (Madison, Wisc.: Dembar Educational Research Services, 1973), p. 228.

51. Keith R. Stamm and James E. Grunig, "Communication Situations and Cognitive Strategies in Resolving Environmental Issues," *Journalism Quarterly* 54 (1977):713–720; James E. Grunig and Keith R. Stamm, "Cognitive Strategies and the Resolution of Environmental Issues: A Second Study," *Journalism Quarterly* 56 (1979):715–726.

ADDITIONAL READING

Grunig, James E., "Communication Behavior and Attitudes of Environmental Publics: Two Studies," *Journalism Monographs* No. 81 (March 1983).

Grunig, James E., "Review of Research on Environmental Public Relations," *Public Relations Review* 3 (Fall 1977):36–58.

Grunig, James E. (ed.), *Decline of the Global Village: How Specialization is Changing the Mass Media* (Bayside, N.Y.: General Hall, 1976).

McGuire, E. Patrick, *The Consumer Affairs Department: Organization and Functions* (New York: The Conference Board, 1973).

Newsom, Doug, "Communication Theory and the Consumer Movement," *Public Relations Review* 3 (Fall 1977):59–70.

Ray, Michael L., *Advertising and Communication Management* (Englewood Cliffs, N.J.: Prentice-Hall, 1982).

Rubin, David M. and David P. Sachs, *Mass Media and the Environment* (New York: Praeger Special Studies, 1973).

EDUCATIONAL RELATIONS AND ECONOMIC EDUCATION

For many years, public relations practitioners have used the domino theory to organize programs to "educate" students, teachers, employees, stockholders, and members of other publics. If people do not buy your product, have negative attitudes about business, oppose nuclear power, these practitioners believed, it is because they do not have sufficient knowledge about the product, organization, or business in general.

Economic-education programs, for example, "were based on the premise that greater knowledge of the enterprise system and economic principles results in greater support for business and the system."[1]

The trouble with many of these "educational" programs, however, is that they have used the press agentry model to promote products in school classrooms, proselytize for right-wing views, or to give one-sided information on crucial issues such as nuclear power. Consider the following examples:

In the early 1960s, the Quaker Oats Company dressed up an actor to look like the Quaker on its oatmeal box and sent him to schools to lecture children on the dangers of communism. He talked to over two million children before the program was stopped.[2]

The New York State Electric & Gas Company took "Larry, the Talking Garbage Can" into schools to discuss energy issues. A public relations man talked with Larry—a garbage can fitted with tape recorder, light effects, and other gimmicks. Larry "never failed to make the kids laugh" as he told them the country is running out of oil and natural gas, that solar and wind energy won't work, and that nuclear power will solve our energy problems.[3]

From 1972 to 1973, General Motors distributed 2.1 million copies of a comic book entitled "Professor Clean Asks . . . What is Air Pollution" to 8,000 schools around the country. Cartoon characters "Charlie Carbon Monoxide" and "Harry Hydrocarbon" told children not to fear health hazards from air pollution. Although the booklet said too much Charlie is not a good thing, it described Harry as a "harmless demon." "In the end, Professor Clean assured the students that air pollution will 'no longer be a problem' with the 'addition of new devices in the near future'—devices to meet government emission standards . . . which the auto industry had resisted."[4]

From the 1940s on, corporations have sponsored "economic education" programs that have warned people about a supposed threat to the free enterprise system from radicals, Communists, and Socialists. The programs equated capitalism with democracy and socialism with totalitarianism. They argued that criticism of the performance of the economy results from leftist political beliefs. "America, love it or leave it!" was a popular slogan.[5]

According to a 1979 report on corporate economic education programs written by the consulting firm of Towers, Perrin, Forster & Crosby (TPF&C), these latter programs have "accomplished very little," and "their combined cost may be classified as American business's greatest marketing disaster, far exceeding the combined losses incurred by the Edsel motor car and 'Corfam,' two expensive and unsuccessful products."[6]

The TPF&C group examined over a thousand current pieces of economic education material—articles, brochures, posters, pay-envelope stuffers, motion pictures, videotapes, etc.—and rated most of them "fair to poor" and "only a handful . . . good to superior."[7]

Some Definitions

Like most of the programs discussed thus far in Part III, educational relations and economic education programs generally are more common in corporations and business trade associations than in other kinds of organizations. But government agencies, hospitals, and associations of nonprofit groups could use the business model of communicating with students and teachers.

We define educational relations as *programs in which public relations practitioners facilitate communication between their organizations and students and teachers*. When educational relations programs discuss economics and the workings of business firms, they subsume one kind of economic education program—those aimed at students and teachers.

Economic-education programs generally aim toward additional publics, however—most often employees, stockholders, and members of the "general public." Thus, economic education programs can be defined as *any educational effort designed to upgrade knowledge and understanding of the economic system and of business in particular*.[8]

Critics and Supporters

Many critics would like to keep sponsored educational materials out of public schools. Sheila Harty, of the Center for the Study of Responsive Law, has argued, for example, that "curriculum materials, like teachers' salaries, should come from public monies—free of intervention from vested interests—in accord with the principle of our tax-supported schools."[9]

Walter Purdy, a former teacher who became manager of educational services for the Edison Electric Institute, the association of utility companies, replied that curricular materials produced by business and associations—especially in science and social studies—can help to alleviate acute budgetary problems in schools.[10]

He added that utilities—which he represented—use panels of educators and advisory groups to avoid bias in the educational materials they provide and that educators and students can easily recognize bias in the materials. "It would be unfair—even unknowledgeable—to conclude that the use of business-sponsored materials will brainwash or con students."

Then he added:

Our nation's future depends on an informed population capable of digesting vast amounts of information and making logical decisions. Educators will require assistance from all segments of society to carry out the vital task of preparing today's students to be tomorrow's decision makers. Hopefully, educators and businesses will get together in communities where cooperative programs do not exist.

Subsidized Information vs. the Symmetric Model

Communication theorist Oscar Gandy has argued that public relations departments provide "subsidized information" about their organizations.[11] It costs people money to gather information to make decisions, and organizations are willing to subsidize this information search by providing free information about the organization, its products, its research, or its services.

The concept of subsidized information fits educational relations especially well, because organizations are willing to subsidize the production of information that schools and other educational services provide to people—believing that people who understand their organization will treat it fairly.

Subsidized information may be blatantly biased toward promoting the organization's interest, as the above examples of educational relations programs show. More often, however, subsidized information is reasonably accurate—along the lines of the public-information model. But the subsidized information will usually be limited to what the organization is doing or knows from its work. Subsidized information does not go beyond the perspective of a single organization to compare the information from that organization with that of others. The U. S. Chamber of Commerce, for example, does not compare its view of government regulation with that of an environmental group and does not discuss research that shows both the benefits and the damages from regulation.

Educational programs that go beyond the press agentry model, in other words, too often confine themselves to the public-information or two-way asymmetric models. Such programs do not help to truly educate people to perceive and evaluate different alternatives to complex problems. Only the symmetric model can do that. Thus, we would argue that organizations should enter into educational relations programs only if they practice the two-way symmetric model. Other programs interfere with, rather than enhance, the educational process.

Let's look more closely, then, at educational relations and economic education programs.

EDUCATIONAL RELATIONS PROGRAMS

In most educational relations programs, public relations practitioners develop materials related to the work of their organization to supplement existing curricular materials. These materials may consist of booklets, comic books, filmstrips, films, booklets, mimeograph or ditto stencils, workbooks, or complete kits of these materials.

Often, the organization may contract the production of these materials to outside consultants or educators—and ask consultants to do formative research on students to see if the materials are appropriate.

Once the materials have been produced, the public relations people announce the materials to educators through educational journals, such as *Today's Education*, or sourcebooks of free materials, such as *Educator's Guide to Free Films* or *Elementary Teachers Guide to Free Curriculum Materials*. Other practitioners have the responsibility for contacting teachers to acquaint them with materials, ask them to use them, and to gather teacher evaluations of the materials.

Educational relations specialists also try to place speakers in classrooms to talk about their organization, to engage in a dialogue with students and teachers, or to supplement the curricular materials with examples of actual business or organizational practice. Many nonbusiness organizations also sponsor science fairs or take students on tours of a hospital, research facility, theater, or museum.

Educational relations programs can be developed for all levels of education—elementary, junior high, high school, or college/university. Many aim only at teachers, hoping to provide them with information they will pass on to students.

Some Examples

Many educational relations programs teach students how to use an organization's products or services. Here are some examples.

Bell System telephone companies provide schools with Telezonia, a multimedia program on proper use of the telephone for students in kindergarten through sixth grade.

The National Consumer Finance Association—which represents small loan companies—believed loan companies develop a poor reputation because people do not know how and when to use credit, and then blame the loan company when they default on loans. Thus, the association developed workbooks, films, and tapes for two-week courses on finance, budgeting, and borrowing for elementary, junior-high, and high schools. It also developed similar materials for ministers to use when troubled couples come to them seeking marital advice—frequently for problems resulting from poor financial planning.

Most major newspapers have "newspaper in the classroom" programs, devised by the American Newspaper Publishers' Association. Newspapers provide schools with copies of the daily paper at a discount, along with supplementary materials to be used by teachers to enhance reading and understanding of newspapers.

Other programs strive to help students make intelligent career choices. For example,

the Goodyear Tire and Rubber Company set up a summer work program for high school guidance counselors. In the program, counselors worked in several company jobs that would be available to the students they counsel when they graduate from high school.

Still others stimulate dialogue between company representatives and students and teachers. For example, the Conoco Oil Company has set up three-day dialogues at university conference centers, with a third of the participants coming from Conoco, a third from university faculty, and a third from government agencies or activist groups. In these sessions, participants debate such topics as "Does the Clean Air Act Need Revision?".

Similarly, the American Iron and Steel Institute sends young professionals who work in the steel industry into university classrooms to discuss current topics such as the environment, import policy, business ethics, or equal employment opportunity. Whenever possible, the speakers go to the college or university from which they graduated.

The Big Four Topics

In 1979, Sheila Harty of the Center for Responsive Law in Washington had teachers request educational materials from the Fortune 500 industrial companies, Fortune 300 non-industrial companies, 124 national trade associations, and 90 large electric utilities.

The materials that Harty received fell predominantly into four subject areas:

Nutrition.
Energy.
Environment.
Economics.

Nutrition Materials • Let's look at some examples of these programs to show what organizations do for educational relations.

In the nutrition area, food producers particularly go after home-economics, nutrition,

EXHIBIT
16–1

A *dialogue* to...

stimulate an exchange of ideas between the academic community and the steel industry. The *Steel Fellows Program* brings young professionals from the steel industry to campus to raise issues in your classroom, exchange ideas with you and your students, and answer questions about the world of industry.

enrich the learning environment by introducing another perspective on the ideas you discuss with your students. Steel Fellows are a *resource* offered to you by the iron and steel industry.

promote understanding of the practices of the business world for college students—whether in business, economics, political science, engineering, the physical sciences, or the humanities. Steel Fellows have made good starts in their career and have been selected on the basis of their broad knowledge and ability to discuss issues responsively.

A *dialogue* of...

young professionals Steel Fellows, men and women not long away from the college campus themselves, await your invitation to return to the classroom—your classroom—to discuss issues, answer questions, and provide the perspective of the business world to your students. They do not come to campus with "canned" presentations. They seek to communicate a sense of what the business world is—its pressures and challenges, its rewards and difficulties.

students Today's students are searching for answers to difficult questions, questions of the quality of life and environment, the role of industry in our society, business ethics, and equal employment opportunity. Steel Fellows share those concerns and are ready to discuss their perspectives as a result of their experience in the business world.

academic community Faculty members can also benefit from inviting a Steel Fellow to campus. The Steel Fellows Program is not a speakers bureau. Steel Fellows will work with you to design a special program suited to your curriculum. They will arrange their schedule to yours, and as they serve you they will also be working towards the goals of your class.

SteelFellows Program

an education cooperation
service of the
American Iron and Steel Institute

The American Iron and Steel Institute announces its Steel Fellows Program by sending a brochure to college and university professors. The program brings young professionals from the steel industry into college classrooms to engage in a dialogue with students and faculty. (Courtesy American Iron and Steel Institute) and health classes. Most want to identify their products with good nutrition. Most stretch the connection, according to Harty. Some examples:[12]

McDonald's Corporation produced a "nutrition action pack," with golden arches on each of the included mimeograph stencils.

Kellogg's distributed Tony the Tiger posters to promote eating of breakfast, posters designed to be displayed in school cafeterias.

The National Dairy Council distributed a film entitled "The Day Milk was Turned Off," materials to help preschoolers identify foods, and a nutrition curriculum for elementary students.

Campbell Soup Company bought physical education equipment for schools whose students collected a specified number of soup labels.

Colgate Palmolive provided teaching materials on dental health.

The National Soft Drink Association distributed a booklet, "The Story of Soft Drinks," which claimed that the water in sodas is of major nutritional value, but did not mention excessive sugar, artificial colorings, and additives.

Energy Materials Push Nuclear Power • Harty found electric utilities to be most active in providing energy materials, such as films and comic books, which she said contained cartoon graphics and simple phrasing.[13] Most strongly advocated nuclear power.

For example, New York's Commonwealth Edison Company produced a comic book in 1977 called "The Atom, Electricity, and You." On page 2, a boy and his parents were about to enter an exhibit on nuclear power. The boy told his parents, "I've heard it's [the exhibit] the greatest, Dad—all about nuclear energy and what it can do for all the folks who use electric power." On the last page, a man concluded, "But there is an answer to the fuel problem—and that answer lies in the use of nuclear energy in the generation of electricity! Nuclear energy, the miracle product of the splitting of the atom!"

Seldom, Harty added, do the energy materials discuss the economics of constructing nuclear plants, the health effects of low-level radiation, or the problem of disposing of nuclear waste. (See Chapter 3 for a discussion of the shortcomings of such a program by Metropolitan Edison Company of Pennsylvania before the Three-Mile Island nuclear accident.)

Oil companies and their trade association, the American Petroleum Institute, also produce energy materials. Most do a reasonably balanced job of discussing energy shortages. But they also have blamed price increases on the Arabs and stressed that the oil industry is competitive (no doubt with a fear of divestiture in mind).

One of the most symmetric of the energy-education programs is a series of "energy economics forums" held for secondary school teachers by the American Petroleum Institute. Teachers participate in one-day programs and hear speakers from oil companies discuss such topics as offshore drilling, petroleum marketing and refining, and energy economics. Time is allowed for participants to question and argue with the speakers.

Environmental Education • As one might expect, companies or industries that are most often accused of polluting frequently produce environmental education materials. Harty reviewed materials produced by three associations.[14]

The American Iron and Steel Institute produced a comic book, "Mark Steel Fights Pollution"; a booklet, "Economics of the Environment"; a leaflet, "The Story of Environment and Industry"; a film, "Steel & America: A New Look," featuring Donald Duck; a multimedia package, "Economics of the Environment: An Activity Master Program for High School Students"; and an audiovisual teaching kit that explains the production of steel, "The Iron & Steel Cookbook." As might be expected, these materials downplay pollution and stress the costs of reducing pollution.

The American Forest Institute developed a curriculum program, "Project Learning Tree," in cooperation with the Western Regional Environmental Education Council and the public relations firm of Education/Research Systems, Inc. of Seattle, Washington. The institute also involved principals and teachers in the development of the materials, and used resource persons from environmental organizations such as the Sierra Club, Friends of the Earth, the National Audubon Society, and the National Wildlife Federation. Formal evaluation was done by the Bureau of School Service and Research at the University of Washington.

The Manufacturing Chemists Association, which represents firms producing considerable industrial waste, has produced educational materials that stress the efforts of chemical companies to clean up pollution; they underplay the damages caused by chemical waste—such as cancer, birth defects, neurological disorders, and other chronic diseases.

The fourth kind of educational materials found in Harty's survey—on economics—is usually produced by economic-education programs. We turn to those programs next.

Economic-Education Programs

In 1977, the management consulting firm of Towers, Perrin, Forster & Crosby, led by TPF&C's director of economic education, Myron Emanuel, surveyed 1,250 large corporations to find out what they had done in economic education since 1970.[15] As stated at the beginning of this chapter, the TPF&C research group rated most of the materials as "fair to poor."

Emanuel and his colleagues traced economic-education programs to the Great Depression of the 1930s and subsequent "assaults" on business—the rise of labor unions, wage and hour laws, antitrust activity, and recognition of the Soviet Union.

Business leaders thought the future of the capitalist system was threatened by these "assaults" and developed economic education programs to counter them. Economic education programs took two directions. Some actually provided education about economics. Most, however, provided political propaganda in support of free enterprise:

> Thus, for many years, interrupted only by World War II, the U.S. public saw a succession of ads in newspapers and magazines, on radio and TV; a profusion of brochures, articles, speeches, meetings and seminars, motion pictures and slide shows devoted to defending and "explaining" the free enterprise, or the free market, economy, or the profit system (as the U.S. economic system was variously described) and the essential role that business and business people played in its dynamic and beneficial growth. The word "capitalistic" was rarely used. It was thought to have negative connotations.[16]

These economic education programs were a marketing disaster much greater than the Edsel, according to the Emanuel group, because they emphasized the wrong issue. Americans had few doubts about the free-enterprise system but were increasingly concerned with the consequences business has on them.[17] A 1977 Yankelovich, Skelly, and White poll showed, for example, that more than 90 percent of Americans support the economic system and believe the public should be willing to sacrifice to save it.

Business leaders today make much of a decline in confidence in business that appears in national polls. In a Harris survey in 1979, for example, only 18 percent of the people interviewed said they had high confidence in business, contrasted to 55 percent in 1966.[18] But other American institutions have suffered a similar decline in confidence—e.g., a decline from 42 percent high confidence to 18 percent for Congress and 61 percent to 29 percent for the military.

The polls also show the decline in confidence has not come from a loss of faith in free enterprise but from dissatisfaction with business performance: "bankruptcy of giant concerns (Penn Central), near bankruptcy of others (Lockheed), Watergate, illegal political bribes and payoffs, recession, unemployment, inflation."[19]

Mass economic-education efforts by business have done little to change these negative evaluations. Yet, according to the TPF&C research team, most economic education programs have changed little:

> The far greater number, as our survey shows, is still addressing the problems and concerns of the 1930s and 1940s—the survival of the free enterprise system, the danger of "creeping socialism," the ideological struggle between democracy and communism—rather than the dominant questions people seem to be asking of business in 1978: "What are you doing to make this system work better for me?" "What can I do to help?"[20]

Newer Programs Are Symmetric • The TPF&C group found, however, that many newer economic-education programs address contemporary problems and are aimed at key publics. These programs are "sharply focused in two critical areas":

> Winning support from key "constituencies"—especially employees and stockholders.
>
> Addressing the legitimate concerns of publics considered important to the organization sponsoring the program.[21]

The newer economic-education programs are a lot like other public relations programs such as public affairs, employee relations, and environmental relations. They attempt to facilitate symmetric dialogue between the organization and key publics about the consequences of business behavior. In discussing these consequences, economic-education specialists hope to achieve an understanding of how the business system operates and what it is doing to correct poor performance.

TPF&C's study found the most frequent target publics of economic-education programs to be employees. Its list of target publics shows that economic education crosses paths with many other public relations programs. In descending order of importance, the target publics were:[22]

Employees.
The "general" public.[23]
Students.
Employees' families.
Shareholders.
Opinion leaders.
Teachers.
Managers.
Retirees.
Consumers.
Community.

Most Topics Relate to the Economic System • What distinguishes economic-education programs from other public relations programs is their emphasis on the function of the capitalist economic system and its relation to government. TPF&C found the following topics, in order, to be discussed most frequently in the programs. The most popular relate to the economic system in general, but many topics delve into business consequences and the performance of business in dealing with those consequences:[24]

Profits.
Free enterprise system.
Government regulation.
Taxation.
General economic principles.
Productivity.
Inflation.

Annual report on state of sponsor's business.

Competition.

Energy.

Employee benefits.

Capital investment.

Consumerism.

Employee compensation.

Divestiture.

Job security.

Wage/price controls.

Business cycles.

Environment.

Financial planning.

World economic systems.

Financial definitions.

Stock market.

Company policies and their progress.

Exports.

Interest.

Retained earnings.

Product and service quality.

Many Methods and Media Used • The TPF&C research group also classified about a thousand pieces of economic education materials it received into categories that show the range of techniques used. The categories included:[25]

**EXHIBIT
16–2**

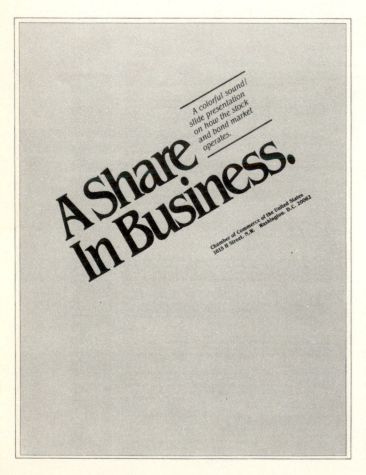

The Chamber of Commerce of the United States has produced an Economics for Young Americans series that is purchased by local chambers of commerce and distributed to schools. This exhibit shows some of the pictures and the text of a taped narration from the filmstrip series, ''A Share in Business . . . How the Stock and Bond Market Operates.'' (Courtesy Chamber of Commerce of the United States)

EXHIBIT
16–2
(Continued)

Slide 1
Music Up
Music Under

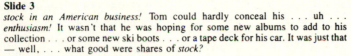

Slide 2
It was Tom Davis' eighteenth birthday — and good old Aunt Martha had come through again. She had given Tom great gifts before — but *this* birthday was special, she said, and she was giving him something really exciting! . . .

Slide 3
stock in an American business! Tom could hardly conceal his . . . uh . . . *enthusiasm!* It wasn't that he was hoping for some new albums to add to his collection . . . or some new ski boots . . . or a tape deck for his car. It was just that — well, . . . what good were shares of *stock?*

Slide 4
But the fact of the matter is — Tom soon found out that Aunt Martha had introduced him to a new world that really was exciting — the world of *business securities.*

Slide 5
Her gift made him one of 25 million Americans who own shares of businesses. What he was yet to learn was that stock ownership by a wide segment of the public is one of the great strengths of the American economic system.

Slide 6
It all has to do with *capital.* Capital is really money that people have decided to *save,* and invest, rather than spend. This money — as *capital* — is put to work. Businesses need capital to invest in

Slide 7
developing new products, building new plants, and buying new, more efficient machinery and processes. This helps them become more productive, stay competitive with other companies here and abroad, remain economically healthy, and grow.

Slide 8
Businesses acquire capital four ways — from retaining a portion of their own profits, by borrowing from banks and other financial institutions, by borrowing through issuing bonds, or by selling shares of ownership in their companies. In a free economic system such as ours, the ownership of stock in business is only one of several kinds

Slide 9
of financial investment open to people with money they have saved. Financial investment is defined as the purchase of securities — as opposed to *business* investment which involves the purchase of productive plants or equipment.

Slide 10
People who have saved can also put their money in banks, savings and loan associations, certain types of insurance policies, credit unions, government bonds, corporate bonds or short-term securities in the money market. Each of these financial investment opportunities offers a return on investment to the saver —

Slide 11
with the *rate of return* based on the *risk.* A savings account in a bank, or savings and loan or a short-term Treasury security offer very little risk to the saver — so the rate of return is relatively low. Other opportunities to invest may provide higher returns — but will usually require a greater risk, a commitment of funds for a longer time, or a greater investment.

Slide 12
An investor in business securities has a variety of risk opportunities to consider. The return on investment depends on factors such as the industry in which the company he or she selects to invest is located, the company's financial record, its current financial condition, what can be expected of it in the future — as well as general national conditions that affect the entire economy. There are several ways to judge the investment potential of a stock —

One-time publications:
    Articles.
    Annual reports.
    Special publications or kits.
    Curriculum or meeting leader guides.
Ongoing series of publications:
    Articles.
    Leaflets, posters, brochures.
Audiovisual materials.
Multimedia materials.

There are many sources of case study programs in economic education.[26] You can pursue more of these case studies on your own, but let's look at a few examples.

Programs for Students and Teachers Extend Educational Relations • One major target of economic education programs is students and their teachers—also one of the big four areas of educational relations found in the Sheila Harty study. For example:

The Chamber of Commerce of the United States has produced a two-part kit, "Economics for Young Americans," with filmstrips, tape cassettes, a teacher's manual, and ditto masters to produce student activity sheets. The Phase II kit (for junior high students) covers four topics: "The Business of Competition," "Why the Price?" Check Your Paycheck," and "The Sense of Saving." The Phase III kit (for high school students) covers four topics also: "A Share in Business . . . How the Stock and Bond Market Operates," "Getting A Job . . . It's Your Move," "Economic Systems . . . What's the Difference," and "The Case for Interdependence" (Exhibit 16–2).

There are also examples of symmetric programs for students and teachers—e.g., the Steel Fellows program and the American Petroleum Institute faculty forums, discussed under educational relations programs. In addition:

The Ryerson Steel Company hired teachers to work in the company during the summer and gave them free rein to ob-serve how a business operates. The teachers sat in on meetings, rode on delivery trucks, and reviewed income and expense statements.

Special Programs for Journalism Students • In Chapter 11, we discussed the belief, prevalent among business leaders, that the media have a bias against business. Because corporations classify media representatives as part of the "opinion leader" public for economic education programs, some companies have sponsored special economic education programs for the media. For example:

The Sperry Rand Corporation held a symposium for the international business press in which sixty journalists participated in dialogues on such issues as multinational business; world business and world politics; and industry, energy, and society.

Corporations have been particularly interested in journalism students, because they will make up the next generation of journalists. Some examples:

General Motors sponsored an intercollegiate business-understanding program in 18 leading schools of journalism. Teams of student journalists competed for prize money by developing a treatise on "Business and the News Media—What are the Roles of Each?"

The National Association of Manufacturers conducted a dialogue program in selected schools of journalism between students and business executives from companies in the geographic area of each school.

"Educating" Employees • Employees share in profits and losses of business, and employee economic education programs strive for an understanding of that shared interest. Two examples:

Allied Corporation has put out an annual report to employees since 1973. Allied extracts financial information of special interest to employees from its annual report to stockholders for the special report. Topics include employee benefits and compensation, financial planning, profits, and taxation.

Green Giant Company ran a series of six articles in its employee magazine *Giant* on economic topics—business cycles, capital expenditures, and financial planning.

Another example shows how the symmetric model can work in an employee program:

Dow Chemical Company held unrehearsed dialogue sessions between a small group of employees and the company's chief executive officer. Most of the discussion was about decisions made by top management and economic topics, such as the effects of government regulation. The sessions were taped in the company's Midland, Michigan, offices and then shown in other company locations.

Advertising for the "General" Public • Corporations and trade associations have used advertisements over the years to promote the free-enterprise system to external corporate publics—and have wasted enormous amounts of money in doing so.

In 1974, the Advertising Council, a nonprofit organization sponsored by advertising agencies to conduct public service advertising, began what has probably been the "most extensive and most expensive" economic education program in U. S. history.[27] In contrast to previous advertising campaigns, the council used research to identify a more realistic approach to mass economic education.

The council began the project by hiring the research department of the Compton advertising agency to find out what the public thought about the economic system. The study showed, as discussed above, that people value free enterprise and do not want fundamental changes in the economic system. But it also showed that people have complaints about inflation, taxes, monopoly, and other business abuses; and that they favor government intervention as a solution more often than not. Most people surveyed, however, had only a fragmentary knowledge of how the economic system operates.[28]

The council defined its objective as informing and educating Americans on how the economic system works. It used advertising as part of the effort—for example, ads containing test questions to measure a person's EQ (economics quotient).

But the council realized advertising alone couldn't create knowledge. Thus, it developed a booklet in cooperation with economists, representatives of the Joint Council on Economic Education, and other business associations. The booklet was illustrated by Charles Schulz, creator of the "Peanuts" comic strip. It was offered free in single copies in the first wave of national advertising. Several newspapers reprinted the booklet in serial form.

In addition, the council developed supplementary materials, including films, filmstrips, teaching and training guides, instructional kits, feature articles, news releases, bulletins, and supplementary booklets on specific subjects.

In spite of the detailed planning for this program, however, many critics have questioned whether economics can be taught through advertising and simplified booklets. And Ad Council research shows that only one in three people who sent for the booklet read it.[29]

Such arguments make sense when one thinks of our theory of active and passive publics. Mass campaigns reach passive, information-processing publics who seldom develop organized thoughts—knowledge. Whether passive information processing justifies the cost of mass campaigns requires a budgetary decision by the manager of an economic-education program (see Chapter 8).

To help make those decisions, let's turn now to the objectives and publics of educational programs.

OBJECTIVES AND PUBLICS FOR EDUCATIONAL PR PROGRAMS

We began this chapter by stating that organizations have typically used the domino theory to develop educational-relations and economic-education programs: they have strived for changes in attitudes and behavior. And, in the past, they have not been shy about using press agentry or two-way asymmetric—persuasive—techniques to try to achieve their objectives.

Those objectives and techniques have almost always failed, and they have antagonized teachers, parents, and members of other publics.

For example, Thomas Ris, president of a Seattle, Washington, public relations firm that produces educational relations materials, found that over half of eighty-eight educators he surveyed thought industry-sponsored educational programs were not factual.[30] In fact, 47 percent thought the materials were one-sided and lacking in objectivity. Similarly, Sheila Harty found that about half of 132 teachers she surveyed thought that corporate educational materials were product-oriented and that they could perceive bias in the presentations.[31] In both studies, however, teachers said they were satisfied with the materials, and that they used them.

The Towers, Perrin, Forster and Crosby study of economic education programs identified five "pitfalls" in those programs, the first three of which suggest that the domino theory doesn't work:[32]

Lack of objectivity.
"Flag-waving."
Failure to meet audience needs.
Failure to limit subject matter.
Failure to consider graphic design.

Communicating and Understanding Are Basic Objectives

In developing any kind of educational program, always remember that the basic purpose of education is to educate, not to propagandize. That is, a good teacher communicates with his or her students, helps them to retain the message, and has enough credibility so that students believe that what he or she says is factual (message acceptance). Those should also be the objectives of educational relations efforts.

First, you must communicate with students, teachers, employees, or other publics.

For school programs, that means teachers must use your materials. To gain that acceptance, you must involve teachers in producing the materials and in reviewing them for accuracy and balance. You should also involve antagonists of your organization—such as environmentalists and consumerists—in producing materials to ensure the balance necessary for classroom acceptance.

To get students, employees, television viewers, or stockholders to use, remember, and believe your materials, you must address topics that are relevant to these publics. Dialogue programs work well because members of the publics can bring up topics that interest them.

For other types of programs, however, you will have to address the shortcomings of your organization—because they usually involve publics—as well as abstract topics such as free enterprise, government spending, corporate profits, or competition.

Reviewing the Study of Journalism and Business Students

In Chapter 11 on media relations, we discussed a study of journalism and business students that was designed to identify the publics of economic-education programs directed at journalism students.[33] This study, which was based on the situational theory of publics, showed that student publics will only passively process materials from educational-relations and economic-education programs—unless they relate to topics that involve the students.

Recall that the study measured problem recognition, level of involvement, and constraint recognition for three sets of issues:

Three basic economic issues covered in most economic education programs (size of profits, capitalism vs. socialism, and supply and demand).

Three governmental relationships also discussed in most programs (regulation of business, taxation of business, and government spending).

Three secondary consequences of business (quality of goods and services, prices of goods and services, and pollution).

Statistical analysis identified two publics: one consisting mostly of journalism students and one consisting mostly of business students. The business students were an active public on all nine issues, but the journalism students were active only on the three issues that represented secondary consequences of business behavior.

The implication is clear. Students will only passively process information contained in public-relations material unless it addresses questions that affect them. That is why the modern, symmetric educational relations programs are so important. They discuss issues relevant to students. They do not propagandize about free enterprise and the evils of government regulation.

Other studies on employee publics (Chapter 12) and public affairs publics (Chapter 14) show these same conclusions also apply to nonstudent publics of economic education programs.

Given this understanding of objectives and publics, let us conclude by looking at means of evaluating educational programs.

EVALUATION OF EDUCATIONAL PROGRAMS

Educational relations and economic education programs for teachers and students can be evaluated in three stages.

First, materials should be pretested experimentally with students or teachers who will use them. Students should be asked whether the topics are relevant or interesting to them. And test questions should be administered to measure message retention and acceptance. These questions are familiar. They are used to test students in most classrooms.

The General Telephone and Electronics Company, for example, developed message-retention questions to evaluate its employee economic-education program. It asked the following multiple-choice question:[34]

An increase in the money supply has the effect of:

(a) Raising prices and lowering the value of money in circulation.
(b) Putting extra dollars in everyone's pocket.
(c) Stabilizing government deficit spending.
(d) Reducing the effect of shortages.
(e) I don't know.

The correct answer is (a).

Dart Industries developed the following message acceptance (belief) question:[35]

A fault of the business system in this country in that owners (stockholders) get too much of the money companies make, compared to what employees get.

—Agree
—Disagree
—No opinion

Once you have determined that your materials can achieve message retention and acceptance, then you should evaluate the materials for balance and fairness by asking representatives of government agencies, activist groups, or other antagonists to evaluate the materials and suggest what they should include.

After these two steps, you can measure the communication objective by counting the number of students or teachers that use the materials. In the Bell System, for example, educational relations specialists must report the number of teachers they contact and the number of students who use the company's materials. This final step allows you to estimate how many students or teachers have communicated with your organization. Combined with the first step, it tells how many have retained or believed your message.

For employee, public-affairs, or special-interest publics that are also targets of economic-education programs, use the evaluation techniques described in Chapters 12, 14, and 15.

NOTES

1. Chamber of Commerce of the United States, "Business and Economic Education Manual" (Washington, January 1980), p. 4.
2. Sheila Harty, *Hucksters in the Classroom: A Review of Industry Propaganda in Schools* (Washington: Center for Study of Responsive Law, 1979), p. 108.
3. Harty, p. 126.
4. Harty, p. 12.
5. Myron Emanuel, Curtis Snodgrass, Joyce Gildea, and Karn Rosenberg, *Corporate Economic Education Programs: An Evaluation and Appraisal* (New York: Financial Executives Research Foundation, 1979), pp. 6–7.
6. Emanuel, et al., p. 7.
7. Emanuel, et al., p. xiv.
8. Chamber of Commerce of the United States, p. 4.
9. Sheila Harty, "Commercials in the Classroom," in Point/Counterpoint section, *Energy and Education* 3 (April 1980), p. 4.
10. Walter Purdy, "Education and Industry Cooperation," in Point/Counterpoint section, *Energy and Education* 3 (April 1980), p. 5.
11. Oscar H. Gandy, Jr., "The Economics of Image Building: The Information Subsidy in Health," in Emile G. McAnany, Jorge Schnitman, and Noreene Janus (eds.), *Communication and Social Structure* (New York: Praeger, 1981), pp. 204–239.
12. Harty, *Hucksters in the Classroom*, p. 15.
13. Harty, *Hucksters in the Classroom*, p. 40.
14. Harty, *Hucksters in the Classroom*, pp. 63–75.
15. Emanuel, et al., pp. 6–7.
16. Emanuel, et al., p. 7.
17. Emanuel, et al., p. 8.
18. Chamber of Commerce of the United States, p. 6.
19. Emanuel, et al., p. 8.
20. Emanuel, et al., p. 12.
21. Emanuel, et al., p. 11.
22. Emanuel, et al., pp. 23–24.
23. Whenever we quote a reference to a "general" public, we put it in quotes. According to our definition of a public, a "general" public is a logical impossibility. Publics always have a specific problem in common.
24. Emanuel, et al., pp. 22–23.
25. Emanuel, et al., p. 24.
26. Emanuel, et al., contains one short case study for each of the above media categories and an additional 25 long case studies. The Chamber of Commerce of the United States (see note 1) contains twelve case studies. Three longer directories of economic-education programs also are available: "CONTACT: A Directory of Interpreting Business/Economic Education Programs" (Washington: Chamber of Commerce of the United States); "Economic Education Programs and Resources Directory" (Washington: National Association of Manufacturers); "Organizations Providing Business & Economic Education Information" (Chicago: Standard Oil Company [Indiana]).
27. Emanuel, et al., p. 316.
28. Emanuel, et al., p. 309.
29. Emanuel, et al., p. 315.

30. Thomas S. Ris, ''Report Card on Industry's Educational Materials,'' *Public Relations Journal* 33 (June 1977):8–11.
31. Harty, *Hucksters in the Classroom*, pp. 169–170.
32. Emanuel, et al., pp. 41–45.
33. James E. Grunig, ''Developing Economic Education Programs for the Press,'' *Public Relations Review* 8 (Fall 1982):43–62.
34. Emanuel, et al., p. 175.
35. Chamber of Commerce of the United States, ''Business and Economic Education Manual,'' p. 15.

ADDITIONAL READING

Chamber of Commerce of the United States, ''CONTACT: A Directory of Interpreting Business/Economic Education Programs'' (Washington, D. C.).

Chamber of Commerce of the United States, ''Strategies for the 1980s: Business and Economic Education Model Programs'' (Washington, D. C.: 1980).

Chamber of Commerce of the United States, ''Pre and Post Testing: A Manual for Determining the Impact of Interpreting Business/Economic Education Programs on Public Attitudes Toward Business'' (Washington, D. C.).

Emanuel, Myron, Curtis Snodgrass, Joyce Gildea, and Karn Rosenberg, *Corporate Economic Education Programs: An Evaluation and Appraisal* (New York: Financial Executives Research Foundation, 1979).

Grunig, James E., ''Developing Economic Education Programs for the Press,'' *Public Relations Review* 8 (Fall 1982):43–62.

Harty, Sheila, *Hucksters in the Classroom: A Review of Industry Propaganda in Schools* (Washington, D. C.: Center for Study of Responsive Law, 1979).

17

FINANCIAL PUBLIC RELATIONS

The financial public relations man is basically a communicator of information. Through his expertness in communications, he helps many people reach the decision to buy or hold his company's stock. His success can be measured in many ways but is best reflected in a realistic appraisal of his company and of its securities. To accomplish this, the public relations man must be professional and have a high regard for truthfulness and accuracy and lean on the side of conservatism in discussing future developments of his company.[1]

This paragraph shows well why financial public relations specialists have fewer options when they design their programs than other public relations specialists.

First, legal requirements for adequate and timely disclosure of financial information essentially limit financial PR specialists to the public-information or two-way symmetric models of public relations. Two agency financial PR specialists, William Dunk and G. A. Kraut, have pointed out, for example, that some financial PR people with ''advertising talents'' want to ''sell the organization's

stock. They would have the public buying shares like shaving cream—and get the company in hot water,'' Dunk and Kraut added. ''Touting stock is illegal.''[2]

Second, financial PR people deal almost exclusively with active publics—people who are going through our entire behavioral molecule to make decisions about whether to buy stocks or bonds or to give advice to others about such purchases. Active publics seek information rather than process it. And they seek it from many different sources. They can't be fooled easily.

Third, financial public-relations people must strive to achieve the communication, message-retention, and message-acceptance objectives. Translated into the opening quote of this chapter, that means they should communicate financial information to key publics, help those publics understand that information, and try to get those publics to believe what they are told.

The PR person has little control over how active publics evaluate the company (their attitudes) and whether they buy securities (their behavior). Members of publics control their own attitudes and behaviors. Financial PR people can only provide them the information they need for evaluations and decisions.

Financial public relations is strictly a business public relations function—for businesses that sell their stock to investors. It is a highly specialized field that often requires the practitioner to have knowledge of corporate finance, law, and economics as well as public relations.

According to business professor Eugene Miller, the "financial public relations man trying to discuss cash flow with a security analyst without some knowledge of accounting and corporate finance would be in somewhat the same position as a blind person trying to discuss the relative merits of the color red versus green."[3]

That's financial PR in a nutshell. Now let's look at it in more detail.

OBJECTIVES OF FINANCIAL PR

Financial public relations is the one area of public relations in which the objectives are set by regulatory agencies. In Chapter 10, Legal Constraints, we discussed the disclosure rules of the Securities and Exchange Commission and the New York and American stock exchanges. A complete and updated version of all the disclosure requirements can also be found each year in the April issue of *Public Relations Journal*—a special issue on investor relations.

In essence, disclosure requirements force the communication objective upon the financial PR specialist. And they restrict him or her from using the tricks of the press agent or the limited disclosure of information practiced by the two-way asymmetric practitioner.

In *Lesly's Public Relations Handbook*, Eugene Miller capsulized disclosure requirements into a "few simple, common-sense policies."

Release immediately any news that might have a material effect on the price of the company's securities, including merger or acquisition negotiations past the top secret stage, imminence of a labor strike, discovery of new resources, death of a top officer, and so on.

Maintain adequate security on confidential information until it is ready to be released, or until it goes beyond a small group of top management of the company.

Act promptly to dispel unfounded rumors that result in unusual market activity or price variations.

Avoid premature announcements, whenever possible, unwarranted claims, and overly optimistic forecasts.

Avoid providing one inquirer with information that would not be given to another.

Insure that news is handled in its proper perspective by avoiding over-optimism or unwarranted conservatism and by supplementing news releases when changing circumstances require it.

Most important, when in doubt . . . DISCLOSE.[4]

Conference Board Identifies Common Objectives

In 1974, the Conference Board—a nonprofit business research group whose research we have discussed in other chapters of Part III—conducted a study of investor relations programs in 119 major companies. Among other questions, the survey asked respondents to name their objectives.[5]

Respondents frequently used the words "factual," "pertinent," and "timely" to describe their objectives in providing financial information—which could suggest the public-information model at work. But, they also talked about "establishing good working relationships, based on credibility, with the professional investment community. . . . They are aware that analysts hate surprises, and so they work to achieve a clear channel for communication." One respondent said, for example, that his objective was to "give professional investors the opportunity to discuss publicly disclosed information with management'' and ''to respond to the analyst's 'need to know' and to form an impression of management.'' Those responses definitely suggest the two-way symmetric model.

The literature on financial public relations suggests that many of its practitioners use the two-way symmetric model. That literature describes ample use of interpersonal communication between stockholders, analysts, company executives, and investor relations specialists. And it shows that many financial PR people use surveys of stockholders and analysts to determine how these members can be served better.

Another study of 400 corporations, described by two Harshe-Rotman & Druck agency executives, showed that only 22 percent of the corporations had an organized program for soliciting opinions from stockholders.[6] These executives, Ronald Millman and James Horton, concluded that corporations do a lot more telling than listening in their financial relations—suggesting that the public information model may be more common than the two-way symmetric model.

The objectives of these two models do not differ greatly, however. The major difference is whether the communication, message-retention, and message-acceptance objectives are symmetric or asymmetric (see Chapter 6).

Translating Our Objectives for Financial PR

The Conference Board study helps to translate our first three objectives into the language of financial relations. Five objectives were most frequently mentioned by respondents to that survey:

1. Good communications. Nearly half of the participants in the survey thought that if ''good communications exist . . . other goals will fall into place.''

2. Building a strong, ongoing relationship with analysts—the symmetric communication objective on a long-term basis.
3. Developing an informed market—adding the message-retention objective. With an ''informed market,'' investors make ''intelligent and well-founded judgments about a company's prospects.'' One corporate vice president, for example, described this objective as developing ''a better understanding of the operating characteristics of our particular company so that its investment worthiness can be judged on its own merits and not be the by-product of rumor, hearsay or incomplete information.''
4. Establishing credibility—adding the message acceptance, or belief, objective. With this objective, a company makes a concerted effort to convince the investment community that information released is totally reliable—by being honest in all its relationships with investors or analysts.
5. The price of the stock or the price/earnings ratio—the behavior objective on a long-term basis. About a third of the companies responding said they measured their success by the ratio of the price of their stock to its profit level. These companies were realistic enough to know, however, that public relations alone cannot increase this ratio. As one executive stated, ''Investor relations won't increase the P/E, but it will make it what it ought to be.'' If the communication, message-retention, and message-acceptance objectives are achieved, in other words, investors will have the information they need to make realistic decisions about a company's stock.

More Than Disclosure

Two financial PR specialists we cited earlier, Dunk and Kraut, add that the objective of financial public relations should be more than disclosure—more than ''disgorgement'' of information, in their terms.[7] It's easy to release all information with little interpretation, but message retention and acceptance requires interpretation and simplification—especially for the nonprofessional small investor.

For advice on how to simplify and interpret financial information, see the discussion of financial writing in Chapter 31.

FINANCIAL PUBLICS

Like all publics, financial publics have consequences on a corporation, or the corporation has consequences on them. Investors' decisions to buy or sell stock affect the selling price of the stock—an important consequence on the corporation. How well a corporation fares from quarter to quarter or year to year affects the investor's finances.

Four Groups of Financial Publics

Financial publics for a business firm can usually be identified from four groups.[8] Members of each of these groups of publics either invest money themselves or are in the business of providing information to others who invest money:

>Current shareholders.
>Prospective shareholders.
>The financial community: bankers, brokers, investment advisers, trustees, security analysts, and managers of mutual funds, insurance companies, and pension funds.
>Financial media: journalists working on specialized media such as the *Wall Street Journal* or *Barron's*, for the financial sections of newspapers or newsmagazines, or for radio and television programs such as *Wall Street Week*.

High-Involvement Problem-Facing Publics

Although we have no studies of financial publics available that have utilized our situational theory of publics, we can deduce what such a study would show.

Financial publics almost always will be *involved* with the company's financial status.

They own shares, are considering owning shares, or advise others who buy or sell shares.

Financial publics also will be high on *problem recognition*. They will be "thinking about" an investment they have already made or might make. Few people invest their money without thinking about it, or work in investment analysis and advising without a high level of problem recognition.

Most, but not all, financial publics will be low on *constraint recognition*. Few people consider investing money if they have no money to invest. And smaller investors will be constrained from making some kinds of investments. Investment counselors work with people who can afford to invest.

In other words, almost all financial publics will be active publics. If our analysis is correct, they most often would fit into the high-involvement problem-facing category, less often into the high-involvement constrained-behavior category.

Two Conference Board studies include statements that support this analysis—at least for securities analysts. In one report, "Communicating with Professional Investors," McGrath quoted a "respected security analyst" as stating that "it is in the nature of his function that the analyst reads everything."[9]

In a report on disclosure of financial forecasts, McGrath and Walsh added, ". . . an analyst who makes a prediction of a firm's earnings, say for the coming year, enjoys a greatly enhanced reputation if his forecast proves accurate and the price of the company's stock behaves as expected."[10]

"Aunt Jane" or the Institutional Expert?

What about the individual investor, however? In the 1950s and '60s, the individual investor made up a large share of the investor publics. That investor was stereotyped as "Aunt Jane," an investor who bought a few stocks and habitually kept them for years on end—without buying and selling as the market changed.

Aunt Jane would be a member of what we call a routine-behavior public—people who do not think about their investment and look mostly for good news about the company to reinforce the decision they made years ago.

In the 1970s, the number of individual investors began a drastic decline—from a peak of 35 million in 1969 to 25 million in 1980.[11] The Aunt Janes of the world were rapidly replaced by large institutional investors, who are sophisticated and who demand extensive, accurate information from a business firm—the highly active publics we just described.[12]

In the 1980s, however, the individual investor seems to be making a comeback—spurred by legislation that gives a tax break to small investors and by computerization of brokerage operations that make it more profitable to service small investors.[13]

Does that mean there will be fewer active financial publics in the 1980s? Probably not, if a small-scale qualitative study of individual investors is accurate.[14] Aunt Jane has been replaced by ''Savvy Sue,'' an individual investor who manages her own portfolio and is a ''spirited, venturesome'' investor—a member of an active public.

FINANCIAL RELATIONS PROGRAMS

In most corporations, investor relations is not strictly a public relations function. Instead, it is a hybrid of public relations and corporate finance.[15] In many corporations, the public relations executive has responsibility for investor relations. In other firms, the responsibility goes to the chief financial officer.

The 1974 Conference Board study also showed a growth in the number of companies that put an investor relations executive in charge of the function—independent of fi-

nance and public relations, but using the expertise of both.

In addition, corporations may use independent financial public relations firms to manage some or all of their financial relations. Smaller firms most often turn their entire program over to an outside firm. Larger firms use outside agencies for special services, especially (in order of use):[16]

Surveys of financial analysts.

Counsel.

Analyst meetings.

Preparation or distribution of financial news releases.

Annual reports.

Special assignments.

Media placement and press relations.

Proxy solicitations.

Counseling Top Management

Financial public relations specialists have responsibility for keeping top management informed about the status of the company's stock on the market. In the Monsanto Company, for example, the financial relations office performs the following functions:

Analyzes and reports on changing trends in the character of sales and purchases of Monsanto Company's common shares, with explanations and interpretations of reasons for significant changes. . . .

Plans and recommends to the Group Vice President—Administrative Staff, a continuing program for financial relations that is effective and expressive of Monsanto Company's business principles and morality.[17]

Shareholder Communication

In addition, financial PR specialists have the responsibility for communicating with shareholders, including:[18]

Printed materials—newsletters, magazines, quarterly reports, special letters, annual reports, company biographies, and booklets describing the company's products and operations. Of these, the annual report to stockholders usually is the cornerstone of the stockholder relations program (see Chapter 31).

The annual meeting of shareholders and reports on the annual meeting to shareholders who could not attend.

Proxy fights and tender offers. In a proxy fight, a new slate of officers tries to replace existing management by soliciting the proxy votes of shareholders. In a tender offer, a buyer tries to purchase shares from shareholders to gain control of the company. In both cases, financial relations specialists help existing management resist the takeover attempt.[19]

Surveys of shareholder opinions.

Financial Media Relations

Next, financial PR people handle financial publicity—usually for the financial media. They write press releases, for example, on new offerings of stock, profit and loss reports, or significant discoveries or new products that might affect the price of the company's stock. And they arrange interviews with the chief executive officer or the chief financial officer to discuss the company's financial status.

Communicating with Professional Analysts

In what is perhaps their most important function, financial relations specialists take responsibility for communication with profes-

Financial specialists want firsthand information about a company's plans and prospects. Here TRW Inc. Chairman of the Board and Chief Executive Officer R. F. Mettler talks informally with securities analysts in Dallas. (Courtesy TRW Inc.)

sional analysts. Some of this communication takes place through printed media. The bulk of it is one-to-one communication. In the Monsanto Company, for example, the financial relations executive is one of four authorized contacts for analysts who visit or communicate with the company. The other contacts are the chairman of the board, the president, and the group vice president—administrative staff.

The most common communication contacts with analysts include:[20]

Telephone inquiries following up an annual report, a news release, or tips about the company.

Visits by individual analysts, to discuss the company with the chief executive officer, the financial relations managers, or other knowledgeable experts.

Group meetings and seminars for analysts, to discuss the company's performance or plans.

Presentations at meetings of societies of analysts.

Travel to meet analysts outside the New York financial community.

Plant tours or field trips for analysts.

Special presentations for analysts at the annual meeting.

Fact sheets, fact books, or other special publications for analysts.

Dissemination of financial news that also goes to the press.

International Investors

Finally, many companies list their stock on foreign stock exchanges. Thus, financial PR people must also make presentations to foreign analysts who are in the United States and travel abroad to meet these analysts.[21]

EVALUATION OF FINANCIAL RELATIONS

Although many writers who contribute to the public relations literature point out that fi-

nancial PR people do little to evaluate their own programs, many companies do use adequate methods to measure the communication, message-retention, and message-acceptance objectives.

The Conference Board study showed that companies use five methods to evaluate their programs for professional analysts:[22]

Analyst surveys. Companies either do survey research themselves or contract with research firms to determine whether analysts are satisfied with the company's financial relations efforts. They ask respondents to rate how well their inquiries were handled or how valuable are their special publications for analysts—a measure of the communication objective. Other questions ask respondents to rate the company's earnings, management, or marketing—measures of message acceptance. Factual questions could also be included to measure message retention (see Chapter 9 for examples).

Feedback from analysts. Financial PR specialists also use informal methods of contacting analysts—either by informally observing how analysts respond to financial relations efforts or by conducting formal interviews of selected analysts. These informal methods work well as long as the observer looks for indicators of the three relevant objectives (see Chapter 9 for a discussion of qualitative research).

Some financial PR people read the reports analysts write about their company's prospects—an excellent measure of the message-retention and -acceptance objectives.

Other financial PR specialists look at the stock's price/earnings ratio or at whether institutions purchase their stock. These measures of behavior are useful, but they are affected more by the performance of the company than by financial public relations. Thus, they should never be used as the principal criterion for evaluating financial relations.

Finally, some respondents said they used awards from societies of financial analysts or financial communication specialists to evaluate their programs. Awards are nice, but usually they offer no measure of the accomplishment of specific communication objectives.

Evaluating Shareholder Communication

Many companies do surveys of shareholders, but those are often general attitude surveys that measure overall evaluation of the company. It is important to measure the communication, retention, and acceptance objectives with shareholders as well as analysts.

Measures can be taken with mail questionnaires, telephone surveys, or questions at shareholder meetings (although shareholders at a meeting will not be a representative sample). Questions should measure exposure to shareholder media (communication), whether shareholders remember that information (retention), and whether they believe that information (acceptance). Chapter 9, again, contains sample questions to measure these objectives either quantitatively or qualitatively.

NOTES

1. Eugene Miller, "Financial Public Relations I. Basic Planning and Programs," in Philip Lesly (ed.), *Lesly's Public Relations Handbook*, 2d ed. (Englewood Cliffs, N.J.: Prentice-Hall, 1978), pp. 105–135.
2. William P. Dunk and G. A. Kraut, "Investor Relations: What It Isn't," *Public Relations Journal* 38 (Spring 1982):12–14.
3. Miller, p. 110.
4. Miller, pp. 133–134.
5. Phyllis S. McGrath, *Communicating with Professional Investors* (New York: The Conference Board, 1974), pp. 5–19.
6. Ronald B. Millman and James L. Horton, "Is Anyone Listening?" *Public Relations Journal* 35 (April 1979):10–12.
7. Dunk and Kraut.
8. Miller, pp. 107–108, 111.
9. McGrath, p. 3.
10. Phyllis S. McGrath and Francis J. Walsh, Jr., *Disclosure of Financial Forecasts to Security Analysts and the Public* (New York: The Conference Board, 1973), p. 1.
11. Thomas E. O'Hara and Donald P. Durocher, "The Decade of the Individual Investor," *Public Relations Journal* 36 (April 1980):14–16.
12. Alexander B. Trowbridge, president of the Conference Board, "Preface," in McGrath.
13. O'Hara and Durocher.
14. Louis Capozzi and Hank Walshak, "Is It 'Aunt Jane' or 'Savvy Sue'?" *Public Relations Journal* 36 (April 1980):18–21.
15. McGrath, pp. 36–53.
16. McGrath, pp. 54–59.
17. McGrath, p. 39.
18. Miller, pp. 112–128.
19. Philip Lesly, "Financial Public Relations II. Takeover Efforts and Disclosure Regulations," in Lesly, pp. 136–155.
20. McGrath, pp. 20–35; Miller, pp. 129–130.
21. McGrath, pp. 60–64.
22. McGrath, pp. 10–19.

ADDITIONAL READING

Dunk, William P., and G. A. Kraut, "Investor Relations: What It Isn't," *Public Relations Journal* 38 (Spring 1982):12–14.

Lesly, Philip, "Financial Public Relations II. Takeover Efforts and Disclosure Regulations," in Philip Lesly (ed.), *Lesly's Public Relations Handbook*, 2d ed. (Englewood Cliffs, N.J.: Prentice-Hall, 1978), pp. 136–155.

McGrath, Phyllis S., *Communicating with Professional Investors* (New York, The Conference Board: 1974), pp. 5–19.

Miller, Eugene, "Financial Public Relations I. Basic Planning and Programs," in Philip Lesly (ed.), *Lesly's Public Relations Handbook*, 2d ed. (Englewood Cliffs, N.J.: Prentice-Hall, 1978), pp. 105–135.

Werba, Gabriel, "What Analysts Want to Hear," *Public Relations Journal* 38 (April 1982):18–20.

Wilson, Mollie Haley, *The Corporate Investor Relations Function: A Survey* (Ann Arbor, Mich.: UMI Research Press, 1980).

18

PROMOTION, FUND RAISING, AND PUBLIC COMMUNICATION CAMPAIGNS

The three categories of public relations programs discussed in this chapter often are the most mindless of PR programs. The majority are managed according to the press agentry model; the more sophisticated, according to the two-way asymmetric model.

Here are just a few examples:

A blimp circles a sporting event.

A hot-air balloon rises in Grand Central Station to promote a fast-food chain.

A press release announces a new screw thread.

Sports reporters are wined and dined at half time of a basketball game.

A new corporate logo is announced with frenzy and flourish.

The mayor of a major city takes a bath on the street in front of City Hall to promote an antilitter campaign.

Is Promotion Public Relations?

Although much of the world outside of public relations equates promotional activities with public relations, there is much debate inside public relations circles about the relationship between the two.

Many public relations practitioners—mainly those who are communication technicians—also equate promotion and publicity with public relations. In a book on public relations in business, for example, Jacqueline Peake talked about ''using the principles of public relations, publicity, and promotion (three terms for the same set of skills) . . .''[1]

Some practitioners recognize that public relations has evolved substantially beyond promotions, but they continue to do promotions work because there is a demand for it—especially in public relations agencies associated with an advertising ageny. Paul Alvarez, chairman of Ketchum Communications, New York, for example, told public relations educators at the 1982 convention of the Association for Education in Journalism and Mass Communication that half the business of his agency is still product publicity.

Other practitioners, and the majority of public relations educators, argue that there is no relationship between public relations and promotion. To them, promotion is a marketing, not a public relations, function.[2]

PR Services for the Disposal Subsystem

We can put the promotion-related activities discussed in this chapter in proper perspective if we recall our discussion in Chapter 1 of the relationship between the public relations subsystem and other organizational subsystems. Public relations, we said, helps other subsystems communicate with each other and with systems in the environment.

Public relations people engage in promotions-related activities when they help the disposal subsystem—essentially the marketing department—communicate with environmental systems to facilitate the disposal of products, such as hamburgers or plays, or services, such as hospital care or university courses.

Marketing people also are communicators, so they don't rely on public relations for all of their communication work. The marketing people handle research, advertising, and sales promotion (shelf displays, packaging, etc.). They use public relations mostly for media relations and printed materials—press releases, press conferences, feature articles, newsletters, photographs, films, and tapes.[3]

Public relations people certainly can perform these techniques (all are described in Part IV of this book), so PR technicians can be useful to the marketing department. It is shortsighted, however, to believe that marketing support *is* public relations. Marketing support should be a minor part of an organization's public relations effort.

Public relations technicians who do promotions-related work usually do so under the direction of marketing managers rather than of public relations managers—especially in business firms. Their work contributes to "marketing communication," which includes advertising, sales promotion, and publicity (Figure 18–1). Thus, it is logically more meaningful to study promotion and publicity as a part of a course in marketing rather than as part of a course in public relations.

Have We Talked Ourselves Out of a Chapter?

By now, you may wonder why we need to continue with this chapter—if promotion activities are really part of the marketing function. There are three good reasons to continue.

Many PR people continue to do promotions work without understanding their role in the organization—often, without understanding modern marketing. You may end up in a promotions role and need to know how you fit into both public relations and marketing.

Many nonprofit organizations—especially colleges and universities, hospitals, and

FIGURE 18–1

The Three Sides of the Marketing Communication Triangle

From Brooke E. Poirier, "How to Develop a Promotion Strategy," reprinted with permission from the March 1979 issue of the *Public Relations Journal*, copyright © 1979.

even government agencies—do what marketing people call "social marketing" under the direction of a public relations manager. Because marketing is part of the public relations role in these organizations, public relations people working in that setting need to understand marketing theory as well as public relations theory.

Most public relations technicians—especially those with no training in marketing—do promotions work with the press agentry or two-way asymmetric model as their guide. The two-way symmetric model can work in marketing as well as public relations—and modern marketing theory stresses just such a model. Indeed, most marketing theorists define marketing as an *exchange relationship* between buyer and seller.

The two-way symmetric model is evident, for example, in the following passage from William Nickels' book on marketing communication and promotion:

> Too much of the marketing literature today emphasizes promotion management for *sellers*. This causes readers to think of marketing communication as something sellers do *to* buyers. Promotion is then viewed as one tool the seller uses to dominate the buyer. But marketing communication is something sellers do *with* buyers. Promotion, in reality, is a tool available to both buyers and sellers. Buyers may use promotion to convince sellers to change their policies and practices, and sellers may try to change buyers. Marketing is not a game to be won by being most persuasive. Rather, it is a technique for facilitating the creation and maintenance of mutually beneficial exchanges. Communication helps *both parties*, not just the buyer or seller.[4]

The two-way symmetric model has many implications for promotion, fund raising, and public communication campaigns. For example:

> Giving away bats or T-shirts may get people to come to a baseball game—once or twice. But if the team performs poorly or if the ticket prices are too high, baseball fans won't get enough entertainment in exchange for the price of their ticket—and they probably won't come back again.

> Donors won't contribute to a fund-raising campaign if they don't think their donation will make much difference. They will give if they get satisfaction or recognition—or a tax break—in exchange. Donors can be cultivated: They want to help make plans for the project to which they contribute.

> People won't wear seat belts after hearing a public communication campaign promoting the use of seat belts if they think the probability of being in an accident is so small that it does not make up for the inconvenience of putting on and wearing the belts. If asked, however, people may have ideas about how to make seat belts more convenient.

Let's look, then, at some examples of promotion, fund raising, and public communication campaigns—three similar and often interrelated kinds of promotional programs.

PROMOTION PROGRAMS

To promote an organization or its products and services is to "make public" that organization, product, or service. "To make public" is the definition of publicity. One cannot market anything unless the potential buyers know about the product—unless it is on the public agenda.

Many kinds of organizations hire PR technicians to publicize themselves. For example:

> Professional and college sports teams have directors of promotion—to help fill their arenas or stadiums.

> Theatres, dance companies, art museums, and orchestras promote concerts and shows.

> Colleges and universities promote their faculty, facilities, and major fields of study to potential students.

Newspapers and radio and television stations have promotion departments to increase their audience—usually in the hope of securing higher advertising rates.

Park and recreation departments of local governments promote use of their facilities and programs.

Community groups hold special events—band concerts, community fairs, jousting tournaments, ethnic days, art fairs—that must be promoted if anyone is to attend.

Hospitals market their services and facilities through open houses, health and medical fairs, seminars and lectures, and health information provided to the media.[5]

Corporations have general promotion programs to establish a corporate identity. The most famous is the Goodyear Tire and Rubber Company's four blimps that help with the televising of major sports events, attend air shows and community events, and help in studies of noise pollution, traffic, or marine life.[6]

Corporations use promotional techniques most often, however, in product publicity work. Staple product-publicity techniques are new-product press releases and new-product introductions/press parties. The most extensive of the new-product introductions usually are those that automobile companies put on to introduce new models each year.

Two cases should provide you with some of the flavor of product publicity.

The Genie Garage Door Opener

The Alliance Manufacturing Company, part of the North American Phillips Company, had dominated the market for home garage door openers with its Genie line.[7] Because of a boom in the market for garage door openers, however, other companies introduced competing products and gained more media attention than Genie.

Genie also had introduced a do-it-yourself model of door opener—which could be installed in three hours—to complement its older model, which had to be installed by a professional. Genie hired the Cleveland PR firm of Hesselbart & Mitten/Watt to develop a promotional program for Genie. Here's what the firm did:

Developed a press kit for use at a home center show in Chicago that was attended by members of the trade press.

Established a consumer hotline number for do-it-yourselfers to call if they had trouble installing the Genie.

Distributed drawings, photographs, and an informative article on how to install a Genie to more than 100 newspapers around the country. Articles appeared in respected newspapers such as the New York *Times* and Denver *Post*.

Appealed to female consumers by sending the media a photo of actress Lily Tomlin installing a Genie opener in the movie *Nine to Five* (Exhibit 18–1). A story accompanied the photo explaining how easy it is to install the device and stressing that an automatic opener provides a woman more security near her home. The story quoted statistics that 32 percent of all attacks occur near the home. (The female angle to this promotion is clearly an example of the two-way asymmetric model: describing a product in terms that the potential buyer most wants to hear.)

Tried to keep good relations with dealers who install Genie openers while promoting the do-it-yourself market. A Genie man—a giant, vivid blue character—was made available for dealers to use at special promotional events, such as the Pro Football Hall of Fame Parade in Canton, Ohio.

Burson-Marsteller Brings "Good Things" to GE

In 1982, the General Electric Company gave the Burson-Marsteller PR agency the assignment of developing a public relations campaign to complement its advertising campaign, "We Bring Good Things to Life."[8] The

GENIE News

automatic garage door opener systems

The **ALLIANCE** Manufacturing Co., Inc.
Alliance, Ohio 44601
A NORTH AMERICAN PHILIPS COMPANY

Contact: Norbert J. Hobrath or
Berenice E. Kleiman
(216) 566-7019

GARAGE DOOR OPENER ASSEMBLY
FROM THE FEMALE PERSPECTIVE

ALLIANCE, OHIO, November 6, 1981 -- Women are increasingly asserting
independence along many formerly nontraditional fronts, from vying for
competitive career opportunities to undertaking home do-it-yourself projects.

Among these new frontiers is the challenge of installing an automatic
garage door opener system. With astronomical mortgage rates and mounting
service and maintenance costs, garage door opener installation not only
contributes to home improvement economics but personal pride, as well.

Women, in greater numbers than ever before, have been sharing the
home toolbox. Lily Tomlin in the recent 20th Century Fox film "Nine to Five"
captures this assertive role in a delightful sequence where she installs
an automatic garage door opener system by following the easy step-by-step
directions. Tomlin does the job and scores for female consciousness, showing
that "nuts and bolts" mechanics no longer belong exclusively to the male-
dominated sphere.

CONVENIENCE AND SECURITY FOR WOMEN

Whether by professional or do-it-yourself installation, the automatic
garage door opener, operated by remote control transmitter from inside the
car, not only eliminates the need to get out on a rainy, snowy or windy day

- more -

EXHIBIT 18–1

The Hesselbart & Mitten/Watt
public relations firm of
Cleveland used a photo of
actress Lily Tomlin installing a
do-it-yourself Genie garage
door opener to promote the
product for its client, the
Alliance Manufacturing
Company. The photo illustrated
the ease of installing a Genie
and promoted its benefits to
women. (News release and
photo caption courtesy
Hesselbart & Mitten/Watt, Inc.
Photo courtesy 20th Century
Fox, IPC Films)

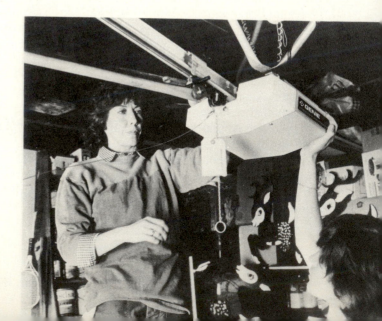

Lily Tomlin, in the recent 20th
Century Fox film *Nine to Five,* shows
how easy it is to install a Genie
garage door opener system.

Burson-Marsteller program did publicize products, but it also developed symmetric communication programs for consumers.

First, the product publicity:

A microwave cooking contest that attracted several thousand entries.

A promotion for the 25th anniversary of GE's Toast-R-Oven.

A half-time cooking contest at pro football games with players' wives as contestants.

Videotaping joggers running on a treadmill before and after Tampa's Gasparilla Distance Classic to publicize GE's video camera and cassette recorder.

A 360-degree, multimedia presentation at major trade shows highlighting GE's solutions to consumer concerns.

In addition, Burson-Marsteller developed these symmetric programs for consumers:

A business leadership program to find out what information consumers need and how to simplify it for them.

A GE Answer Center—with a computer data base on GE products—for consumers to call on a toll-free telephone number when they have questions or problems.

FUND-RAISING PROGRAMS

Nonprofit organizations maintain their functional linkages (see Chapter 7) with the users of their services by using the promotional techniques described in the previous section. But many must also maintain a critical enabling linkage with sources of funds if they are to survive. Among the organizations that must raise funds are colleges and universities, nonprofit hospitals, charities, "disease" organizations (such as the American Cancer Society), community service groups, and research organizations.

These organizations frequently call their fund-raising efforts a "development" program. Some organizations keep this function independent of public relations. Most place it within the public relations department.[9]

Typical Fund-Raising Campaigns

Nonprofit organizations generally raise money through the following kinds of campaigns:[10]

The Capital Program • Usually this is a massive effort to raise a targeted amount of money for a major building or similar project within a specified period of time. For example, Iowa State University conducted such a campaign to raise money for its C. Y. Stephens cultural center in the late 1960s. Churches may organize a capital campaign to finance a new building, or hospitals, a new wing. University departments may stage a campaign to renovate a building or update their equipment and facilities.

Campaigns for Annual Support • Many organizations must hold a campaign each year to pay their annual operating expenses. The American Cancer Society, the Red Cross, the Heart Association, the United Givers Fund, and university alumni organizations all stage such campaigns. Annual support programs may be conducted throughout the year (such as most alumni programs—Exhibit 18–2), in one intensive community drive (such as the Community Chest or United Givers Fund), or through direct mail or telethon campaigns (such as those conducted by public television stations).

Raising Funds from Foundations • Organizations solicit funds for specific projects from about 26,000 foundations that give money for worthy projects. To solicit funds from a foundation, fund raisers do research to identify the best foundation for a proposal, write letters and a formal proposal to the foundation, and confer with foundation representatives to present or clarify the proposal.

Seeking Corporate Support • Nonprofit organizations seek support from corporations—the flip side of the coin of business charitable contributions that we discussed in Chapter 13 on community relations. Robert

**EXHIBIT
18–2**

1982 Annual Fund

University of Wisconsin Foundation
702 Langdon Street
Madison, Wisconsin 53706
Telephone: 608/263-4545

February 1982

Dear Friend of Wisconsin:

In our effort to gain your support for the 1982 Annual Fund, we cannot avoid "spending money to make money." But here are some straight facts we hope will mean more economy in bringing your vital gift to the University of Wisconsin-Madison.

If you send your contribution now, you will not receive any University of Wisconsin Foundation appeals for the rest of 1982. However, you will receive the UW Foundation's Annual Report and one special message from your school or college. By sending your tax deductible contribution in the enclosed envelope, you will help the UW Foundation put valuable resources to work for the University now, instead of towards asking for your support throughout 1982.

You can also decide to give later in 1982. Just check the appropriate box on the enclosed card, and we'll send you a reminder whenever you choose. Or you may opt for the perma-pledge system, which greatly minimizes mailing and handling costs because no regular UW Foundation appeals will be mailed to you. In 1981, over 4,000 contributors gave through this system. We're hoping for even more in 1982.

The UW Foundation is proud of its record of cost-containment. With your help we can trim the cost of our efforts even more and at the same time achieve our most important goal--to stimulate giving for the benefit of the University of Wisconsin-Madison.

The UW Foundation helps to bridge the gap between available state and federal funds and the financial support needed for educational excellence. We exist to encourage private gifts and to guide them to hundreds of areas where they are needed.

The need for your help is increasing and so is the need to keep our costs down. Please let us hear from you soon.

Sincerely,

Robert B. Rennebohm

Robert B. Rennebohm
President

Letters are a staple technique of fund raising. This one urges University of Wisconsin alumni to give to the University. (Courtesy University of Wisconsin Foundation)

S. Cole, for example, placed the "giving and getting" of charitable contributions into one chapter of his public relations handbook.[11] Fund raisers seek funds from corporations as they would from a foundation. Organizations most often get support from corporations in their geographic area or with interest in the work of the organization—such as a specific university department. Some corporations also match gifts made by their employees.

Deferred Giving Programs • These programs seek gifts from individuals who will gain a tax advantage from giving part or all of their estate to a chosen organization. Many individuals write their wills to give property, equipment, or money to an organization at the time of their death. Other deferred givers transfer their money or property during their lifetime in exchange for some form of retained life income.[12]

Fund-Raising Techniques

Fund-raising specialists use many of the techniques described in Part IV of this book, especially:

Media relations techniques to announce and promote a campaign.

Letter writing and direct mail solicitation of prospects.

Writing of proposals to foundations or corporations.

Intensive campaigns that feature such techniques as media promotion, staged events, telethons, and celebrity support.

Provision of ongoing information to donors or prospective donors through magazines, newsletters, or annual reports.

Speeches to donor groups.

Interpersonal contacts with key prospects.

Critical Segments of a Fund-Raising Program

Fund-raising specialists manage their programs in steps that are quite similar to those of the behavioral molecule used throughout this book. The terminology differs only a little. In his book on fund raising, Thomas Broce stressed these segments of a program:[13]

Establishing organizational objectives and using those objectives to determine what kind of fund-raising program is needed (*detect* and *construct* segments of the behavioral molecule).

Identifying and researching "natural prospects"—likely active publics—for targets of the campaign (*construct*).

Writing a "case statement." Fund-raising specialists write a statement "making a case" why the organization needs funds and showing why prospects should contribute to the cause. The case statement should show clearly why the organization is not simply begging for funds (*construct*).[14]

"Cultivation" of donors and prospective donors. Visiting prospects, holding special events, sending information to prospects to help them identify with the organization (*behave*, but also part of the *select* and *confirm* segments—to determine the best method of solicitation.

Solicitation. Actually asking prospects to give money (*behave*).

Most books and articles on fund raising stress the importance of research—identifying prospects in the *construct* segment, evaluating the program in the second *detect* segment. In fact, however, fund raisers do little research, although they keep extensive records of prospects and donations that could be used as raw data for research.[15] In addition, formative research with prospective donors would make fund raising more symmetric by including donors in the formulation of objectives and preparation of the case statement.

PUBLIC COMMUNICATION CAMPAIGNS

Public communication campaigns—or public-information campaigns, as they are also called—have been waged over the 200-year history of the United States. Stanford University's William Paisley has described many of the early public relations campaigns discussed in Chapter 2—for example, Thomas Paine's campaign for independence and Hamilton and Jefferson's campaign for ratification of the Constitution—as public communication campaigns.[16]

Public communication campaigns are media campaigns—with radio or television public-service announcements, posters on trash cans or in buses, pamphlets made available by mail. Almost all of these campaigns try to reform the behavior of a target public in some way.

Public communication campaigns use marketing strategies similar to those used to publicize products or fund-raising programs. Public communication campaigns also are "social marketing" programs that are used to gain acceptance of a social idea or practice rather than to facilitate a commercial transaction.[17] Frequently, the objective of a social-marketing campaign is to get people to *stop* doing something—such as smoking or using drugs—rather than to begin doing something—such as buying a product.

You have, no doubt, seen a picture of an Indian on a trash can with a big tear on his cheek urging you to stop pollution, or Smokey the Bear urging you to prevent forest fires. Here are a few other examples of public communication campaigns:[18]

The extensive campaign by the National Institute of Mental Health against drug abuse.

The antismoking campaigns by the U. S. Office on Smoking and Health, the American Cancer Society, and others.

Community heart-disease-prevention programs.

Campaigns for family planning and against venereal disease.

A campaign by your local utility or another group to promote energy conservation.

Campaigns to encourage people to drive safely, especially on holiday weekends.

Campaigns to encourage people to use seat belts.

Campaigns to encourage people to "fight cancer with a checkup and a check."

Campaigns to gain compliance with the 55-mph speed limit.

All Four Models Show Up in Communication Campaigns

Beginning with the first public communication campaign, campaign planners have had reform of behavior as their objective. In many cases, these planners have used communication as a simple substitute for more difficult—and more effective—ways of affecting behavior. It's much easier, for example, to run television public service announcements telling people to drive 55 mph than to have the state police stop and fine all the drivers who exceed that limit.

Many planners of public communication campaigns have used the press agentry model to sell seat belts or nonpolluting behavior the way P. T. Barnum sold a 150-year-old nurse or a "Swedish Nightingale."

Many others have followed the public-information model—as the earlier title of "public-information campaigns" suggests—by disseminating information related to a desired behavior with little knowledge of whether anyone would use or did use that information. The more sophisticated planners have used attitude research to mount two-way asymmetric campaigns.[19]

Beginning in the 1940s, research began to show that public communication campaigns have had little impact on behavior—as did most mass communication research at that time (see Chapter 6 for a review of this research). Two heavily cited journal articles brought together evidence that information campaigns affect behavior little: Hyman and Sheatsley's 1947 article, "Some Reasons Why Information Campaigns Fail,"[20] and Raymond Bauer's "The Obstinate Audience" (1964).[21]

In 1973, however, the University of Denver's Harold Mendelsohn countered with an article entitled, "Some Reasons Why Information Campaigns Can Succeed."[22] His article can be compared to the parable of the chicken and the golden egg described in Chapter 6. Mendelsohn argued that information campaigns alone may not create golden eggs—changes in behavior. But he argued that information campaigns based on solid mass communication research of publics and messages can increase knowledge and understanding and that some people may eventually use that knowledge and understanding to change their behavior.

No One Considers Himself a "Bad Driver" • Mendelsohn pointed out, for example, that research had shown that highway-safety campaigns to reach "bad drivers" and to eliminate accidents failed because 80 percent of all drivers considered themselves good or excellent drivers. In fact, most drivers ignored the over 300,000 persuasive traffic safety messages that appeared each year in the print media alone.

A campaign had to be devised to make people aware of their driving deficiencies. Straightforward messages about those deficiencies wouldn't work. So, in 1965, CBS television ran a special program, *The National Driver's Test*, just before the Memorial Day weekend. Some fifty million test forms were distributed before the program was broadcast.

Thirty million people watched the program, and 40 percent of those who completed the test failed it. Thus, about 600,000 people learned of their driving deficiencies. A small percentage of the total who failed the test—35,000 people—changed their behavior by enrolling in driver-improvement courses. Although only about 6 percent of the people who failed the test took courses, the total enrolled in such courses was three times the number enrolled the previous year.

Note here how closely these results fit our behavioral molecule and situational theory of publics. A public communication campaign can get people to *detect* a problem and get some of those people to develop ideas of what to do about the problem. A few people will decide to *behave* to correct the problem. However, our two theories make it clear that the communication campaign did not change their behavior. Each person changed it him- or herself. The campaign made many people aware of the problem and helped them develop the cognitions that are *necessary* but not *sufficient* conditions for a change in behavior.

The Three "E's" of Campaigns

After planners of public communication campaigns learned that communication alone could not reform behavior, they began to look for complementary techniques to guide and channel behavior—mostly in the form of behavioral constraints.

The U. S. Forest Service, for example, built a program to prevent wildfires around three "E's"—education, enforcement, and engineering:[23]

> Education: the role played by the communication campaign—informing people about the dangers of fire and what they can do to prevent one.
>
> Enforcement: enforcing fire laws—another set of constraints on undesirable behaviors. For example, laws can prohibit campfires outside specified campgrounds.
> Engineering: structuring the physical environment—putting in constraints on undesirable behaviors—to make it more difficult for people to start fires. For example, enclosures can be built to keep campfires from spreading.

The Chessie Safety Express • The Chessie System railroad also used these three "E's" in a campaign to reduce the number of accidents at highway grade crossings:[24]

Education. A national communication campaign was centered around a "Chessie Safety Express," a train pulled by a steam locomotive that brought information on railroad safety to communities throughout the Chessie System.

Enforcement of laws designed to protect motorists and pedestrians at grade crossings.

Engineering of grade crossings to make them as safe as possible, and making improvements when necessary.

Interpersonal Support Vital

Researchers have also learned that interpersonal support provides an essential backup to a communication campaign, especially in antismoking, heart-disease prevention, and other health programs.[25]

People cannot easily break poor health habits. A campaign can make people aware that they have a problem. But they usually cannot change their behavior without the support of groups such as Alcoholics Anonymous, Weight Watchers, or antismoking groups. People must also be trained in how to set up an environment that supports a decision to change a behavior.

Servicing People's Information Needs

Planners of public-communication campaigns also are beginning to learn how to use the two-way symmetric model in a campaign. Most campaigns begin with planners deciding what target publics need to know about safety, smoking, or wildfires.

With a symmetric approach, campaign planners ask people what kind of information they used when they confronted a troublesome situation—such as a health problem—and what kind of information they could have used.[26] Then the planners can develop a campaign to help people get information that they perceive they need.

OBJECTIVES AND PUBLICS

Although the eventual goal of any promotional program is to affect behavior, our discussion of the change of thinking about public communication campaigns should have made clear that other objectives frequently are more reasonable for planning and evaluating most of these programs.

Your objective depends heavily upon the nature of the public to which the campaign is directed and your organization's goal.

If your organization must fill seats, sell products, or raise funds—i.e., if bringing about a behavior is a must—then you should do research to identify the people who are already active publics for the behavior you want and communicate to them what you have to offer. To fill seats for football games, communicate to the active football fans, and forget those who have no interest in the sport. To raise funds, identify, cultivate, and solicit publics that have money to give and take interest in your organization. To sell a product, promote the product only to those who need it (don't try to sell dog food to people without dogs!).

If your organization's goal is to reform the behavior of passive, generally disinterested publics—such as getting people to buckle up their seat belts—then your objective should be message retention and acceptance. You should get them to recognize that a problem such as automobile safety or smoking affects them. Then, to change the behavior of a public, you will have to communicate symmetrically to make the behaviors you recommend more relevant. And, you will have to use engineering and enforcement techniques to reinforce the communication program and to eliminate the conditions that make the undesirable behaviors possible.

Let's look at two studies based on the situational theory of publics that illustrate these two relationships between objectives and publics.

Identifying Active Donors for a Fund-Raising Program

Kathleen Kelly used a statistical technique called discriminant analysis to identify the alumni of the University of Maryland's College of Journalism who were most likely to give money in the college's annual fund-raising drive.[27] Her findings suggest how promotional specialists might identify active publics when they need them to meet an organizational goal of more sales, more donations, or more attendance.

Discriminant analysis allows a researcher to determine which characteristics ''discriminate'' one type of person from another. Kelly used the technique to determine the characteristics that donors have but nondonors do not. This information then allows a fund raiser to spend money to solicit contributions only from the people most likely to give money. Similarly, promotions specialists could direct their appeals only to those publics most likely to attend a concert or football game or to buy a new automobile or stove.

Constraint Recognition Stands Out • Kelly's results showed the importance of constraints in identifying active publics. Many of the journalism alumni had a high level of concern about the college's problems and felt involved with those problems. But they gave no money because they perceived constraints to giving money: They were young alumni who did not have enough money yet to donate.

The donors were not especially likely to recognize the problems of the college or to feel involved with it. But they had more income, more often paid dues to the alumni association, and more often gave money to other charitable causes—in sum, they perceived fewer constraints to helping the college.

For people to give money to a cause, the study suggests, they have to feel their contribution will make a difference. If a struggling young couple is asked to give $25 to help build a new stadium at their alma mater, for example, they probably will feel their contribution will make little difference to whether the stadium is built. But the $25 will buy their child a pair of shoes that he or she needs badly. Thus, they will not donate the money even though they recognize the need for a new stadium and feel quite involved with the team.

Daniel Conrad's fund-raising book also expresses the importance of constraints quite well:

> Take the case of hospitals that want to add a new wing to increase capacity. Invariably they create a brochure which discusses the new wing in much detail. There are schematic drawings, rooms labeled individually, huge lists of equipment (whose functions are unknown, perhaps even unknowable), followed by cost figures for that equipment which would stagger the average donor, and much talk about the cost of the whole project.[28]

Extending the Same Idea • Kelly's study did not show problem recognition to discriminate donors from nondonors because the two groups were at about the same level on that variable. The situational theory suggests that people must think about and be interested in a sport, product, university, or hospital before they attend, buy, or give money—the theory suggests, that is, that problem recognition is a necessary condition for behavior.

But problem recognition alone is not enough for people to *behave*—it is not a sufficient condition. Recognition of constraints stops many people from behaving in ways they would like to behave.

Take sports promotion, for example. In 1983, it cost about $12 a ticket to attend a professional basketball or hockey game. To take a family of five to a professional game would cost $60 plus parking and snacks. For most people, that price constrains them from attending many games.

Family discount plans or dollars off special tickets purchased from supermarkets or fast food chains, however, make a big difference. Those promotional techniques work because they help to remove constraints—but only if the team is good enough to offer entertainment in exchange.

On the practical side, therefore, this research suggests that promotional appeals must either be limited to people who are unconstrained from behaving in the desired way. Or, it suggests that something must be done to lower the constraints to enlarge the active public.

Promotional Programs Aimed at Passive Publics

Although we have suggested that campaigns for which a behavioral effect is an absolute necessity should be limited to active publics, there are many other promotional campaigns for which the objective is to reform or initiate behavior by passive publics that have little interest in the topics of the campaign—such as highway safety, seat belts, or drunken driving.

Those are the campaigns for which objectives must be scaled down to communication (exposing people to the campaign) and to message retention and acceptance. It was the recognition of the passive nature of the publics for these campaigns that led Mendelsohn to conclude in 1973 that information campaigns can succeed if the behavior objective is dropped or limited to a small part of the public.

In Chapter 6, we explained why low-involvement, passive publics will process but not seek information.[29] A communication campaign, therefore, can alert members of a passive public to a problem. A few members of these passive publics may begin to seek information actively after recognizing the problem, and eventually change their behavior—exactly what happened in the National Driver Test campaign. Most members of the passive publics, however, will not turn into members of active publics after retaining, or even accepting, the message of a public-information campaign.

Effects of a Campaign Against Drunken Driving

Grunig and Ipes conducted a two-stage study of campaigns on the drunken-driving issue that confirmed the conclusions in the previous paragraph.[30]

Drunken driving had been in the news and the subject of many communication campaigns, both in Maryland and nationally, for about a year before the first stage of the Grunig-Ipes study in January 1982. When researchers interviewed 100 residents of Prince Georges County, Maryland, they found nearly all of the respondents had a high level of involvement and problem recognition for the issue—apparently caused by the campaigns on the issue the previous year. At the same time, however, most of the people sampled also had a high level of constraint recognition.

About a month after the first survey, the researchers sent each respondent a packet of articles that had been published in local newspapers on the drunken-driving issue—to reinforce the intensive media coverage of the issue that had occurred since the first interview. They also included a form that the respondents could use to send for additional publications on the issue, thus providing respondents with a chance to actively seek information.

Two months after the initial survey, researchers interviewed the same people again. Problem recognition and involvement remained high, but constraint recognition had not fallen even though articles sent to people discussed what they could do to remove the constraints.

The people interviewed also did not develop more organized ideas about what to do about drunken drivers, and only a few remembered the mailing they had received. Only one person actually mailed in the request form for more information. Apparently, the information campaign had little additional effect after it raised problem recognition and level of involvement.

What the Study Suggests • The study suggests, therefore, that the major effect that a public-communication campaign has on a passive public is simply to put the problem on that public's agenda. Only. a few people then move on to other segments of the behavioral molecule—to construct cognitions, attitudes, and behaviors.

The Grunig-Ipes study, like the Kelly study of fund raising, also showed the importance of constraints in stopping people from moving on through the molecule to behavior. Something must be done to remove constraints if people are to be moved—something like the interpersonal support provided by organized groups. In Maryland, a group called MADD (Mothers Against Drunk Driving) provided that support to a few people. (See the discussion of size and cohesion of publics in Chapter 7.) Or, the study suggests, engineering and enforcement must be used to move people, because education alone won't do it.

Promoting Low-Involvement Products

There are situations, however, when low-involvement, passive publics will move to the *behave* segment of the behavioral molecule directly from the *detect* segment without the organized thought and evaluation that takes place in the segments between these two. Those low-involvement situations require a different strategy for the promotion of some products or issues.[31]

If a product costs little or the consumer does not perceive one brand of a product to be much different from another, the consumer will often purchase the product after simply hearing about it. That's why television advertising works so well for low-involvement products such as toothpaste, mouthwash, or hair cream. The more often consumers hear the message, the more likely they will be to remember the product when they are in a store.

After buying the product, habit may set in. Remember that the behavioral molecule then becomes *detect . . . behave . . . detect . . . behave*. Some consumers may rationalize a purchase after they make it—*construct* a cognition after the fact. In either case, publicity alone may be sufficient to get people to buy low-involvement products, to vote for political candidates running for lesser offices, or to recognize the names and attributes of uninvolving organizations.

That explanation tells us why hot-air balloons, blimps, or staged events often achieve name recognition (message retention), followed by a habitual kind of effect upon behavior. But, remember, an unthinking change in message retention and behavior occurs only when the product or issue makes little difference to the receiver of the message.

EVALUATION OF PROMOTIONS AND CAMPAIGNS

Promotional campaign strategists—who almost always choose an effect on the behavior of a public as their long-term objective—frequently err by measuring nothing other than behavior to evaluate their campaign. They may monitor changes in product purchases, traffic accidents, drunken driving offenses, enrollments in driving classes, or number of heart attacks.[32]

It's important to measure behavior, but as we have seen in this chapter, measures of behavior alone may make it appear that the campaign has failed when it has been as successful as possible for a particular public.

For the three kinds of promotional campaigns discussed in this chapter, therefore, it is important to measure all of the objectives discussed throughout this book. And as promotional campaigns become symmetric as well as asymmetric, it becomes important to measure the coorientational version of these effects—described in Chapter 6—as well. Measures for all of these objectives can be taken from the samples in Chapter 9.

Learn More About Marketing

Throughout this chapter, we have been giving you what is essentially a brief course in marketing and marketing research, so that you can understand the disposal subsystem when public relations is asked to support it.

If you work in a public relations subfield that includes or supports marketing—such as product publicity or nonprofit public relations—you will need to understand marketing as well as public relations. For that purpose, we urge you to seek further training at your school of business.

NOTES

1. Jacqueline Peake, *Public Relations in Business* (New York: Harper & Row, 1980), p. 5.
2. William Ehling, ''Toward a Theory of Public Relations Management: Applications of Purposive and Conflict Theories to Communication Management.'' Paper presented to the Association for Education in Journalism, East Lansing, Mich., August 1981.
3. Michael Ray, *Advertising and Communication Management* (Englewood Cliffs, N.J.: Prentice-Hall, 1982), p. 17.
4. William Nickels, *Marketing Communication and Promotion*, 2d ed. (Columbus, Ohio: Grid, 1980), p. 15.
5. Dorothy L. Zufall, ''How to Adapt Marketing Strategies in Health-Care Public Relations,'' *Public Relations Journal* 37 (October 1981):15.
6. ''Behind the Scenes with The Goodyear Blimp—Public Relations Ambassador Extraordinaire,'' *PR Casebook* 3 (May 1982):11–14.
7. ''Awakening Interest in a Well-Known Product,'' *PR Casebook* 3 (March 1982):3–5.
8. ''B-M Brings 'Good Things' to GE,'' Marsteller, Inc./Burson-Marsteller *Viewpoint*, March 1982.
9. For a description of how a Seattle, Washington, hospital integrated fund raising, public relations, and marketing, see Nancy J. Hicks and David T. McKee, ''Integrated Strategies: A Successful Approach to Hospital Public Relations,'' *Public Relations Journal* 37 (October 1981):14–16.
10. Thomas E. Broce, *Fund Raising: The Guide to Raising Money from Private Sources* (Norman: University of Oklahoma Press, 1979).
11. Robert S. Cole, *The Practical Handbook of Public Relations* (Englewood Cliffs, N.J.: Prentice-Hall, 1981), Chapter 10.
12. Broce, p. 137.
13. Broce, p. 137.
14. Stephen Wertheimer, ''On Thinking About . . . The Need for a Case Statement: Part I,'' *Fund Raising Management* 9 (November/December 1978):37–39.
15. Kathleen S. Kelly, ''Pass the Alka-Seltzer: How Market Research Eases the Pain of 'Gut-Feeling' Solicitation,'' *Case Currents* (May/June 1982):32–36.
16. William J. Paisley, ''Public Communication Campaigns: The American Experience,'' in Ronald E. Rice and William J. Paisley (eds.), *Public Communication Campaigns* (Beverly Hills, Calif.: Sage, 1981), pp. 15–40.
17. Douglas S. Soloman, ''A Social Marketing Perspective on Campaigns,'' in Rice and Paisley, pp. 281–292.
18. Detailed descriptions and analyses of many of these campaigns can be found in Rice and Paisley.
19. For a theoretical conceptualization of the two-way asymmetric approach to public communication campaigns, see William J. McGuire, ''Theoretical Foundations of Campaigns,'' in Rice and Paisley, pp. 41–70.
20. Herbert H. Hyman and Paul B. Sheatsley, ''Some Reasons Why Information Campaigns Fail,'' *Public Opinion Quarterly* 11 (1947):412–423.
21. Raymond Bauer, ''The Obstinate Audience: The Influence Process from the Point of View of Social Communication,'' *American Psychologist* 19 (1964):319–328.
22. Harold Mendelsohn, ''Some Reasons Why Information Campaigns Can Succeed,'' *Public Opinion Quarterly* 37 (1973):50–61.

23. Eugene F. McNamara, Tony Kurth, and Donald Hansen, ''Communication Efforts to Prevent Wildfires,'' in Rice and Paisley, pp. 143–160.
24. Lloyd D. Lewis, ''Chessie's Safety Express,'' *PR Casebook* 3 (April 1982):9–12.
25. See, for example, Alfred McAlister, ''Anti-smoking Campaigns: Progress in Developing Effective Communications,'' in Rice and Paisley, pp. 91–103.
26. Brenda Dervin, ''Mass Communicating: Changing Conceptions of the Audience,'' in Rice and Paisley, pp. 71–87.
27. Kathleen S. Kelly, ''Predicting Alumni Giving: An Analysis of Alumni Donors and Non-Donors of the College of Journalism at the University of Maryland,'' master's thesis, University of Maryland, 1979.
28. Daniel Lynn Conrad, *Techniques of Fund Raising* (Secaucus, N.J.: Lyle Stuart, 1974), p. 20.
29. For a similiar line of theoretical reasoning, see Charles K. Atkin, ''Mass Media Information Campaign Effectiveness,'' in Rice and Paisley, pp. 265–279.
30. James E. Grunig and Daniel Ipes, ''A Theoretical Anatomy of a Public Communication Campaign.'' Paper presented to a session sponsored by the Foundation for Public Relations Research and Education and the Educators' Section of the Public Relations Society of America at the PRSA annual convention, San Francisco, November 1982.
31. For research to support the following discussion, see Michael L. Ray, ''Marketing Communication and the Hierarchy-of-Effects,'' in Peter Clarke (ed.), *New Models for Communi-cation Research* (Beverly Hills, Calif.: Sage, 1973), pp. 147–173.
32. Brian R. Flay and Thomas D. Cook, ''Evaluation of Mass Media Prevention Campaigns,'' in Rice and Paisley, pp. 239–264.

ADDITIONAL READING

Broce, Thomas E., *Fund Raising: The Guide to Raising Money from Private Sources* (Norman: University of Oklahoma Press, 1979).
Dervin, Brenda, ''Strategies for Dealing with Human Information Needs: Information or Communication?'' *Journal of Broadcasting* 20 (1976):324–333.
Hicks, Nancy J., and David T. McKee, ''Integrated Strategies: A Successful Approach to Hospital Public Relations,'' *Public Relations Journal* 37 (October 1981):14–16.
Kotler, Philip, *Marketing for Non-Profit Organizations* (Englewood Cliffs, N.J.: Prentice-Hall, 1975).
Mendelsohn, Harold, ''Some Reasons Why Information Campaigns Can Succeed,'' *Public Opinion Quarterly* 37 (1973):50–61.
Nickels, William, *Marketing Communication and Promotion*, 2d ed. (Columbus, Ohio: Grid, 1980).
Ray, Michael, *Advertising and Communication Management* (Englewood Cliffs, N.J.: Prentice-Hall, 1982).
Rice, Ronald E., and William J. Paisley (eds.), *Public Communication Campaigns* (Beverly Hills, Calif.: Sage, 1981).

Welcome
Shareowners

IV

Managing Public Relations Techniques

Part IV moves down one additional level of management to the day-to-day skills and techniques used in the public relations programs described in Part III. The first three parts of the book concentrated on the management and conceptual skills needed to be a public relations professional. Part IV now discusses the technical skills needed to put those conceptual skills to practical use.

Part IV, in theoretical terms, takes you into the *behave* segment of the behavioral molecule that has been used as a management model throughout this book:

. . . Detect . . . Construct . . . Define . . . Select . . . Confirm . . . Behave . . . Detect . . .

The behavioral molecule should make it clear that a behavior—here the use of a communication technique—should be planned: constructed, defined, selected, and confirmed. Thus, the fifteen chapters of Part IV discuss how communication skills are used in public relations and special problems encountered in using these communication techniques. They also discuss "how to do" the technique. The chapters also tie public relations techniques to the management concepts of Parts I and II. They discuss when it is appropriate to use each technique and how to evaluate whether the technique has accomplished what you wanted it to.

19

PUBLIC RELATIONS WRITING

In another of its many public-spirited gestures, the Goodall Company has announced that once more it will take the lead in community betterment by donating a generous gift of $10,000 worth of playground equipment to the city so that the little children of the low-income Helmsley housing development can enjoy their summer. . .

The donation of playground equipment certainly is a newsworthy occurrence. Most media gladly would give the story space—unless, that is, they learned of the event through a news release filled with such puffery as "public-spirited gesture," "taking the lead once more," and "generous gift." The gratuitously sentimental image of "little children enjoying their summer" only compounds the error.

News editors rankle at such blatant and self-serving phrases. On a slow day, they might be willing to edit the offending news release. But, then again, they might not have the time or the inclination. It is up to the writer of the news release to know what the editor is looking for in style and format.

Getting legitimate news stories published or broadcast in the community news media is a major public relations goal for any organization. It's no wonder, then, that newswriting experience is a prime requisite for a well-rounded practitioner. A 1980 study of 200 PRSA members showed that 90 percent of the professionals in the field say basic newswriting is the most important course required of the PR student, even ahead of the basic introduction to public relations course.[1]

Not all public relations techniques require writing skill, but the majority of them do. In addition, writing represents a crucial skill in each of the four models of public relations practice introduced in Part I of this book.

Many of the practitioners who stress the importance of writing practice the public-information or press-agentry models. Writing is critical to practitioners of those models whose main objective is to place stories in the news media—where unclear writing cannot be tolerated—or to produce brochures and other publications.

Yet writing is equally critical for the two-way asymmetric and symmetric models. The persuasive communicators of the asymmetric model often look for motivations of readers or for writing devices that will make persuasion possible. What they ignore is the simple fact that people cannot be persuaded to accept an idea unless they understand it—and that clear writing is a key to understanding.[2]

In the two-way symmetric model, the public relations person uses many interpersonal communication channels. But even in this model, practitioners communicate most often with their publics through print or broadcast media, and those messages must be written. Messages to management about publics generally are written, too, as memos or reports. A two-way symmetric practitioner who wants to be understood—the purpose of the model—must be able to write well.

Several specific categories of public relations writing will be examined in later chapters, including press releases, speeches, radio announcements, and scripts. At this point, however, it is useful to take a general look at the special requirements of the field, including maximum objectivity, source review, long-range implications, consistency, achieving maximum impact, and special style considerations.

Although we speak frequently of public relations writing as if it were a subfield of its own, we must acknowledge that the best PR writing blends into context by adopting a style and tone consistent with the medium chosen for its dissemination. The practitioner must learn to emulate straight news style for a basic news release, then shift gears into a "feature" style for a magazine article or a conversational tone for the script of a welcoming speech. In other words, PR writing is doing its job when the audience never stops to think, "This is good PR writing!"

WRITING OBJECTIVES

In Chapter 6. we outlined five effects of communication that can serve as objectives for public relations: communication, retention of the message, acceptance of cognitions, formation or change of an attitude, and overt behavior. You should keep these objectives in mind when you write even the simplest public relations message. Remember, however, that the most likely effect of your writing will be retention of the message: if you write well, people will remember what you write. Strive for that effect, because the others cannot be achieved through writing alone. Here's why:

Communication • You can't control whether people will expose themselves to your message. If they don't read the message, there's no way your writing can cause them to read it!

Acceptance of Cognitions • People will see your organization or its behavior the way you see it more often if you have explained the organization well and the people have retained your message. But retaining your message doesn't always mean they will accept it. Sometimes people simply don't believe what you say. Writing alone won't change that fact.

Formation or Change of Attitude • Writing, by itself, will not accomplish this objective either. People evaluate your organization positively or negatively for many reasons. Good writing helps them to base that evaluation on an accurate picture of the organization. But sometimes they just don't like the picture.

Overt Behavior • In contrast to what many people think, you cannot change or cause behavior by skillfully writing to appeal to hidden motivators. Most people base their behavior on what they believe. You can tell them what you want them to believe and do; that's the effect of writing. But people themselves decide what to believe and do; writing cannot control them.

What does this tell the public relations writer? It indicates that the aim should be to be objective . . . to give people the facts, help them to retain those facts, and then let them decide for themselves how to think and behave.

MAXIMUM OBJECTIVITY

Objectivity sounds like an absolute: A writer either is biased or unbiased. But the best news reporter or editor knows that every sentence is a compromise. Every choice of adjective presents a problem of drawing a completely "accurate" picture of the truth.

The beginning reporter is taught that objectivity begins with keeping himself out of the story. Instead of writing, "I observed an oddly dressed procession outside the courthouse," which suggests a response based on personal values, one learns to write, "Eleven young men dressed as colonial elders marched up the steps of the courthouse carrying anti-taxation placards." The reader can decide whether that scene is "odd," or moving, or whatever.

Reporters may keep their own views out of a straight news story, but they are often identified with a byline. That simple device has the effect of informing the reader that one person's eyes and mind have filtered the facts in the article. But the public relations writer works anonymously. PR writing must stand on its own merits, divorced from the identity of the author. For the reader to accept anonymous information, the words and sentences must carry self-evident authority and integrity.

How do PR writers reconcile the need for credibility with the need to be loyal to their employer? It is a matter of keeping the employing organization in mind when gathering the information, and then keeping the editor—and, by extension, the reader—in mind when organizing the information and writing it for publication.

In other words, the writer who is planning an article on new engine developments for General Motors probably would gather information only from GM's research and testing facilities, whereas the newspaper reporter would be obligated to interview GM's competitors as well as independent researchers and auto industry critics such as Ralph Nader. However, when the PR writer sits down to assemble the article, the information is developed in the same way as the news reporter would do it, looking first for a lively angle to get the readers thinking about what sort of car they'll be driving in a decade, and then summarizing the types of propulsion envisioned by the engineers.

Both the news reporter and the PR writer would rely on the same elements to carry the story along: visual description, anecdotes about testing of the new systems, quotes from engineers who know the capabilities and drawbacks of the test engines, and simple statistics that give an idea of the cost savings or other benefits of the technological developments.

SOURCE REVIEW

Despite deadline pressures, material written by the news reporter is subjected to some scrutiny before it is printed. A city editor or news editor reads the piece to ensure that the content is complete, adequately explained, free of libel, and attributed properly to knowledgeable sources. Next, a copy editor checks spelling and grammar, verifies addresses and proper identification of sources, attempts to remedy any lack of clarity that results from careless or complex writing, and, finally, assures that the newspaper's style for figures, quotations, titles, and punctuation has been followed. Rarely does an editor double-check the reporter by telephoning a source to verify a fact or a quote. The assumption is made that the reporter got the basic facts straight. If the source complains, the remedy may be a small correction notice the next day or a subsequent story that clarifies the matter. If the editors feel no great harm was done by the slight inaccuracy or misplaced emphasis, nothing will be done.

The PR writer finds a different reality. One professor puts it this way:

> It is considered a breach of journalistic ethics for the source of a story to review the copy prior to publication. Journalists do not wish to render themselves vulnerable to pressure from the source, even at the risk of getting the facts wrong.
>
> In public relations, on the other hand, review of written copy by a source is frequent. It is one reason that the factual accuracy of press releases is far superior to media-generated stories; press releases have been checked by someone other than the writer who is thoroughly familiar with the facts. Most practitioners know by experience what embarrassment such checking can save them.[3]

So, in addition to the omission of a byline as a reward, we now note that the PR writer's pride of authorship must be subjected to another burden—the approval of others who may not be appreciative of good writing. One of the crucial interpersonal skills a PR practitioner must develop is the ability to take the criticism of a piece of writing from a superior who knows the technical facts better than the writer does, incorporate the necessary changes into the written message, and still maintain the style, interest, and integrity of the words so they will attract a media audience.

To sensitize nonwriters in an organization to what you are doing, it may be useful to show them models of media stories you intend to emulate in order to get space in the news media. A superior who has no mental picture of the final product may instead visualize a dry technical report. If, on the other hand, you can show examples of the kind of ''spread'' you're aiming for, the superior may grant the creative leeway you need in order to write an article that will attract an editor's attention.

LONG-RANGE IMPLICATIONS/CONSISTENCY

Newswriting is ephemeral. The reporter usually worries only about the current twenty-four-hour cycle of news production. If the facts appear to change tomorrow, it's simply a matter of updating the story by ''finding a new angle.''

The PR writer enjoys no such luxury. Access to the public media cannot be taken for granted. And when a story does appear, the impression it leaves with the public may last until such time as it is again your organization's ''turn'' to get news space, or until you have another item of fresh and legitimate news interest. The PR writer must review past articles about the organization, determine how the public perceives the organization or program, and then write a piece that will be consistent with how the writer wants the public to view it. Advertisers talk of ''maintaining market position'' for a product. Similarly, it is useful for the PR writer to view articles in the media as a way of maintaining position in the marketplace of ideas, or of ''repositioning'' the organization's programs, if that is needed.

Another parallel between advertising and public relations writing is the need for consistency, so as to reap the effects of repetition. Imagine if the Coca-Cola people said ''Things go better with Coke'' one time and ''Coke makes everything taste better'' the next time. You have to work hard to get an idea to remain in the reader's mind after the act of receiving the message is over. Develop a concept, work out the written expression of it, and then use it faithfully without alteration.

For example, the publicist, the director, and the president of the board of trustees of a museum must agree to refer to the institution in all public messages as "a regional arts facility serving the citizens of the tri-county area," if they want to implant the notion that the museum does not belong to the city in which it is located, and is not restricting itself to use by cultural elites. The payoff comes when the organization notes in articles and editorials initiated by news media personnel that the phrase has caught on as the proper identification. Sometimes the goal may seem simple, like making certain that people say "Health Systems Plan" instead of merely "Health Plan" when they refer to an agency. But the discrimination may be subtly important in terms of the public's ability to identify the role and contribution of that agency.

You'll especially want to use repetition when your analysis of publics shows that people will be passively processing rather than actively seeking out the message you have written (see Chapter 7). People who actively seek information tend to remember it because they need to use it to guide their behavior. But when they don't really need the information—which is true of most public relations messages—they will not go out of their way to remember what you said. You have to repeat your message over and over so that they not only process the message, they remember some of it as well.

ACHIEVING MAXIMUM IMPACT

Simplicity versus completeness.

That, in a nutshell, is the dilemma PR writers face every time they sit down at the keyboard.

Simplicity is vital because "the news system is a relentless process of progressive simplification and oversimplification," as one PR consultant has pointed out.[4] Faced with thousands of worthy stories competing for attention each day, editors and readers alike distill it all down into bite-sized chunks:

The local hospital has a new CAT-scanner that will save many lives through faster, better diagnosis.

Poor people can get help with their rent from the county housing authority.

The local auto assembly plant expects rising car sales to result in the recall of laid-off workers.

In reality, each of those important stories is much more complicated. Because the hospital was designated to house the CAT-scanner, it will not be given permission by the state to become a center for cardiac analysis and therapy. The requirements for county rent aid are complex, and it may be more advantageous for low-income tenants to receive pass-along rent savings from a landlord who qualifies for renovation assistance under a less-well-known federal program. The return to full auto employment may be temporary, pending the manufacturer's long-range plans to phase out the local facility.

Simplicity or completeness? The PR writer tries to have it both ways by giving the news media a concise and understandable twelve-paragraph press release summarizing the story in a way that is readable and interesting (Exhibit 19-1). And then the reporter or editor is provided with an accompanying press packet that includes fact sheets that go into greater detail about specifics (see Chapter 25).

The hope is that the news organization, once it has used the succinct version of the story, will see the need for an in-depth report and will use the press packet as background for a Sunday feature or magazine piece. Another technique is to distribute the simplified press release at a news conference where organization officials with the necessary expertise are ready to answer the press's more probing questions. If the media want to go with the concisely digested version, fine. If they want depth and breadth, the opportunity is there.

Publics learn about events when writers in the public relations department prepare and distribute news releases. When New Brunswick, N.J., community leader Richard Sellars spoke at a news conference announcing plans to construct a major new hotel in the revitalized city, Development Corporation (DevCo) personnel already had their article ready to pass out to journalists. (Photo and news release courtesy of DevCo)

New Brunswick DEVELOPMENT CORPORATION

Contact: Angelo V. Baguvo
                  201-624-2758
         (home) 201-687-0291

          Robert V. Andrews
                  201-524-6925
         (home) 201-431-1009

                                            12980

                              FOR IMMEDIATE RELEASE

     New Brunswick, N.J. -- Ground was broken today (Monday, Sept. 29) for construction of a $28 million downtown Hyatt Regency Hotel and conference center before a large group of local, State and Federal dignitaries.

     The ceremony marked another milestone in the physical, economic and social revitalization of the City spearheaded by a private-public-community partnership known as New Brunswick Tomorrow.

     Richard B. Sellars, Chairman of the New Brunswick Development Corporation (DevCo), sponsor of the hotel project, presided at the ceremony. Participants included James E. Burke, Chairman and Chief Executive Officer of Johnson & Johnson; State Attorney General John J. Degnan, representing Governor Brendan T. Byrne, and Mayor John A. Lynch Jr.

     The groundbreaking took place on a cleared site at Albany and Neilson Streets, the gateway to downtown New Brunswick, against a backdrop of several hundred million dollars worth of construction.

     Directly across Albany Street, the new $50 million worldwide corporate headquarters for Johnson & Johnson, the health care products manufacturer, is under construction. A few blocks away, the $60 million expansion of Middlesex General Hospital as a regional medical center and teaching hospital for Rutgers Medical School, CMDNJ, is under way. One block away, a key transportation project, the State-sponsored extension of the Route 18 expressway, is under construction.

390 GEORGE STREET NEW BRUNSWICK, NEW JERSEY 08901, (201) 249-2220

**EXHIBIT
19-1**

A MATTER OF STYLE

By this point, communicating with some sort of flair may seem to be totally out of the question, so complicated is the PR writer's task. But no. Once all those other thorny problems are addressed, PR writing, like all good writing, must capture the attention of the reader, engage the imagination, and eventually, one hopes, gain approval.

Begin any writing task by identifying—and then identifying with—the readers. In an institutional advertisement sponsored by the International Paper Company, author Kurt Vonnegut pleaded with writers:

> Pity the readers. They have to identify thousands of little marks on paper and make sense of them immediately. They have to read, an art so difficult that most people don't really master it even after having studied it all through grade school and high school—twelve long years.[5]

People tend to read or listen to messages for one of two reasons. Sometimes, the message has practical relevance to them. At other times, the message has no relevance, but if it is written well, they will read it because the message arouses interest or curiosity.

Let's look at the idea of relevance first. In the theoretical terms of Chapter 7 on organizational linkages to publics, a message will be relevant if it talks about something that has a high level of involvement for your reader. As you remember from that chapter, some people seek, rather than just process, information about things that involve them.

What involves your readers? How will a development change their lives? What's in it for them?

An article that introduces a new product shouldn't focus on the fact that the company "has announced" marketing of the product. It should focus on what the product can do for the consumer: "The drudgery of fertilizing the lawn can be greatly reduced with a spreader attachment that spreads pellets at the same time the homeowner is mowing the lawn. Introduction of the GREEN-SPRED device was announced this week by. . .''

You got the reader's attention by bringing the story close to home, literally and figuratively. Keep that attention by humanizing the story, which means having people talking. Use quotes from those who are most affected by the program or product your organization is promoting. Don't let them ramble; synthesize what they have to say into a brief, memorable sentence or two: "My customers used to groan when I told them it was time to attack the dandelions," smiles hardware store owner Hy Becker, "but GREEN-SPRED means they can do two jobs at once and not drop over from exhaustion."

If there is really no way to show the relevance of your message because the reader's involvement is low, then you've got to simplify and brighten your writing. Packaging information in digestible portions makes the message more palatable. The writer may find that a forty-word sentence in a memo to the boss has the effect of adding importance and apparent substance to the message. But a forty-word sentence in an article may be just the turnoff the reader needs in order to justify returning to the program on the tube.

So, write short. Short words. Short sentences. Short paragraphs . . . with an occasional long one for variety.

Read your material out loud, and punctuate where the sentence compounds or where you insert an explanatory phrase. The resulting "visual relief," which supplements the required structural punctuation, helps the reader's eye.

Avoid overcapitalization. Organizations have a tendency to capitalize the name of every little subcommittee and program. The news services, in the interest of speed and clarity, have taught us to expect only proper names and the names of full organizations to be capitalized. (Consolidated Edison, for example, but ''Con Ed's rate advisory board'' rather than ''Rate Advisory Board.'')

Virtually every journalism and public relations writing course requires students to use the Associated Press style manual, which mandates form and usage for newswriting. Obviously, a news release that follows the AP style rules will please an editor . . . and its chances of being used in the media will be enhanced.

When you have written enough, don't be afraid to end neatly and swiftly. Like this.

EVALUATING YOUR WRITING

Many people think that writing is an art . . . that it can't be evaluated. Don't be misled. Only stream-of-consciousness writers fail to evaluate their work.

Because the principal objective of writing is message retention, you can evaluate your own writing by putting it aside for a few days and then reading it over by yourself. Have you retained your own message? Do you understand what you want to say? Ask someone else to read what you have written and tell you what you said. You'll be surprised at how often the other person fails to retain the message.

If you want to use formal evaluation devices, refer to Chapter 9 on evaluation research. The readability tests outlined there will help you to determine whether you have written simply enough for your audience. You'll probably find the signaled stopping technique (SST) to be the most useful technique to evaluate your writing. That's where you or someone else reads your writing, and whenever you or the reader feels like stopping, you or he note the reason for stopping—such as confusion, rereading, or dis-

agreement. It's an excellent technique for finding what goes on in the reader's mind (or your own mind). The reasons given for stopping will help you when you rewrite or edit your work.

Remember this axiom: Good writing is not merely written . . . it is rewritten.

NOTES

1. Mike Shelly, ''PR Professionals Pick News Writing as Priority Course,'' *Journalism Educator* (January 1981): 16.
2. See, for example, Richard E. Petty, Thomas M. Ostrom, and Timothy C. Brock (eds.), *Cognitive Responses in Persuasion* (Hillsdale, N.J.: Lawrence Erlbaum Associates, 1981).
3. John S. Detweiler, ''Public Relations Writing Is Different.'' Paper presented to the Association for Education in Journalism, Boston, 1980, p. 16.
4. Richard M. Detwiler, ''Executives Make 10 Great Mistakes Mis-Coping with News,'' *Public Relations Journal* (December 1975): 17.
5. Kurt Vonnegut, ''How to Write with Style,'' reprints available from International Paper Company, Dept. 5-T, P.O. Box 900, Elmsford, N.Y., 10523.

ADDITIONAL READING

Douglas, George A., *Writing for Public Relations* (Columbus, Ohio: Charles E. Merrill, 1980).

Flesch, Rudolf, *The Art of Readable Writing* (New York: Harper & Row, 1974).

Gunning, Robert, *The Technique of Clear Writing* (New York: McGraw-Hill, 1968).

Newsom, Doug, and Tom Siegfried, *Writing in Public Relations Practice* (Belmont, Calif.: Wadsworth, 1981).

Strunk, William, and E. B. White, *The Elements of Style*, 3d ed., (New York: Macmillan, 1979).

Zinsser, William, *On Writing Well* (New York: Harper & Row, 1976).

20

PRESS RELEASES

Four members of management have just been named vice presidents. That's newsworthy to the readers of weekly newspapers in the various suburban communities where each of the officers lives. It also is of interest to those who keep up with your field through a biweekly trade journal.

Your company has shifted to a new advertising agency in preparation for bringing out a new line of products. Advertising trade columnists will want to know about it, and the products also should be written up in the public media.

Plans for modernizing your plant mean profitable construction contracts for many other area firms—a development that will be important news in the regional Chamber of Commerce magazine.

Other occasions for issuing news releases include:

Milestones, such as anniversaries of the company's existence, the one-millionth customer, or a decade since the introduction of a successful product or service.

New savings or economies, such as institution of an energy-conservation or recycling program, or the achievement of productivity goals.

Selection of the company by another institution or by a government agency to produce a component or service a new program.

The winning of achievement awards by the company or its individual employees. Also, completion of training programs by managers or other employees.

Opinions of company officials regarding the economy, pending legislation affecting business, or other public issues in which the firm has an interest.

The results of research.

Announcement of a contest.

The list could be virtually endless . . . and so far it includes only good news. Obviously, it also may be useful to issue a press release if you fire four vice presidents, lose an anticipated contract, decide to close a plant instead of modernizing it—or if your plant burns down and the fire chief is blaming it on allegedly improper storage of combustible materials.

At holiday time, the Seagram Company distributes a feature release describing how to stock a bar for entertaining large groups of people, complete with a photograph depicting the ideal setup (with Seagram products prominently displayed, of course). Any company involved in high technology probably can arrange for a panel of its scientists and engineers to predict the future a decade or a century hence, resulting in a fascinating article that will interest the Sunday newspaper editor.

Editors Depend on Releases

Some editors say they never look at the piles of "handouts" that cross their desks each day.[1] But usually even the largest news organizations sort out the releases that offer tips, ideas, data, or other starting points for staff reporters, who will assemble and write a story in their own style. Routinely, certain columns in almost every paper are put together by pasting up news releases: business promotions, military personnel activities, cultural and entertainment events. Similarly, many of the short "bulletin board" items about meetings and social events carried by local newspapers and radio stations come to them as news releases.[2]

Most weekly and small daily newspapers with limited resources depend heavily on news and features provided by governments, educational institutions, industry and trade associations to fill their columns. Similarly, radio station news personnel receive taped feature materials from public relations departments, and they have the phone numbers of "daily feed" systems that permit them to tape a minute or more of "live quote" information from spokespersons for various organizations. (See Chapter 22.) The amount of information in the media that has its origins in news releases cannot be underestimated.

After looking at management considerations related to the use of news releases, we will look at the format for the standard news release. Then we shall examine the difference between broadcast and print releases, the matter of timing a release, and how to submit it.

MANAGEMENT CONSIDERATIONS

We have stressed throughout this book that public relations techniques should not be used unless there is a solid management reason for using them. Press releases tend to be the most overused device, because practitioners often write them when they don't know what else to do. Let's look at some things you should think about before you write a release.

Model of Public Relations

You will recall from Chapter 2 that the press release originated in the last half of the nineteenth century, when the press-agentry model was in its heyday and the public-information model was developing. Even today, the practitioners of these two models consider the press release to be their principal tool—often their only tool. Practitioners of the two-way asymmetric and symmetric models also use press releases, but they use them more selectively. Whatever the model, make sure there is a good reason for communicating a message before you issue a press release.

Objectives

Is there really a good reason for your publics to be exposed to and to retain your message? Does the community really need to know, for example, that a long-time employee was given an award for 25 years of service? Are the mass media the best way to communicate that fact?

If both answers are yes, then think of the first two objectives listed in Chapter 6. The first objective of your release is to communicate with members of a public. To meet that objective, your release first must pass the media gatekeepers and be placed on the media agenda. (You will recall from the chapter on media relations that communication researchers now perceive ''agenda-setting'' as the major effect of the media.) To get on the media agenda, your release must meet journalistic standards. The second objective is message retention. That means your release must be written so that it is clear, complete, and interesting.

Which Programs?

Most of the specialized public relations programs discussed in Part III use news releases as part of media relations. Public-affairs and government-relations people announce their companies' positions with releases. News releases are sent to media serving activist publics, such as the Sierra Club newsletter for environmentalists. Most financial news is distributed through news releases.

In addition, many organizations send copies of the same releases they plan to distribute to the press to their own employees as well, in order to keep them informed about the organization's news. Reprints of published releases may also be distributed internally to build good employee relations.

Communication Behavior of Publics

Whether the target public for a release will be most likely to actively seek or passively process the story that results depends mostly on the kind of medium to which the release goes. For most people, general circulation newspapers, radio, and television tend to contain mostly low-involvement information.[3]

Readers of trade publications and other specialized newsletters and magazines tend to seek information actively from those media. Thus, your story there can be more straightforward; perhaps it actually would appear dull to those not involved with the topic. A story about a new tank truck, for example, will interest readers of *Modern Bulk*

Transporter magazine no matter how it is written.

Cost in Time and Money

Press releases often are called free advertising because the public relations person does not have to pay for the space in the media. It does take time to produce a release, however, and that cost should be considered when you decide to write one. Is the cost of postage justified? Could your time be better spent on a different release or technique?

Timing is critical. Thus, the time-budgeting techniques from Chapter 8—Gantt charts, PERT, critical-path method—can help you to make sure your release arrives at the optimal time.

Evaluation

Find out if your two major objectives, communication and message retention, have been satisfied. Use a clipping service or check the media yourself to see if your releases have been used. Compare releases the media did use with those of yours they didn't use. Ask editors why they don't use your releases. From time to time, use the formal readership and retention studies discussed in the chapters on evaluation research and media relations.

THE NEWS RELEASE

A small electronics company was proud of its letterhead, printed on a cream-colored, heavy linen paper with burgundy ink. The firm's officers were listed down the side of the stationery, and superimposed in the middle of the sheet was the faint image of a computer data display. It was enough to make recipients of a letter squint. When an unsophisticated public relations person decided to use the letterhead to carry news releases, it made editors see red.

Ideally, a release is prepared so that the news editor can hand it quickly to a rewrite

EXHIBIT
20-1

news release

News Bureau • International Airport
St. Paul, Minn. 55111 • AC 612/726-2331

NORTHWEST ORIENT

M. JOSEPH LAPENSKY

PRESIDENT AND CHIEF EXECUTIVE OF

M. Joseph Lapensky, a lifelong native of
Minnesota, joined Northwest Airlines as an
after graduating in business administration
College in St. Paul, Minnesota.

He served in a n
financial area of th
until 1960.

In June 1960,
in 1966 vice pres
vice president of
was active in t
of NWA. In 19
treasurer.

Northwe
president a
was named
1, 1979.

news release

News Bureau • International Airport
St. Paul, Minn. 55111 • AC 612/726-2331

NORTHWEST ORIENT

NORTHWEST ORIENT AIRLINES

A Brief History

The history of Northwest Orient Airlines is one of pioneering --
over rugged mountains and vast oceans -- and of the development of an
international airline from a small, regional airmail carrier.

The second-oldest air carr
tinuous
1926,

Airways,
men in
Twin

vice

it
ld's

news release

News Bureau • International Airport
St. Paul, Minn. 55111 • AC 612/726-2331

NORTHWEST ORIENT

NORTHWEST AIRLINES TO ADD

FOUR MORE EUROPEAN CITIES

TO 1980 TRANS ATLANTIC SCHEDULE

Minneapolis/St. Paul -- Four more major European cities --
Oslo, Hamburg, Shannon and London -- will be added to Northwest
Airlines' 1980 trans Atlantic schedule, the company announced
today.

Northwest's schedule for summer, 1980 on the trans Atlantic
will be implemented in several phases:

. Beginning April 27, 1980, Northwest will inaugurate
flights 34 and 35 between Boston and Shannon with one
747 nonstop flight weekly (on Tuesday) in each direction.

In addition, Northwest will inaugurate flights 38 and 39
between New York and Shannon with two nonstop 747 flights
weekly in each direction (on Thursday and Saturday).

. Beginning May 29, 1980, Northwest will increase its
Boston to Shannon service from one nonstop flight weekly
to three nonstop flights weekly (Tuesday, Wednesday and
Friday).

-more-

M. J. Lapensky
President and Chief Executive Officer
Northwest Orient Airlines

News releases issued by Northwest Orient Airlines are headed by the company logo in red. The press kit issued when Northwest inaugurated four new trans-Atlantic routes included an all-purpose release, profiles of company officers, a history of the company, several photographs, as well as copies of the firm's annual report and in-flight magazine. Northwest does not put the name of the contact on the release, preferring that queries go to whomever is on duty at the line's "news bureau" at company headquarters. (Courtesy Northwest Orient Airlines) person for light editing. The copy desk then quickly writes a headline in the available white space left at the top of the first page. Radio newscasters prefer a concise, one-page release—preferably written in large, all-capital letters, so they can mark it rapidly for reading on the air.

The Northwest Orient Airlines press kit (Exhibit 20–1) is slickly done, and the accompanying mug shot of the CEO enhances the chances that the news release will be used. But note that the release itself is a model of simplicity.

Use the following checklist to evaluate a news release.

News-Release Checklist

1. Print on one side only of plain white mimeo paper. High-quality mimeo is preferred, although purple-inked duplicator is acceptable. If only one or two copies of a release are to be distributed, crisp photocopies of the typewritten original may be made.

2. Double-spacing is standard for news copy, and triple-spacing is not uncommon. In order to conserve the taxpayers' money, some governmental agencies double-space the first few paragraphs and then single-space, on the theory that a rewrite person will rework the information in any case. Keeping the release on one page also permits the editor to see all of the information in one glance.

3. Use a standard, clean typewriter face. Carbon or mylar (film) ribbons on office model typewriters yield the darkest and most flawless impression. If your release is for radio use only, you may wish to render it in the quarter-inch-high typeface that is available only on special typewriters. This makes the copy easily readable for the "talent," or newscaster.

4. The heading across the top of the page may be distinctive, but it should not be cluttered. Amounting to approximately one-fifth of the page, it usually includes:

a. The large single word NEWS in plain, black letters.

b. In typescript, the words "For immediate release" or, if necessary, a release date such as "For release at 6 p.m. EST Friday, Oct. 23." If you want to indicate that it is for release in time for morning newspapers and drive-time radio, say: "For release AMS Tuesday, May 3." (The appropriateness of such an "embargo" is discussed later in this chapter.)

c. The name, address, and phone number of the person to contact for additional information.

d. (Optional) The date and serial number of the release, which is useful in situations where a public relations office generates several releases every day or week. This facilitates quick reference when reporters or editors call for additional information or clarification.

5. A sample headline. The sample head occasionally is used by a newspaper, so it should be simple, direct, and written in the active voice:

WHEELING STEEL APPOINTS LOCKE
TO HEAD PITTSVILLE FOUNDRY

Usually, however, the newspaper editors will write a headline to fit their own specifications, so the sample is primarily a way of summarizing the main point of the release. If no headline is provided, leave approximately one-fourth of the page blank to allow the editor space to write one. Often, the decision on whether or not to use a marginally newsworthy release is simply the ease with which it can be processed by the editor.

6. Start the story with a so-called dateline, which no longer carries the date, but merely the name of the town from which the news emanates. While many newspapers will move the name of the town into the body of the story, others still prefer the dateline. Some organizations capitalize the names of towns mentioned throughout the article—not because they will appear that way in final

print, but in order to highlight them for editors who skim through looking for local names and places. The alert organization may even fold a release and mark it with red ink in such a way that mention of Bellville on the second page of a list of promotions and appointments or awards will jump out at the editor of the weekly *Bellville Bugle*.

7. Standard newspaper copyediting marks and symbols should be used throughout. Use the Associated Press Style Manual. If the release runs more than one page, the word "more" should appear at the bottom of each page except the last. An end sign such as "30" or "#" indicates that there are no more pages. The second and successive pages should be "slugged" at the top in the following manner:

PROMOTIONS—add one
PROMOTIONS—add two

The slug word ("Promotions," in this case) is selected from the first paragraph of the story and keys the most important aspect of the news.

BROADCAST RELEASES

We already have noted that the requirements of radio differ from those of the print media. Radio has much tighter space-time requirements than print. News items are usually only a few sentences long.

Here are the requirements of the broadcast release:

Type the information entirely in large capital letters to facilitate reading.

Keep the item to no more than 200 words, which is about one minute of reading time.

Use short paragraphs; it may be useful to display each sentence as a separate paragraph.

Separate clauses, or the parts of long sentences, with ellipses (. . .) to give the newscaster an indication of where to pause or take a breath.

Avoid contractions, hard-to-pronounce words, abbreviations, or anything else that may trip the tongue.

Provide pronunciation help in parentheses immediately following any unfamiliar word or name: Tomas Arguea (toe-MAS ar-GWAY-ah). Note how the accented syllable is indicated.

Do not put names, figures, or other critical information in the opening phrase or sentence. The first sentence should "index" the story for the listener and catch attention by naming the general topic.

Wrong: Deputy Director of Finance Hiram Williams today submitted a $4.2 million budget to city council . . .

Right: It will cost less to run the city next year.
A budget of over four million dollars was . . . etc.

Make a Spokesperson Available

One of the things that may "sell" a release to radio is the availability of a spokesperson who is willing to be interviewed over the phone. At the bottom of the release or on an attached page, indicate if the person named in the release is "available for phone interview" and provide the telephone number. Make sure the spokesperson has been provided with a copy of the release and an outline of material that might be discussed in the interview. Typically, a reporter from the radio station will conduct the interview in just a few minutes, using the phone "beeper" system.

If your source is available for an appearance on a radio or television talk show or public-affairs program, attach a very brief note to the release summarizing the spokesperson's expertise and availability, and include your number so that you can arrange the appearance.

TIMING THE RELEASE

When an important event happens, or when something will be newsworthy for only a day, you might have to phone local editors and send a courier quickly to carry a "perishable" release to the media. Ordinarily, however, sufficient lead time must be allowed when submitting a news release, especially if it is accompanied by photographs. Only when you have alerted an editor or news director in advance are you likely to get a major news item in the paper or on the air with a lead time of less than a day.

That means anticipating an event with positive PR value. You must allow yourself ample time for preparing the release and processing photographs. Plan at least two or three days for mail delivery, unless the release is important enough to deliver by courier. Then allow two or three days for the media to process the material.

Using an "Embargo"

In order to have information in the hands of the media at the proper time, it may be necessary to divulge facts before your organization desires to have them distributed. The names of scholarship or contest winners, destined to be announced on a certain date, must be provided to the newspapers ahead of time if the long list of names, addresses, and hometowns is to be set in type. Drawings and charts depicting the plans for a new plant and its impact on the community must be in the hands of the newspaper's art department early in order to have suitable illustrations ready on the day when the expansion is announced to the public at a news conference.

In such situations, it is understood by the news organization that the preparer of the news release will "embargo" the item, meaning that a release date is put on the material, and the media are expected to hold the information until that time. The public relations department must be extremely sensitive to the requirements of all the media when using an embargo.

A reasonable embargo that most media would agree to observe would be the 6 A.M. release, which means that the item could appear in all morning papers and be included in the drive-time radio broadcasts. An embargo for almost any time of the day is acceptable when the press release is based on the text of a speech, as long as it is made clear that the release time coincides with the precise time when the speaker will be appearing before the audience. Similarly, a "September 15" embargo on the results of a research study is understandable when the release indicates that the findings will be presented at a conference on that date.

Unfortunately, some organizations arbitrarily assign release dates to items for no apparent reason. The media may ignore such an embargo or, more likely, simply toss the release in the wastebasket.

Hand Delivery May Be Necessary

Some releases call for extraordinary handling. When announcements of major personnel changes mean that some people will be big winners and others big losers within the organization, it is not unusual for the head of the public relations department personally to write and reproduce the press release, hold it for safekeeping, and hand deliver it to the media when word comes from the chief executive officer that the affected parties are being notified.

Similarly, in crisis situations, such as when a company has been charged by the government with wrongdoing, or when an accident destroys a facility and causes injuries, the rules change. The press shows up at the organization's doors, and the public relations chief must set up a press briefing and issue a statement. The underlying facts and the essence of the statement should be ready for distribution in the form of an on-site press release:

A spokesman for the Acme Rubber Products Company today denied charges that the firm had engaged in price-fixing. Public relations director Carl Baker called a press conference at the main plant on Fordam Road and distributed information showing that Acme has engaged in a vigorous competition for its approximately 25 percent share of the market in sports diving equipment.

We have focused mainly on the daily news media. Except for weekly trade publications, which function much like newspapers, most magazines have deadlines of two or three months, rather than days or weeks. Releases about new product lines or seasonal material must be prepared far in advance if they are to be of use to magazines.

SUBMITTING THE PRESS RELEASE

If your press release is aimed at all of the media in the area, you can find the addresses in standard directories, such as the *Editor and Publisher Yearbook* for newspapers and the *Broadcasting Yearbook* for radio and television stations. Address the release to "Editor" for the print media and "News Director" for broadcast media.

Because of the large volume of releases, however, it is useful to target the release more specifically when possible. On most daily newspapers, the managing editor oversees the daily operation of the newsroom, and the city editor is in charge of local coverage. It is worthwhile to check the yearbook for listings of specialized editors. If your news belongs on the business page, aim it at the business editor. Your item may get better play on the education page or from the women's editor. Familiarity with the paper is useful.

When to Be Selective

Ordinarily, it is of no particular help to contact the media personally if your release is a routine one that you are sending to dozens of outlets. However, if you are being selective

and sending the release to only a handful of media with a particular interest in the story, or if you have taken the time to prepare a special article or photo for each paper, it is useful to alert the editor by phone about the "exclusive" material. Over time, the editor will come to recognize and appreciate when you provide material that is different from what the general media are receiving.

Always analyze the benefits of selective mailings of releases. Features about people or programs in your organization can get major play if the editor senses exclusivity. On the other hand, routine announcements should be sent equally to all media in order to keep your organization's name in the minds of all publics and all editors. The PR director of a state-run summer arts facility, for example, sends the same release to every paper, but selects different shots and poses of the star celebrities for use in various competing media. That way, no afternoon daily editor jettisons the picture, and the release along with it, simply because the same shot appeared in the morning papers.

Note that the role of "art"—photographs, tables, graphs, or diagrams—in selling a news release cannot be underestimated. See Chapter 27 for information on how to prepare photographs and cutlines for submission along with the print release.

USING THE PR WIRE

Distribution of press releases involves maintaining an up-to-date mailing list, mimeographing, addressing and stuffing envelopes, and affixing postage stamps. As we noted above, the *Editor and Publisher Yearbook* and regional media directories are useful for finding addresses of weekly and daily newspapers, but names of department editors listed in such directories can get out of date quickly. And what if a release sent to a particular editor sits in the in-basket past the point of usefulness simply because the editor is on vacation? Yet another problem facing the PR department is the often undependable service of the increasingly expensive U. S. Postal Service.

For the PR department that regularly sends out news releases with ''time value,'' the answer may be to use the PR Newswire service or a regional service such as the Southeastern Press Relations Newswire, which serves twelve Southern states.

How the Service Works

For a fee, PR Newswire and the various regional PR wire services process your organization's news releases for electronic transmission to computer terminals and/or high-speed teleprinters at many of the leading news and business media. Your news can be transmitted to the PR Newswire by messenger, Telex, facsimile, or telephone dictation. It can be held for transmission at a specific time, or if it has instant news value, it will go out at once. The release can be distributed to all media or only specialized publications.

PR Newswire's special Investors Research Wire carries news about publicly owned corporations to banks, investment firms, and financial publications. The instant and simultaneous transmission of such news by electronic means helps to meet the requirements for ''timely disclosure'' discussed in Chapters 10 and 17.

The Information-Retrieval Link

News releases distributed through PR Newswire may also become part of a computer-stored data base used for information retrieval by researchers in PR, the news media, and specialized business and industrial publications. The NEXIS data base is a news-retrieval service that includes a backlog of information carried in the Washington *Post*, *Newsweek*, *Congressional Quarterly*, the Associated Press, PR Newswire, and many other services and publications.

Using the service, a researcher is able to scan not only news stories and fact sheets concerning an organization, but also the organization's own news releases and statements about its stock offering, new products, management decisions, or plans for expansion. The president of PR Newswire has pointed out a particularly attractive feature of NEXIS: storage of a press release in the news retrieval system is analogous to publication. In other words, even if no medium prints the story, it still is available to researchers.[4] Clearly, the computer age has provided new and expanded uses for the traditional PR news release.

THE LAST WORD

The last word in public relations should be ''thanks.''

If you send or phone a thank-you after the publication or broadcast of every little release, the editors probably will consider you a nuisance. However, when you feel genuine gratitude for a spread or program that really benefited your organization, a call or a note is a good way to reward the journalist. In fact, given the ethics of both PR and journalism, it's really the only way you have of providing an incentive to repeat the favor.

NOTES

1. See, for example, Chuck Honaker, ''News Releases Revisited,'' *Public Relations Journal* (April 1981):25–27; Chuck Honaker, ''Why Your News Releases Aren't Working,'' *Public Relations Journal* (March 1978):16–19; Ed Zotti, ''Journalists Gripe: Too Much, Too Little,'' *Advertising Age* (January 5, 1981):S6–S7; Gerald Powers, ''For Immediate Release: View From the Editor's Desk,'' *Public Relations Journal* (September 1971):18.
2. See James E. Grunig, ''Time Budgets, Level of Involvement and Use of the Mass Media,'' *Journalism Quarterly* 56 (1979):248–261.
3. A. E. Jeffcoat, ''A Touch of Amazement,'' *Public Relations Journal* (May 1981):34–36.

4. David Steinberg, letter to the editor, "Press Relations: a New Dimension," *Public Relations Journal* (July 1981):8.

ADDITIONAL READING

Douglas, George A., *Writing for Public Relations* (Columbus, Ohio: Charles E. Merrill, 1980).

Lendt, David L. (ed.). *The Publicity Process* (Ames, Iowa: Iowa State University Press, 2d ed., 1975).

Newsom, Doug, and Tom Siegfried, *Writing in Public Relations Practice* (Belmont, Calif.: Wadsworth, 1981).

Weiner, Richard, *Professional's Guide to Publicity* (New York: Richard Weiner, Inc., 1975),

21

CATERING TO THE PRESS

Jeff Greenfield, who covers politics and the media for CBS, suggested in one of his commentaries that the press must be treated as "a dangerous, but potentially valuable, animal. You must house it, feed it, pet it once in a while. You must never show it fear, or it will turn on you. You must gently, but firmly, guide it in the way you want it to go."[1]

Catering to the press—housing, feeding, and petting—is only an occasional task for most public relations departments. As a matter of course, both sides find it easier to depend on news releases for transmitting routine information. The press conference should be used when it is clear that giving the press an opportunity to question expert sources will result in more meaningful and effective news coverage. The press party, festive cousin to the news conference, is appropriate when an organization has genuine reason to mark some sort of milestone, such as an anniversary, or when the attendance of celebrities is a cause for excitement, as when astronauts pay a visit to a government contractor.

Some other examples:

The Bank of America, whose Broad Street offices are just around the corner from the New York Stock Exchange, regularly calls in the business press for briefings by company economists on topics ranging from interest rates to trends in banking methods. It's a low-key coffee-and-donuts affair, and the emphasis is on providing background information to the writers rather than providing a headline item.

American Express, which sponsors a weekly half-hour television program featuring NFL film highlights, invites sportswriters and other journalists to a cocktail party at a New York restaurant associated with the sports scene. A short reel of highlights from upcoming programs is previewed, and then the members of the press have an opportunity to talk individually or in groups with a dozen or so top-name players and coaches, the producers of the films, or perhaps even NFL commissioner Pete Rozelle. Press packets that include stills from the films and biographies of the narrators are distributed.

Dr. Albert Sabin, developer of the oral polio vaccine, is often a featured panelist at national medical conventions, and the press is interested in hearing his views on new developments in medicine. Sabin usually is eager to meet with the press, and he may forgo his lunch hour so that local newspapers and television stations can interview him in a press conference.[2]

There are many ways for a press event to turn into a disaster. The news value may be so weak that the reporters feel duped. The release announcing the news conference may contain all the information the press needs, so reporters don't show up, and the guest or interviewee is embarrassed. The guest or interviewee may not perform as expected, and the press wonders why it was summoned. The timing may be wrong, or a breaking news event may preempt the attention of the press. The broadcast press, with its lights and microphones, may sour the print press, resulting in negative publicity. All of these potential miscues should be weighed before making the decision to proceed with a press event.

MANAGEMENT CONSIDERATIONS

Generally, public relations managers can apply the same management considerations when they set up events to help the press develop its own stories about their organizations as they apply to their own press releases. There are just a few differences to remember.

Model of Public Relations

Although used in all four models of public relations, press conferences and similar events work especially well in the two-way symmetric model. That model emphasizes dialogue. Press events facilitate dialogue with the press because reporters can probe and question, and they can set the agenda for their own stories.

Be careful if you use press events for press agentry or two-way asymmetric purposes.

With those models, the public relations practitioner often tries to control the information going to reporters, which may alienate the press and result in adverse publicity.

The press event is a reasonable way to disseminate information in the public-information model. With that model, the reporters usually get less of a chance to set the agenda for discussion. More often, they can only ask questions to clarify statements made by organizational representatives.

Objectives

With press releases, your objectives are communication (placing a story on the media agenda) and retention of the message. With press events, you have little control over the retention objective because somebody else writes the story. Your objective, therefore, should be to get your organization's point of view on the media agenda. Anything else is out of your hands.

You can monitor the message retention variable, however, by checking the accuracy of media coverage of your organization that results from press events. Give additional information and clarification to reporters who do not accurately report your organization's position. But don't try to badger them into accepting your organization's position (the ''acceptance of cognition'' objective) or into evaluating that position favorably (the ''attitude'' objective).

Which Programs?

Press events cannot be used in quite so many programs as can press releases. They can be used, however, in general media relations, when the organization has news of consequence or wide interest to the public. In larger cities, community relations workers can hold press events. In smaller communities with fewer media, it is best to meet with individual reporters from those few media.

Press events can be held to announce policy positions in public affairs and government

The revitalization of downtown New Brunswick, N.J., is marked by a press event that may involve mere press agentry or two-way communication. The town's mayor and the sales director for the new Hyatt Regency hotel watch (right) as the building is "topped out" with a flag. The press is allowed to question the president of New Brunswick Tomorrow (standing, below), who also is an officer in the town's largest corporation. Reporters will also have an opportunity to question internationally famous architect I. M. Pei (seated at right) about his plans for land use. (Courtesy New Brunswick Tomorrow)

relations programs and to meet with media serving activist publics. They can be called to release financial information. Specialists in promotion frequently use press events to publicize new automobile lines, sports events, or fund-raising drives.

Communication Behavior of Publics

Press events can be used for media that serve both high- and low-involvement publics. Be careful not to mix the two at the same time, however. Detailed, technical information will be necessary for the trade press or media serving activist publics. Simplified information will be needed for general assignment reporters worked for the mass (low-involvement) media.

Cost in Time and Money

Press events cost more than press releases. You must rent a room, buy refreshments, and rent equipment. So be sure to budget for those items. And be sure the press event serves a legitimate purpose before spending the additional money.

Press events also require careful timing. Devices such as Gantt and PERT diagrams can be especially useful.

Evaluation

Evaluate a press event by determining whether it resulted in increased press coverage of your organization, and by the accuracy of that coverage. You can measure both effects by content-analyzing press clippings, as described in Chapter 11 on media relations. When possible, ask reporters for formal or informal reaction to your press event. Remember, though, that you have more control over getting reporters to your event and helping them to cover the story than over what they write. Evaluate your performance accordingly.

If you do have an event of interest and news value, you are ready to address several logistical considerations: whom to invite, how to issue the invitation, where to hold the event, what amenities to offer, and how to assure that the members of the press are able to gather and transmit the information with the greatest possible ease.

WHOM SHALL WE INVITE?

At first, it might seem easy. But deciding whom to invite to a press conference isn't automatic. If we send an invitation or release to the managing editor or the city editor, a general-assignment reporter might be sent to the event—that is, a less experienced writer who just happens to be available. It's far wiser to invite business editors if our story involves economics, political writers if we are involved in a legislative matter, the entertainment columnist if we are sponsoring a cultural event, or a member of the ''lifestyle'' staff if our organization is running a summer camp for underprivileged children.

Shall we invite bona fide reporters only, or a wider list of journalists? If the story has legitimate spot news interest, the presence of press hangers-on may interfere with reporters who must meet a deadline. On the other hand, if our news conference is intended to suggest a continuing story that deserves prolonged coverage, it may be wise to invite managing editors and editorial writers, who have the responsibility of planning long-range news policy.

Should print and broadcast press be invited to the same conference? If so, how can we assure that both are adequately served? Early morning and late afternoon are good times for the print press, but midday usually is better for television. Moreover, if television crews arrive in full force with their lights and microphones, the print press may be pushed to the side. The television reporters may want only a crisp, concise one-minute statement, preferably with visual interest, while the print reporters may prefer to probe for the in-depth stories they have the time and space to cover.

Grumman's public relations department makes sure that television and press photographers have something lively and colorful to shoot whenever the firm wins a major government contract or has other good news to announce. Here a "Spirit of '76" fife and drum corps and flag bearer lead the company's board of directors into a hangar where employees have rallied to celebrate their "independence" after Grumman fended off a hostile takeover attempt by another firm. (Courtesy Grumman Corporation)

One solution to the dilemma posed by the different needs of the various media may be to hold a split conference, with the television cameras invited for one segment, and the print people given exclusive access to another segment.[3]

Avoid Embarrassing Silences

A news conference may be jeopardized if no reporter is willing to ask the opening question, or if the press—through ignorance or laziness—fails to explore all of the available topics.[4] Some organizations routinely seat one or two members of their own public relations staff or the editor of the organization's magazine with the working press to raise additional questions at the appropriate time, and generally to "keep the ball rolling." Of course, such a maneuver must be handled in a way that is perceived as helpful by the news media, not as a heavy-handed job of "shilling." It probably is better to prepare your speaker to raise and answer his own questions if the press is remiss.

If your organization provides a spokesperson who is not adequately prepared, or who does not know how to handle questions from the press, the conference quickly falls apart. Until the Nuclear Regulatory Commission appointed a qualified "point man" to brief reporters covering the Three-Mile Island incident, the press complained of "conflicting and contradictory statements" about the nuclear emergency, and the result was confusing and incomplete news coverage.[5]

You must be prepared, too, for reporters who refuse to attend a press conference because, in the words of one journalism newswriting textbook, they "dislike working with precisely the same clay their competitors are using."[6] Some print reporters flatly refuse to raise questions while television cameras are running, saying, "Why should I let my questions get answered on TV before I can put them in print?"[7] If coverage by the reporters who complain is important to you, be pre-pared to make special arrangements so that they can interview your speaker or obtain the information in another manner.

HOW TO ISSUE THE INVITATION

An editor who is contacted the day before a press conference: "Look, all my reporters are busy . . . you've got to give me greater lead time if you want coverage."

An editor who is contacted well in advance: "Two weeks from now? You know we work on a day-to-day basis. Give me a call the day before . . ."

Thus, it is difficult to time an invitation. To that, add this dilemma: for every editor who insists on a written record, another runs his entire operation verbally over the phone. The only compromise seems to be sending out a press release (combined with an "invitation" and an RSVP postal card, if you wish) about ten days before the event. Then, plan to call the editor the day before to confirm whether or not a reporter will be sent. Some PR practitioners who feel that their personal persuasive abilities are their main strength may reverse the process, making the phone contact ten days ahead to alert the editor about the upcoming event, then timing the written reminder to arrive just a day or two ahead of the workshift in which the reporter will be assigned.

Dealing with Journalistic Ethics

When issuing invitations to a press party or social event, special consideration should be given to the ethics codes subscribed to by many newspapers, such as the Associated Press Managing Editors code. An important clause of the Code of Ethics of the Society of Professional Journalists, Sigma Delta Chi, states: "Nothing of value shall be accepted."[8] This is generally interpreted to mean gifts having intrinsic value (but excluding premiums or mementos such as imprinted ball-point pens).

Most journalists feel that attendance at a social function where an ordinary hotel-style dinner, preceded by a cocktail hour, is served will not compromise their integrity. However, it is increasingly common for larger papers to require that the charge levied on paying guests be applicable to journalists, with the paper picking up the tab. It is wise for the public relations practitioner to be sensitive to this trend, even though it may mean that some journalists are paying and others are availing themselves of a free meal.

Ethical considerations also dictate that an invitation not be sent to the private home of the journalist, thereby confusing the issue of whether the reporter is being invited in a professional or a private capacity. Similarly, the invitation of the spouse to attend may raise ethical questions, unless the nature of the event—such as a dinner-dance—clearly dictates that attendance by couples is the norm.

WHERE TO HOLD THE EVENT

If your organization has a large boardroom, auditorium, or general-purpose facility that is equipped with a public-address system and is available to you for at least half a day, you may be able to hold a press conference in your own facility—provided, that is, that you are located within a short drive of the media, and you have adequate parking available.

Aside from the convenience of using your own facilities, there may be another valid reason for bringing the press to your site. If the point of the event is to show off a new plant or piece of equipment, then some inconvenience on the part of the press may be warranted. You may even arrange for the press to congregate at a convenient central location to be bused to the site of your event, but that presupposes an attraction of genuine interest or novelty.

Not surprisingly, hotels, motels, and restaurants frequently are used for press conferences, simply because they are centrally located, offer a full range of catering services, and can provide basic amplification and audiovisual equipment. (How many times does the first item in the evening television news consist of a speaker behind a lectern bearing the name of a well-known hotel!)

Check the Facilities

Representatives of the PR department should make at least one on-site inspection, accompanied by a sales representative of the facility, to check for items such as:

Adequate electrical outlets for audiovisual equipment.

Sufficient water pitchers and drinking glasses.

Ashtrays, and provisions for a nonsmoking section.

Phone booths outside the room. (If none or too few are available, you can arrange with the phone company to bring in a temporary portable unit.)

Comfortable seating and, if appropriate, tables for writing or for displaying handouts and brochures.

One sure way to ruin the effect is to rent half of a partitioned room, only to find out that a hog-calling contest or a demonstration of stereo speakers has been scheduled for the space on the other side of the flimsy partition. Rent the entire room. You'll not only assure peace and quiet for your meeting, you can arrange to open or shut partitions as necessary to make your meeting appear well attended but comfortably uncrowded.

And finally, if you determine on your scouting trip that the layout of the conference area is confusing, have your art department prepare plenty of signs pointing the way to the proper outside entrance, the conference room, the phones, and, of course, the restrooms. Keeping reporters from getting irritated over logistics is part of what Greenfield means by "petting" the press.

WHAT AMENITIES TO OFFER

We already have noted that offering gifts or lavish entertainment to journalists may constitute a breach of journalistic as well as PR ethics. However, it is never inappropriate to provide coffee and soft drinks, along with donuts and cookies, in recognition of the fact that those attending a press conference may have hurried from another assignment without time to stop for refreshments.

Similarly, most news reporters carry their own paper and pencils, but it is useful to have a supply on hand at a press table for the benefit of those who have exhausted or misplaced their supplies.

Anticipate the special needs of journalists. Radio people often wish to record a speech or presentation, and even print journalists use portable tape recorders as a backup note-taking device. Prevent the scramble that occurs when they all try to place microphones around the lectern. Avoid discomfort to your speaker, and leave the view uncluttered for photographers, by arranging to have a single microphone leading not only to the public address system, but also to a box below the platform or on a table to one side where each journalist can "jack in" to the sound source. That way, those who need to pop up and flip cassettes every thirty minutes won't distract the speaker or destroy the decorum.

Offer Helpful Handouts

The issue of how much printed material to provide, and where and when to distribute it, is always a complex one. If you pass out transcripts of the presentation and plenty of background data, the press will be pleased—but they may also disrupt the proceedings with their paper-shuffling, or, worse, they may determine that they can get a story from the handouts and decide to leave early. On the other hand, they may be irked when they realize they have taken copious notes throughout the presentation, only to be presented with a transcript immediately afterward. The answer may be a combination of techniques: a one-page outline of material to be covered (placed on every chair), a selection of fact sheets (placed on the press table), and a text of the main speaker's prepared statement (passed out at the door as reporters leave).

In addition to smoothing the way for reporters, you must keep your own selfish interests in mind: Did everyone attend, and did they get all of the information? By stationing a member of the PR staff at the door with a checklist of invitees and an envelope of prepared material, it should be possible to keep track of which media received the material. An important part of the press conference plan should be to assure that, as soon as possible, all printed materials get in the hands of invited reporters who did not attend—by courier delivery, if necessary.

PROVIDING A PRESS ROOM

We would be remiss if we failed to mention that something called the "hospitality room" frequently is set up in a suite adjacent to the area where the press is covering a conference, convention, or the proceedings of an organization. Typically such a room is well stocked with ice and a variety of beverages. It is "the American way of doing business," and the custom wouldn't be continued if all parties didn't find it advantageous. Reporters enjoy talking informally with sources and other journalists in such an atmosphere. The result frequently is a frankness that can't be found on a convention floor or in the formal atmosphere of a press conference. From the PR practitioner's point of view, the value of the social situation cannot be discounted, but it is generally useful to follow up any discussions in the hospitality room with a more businesslike contact.

Whenever journalists are required to spend a prolonged period far from home base, they need the services of a temporary press facility—the working press room. Of course, at large political conventions the major media set up their own operations, with direct electronic links to home base. But for other events—including trade shows or expositions, professional or union conventions, and natural disasters or calamities such as Mount St. Helens and Three-Mile Island—the press expects the sponsor of the event, or the organization most closely involved with it, to set up a press room . . . sometimes on the spur of the moment.

Organizations such as the military, public utilities, and large corporations that routinely hold events far afield find it advantageous to equip a trailer or bus with phones, typewriters, water cooler, and perhaps even bunks for quick naps. Typically, though, space is rented from a hotel. Or arrangements may be made to use a public facility in order to set up a temporary news operation with links to the wire services and major media.

PR Staff Relations with the Press

Occasionally, the room where convention materials are mimeographed for distribution to delegates must double as the press room. That gives reporters the advantage of getting information as it rolls off the machines—though this may not serve the interests of the public relations department. In addition, the working habits of the organization's public-information staff and the working press may not coincide. So, it is best to have a separate room for each function. As we have already noted, television and print press have different needs, so it also is advantageous to set up a room separate from the print people where TV crews can store their equipment and hold electronic interviews.

It is a good idea to designate one or more members of the PR staff to be available in the press room regularly—holding briefings, providing background information, or simply hearing the suggestions and complaints of the reporters concerning services they need.

It is extremely important that knowledgeable members of the PR staff be assigned press-room duty, not just go-fers and clerks. Having good-quality information available to the press is important, and the staff also must have the authority to cut red tape and expedite access of the press to important sources.[9]

As far as equipment is concerned, even a minimal press room should be equipped with typewriters, telephones, typing paper, pencils, storage space, a dictionary, press kits, publicity photos, drinking water, and—if the budget permits—envelopes, stamps, and simple refreshments.[10]

FOLLOW-UP IS IMPORTANT

Carefully keep track of those who attend every event or press conference. Good records help you decide whom to invite to your next briefing, press conference, or special occasion.

Be sure that each person who attends one of your organization's events has been greeted properly by a member of the organization, and either introduced to a sufficient number of other guests or provided with an identification badge. Similarly, assure that someone is at the door to offer a farewell to each guest and to determine if transportation has been arranged.

For the PR department, the event does not end as the press departs. Whether it was a simple news conference or a one-hundredth-anniversary ball, the next morning the staff should conduct a full review of the event's success or problems. A checklist with the names of every member of the press should be maintained to note who attended, who did not, and what reasons were given. Follow-up mailings should be ready to go within days, along with additional fact sheets in the case of a developing news story, and perhaps souvenir photographs in the case of a gala reception.

And finally, the media must be monitored to find out whether the event generated news coverage (and thus is worth repeating in the future).

NOTES

1. Jeff Greenfield, ''A Charm Book for Candidates,'' *Columbia Journalism Review* (July/August 1980):34–37.
2. John L. Normoyle, ''Split Media Press Conferences,'' *Public Relations Journal* (May 1979): 14–15.
3. Normoyle; see also Gary B. Bassford, ''The Tube vs. the Pencil Press,'' *Public Relations Journal* (May 1979):16–22.
4. Lou Cannon, ''Nessen's Briefings: Missing Questions (and Answers),'' *Columbia Journalism Review* (May/June 1975):12–16.
5. Peter M. Sandman and Mary Paden, ''At Three Mile Island,'' *Columbia Journalism Review* (July/August 1979):43–58.
6. Mitchell V. Charnley and Blair Charnley, *Reporting*, 5th ed. (New York: Holt, Rinehart and Winston, 1979), p. 281.
7. Charnley, p. 222.
8. Adopted by the national convention of SPJ-SDX, Nov. 16, 1973. See also Todd Hunt, ''A Study of Ethics Codes in New Jersey Daily Newspapers,'' Institute of Communication Studies monograph, Rutgers University (1977).
9. R. Stanwood Weeks, ''Setting up the News Room,'' *Public Relations Journal* (December l969):18.
10. Weeks.

22

USING RADIO

Radio is another person talking to you. Radio is local. And the cost of radio is comparatively inexpensive per message, which permits an organization to repeat something until it sinks in.

Radio, in other words, is a very important medium for the public relations practitioner to consider.

Let's begin our discussion of the way radio fits into the public relations campaign by analyzing the formats it offers, from paid advertisements to public-service spots.

RADIO INFORMATION FORMATS

Paid Advertisements

If you want to dictate the precise content, time, and date of your message, you'll have to pay for advertising space. The size of your budget will determine what kinds of paid spots you can afford. It costs more to buy drive-time spots, when millions of commuters are listening to the radio, than it does to buy late-night time, when insomniacs are the main audience. It costs more to position your spots before the local news broadcast each evening than it does to buy a package deal for thirty or forty repetitions of the same spot when the radio station selects the positions—perhaps guaranteeing that a certain percentage of them will fall in prime time.

Although there are many attractive and useful ways to gain access to radio, the paid announcement is effective enough to be used by such diverse organizations as Planned Parenthood, Inc., the National Milk Council, the International Ladies Garment Workers Union, and the U. S. Postal Service.

Perhaps radio's greatest attribute is its utility in sudden or emergency situations, when it is necessary to get a quickly prepared message to the general public or specialized publics on short notice. When the air traffic controllers' union went on strike early in 1981, seriously disrupting air service across the nation, the airlines quickly bought time to broadcast simple spots in which a calm and authoritative announcer explained which flights would be operating normally, which service would be curtailed, and what telephone numbers area residents should call for various types of information—one number for flight crews, another for ground personnel, another for passengers with flights scheduled on that particular day, and still another number for general information.

Public-Service Announcements

In order to get their broadcast licenses renewed, commercial stations must demonstrate that they have provided the public service of distributing useful information to the community from government agencies, charities, and community betterment groups. When the information is carried in the form of a free advertisement, it is known as a public-service announcement, or PSA.

Often the PSA is as slickly and as expensively produced as any paid advertisement and arrives through the mail from national organizations such as those organized to raise research funds to combat diseases or social problems. Other PSAs may come to the station in the form of scripts. Or a spokesperson from the organization may come to the studio and record the spot. Stations also take information from news releases or letters and rewrite it into radio format for reading by the station announcer.

Usually only nonprofit groups may expect to get PSAs on the air, although consumer information offered by power companies and professional associations is included in this category. Not surprisingly, the organization that submits a PSA in any form should expect to hear it aired mainly in time periods when paid advertising cannot be sold—which is to say, when only some segments of the radio audience are listening.

Usually, more than one version of a PSA is submitted to the station, both to provide variety for the listeners and to give the station flexibility in scheduling spots.

Community Bulletin Board

Many stations offer a variation on the PSA, variously called "Community Bulletin Board," "Around the Town," or "In (our town) Today." For decades, citizens of the Minneapolis-St. Paul area have tuned to CBS affiliate WCCO around 9 A.M. every morning to hear a cheery woman read a listing of fund-raising events, free senior citizen attractions, health clinics, the Bloodmobile schedule, and educational or cultural goings-on. Most stations limit the bulletin board to nonprofit organizations or to nonprofit events sponsored by businesses.

In the largest markets, bulletin board announcements usually are limited to county-wide events, and are sprinkled at random throughout the day's programming rather than being assigned a specific time slot. In any case, it is easy for a public relations department to get an item read in the bulletin board format because a simple letter to the station manager will do. It may even be possible to telephone the item in to the promotion manager or to the news desk of the station.

Local News Broadcasts

We saw in the preceding chapters that the press release, especially when it is geared to radio's special needs, can gain you air time when you have a legitimate news story. The staged event is another way to create free news coverage, when the publicity/press agent model is appropriate. On a slow news day, it is not unusual for a midday radio broadcast to devote two or three minutes to a live report from the intersection of Main and Broadway, where a man dressed as a chicken is climbing a light pole. When the ensuing interview reveals that the stunt is promoting "Eat More Chicken Week," everybody has a good chuckle, and the press agent for the poultry association chalks up a success.

Talk Shows

Radio must fill endless hours with sound, and one of the cheapest sources of programming is the listener call-in show. The format varies widely. Sometimes, the host announces one or more topics for the day; other times, it's "open mike." Typically, the participants call in, are placed briefly on hold, then go on the air with a seven-second tape delay, which permits the station to cut off profanity or slander.

Some of the callers are articulate and informed, some are rabid advocates of extreme positions, and others are merely blabbermouths. The longevity of the format attests to the fact that the mix usually is interesting, if only as a barometer as to what the "common person" is thinking and saying. (Research shows that some listeners/callers are strongly motivated by a desire to motivate others to action,[1] while others apparently tune in purely out of loneliness.[2])

The programs can serve a public relations function. Thus, many organizations assign at least one well-informed member to monitor each broadcast. That way, if the conversation turns to gun control, birth control, self control, or whatever falls within the purview of the organization, an opportunity is provided to offer the group's standard line: "This is Elissa Dandridge from the Lee County Adoption Service . . . I'd just like to reply to the woman who called earlier to say that she had heard there is a two-year wait for adoption. Fortunately, that isn't the case if the party is willing to consider adopting a minority child or a child with a minor birth defect. Anyone who is interested should call this number for information about adoption . . ."

Some radio talk shows use guest panelists to begin the discussion and act as respondents to the callers. Government and social agencies can take the opportunity to get their views across by providing panelists. When topics are announced in advance, it may also be useful to assign members of your organization to join the ranks of the callers.

Public-Affairs Programming

As another way of fulfilling the FCC's public-service requirements, most stations air two or three programs a week in which a member of the news staff or station management interviews a newsmaker, a representative of government, a spokesman for a community group, or a public relations person from industry. A call or letter to the station manager proposing a program or a segment on a weekly show usually will get a reply. Most of the programs are aired late in the evening or early Sunday morning, but the radio audience is large enough even at those times to deliver thousands of listeners.

Deejay Chatter

Disk jockeys love to "chat" with their listeners while changing records. Most of them command loyal followings. Deejays need new material all of the time and often seize upon an unusual tidbit of information. If you have something intriguing, just phone or drop a short letter.

"Equal-Time" Reply

The FCC's Fairness Doctrine requires broadcast stations to offer the right of reply to anyone who has been criticized on the air. Under the personal-attack provision, the station must notify the person or persons of their right of reply and furnish them with a copy of the original script.

Many stations voluntarily broaden the concept to permit "responsible groups or persons representing differing viewpoints" to reply to any opinions put forth by the management in the form of an editorial. The "editorial reply" segment usually is broadcast in the same general time slot and in the same format as the original broadcast, and the station provides its engineer and a director to assist whoever wishes to reply.

Other stations, acknowledging that there

may be many opinions differing with the one broadcast by management, prefer to read listeners' letters, or to splice together excerpts from telephone calls from citizens who have voiced their viewpoints. Whatever the system, organizations with political, social, or public-affairs positions should monitor local stations and be ready to make use of the access.

Specialized Opportunities

Radio stations often use programs prepared by others as public information. Universities, for example, call on professors and agricultural-extension agents to discuss topics in which they have expertise. The taped programs, a staple of weekend mornings on many stations, enhance the reputation of the educational institution. Trade and professional organizations provide public-affairs programs about careers, and businesses provide consumer information. Just as large corporations underwrite cultural programming for public television, they also provide the funding for public radio, in return for a credit at the beginning and the end of the program.

MANAGEMENT CONSIDERATIONS

There are four factors to keep in mind when you are deciding whether or not to use radio to communicate a public relations message:

> Radio offers many formats, making it a flexible medium.
> Radio is primarily a local medium.
> Radio has specialized stations with specialized audiences.
> Nearly all publics use radio.

Let's see how these generalizations translate into specific management considerations.

Model of Public Relations

There is a radio format to fit each of our four models of public relations.

Paid advertisements, deejay chatter, talk shows, and some public-service and community-bulletin-board announcements provide the press agent/publicist with a means to announce an event or service or to publicize an organization.

Public-information specialists use local news broadcasts, PSAs, public-affairs programs, and the specialized opportunities we discussed previously to inform their publics.

Two-way asymmetric practitioners frequently purchase paid announcements to promote their view. Many also can use PSAs—especially when they want to promote a socially desirable cause, such as a campaign against smoking, drugs, or heart disease. They also can get their advocate on a talk show or a public-service broadcast.

Two-way symmetric practitioners can use all of the radio formats to communicate the organization's message. But they should find talk shows and other kinds of dialogue to be especially useful. Members of management who appear on a talk show or call-in show with members of active publics can learn from those public representatives, and they can try out new ideas. Publics listening in can hear the management representatives discuss issues, present their arguments, then negotiate and compromise with public representatives. Radio, in other words, allows members of publics to listen in on symmetric dialogues. Remember, though, to advise your management representatives to bargain and negotiate on the air, not to try to bulldoze the other side into submission.

Objectives

Generally, you would choose the same kind of objective for radio that you would for print media. You want your organization on the agenda of radio, so that people can hear your message.

You also want them to retain your message. Thus, the hour at which a station airs your message makes a great difference. A half-hour talk show at 5:30 A.M. on Sunday doesn't reach anyone except parents with babies who wake up early or those rising for early religious services. But if you want to communicate with professionals, try to get on the air during drive time. To reach housewives, try for the daytime hours. Teenagers? You can reach them after school on pop and rock stations.

You can't control air time for most of the radio formats we've discussed, but often you can predict it. If you don't think it's likely your target public will hear—and retain—your message when it's most likely to be aired, then choose another medium.

Paid advertisements allow you to try to change some aspects of people's attitudes and behavior. Remember, though, how difficult those effects are to attain. Strive for communication, retention, and understanding of your advertisement. The announcements that achieve those objectives usually are the most persuasive.

Which Programs?

Radio can be used to reach the publics targeted by all of the programs discussed in Part III. It is most effective, however, for public relations programs aimed at local publics.

Radio has obvious strengths for community relations. It also can be used for local promotion and fund raising. If you employ enough people, stations will air announcements aimed at employees. And you can place financial news on business programs.

Nearly everyone listens to radio, but most members of high-involvement publics listen to selected stations at specific times. Plan carefully, and you can communicate about specific organizational concerns with aware and active publics.

Cost in Time and Money

Radio is inexpensive if you send a press release to a station or get your representative on a talk show, public-affairs program, or equal-time reply. But even if these formats don't cost much, they may take considerable time to arrange.

Radio will be more costly than print if you produce a public-service announcement or paid advertisement. You'll have to hire talent, buy music rights, produce and distribute audio tapes, and buy time on stations. Audio formats also require planning and coordinating with a Gantt chart or network diagram.

Evaluation

To evaluate the effect of a radio message as to the communication and retention objectives, you'll want to know if a station used your material, if anyone listened, and if listeners remember your message.

Because of the ephemeral nature of the radio broadcast, it is difficult to maintain a record of what was put on the air and how listeners reacted. There are no clippings to file, no mailed-in coupons to measure response. In major markets, you may be able to subscribe to a service that monitors broadcasts and maintains "air check" logs verifying which items were used at what times.

If you call a station within a day or two of an airing, the promotion director should be able to locate the script and make a copy for your records. Of course, if you have cultivated a contact at the station, that person can make sure you receive pertinent transcripts immediately after the airing. With PSAs, it is customary for the station to send the submitting organization a confirmation in the form of a bill marked "Paid"—to document for the FCC that advertising time has been donated by the station.

In order to ascertain whether anyone heard your message, you might include in your radio spots an address or phone number that is different from the one you use in your print releases. Another device is to include a key phrase in the radio message, again, one that is different from your print messages.

This will indicate whether an audience member who subsequently communicates with you has heard your radio version.

Of course, listeners may have retained your message even if they don't communicate with you right away. For some radio formats, you may want listeners to accept the message, form or change an attitude, or behave in a certain way. A phone survey following the broadcast can help you to determine whether your message had the desired impact.

PREPARING THE RADIO SPOT

Journalists and copywriters who are practiced at writing for the eye eventually must learn that writing for the ear is something quite different. Rarely is a message that appeared in print directly translatable to the audio media. Because time is money, audio messages must be more economical. And they must be written in a more conversational style rather than following the more formal structure required by print. Note in Exhibit 22–1, for example, that Long Island Lighting Company Chairman Charles Pierce refers to himself as "Charlie."

At its simplest, the radio spot consists merely of an announcer speaking:

> ANNCR: Today the Red Cross Bloodmobile will visit the Ford Motor Company plant in Edison. Employees and family members will find it in the south parking lot from 8 A.M. until 2:30 in the afternoon. If you have Type O blood, your donation is especially urgent. Help alleviate the critical shortage in our Tri-County area. Donate today!

Every radio station is prepared to have an announcer read any material that is accepted for airing. Many stations also are willing to help advertisers, and perhaps even nonprofit organizations, to add other elements to improve a spot, including voices of actors or "real people" previously taped or recorded in the studio. Most stations have a library of sound effects for which they have been granted radio rights, having paid for them at the time of original purchase. If a script calls for a "lead-in-and-fade-under" of quiet pastoral music or an uptempo "city beat," the engineer can find it quickly in the library of standard music.

These basic elements are readily available for the simple PSA or commercial spot that does not require elaborate sound mixing or split-second timing. But don't expect your local station to help you produce slick spots like those featuring the snappy dialogue of Jerry Stiller and Anne Meara, or Dick (Orkin) and Bert (Berdis). Those award-winning spots are created in special studios with a director and a battery of engineers, and then distributed in recorded form to individual stations.

Getting It Timed Right

Once the basic sound elements have been selected, the critical limiting factor is time. Whereas the print writer may be able to use 900 words to get across the message, and the advertising copywriter may be able to "fudge" a bit through the manipulation of type size, the radio writer must live with formats as short as thirty seconds (a typical time for PSAs) that cannot be stretched to forty or fifty seconds.

Sixty seconds of copy, read at moderate speed, is about 140 words. Some writers find that fifteen typed lines of seventy characters come out to just a minute of air time. But short, rapid-fire phrases may shrink the reading time, and polysyllabic mouthfuls may slow the announcer down. Thus, the only dependable system is to ask one or two other people to read the script aloud. Be prepared to pare out or add several words or phrases after trial readings and rehearsal in the studio.

The time limitations mean that often an entire idea must be expressed in a single ad-

EXHIBIT 22-1

```
ACCOUNT:.                                    TITLE: " OPENING SCRIPT"    P. 1

Identification #:  1                         Length: 90
RADIO

CHARLES PIERCE:

THIS IS CHARLIE PIERCE, CHAIRMAN OF THE LONG ISLAND LIGHTING COMPANY.

THIS IS THE FIRST IN A SERIES OF PROGRAMS LILCO IS SPONSORING.

THE REASON FOR DOING SO IS SIMPLE.

THERE ARE A LOT OF TOUGH ISSUES FACING LILCO AND THE PEOPLE OF LONG ISLAND.

AND WE BELIEVE WE SHOULD FACE THEM TOGETHER.

BECAUSE THE DECISIONS WE FACE AFFECT EACH AND EVERY ONE OF YOU.

AND THEY AFFECT LILCO TOO, BECAUSE WE'RE ALSO A PART OF THE LONG ISLAND

COMMUNITY.

I'M NOT JUST TALKING ABOUT YOUR UTILITY BILL, ALTHOUGH THAT'S ONE OF THE

ISSUES WE'LL BE DISCUSSING ON THESE PROGRAMS.

THERE ARE OTHER KEY AREAS: THE ENVIRONMENT, THE LOCAL AND NATIONAL ECONOMY

FUTURE INVESTMENT, NUCLEAR ENERGY, CONVERSION FROM OIL TO COAL, AND

UTILITY MANAGEMENT.

I ALSO WANT TO USE THESE PROGRAMS TO REVIEW PAST POLICIES, ANNOUNCE NEW

PROGRAMS, AND GENERALLY KEEP YOU INFORMED WITH NEWS ANNOUNCEMENTS.

YOU MAY NOT AGREE WITH EVERYTHING WE HAVE TO SAY.  OR EVERYTHING WE HAVE

TO DO.  BUT I WILL GIVE YOU THE FACTS.

WE'LL TALK ABOUT THINGS WE'VE DONE IN THE PAST AND WHAT WE'LL DO IN THE

FUTURE.  AND WE'll EVEN TALK ABOUT SOME MISTAKES WE'VE MADE.

I ALSO INTEND TO INVITE PEOPLE WITH OPPOSING POINTS OF VIEW TO SPEAK ON

THIS PROGRAM,AND I MAY NOT AGREE WITH WHAT THEY SAY.

BUT THERE'S A TREMENDOUS NEED TO DISCUSS OUR PROBLEMS OPENLY AND IN

PUBLIC, AND WE DON'T THINK OUR CUSTOMERS SHOULD HAVE TO PAY FOR IT.

THAT'S WHY THESE PROGRAMS WILL BE PAID FOR BY OUR SHARE HOLDERS

THANK YOU FOR LISTENING.

THIS IS CHARLIE PIERCE FOR LILCO.

(:84)
```

In 1981, Lilco, the Long Island Lighting Company, began airing a series of ninety-second to two-minute radio spots featuring ''straight-talk'' messages read by Chairman and Chief Executive Officer Charles R. Pierce—''Charlie Pierce'' as he identifies himself in each spot. The ''continuing program'' has placed heavy emphasis on tough issues facing the utility industry, including nuclear power, coal conversion, and rate increase requests. As indicated by this initial script from the successful series, the company's critics have also been provided free air time by Lilco. (Courtesy Long Island Lighting Company) jective. You might like to explain the reason for the blood shortage mentioned in the spot above, but you have to hope that the adjective "critical" will impress the listeners enough to make them believe the appeal without hearing the specific reason.

It also may mean resorting to stereotypes: a few bars of campfire music, hand-clapping, and the line "Welcome to Camp Wanatsha" may have to set the scene in the listener's mind for a YMCA spot. A picture can be telegraphed to the listener by having the announcer or the first speaker in a dialogue spot use descriptive words:

> "You there in the jogging suit . . . have you outgrown your need for milk?"
> "(Puff-puff) . . . No!"

Variation of the Spot

Usually, different versions of the radio spot are written to fit the various standard time slots, from sixty seconds down to ten seconds. In the case of the paid announcement, cost savings can be realized by introducing the campaign with full sixty-second spots, and then achieving the desired repetition using thirty- or twenty-second spots that contain all of the main elements but that have been condensed.

When a nonprofit organization prepares PSAs, it is a good idea to offer ten-, twenty-, thirty-, and sixty-second versions so a station can choose the versions that best fit its format. Here, for example, are different versions of the same PSA written for the George Street Playhouse, a regional nonprofit professional theater:

ANNCR: The spotlight is on the George Street Playhouse. Make sure you get the best seat in the house. Subscribe now. Call 246-7717. (10 sec)

ANNCR: The spotlight is on the George Street Playhouse. You'll see *Tobacco Road, Jacques Brel, Private Lives,*

Shakespeare, and two great new American plays. Subscribers have the best seats in the house. To reserve your season tickets, call 246-7717 now. (20 sec)

ANNCR: The spotlight is on the George Street Playhouse. The season begins in September with *Tobacco Road.* You'll thrill to the delightful musical *Jacques Brel.* Rounding out the season are Noel Coward's wonderful and witty *Private Lives,* William Shakespeare's moving *Henry the Fourth,* plus two great new American plays. Our subscribers enjoy the best seats in the house. Reserve your season tickets now. Don't wait. Call 246-7717. (30 sec)

Notice that the extra time is not used to make quantum jumps in the amount of information, but rather to flesh out the basic ideas of the shorter spots by offering more adjectives, filling in a few particulars, and engaging in greater familiarity with the listener.

SUBMITTING THE MATERIAL

Time constraints dictate that most radio stations must be selective about which PSAs they use. The main reasons for rejecting a PSA are:

> The material is too dry or dull.
>
> The spot lacks a local angle.
>
> The tone of the spot does not "blend" with the station's format.
>
> The tapes submitted are not up to the standards of technical quality required by the station.[3]

Material that is to be submitted to radio stations in tape form should be produced with studio-quality equipment on clean, quarter-inch magnetic recording tape. If only one copy is needed, cut the tape from the master recording reel and rewind it on a small plastic reel. If the station plans to make repeated use of the spot, they will transfer it to a plastic cartridge, or "cart," so that it can be played automatically merely by punching a button.

If duplicates are needed, take the master tape to a studio equipped with a multiple duplicator. The high-speed machinery simultaneously makes as many as half a dozen copies, which can then be rewound on individual reels or carts. PSAs distributed in large quantities for frequent use should be packaged in carts to increase the chances that a station manager will okay the spot because it is conveniently ready to go.

If you are submitting a PSA or other taped information for radio use, and if you have no familiarity with station management, the material may be directed to the general manager, which is the equivalent of sending it to the editor of a newspaper. If it is newsworthy, it will be routed to the news director. If it fits better in another format, it will be routed to the program director.

The organization that plans to make frequent use of radio should endeavor to cultivate a contact in both the news and programming departments in order to be able to deliver material to someone who is directly concerned. Make sure that the name, address, and phone number of someone in your organization who can answer questions or provide additional information is included at the top of the covering letter, on the script, and on the tape reel itself—you never know which they'll have in hand at the moment they decide to call you. Anyone who is unsure of how to submit material, or to whom, usually will be granted a short interview and orientation merely by coming to the reception desk of the station. Because of the FCC requirements, radio stations tend to be more responsive to callers than are newspapers.

RADIO FONE-FEED

When a public relations department begins to notice that it is dealing with radio stations on almost a daily basis—providing quotes from spokespersons within the organization on such topics as the economy, energy, safety, or research—perhaps it is time to institute an "audio feed" system. Then radio stations can call a special number to tape one or two minutes of material recorded for continuous automatic sending. In effect, the radio station's tape recorder listens to and copies the PR department's tape recorder. The advantage to the station is that it receives "live interview" material with only a few minutes of effort and no special arrangements.

Obviously, the feed is not worthwhile for many organizations, but it works well for, say, a sports team that is telephoned daily by dozens of broadcast media people for a word or two from the coaches on the upcoming game. A major university that issues print press releases at the rate of four or five a day finds it natural to offer a supporting audio feed to the many radio stations in the state or region.

Perhaps the most vigorous users of Fone-Feed services are the departments of the federal government. Nearly every agency in Washington has a well-publicized number that reporters can call for transmission of program material. In fact, the practice is so widespread that the Washington *Post* has listed some of the numbers in mockingly humorous stories about the varied materials available at the broadcaster's fingertips.

To be successful, the feed system must be promoted vigorously when it is initiated. Essentially that is done by making personal phone calls to the news directors of all area radio stations, explaining to them how the system works, and then playing sample tapes to them over the phone. A follow-up letter is sent to the station, and along with it a reminder card (or self-stick adhesive label) to be placed next to the news desk phone, listing the special number.

Preparing the Tape Loop

The sender must be prepared to provide one or two short items each day. Usually, these are feature items, but if a spot news story breaks, the feed may be used to provide a statement to the press from the president, the manager, or whichever official is in a position to speak for the organization.

The message is put on a loop of audio tape in playback equipment that is attached to the phone in such a way that it is activated by an incoming call. It automatically rewinds when the connection is terminated. The message consists of two parts, an introduction, and the voice "actuality." Note that the following script is written in the all-capital-letters format favored by radio news personnel.

THIS IS ROBERT ROBBINS, SPORTS INFORMATION DIRECTOR FOR STATE UNIVERSITY. THANK YOU FOR CALLING STATE U FONE-FEED. TODAY WE HAVE A 40-SECOND STATEMENT FROM FOOTBALL COACH ALEXANDER ANDERSON ON HIS CHOICE OF STARTING QUARTERBACK FOR SATURDAY'S GAME WITH CENTRAL TECH, AND A 50-SECOND STATEMENT FROM UNIVERSITY PRESIDENT HOWARD H. HOXIE SPEAKING IN SUPPORT OF THE BOND AMENDMENT TO BUILD A NEW FIELDHOUSE. IF YOU DESIRE FURTHER INFORMATION, PLEASE CALL ME AT 999-9999. THE FONE-FEED WILL COMMENCE AT THE SOUND OF THE TONE.

(Five-second pause, followed by a "beep.")

WE . . . UH . . . WE'VE DECIDED TO GO WITH LANCE LARSON FOR THE TECH GAME BECAUSE THEY HAVE SHOWN A STRONG DEFENSE AGAINST THE RUNNING ATTACK, BUT WE THINK THEY'RE VULNERABLE TO THE PASS, AND LANCE IS OUR . . . (etc.)

An organization that regularly puts out feature print releases may find that the feed system will help place more of those stories on radio. If the tape recorder carries voice actualities to "illustrate" a print release, radio stations should be alerted by a special box at the top of the release:

> RADIO NEWS DIRECTORS, CALL FONE-FEED AT 999-9999 FOR SPOKEN VERSION OF MAJOR QUOTES IN STORY BELOW.

To make an audio-feed system work, the public-information department must make careful advance plans, and one member of the staff must be designated to prepare the tapes and maintain the equipment. Some organizations find that it is not feasible to offer the daily feed year-round, but it is a useful adjunct at specific times, such as a convention, a state tournament, or another annual event where the media demand extra servicing. In New Jersey, the governor's communication office provides audio feed on the two days each week when the state legislature meets and, toward the end of the session, on days when the governor is scheduled to sign major bills.

NOTES

1. John Crittenden, "Democratic Functions of the Open Mike Forum," *Public Opinion Quarterly* (Summer 1971):200–210.
2. Jeffrey Bierig and John Dimmick, "The Late Night Radio Talk Show as Interpersonal Communication," *Journalism Quarterly* (Spring 1979): 92–96.
3. See, for example, William B. Toran, "Radio: Fertile Ground for Nonprofit Public Service Spots," *Public Relations Journal* (August 1977): 24–25.

ADDITIONAL READING

Broussard, E. Joseph, and Jack F. Holgate, *Writing and Reporting Broadcast News* (New York: Macmillan, 1982).

Guimary, Donald L., *Citizens' Groups and Broadcasting* (New York: Praeger, 1975).

Hilliard, Robert L., *Writing for Television and Radio*, 3d ed. (New York: Hastings House, 1976).

Stephens, Mitchell, *Broadcast News* (New York: Holt, Rinehart and Winston, 1980).

23

TELEVISION
AND VIDEOTAPE

Is the notoriously wicked J. R. Ewing, villain of CBS's *Dallas*, typical of American businessmen?

In May 1981, a study entitled "Crooks, Conmen and Clowns: Businessmen in TV Entertainment" reported that the majority of corporation heads portrayed on television committed illegal acts, while only three percent were depicted as engaging in socially productive behavior. In one of its public issues advertisements headlined "Does the TV Camera Distort Society?" Mobil Oil questioned this view of businessmen and suggested that "television does owe the American people more than the social and economic views of a small group of individuals."[1] (The nonprofit Media Institute, which conducted the study, is supported by 300 individual and corporate members . . . including Mobil.)

Only a few seasons earlier, the president of the International Association of Machinists asserted that television portrays the union worker as "an Archie Bunker type—a shiftless, indigent lout." To fight such stereotypes, the Machinists decided to document negative portrayals of blue collar workers through an extensive television-monitoring campaign.[2]

Television arouses passions across the entire spectrum of society's pressure groups, not only because the medium's images are so vivid, but also because the medium is pervasive. If you get a bad image on TV . . . well, you've got a bad image.

TV Provides Recognition

Television is courted by all segments of society as the medium whose blessing of attention can prove the open-sesame to public recognition and approval. Many of the award winners in the Public Relations Society of America's Silver Anvil competition cite the importance of television to their successful campaigns:[3]

When Coca-Cola used an ice-skating robot to publicize its involvement with the Lake Placid Winter Olympic Games, it released two television film clips, which were carried by 136 television stations in 119 cities for a total of 214 telecasts that reached a projected thirty-seven million households. A twenty-three-city tour by the robot attracted further coverage: 125 minutes of television time, reaching an audience of thirty million.

The British Post Office marked the issuance of a Pony Express commemorative stamp by re-creating the original Pony Express ride from St. Joseph, Mo., to Sacramento, Calif. A ninety-second TV news clip, entitled "High Noon in Sacramento" and produced by Carl Byoir & Associates, showed the start and end of a race along the Pony Express Trail. The film was used by 185 stations in North America.

The Houston Parks Department made a persuasive case for increasing park acreage and funding by financing a twenty-minute documentary videotape, "No Room at the Park," which was aired in prime time by public television.

Among the many means Pan Am used to promote its merger with National Airlines was the preparation of three television features that were distributed nationally for use on talk shows as well as news programs.

Burger King's "spokesman" for its fire-safety program aimed at children is "Snuffy," a scaled-down replica of an antique fire engine. Following a campaign that included appearances on sixty television shows, and a PSA run by 105 television stations with an estimated audience of 115 million, nationwide market research by Burger King showed that 74 percent of children under age thirteen were aware of the talking fire engine.

When an Air Force Academy cadet was selected to chaperone a Colorado competitor in the International Special Olympics, the service academy's public affairs office assigned a PR practitioner full-time to assist ABC in preparing a television feature on the relationship between the cadet host and the handicapped athlete. The human-interest angle was a major part of the network's nationwide coverage of the event on its popular *Wide World of Sports*.

PUBLIC-SERVICE ANNOUNCEMENTS FOR TV

We saw in the preceding chapter that the radio PSA is an important public relations tool. The FCC also requires television stations to provide time for nonprofit public-service messages. Some, such as the armed services recruiting pitches and the antilittering spots donated by the Advertising Council, Inc., are as slickly and expensively produced as those for commercial products. On the other hand, the no-budget PSA may be as basic as an announcer reading a 200-word script while a title card with the name and phone number of the service organization is shown on the screen.

A series of PSAs prepared for the Summit County (Ohio) Association for Retarded Citizens sought to dispel myths about mentally handicapped people by employing new words to describe and depict them, by differentiating between mental illness and mental retardation, and by giving mentally handicapped persons a chance to speak for themselves in the public media—a powerful use of television:

> A major step in the production process was the use of a 15-person focus group. Eight TV storyboards and scripts were produced and submitted to the focus group for review and discussion. Based upon these findings, amendments were made and final production undertaken. Of greatest significance was the finding that PSAs were most succesful if they avoided preaching and stimulated new thinking about mentally handicapped people.[4]

The PSAs were used in conjunction with a complete media program that also included talk shows and news programs (see following section). Seven television stations aired the PSAs an estimated 133 times during the one-month campaign.

Some Stations Produce PSAs

Before planning the television PSA, it is wise to make contact with area stations to find out what special formats they make available free of charge. In the New York metropolitan area, for example, Metromedia's flagship station, WNEW, produces a series of "Big Apple Minutes"—news-features using the station's own personalities and production crews to highlight attractions such as museums, exhibits, and historic programs. The station prepares spots that would cost the nonprofit organizations thousands of dollars to produce independently.

Television is a highly specialized medium. Producing a PSA can take a huge bite out of your PR budget. That's why, after carefully weighing the expected benefits of a PSA, most organizations use an outside agency to arrange with a specialized film or video firm to produce the spot.

If your organization does decide to write, produce, and distribute its own television spots, you will need to start the preproduction planning by writing a script with the visual material described in full on the left side of the split script, and the dialogue or narration provided on the right side. Numerous story conferences will be necessary. First, you must assure that each precious word of the thirty- or sixty-second script conveys important information. Next, you must work with technicians to arrange for sound, cameras, actors, props, and setting. Finally, you must estimate the price of the entire project.

GAINING ACCESS
TO COMMERCIAL TELEVISION

We noted in our discussion of PSAs above that a complete media program seeks every possible access to television, including news coverage and talk shows, as well as cable coverage. In the case of the Summit County Association for Retarded Citizens, the campaign was labeled Project Dawn. The help of radio, television, and print professionals was enlisted to form a media consortium to advise the association how to gain access to the media. Each of the television stations serving the county was contacted, and visits were arranged so that volunteers and the PR firm engaged by the association (Meeker-Mayer) could learn how best to place information in the electronic media. The organization did not pressure the media. Instead, it sought to find out how material could be tailored to the media's needs, in order for the association to achieve greater acceptance and usage.

A variety of background material was provided to talk show hosts, and assistance was given in finding mentally retarded people to appear on the shows as spokespersons. Eventually, six television talk-show appearances were booked, providing a large share of the more than four hours of television coverage in a single month.

Such cooperation is extremely important for an organization that wants to make an impact on television. Often, a failure or unwillingness to accommodate the special needs and desires of television means the loss of valuable exposure. Although the American Academy of Family Physicians received volumes of print coverage for its observance of the tenth anniversary of the establishment of family practice as a medical specialty, it forfeited valuable exposure on both the *Today* show and *Good Morning America*. Why? Because it declined to offer either show an "exclusive" prior to release of a major health-care research report at a press conference open to all of the news media.[5]

Let's look briefly at three ways to get a story on television:

Television Handout

The print-press release is relatively inexpensive to produce and distribute. But several seconds or minutes of film or videotape may cost a thousand dollars or more for the original, and hundreds more for a few copies. Obviously, you cannot produce pieces of visual material indiscriminately. You'd better be sure you have a very good chance of placing it on the screen.

A recent report by an executive of a film service indicates that news films supplied free to television stations average about 45 percent usage, at a cost of less than sixty cents per thousand audience members. He found that films related to sports are in top demand, with women's news, energy-related information, and depictions of new technology also likely to be aired.[6]

Increasingly, visual material prepared for distribution to broadcast and cable television outlets is being packaged on three-quarter-inch videotape cassettes. Small cable outlets may use them in that format; others have the equipment to convert them to one-inch or two-inch tape. Tape cassettes are cheap to produce and copy, convenient to mail, and easy to preview on a playback unit.

Film is still used by some organizations. PR films should be shot in 16-mm color. (Super-8 and most small video formats are not considered to be of broadcast quality.)

Some stations prefer silent material, so their news department can script narration to be read by an anchorperson. But a surprising number of stations are willing to use tape or film in which narration and background music are provided on the sound track. One media consultant suggested that every company should provide area television stations with background stock footage on the firm's key operations, as AT&T does through six five-minute films on how long-distance dialing works, and other basic operations. He also recommends that a stand-up reporter just like the ones on television news programs be used in PR film handouts—on the theory that television editors want "handouts" to blend in as smoothly as possible with the usual material.[7]

Getting on the Talk Shows

A broadcast news item may last only a fraction of a minute and get lost among a dozen stories squeezed between two commercials. But get a spokesperson for your organization on a talk show, and you are virtually assured of ten minutes of leisurely and uninterrupted attention. And if the host is a major personality who takes a liking to you or your organization's cause, you can garner an extremely influential "testimonial" at no cost.

Of course, an appearance with Johnny Carson on NBC's *Tonight* show is the top target. The syndicated Phil Donahue and CBS's Dinah Shore are also considered prime spots. In addition to the dozens of network and syndicated national shows, local stations have their own formats, including "Dialing for Dollars" programs that mix visiting celebrities and interesting local people with viewer promotions and contests, and perhaps even variety acts or performances by the host talents. The charge can be made that many of these shows are corny and that they deliver lowest-common-denominator audiences. But the cost is low, and the numbers reached are high, which makes them attractive when you are working in the press-agent or public-information model.

Most talk shows have talent coordinators or assistant producers in charge of screening suggestions for guest spots. One survey of these gatekeepers showed that most prefer to be contacted by telephone, so that they can save time by giving the public relations person an immediate reaction to a proposed guest or topic. If they are interested, they'll ask for a written proposal summarizing what is interesting about the guest. Phil Donahue's producer stresses that all ideas are kept on file in case a guest might fit in well on a later show.[8]

Before grabbing the phone, the PR person should study the format of the target show carefully. Some shows use only celebrities or oddities. Some are so frivolous, or the hosts so inane, that they may not provide a good showcase for your spokesperson. Others may be preferable because they regularly provide a consumer-oriented spot or a serious segment involving representatives of all sides of a current issue. You have a better chance of getting on some shows if you're willing to take a controversial stand. Other shows put a premium on the visual aspect, such as whether a guest is good looking or whether he or she can bring something to the studio to show or demonstrate. (In Chapter 24, Preparing to Speak, we look at ways you can help your spokesperson to perform well on television.)

Most talk shows shy away from guests who want to use the opportunity for obvious and heavy-handed product publicity. But they don't mind if someone works in a few "plugs" while discussing trends, consumer issues, technology of the future, or public issues. Many local shows have regular features where new products, unusual gifts, and other innovations are demonstrated.

Placing Longer Features

News programs and talk shows may be the most important forms of television communication, but there are plenty of hours to be filled outside of prime time, and millions of viewers watching. If your organization can afford the $20,000 to $100,000 it costs to produce a television-quality 16-mm sound and color film (including five to ten prints, plus distribution and promotion costs), your message may gain air time worth many times that amount.

Here is a sampling of film features, prepared by PR departments and provided free to local broadcast and cable stations, that can be viewed on a weekend morning:

A depiction of "air strike readiness," with exciting action footage showing pilots

When a spokesman for the Standard Oil Company of Indiana is interviewed by a television reporter, the company's Media Relations Section has coordinated the contact. (Courtesy Standard Oil Company of Indiana)

scrambling to their planes and flying in formation—prepared, of course, by the U. S. Defense Department.

A travelogue depicting life on the arctic tundra, with a soft-sell pitch for the trans-Alaska pipeline—produced by a major oil company.

An exploration of "miniaturization" in industry, with fascinating microphotography and stop-action sequences—provided by a manufacturer of computers and other high-technology products.

A dramatic documentary of the life of Alexander Graham Bell—as recounted by (who else?) the Bell System.

These are familiar topics and sponsors, of course, but even a smaller organization can prepare television features. Nonprofit groups, especially, may be able to work with donated equipment and volunteer personnel. An organization can virtually assure itself of local air time if it prepares a historical documentary on the area or a look at a regional public-service program such as Meals on Wheels or a halfway house for drug rehabilitation. Typically, these public-service tapes and films feature the name of the sponsor only at the beginning and the end, although it may be possible to work in subtle identification of the firm when its employees are shown working as volunteers in the program, or when its donated equipment is being used.

Your chances of getting a feature film used are enhanced if you aim for a length of approximately 24 minutes, which allows for several advertisements, PSAs, and station announcements during the half-hour slot. You can contact the station manager by phone or letter, and your chances may be enhanced if you have prepared a brochure or fact sheet to promote the tape or film, complete with representative still shots and a synopsis of the content, along with notations about running time, format, and narration.

Cable and broadcast stations may also be interested in scheduling the showing far enough in advance so that your organization can promote it in local advertising, stuffers mailed out with monthly bills, and articles in the employee house organ.

TV AS ADVERSARY

As we saw in Chapter 10, the Fairness Doctrine enables organizations that have been criticized on television to gain access to the airwaves for purposes of reply. The right is easily exercised when the criticism comes in the form of an editorial by a local station's management, since the format usually makes provision for replies of the same length and in the same time slot. But the national networks have not been nearly so generous or sympathetic to organizations that ask for "equal time" to rebut charges made on magazine-format investigative shows. The two cases that follow illustrate the lengths to which public relations departments may go to seek redress and offset negative publicity.

Illinois Power Company vs. CBS'S 60 Minutes

In November 1979, the popular *60 Minutes* aired a report by Harry Reasoner on alleged overcharging of customers by the Illinois Power Company, which supplies power to one third of that state. The report, which used three former employees of the utility as informants, charged that the company was inexperienced in the nuclear field, made no effort to control costs, engaged in slipshod internal reporting, and fabricated estimates of construction-completion timetables—all of which cost the consumer.[9]

The Monday following the program, the company's stock fell in the busiest trading day in its history. Illinois Power's public-affairs division realized the potential magnitude of the damage and set out at once to offset the blow with a technique it labeled "defensive videotaping." The company obtained a copy of the complete *60 Minutes* segment as well as additional footage of CBS interviews with the president and other executives. Using the *60 Minutes* technique of a ticking stopwatch and a blunt, straightforward narrator, Illinois Power prepared a 44-minute videotape, *60 Minutes/Our Reply*, intended for an audience of the company's employees, customers, and stockholders. Point by point, the tape rebuts each of the assertions made by the television program.

When the tape was released, the company found that it had a much wider audience. By the end of 1980, more than 2,000 copies had been distributed to legislators, corporate executives, journalists, and educators.[10] Dissemination of the tape has been further promoted by the Media Institute, a business-oriented research group, which issued a widely publicized booklet that included the complete transcript of the Illinois Power videotape and copies of correspondence between CBS and the utility. The booklet's copy is clearly slanted in favor of Illinois Power—in the first sentence of the copy, *60 Minutes* is referred to as "champ of the TV ratings brawl," and efforts by other companies to use "defensive videotaping" are lauded.

CBS noted in its correspondence with Illinois Power that the company had violated copyright restrictions by using the segment from *60 Minutes.* The utility replied that it was making "fair use" of the material in order to defend its reputation. A year after the original broadcast, *60 Minutes* aired a short "update" segment in which it reviewed and renewed its charges that costs were out of control at the utility.

Clearly, the network did not back down. Whether the utility's efforts will help meet its long-range goals of gaining support from ratepayers, acceptance by government regulators, and higher profits remains to be seen. But Illinois Power set a precedent of striking back at adversarial television, as we can see in the following case.

Kaiser Aluminum vs. ABC'S 20/20

In April 1980, a segment on ABC's *20/20* produced by investigative reporter Geraldo Rivera alleged that Kaiser Aluminum had knowingly marketed an unsafe product, aluminum residential electrical wiring. Insisting that its report was accurate, ABC first agreed to let Kaiser submit a four-minute tape for airing on *20/20*, but later decided that the network's late-evening *Nightline* news program was "the appropriate forum for a full airing of both the subject of aluminum wiring safety and the broader issues of 'response time' and 'access.' "[11]

Kaiser found the ABC response unacceptable. The company not only felt that the tape it had prepared should be aired in the same forum as the original charges, it also demanded a "satisfactory retraction" from the network. Ronald E. Rhody, corporate vice president for public relations and advertising, decided the case was important enough to warrant a major counterattack. The company took full-page advertisements in leading newspapers with the banner headline "Trial by Television." The ad questioned many of the practices of television investigative journalism and called on citizens to write their elected representatives to protest. Kaiser also vowed to seek hearings before the FCC and the House subcommittee on communications.

Carrying the campaign still further, Kaiser's PR department turned out a slick twenty-four-page booklet with the look and feel of an annual report. Entitled "At Issue: Access to Television," it simultaneously lauded the history and growth of television (pictures of Howdy Doody and the Mouseketeers) and questioned the impact of television on society (charts, bar graphs, quotes from various Supreme Court justices, and an assertion that Richard Nixon had been convicted by public opinion created through unfavorable television coverage). Seeking the widest possible audience for its booklet, Kaiser distributed it to teachers throughout the country, including instructors of journalism and public relations.

Kaiser had three goals in moving to counter the television report:[12]

To rebut specific charges made on the program.

To raise the issue for government officials and the public as to whether television does a disservice in its investigative reporting.

To reaffirm the company's policy of speaking out when it feels it has been wronged, and to urge others to do the same.

Kaiser has been vigorous in offering company officials as speakers before media and public-policy groups. While no apology or retraction has come from ABC, Kaiser believes that letters from the public, statements by congressmen, and indication of support from leaders of other companies all indicate that more careful scrutiny of media coverage of business has been placed successfully on the agenda for public discussion.[13]

Kaiser and the television networks also ran afoul of one another when the company attempted to run a series of advertisements with political overtones. All three major networks rejected some of the spots as too controversial, assuming that Kaiser's opinions would occasion demands for ''equal time'' under the Fairness Doctrine. When Kaiser did not get its spots aired, it reproduced parts of the storyboards for the TV ads in a print ad that asked, ''Can a corporation speak its mind in public?'' Clearly, Kaiser means to make a continuing issue of its ability to gain access to television.

OTHER OUTLETS FOR VIDEO MESSAGES

Fortunately, organizations no longer are limited to commercial television media in order to distribute their video messages. Other newly emerging outlets include:

Public-access channels on cable television. As a condition of their franchise, most cable companies must reserve times and channels for community groups. Prepackaged tapes may be shown, or the cable company may make one of its own studios available for production of program materials.

Video playback units. Although the cost of videodisc units and home video recorders is still high, they are becoming commonplace in public institutions and affluent homes. PR departments that place informational tapes in schools and libraries may expect them to find wide exposure among certain target audiences. Health-care information is just one area of public relations where video dissemination for individual playback has great possibilities.

Nonprofit public television usually is more open to innovative programming ideas than commercial television. To present the results of its biennial survey of working families, conducted by Louis Harris and Associates, General Mills worked with the public broadcasting station in New York-New Jersey to set up a two-way electronic teleconference. Reporters watching at eighteen other public broadcasting stations around the country were able to ask questions of Harris and the head of General Mills.[14]

NEW ROLES FOR CORPORATE VIDEO

By the beginning of the 1980s, U. S. businesses and nonprofit organizations were producing more television programs for their own use than the programming carried by the networks and public broadcasting combined. Hundreds of organizations produced over 46,000 video programs, totaling some 15,000 hours of viewing time, in 1977.[15]

Businesses first adopted video as a training tool, and responsibility for making and distributing tapes initially rested with the personnel department of many corporations. But increasingly, management is appreciating the potential of video communication, and corporate communication departments are taking greater responsibility for it. Video capability is no longer considered a luxury enjoyed by only the largest organizations: The typical user is a medium-sized company working with a budget of $100,000 and a production staff of two or three people.[16]

One of the attractions of video is that it has many of the elements of "face-to-face" communication, but it cuts down on the cost and wasted time of sending managers all over the country or the world. Johnson & Johnson, the health-care company, sends talks by company officers and reports on new developments to its 150 companies and divisions through a worldwide video network. The average cost per program is $10,000—far cheaper than sending company representatives to 150 locations. The programs are distributed on three-quarter-inch videotape cassettes. The home-office public relations department suggests appropriate audiences, but each division has its own video coordinator who decides when, where, and how each tape will be used. The video network is especially useful for announcing personnel changes: Managers in the company's many outposts have an early opportunity to hear and "meet" the new person on videotape.[17]

It is even possible to set up a long-distance video conference using phone lines to carry closed-circuit television. Usually, when a company is about to make a new stock offering, its top executives travel around the country talking to brokers and major investors in key cities about the move. But when AT&T was planning a new offering in 1981,

its executives appeared on a closed-circuit show carried to twenty cities simultaneously, and viewers were able to phone in their questions during the program.[18]

Video offers an opportunity to bring the annual report to life. In 1980, Emhart Corp., a metal parts and chemical firm, produced a twenty-two-minute videotape version of its annual report for use on cable stations in eight states. The tape, which cost less than $10,000 to produce, presented company executives, not actors, and gave stockholders a glimpse of components being manufactured in its various plants. Company officials felt the taped report gave a better picture of the firm's activities than could be obtained from still pictures and written copy. The firm's specific public-information goal was realized when an estimated audience of 250,000 viewers in fifty-one communities saw the program.[19]

It might even be advantageous for a company to allow its annual meeting to be carried on cable television, with prepared "documentary" film footage inserted. Many stockholders are already accustomed to receiving information about companies on home microprocessors merely by paying a monthly fee and using a telephone hookup to access a satellite that transmits the Dow Jones News/Retrieval service. A logical next step would be for companies to prepare their own materials for direct electronic transmission to the home.

Many companies already use video-cassette systems for training employees. Usually, the workers come to a meeting room for playback of the prepared lessons. But there is even greater potential for employee communication: video monitors placed in the lunchroom, so that the employee house organ may be a weekly television program instead of a monthly printed publication.

WHAT DOES IT TAKE
TO PRODUCE VIDEO?

Of course, many organizations have decided they do not have the budget or the personnel to produce video messages, and some organizations have found that television does not address enough of their goals to warrant the high cost.

Approximately 90 percent of those organizations regularly using video have invested in their own in-house production facility. One third spent less than $50,000 on a studio, and one third spent more than $200,000.[20] While the cost of video equipment exceeds the cost of making and showing slide shows and films, duplication costs are much less, since copies can be made on any recording and editing equipment—it is not necessary to send away to a specialized studio.[21] Although technology is changing rapidly, the most popular video format is the three-quarter-inch cassette, which loads as easily into a playback unit as an audio tape cassette loads into a tape recorder.

What does it take to produce video? The sections that follow describe the various components of the corporate video system.

The Studio

It is not necessary to construct or remodel a huge space in order to have a workable video studio. Ideally, it is useful to have twelve- to fifteen-foot ceilings from which you can hang lights, but lighting can be mounted on tripods or wall fasteners. The studio space should be at least 300 square feet (15 by 20) to permit movement by two cameras mounted on rolling tripods. Yet, one East Coast medical center manages to produce acceptable live programming for its in-house channel using a room measuring no more than 12 by 12—less than 150 square feet.

You'll want to provide the studio space with sound-absorbent material such as acoustic tiles or cork. The velvet curtain you hang on a track or against one wall to form a neutral background will also serve to soak up studio noises. Furniture should include a desk or table, two straightback chairs for formal narration, and two easy chairs for more con-versational settings. Visual-aid equipment should include an easel and a blackboard.

Today's lightweight video cameras can free you from the confines of the video studio. The PR department should look upon the entire physical plant as its studio. Instead of "talking heads" taped in a static setting, strive for real-life situations that show employees on the job.

Cameras

The standard small-format camera is a miniaturized version of the huge cameras the networks use. Mounted on similarly scaled-down rolling tripods, it enables you to duplicate most of the zooms, pans, dolly shots, and switches from general to close-up shots that you are accustomed to seeing on television news and talk shows. Using a two-camera studio setup, you can vary the presentation so that a recorded fifteen-minute talk by your president or the director of training will be visually interesting.

The real excitement in small-format video, however, comes from the Porta-Pak or ENG (electronic-news-gathering) units, which enable a crew of two or three to wander at will in search of information that is live and visual. Battery-powered camera and recorder are housed in portable units connected by cables. The taped material is brought back to a studio for editing.

Recording and Editing Equipment

Unlike motion pictures, where the visual image is recorded on film (and where you can view the images frame by frame), video images are scanned by the television camera and converted into electronic information that can be stored on magnetic tape. No image is visible on the tape. In order to reconstitute the image (and the sound that was recorded simultaneously), it is necessary to place the tape (on a loose reel or in a packaged cassette) in a playback unit connected to a monitor. During production, the same "deck" can be used to record the original material and to view it. To ensure quality, more expensive editing equipment should be used to edit the final version.

Special effects such as dissolves from one shot to another, optical effects such as split-screen or the "wipe" transition, and even overlapping images can all be created during recording or editing with the use of a special-effects generator (SEG), the most sophisticated and most costly piece of equipment in the small-format video studio.

Editing of taped video material can be accomplished with splices, but the preferred system is electronic editing, where various sounds, scenes, and images, including superimposed titles, are assembled electronically by moving each piece of recorded material from the reel on which it was shot and stored to a master finished reel, which can be duplicated for distribution.

Sound mixers enable background music, separately recorded narration, and other effects to be joined on the single sound track found on standard videotape.

Lighting and Sound

Small-format video doesn't require exotic or expensive auxiliary equipment in order to make a credible product. The standard video lens system is sensitive enough to use in normal lighting conditions. The result is an acceptable cinema verité feeling that we are accustomed to in film documentaries. Most video crews carry one or two light-weight sources of illumination—high-intensity lamps with reflectors, mounted on slender tripods or clamp-on devices—so that they can wipe out shadows, provide good general illumination, and "key" on the faces of speakers.

The standard camera-recorder outfit sold by most video manufacturers includes a unidirectional microphone, with a lavaliere cord to hang it around a speaker's neck or a simple mounting stand to hold it in place on a table.

It is also useful to obtain other microphones, including an omnidirectional one for recording general sounds, crowd noise, or multiple speakers. For recordings of panel discussions or meetings, it is wise to provide all speakers with their own mikes, all jacked into a microphone switcher—a device that enables several sound sources to be picked up by the sound track on a single recorder.

Playback Equipment

To show video to a small audience, your organization needs a suitcase-sized playback unit that accepts the reel or cassette, and a standard television set or monitor equipped with an input jack. For audiences of more than ten, you can link several monitors together with cables so that no one person sits more than ten feet from a screen, or you can use special optical equipment that enlarges the image and throws it up on a movie screen for viewing by large audiences of as many as 100. Usually, the image is brighter and better focused if it is viewed on the glass-screen monitor.

MANAGEMENT CONSIDERATIONS

Television commands huge national audiences for network programs, and large community audiences for local programs. Videotapes can add the glamour of television to internal communication. The question is: Do the huge audiences and the visual impact justify the cost? Frequently, the target publics for a public relations program won't be in the television audience. Or your public may be only a small part of that vast audience.

Television is not the solution to every PR problem. Let's examine situations where it might be a useful tool.

Model of Public Relations

Like radio, television can be an effective technique for each of the four models of public relations.

Press agents and publicists positively drool at the thought of the large TV audience and the attention they can get for their organization with the visual medium. They can sandwich their messages into entertainment and news programs—by paying for ads, getting items on news programs, placing personalities on talk shows, or by submitting PSAs. The audience, which does not have to work at seeking out the message, passively processes it from television without much resistance.

Public-information specialists prepare television handouts that get extensive play on local news programs. They also can get specialists onto talk shows and prepare documentaries and PSAs. They use videotape to inform employees and community residents.

Two-way asymmetric communicators make heavy use of paid advocacy advertisements on television, and they use what we call adversary television in an attempt to persuade publics to accept their points of view.

Two-way symmetric practitioners can use TV much as they use radio. Managers who participate in talk shows and TV news specials with representatives of active publics can learn of the consequences the organization has on publics. Adversary television and TV advocacy advertising can promote public dialogue on major issues—even though the organization strongly argues only its point of view. Paisley calls such debates ''proactive'' information campaigns, as opposed to ''reactive'' campaigns.[22]

Asymmetric communicators generally run reactive television campaigns: they try to get rid of existing policies their organization doesn't like, or to preserve policies it does like, after a decision has been made. Symmetric communicators, in contrast, argue their organization's point of view before decisions are made on such issues as the energy shortage or the Clean Air Act. Representatives of other organizations and of publics argue their views. As a result, both organiza- tions and publics benefit from an open and free-wheeling debate on the issue.

Objectives

Many public relations practitioners believe television messages have great impact upon cognitions, attitudes, and behaviors. They worry about their organization being discussed unfavorably on *60 Minutes* and subsequently being flooded with letters and calls of protest.

It's easy, however, to overestimate the effect of television. Many people may write letters to protest what they learn on *60 Minutes*. But many, many more people will do nothing. In fact, there's much evidence that people retain very little of what they see and hear on television, unless they hear it over and over again.[23]

Television news introduces issues to the public agenda. But television news stays with issues for a shorter time than the print media—usually not long enough to fix the issues on the public agenda.[24] Television commercials, similarly, must be repeated many times before people remember them.

Television, in other words, seems to make it possible to meet the objective of communicating with millions of people all at the same time. Communicating with large audiences is indeed the strength of the medium. Yet, many public relations practitioners overestimate the extent to which they can communicate with members of target publics through television. Their messages may reach millions of people, but only a few thousand may be members of a target public.

Television also may not be as effective as print media in achieving PR objectives other than communication. You can put a message before millions of people, but they may not retain the message. And, the cognition, attitude, and behavior objectives rarely can be achieved through television.

We also should look at the effect of television from a slightly different perspective—

its visual nature. People react with more feeling and emotion to something they can see. When they first receive a message from television, they may only passively process the information. But the visual portion of the message may create an emotional response. Seeing a problem may change them from passive to actively communicating publics. There is evidence that television sometimes can have this dramatic effect on publics. But there also is evidence that, for most people, it usually does not.[25]

Which Programs?

Broadcast television, cable, videotape, and videodiscs can be used to reach publics targeted by most of the specialized public relations programs discussed in Part III.

Media-relations programs must cope with broadcast television. We have also provided examples of how videotape can be used in employee communication. It also can be used for open houses and tours in community relations programs.

Public relations people use televison extensively for public affairs campaigns and for debates with activist publics. They also run PSAs on television as part of economic-education programs. In addition to using video at stockholder meetings, financial PR specialists must monitor and be ready to respond to information dispensed on *Wall Street Week* and similar investment programs on television. Finally, fund-raising specialists find the large audiences of television particularly enticing for their appeals.

Communication Behavior of Publics

When we discussed the possible objectives of a television message, we argued that television effects are relatively weak because television reaches primarily low-involvement publics.

Public relations practitioners like to use television because they can sandwich their messages into programs watched by millions of viewers. But the viewers do not seek out the PR messages. They process them because it would be difficult to avoid hearing the messages without leaving the room or shutting off the set. Even employee and community publics seldom seek out videotapes prepared by public relations people. Usually the tapes are shown as part of some other event or exhibit. Videotapes shown in employee lunchrooms probably receive only partial attention.

Television offers the possibility of communicating—if only passively—with low-involvement publics that otherwise could not be reached. Most often, the publics reached will retain only a vague idea of the message.

Cost in Time and Money

Producing a message for television costs more money and takes more time than most other PR techniques. Yet, if the audience is large, the cost per thousand of a television message may be relatively small. Again, however, if you want a meaningful comparision with other media, remember to calculate the cost per thousand of your target public that sees the message on television—not of the total television audience.

With television, it is essential that you use the money and time budget techniques outlined in Chapter 8. It also is imperative that you do formative and evaluative research to determine whether the effect of the television message merits the cost.

Evaluation

Numerous rating services provide data that can be used to measure the communication objective—the number of people seeing a televised message. If you can get demographic information on the viewers of a particular program, you also may be able to match the characteristics of the viewers with those of your target public. But remember that members of target publics do not necessarily have common demographic characteristics. Thus, the ratings often do not provide the data you need.

To perform an adequate evaluation, you will need to survey members of your target public shortly after your message appears on television. Ask survey respondents if they remember seeing your message. Then use questions such as those described in Chapter 9:

Did you happen to hear a message about TRW on television last night?

(If yes) Can you tell me what you remember about that message?

(Follow-up) Anything else?

If you feel that your message may have had an effect on acceptance, attitude, and behavior, you also can attempt to measure those changes using techniques discussed earlier.

NOTES

1. *Crooks, Conmen and Clowns: Businessmen in TV Entertainment* (Washington: The Media Institute, 1981). Cited in Mobil advertisement "Does the TV Camera Distort Society?" *New York Times* (May 14, 1981), p. A–27.
2. "How Unions Try to Clean Up Their Image," *U.S. News & World Report* (Oct. 22, 1979): 69–70.
3. All cases listed here are 1980 PRSA Silver Anvil Award winners.
4. The Summit County program was another 1980 Silver Anvil Award winner. These remarks are excerpted from the winning entry.
5. Ibid.
6. Don Phelan, "TV Film Handouts Can Work," *Public Relations Journal* (January 1976): 32–33.
7. Phelan.
8. Kathy Rand, "How to Work with TV Talk Shows," *Public Relations Journal* (March 1977): 20–21.
9. *Punch, Counterpunch: "60 Minutes" vs. Illinois Power Co.* (Washington: The Media Institute, 1981).
10. *Punch, Counterpunch.*
11. Tony Schwartz, "Kaiser to Ask FCC Action on ABC News," *New York Times* (February 5, 1981):C–22.
12. Kaiser Corp., "Trial by Television," documentation supporting winning entry in "Emergency Public Relations" category, 1981 PRSA Silver Anvil Award competition.
13. "Trial by Television," Kaiser Corp.
14. Jane E. Ferguson, "A First for Teleconferencing," *Public Relations Journal* (September 1981): 26–29.
15. Judith M. and Douglas P. Brush, "Corporate Video: Burgeoning Role for PR," *Public Relations Journal* (October 1977):14–16.
16. Brush and Brush.
17. Robert Andrews, Public Relations Department, Johnson & Johnson, personal interviews.
18. Karen W. Arenson, "Anatomy of AT&T's Offering," *New York Times* (June 10, 1981):p–1, D–5.
19. Barbara Frankel, "Company Annual Reports, Once Dull, May Be Brightened on Cable TV," *The Home News* (Nov. 25, 1980):20.
20. Brush and Brush.
21. Ronald S. Posner, "A/V Comparisons: Video vs. Film vs. Slides," *Public Relations Journal* (September 1978):45–48.
22. William J. Paisley, "Public Information Campaigns: The American Experience," in Ronald E. Rice and William J. Paisley (eds.), *Public Communication Campaigns* (Beverly Hills, Calif: Sage Publications, 1981), p. 39.
23. Mark R. Levy, "The Audience Experience With Television News," *Journalism Monographs* No. 55 (April 1978).
24. Maxwell McCombs, "Agenda Setting Function of Mass Media," *Public Relations Review* 3 (Winter 1977):61-82.
25. James E. Grunig, "A Simultaneous Equation Model for Intervention in Communication Behavior." Paper presented to the Theory

& Methodology Division, Association for Education in Journalism, Houston, August, 1979.

ADDITIONAL READING

Barnouw, Eric, *Tube of Plenty* (New York: Oxford University Press, 1975).

Cantor, Muriel, *Prime-Time Television: Content and Control* (Beverly Hills, Calif.: Sage, 1980).

Foster, Eugene, *Understanding Broadcasting* (Reading, Mass.: Addison-Wesley, 1978).

Gans, Herbert J., *Deciding What's News* (New York: Pantheon, 1979).

Goldsen, Rose K., *The Show and Tell Machine: How Television Works and Works You Over* (New York: Dial Press, 1975).

Johnson, Nicholas, *How to Talk Back to Your Television Set* (Boston: Little, Brown, 1970).

Lee, Robert, and Robert Misiorowski, *Script Models: A Handbook for the Media Writer* (New York: Hastings House, 1978).

Maloney, Martin, and Paul Max Rubenstein, *Writing for the Media* (Englewood Cliffs, N.J.: Prentice-Hall, 1980).

Newcomb, Horace (ed.), *Television: The Critical View* (New York: Oxford University Press, 1976.)

24

PREPARING TO SPEAK

The same person who supervises the preparation of news releases and broadcast messages is likely, at any given time, to be working on one or more of the following nonmedia tasks:

Preparing the head of a department to brief the press on a new program.

Writing a "stock speech" for delivery to any visiting group before beginning a plant tour.

Rehearsing the president of the firm for an appearance before the Chamber of Commerce.

Setting up a speaker's bureau to provide presentations on nontechnical topics of interest to community, professional, and educational groups.

Drafting the question format for interviewing employees' children who are candidates for company scholarships.

Making arrangements for a dialogue session that will bring company officials together with community members to discuss problems of pollution and waste disposal.

All of these events have one thing in common: Someone will have to be prepared to speak on behalf of the organization.

Speaking vs. Writing: Differences and Similarities

It is useful to understand the ways in which speaking differs from other communication skills, and the ways in which it is similar. First, two important differences:

While a written message such as a newsletter, brochure, or advertisement is somewhat impersonal, the spoken word carries the credibility of the speaker. Enthusiasm, concern, tolerance, understanding, and empathy are all best demonstrated through the verbal and nonverbal act of meeting an audience in person.

The speaking situation is flexible and can be altered to fit the response of the audience. With the print or audiovisual message, you fire your shot and hope it hits the target. In a speaking situation, you can make mid-course corrections.

But, in some very important ways, the speech is similar to other public relations messages:

It must be consistent with other messages disseminated by the organization. The speaker must be familiar with positions taken in written communication, and must strive to articulate them in a personal style that is consistent with the view of the organization.

Careful and complete preparation is necessary in order to avoid embarrassment. The speaker must have all the facts straight. He or she cannot hope to merely "wing it" on personal charm alone.

The speaking situation poses the usual "packaging and delivery" questions for the PR department: Is this the best forum for reaching the target audience? Will it help us to achieve our goals? Is it the best use of resources? Should it be reinforced with other channels of communication? Will we be able to measure the effect?

MANAGEMENT CONSIDERATIONS

Most of the people who developed the profession of public relations used the skills of the print journalist more than they used speaking skills. Today, however, PR people use—or help others use—speaking skills as often as they use writing skills. Speaking allows more two-way communicating than writing. It also leads to different effects. Let's look at those differences.

Model of Public Relations

Although P. T. Barnum used speaking skills extensively when he promoted his museum and circus, the press agents and public-information specialists who followed him practiced written PR. Their objective was to place articles in the mass media. Even today, press agents, publicists, and public-information specialists rely primarily on their writing skills.

With the two-way asymmetric and symmetric models, however, public relations people strike much more of a balance between writing and speaking. More feedback is possible when the speaker and audience meet face to face. Feedback is especially important for persuasion in the asymmetric model. Oral communication also makes dialogue and interaction much easier than they are when messages must be written and exchanged. Thus, speaking skills are especially useful in the symmetric model.

Objectives

For most of the techniques discussed previously, we cautioned you to limit your objectives to communication with a public and, sometimes, to the public's retention of the message. When messages are spoken skillfully, however, sometimes you can expect to achieve acceptance of the message, formation or change of attitude, and even behavior.

The nonverbal feedback in face-to-face interaction helps the speaker to correct and repeat messages that members of the listening audience do not understand. Questions addressed to a speaker or the give-and-take of dialogue also help to make understanding—acceptance of a message or the construction of a shared cognition—possible.

Even with face-to-face communication, you won't be able to attain the attitudinal and behavioral objectives as often as you will the cognitive objective. But you will be able to attain them more often than with other forms of communication. When you communicate face to face with members of publics, you can sense when they disagree, when they agree, and when they are silently at odds with you. You even can ask how they react to your message or what they would like you to know. Then you can take a position that is more acceptable to your listeners. Often, you or the managers you coach will even be persuaded to agree more with the public with whom you are speaking.

Remember, also, that interpersonal skills have great importance when you are trying to communicate the public's point of view back to your management. You will want to help management understand the public's position. It is even possible that your spoken argument will enable management to evaluate the public's view positively and to behave in a way that is consistent with what we call the public interest.

Which Programs?

Speeches and interpersonal communication skills have a place in all of the programs aimed at specific publics, especially when the programs have the two-way symmetric model of public relations as a framework. Some examples:

You and your managers prepare to meet personally with the press and hold press conferences—essential to symmetric media relations.

Members of your organization give speeches to community groups. They also have face-to-face interviews and dialogue sessions with community leaders and other citizens.

You speak at tours and open houses, help dedicate community facilities, visit school classes, and put on events for scouts and other youth groups.

Public relations practitioners and managers meet directly with members of activist publics, trying to negotiate compromise solutions to conflicts with consequences for the organization.

Government relations specialists meet with officials and members of key constituencies to present their organization's positions on policy issues. They also give numerous speeches to civic, professional, and political groups.

Specialists in educational relations and economic education set up speeches and small group sessions to facilitate interaction between students and organizational representatives.

Financial PR specialists talk with stockbrokers and give speeches to members of the financial community. They also plan the extensive spoken communication that takes place at the annual stockholders' meeting.

The fund raiser finds that personal contacts, speeches to alumni and supportive publics, and telephone calls are essential for raising money.

Communication Behavior of Publics

You or your organization's representative are likely to speak with members of all kinds of publics—high- and low-involvement; latent, aware, and active. Thus, it is important to know what kind of public you have before planning what you or the manager you coach will say.

Low-involvement publics will listen to someone speak if the presentation is entertaining, brief, and not too technical. Aware and active high-involvement publics can tolerate longer, less dramatic, and more technical speeches or discussions. They want the information. They listen carefully.

You may give limited attention to the teacher of a course outside your major who is not entertaining. But you probably approach a course in your major differently. If you believe that someday you will have to manage a public relations program, you listen fairly carefully to your PR instructor . . . even if he or she is having an off day.

Cost in Time and Money

The old saying ''words are cheap'' can be applied to spoken communication. Contrasted to messages prepared for the electronic media and for brochures or booklets, speeches and other oral messages don't cost a lot of money. Most of the expense comes from hiring the speechwriters.

At the same time, preparation of spoken messages can take considerable time. Look at the preparations we have suggested for a speech or press session. These activities must be planned and coordinated. Thus, you will find time budgeting techniques especially useful in planning spoken communication.

Evaluation

Because all of the communication effects described in Chapter 6 may be possible to achieve with spoken forms of communication, you may want to use all of the measures of these effects described in Chapter 9.

To measure whether communication took place, for example, you might:

Count the number of people who hear the speech.

Review the content of the press clippings that result from the meeting between the manager you coached and the press.

Keep track of the kinds of people who attend dialogue sessions.

Record the number of times you articulate the view of a public to your management.

In measuring the communication objective, you might also measure the quality of the speaker's presentation. Later in this chapter, after we have discussed how to prepare and deliver a speech, we will look at some methods for helping your speakers to improve their performance.

If you want to measure the four effects of communication—message retention, message acceptance, formation or change of an attitude, and behavior—you might administer a questionnaire to people who attend a speech or dialogue session. You could administer it right after the speech, you could mail it out later, or you could ask the questions in a telephone interview.

If you aren't able to use a questionnaire, take some informal measurement. Circulate among the audience after a speech. Listen to what people are talking about. Ask them

questions. If you are known to the audience, let an assistant who is not known ask the questions.

To evaluate the effect of your oral communication with management, listen to what your managers say to others. Do they remember what you said? Do they understand the public's view? Do they behave in ways that are consistent with the public's view?

To evaluate the effect of a press session, examine the content of the media to see if the message was communicated accurately and with understanding. Code articles to indicate whether the writer attached a positive, negative, or neutral evaluation to what your speaker said.

RESEARCHING AND ORGANIZING THE SPEECH

In a perceptive article on the "Care and Feeding of Speechwriters," Westinghouse public relations manager Jean Pope, formerly a speechwriter for Hill and Knowlton, offered a scenario of what too often happens:[1]

The chief executive officer tells the secretary, "I'm speaking to the Management Club March 14 on the future of business-labor relations in Britain. Have Bob prepare a speech for me by next week." The secretary dutifully calls the vice president for public affairs, who passes the job to the public relations manager, who assigns the task to a second-stringer in his department, who fails in her attempts to get an appointment with the CEO. Laboriously and without direction, she comes up with something she hopes is satisfactory. When the CEO finally gets around to reading the speech, he reworks it and gives it to the secretary to type half a day before he delivers it.

The speech, needless to say, is lackluster and completely forgettable. Says Pope: "The writing-by-committee has mangled the best parts of the speech. What's more, unrehearsed, it comes across flat and lifeless."[2]

The moral of the story is that:

1. Adequate planning must precede speech-making.
2. Writing and reviewing it are important group tasks.
3. The speechwriter must have access to the speaker.
4. Presentation of the speech should be rehearsed to assure that it will have the desired impact.

Let's look at the many facets of the job in greater detail.

Research

Anyone who has prepared a term paper has experienced the first phase of speechwriting: library research. Statements made about the topic should be reviewed in order to know what the main arguments are and what raw data are available. In addition to books and periodicals, make sure you check professional or trade journals and government publications for statistics and informed opinions that can lend credence to your presentation. Your own files are also important: You should be able to put your hands quickly on everything your organization's managers have written or said on the topic.

What's the "Big Idea"?

After you've gathered the data, but before you prepare an outline, the all-important question is, What is the main point we want to make with this speech? Just as the advertising copywriter must be able to reduce the entire message to a phrase, a slogan, or a headline, the speechwriter should be able to summarize the big idea of the speech in a single line: "XYZ Corporation believes high property taxes are driving business out of Central Valley" or "The main goal of the state Environmental Protection Agency during the next year is to clean up the air in our cities."

Deciding on that single thrust will help you to weed out information that may be interesting but that does not support or illustrate the main point. It may cause some tension with your spokesperson, since there may be pressure to "tell them about all of the wonderful things we're doing and all of the problems we think are important to overcome." Certainly, you should try to work in some background about the organization and its many concerns, but as one professional PR speechwriter succinctly puts it, one of the simple but hard-and-fast rules is to "keep your eye on the ball" at all times.[3]

Organizing and Outlining

To say that a good speech has an introduction, a body, and a conclusion is to say that, once again, it must be outlined the way you would organize a term paper or article. The concept can be summarized by that old saw: "Tell 'em what you're going to tell them; then tell 'em; and finally, tell 'em what you told them."

If a one-page outline—with the classical I., A., 1. a. format for arranging main and subordinate points—is submitted to the speaker for discussion and refinement beforehand, the writing task will be easier, and fewer alterations will have to be made on the completed script.

Working with the Speaker

By this point, it should be clear that the speechwriter must work with the speaker on every phase of developing the speech. The word choices, even the length and rhythm of the sentences, must be appropriate to the individual speaking style. The speaker must feel familiar enough with the supporting data to field questions and defend his or her views. And finally, the speaker must have a general confidence in the speech in order to give it with conviction. Ideally, the person selected to write a speech should have worked for some time in close conjunction with the speaker. If that is not the case, then the writer must have access to the speaker to go over the information, and there must be at least

The annual meeting, at which corporate officers must deliver prepared remarks and then field questions from the audience of stockholders. (Courtesy of Warner-Lambert)

one session in which the writer hears the script read by the speaker. That way, the words can be tailored to the speaker, and the speaker can develop the necessary trust in the writer.

The All-Important Introduction

"A funny thing happened to me on the way to the hotel tonight . . ."

Oh, yeah?

A funny thing happened to speechwriting in the past few decades: Speakers learned that audiences don't howl anymore over jokes lifted from books like *A Thousand and One Stories for Every Occasion*. We get enough formula jokes and canned laughter on television. And the contemporary audience is cynical enough to doubt that the quotation from Aristotle, Will Rogers, or John F. Kennedy is really one of the speaker's favorites, rather than something the speechwriter dug up for the occasion.

"The rule of thumb concerning a joke is threefold: the speaker can deliver it effectively; it flows out of the experience of the speaker; it is appropriate to the subject."[4] If those tests can be met, then certainly a moment of levity is an effective way to gain the attention and the empathy of the listener. The speechwriter might draw out an anecdote from the speaker during the first interview and attempt to shape it into a lively opening remark. If it falls flat in rehearsal, or if the speaker wants to open with something ad lib that is appropriate to the moment, then the humorous story is best left out of the script.

If the speech is to be serious in tone, an ominous opening statement might be appropriate: "Central Valley may be a ghost town ten years from now . . ."

Intriguing little-known facts can raise the curiosity of the listeners: "Every year, twenty-seven pounds of soot and dust particles fall on each of the citizens living in Central City. Fortunately, it falls a little at a time, and not all at once!''

Still another effective device is the revealing bit of personal history: ''This is the first time I've been back to Bloomington since I was graduated from college, and I have to admit the circumstances are a bit happier this time. Now I'm working for the government. When I left, the government wasn't so happy with me—as a student, I ran up a small fortune in parking fines right here on Campus Drive.'' (If it doesn't get a big laugh from the audience, at least it may help put the speaker at ease.)

How Much to Say?

A professional speechwriter put it succinctly: ''No one will get mad at a speaker who made a twenty-minute speech when he was scheduled for twenty-five minutes.''[5] The tolerance level of the typical audience, conditioned by half-hour television sit-coms, is not what it used to be. Even captive audiences (employees, fellow professionals . . . students in classrooms!) become restless when the big hand on the clock completes a full circle. If you've narrowed your topic sufficiently, you can be complete and still be brief. If you've been commissioned to fill an hour, why not plan to devote half of it to fielding questions?

DELIVERING THE SPEECH

When managers are going to address a friendly and familiar audience, they probably will not ask the PR department for help in preparing the speech. On the other hand, many managers attained their positions because they were superb engineers, planners, or economic analysts, not because they have a knack for getting an audience in the palms of their hands.

Even when the manager is a competent speaker, making an effective speech is not merely a matter of turning on the charm or reaching into a bag of oratorical tricks. One of the most important contributions the PR department can make, for example, is to re-

The internal training session, in which the department head prepares others to carry out company programs. This conference-seminar room in AT&T's Communication Center at Basking Ridge, N.J., makes use of visual aids and facilitates exchange of ideas among participants. (Reproduced with permission of AT&T)

search the composition of the audience in order to advise the speaker who the listeners are, what their interest level is, what they already know about the subject, and what kinds of questions they are likely to ask.

Provide Coaching

Some executives welcome coaching and preparation. Others are insulted to think they must be rehearsed and trained in order to perform adequately. It may be advisable, therefore, to make it official management policy that all speakers undergo a "prep session." Professional speech consultants, using videotape, are available to conduct such training.

One consultant suggests that the checklist for preparing a speaker begins with a discussion of the proper attire for the occasion.[6] Perhaps the topic can be overlooked in the case of a senior executive who routinely dresses in a three-piece pinstripe suit and silk tie. But it may be necessary to suggest that a scientist leave his loud sportcoat in the lab and venture out to speak at a professional meeting wearing a dark blazer and coordinated slacks. The PR department must do its homework: at certain conferences held in tropical resort areas, it is customary to wear good-looking golf attire, and the speaker in urban work clothes may make the audience and himself ill at ease.

Some managers allow that old bugaboo stage fright to become a self-fulfilling prophecy. They expect to be nervous and to stumble, and so they do. It may be so severe that the speaker experiences momentary paralysis. The public speaking volumes listed as Additional Reading at the end of this chapter all agree that a certain amount of apprehension is useful, because it gets the adrenalin running and pumps the speaker up to perform. If your manager has severe apprehension, a speech consultant may be used to teach him or her helpful relaxation techniques.

Polish During Rehearsal

During the rehearsal of a speech, help the speaker to slow up delivery of the first few lines. Mark the script to indicate where a breath can be taken. Try to implant a substitute self-fulfilling prophecy: "You're going to do great, because this is a well-prepared speech tailored to your style, and it's got some information that the audience really wants to hear."

Give the speaker an opportunity to perform before an in-house group, such as a regularly scheduled department meeting. Some organizations routinely make use of their video studios to tape dry runs of presentations, thus providing the speaker with valuable instant analysis. Stored copies of trial runs can also be used to train speakers in the future.

USING VISUAL AIDS

Notice that we didn't discuss visual aids earlier as a device for helping the speaker to overcome stage fright. Visual aids shouldn't be thrown in to compensate for a mediocre speaker. Visual aids should be used primarily because they make the presentation clearer, and second because they can add interest and variety.

The time to decide whether a visual aid will be useful is after the research and first draft are completed. Then the speechwriter must analyze whether some data lend themselves to graphic display, or if a slide show, film, or videotape might make a major point come to life.

Another major concern is whether the visual aid will be appropriate for the meeting room where it is to be used. If you plan to show sales figures and research expenditures using graphics on slide transparencies, make sure the room can be fully darkened. If charts and graphs are to be used, provide the speaker with an easel and cardboard-backed signboards that are nonreflecting so that they can be read no matter how harsh the lighting. (The best professional easels have a light source hanging from the top.)

Misuse of Visual Aids

Nothing is more annoying than the misuse of visual aids. Does the one card left on the easel for thirty minutes carry routine information that the audience didn't need to "see" in order to understand? This kind of presentation can insult them and lead to boredom. Conversely, is there so much information on the cards that the speaker must flip them before the audience has had a chance to digest the ideas? This can be especially upsetting.

Do the audience members or the speaker have difficulty in seeing the graphics and interpreting them from where they sit or stand? Maybe using a flip pad of blank paper and a felt tip pen to create fresh material would make the audience feel that the presentation was geared especially to its interests.

And remember, if your speaker is a dynamic person with a personality that can rivet the attention of the listeners, visual aids may actually detract from the presentation.

FEEDBACK AND EVALUATION OF THE SPEECH

With speakers who are so mechanical in their presentation that they can't or won't vary a word, then the PR department might as well use videotape to disseminate the message. One of the principal benefits of using a live spokesperson is that feedback received from listeners during the speech can be acknowledged and used to improve the audience's understanding of the topic.

During rehearsals, note whether the speaker is able to read perplexity on the faces of the audience. Help the speaker learn to stop and say, "Are you all familiar with the concept of 'front-end-loaded' funds? Let me explain briefly." Some speakers also need practice in order to avoid unwanted interruptions by perpetual question-raisers. Teach them a phrase such as, "I know this is a complicated subject, but I think it will be much clearer when I explain step by step, so I'll ask you please to hold your questions for just a few moments." These may seem like obvious devices to the practiced speaker, but it's surprising how many people have to be coached in order to master them.

PR students who have taken public speaking courses know that a speech-evaluation checklist can be a useful analytical tool. While it may not be politic to present your CEO with a "report card," the checklist can help the PR department to evaluate the speeches it prepares. Extra space or wide margins should be left after each item, so that additional specific comments can be added by the evaluator. You should tailor the form to your organization's specific needs, but an example is given in Exhibit 24–1.

Rarely will feedback be useful unless it is provided immediately and in an organized way. That's why the speech-evaluation form often works better than the verbal briefing you never seem to find time to hold until too many days later.

GETTING MORE MILEAGE FROM THE SPEECH

You may have followed every suggestion to the letter, and your speaker is ready to dazzle an audience . . . when an unpredicted ice storm makes travel hazardous, and two-thirds of the expected guests stay at home. If the speech was your total PR message, then you probably will end up far short of your objectives. But if you have planned multiple uses of the prepared material, success can still be yours.

As soon as the speechwriter has completed the final draft, for example, preparation of a simultaneous print press release

**EXHIBIT
24-1**

Speech Evaluation

Date   Audience

----------------   --------------------------------

Speaker   Evaluator

    --------------------   -----------------------

Room was properly set up for presentation.

Introduction of speaker was clear and adequate.

Speaker's dress and bearing were appropriate to occasion.

Voice level was satisfactory to the audience.

Speaker established rapport with audience.

Credibility of speaker was established.

Eye contact was maintained.

Overdependence on prepared script was avoided.

Opening section got attention.

Topic area and main point were clearly established.

Main points were repeated and emphasized.

Topic was clearly summarized and point driven home.

Ending section left audience with desired reaction.

Audience was engaged throughout speech.

Feedback was acknowledged and corrections made.

Opportunity for questions was provided.

Visual aids were properly set up and used.

Visual aids provided desired emphasis and clarity.

Speaker was comfortable using visual aids.

Audience reaction to visual aids was positive.

Additional suggestions:

should begin. (One speechwriter even suggests that the press release should be written before the speech, in order to force the speaker and the speechwriter to come up with key thoughts that can be packaged as news.[7]) The release, along with a text of the speech, can be provided to the wire services and other news organizations in the area ahead of time. The PR person should be prepared to put the speaker in phone contact with the media immediately after the speech, especially if reporters who had expressed an interest in attending were not able to be there.

And don't forget the reprint value of a speech. If the names of those attending a convention where your spokesperson appeared are available from the sponsors, you may want to send a reprint to each, with a cover letter reminding them of the impact the presentation had on the convention. A device that has special impact is the reprinting of the speech in a quality booklet format, with a picture of the speaker preceding the text. A commencement speech by your CEO, or a keynote address to a professional or trade meeting, might warrant such prestigious treatment.

ORGANIZING A SPEAKERS BUREAU

At some point it's going to hit you: "We're sending somebody out there to speak to some organization almost every week." Maybe it's time to set up a speakers bureau. Here's what it takes to set up an ongoing service for presenting your organization's ideas to other organizations through a team of trained speakers:

A program to identify managers in your organization who are willing speakers. They must not only do the job well, they also have to enjoy going out to meet with Kiwanians, Daughters of the American Revolution, or the Association of Professional Whatevers.

A set of topics suitable for any and all groups: "The New Technology" . . . "The History of Mining" . . . "How to Prepare for a Job in the Aerospace Industry" . . . "Why We Must Explore Outer Space." All of these topics, of course, must relate to your organization's goals and interests. The target group expects some sort of "sell," although they expect it to be "soft."

A system of publicizing and promoting the speakers and their topics. In most parts of the country, the phone company's bill-stuffer newsletter includes an occasional item about "interesting programs for your club—just call your local Bell office to arrange a speaker." Utilities, along with the monthly bill, also promote "science magicians" and experts in various fields for school and club appearances. Another good device is to mail flyers to school superintendents and principals, who are always looking for free educational programs. National headquarters of professional and fraternal organizations usually are willing to provide mailing lists of presidents or program chairpersons of local chapters, making it easy for you to get your descriptive brochure to them.

A booking person. One secretary or administrative assistant in the public relations department should be responsible for handling all speaker requests and assuring that obligations are fulfilled.

Most universities maintain a list of professors and their interest areas, so that groups requesting presentations on very specialized topics of interest can be matched with speakers. Large corporations provide speakers in wholesale quantities: the Western Electric Company has 500 speakers working out of fifty-two local bureaus around the country.[8]

Dealing with Brushfire Topics

Sometimes a special speaker service is set up to deal with a very limited public relations situation. When the state legislature is considering a bill that would limit duck hunting, sportsmen's organizations may set up a special task force to go around the state speaking on "Our American Heritage: The Sport of Duck Hunting." Whenever First Amendment guarantees are threatened, journalism and public relations groups usually field speakers to address civic and school groups about "Our American Heritage: Freedom of the Press."

When the speakers bureau is set up on a "brushfire" basis, phone contacts with school administrators and civic groups listed in the telephone directory can be used to arrange several quick bookings for speakers.

Use by the Military

Speaker materials are provided to all military commanders in order to increase the visibility and reputation of the military in the community. Each service branch has an information office that prepares stock speeches and speaker materials for use on Veterans Day, Memorial Day, the Fourth of July, and other special occasions when military personnel may be called upon to speak. While many college students may never have had an opportunity to hear such speeches, they are regular fixtures of public gatherings in thousands of communities around the country where military bases and large government contractors are prime employers.

PREPARING MANAGERS FOR PRESS CONTACTS

Given the choice between speaking to 500 Rotarians or just half a dozen reporters, most managers would choose the vast audience of 500. There may be an awful lot of them, but at least you know they won't bite.

As awesome as a major speaking engagement may seem, the speaker has a great deal of control over the situation. The press, on the other hand, insists on making its own rules. And, the impact of speaking to a half

dozen reporters is potentially much greater than addressing a huge hall full of people. It can be even riskier than a formal debate, because the rules seem to be made up as the interview or press conference goes along.

Frederick Knapp, president of a consulting firm that specializes in preparing executives to appear in public, calls the media interview the most challenging of speaking appearances because of the probing questions and the necessity of thinking clearly under pressure.[9] Keeping the main point in mind and avoiding getting sidetracked takes concentration.

Another key problem is the fact that most managers can't visualize what a story will look like in print or sound like on the air. The PR practitioner should keep clips showing the results of interviews where the spokesperson for an organization understood the task and provided quotes that worked well for the organization, along with other articles that illustrate how the speaker's ineptitude led to embarrassing coverage in the press.

After reviewing the clips, you can stage a mock interview or press conference for your manager, using PR department personnel as reporters. Throw a little of everything at the speaker: rudeness, interruptions, hostile questions, no-win questions ("When is your company going to stop polluting the river?"), and incessantly returning to previous topics the speaker feels have already been addressed. If you try everything imaginable on the speaker in practice, the actual interview may seem more tolerable and manageable.

Before and after the mock interview, try to impress the following guidelines upon your spokesperson:

1. Be brief. Print reporters who take longhand notes will choose quotes that are succinct and to-the-point. Broadcast reporters need to tape only a few sharp sentences for use. Interviewees who ramble on will be "paraphrased" instead of quoted directly—if they are quoted at all.

2. Avoid being "cagey" about information. Don't ask that something be "off the record"—nobody can guarantee it. "No comment" makes the speaker look evasive. Better to say, "I am not at liberty to release that information at this time," giving the reason, if possible. If you don't know something, instead of pretending to be secretive, tell the reporters you aren't sure of the facts or figures, but you'll have your PR staff check it out and get in touch with the press as soon as possible. Most important of all, don't get caught telling a half-truth. An enterprising reporter may check it out and find that you were revealing only part of the story.

3. Maintain a firm but cordial stance. If the reporters are on a first-name basis with you, address them by first name, too. Otherwise use Mr. or Ms. Don't show favoritism to one reporter who is a friend or who represents a "friendly" news medium: The other reporters may unconsciously or consciously retaliate for being put on less-favored status. Above all, don't lose your temper, no matter how boorish a reporter may become. If you threaten a member of the press in any way, that fact will probably become the lead of the news story, not the information about your organization that you hoped to present.

4. When asked a negative question, don't give a knee-jerk, defensive response. Think quickly about the topic raised by the question. What relevant facts can you discuss about your organization's performance in this area? As we have stressed, in the symmetric model it is important to answer negative questions honestly, truthfully, and fully. If your organization has done something wrong, explain what happened and tell what is being done to rectify the situation. Without ignoring the substance of the question, try to turn the main substance of the reply into a "plus" for your point of view.

5. Keep calm and try to manage a smile: You're only doing your job, and the reporters are only doing theirs.

EFFECTIVE INTERPERSONAL COMMUNICATION

In an award-winning series of institutional advertisements, the Sperry Rand Corp. emphasized the importance of training its employees to be good listeners.[10] As more organizations embrace the two-way symmetric model of communication, they realize that listening is a communication skill that is as important as speaking effectively.

What this means is that PR departments, which traditionally have viewed themselves as disseminators of public information, must devote more energy to facilitating genuine two-way communication, both within the organization and between the organization and its many publics. One PR expert suggests that corporations may have to depend on a third party—a consulting firm specializing in group discussions—to open a true dialogue with a suspicious and frustrated public.[11]

There are several activities a consultant might help the PR department institute to encourage better interpersonal communication, including:

Small group sensitivity training within departments.

An ombudsman program to handle complaints and suggestions both from employees and individuals outside the organization.

Focus sessions in which representatives of a public are encouraged to discuss their impressions and questions about the organization and its role.

One of the problems with spoken communication between any two parties is that verbal understandings must be translated into action. The competent PR practitioner must learn to write a "confirming letter" that provides a written record of an interview, conference, or meeting, and that helps the practitioner to assure that the organization's objectives are being achieved. Those who become adept at such correspondence usually find that they have a hand in the "creation of reality" within their organization—and that translates to power and influence!

In addition to the public speaking course available at most universities, students who plan to enter the field of public relations can benefit from a course in human relations offered by a communication department. In such a course, students learn how they are perceived by others, how to develop interpersonal relationships, and how to work within a group to perform a task and to realize a common goal.

NOTES

1. Jean Pope, "Care and Feeding of Speechwriters," *Public Relations Journal* (May 1979):6–9.
2. Pope.
3. Edwin F. Brennan, "Five Rules for Speechwriters," *Public Relations Journal* (May 1979):10.
4. Pope.
5. Brennan.
6. Frederick J. Knapp, "Prepare Your CEO to Meet his Publics," *Public Relations Journal* (May l979):11–13.
7. Nariman N. Karanjia, "The Nitty-Gritty of Speechwriting," *Public Relations Journal* (May 1980):17–19.
8. "Speakers Bureaus Can Amplify PR Impact," *IABC News* (December 1980):1, 5.
9. Knapp.
10. Sperry Rand Listening Program, 1981 PRSA Silver Anvil Award winner.
11. Kendrick E. Fenderson, "Telling Is Out, Dialogue Is In," *Public Relations Journal* (July 1979):32–34.

ADDITIONAL READING

Baird, John E., Jr., *Speaking for Results: Communication by Objectives* (New York: Harper & Row, 1981).

Barrett, Harold, *Speaking Practically: An Introduction to Public Speaking* (New York: Holt, Rinehart and Winston, 1980).

Brooks, William D., *Public Speaking* (Menlo Park, Calif.: The Benjamin/Cummings Publishing Co., 1980).

Burson-Marsteller, *The Executive Speechmaker: A Systems Approach* (New York: Foundation for Public Relations Research and Education, 1980).

Hunt, Gary T., *Public Speaking* (Englewood Cliffs, N.J.: Prentice-Hall, 1981).

Minnick, Wayne C., *Public Speaking* (Boston: Houghton Mifflin, 1979).

Rein, Irving J., *The Public Speaking Book* (Glenview, Ill.: Scott, Foresman, 1981).

Verderber, Rudolph F., *The Challenge of Effective Speaking* (Belmont, Calif.: Wadsworth, 1979).

25

BROCHURES, FACT SHEETS, AND DIRECT MAIL

Advertising, promotions, posters, displays, and special events are used to alert the public to ideas and programs. Brochures and fact sheets are designed to go into greater detail about the issue. They provide information that can be saved, stored, referred to, and acted upon. In previous chapters we mentioned the desirability of passing out or making available brochures and fact sheets to reinforce information presented through the press briefing, the speech, or an audiovisual presentation. Another important channel is the postal service, which is used for direct-mail distribution of mass messages.

The mailing list is one of the most valuable tools a PR department can use. The mass media deliver thousands of unwanted members of subpublics that do not interest your organization. But mailing lists target much more precisely the audience you want to reach: homeowners, apartment dwellers, boating enthusiasts, hunters, coin collectors, registered voters, users of credit cards, opera patrons, senior citizens, supporters of women's liberation, opponents of women's lib-

eration, conservationists, left-handed bowlers.

Some mailing lists cost thousands of dollars, especially those that identify high-income families with special characteristics. Other lists can be bought more cheaply from magazines aimed at hobbyists or regional audiences. Many organizations, such as noncompeting arts and cultural organizations, routinely exchange mailing lists at no cost to either organization. Commercial direct-mail houses, for a handsome fee, will take care of everything from obtaining the appropriate mailing lists to stuffing and mailing the envelopes for you.

Of course, any organization should carefully develop its own mailing lists by making sure that every person participating in an event sponsored by the organization, every citizen who writes the organization for information, every contributor, every customer, every personal friend of management, every elected official is put in a card file or on a computer list to receive mailings that fall in his or her interest areas.

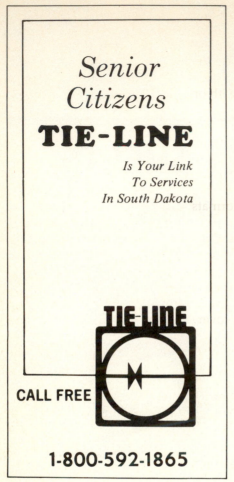

Brochure for the South Dakota Tie-Line, shown with related materials rendered in similar graphic style. (All materials produced for the Tie-Line were prepared by Media One Inc. of Sioux Falls, S.D.)

Varied Names

The range of names for direct-mail items suggests the variety that is possible: circulars, folders, booklets, pamphlets, monographs, tracts, catalogs, packets, portfolios, bulletins, broadsheets, manifestos—not to mention pseudo-magazines, pseudo-newspapers, and pseudo-newsletters. Because so many of these terms are associated with the hoopla of marketing and promotion, public relations practitioners working for government depart-

ments, public utilities, and regulated industries often prefer to use the more dignified term ''fact sheet'' to identify any printed matter that provides background information about the organization and/or one of its projects.

Some examples of fact sheets:

The state government of South Dakota distributes a four-page brochure at meetings of senior citizens to describe a special phone service that enables the elderly to call the state capital on a no-charge 800 number for information about Social Security benefits, consumer fraud, homemaker services, taxes, Medicare, and legal services. As shown in Exhibit 25–1, included with the brochure are a wallet card and a gummed sticker so that the number can be affixed to the telephone.

Branches of the armed services issue fact sheets in convenient, three-hole-punched, looseleaf format, on such varied topics as "The Chaplain Service" and "Burial in a National Cemetery."

The National Bureau of Standards issues regular bulletins on the progress of research and development on such projects as cardiac pacemaker batteries, natural gas pipelines, and resistivity standards for silicon power devices.

Federal and state health agencies, as well as hospitals, health-maintenance organizations, professional medical organizations, and insurance companies, offer printed material on every disease, physical ailment, or mental problem imaginable.

Common Formats

The format you decide on depends upon the needs of the occasion, the creativity of the PR department, and, of course, the size of the budget (see Exhibit 25–2).

Because the standard "legal-size" mailing envelope is approximately 4 1/4 by 9 1/2 inches, and the most common precut sheet size used in duplicating and quick-print processes is 8 1/2 by 11 inches, it is not surprising that the most popular mailer is what printers call a "two-fold folder" consisting of six panels, each 3 5/8 inches wide and 8 1/2 inches high. When a standard printing press and the standard 23-by-45-inch paper stock are used, a printer can neatly fit ten such brochures per sheet with a minimal loss of paper through trimming.

A common variation is the four-panel single-fold brochure. Another configuration favored by the travel business is the 8 1/2-by-22-inch sheet, which appears to be the standard six-panel format until it is fully opened to reveal a "poster-sized" inside spread. Still another option is the two-fold, six-panel folder with one of the end panels trimmed to as little as 1 1/2 inches so that it forms a "teaser" flap that partly overlaps another page. Price information or copy that intrigues the readers enough so that they will continue reading inside, might be placed on this small surface. Exhibit 25–2 shows the common brochure formats, how they fold, and how the panels can be numbered for easy reference.

Typically, the right-hand panel on one side of the 8 1/2-by-11 sheet is designed as the cover. The left-hand panel on the same side of the sheet folds around to become the second panel seen by the reader after opening the cover. The middle panel of the same side of the sheet thus becomes the "back" side. Because it occupies the least advantageous position, it may be used for supplementary information. Or it may be left blank, except for a return-address section, so that the brochure can be mailed without an envelope.

The three panels on the reverse side of the sheet read in one of three ways:

As a single "poster" spread.

As a left-hand single page seen first in conjunction with the inside cover flap, then in conjunction with a two-panel spread at center-right.

As three separate and individual panels reading left to right.

The decision, of course, depends on the amount of information, the personality of the design, and whether or not you want the information to be presented in a linear or random fashion.

When the object is to keep the cost down to between five and fifteen cents per brochure and to present the reader with a familiar artifact, the formats above work best.

EXHIBIT 25-2

8½ ×11 Brochure Formats

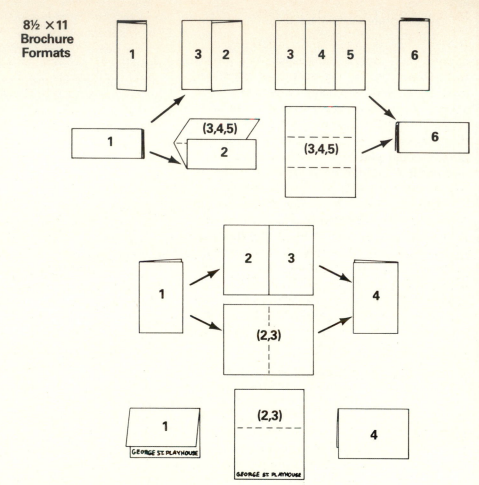

Here are some standard formats for brochures, all using 8½ by 11 sheets of paper. The two-fold, six-panel format may be horizontal or vertical. When the one-fold, four-panel format is used horizontally (bottom), an off-center fold provides a "teaser" that is visible when reading page 1 as well as when viewing the pages 2–3 center spread.

If you wish to intrigue the reader or achieve a lavish feeling with your message, you may decide to work with a printer to develop a nonstandard format. A particularly intriguing, if expensive, format is the standard two-fold brochure with an extra flap glued on the right-hand inside panel to form a pocket that holds a sheaf of single sheets in varied heights and colors.

The single-sheet, unfolded broadside is preferable for meeting announcements, grand openings, sale promotions, and handbills to be passed out at rallies. The uncomplicated format suggests a certain directness, urgency and lack of pretense. Conversely, any multipage format that is glued, stitched, or stapled at the back becomes a booklet and has a sense of permanency. Having attracted an audience to a meeting with handbills, you might then put a durable pamphlet into their hands for more careful consideration.

MANAGEMENT CONSIDERATIONS

Public relations practitioners often call brochures, fact sheets, and direct mail ''controlled'' media. The practitioner does not have to tailor the message to pass the gatekeepers of news media such as newspapers or television. The organization's public relations objectives need not be compromised. In other words, you can write what you want and put it directly in the hands of the person who wants to read it.

Thus, the practitioner always can select ''retention'' as an objective for one of these printed media, as well as the ''exposure'' to the message, the objective we have termed most realistic for communication through various media. When the brochure or fact sheet reaches an aware or active public, the practitioner also can expect it to affect the cognitions of the readers, and sometimes their attitudes and behaviors.

Best for Actively Communicating Publics

These printed publications provide an excellent way to get a message to actively communicating, information-seeking, publics. But they are an ineffective way to reach passive publics. Readers generally must send for the publications or seek them out and pick them up from information racks, exhibits, or display tables. Members of active publics will do that, but members of passive publics seldom take the initiative.

When sent through the mail, brochures and fact sheets may reach passively communicating publics. However, passive publics must exert more effort to read a direct-mail piece than they would listening to radio or television. They may open what they consider junk mail, and then simply not read it.

A Staple of the Public-Information Model

Like most public relations media, brochures and fact sheets can be used with any of the four PR models. Because of the informational nature of these formats, however, practitioners of the public-information model probably use them most. The National Institutes of Health, for example, produce numerous brochures to inform people about nearly every disease.

Brochures and fact sheets also have great value in the two-way asymmetric model, as a way of communicating the organization's position to an activist public. The Hooker Chemical Company produced several brochures about the Love Canal problem, for example, and sent them to environmental and governmental publics.

The symmetric practitioner must remember that the position stated in a fact sheet or brochure should not be the organization's final position. A tentative position can be stated in a printed publication that is sent to adversary publics. The organization should be willing to negotiate that position, however, after the active public has had a chance to respond.

Brochures and fact sheets are versatile enough to be used in all types of specialized programs. Brochures describe benefits that are part of an employee relations program. They are placed in press kits to give reporters background information as part of media relations. They are given to educational and community publics who tour a plant or office. And they can be used to give financial information to stockholders and brokers.

A Moderately Costly Medium

Brochures and fact sheets must be printed, and that means more cost and time for preparation than, for example, press releases or audio tapes. But they are not as costly as many other media, such as videotapes, magazines, or newspapers. You must budget money and time needed, but the preparation of brochures and fact sheets won't overtax your resources.

Brochures and fact sheets are no exception to the rules for evaluation. Use a readability formula or signaled stopping technique to see if your publication is right for the target public. Measure retention, acceptance, and effect on attitudes and behavior using the methods described in Chapter 9.

DEVELOPING THE LAYOUT

Arranging information for multipanel presentation creates many design situations that don't occur when you're dealing with the single rectangle of the poster or advertisement. If the brochure is to be disseminated from a rack or holder where it shares space with similar messages, the front cover must be arranged with title or "teaser" on the top third of the front panel—just as magazine cover designers have to put intriguing information at the top, where it can be seen peeking out over its competitors for attention. While the cover should be unique in some respect, the designer cannot forget that it must be related stylistically to the remaining panels through consistent use of a related type and art materials.

Organizing the text presents another challenge. Essentially, you write the copy to make a complete message in linear form, as for a news release or a feature article. Then it must be divided into suitable segments for each panel. Key sentences should be highlighted by placing them in display type instead of regular text. Care must be taken to keep the presentation balanced, with approximately the same number of titles or headlines on each panel, or a multipanel overline holding the text together.

Selecting the Art

Depending on how many appeals or how many examples you want to provide in one publication, you may decide to use several small pieces of art—line drawings or photos— or you may feel that the impact of a single picture will carry the entire message. For a leaflet decrying the fact that many unwanted pets must be put to death each year because nobody will adopt them, the startling statistic ("One out of three cats in Ourtown will be 'put to sleep' this year") might be most effective if reversed (light lettering over dark image) and placed right over the picture of a cute, furry little kitten.

Will you need to include a coupon, so that the reader can request more information or mail in a contribution? Ideally, it should be on a separate slip of paper, so that the main message will not be mutilated once the coupon is removed. Make sure that the type, the art, and the slogan of the main brochure are echoed on the insert. That way they will relate stylistically when they are together, but each also can stand alone. If the budget dictates that the coupon must be torn from the brochure, put it on the flap farthest from the cover, and make sure no important information is removed from the main message when the coupon is torn out.

Some Do's and Don't's

There may always be good reasons for ignoring accepted rules and practices of design. Nonetheless, the following advice can spare you considerable trial and error:

Resist the temptation to design an entire brochure so that it reads sideways—that is, so that the 8 1/2-inch measure is the width and the pages are flipped from the bottom. The format is useful when you must present statistical information in tables that are wide because there are many columns of figures. But, ordinarily, it is perceived as "odd" and rather annoying. Never mix horizontal and vertical makeup if you want the reader to get all the way through the multipanel layout.

Don't tilt the main title on the cover panel ninety degrees, unless it is one or two simple and easy-to-recognize words such as "We need you" or "Go Navy!" A complex title such as "Ten Reasons Why You Must Support Land Reform" should be run in orthodox fashion. At most, tip it at a thirty-degree angle if a bit of excitement is desired.

The information on the cover should either intrigue the reader or clearly label the topic of the contents. The development of the concept begins through the text that is inside. Usually, the cover is most effective if it is approximately one-third type and two-thirds illustration or visual relief (white space). Sometimes, of course, impact is achieved by totally filling the cover space with super-sized type that boldly confronts the reader: "The five minutes you spend reading this pamphlet could save your life!"

Some element on each and every panel should "pull" the reader on from the previous panel: an illustration, a headline, a boxed item, a statistical table, or a variation in the layout. Reading an all-text message is hard work; the reader needs incentive.

Strive for equilibrium. A brochure should not be top-heavy, bottom-heavy, right- or left-heavy, front-loaded, or crammed at the back. If your only copy adds up to the equivalent of three pages of text, use white space and wider margins in order to spread it out evenly. Avoid the device of dumping a gratuitous piece of art in at the end in order to fill.

Is this one of a "family" of messages from your organization? If so, don't forget to use devices that will make the family resemblance obvious: the organization's logo and slogan, distinctive color or border devices, and familiar typefaces.

Liven the presentation with separate boxed or bordered items such as maps, directions, "how-to" explanations, and lists. A brochure is supposed to have a longer lifetime than other messages. Nothing assures longevity more than the inclusion of vital information that the recipients realize they may need to use at a later date.

The question-and-answer format never seems to outlive its usefulness. It is just about the simplest and most recognizable way to draw the reader in to the material. It is especially effective when the Q. lines appear in larger or bolder type. Questions should be written in an intriguing, punchy style, with a "What if?" or "How come?" aspect that the reader absolutely must resolve before going on. The Q-and-A format may fall flat, however, when the questions are loaded or petty. ("Why don't the conservatives care about the little man?")

If you can afford to spend a bit more, spot color will dress up a brochure . . . unless you splotch it around with wild abandon. Try using a dark-blue ink throughout for instance; render a title in red for emphasis; or obtain a shading effect by having the printer back one entire panel with a halftone screen to give the brochure extra snap. Restraint and good taste are usually preferable to gratuitous excitement, however. When in doubt, have your printer show you examples of work done in the past. If it has a quality look, you might want to try colored paper stock or spot color on some of your text. Exhibit 25-3 shows some examples of impressive and varied brochures and fact sheets.

WORKING WITH THE PRINTER

Since almost every PR practitioner must design print messages, a working acquaintance with typography and printing is helpful—as we can appreciate both here and in the next chapter.

It is a waste of both your time and the printer's if you have not sufficiently thought out what it is you want printed. It helps greatly if you have in hand rough layouts or samples of jobs similar to what you are looking for. On the other hand, the worst approach you can take, unless you have an unlimited budget, is to come to a printer with the job so firmly worked out in your mind

EXHIBIT
25-3

PHILIP MORRIS INDUSTRIAL

8901 NORTH KILDEER COURT   P.O. BOX 23900   BROWN DEER, WISCONSIN 53223   TELEPHONE (414) 352-3500

FACT SHEET

PHILIP MORRIS INDUSTRIAL

Headquarters: Brown Deer, Wisconsin
President & Chief Executive Officer: William D. McCoy

Philip Morris Industrial Incorporated is one of the six operating
Incorporated and consists of eight companies in the chemical, pa
dustries. These companies operate 14 plants in the U.S. and on
panies are: Polymer Industries; Armstrong Products Co.; Wikolin P
Paper Co.; Plainwell Paper Co.; Wisconsin Tissue Mills; Milprint an
companies operates in highly specialized markets. PMI's total e
the companies range in size from $8 million to $90 million. Phili
four groups.

CHEMICAL GROUP
Polymer Industries

Headquarters: Greenville, South Carolina
Plant Locations: Greenville, South Carolina; Stamford, Conr
Vice President & General Manager: Bartholomew J. Twome

Polymer produces   micals for the textile indust
in   clude coatings and adhe
                           re sensitive packaging, o

                    rsaw, Indiana
                  : Thomas J. Scattolo

                r coatings that car
              d on such items as
                ms of cans for fo
                ant than a galva
              rmstrong also pr
              hlike the plants
              o polutants int

            n, West Ge
          f L. Kritzle

            atings to
          rs, a fe
          de pro

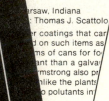

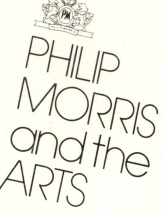

PHILIP MORRIS and the ARTS

Remarks by
George Weissman
Chairman of the Board and
Chief Executive Officer

that you are totally inflexible. Printers will accommodate you, but it may mean jobbing out parts of the project that they can't handle, and you will pay a premium price.

Contact three or four printers far in advance of the time when the work must be done, and obtain samples of their work. You may find one printer who is already doing jobs similar to what you want, which translates into cost savings. Find out what typesetting and other services each printer handles in the shop and what has to be sent to an outside supplier. Time is lost and the price increases every time something must be sent outside. The printer may not want to divulge this information, but if you obtain two or three competitive bids, it will show up in disparities between fairly standard items such as typesetting and binding.

Be sure to let the printer know if it's a one-shot job or whether you will bring similar work periodically. You may get a better price on return business, especially if the printer can save certain graphic materials you intend to reuse.

The printer will need a day or two to work up the bid. Estimating is a fairly exact business, taking into account the normal office and plant overhead that must be apportioned among all the jobs, plus hourly costs of running each piece of machinery involved in your job. It is always useful to ask for a "breakdown bid," which indicates how the price differs depending upon the grade of paper, the type of ink, the number of pictures, the multiples of thousands of copies, and the use of spot color. If you have a limited budget, you may have to play off one item against another: Take a better grade of paper and sacrifice the second color of ink, for example.

Write a Careful Contract

Before signing the printer's contract, check three important areas:

1. How much time will it take from the day you deliver all the copy until you receive the printer's proofs? How long will you have to correct and return the proofs? Make sure you will have an opportunity to make a final check of the corrected material before it goes to press. To guarantee that you and the printer understand what you expect in terms of turnaround time, work out a production schedule that shows how many days each of you has for each step in the typesetting, layout, and checking process.
2. How much material can you correct or change without paying extra? Some printers allow up to 10 percent without penalty. Others charge for everything. You should be able to make "normal" corrections, plus a few changes of headlines that don't please you, without paying extra.
3. Where is the job to be delivered? If the contract doesn't specify, then the probable answer is the end of the printer's loading dock. If your publication is to be mailed, you may wish to contract with a printer who has the capability of preparing material for postal delivery and mailing it, thus saving you the bother.

Learn the Basics

You'll be able to work much more closely and effectively with your printer if you learn the basics of typography and printing by taking a graphics course while you are in college. You can teach yourself the basic nomenclature using the additional readings at the end of this chapter.

A selection of brochures and fact sheets distributed by Philip Morris and its subsidiaries shows the great variety of formats possible, depending upon the audience and the function of the publication. Fact sheets describing industrial subsidiaries and the parent company's involvement in the arts are modest black-and-white sheets presented in a straightforward manner. Brochures promoting product lines are much more imaginative, using color, cut-outs, and odd folds—one brochure for Miller beer even has small packets of barley, corn grits, and hops glued to the inside back cover. (Courtesy Philip Morris Incorporated)

FLASH

ABCDEFGHIJKLM
NOPQRSTUVWXY
Z abcdefghijklmn
opqrstuvwxyz 12
34567890&?!$ß
£《()》~°° ˉˉ

FOLIO LIGHT

ABCDEFGHIJ
KLMNOPQRS
TUVWXYZ ab
cdefghijklmnop
qrstuvwxyz123
4567890&?!ß£$
˘ ;○《 ˉˉ

FOLIO MEDIUM

ABCDEFGHIJ
KLMNOPQRS
TUVWXYZ ab
cdefghijklmnop
qrstuvwxyz123
4567890&?!ß£
$()˘˘˘ˉ

EXHIBIT
25–4

Folio Light Bauer

E1 a E1 a E1 a
35-66-CN   35-66-L   35-54-CN   35-48-CN   35-48
(421)   (422) B   (431) B   (441) B   (19

Folio Medium Bauer

E1 a E1 a
31-66-CN   31-66-L   31-54-CN   31-54-
(434) N   (435)   (436) N   (437)

Folio Medium Extended Bauer

E1 a E1 a
75-66-CN   75-66-L   75-54-CN   75-54-
(447) B   (448) B   (449) B   (450) B

Folio Bold Bauer

E1 a E1
32-66-CN   32-66-L   32-54-CN
(460) B   (461) L   (462) B

Folio Extra B

ABCDEFG
KLMNOP
TUVWXY
bcdefgh
nopqrst
xyz 123
90&?!ß

35 FOLIO ME

Flash Ea1 Ea1
       36-CLN 36-24-CLN
       (77) B

Ea1 Ea1 Ea1 Eat Eat
35-14-CLN 35-12-CLN 35-10-CLN 35-8-CLN
(432)   (19531) B (19534)

Artists

AR

FAR–1

Farming

You'll want to have a working knowledge of printing methods, artwork reproduction, typesetting, and type characteristics.

Printing Methods • Offset, the predominant method used today, gives a flat, even image, and reproduction of art is inexpensive. Letterpress—which some specialized printers still provide—gives a sharper, glossier look. Gravure is used for large jobs where high-quality reproduction of color photographs is important.

Artwork Reproduction • Line drawings, which have no intermediate tones of gray, can be reproduced quickly and cheaply in photo offset, and they can be put directly on the final layout. However, continuous-tone art, including photographs, must be made into a halftone screen, so that the image is created by a pattern of dots that will ink properly.

Typesetting • Some special display types are still set mechanically or even by hand. But most text and display type today is handled through an electronic process called phototypesetting. The material is typed into a computer, which takes care of all spacing and word division, and the finished type comes out of a printer on strips of paper, ready to be pasted directly onto the layout sheet.

Type Characteristics • Every typeface has special characteristics: plain, fancy, bold, light, *italic* (slanted), or roman (straight up and down). Each has a "personality" as well: masculine, feminine, humorous, serious, pompous, dignified. And most types belong to a "family" that includes bold, bolder, boldest, light, lighter, lightest, italic, and roman variations on the same basic design. To the person just getting acquainted with type, the printer's specimen book is as exciting to peruse as the Sears, Roebuck "wish book." Exhibit 25–4 gives an idea of that excitement.

ADDITIONAL READING

Craig, James, *Designing with Type: A Basic Course in Typography* (New York: Watson-Guptill, 1971).

Hanson, Glenn, *How to Take the Fits out of Copyfitting* (Ft. Morgan, Colo.: Mul-T-Rul Co., 1967).

Hodgson, Richard S., *The Dartnell Direct Mail and Mail Order Handbook* (Chicago: Dartnell Corp., 1976).

International Paper Pocket Pal, 12th ed. (New York: International Paper Co., 1980).

Jones, Gerre, *How to Prepare Professional Design Brochures* (New York: McGraw-Hill, 1976).

Nelson, Roy Paul, *The Design of Advertising* (Dubuque, Iowa: Wm. C. Brown, 1977).

Turnbull, Arthur, and Russell Baird, *The Graphics of Communications* (New York: Holt, Rinehart and Winston, 1975).

Examples of type specimen books and line art (clip art) services. (Top left courtesy Letraset USA, Inc.; bottom left courtesy the Ron Gablon Graphic Archives)

26

NEWSLETTERS, NEWSPAPERS, AND MAGAZINES

Industry and government have long appreciated the need to inform their workers, their customers, and their fellow professionals about what they are doing. They do so through publications modeled after the most successful public media, particularly newspapers and newsmagazines.

Organizations such as the International Association of Business Communicators are working to improve business, industrial, and government publications through workshops, professional meetings for editors and writers, and newsletters. (In fact, the IABC's *Communication World* is a newsletter that carries articles about how to improve newsletters.)

Today, almost every company and organization publishes at least one newsletter or magazine, and some have as many as a dozen aimed at various internal and external audiences. The "house organ" or employee publication is a newspaper or magazine designed principally for an internal audience. Industrial publications, company publications, and

"the business press" are terms usually associated with vehicles packaged primarily for external audiences. Trade publications are aimed at segments of the professionals in a specific area of manufacturing or service, such as *Toy Trade News*, *Hardware Age*, and *Office Products Industry Report*.

Publications issued by nonprofit organizations usually must manage simultaneously to look competent and yet not too extravagant. Their editors often prefer merely to call them newsletters. Typically, they have an audience composed of a combination of alumni, academics, contributors, legislators, lobbyists, bureaucrats, industrial leaders, and clergy.

Often the word *News* or *Newsletter* is simply appended to an organization's name to create the publication title. Or the word *Weekly* or *Monthly*. Other commonly used names strive for generality, universality, or all-inclusiveness: *Update*, *Outlook*, *Overview*, *Action*, *Perspective*, *Reporter*, *Scene*, and *Review*.

Whatever the name, the publication usually has two well-defined roles:

1. To present special information to a special audience (the term ''special-audience publication'' is used by some magazine specialists).
2. To positively reinforce cognitions and attitudes about the sponsoring organization.

SELECTING THE FORMAT

Many PR departments have been putting out their special-audience publications in the same formats for so long that they haven't considered the options. Not that change for the sake of change alone is good. But each format has its strong points.

Newspapers

The tabloid four- or five-column newsprint format is relatively inexpensive and easy to produce. It is well suited to organizations that have plenty of ''hard'' news items to report, and a single staff member responsible for most of the writing, photography, and editing. If advertising and notices, as well as columns of information concerning the activities of employees or members, are to be carried, the presentation may be modeled directly after the standard weekly suburban newspaper.

Magazines

When longer articles of a feature nature are to be illustrated with color photographs, or when a more durable and prestigious product is desired, the commercial magazine printed on slick, heavy paper is the model. *Exxon USA* is the oil company's flashy way of demonstrating a mutual concern for ecology and productive exploration for new energy sources. In the *Dodge Adventurer*, the motor company offers travel articles, historical pieces about the role of the automobile in American life, and, of course, the same mul-

tipage, full-color Dodge ads that run in national magazines. In most states, the external publication circulated by the local or regional Bell System company to leaders of business, industry, education, and government contains photo features in full color, illustrations by area artists, and articles on progress in the state or area, often with no discernible tie-in to Bell's products or programs. The so-called *Time* magazine size is most common—approximately 8 1/2 by 11 inches, but some firms go to 9 by 12 for more impressive impact. Often, the magazine is mailed in an envelope or brown paper sleeve, rather than having a gummed mailing sticker affixed. Again, the special treatment is part of the prestige factor of magazine.

Minimags

The half-size (approximately 5 1/2 by 8 1/2 inches) magazine says, in effect, ''Go ahead, give me a look. Even though you didn't plan on receiving me, a quick browse will be easy.'' *Everybody's Money*, circulated to federal credit union members throughout the nation by the Credit Union National Association, looks like a particularly bright and colorful slim edition of the *Reader's Digest*. The compact two-column format means that half a dozen short features on personal and family finances can be included in each thirty-two-page issue, along with two or three easily read columns and regular features. The Grumman Corporation's *Overview* packs four or more 500-word features with dramatic black-and-white photographs into a tidy sixteen-page minimag directed at stockholders, subcontractors, and government officials. It is also a handy and effective vehicle for the firm's quarterly report. *Voter*, sent quarterly to all members of the national League of Women Voters, is a two-column, digest-sized magazine printed in black-and-white with spot color. The format includes articles, a news column, one-page reports on important issues, a photo spread highlighting a national or regional meeting, and a regular report from Capitol Hill on developments in important legislation.

Maganews or Magapapers

An imaginative and flexible hybrid format that has emerged in recent years is the maganews or magapaper. With its magazine layout (at least on the first few pages) and generous use of white space, it presents engaging modern graphics. Usually printed in black-and-white offset on newsprint or quality white stock, it blurs the line between both of its typographical antecedents by mixing newspaper column presentation with the more open magazine layout. The *St. Regis News*, employee publication of the paper company, leads with a full-page picture on the cover, then reverts to a fairly orthodox four-column newspaper format inside. *Perspective*, published for the employees of the Prudential Property and Casualty Insurance Company, also leads with a full-art cover. Inside, the features and employee news items are presented in a wide-open style patterned as much after modern corporate advertising as magazine or newspaper layout. Tipped type and generous use of white space are complemented by stark black-and-white photography and drawings.

The 8 1/2-by-11 Offset Newsletter

This is one of the most popular formats, because it opens up to magazine size, yet it can be folded for mailing in a standard 4 1/4-by-9 1/2-inch business envelope. The newsletter's popularity can be attributed in part to the fact that, depending on expertise and the availability of certain basic equipment, the editorial staff can set some or all of the type, including headlines, and prepare the "camera-ready" pages, except for halftones of the photographs. The printer makes the halftones, shoots the page negatives, makes the plates, and does the printing. In more mod-

est operations, the editor merely gathers and edits all of the material, prepares a final dummy for the entire publication, and depends on the printer's makeup staff to prepare the final, comprehensive layout. Because the new member of the PR staff is most likely to be assigned responsibility for this type of publication, in a later section we'll look more closely at how the editor prepares the layout for an 8 1/2-by-11 offset newsletter.

MANAGEMENT CONSIDERATIONS

Generally, regardless of which of the four models of public relations a manager practices, he or she will make use of newsletters, newspapers, and magazines. Like brochures and fact sheets, however, these publications are the staple of the public-information model, and they frequently share the faults of that model. Practitioners publish them without doing research to find out if there is a public that needs the information or finds it relevant.

A "Controlled" Medium

Because newsletters and other publications are controlled media, public relations writers can say exactly what they want. That means the writer has more control over the quality and content of the writing, and thus more control over accomplishing the message-retention and message-acceptance objectives. It is possible to write a message designed to change attitudes or behavior in the controlled publication that a gatekeeper would cut out of the uncontrolled medium.

In general, however, an organization's newsletters, newspapers, and magazines have effects similar to those of the commercial print media. They're good for meeting the communication and message-retention objectives—getting messages to people that put your organization on the public's agenda. But because the members of the public often have no strong reason to read one of these printed publications, they cannot be expected to form or change cognitions, attitudes, or behaviors.

Useful for Active and Passive Publics

You can go into more detail with print publications than you can through interpersonal communication or use of the broadcast media. Thus, they are useful for reaching active publics, whose members can read carefully, reread, and keep the publication for future reference. Association members eagerly await their monthly magazine, employees scan the company newspaper for news affecting their job, and stockholders look for newsletters to see how well their investment is doing. For such actively communicating publics, the publication can be a simple black-and-white newsletter with modest graphics, rather than the slick four-color magazine needed to attract low-involvement publics.

At the same time, however, organizations often send publications to those having no involvement with the organization or with the specific topics discussed in the publication. Many external magazines go to the presidents of universities or corporations, who in turn place them on tables in waiting rooms. Slick, attractive four-color magazines may attract the attention of important people, who will process their content while waiting for an appointment.

Other organizations produce specialized magazines for both actively and passively reading publics that use the organization's services. For example, until 1982, the National Bureau of Standards published *Dimensions/NBS*, a magazine aimed primarily at industry managers who could use the results of the bureau's research—an active public. A readership study showed that these readers did read the publication to learn about research results they could use.[1] But, for any given issue, most of the content was not relevant to the work of the managers. They read it anyway, processing the information out of general curiosity about the research conducted at the bureau—an example of high problem recognition combined with low involvement. Depending on the topic of each article, the reader either actively sought out or passively processed the information.

An organization's employees passively process the information in their employee publications more frequently than they actively seek it out. Another study at the National Bureau of Standards, for example, showed that employees spent only about a half an hour a week reading twenty-one employee publications.[2] Unless an article related to their work or showed how management decisions affected them, the employee publics only processed—they did not seek out—the voluminous messages directed at them.

Organizations often produce expensive publications in the belief that the publics to which they are sent will read the publications eagerly. Often, however, those publics process the information only when they have time. If your intent is to communicate with passively communicating publics, the controlled print media will work better than uncontrolled commercial media. Don't make the mistake of believing, however, that the audience actively reads them. If you cannot demonstrate that a publication's audience is active, make certain you can justify the expense of reaching a passive public.

Costly in Money and Time

Slick color magazines are very expensive, while offset newsletters can be relatively inexpensive. All take time to produce, however. Budget a publication carefully before you commit your organization to its production. Get estimates from printers and typesetters. Consult with editors in other organizations to determine production costs, along with the number of people and the time needed to produce such a publication.

Evaluate with a Readership Study

Because the communication objective is the most realistic one for a print publication, a readership study—which measures that objective—is usually the most appropriate evaluation technique. You will also want to use the signaled stopping technique to determine if your audience can retain the message.

LAYOUT

Designing, or laying out, a print publication is a challenging job. It can be vexing because so much information must somehow be fit in limited space. But it also can be rewarding when the results are pleasing to the eye and focus attention on the desired pictures and articles. We will discuss newsletters in this section, but the principles apply also to magazines and other print formats.

Placing the Basic Elements

Your printer or office-supply firm can provide layout sheets marked off in fractions of inches, so that you can plan each page or spread (pair of facing pages). The lines on the layout forms are blue, and the editor makes all of the sketches and notations with a light-blue pencil. Why? Because light blue does not photograph in the offset process, and thus the color is "invisible."

Layout means placement of the four basic elements of typographical design:

1. Body type (text).
2. Display type (headlines, titles, "teasers").
3. Art (photos, drawings, graphic elements).
4. White space (air, or "visual freedom").

Each page or two-page spread goes through three phases of preparation:

1. Rough layout or dummy, in which the editor sketches in the four basic elements to help visualize the final product.
2. Comprehensive layout, or "comp," which is a mock-up precise enough for the printer and the editor to measure the exact space needed for each item.

3. Mechanical layout—a paste-up of the type and halftones into a camera-ready layout suitable for photographing and making into a printing plate. If you have a light table, cutting and pasting tools, and a supply of graphic materials, you can develop the skills necessary to prepare your own mechanicals. Most editors, however, prefer to let the printer take over once the comp has been approved.

How Many Columns?

When you first sit down to design the format for your newsletter, the initial decision involves the number of columns per page. A single full-width column of type is difficult to read. The single-column newsletter format is only feasible for "news-flash" business letters and economic forecasts, which break the text up into short, one-paragraph items.

The two-column format allows plenty of room for type, since only a small amount of space is lost to the "gutters," or white space between columns. But there are few layout variations in two-column format, and it will be difficult to make each issue of the publication look fresh. That's why the three- and four-column formats are so popular. They permit all sorts of combinations of one-, two-, and multiple-column items. Following the lead of the major national newsmagazines, which reintroduced thin lines called "rules" between the columns, some newsletters have gone to four-column format, with slightly smaller type. The examples in Exhibit 26–1 will give you an idea of the variety in layout that is possible if you have imagination and don't get stuck with an inflexible basic format.

One reason so many editors prefer the three-column format is that the editor can use one-column "mug shots" for pictures of individuals, two-column shots for a small number of people, and three-column display for special art that is worthy of major attention. The choice of three headline widths also helps the editor to ''grade'' the news better and to offer greater variety in sizes of type.

Another currently popular layout development is basically the three-column format modified to a ''one-and-two'' style, with the outside column (left on a left-hand page, right on a right-hand page) run as a single column, and the other two columns set double-width. *Hope News*, the quarterly publication of Project Hope, follows basically a two-column format, but uses three columns for picture spreads and news-notes sections on the top two-thirds of single pages—proving that an editor can even mix-and-match formats with success.

The three-column format has also been transmuted into a kind of one-column format where the single main column is at least as wide as two-thirds of the page, with all headlines and pictures stacked in the free column at the left. It's an idea that calls for generous use of white space and careful planning, but it pays off as an attention-getter. Whenever the editor goes to multiple columns, white space must be added, and thus there is shrinkage in the amount of copy that can be included in the standard number of pages. The narrower columns can lead to more hyphenation and odd spacing of letters. But most editors feel the flexibility gained makes the tradeoffs worthwhile.

As the layout for an issue of a newsletter takes shape (Exhibit 26–2), the editor must assure that the edited material precisely fits the assigned space on the layout sheet. ''Copyfitting'' means developing a counting and estimating scheme for headlines and text. Several of the additional reading suggestions for this and the preceding chapter explain the systems for estimating type.

Graphic Elements

The logo, slogan, and proprietary color selected to represent the organization (Kodak's yellow and Campbell Soup's red-orange, for example) should appear prominently in every publication's nameplate. In fact, the announcement of any changes in such corporate identity elements usually is made first in a newsletter article and picture.

If your organization publishes several publications for special audiences, the family tie should be apparent in typeface and graphic styles. People who come across a publication for which they are not the usual target should nevertheless recognize the organization's personality and style.

SETTING THE PRODUCTION SCHEDULE

We saw in Chapter 8 that a Gantt chart can help the manager to plan use of time and resources. The publication editor must develop a production schedule to assure the organization's ability to publish one or more periodicals on time. The lead time for a publication—the time needed to develop article ideas, make assignments to writers and artists, and allow the printer to set type, make up pages, and do the complete printing job—typically is two to three months. This means that an editor may be working on the phases of three different issues of a monthly publication at any one time.

Of course, the production schedule for a weekly newspaper may be as little as ten days, while the annual report's preparation literally takes an entire year. Whatever the period of time, the editor must spell out which activities take place, in what order, and with what time separation. Here, for example, is an abridged production schedule for a monthly magazine (numbers indicate how many days prior to the mailing date, which is the twenty-fifth day of the month preceding the month of the issue):

Don't underestimate the ability of such basic graphic elements as cutoff rules and border treatments to create the style and ''feel'' of your publication. Study the illustrations accompanying this chapter, and you will note that one newsletter uses a single

the alcoa news

Volume 50/Number 2

1979 February

At Rockdale

15 Alcoans join city medical service

"One and two and three and four and five and one and two and three and . . ."

That is what 15 Rockdale Works Alcoans have been quoting faithfully the past few weeks while training for the newly formed Rockdale Emergency Medical Service. The sequence of numbers, familiar to those already trained, is part of the life-saving pattern

cal physician to investigate possibilities for an area ambulance service. Dr. John Weed of Rockdale gathered a committee of citizens including Alcoans Nelson Mueller and Alan Parker. Together, they came up with a design to meet the city's needs.

The plan was to recruit 30 volunteers and devote 36 attending the plus two each month.

egan.

ale Alcoans not only volut also of courses. rman, R.N., y al engi- Jimmy (o Page 3)

Seaport Bulletin
A Calendar of Events and Projects
at the South Street Seaport Museum
Volume 5, Number 5
December 1980–February 1981

Bulletin

Schermerhorn Block Plans Are Approved

In early September, the city's Landmarks Preservation Commission approved the restoration plans for the Schermerhorn Row block prepared by the firm of Jan Hird Pokorny, Architects & Planners, New York State—owner of the block—and the Restoration Committee of the South Street Seaport Museum wanted their varied histories and retain the architecturally and historically interesting elements that have evolved since their original 1811-1813 construction.

The architect's approach has been to examine the existing elements in each building—as documented by the New York State Division for Historic Preservation and by the architects—and incorporate them in a sympathetic and appropriate design. Most of the restored storefronts will contain architectural elements dating from 1868-1920, but certain earlier elements will be retained where still extant. For example, in October some stucco was removed from the front of No. 14 Fulton Street, uncovering what are thought to be the remains of the original

1812 arched and brownstone-quoined door, and this surprising survival will be retained in the building's restoration. The mansard-roofed former Fulton Ferry Hotel, at No. 2 Fulton Street and Nos. 92-93 South Street, will retain its raised 1868 roofline, and the well-preserved hotel rooms contained in its upper floors will one day be restored as an example of the hotels that were common-place in this neighborhood. The overall unity of Schermerhorn Row will be reinforced by a new slate roof, restored cornices, and rebuilt high-standing chimneys.

The restoration work will be overseen by the State's Urban Development Corporation and is slated to begin in the spring of 1981. When complete, the buildings will once again be filled with life—some with commercial enterprises, Nos. 12 and 14 with the Museum Visitors Center, and others with Museum exhibition space. But the buildings themselves will become one of the Museum's most important exhibits; with care for scholarship and thought toward education, the restored block will present historic buildings that show their age and traces of their manifold pasts, including this newest layer of change.

The Peck Slip facade of the 1807 W... House (at right) in the early stages... toration (photograph by Callie La...

ox, po...ngi... power... ...ive the victim, a n... Alcoan, cardiopulmonary... citation (CPR), while the... Ron Homce, construction... partment, persuaded the b... driver to drive to the near... lice station and a waiting a... lance.

Through their efforts, the vi... was kept alive prior to advan... medical support. Unfortunate... the victim died a week later i... the hospital.

HOPE NEWS

/ Millwood, Virginia 22646

VOL. 19, NO. 1/1981

A publication of Project HOPE, The People-to-People Health Foundation, Inc.
Editor: Anson B. Campbell

ST. LUCIA/HOPE IS "AN IMPORTANT NEW INITIATIVE"

Project HOPE, with a U.S. Agency for International Development grant, will now provide St. Lucia and other Eastern Caribbean countries assistance for the training of public health inspectors, environmental health assistants, dental nurses and hygienists, pharmacists, and child care specialists. Over a five-year period HOPE will be training participants from eight nations of the Eastern Caribbean in facilities provided by the government of St. Lucia.

Signing on behalf of the United States were Ambassador Sally A. Shelton and Director of United States Agency for International Development in the Eastern Caribbean, William B. Wheeler, while Dr. Nicholas Allard, HOPE's Program Director, signed on behalf of the Project. St. Lucia's Minister of Health, Bruce Williams, also participated in the signing ceremony.

Speaking during the ceremony, Ambassador Shelton noted that while the nations of the Caribbean have made great strides towards meeting the health care requirements of their populations, a continuing commitment is required on the part of governments and

individuals to provide services that are at once accessible, affordable, and appropriate for the needs of the people being served.

The Ambassador noted: "Shortages of skilled health manpower exist throughout the Caribbean but are felt most acutely by the smaller states. While shortages of physicians and other highly specialized personnel are serious, tremendous shortages also exist in the numbers of allied public health personnel who are the backbone of the health care system.

"Through this grant a program can be initiated to assist in alleviating some of these manpower shortages, particularly in environmental health, dental health, and child health services. The United States is highly supportive of the efforts being undertaken by the countries of the Caribbean to meet the health needs of their populations."

Mr. Wheeler noted: "This grant with Project HOPE is an important new initiative from two perspectives. First, it directly addresses the shortages of key allied
(Continued on Page 8)

International Interchange for Nursing Enrichment Is Proposed

A meeting to explore an initial proposal to establish an International Interchange for Nursing was held in mid-November at the HOPE Center.

The intent was to follow-up the recommendation of last fall's (1979) International Nursing Conference that such an interchange be established in the United States, possibly at the Project's international hea...
(Continued on Pag...)

Six hundred and fifty nurses have served with HOPE.

EXHIBIT 26–1

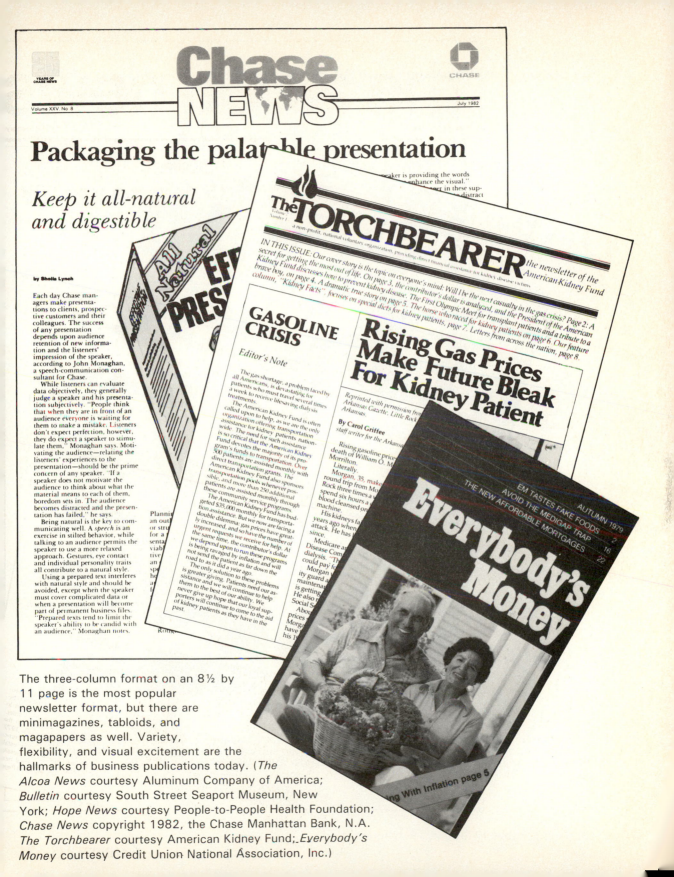

25 YEARS OF CHASE NEWS

Chase NEWS

Volume XXV. No. 8

CHASE

July 1982

Packaging the palatable presentation

Keep it all-natural and digestible

by Sheila Lynch

Each day Chase managers make presentations to clients, prospective customers and their colleagues. The success of any presentation depends upon audience retention of new information and the listeners' impression of the speaker, according to John Monaghan, a speech-communication consultant for Chase.

While listeners can evaluate data objectively, they generally judge a speaker and his presentation subjectively. "People think that when they are in front of an audience everyone is waiting for them to make a mistake. Listeners don't expect perfection, however, they do expect a speaker to stimulate them," Monaghan says. Motivating the audience—relating the listeners' experiences to the presentation—should be the prime concern of any speaker. "If a speaker does not motivate the audience to think about what the material means to each of them, boredom sets in. The audience becomes distracted and the presentation has failed," he says.

Being natural is the key to communicating well. A *speech* is an exercise in stilted behavior, while talking to an audience permits the speaker to use a more relaxed approach. Gestures, eye contact and individual personality traits all contribute to a natural style.

Using a prepared text interferes with natural style and should be avoided, except when the speaker must cover complicated data or when a presentation will become part of permanent business files. "Prepared texts tend to limit the speaker's ability to be candid with an audience," Monaghan notes.

...speaker is providing the words ...enhance the visual." ...ver in these sup- ...distract

All Natural EFF... PRES...

Planning... an outl... or stru... for a s... senta... viab... tive... an... spe... he... a... f...

Rou...

The TORCHBEARER

Volume 1 Number 1

a non-profit, national voluntary organization, providing direct financial assistance to kidney disease victims

the newsletter of the American Kidney Fund

IN THIS ISSUE: Our cover story is the topic on everyone's mind: Will I be the next casualty in the gas crisis? Page 2: A secret for getting the most out of life. On page 3, the contributor's dollar is analyzed, and the President of the American Kidney Fund discusses how to prevent kidney disease. The First Olympic Meet for transplant patients of the American brave boy, on page 4. A dramatic true story on page 5. The horse who raced for kidney patients on page 6. Our feature column, "Kidney Facts," focuses on special diets for kidney patients, page 7. Letters from across the nation, page 8.

GASOLINE CRISIS

Editor's Note

The gas shortage, a problem faced by all Americans, is devastating for patients who must travel several times a week to receive lifesaving dialysis treatments.

The American Kidney Fund is often called upon to help, as we are the only organization offering transportation assistance for kidney patients nationwide. The need for such assistance is so critical that the American Kidney Fund devotes the majority of its program's funds to transportation. Over 500 patients are assisted monthly with direct transportation grants. The American Kidney Fund also sponsors transportation pools whenever possible, and more than 250 additional patients are assisted monthly through these community service programs.

The American Kidney Fund has budgeted $35,000 monthly for transportation assistance. But we now are facing a double dilemma: gas prices have greatly increased, and so have the number of urgent requests we receive for help. At the same time, the contributor's dollar is being ravaged by inflation and will not send the patient as far down the road to as it did a year ago.

The only solution to these problems is greater giving. Patients need our assistance and we will continue to help them to the best of our ability. We never give up hope that our loyal supporters will continue to come to the aid of kidney patients as they have in the past.

Rising Gas Prices Make Future Bleak For Kidney Patient

Reprinted with permission from Arkansas Gazette, Little Rock, Arkansas.

By Carol Griffee
staff writer for the Arkansas...

Rising gasoline prices... death of William O. M... Morrilton.

Literally.

Morgan, 35, make... round trip from Mo... Rock three times a... spend six hours a... blood cleansed on... machine.

His kidneys fa... years ago when... attack. He has l... since.

Medicare an... Disease Com... dialysis. "T... could pay fo...

Morgan... ity guard a... maintenanc... is getting... He also r... Social Se...

About... prices a... Morgan... have s... his re...

AUTUMN 1979

EM TASTES FAKE FOODS 2
AVOID THE MEDIGAP TRAP 16
THE NEW AFFORDABLE MORTGAGES 22

Everybody's Money

...ng With Inflation page 5

The three-column format on an 8½ by 11 page is the most popular newsletter format, but there are minimagazines, tabloids, and magapapers as well. Variety, flexibility, and visual excitement are the hallmarks of business publications today. (*The Alcoa News* courtesy Aluminum Company of America; *Bulletin* courtesy South Street Seaport Museum, New York; *Hope News* courtesy People-to-People Health Foundation; *Chase News* copyright 1982, the Chase Manhattan Bank, N.A. *The Torchbearer* courtesy American Kidney Fund; *Everybody's Money* courtesy Credit Union National Association, Inc.)

EXHIBIT 26–2

Six Stages in the Preparation of an Article for an Employee Newspaper

(1) After editing the text, the editor selects pictures to accompany the article, crops them to fit the columns, and then types and edits photo captions and headlines for the full-page spread. (This article, from p. 6 of the Warner-Lambert *World* for September 1982, discusses the company's contribution to cancer research.)

7-A

(2) The string of ''galley proofs'' must be read carefully by the editor. Necessary changes and corrections will appear on a second set of galleys, if there is time. Otherwise corrections appear at the time of full-page proofs.

Copy being reset at Elizabeth

—0007—

⊐, reset 9/3

no extra line

Cancer
for September WORLD

Ann Arbor, Mich.—Cure. Increasingly this word is being heard when scientists, physicians, patients and their families discuss the most feared disease of our time. That disease, of course, is cancer, and approximately 835,000 Americans will be diagnosed as having it this year.

Twenty years ago, only one patient in four survived cancer for at least five years. Today the rate is about one in three. If all skin and cervical cancers are considered, one in two will survive for at least five years, according to the latest information from cancer research centers.

Promising developments

Progress against cancer, although hard-won, has been significant. And today advances are coming on many fronts. Some hopefully promising developments in cancer chemotherapy are being reported by Warner-Lambert, where an accelerated cancer research program has been under way since late 1979.

More than 65 company scientists now focus full energies on new drugs to treat major solid tumors that remain resistant to cure, including colorectal, lung, breast and gastric cancers.

The focal point for company cancer research is Ann Arbor, Michigan, where two months ago a new $4 million cancer chemotherapy laboratory building opened.

At July dedication ceremonies, a leading scientist from the National Cancer Institute (NCI) called the new laboratories "a landmark in the history of private industry involvement in cancer research." He characterized the project as consistent with the trend toward more private involvement, one which the NCI favors and supports.

His reference was to the movement of companies like Warner-Lambert from the periphery of cancer research to the real battlefront. Cancer research has attracted greater private enterprise participation as knowledge of the biological processes that underlie the disease has grown and, along with improved opportunities for cures.

The Ann Arbor research laboratory, Warner-Lambert's latest commitment to the battle against cancer, houses the important soil screening or fermentation facet of the cancer program, as well as anticancer antibacterial testing. Many of the stages essential to the identification, testing and small-scale production of anticancer compounds occur here, including culture isolation, fermentation in varying sc... and testing for cancer-causing poten...

Progress in chemotherapy

An in-house pilot plant produces anticancer antibiotics in sufficient bulk to satisfy the requirements of human trials. At the approach of the marketing stage, the plant develops methods and systems for producing these drugs in mass quantities.

The research program concentrates on chemotherapy, the application of chemical compounds against malignancies. In recent years, chemotherapy has come of age. At least 12 types of cancer are curable today mainly because of advances in chemotherapy.

Chemotherapy, while highly effective in many cases, needs further development and refinement, namely the discovery of more effective, specific, less toxic agents. This is especially true for solid tumors, Warner-Lambert's primary interest.

Warner-Lambert scientists are searching not for the "magic bullet" cure sought by the cancer pioneers, but a battery of new drugs, each with a specific function. Combination therapy has become the approach of choice today. Doctors use radiotherapy and surgery for removal of large, primary tumors while chemotherapy deals a blow to cancerous cells that have spread or metastasized through the body.

Collaborative programs

...complexities are so overwhelm... ...now relies on a number ...programs which ...anding

---

88 JOB 54806-0010-05 W-L D1-4
REV:08-26 EXP:08-24 SW SIZ: 51

54806-100 from 54806-10
54806 L P THEBAULT w/l newsletter
rs 8-24-82 cc-4
rev 8-26-82 sw 202 cc-3
Electronically Composed By:
ELIZABETH TYPESETTING COMPANY
26 North 26th Street, Kenilworth, New Jersey, (201) 241-6161

I ⊗

Elslager
for September WORLD

An interview with Dr. Edward F. Elslager on cancer Dr. Elslager is vice president of research, Pharmaceutical Research Division.

Q. The medical profession has in its arsenal radiation, chemical and surgical techniques for cancer treatment. How important are chemotherapeutic approaches today?

A. Chemotherapeutic approaches to cancer treatment are becoming increasingly important with the advent and acceptance of the combined modality approach to the treatment of solid tumors and lymphomas. Conceptually, this utilizes the best features of all available therapeutic modalities, including surgery, radiation therapy and chemotherapy, combined rationally to exert maximum lethal effects on the tumor. Each form of treatment has specific attributes and limitations. Systemic chemotherapy has the potential to eradicate microscopic residual disease and secondary tumors but, with a few exceptions, cannot eradicate large tumors. A decade ago only 25 percent of cancer patients were treated with chemotherapy. Today, 35 percent of patients receive chemotherapy, and it is projected that 45 percent will be treated with drugs within the next decade.

Q. In recent years, what notable advances have been made in cancer treatment, particularly chemotherapy?

A. Perhaps the most significant advance in cancer chemotherapy in recent years has been the evolution and acceptance of the concept of combination chemotherapy. Thus, anticancer drugs with different mechanisms of action, cell cycle actions, toxicities and times of onset of toxicity are combined to enable maximum tumor cell kill while minimizing host toxicity. Significant newer drugs include duroxorubicin, platinol, and tamoxifen.

Q. Why has the cancer fight been so protracted?

A. Because it has proven to be a multifaceted disease almost as complex as life itself. It is now recognized that cancer is not a single disease, but rather comprises a group of more than 100 diseases with different characteristics. Also, we have been unable to identify any fundamental differences between normal and cancer cells which would allow for the design of new drugs absolutely selective for the neoplasms (tumors). Consequently, it has been necessary to rely primarily on cytotoxic drugs which not only kill rapidly dividing tumor cells, but also destroy rapidly dividing normal cells. In spite of early diagnosis and surgical removal, patients may already have many established and undetected microscopic metastases which become apparent only after the disseminated disease is measurable. At this time the tumor contains at least one billion cancer cells, and presents a formidable challenge to any cancer chemotherapeutic agent.

Q. What are the most promising avenues of research and do you foresee any possibilities for significant breakthroughs?

A. In the immediate future, continued progress will be made in the development of new and useful cytotoxic drugs utilizing traditional enlightened semi-empirical approaches. New drugs with unique chemical structures will be developed which will possess novel biochemical mechanisms of action, selective activity against solid tumors, greater specificity for tumor cells, lower host toxicity, improved activity against drug-resistant tumors and greater therapeutic effect when used in combination therapy. Over the next decade, I believe that revolutionary developments in cell biology will enable a better understanding of fundamental biological processes in cancer and provide more rational approaches to new drug design and testing. Rapid progress in genetics, recombinant DNA technology, monoclonal antibody techniques and biochemistry already signal novel approaches such as cell membrane active drugs, differentiating agents, oncogene product inhibitors, tumor-associated monoclonal antibody complexes, and immunoreactive agents.

Copy being reset at Elizabeth

AA

K12C

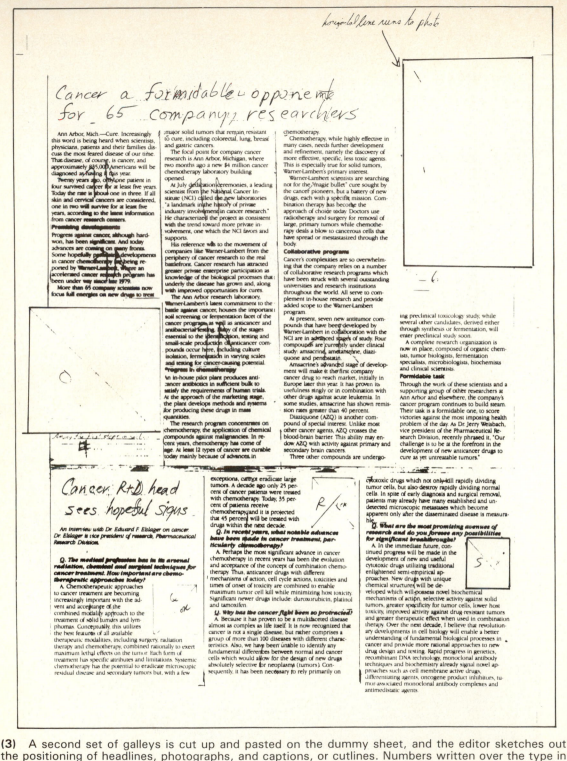

horizontal line runs to photo

Cancer a formidable opponent for 65 company researchers

Ann Arbor, Mich.—Cure. Increasingly this word is being heard when scientists, physicians, patients and their families discuss the most feared disease of our time. That disease, of course, is cancer, and approximately 835,000 Americans will be diagnosed as having it this year.

Twenty years ago, only one patient in four survived cancer for at least five years. Today the rate is about one in three. If all skin and cervical cancers are considered, one in two will survive for at least five years, according to the latest information from cancer research centers.

Promising developments

Progress against cancer, although hard-won, has been significant. And today advances are coming on many fronts. Some hopefully promising developments in cancer chemotherapy are being reported by Warner-Lambert, where an accelerated cancer research program has been under way since late 1979.

More than 65 company scientists now focus full energies on new drugs to treat major solid tumors that remain resistant to cure, including colorectal, lung, breast and gastric cancers.

The focal point for company cancer research is Ann Arbor, Michigan, where two months ago a new $4 million cancer chemotherapy laboratory building opened.

At July dedication ceremonies, a leading scientist from the National Cancer Institute (NCI) called the new laboratories "a landmark in the history of private industry involvement in cancer research." He characterized the project as consistent with the trend toward more private involvement, one which the NCI favors and supports.

His reference was to the movement of companies like Warner-Lambert from the periphery of cancer research to the real battlefront. Cancer research has attracted greater private enterprise participation as knowledge of the biological processes that underly the disease has grown and, along with improved opportunities for cures.

The Ann Arbor research laboratory, Warner-Lambert's latest commitment to the battle against cancer, houses the important soil screening or fermentation facet of the cancer program, as well as anticancer and antibacterial testing. Many of the stages essential to the identification, testing and small-scale production of anticancer compounds occur here, including culture isolation, fermentation in varying scales and testing for cancer-causing potential.

Progress in chemotherapy

An in-house pilot plant produces anticancer antibiotics in sufficient bulk to satisfy the requirements of human trials. At the approach of the marketing stage, the plant develops methods and systems for producing these drugs in mass quantities.

The research program concentrates on chemotherapy, the application of chemical compounds against malignancies. In recent years, chemotherapy has come of age. At least 12 types of cancer are curable today mainly because of advances in chemotherapy.

Chemotherapy, while highly effective in many cases, needs further development and refinement, namely the discovery of more effective, specific, less toxic agents. This is especially true for solid tumors, Warner-Lambert's primary interest.

Warner-Lambert scientists are searching not for the "magic bullet" cure sought by the cancer pioneers, but a battery of new drugs, each with a specific mission. Combination therapy has become the approach of choice today. Doctors use radiotherapy and surgery for removal of large, primary tumors while chemotherapy deals a blow to cancerous cells that have spread or metastasized through the body.

Collaborative programs

Cancer's complexities are so overwhelming that the company relies on a number of collaborative research programs which have been struck with several outstanding universities and research institutions throughout the world. All serve to complement in-house research and provide added scope to the Warner-Lambert program.

At present, seven new antitumor compounds that have been developed by Warner-Lambert in collaboration with the NCI are in advanced stages of study. Four compounds are currently under clinical study: amsacrine, amatantrone, diaziquone and pentostatin.

Amsacrine's advanced stage of development will make it the first company cancer drug to reach market, initially in Europe later this year. It has proven its usefulness singly or in combination with other drugs against acute leukemia. In some studies, amsacrine has shown remission rates greater than 40 percent.

Diaziquone (AZQ) is another compound of special interest. Unlike most other cancer agents, AZQ crosses the blood-brain barrier. This ability may endow AZQ with activity against primary and secondary brain cancers.

Three other compounds are undergoing preclinical toxicology study, while several other candidates, derived either through synthesis or fermentation, will enter preclinical study soon.

A complete research organization is now in place, composed of organic chemists, tumor biologists, fermentation specialists, microbiologists, biochemists and clinical scientists.

Formidable task

Through the work of these scientists and a supporting group of other researchers at Ann Arbor and elsewhere, the company's cancer program continues to build steam. Their task is a formidable one, to score victories against the most imposing health problem of the day. As Dr. Jerry Weisbach, vice president of the Pharmaceutical Research Division, recently phrased it, "Our challenge is to be at the forefront in the development of new anticancer drugs to cure as yet untreatable tumors."

Cancer R&D head sees hopeful signs

An interview with Dr. Edward F. Elslager on cancer. Dr. Elslager is vice president of research, Pharmaceutical Research Division.

Q. The medical profession has in its arsenal radiation, chemical and surgical techniques for cancer treatment. How important are chemotherapeutic approaches today?

A. Chemotherapeutic approaches to cancer treatment are becoming increasingly important with the advent and acceptance of the combined modality approach to the treatment of solid tumors and lymphomas. Conceptually, this utilizes the best features of all available therapeutic modalities, including surgery, radiation therapy and chemotherapy, combined rationally to exert maximum lethal effects on the tumor. Each form of treatment has specific attributes and limitations. Systemic chemotherapy has the potential to eradicate microscopic residual disease and secondary tumors but, with a few exceptions, cannot eradicate large tumors. A decade ago only 25 percent of cancer patients were treated with chemotherapy. Today, 35 percent of patients receive chemotherapy, and it is projected that 45 percent will be treated with drugs within the next decade.

Q. In recent years, what notable advances have been made in cancer treatment, particularly chemotherapy?

A. Perhaps the most significant advance in cancer chemotherapy in recent years has been the evolution and acceptance of the concept of combination chemotherapy. Thus, anticancer drugs with different mechanisms of action, cell cycle actions, toxicities and times of onset of toxicity are combined to enable maximum tumor cell kill while minimizing host toxicity. Significant newer drugs include: duroxorubicin, platinol and tamoxifen.

Q. Why has the cancer fight been so protracted?

A. Because it has proven to be a multifaceted disease almost as complex as life itself. It is now recognized that cancer is not a single disease, but rather comprises a group of more than 100 diseases with different characteristics. Also, we have been unable to identify any fundamental differences between normal and cancer cells which would allow for the design of new drugs absolutely selective for neoplasms (tumors). Consequently, it has been necessary to rely primarily on cytotoxic drugs which not only kill rapidly dividing tumor cells, but also destroy rapidly dividing normal cells. In spite of early diagnosis and surgical removal, patients may already have many established and undetected microscopic metastases which become apparent only after the disseminated disease is measurable.

Q. What are the most promising avenues of research and do you foresee any possibilities for significant breakthroughs?

A. In the immediate future, continued progress will be made in the development of new and useful cytotoxic drugs utilizing traditional enlightened semi-empirical approaches. New drugs with unique chemical structures will be developed which will possess novel biochemical mechanisms of action, selective activity against solid tumors, greater specificity for tumor cells, lower host toxicity, improved activity against drug-resistant tumors and greater therapeutic effect when used in combination therapy. Over the next decade, I believe that revolutionary developments in cell biology will enable a better understanding of fundamental biological processes in cancer and provide more rational approaches to new drug design and testing. Rapid progress in genetics, recombinant DNA technology, recently phrased it, "Our approaches such as cell membrane active drugs, differentiating agents, oncogene product inhibitors, tumor-associated monoclonal antibody complexes and antimetastatic agents.

(3) A second set of galleys is cut up and pasted on the dummy sheet, and the editor sketches out the positioning of headlines, photographs, and captions, or cutlines. Numbers written over the type in grease pencil correspond to the printer's galley numbers. At this point, subheadings are written and indicated on the layout. The editor notes that slightly more than 10 lines of copy will have to be cut, and decisions are made to place other graphic elements such as borders and white space.

Cancer: a formidable opponent for 65 company researchers

Ann Arbor, Mich—Cure. Increasingly this word is being heard when scientists, physicians, patients and their families discuss the most feared disease of our time. That disease, of course, is cancer, and approximately 835,000 Americans will be diagnosed as having it this year.

Twenty years ago, only one patient in four survived cancer for at least five years. Today the rate is about one in three. If all skin and cervical cancers are considered, one in two will survive for at least five years, according to the latest information from cancer research centers.

Promising developments

Progress against cancer, although hard-won, has been significant. And today advances are coming on many fronts. Some hopefully promising developments in cancer chemotherapy are being reported by Warner-Lambert, where an accelerated cancer research program has been under way since late 1979.

More than 65 company scientists now focus full energies on new drugs to treat major solid tumors that remain resistant to cure, including colorectal, lung, breast and gastric cancers.

The focal point for company cancer research is Ann Arbor, Michigan, where two months ago a new $4 million cancer chemotherapy laboratory building opened.

At July dedication ceremonies, a leading scientist from the National Cancer Institute (NCI) called the new laboratories "a landmark in the history of private industry involvement in cancer research." He characterized the project as consistent with the trend toward more private involvement, one which the NCI favors and supports.

His reference was to the movement of companies like Warner-Lambert from the periphery of cancer research to the real battlefront. Cancer research has attracted greater private enterprise participation as knowledge of the biological processes that underlie the disease has grown and, along with improved opportunities for cures.

The Ann Arbor research laboratory, Warner-Lambert's latest commitment to the battle against cancer, houses the important soil screening or fermentation facet of the cancer program, as well as anticancer and antibacterial testing. Many of the stages essential to the identification, testing and small-scale production of anticancer compounds occur here, including culture isolation, fermentation in varying scales and testing for cancer-causing potential.

Progress in chemotherapy

An in-house pilot plant produces anticancer antibiotics in sufficient bulk to satisfy the requirements of human trials. At the approach of the marketing stage, the plant develops methods and systems for producing these drugs in mass quantities.

The research program concentrates on chemotherapy, the application of chemical compounds against malignancies. In recent years, chemotherapy has come of age. At least 12 types of cancer are curable today mainly because of advances in chemotherapy.

Chemotherapy, while highly effective in many cases, needs further development and refinement, namely the discovery of more effective, specific, less toxic agents. This is especially true for solid tumors, Warner-Lambert's primary interest.

Warner-Lambert scientists are searching not for the "magic bullet" cure sought by the cancer pioneers, but a battery of new drugs, each with a specific mission. Combination therapy has become the approach of choice today. Doctors use radiotherapy and surgery for removal of large, primary tumors while chemotherapy deals a blow to cancerous cells that have spread or metastasized through the body.

Collaborative programs

Cancer's complexities are so overwhelming that the company relies on a number of collaborative research programs which have been struck with several outstanding universities and research institutions throughout the world. All serve to complement in-house research and provide added scope to the Warner-Lambert program.

At present, seven new antitumor compounds that have been developed by Warner-Lambert in collaboration with the NCI are in advanced stages of study. Four compounds are currently under clinical study: amsacrine, ametantrone, diaziquone and penostatin.

Amsacrine's advanced stage of development will make it the first company anticancer drug to reach market, initially in Europe later this year. It has proven its usefulness singly or in combination with other drugs against acute leukemia. In some studies, amsacrine has shown remission rates greater than 40 percent.

Diaziquone (AZQ) is another compound of special interest. Unlike most other cancer agents, AZQ crosses the blood-brain barrier. This ability may endow AZQ with activity against primary and secondary brain cancers.

Three other compounds are undergoing preclinical toxicology study, while several other candidates, derived either through synthesis or fermentation, will enter preclinical study soon.

A complete research organization is now in place, composed of organic chemists, tumor biologists, fermentation specialists, microbiologists, biochemists and clinical scientists.

Formidable task

Through the work of these scientists and a supporting group of other researchers at Ann Arbor and elsewhere, the company's cancer program continues to build steam. Their task is a formidable one, to score victories against the most imposing health problem of the day. As Dr. Jerry Weisbach, president of the Pharmaceutical Research Division, recently phrased it, "Our challenge is to be at the forefront in the development of new anticancer drugs to cure as yet untreatable tumors."

Early testing of possible antitumor compounds is accomplished using cell cultures, which can be stored indefinitely by freezing in liquid nitrogen-filled tanks, shown here. The company's first major anti-cancer product, Amsidine, was recently introduced in The Netherlands.

Among the first steps in soil sampling phases of anticancer research in the company's new cancer chemotherapy laboratories is the isolation of actinomycete colonies from agar plates.

Cancer R&D head sees hopeful signs

An interview with Dr. Edward F. Elslager on cancer. Dr. Elslager is vice president of research, Pharmaceutical Research Division.

Q. The medical profession has in its arsenal radiation, chemical and surgical techniques for cancer treatment. How important are chemotherapeutic approaches today?

A. Chemotherapeutic approaches to cancer treatment are becoming increasingly important with the advent and acceptance of the combined modality approach to the treatment of solid tumors and lymphomas. Conceptually, this utilizes the best features of all available therapeutic modalities, including surgery, radiation therapy and chemotherapy, combined rationally to exert maximum lethal effects on the tumor. Each form of treatment has specific attributes and limitations. Systemic chemotherapy has the potential to eradicate microscopic residual disease and secondary tumors but, with a few exceptions, cannot eradicate large tumors. A decade ago only 25 percent of cancer patients were treated with chemotherapy. Today, 35 percent of patients receive chemotherapy, and it is projected that 45 percent will be treated with drugs within the next decade.

Q. In recent years, what notable advances have been made in cancer treatment, particularly chemotherapy?

A. Perhaps the most significant advance in cancer chemotherapy in recent years has been the evolution and acceptance of the concept of combination chemotherapy. Thus, anticancer drugs with different mechanisms of action, cell cycle actions, toxicities and times of onset of toxicity are combined to enable maximum tumor cell kill while minimizing host toxicity. Significant drugs include duroxorubicin and platinol.

Q. Why has the cancer fight been so protracted?

A. Because it has proven to be a multifaceted disease almost as complex as life itself. It is now recognized that cancer is not a single disease, but rather comprises a group of more than 100 diseases with different characteristics. Also, we have been unable to identify any fundamental differences between normal and cancer cells which would allow for the design of new drugs absolutely selective for neoplasms (tumors). Consequently, it has been necessary to rely primarily on cytotoxic drugs which not only kill rapidly dividing tumor cells, but also destroy rapidly dividing normal cells. In spite of early diagnosis and surgical removal, patients may already have many established and undetected microscopic metastases which become apparent only after the disseminated disease is measurable.

Q. What are the most promising avenues of research and do you foresee any possibilities for significant breakthroughs?

A. In the immediate future, continued progress will be made in the development of new and useful cytotoxic drugs utilizing traditional enlightened semi-empirical approaches. New drugs with unique chemical structures will be developed which will possess novel biochemical mechanisms of action, selective activity against solid tumors, greater specificity for tumor cells, lower host toxicity, improved activity against drug-resistant tumors and greater therapeutic effect when used in combination therapy. Over the next decade, I believe that revolutionary developments in cell biology will enable a better understanding of fundamental biological processes in cancer and provide more rational approaches to new drug design and testing. Rapid progress in genetics, recombinant DNA technology, monoclonal antibody techniques and biochemistry already signal novel approaches such as cell membrane active drugs, differentiating agents, oncogene product inhibitors and tumor-associated monoclonal antibody complexes.

note: Vertical rules extend to horizontal rule on page bottom

6

(4) While the photographs are being engraved for reproduction, the printer provides the editor with full-page proofs—minus art, but including all type elements. This is the editor's final chance to catch typographical errors or to adjust the positioning of graphic elements.

Cancer: a formidable opponent for 65 company researchers

Ann Arbor, Mich.—Cure. Increasingly this word is being heard when scientists, physicians, patients and their families discuss the most feared disease of our time. That disease, of course, is cancer, and approximately 835,000 Americans will be diagnosed as having it this year.

Twenty years ago, only one patient in four survived cancer for at least five years. Today the rate is about one in three. If all skin and cervical cancers are considered, one in two will survive for at least five years, according to the latest information from cancer research centers.

Promising developments

Progress against cancer, although hard-won, has been significant. And today advances are coming on many fronts. Some hopefully promising developments in cancer chemotherapy are being reported by Warner-Lambert, where an accelerated cancer research program has been under way since late 1979.

More than 65 company scientists now focus full energies on new drugs to treat major solid tumors that remain resistant to cure, including colorectal, lung, breast and gastric cancers.

The focal point for company cancer research is Ann Arbor, Michigan, where two months ago a new $4 million cancer chemotherapy laboratory building opened.

At July dedication ceremonies, a leading scientist from the National Cancer Institute (NCI) called the new laboratories "a landmark in the history of private industry involvement in cancer research." He characterized the project as consistent with the trend toward more private involvement, one which the NCI favors and supports.

His reference was to the movement of companies like Warner-Lambert from the periphery of cancer research to the real battlefront. Cancer research has attracted greater private enterprise participation as knowledge of the biological processes that underlie the disease has grown and, along with improved opportunities for cures.

The Ann Arbor research laboratory, Warner-Lambert's latest commitment to the battle against cancer, houses the important soil screening or fermentation facet of the cancer program, as well as anticancer and antibacterial testing. Many of the stages essential to the identification, testing and small-scale production of anticancer compounds occur here, including culture isolation, fermentation in varying scales and testing for cancer-causing potential.

Progress in chemotherapy

An in-house pilot plant produces anti-cancer antibiotics in sufficient bulk to satisfy the requirements of human trials. At the approach of the marketing stage, the plant develops methods and systems for producing these drugs in mass quantities.

The research program concentrates on chemotherapy, the application of chemical compounds against malignancies. In recent years, chemotherapy has come of age. At least 12 types of cancer are curable today, mainly because of advances in chemotherapy.

Chemotherapy, while highly effective in many cases, needs further development and refinement, namely the discovery of more effective, specific, less toxic agents. This is especially true for solid tumors, Warner-Lambert's primary interest.

Warner-Lambert scientists are searching not for the "magic bullet" cure sought by the cancer pioneers, but a battery of new drugs, each with a specific mission. Combination therapy has become the approach of choice today. Doctors use radiotherapy and surgery for removal of large, primary tumors while chemotherapy deals a blow to cancerous cells that have spread or metastasized through the body.

Collaborative programs

Cancer's complexities are so overwhelming that the company relies on a number of collaborative research programs which have been struck with several outstanding universities and research institutions throughout the world. All serve to complement in-house research and provide added scope to the Warner-Lambert program.

At present, seven new antitumor compounds that have been developed by Warner-Lambert in collaboration with the NCI are in advanced stages of study. Four compounds are currently under clinical study: amsacrine, ametantrone, diaziquone and pentostatin.

Amsacrine's advanced stage of development will make it the first company cancer drug to reach market, initially in Europe later this year. It has proven its usefulness singly or in combination with other drugs against acute leukemia. In some studies, amsacrine has shown remission rates greater than 40 percent.

Diaziquone (AZQ) is another compound of special interest. Unlike most other cancer agents, AZQ crosses the blood-brain barrier. This ability may endow AZQ with activity against primary and secondary brain cancers.

Three other compounds are undergoing preclinical toxicology study, while several other candidates, derived either through synthesis or fermentation, will enter preclinical study soon.

A complete research organization is now in place, composed of organic chemists, tumor biologists, fermentation specialists, microbiologists, biochemists and clinical scientists.

Formidable task

Through the work of these scientists and a supporting group of other researchers at Ann Arbor and elsewhere, the company's cancer program continues to build steam. Their task is a formidable one, to score victories against the most imposing health problem of the day. As Dr. Jerry Weisbach, president of the Pharmaceutical Research Division, recently phrased it, "Our challenge is to be at the forefront in the development of new anticancer drugs to cure as yet untreatable tumors."

Among the first steps in soil sampling phases of anticancer research in the company's new cancer chemotherapy laboratories is the isolation of actinomycete colonies from agar plates.

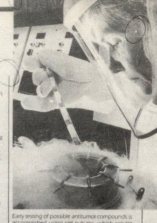

Early testing of possible antitumor compounds is accomplished using cell cultures, which can be stored indefinitely by freezing in liquid nitrogen-filled tanks, shown here. The company's first major anti-cancer product, Amsidine, was recently introduced in The Netherlands.

Cancer R&D head sees hopeful signs

An interview with Dr. Edward F. Elslager on cancer. Dr. Elslager is vice president of research, Pharmaceutical Research Division.

Q. The medical profession has in its arsenal radiation, chemical and surgical techniques for cancer treatment. How important are chemotherapeutic approaches today?

A. Chemotherapeutic approaches to cancer treatment are becoming increasingly important with the advent and acceptance of the combined modality approach to the treatment of solid tumors and lymphomas. Conceptually, this utilizes the best features of all available therapeutic modalities, including surgery, radiation therapy and chemotherapy, combined rationally to exert maximum lethal effects on the tumor. Each form of treatment has specific attributes and limitations. Systemic chemotherapy has the potential to eradicate microscopic residual disease and secondary tumors but, with a few exceptions, cannot eradicate large tumors. A decade ago only 25 percent of cancer patients were treated with chemotherapy. Today, 35 percent of patients receive chemotherapy, and it is projected that 45 percent will be treated with drugs within the next decade.

Q. In recent years, what notable advances have been made in cancer treatment, particularly chemotherapy?

A. Perhaps the most significant advance in cancer chemotherapy in recent years has been the evolution and acceptance of the concept of combination chemotherapy. Thus, anticancer drugs with different mechanisms of action, cell cycle actions, toxicities and times of onset of toxicity are combined to enable maximum tumor cell kill while minimizing host toxicity. Significant drugs include daunorubicin and platinol.

Q. Why has the cancer fight been so protracted?

A. Because it has proven to be a multifaceted, disease almost as complex as life itself. It is now recognized that cancer is not a single disease, but rather comprises a group of more than 100 diseases with different characteristics. Also, we have been unable to identify any fundamental differences between normal and cancer cells which would allow for the design of new drugs absolutely selective for neoplasms (tumors). Consequently, it has been necessary to rely primarily on cytotoxic drugs which not only kill rapidly dividing tumor cells, but also destroy rapidly dividing normal cells. In spite of early diagnosis and surgical removal, patients may already have many established and undetected microscopic metastases which become apparent only after the disseminated disease is measurable.

Q. What are the most promising avenues of research and do you foresee any possibilities for significant breakthroughs?

A. In the immediate future, continued progress will be made in the development of new and useful cytotoxic drugs utilizing traditional enlightened semi-empirical approaches. New drugs with unique chemical structures will be developed which will possess novel biochemical mechanisms of action, selective activity against solid tumors, greater specificity for tumor cells, lower host toxicity, improved activity against drug-resistant tumors and greater therapeutic effect when used in combination therapy. Over the next decade, I believe that revolutionary developments in cell biology will enable a better understanding of fundamental biological processes in cancer and provide more rational approaches to new drug design and testing. Rapid progress in genetics, recombinant DNA technology, monoclonal antibody techniques and biochemistry already signal novel approaches such as cell membrane active drugs, differentiating agents, oncogene product inhibitors and tumor-associated monoclonal antibody complexes.

---

(5) The printer's "blues" are copies of the actual negative that will be used to make the offset printing plate. The editor studies the blueprint carefully and notes where quality is not satisfactory—black or white spots on photos, crooked borders, or areas of the layout that do not appear to be printing evenly. For any changes other than these, the printer's charges will be high.

Cancer: a formidable opponent for 65 company researchers

Ann Arbor, Mich.—Cure. Increasingly this word is being heard when scientists, physicians, patients and their families discuss the most feared disease of our time. That disease, of course, is cancer, and approximately 835,000 Americans will be diagnosed as having it this year.

Twenty years ago, only one patient in four survived cancer for at least five years. Today the rate is about one in three. If all skin and cervical cancers are considered, one in two will survive for at least five years, according to the latest information from cancer research centers.

Promising developments

Progress against cancer, although hard won, has been significant. And today advances are coming on many fronts. Some hopefully promising developments in cancer chemotherapy are being reported by Warner-Lambert, where an accelerated cancer research program has been under way since late 1979.

More than 65 company scientists now focus full energies on new drugs to treat major solid tumors that remain resistant to cure, including colorectal, lung, breast and gastric cancers.

The focal point for company cancer research is Ann Arbor, Michigan, where two months ago a new $4 million cancer chemotherapy laboratory building opened.

At July dedication ceremonies, a leading scientist from the National Cancer Institute (NCI) called the new laboratories "a landmark in the history of private industry involvement in cancer research." He characterized the project as consistent with the trend toward more private involvement, one which the NCI favors and supports.

His reference was to the movement of companies like Warner-Lambert from the periphery of cancer research to the real battlefront. Cancer research has attracted greater private enterprise participation as knowledge of the biological processes that underlie the disease has grown and, along with improved opportunities for cures.

The Ann Arbor research laboratory, Warner-Lambert's latest commitment to the battle against cancer, houses the important soil screening of fermentation facet of the cancer program, as well as anticancer and antibacterial testing. Many of the stages essential to the identification, testing and small-scale production of anticancer compounds occur here, including culture isolation, fermentation in varying scales and testing for cancer-causing potential.

Progress in chemotherapy

An in-house pilot plant produces anticancer antibiotics in sufficient bulk to satisfy the requirements of human trials. At the approach of the marketing stage, the plant develops methods and systems for producing these drugs in mass quantities.

The research program concentrates on chemotherapy, the application of chemical compounds against malignancies. In recent years, chemotherapy has come of age. At least 12 types of cancer are curable today, mainly because of advances in chemotherapy.

Chemotherapy, while highly effective in many cases, needs further development and refinement, namely the discovery of more effective, specific, less toxic agents. This is especially true for solid tumors, Warner-Lambert's primary interest.

Warner-Lambert scientists are searching not for the "magic bullet" cure sought by the cancer pioneers, but a battery of new drugs, each with a specific mission. Combination therapy has become the approach of choice today. Doctors use radiotherapy and surgery for removal of large, primary tumors while chemotherapy deals a blow to cancerous cells that have spread or metastasized through the body.

Collaborative programs

Cancer's complexities are so overwhelming that the company relies on a number of collaborative research programs which have been struck with several outstanding universities and research institutions throughout the world. All serve to complement in-house research and provide added scope to the Warner-Lambert program.

At present, seven new antitumor compounds that have been developed by Warner-Lambert in collaboration with the NCI are in advanced stages of study. Four compounds are currently under clinical study: amsacrine, ametantrone, diaziquone and pentostatin.

Amsacrine's advanced stage of development will make it the first company cancer drug to reach market, initially in Europe later this year. It has proven its usefulness singly or in combination with other drugs against acute leukemia. In some studies, amsacrine has shown remission rates greater than 40 percent.

Diaziquone (AZQ) is another compound of special interest. Unlike most other cancer agents, AZQ crosses the blood-brain barrier. This ability may endow AZQ with activity against primary and secondary brain cancers.

Three other compounds are undergoing preclinical toxicology study, while several other candidates, derived either through synthesis or fermentation, will enter preclinical study soon.

A complete research organization is now in place, composed of organic chemists, tumor biologists, fermentation specialists, microbiologists, biochemists and clinical scientists.

Formidable task

Through the work of these scientists and a supporting group of other researchers at Ann Arbor and elsewhere, the company's cancer program continues to build steam. Their task is a formidable one; to score victories against the most imposing health problem of the day. As Dr. Jerry Weisbach, president of the Pharmaceutical Research Division, recently phrased it, "Our challenge is to be at the forefront in the development of new anticancer drugs to cure as yet untreatable tumors."

Among the first steps in soil sampling phases of anticancer research in the company's new cancer chemotherapy laboratories is the isolation of cancerigenic colonies from agar plates.

Early testing of possible antitumor compounds is accomplished using cell cultures, which can be stored indefinitely by freezing in liquid nitrogen-filled tanks, shown here. The company's first major anti-cancer product, Amsidine, was recently introduced in The Netherlands.

Cancer R&D head sees hopeful signs

An interview with Dr. Edward F. Elslager on cancer. Dr. Elslager is the president of research, Pharmaceutical Research Division.

Q. The medical profession has in its arsenal radiation, chemical and surgical techniques for cancer treatment. How important are chemotherapeutic approaches today?

A. Chemotherapeutic approaches to cancer treatment are becoming increasingly important with the advent of newer and more effective agents. There is growing acceptance of the combined modality approach to the treatment of solid tumors and lymphomas. Conceptually, this outlines the best features of all available therapeutic modalities, including surgery, radiation therapy and chemotherapy, combined rationally to exert maximum lethal effects on the tumor. Each stage of treatment has specific attributes and limitations. Systemic chemotherapy has the potential to eradicate microscopic residual disease and secondary tumors but, with a few exceptions, cannot eradicate large tumors. A decade ago only 25 percent of cancer patients were treated with chemotherapy. Today, 55 percent of patients receive chemotherapy, and it is projected that 45 percent will be treated with drugs within the next decade.

Q. In recent years, what notable advances have been made in cancer treatment, particularly chemotherapy?

A. Perhaps the most significant advance in cancer chemotherapy in recent years has been the evolution and acceptance of the concept of combination chemotherapy. Thus, anticancer drugs with different mechanisms of action, cell cycle actions, toxicities and times of onset of toxicity are combined to enable maximum tumor cell kill while minimizing host toxicity. Significant drugs include daunorubicin and platinol.

Q. Why has the cancer fight been so protracted?

A. Because it has proven to be a multifaceted disease almost as complex as life itself. It is now recognized that cancer is not a single disease, but rather comprises a group of more than 100 diseases with different characteristics. Also, we have been unable to identify any fundamental differences between normal and cancer cells which would allow for the design of new drugs absolutely selective for neoplasms (tumors). Consequently, it has been necessary to rely primarily on cytotoxic drugs which not only kill rapidly dividing tumor cells, but also destroy rapidly dividing normal cells. In spite of early diagnosis and surgical removal, patients may already have many established and undetected microscopic metastases which become apparent only after the disseminated disease is measurable.

Q. What are the most promising avenues of research and do you foresee any possibilities for significant breakthroughs?

A. In the immediate future, continued progress will be made in the development of new and useful cytotoxic drugs utilizing traditional enlightened semi-empirical approaches. New drugs with unique chemical structures will be developed which will possess novel biochemical mechanisms of action, selective activity against solid tumors, greater specificity for tumor cells, lower host toxicity, improved activity against drug-resistant tumors and greater therapeutic effect when used in combination therapy. Over the next decade, I believe that revolutionary developments in cell biology will enable a better understanding of fundamental biological processes in cancer and provide more rational approaches to new drug design and testing. Rapid progress in genetics, recombinant DNA technology, monoclonal antibody techniques and biochemistry already signal novel approaches such as cell membrane active drugs, differentiating agents, oncogene product inhibitors and tumor-associated monoclonal antibody complexes.

---

(6)   The page as it appears in the employee newspaper. (Courtesy Warner-Lambert)

bold line to set off each story, while another uses alternating bold and light rules to add character to the nameplate and to highlight featured articles.

90—Story list completed. Assignments to writers.

70—First drafts due from writers. Conferences.

60—Assignments to photographers and staff artist.

50—Final drafts due from writers. Editing.

40—All art must be in. Prepare rough dummies. All material to printer for typesetting by now.

25—Proofreading. Prepare comprehensive.

10—Printer prepares mechanical. Final corrections.

0—Distribution.

GENERATING STORY IDEAS

Reader surveys may help the editor to know generally what the readers like. But it is the editor's job to generate specific ideas. It is extremely easy for a periodical to get in a rut, to become predictable—and thus irrelevant. This is especially true when the publication runs a scant four pages, and several reports, columns, and departments are "must-run" matter, leaving precious little space for enterprise material.

Here are some ways a good editor gets story ideas:

All meetings held by the organization are potential "story sessions" from the editor's point of view. Most meetings are called to discuss problems and their solutions, new programs, or ways that an organization is responding to its environment. All of these topics can generate articles.

The editor should meet frequently with department heads and committee chairpersons to become familiar with the workings of the organization and to learn about new developments.

An occasional walking tour of the plant or premises will help the editor to see things from an outsider's point of view. Often, physical changes are made without thinking about their news value. Department bulletin boards can yield stories.

Distribution of a simple form for reporting news items can bring in some worthwhile information. It is useful to set up a network of "stringers"—one worker in each department who is responsible for reporting on human-interest items or developments that may not have been discussed in meetings attended by public relations personnel. If the editor can pay $25 for each short article used, the stringers probably will be fairly productive.

The editor should read related publications for story suggestions. A consultant for state dental association newsletters suggests that editors of county and regional dental newsletters might read the state and national journals, then think of ways to "localize" topics by interviewing dentists in their area. Many editors exchange subscriptions in order to keep up with what others in the field are doing.

The editor should affiliate with organizations dedicated to improving house organs, such as PRSA, IABC, and the American Business Press. There are specialized associations for editors of banking publications, Defense Department organs, medical journals, etc. Most hold occasional workshops in major cities.

A postpublication critique, in which the entire PR staff analyzes the effectiveness of the current issue, should generate ideas for the next one. A quarterly planning meeting should be used to generate ideas for the next three or four issues. Both of these devices can enhance the reputation of the newsletter editor within the organization, since outsiders such as department heads can be invited to help strengthen the role and the quality of the publication.

NOTES

1. Gail Lupton Porter, "Why They Read and Who Reads What: Information Utility, Market Segmentation, and the Government Magazine Editor." Master's thesis, University of Maryland, 1982
2. James E. Grunig, "Evaluating Employee Communication in a Research Operation," *Public Relations Review* 3 (Winter 1977):61–82

ADDITIONAL READING

Brigham, Nancy, *How to Do Leaflets, Newsletters and Newspapers* (Somerville, Mass.: Economic Affairs Bureau, Inc., 1982).

Hill, Donald E., *The Practice of Copyfitting* (Huntsville, Ala.: Graphic Arts & Journalism Publishing Co., 1971).

Hill, Donald E., *Techniques of Magazine Layout* (Huntsville, Ala.: Graphic Arts & Journalism Publishing Co., 1972).

Nelson, Roy Paul, *Publication Design, 3d ed.* (Dubuque, Ia.: Wm. C. Brown, 1983).

Reuss, Carol, and Donn Silvis (eds.), *Inside Organizational Communication* (New York: Longman, 1981).

Root, Robert, *Modern Magazine Editing* (Dubuque, Ia.: Wm. C. Brown, 1966).

van Uchelen, Rod, *Paste-Up: Production Techniques and New Applications* (New York: Van Nostrand Reinhold, 1976).

Wales, LaRae H., *A Practical Guide to Newsletter Editing and Design* (Ames: Iowa State University Press, 1976).

27

PHOTOGRAPHS AND ILLUSTRATIONS

We noted in Chapter 23 that the ability to supply or arrange exciting "visuals" increases the chances of placing a story on television. In truth, every medium needs photographs and illustrations. Presented with two articles of equal value, the magazine or newspaper editor is more likely to choose the one that is accompanied by "art."

Since preparing photographs for dissemination to the media is a skill most PR people need at one time or another, we'll examine the ways in which practitioners place art. First, however, let's look at management considerations and the basics of setting up an in-house photo operation. Finally, we'll see how to prepare pictures and illustrations for layouts and displays.

MANAGEMENT CONSIDERATIONS

Photographs represent a basic form of visual communication used in each of the four public relations models and nearly all of the programs described in Part III. Most often, pho-

tographs supplement written or spoken communication, as when they accompany a press release or are found in company publications, exhibits, slide-tape shows, or television and videotape. Sometimes, photographs can carry the entire message, as in a photo display or photo feature story.

Choose a Meaning for Your Photograph

It's important to have a communication objective in mind when you take or choose a photograph. The late film theorist Sol Worth of the University of Pennsylvania's Annenberg School of Communication believed strongly that photographs are more than a window to the world.[1] He believed photographs carry a meaning that a communicator intends to convey.

"Intent" means that the communication objectives we've discussed throughout this book apply to photographs as well as to written or spoken messages. Don't choose a photo just because it is interesting, artistic, or different. Determine what message you intend to communicate with the photo, and whether the person who sees the photo will understand and retain that message. It is difficult to change attitudes or behaviors with photographs alone, so don't expect those effects very often—although a particularly dramatic photo sometimes may change an attitude or stimulate a behavior.

Consider Visual Complexity When Publics Differ

Research on visual communication shows that photographs are more complex than illustrations, graphs, or similar graphic materials—that is, they carry more information. When a visual message is complex, the person who views it can take more and varied meanings from it. If you look at a graph of profits and losses, you probably receive the same message as anyone else who looks at the same chart. But when you look at a photograph meant to depict a retiree who has just completed forty years on the job, you might also see "dangerous working conditions," "capitalistic exploitation of labor" . . . or even memories of your grandfather.

Because photographs are complex—and thus interesting—they're particularly effective in getting and holding the attention of low-involvement, passive publics. But because they are complex, they're also not as useful for communicating difficult ideas. They can carry too much information that is not relevant to the idea you are trying to communicate. Thus, if you want to illustrate financial data in an annual report or research results in a technical report—information most often communicated to active, high-involvement audiences—you may want to use illustrations or graphs that are less complex than photographs.

A study by David Micklos, a graduate student and photography instructor at the University of Maryland, showed this difference.

He compared the visual materials used in two science magazines, *Science 81* and *Scientific American*.[2] *Science 81*'s audience members seek information about science because it arouses their curiosity, while *Scientific American*'s readers tend to be scientists who can apply the information to their work. Micklos found that *Science 81*'s editors use photographs mainly to gain the readers' attention, while *Scientific American*'s editors are much more likely to use graphs and illustrations, without bringing in the extraneous information found in photos.

Of course, photos can make a message more interesting for high-involvement publics, too.

Evaluating the Effect of Pictures

Because you use pictures with the intention of achieving an effect, you can evaluate them just as you can any other type of message. Generally, you will evaluate them as part of a readership study. Ask if people remember seeing a photograph—thus measuring the communication objective. To measure message retention, ask people what message they think a photograph conveyed. To measure message acceptance, ask whether people believe the photograph portrayed a situation the way it actually exists.

If you choose the attitude or behavior objectives, you would apply the measures of attitude and behavior described in Chapter 9, just as you would apply them to written messages. It will be extremely difficult, however, to separate the attitudinal and behavioral effects of photos from the written messages they usually supplement. Thus, seldom should you choose these two objectives for a photograph.

When you send pictures along with press releases to the media, remember that communication is your principal objective. Examine the press clippings and compare your success in getting on the media agenda when a picture accompanies a release as opposed to when a release goes out alone.

Costs Vary Greatly

You can take photographs yourself and pay for little more than the cost of your time, film, and processing. Or you may find it advantageous to hire a talented and expensive free-lance photographer. The costs vary greatly, and budgeting is essential before you choose one over the other. That's why we'll look at the in-house photo operation next.

ORGANIZING THE PHOTO OPERATION

At some point, every public relations department is faced with a decision: Do we commission our photos to be taken by outside photographers, or do we set up our own photo operation, including a fully equipped darkroom? Free-lance photographers may seem expensive, since their charges must reflect considerable overhead and the cost of getting one good print out of scores of shots and dozens of trial prints. Top-flight commercial photographers do not blush at charging $1,000 for a single photograph, when getting it involves half a day of shooting and countless hours in the darkroom working to achieve the perfect print. With experience, a PR department learns to appreciate the value of a good free-lance photographer.

There can be good reasons for setting up an in-house photo operation. In a fairly small PR department, a staff member who has an interest and expertise in photography can add a much-needed dimension to the print media effort. In a larger shop, there may be enough regular work to warrant employing a full-time photographer. The small department probably will need $1,000 to set up a basic darkroom, and it will be worth it. The big-time operator will need $10,000 to set up a darkroom, but it will be worth it. Just consider the $50 to $100 or more per shot that a free-lance must charge, and you will see how quickly a staff photographer can pay off.

Whatever the source of photographs, the PR department must be prepared to organize and keep track of the many photographs it commissions. A numbering and cataloging system should be instituted so that every single picture has its own identification and can be found in the proper place. As each roll of film is shot, negatives are placed in plastic holders, contact sheets are made, and each strip of contacts is serially stamped—84-24 identifies the twenty-fourth set of negatives filed during 1984. The code number 84-24-15 written on the back of a print indicates that it is frame 15 from the 84-24 set. This is the only way to keep track of individual shots in an operation where thousands of pictures are taken each year.

SUPPLYING PHOTOS TO THE MEDIA

Editors of newspapers and magazines usually begin laying out their pages by selecting the pictures that will "anchor" each display. Photos, in other words, are given the best display on the printed page. And that is why they are so important in public relations plans.

Whether a photograph accompanies a story or stands alone, the following specifications are fairly standard:

The 8-by-10-inch photo is the preferred size for submissions to newspapers and magazines that use black-and-white photos, although the 5-by-7 is sufficient for a head-and-shoulders shot of an individual; some PR operations stretch their budget by using the 4-by-5 for mug shots. The larger sizes ensure that the picture will be reduced for publication rather than enlarged, which is easier for the editor and results in better engraving quality. The 35-mm color transparency is the most common format for submitting photos to a magazine that uses color shots.

Seymour Cray (left) and John A. Rollwagen are pictured in a Cray Research, Inc., facility in Chippewa Falls, Wisconsin. In the foreground is a three-dimensional module for the CRAY-2 computer prototype immersed in a tank of clear, inert liquid to demonstrate liquid immersion technology.

It is useful to offer the media two versions of the same photo—one horizontal and the other vertical. Note that the PR agency here (Padilla and Speer, Inc.) has processed the photographs so that the cutline information is printed immediately below the picture on the same sheet of glossy paper. (Photos courtesy Cray Research, Inc.)

Seymour Cray (left) and John A. Rollwagen are pictured in a Cray Research, Inc., facility in Chippewa Falls, Wisconsin. In the foreground is a three-dimensional module for the CRAY-2 computer prototype immersed in a tank of clear, inert liquid to demonstrate liquid immersion technology.

4

The photo should be glossy for submission to any print medium. For television, however, provide a matte-finish print that will not reflect into the television lens. (For glossy finish, dry a photo against a smooth metal surface; for matte finish, dry it pressed against woven cloth.)

Your chances of placing a picture, especially in smaller media with low engraving budgets, are enhanced by providing "camera-ready" halftone reproductions of photographs already cropped to standard two- and three-column newspaper widths. That means you go to the extra expense of having a printer make the halftone and reproduce multiple copies of it on slick paper. But if it induces more editors to use the material because it can be pasted right onto their layouts, the expense is worth it.

Cutline information is typed double-spaced, just like the news release, and duplicated on white paper. Glue or tape is applied to a one-inch fold of the sheet, which is then affixed to the back of the photograph. The remainder of the sheet is folded over to protect the surface of the glossy photo, which is unusable if it becomes scratched or soiled.

Public relations photos do not normally carry a credit line for the photographer, unless the shot is provided by a well-known artist with the agreement that credit be given. It is assumed by the receiving news media that actual or tacit permission has been granted by all identifiable persons in the photograph to use their likenesses for publicity purposes. The public relations value of the photograph would be negated if complications later arose because of a failure to obtain these permissions (see Chapter 10, "Legal Constraints").

WRITING THE CUTLINE

When the cutline is written for a picture that accompanies a news release, the information is kept to a minimum. The meaning of the action in the picture is described in a few words, and all identifiable persons are named, unless it is clear that they are merely "models." For example:

> The terminal of the new computer that enables the company to monitor all traffic in the tri-county area and flash instant reports to police and area news media is operated by Fairbanks Corp. technician Fred Paltzman.

When the picture stands alone, the cutline must give all of the pertinent information that would appear in a short news story:

> TRAFFIC MONITOR. The Fairbanks Corp., located in the Beltline Industrial Park, has completed installation of a new computer that will enable the firm to electronically monitor traffic under a recently awarded federal Department of Transportation grant. Here Fairbanks technician Fred Paltzman operates the console, routing information to computer terminals at area news media and local police departments. Fairbanks President Ronald E. Glazer said the computerized traffic monitor should lessen jams and delays in the tri-county area.

Since the PR department cannot always be sure whether the news media will prefer to use the picture in conjunction with the full press release or let it stand alone with the longer cutline, frequently the practice is to provide both versions on the same cutline sheet.

Photographs are mailed in manila envelopes with a cardboard liner to provide protection. That extra stiffness, along with a "Photo Do Not Fold" warning on the front of the envelope, will ward off all but the most punitive of postal employees. Because of the extra value of photographs, it is also common for PR firms to have them hand-delivered by courier. Do not expect unused photos to be returned, however. The news media just don't have the time or resources. At best, they may file a timeless photo in the library for possible later use.

SELECTING THE SUBJECT

The alert PR person walks through the plant, the office, and the community with an eye toward subjects that will make good photographs. That may mean taking scouting trips to locations such as outlying plants and research areas, visualizing what will make a dramatic or storytelling shot. It means thinking of ways to avoid the standard head-and-shoulders mug shot: How can we show the subject in context, naturally, in an appealing way that doesn't suggest the scene was staged?

Another important skill to develop is selecting shots from the contact sheets. If you look at the contacts along with the photographer who took the shots, try to remain dispassionate. Look at the shots one by one in progression, seeking the single photograph that summarizes the idea found in the series of shots. Determine which picture has the most human interest or emotional appeal—a close-up of a face registering happiness, a gesture that telegraphs the subject's reaction to the situation. Next look for supporting shots that might make a multipicture spread. Then check to see that the pictures you selected are consistently excellent in tonal quality, with proper focus and contrast.

The dilemma of selecting the best picture is this: How can you avoid the cliché that will make the editor groan, yet hit upon the ready appeal of what interests people? The line is fine: A photo of a child discovering the wonder of a small animal is either downright corny or utterly charming. In fact, the corny one and the charming one may be found side by side on the contact sheet . . . if only you can decide which is which.

Editors despair of receiving the same kinds of pictures that have been crossing their desks since shortly after the camera was invented. Here are some standard shots that you should try to avoid:

Person at desk talking on telephone.

Group of retirees (honorees, appointees) standing in semicircle beaming at camera.

One person handing a check (certificate, trophy, plaque) to another.

Speaker standing at microphone on podium, with standard meeting hall decor including drape and potted palm in background.

We have all seen these shots so many times that they hold no interest for us. The photographer must be instructed to try for candid shots that catch the subject more naturally than the stock poses ever can. This can be a problem when the chief executive officer always seems to have one eye cocked on the camera, ready to strike a properly presidential pose. Press photographers know that the secret is to shoot dozens—even scores—of pictures in quick succession, in order to capture that moment when the guard is down and the subject appears ''real.''

CROPPING FOR EFFECT

Every photo gets its first ''crop''—cutting away of extraneous information—when the photographer frames the subject and eliminates unwanted background. When making a print from the negative, the photographer usually improves the picture by cropping still tighter, in order to make the central subject as large as possible. Then the PR specialist, acting as editor, decides whether to make still another crop—either for aesthetic reasons or because a picture of a certain size or proportion is needed for use in a specific layout.

Reasons for cropping a picture include:

To highlight a specific object or to focus on detail. At the time a product promotion picture is ordered, the photographer

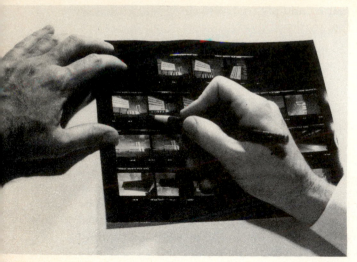

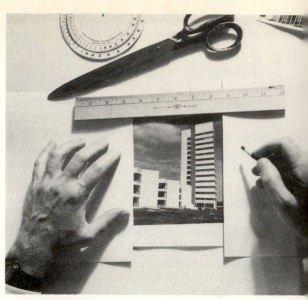

(1) Using the contact sheet prepared by the photographer, the editor selects the shot with the best composition, lighting, and focus. Marks made with grease pen indicate which shots the photographer is to enlarge.

(2) Lacking any aids for cropping pictures, the editor can use blank sheets of paper, moving them around until the desired content is framed in the desired proportions.

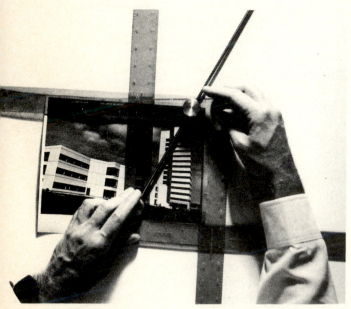

(3) A scaling and proportioning device, sold at art supply stores, enables the editor to crop a picture and ascertain the reproduced dimensions, all in one swift move.

(4) The printer's proportion wheel is a useful device for calculating the precise proportions of the picture when it is reproduced, expressed in both inches and percentage of increase or decrease in size from the original. (Photos courtesy David Kessler) may be told to provide a shot of "a woman modeling the new line of jewelry." When it comes time to select the photos that will be sent along with the news release, you may decide to crop to the hand and arm, eliminating the smiling features of the model's face—perhaps because other photos in the same group have smiling faces, and they are getting a bit repetitious.

To reduce ambiguity or remove distractions. Details that enhance a single photo may be extraneous when the photo is to be used with other shots. Sometimes the line of a hand or leg may lead the viewer's eye away from the most important element of the picture. Or, on a multipicture spread, a hand in one picture may seem to be pointing to something in an adjacent picture, with humorous results. These are situations in which the photo editor exercises the prerogative to chop the person off at mid-torso.

To fit a scheme. The editor may want to make a particular point by juxtaposing two pictures to call attention to similarities or differences. If so, the pictures may need to be cropped to make the parallel clear and to keep subject size consistent. It looks odd, for example, if the head size of the person in one photo is just 10 percent larger than the head of the person in the adjacent shot.

To highlight shapes or direction. The photographer tends to compose within the camera frame, achieving balance and unity. The designer who uses the photograph must work with a new frame: the page, the "spread," or the display background. New horizon and boundary lines may be created by blocks of type or the architectural environment. Thus, it is sometimes necessary to crop a perfectly fine picture in order to bring its shapes and directions in consonance with external elements.

Crop marks may be made by the photographer or designer right on the contact sheets or the glossy print, using an orange or white grease pencil. The simplest device for estimating and planning the crops before making the marks is a pair of cornices—L-shaped cardboard pieces that can be manipulated to create instant frames of any size or shape. In fact, any two sheets of paper lying handy can be used to perform a quick crop.

SIZING PHOTOS FOR REPRODUCTION

When the editor of a newsletter or other PR publication works with a staff photographer, prints of pictures often can be made to fit the precise space on the layout. But more often than not, available pictures have to be adapted to fit the space. That means "sizing" the photo—determining how much the shot must be reduced or enlarged during the engraving process.

Usually editors work with standard column widths, and pictures routinely are ordered two or three columns wide by so many inches "deep." In other words, the width is a common one, and the depth of the picture is the variable. Let us look at a typical sizing situation:

Known quantity:
    width of cropped picture = 8 1/4 inches
Known quantity:
    depth of cropped picture = 6 1/2 inches
Known quantity:
    two-column width on layout = 5 1/4 inches
Unknown quantity:
    picture's depth on layout = "x" inches

8 1/4 is to 5 1/4 as 6 1/2 is to x ($x = 4 1/8$)

The unknown quantity can be found by stating the problem as an algebraic problem and using a calculator to solve it:

8 1/4 is to 5 1/4 as 6 1/2 is to x ($x = 4 1/8$)

Fortunately for editors who are not mathematicians, printing-supply houses sell (or give away as promotional devices) a marvelous little gadget known as the proportioning wheel, which anyone can learn to use. By lining up the known numbers on the two rotating wheels, one finds the unknown quantity lined up opposite the depth of the cropped picture. Another versatile gadget for proportioning pictures is the Scaleograph, which can be used simultaneously for cropping and sizing. The device consists of two clear plastic cornices with ruled scales. The two pieces slide on an aluminum bar and can be tightened into a fixed relationship, once the desired crop is made by framing the desired portions of the picture. When the knobs are tightened, the plastic pieces slide along the aluminum bar. In effect, the Scaleograph mechanically performs the same function as the algebraic equation.

If you have only a ruler (plus a dread of both mechanical devices and mathematics), use a window or light table to shine through the picture so that you can make both your crops and your proportions on the back of the picture with soft pencil. Once you have drawn a full frame around the desired part of the picture, draw a diagonal line across the frame from corner to corner. Place the ruler so that "0" touches the left or right side of the frame, and the desired reproduction width touches the diagonal. (In the example above, place the ruler so that 5 1/4 touches the diagonal line.) Make a mark at that point on the diagonal. Now all you have to do is to take the vertical measurement from the mark you made on the diagonal line to the bottom margin of the cropped area, and that is your "unknown quantity"—the depth of the picture when it is reproduced.

MOUNTING PHOTOS FOR DISPLAY

Prints of photos that are to be published can be used even if they curl or get bent slightly at the corners. But pictures intended for display (see Chapter 30) need more protection.

Generally speaking, every print benefits from being dry mounted—laminated to stiff backing material—before it is framed, attached to a display card, or suspended in any manner. Dry mounting assures that the picture will stay flat. If done correctly, it prevents buckling, creasing, bubbling, or other imperfections that can decrease the impact of the photo.

A photo operation of any size should include a mounting press and associated materials. If yours is a small operation, you'll find that many photography- and art-supply houses provide free use of their press to their regular customers. Supplies you'll need are mounting board and dry-glue tissues, which form the adhesive bond when heat is applied. Also necessary are a small tool called a tacking iron, and a good-quality paper cutter for cropping the photo and the supporting mounting board. Personnel at the supply house where you obtain your equipment will show you how to make a "sandwich" of photo, adhesive tissue, and mounting board, and how to apply just the right amount of heat and pressure to cement them together.

Store mounted pictures in envelopes until you are ready to display them. The same dry-mounting process may be used to attach individually mounted shots to a larger board for a photo essay or display. However, since wrinkling is not a problem when attaching board to board, any other adhesive, such as rubber cement, is satisfactory.

PHOTO STORY LAYOUT

Whether you are planning a two-page magazine spread or a photo display for an exhibit, you will want to try to group the individual pictures so they make a statement greater than the sum of the parts. The editor or designer increases the impact by intriguing the viewer with patterns and positioning, leading the eye.

As you recall from our discussion of how to choose shots from a contact sheet, the goal is to find the all-purpose picture, some emotional human-interest shots, and photos that show the steps leading to the culmination of an event. To these we may add the context-setting shot, which documents the environment in which the events take place, and the reaction shot, which indicates how observers other than the main subject react. These categories are generalizations, of course, but they represent the basic elements of good visual storytelling.

Having selected the shots, rank them in terms of visual effect and storytelling ability. The photo you rank highest is your ''anchor'' picture, which you probably will make twice as large as any other photo in the essay. Place it in the grouping so that the viewer begins and ends by looking at this crucial picture. After all, a photo essay has to have a beginning or end, just like any other story. In order to achieve the PR objective of making a point, the essay must be more than merely a collection of individual shots.

ARRANGING FOR ILLUSTRATIONS

When you need something other than a photograph to do the job, here are some of the alternative sources of illustrations:

Clip-art services, for a monthly subscription fee, will supply voluminous books of simple line drawings of every subject imaginable. Because they are rendered in black-and-white with simple shading, these illustrations can be pasted directly onto the camera-ready offset layout without engraving.

At the other end of the cost spectrum you will find computer-generated graphics—basic pie-charts, bar graphs, and other standard information formats that are programmed into a computer. The software permits you to label the charts, enter your own figures, select colors or shadings, and print out the graphics in precisely the desired dimensions. Large companies may be able to afford their own system. Smaller organizations can order computer-generated graphics—including slides—from graphics services listed in the Yellow Pages.

Between the ''stock art'' of the clip services and the modern technology of the computer, there are, of course, the staff and free-lance artists who can produce illustrations to order. Finding and developing an artist who knows and understands the needs of your publications is a major accomplishment, which is why you probably will stick with the one you are lucky enough to find.

NOTES

1. Sol Worth (Edited by Larry Gross), *Studying Visual Communication* (Philadelphia: University of Pennsylvania Press, 1981), pp. 162–184.
2. David Micklos, ''Visual Complexity and the Function of Graphics in *Scientific American* and *Science 81*.'' Paper presented to the Graphics/Photojournalism Division, Association for Education in Journalism, Athens, Ohio, July 1982.

ADDITIONAL READING

Cherry, David, *Preparing Artwork for Reproduction* (New York: Crown, 1976).

Geraci, Philip C., *Photojournalism: Making Pictures for Publication* (Dubuque, Ia.: Kendall-Hunt, 1976).

Horenstein, Henry, *Black and White Photography: A Basic Manual* (Boston: Little, Brown, 1974).

Kemp, Weston, *Photography for Visual Communicators* (Englewood Cliffs, N.J.: Prentice-Hall, 1973).

Kobre, Kenneth, *Photojournalism: The Professionals' Approach* (Somerville, Mass.: Curtin & London, 1980).

Kodak, *Encyclopedia of Practical Photography* (Garden City, N.Y.: American Photographic Book Publishing Co., 1977).

Nelson, Norbert N., *Photographing Your Product for Advertising and Promotion* (New York: Van Nostrand Reinhold, 1970).

Schuneman, R. Smith (ed.), *Photographic Communication: Principles, Problems and Challenges of Photojournalism* (New York: Hastings House, 1972).

Swedlund, Charles, *Photography: A Handbook of History, Materials and Processes* (New York: Holt, Rinehart and Winston, 1981).

28

SLIDES AND MULTIMEDIA PRESENTATIONS

And now . . . let's turn off the lights and see the slides.

If your skin crawls whenever that sentence is uttered, you probably have watched one too many slide shows that were poorly organized and accompanied by a droning commentary of interest only to the narrator.

And yet, the slide show is one of the most useful systems of public communication available. Prepared and presented properly, it can be a solid public relations device that doesn't need an apologetic introduction.

MANAGEMENT CONSIDERATIONS

Most of the management considerations we discussed in the previous chapter on photographs apply also to slides and multimedia presentations. But because we're now talking about showing groups of photographs on one or more projectors, the technique has somewhat fewer uses and slightly different effects.

Slide shows can be used for each of the four public relations models, although the

communicator's intent would be different for each model:

The press agent most often uses slide presentations to promote products, shows, and events to captive audiences.

The public-information specialist uses slides to disseminate information about an organization or program at seminars, exhibits, open houses, etc.

The two-way asymmetric communicator finds that slide shows—especially those that include multimedia techniques—can be persuasive because they create a sense of involvement and arouse emotion. The Burson-Marsteller agency, for example, used a multimedia presentation of pollution scenes to sensitize oil company managers to pollution problems.

The two-way symmetric communicator wouldn't base an entire program on a slide show. But such a show can be a useful way to make a preliminary presentation of an organization's position and to trigger discussion with aware and active publics in a group setting.

Slide Shows Supplement Face-to-Face Contact

Slide shows can be used in all of the specialized public relations programs discussed in Part III. However, they can be used only when those programs set up group sessions with members of target publics. Thus, public relations people use slide shows most often in these programs:

Community relations—to supplement tours, open houses, speeches, dialogue sessions with community leaders.

Employee relations—in special seminars or presentations, economic-education discussions, presentations on employee benefits or collective bargaining proposals.

Financial relations—to present financial information to shareholders or financial analysts.

Promotion and fund raising—for presentations to buyers, potential donors, publics with particular interests in a service.

Educational relations—for classroom presentations.

You might want to use a slide show for a presentation to the press. But often the press won't "sit still" for slides. Reporters want to ask questions of news sources. Slides may work well for some presentations to the trade press, however, such as new product introductions.

You can also use slides for presentations to activist publics . . . but don't fill the entire dialogue session with slides, because the activists will want to talk and argue, and they will get impatient if the slide show takes too long.

Objectives, Publics, and Evaluation

As you would with other photographs, have an objective and effect in mind when you put together a slide show. Maximize message retention and understanding. Ask yourself what the audience already knows and what you want it to know.

Slide shows rarely change attitudes and behaviors, but they have a slightly better chance of achieving those effects than still photographs alone. Dramatic sequencing of slides can have a more involving, emotional impact than single pictures.

We also said in the previous chapter that pictures, because they are complex, can get the attention and interest of otherwise passive publics—and that they can make instrumental information more palatable for active publics. Slide shows, especially complex multimedia presentations, can increase that effect because of their greater visual complexity. But keep in mind that these complex visual presentations may arouse interest and emotions but not communicate a message. If you want a clear message to come across, don't make your presentation too complex.

While still photos can be evaluated as part of a readership study, it's not so easy to measure the effect of a slide show. It is too obtrusive to hand out a questionnaire to members of an audience that has just seen a slide show.

Instead, pretest the slide show on a sample audience. You can use a questionnaire with questions similar to those described in Chapter 9 to measure each of the objectives. You also can use a variation of the signaled stopping technique to see how the trial audience uses your message. Provide people with a list of slides, and ask them to indicate next to a slide description whenever they feel like stopping for one of the standard reasons—to register confusion, agreement, or understanding.

Budget Your Costs and Time

Slide shows can cost little more than the labor, film, and processing, or they can be quite expensive if you add sophisticated equipment and specialized personnel. Thus, you'll want to look at how often your public relations department will present slide shows before investing in expensive equipment. Think of renting equipment or contracting with outside specialists. Budget carefully, and weigh costs against the frequency with which you will use slide equipment to reach the captive audiences for which slides shows communicate effectively.

As you will see, slide shows take much preparation and planning. Thus, you will find Gantt charts and network analyses especially useful.

PLANNING AND SCRIPTING

When your objectives have been established, outline the major points of the presentation, still not worrying about the exact visuals to be used. The list of main points is the equivalent of an outline for a speech or any other form of mass communication. In other words, the content of the message should be decided before selecting the form. If one starts with visual images, the danger is that objectives never will be set down. The result may be a presentation that is somewhat pleasing aesthetically but that fails to make specific points.

The outline must be broken into two parts:

1. Individual pieces of information—single ideas or concepts.
2. The visual images or series of images that will illustrate those concepts.

At this point, it is helpful to borrow a technique from television production: the split script. Place the concept (single piece of information) on one side of the planning sheet, the visual images on the other side:

Eventually, you must come up with a suggested shot or series of shots for each of the major and minor points in your outline.

Once the outline script and the visuals have been decided upon, the next task is writing the narration. But first, you'll have to make some more important decisions, based on your objectives:

> Will the narration be live, which can make the presentation more personal? Or will it be recorded, which ensures accuracy and proper coordination of sound and visual?
>
> Will the narrator be an authoritarian figure, a professional-sounding announcer, or perhaps a "realistic" protaganist, such as an employee?

When the script has been written, it will become apparent if more shots are needed in order to fill out some sections of the show. Condensation of the visuals may be necessary in order to prevent "stalling" in sections where there is insufficient narration to cover the series of slides.

It should be noted that, on rare occasions, satisfactory results have been obtained merely by gathering together available slides and having someone write a sharp script to read as their accompaniment. A slide may pop up on the screen at the moment when the narrator is making a corresponding point. But, just as likely, a strange juxtaposition of visual image and verbal statement may occur: the narrator talks about the organization's mascot, a mongrel pup, just as the photo of our illustrious president comes up on the screen.

Points to be Made	Visuals
Pelham Corp. is located in Centerville and is part of the business community.	Skyline of Centerville, with successive shots closing in on Pelham's rooftop sign.
Pelham is a clean place to work, a nonpolluting neighbor.	Views of lawn, flowers and picnic tables in employee outdoor lunch area.
Pelham is not a cold, impersonal place.	Shots of executives meeting with group of employees.

The professional-quality show is arranged so that a verb or noun in the narration corresponds to an action or an event on the screen. That "cue" word may be underlined in the script so that the narrator will accentuate the word, making the connection between the visual and the aural:

staff. Look for these common faults of slide shows:

Show Is Too Short • A selection of only a dozen slides, with each held on the screen for two or three minutes, is likely to be boring unless each slide has a great amount of detail to be studied. Audiences do not like to sit in

Narration	Visuals
"Youth in our community need adult guidance."	Counselor with hand on shoulder of teenager.
"Someone must show them useful skills for living."	Counselor holds up copy of auto-repair manual.
"And they need to learn for themselves."	Two young men puzzling over broken auto part.

A slide show should place demands on two key senses, sight and hearing. When both are working in coordination, the chances are greatly enhanced that the intended points will reach their mark.

In order to visualize the slide show before the script has been written and the photographs have been shot, it is helpful to prepare a planning board, which serves the same function as the storyboard in television or film. Using index cards, sketch each individual shot and write below the sketch what point is being made by the visual image. By putting these sketch cards on a board the entire planning team can view, it becomes easier to detect areas of omission or repetition. This device is especially helpful when different people will prepare the script and the transparencies. Gathered around the planning board, the members of the team can arrive at a better consensus on what the finished product will look like.

EVALUATING
THE ROUGH PRESENTATION

Before showing the completed presentation to a preview audience for reaction, schedule a few run-throughs for the public relations

the dark listening to what is obviously a lecture accompanied by a handful of visuals. If there is too little visual information for a slide show, use posters or wall charts instead.

Show Is Too Long • An hour-long slide presentation is successful only if a great amount of information is dispensed, or if the narrator is able to keep the audience interested with lively commentary. Ordinarily, a slide show of ten to twenty minutes, followed by a question-and-answer period, is more enjoyable. Not infrequently, the duration of the show is dictated for the wrong reason: "We can only start the tour every half hour, so the slide show must be twenty-five minutes long." The audience can detect padding and will grow restless.

Pace Is Too Slow or Too Fast • An audience does not appreciate slides that flash by so rapidly that important details are missed. The presenter who thinks that a shotgun approach to projection will assure visual excitement may really only be causing headaches and inviting the audience to tune out. The audience also may grow restless if the pacing is relentless—precisely fifteen seconds for each shot, for example. The pace should be varied from time to time by alternating slides that call for a longer attention span with groups of slides that can be shown in rapid succession. (Self-activated or continuous slide shows in display booths often are programmed at set intervals. In that context, however, the dynamic is different, because the audience is not held captive.)

Slide Selection Is Redundant • A dozen views of a building shot from slightly different angles may keep the information on the screen changing, but it will not necessarily be effective. Twenty shots of children at a playground do not convey the message of ''successful youth program'' as well as two or three technically excellent and well-chosen shots. If one cue word or one line of narration has to account for more than just a few pictures, the entire show may need overhauling.

Major Points Are Inadequately Illustrated • Each major point in the script should be illustrated by a cluster of related visual information. Repetition of key slides may help solve the problem, but the audience feels cheated when multiple use is made of the same images.

TITLES, CHARTS, AND GRAPHICS

Title slides and other graphics such as tables and charts add professionalism to a show. The titles also divide longer shows into manageable sections, provide transition from one subject area to another, and help reinforce major points.

Some graphics-supply houses offer blank slides that can be written or typed upon to create simple titles and tables, but they usually look so crude that they should be used only in emergencies. If you plan your slide presentation carefully, all titles and graphics should be accounted for from the beginning. One index card goes on the planning board for each title, color coded so it can be retrieved in a group and handed over to the person who will make the titles.

All titles and graphics should be shot at the same time, with the same camera and lighting, to assure consistency of color, brightness, and tone. Background colors, typefaces, and other design elements should be harmonious with the photo transparencies. For a show on state parks, use greens and browns, for example. For a new-product introduction, pick up the colors on the packaging or colors associated with the rest of the company's line.

As we mentioned in an earlier chapter, computer-generated graphics, while expensive, are now the ''state of the art,'' and they should be prepared or purchased if they are within reach of your budget.

Keep the Audience in Mind

Never forget the makeup of the proposed audience. A leading midwestern newspaper assembled an informative show on display advertising, with an intended audience primarily of advertising salespersons and retail advertisers. A jaunty little stick-figure character was used on the title cards, pointing at the numbers and grinning at the audience. That was an effective device for the middle-aged male target audience.

But when the slide show was shown to college advertising classes, the students burst out laughing at the little man and his antics, which they described as ''corny'' and ''old-fashioned.'' One instructor remedied the problem by removing most of the slides featuring the silly salesman.

One PR director was advised by his superiors to make his title card lettering look more ''hand-drawn.'' They explained that his presentation was so slick that he was giving off a ''holier-than-thou'' image that might work to the detriment of the information campaign.

Keep Preparation Simple

Even the PR person without art training can prepare title cards, using transfer letters and nonreflective card stock. If you are shooting the titles with a 35-mm camera on a copy stand (see next section), use 9-by-12-inch cards with border lines that reduce the actual title area to about 7 by 10 1/2 inches. With planning, you can figure out which words, phrases, or even entire sections of titles and charts will be repeated on two or more cards. You can then place these elements on movable pieces so that they can be reused each time just by moving them to the next card.

Hard-to-read titles and charts defeat their purpose. Cluttering the slide with too much information, not leaving sufficient borders for visual relief, and choosing type that is too small to be read more than a few feet from the screen are common reasons for illegibility. The Kodak booklets listed as suggested reading at the end of the chapter offer several guidelines for setting the proper ratio between type height and viewing distance. Overly fancy typefaces and insufficient contrast between the graphic elements and the background may also be detrimental.

Some of the points in this section appear to be painfully obvious, and yet the same flaws persistently mar slide shows. The public relations practitioner cannot afford to treat any principle of visual communication as "too elementary."

BASIC SLIDE-SHOW EQUIPMENT

As we noted in the previous chapter, outside free-lance photographers can be hired to shoot pictures. However, the PR department that anticipates making slide shows regularly for training and promotion will want to buy some basic equipment.

Camera • Transparencies usually are made with a 35-mm reflex camera. The through-the-lens viewing of a reflex camera permits precise composition of the frame when shooting. You'll want to equip the camera with a close-up lens, which is indispensable for making titles. A wide-angle lens will solve the problem of making good interior shots in cramped spaces. Also plan to buy a tripod and cable release: Both help ensure a steady, unblurred shot.

Copying stand • For making titles and charts and for copying still photos, the copying stand is a must. It holds the camera steady in relationship to the flat surface upon which the materials to be copied are placed, and it may also be used to hold the necessary lights in the proper position so that there is no reflection from the material being copied. Kodak's Ektagraphic Visualmaker is a relatively inexpensive copying outfit. However, if price is no object, you'll want a professional model that comes with guides and masks for pinpoint cropping and positioning of material, as well as holders for transparent sheets of plastic upon which lettering may be placed for superimposition over background photographs.

Lights • For titling and copy work as well as close-ups and shots taken in confined spaces, you'll need photoflood bulbs and reflectors mounted on their own small tripods. One light can be used to enhance general illumination, while the other fills in shadows around faces or other details.

Editing and Viewing Stand • An editing stand is merely an inclined translucent surface, lighted from behind, with narrow ridges that hold slides in rows for viewing and rearranging. It is worth getting the largest model you can afford, so that you can edit as many as 80 to 100 slides at one time.

Storage • Heat, dust, and temperature extremes are the enemies of the transparency. Slides should be stored in their projection trays in a metal cabinet. Out-takes, duplicates, or slides that have not yet been organized into a show may be stored conveniently in compartmented pages of clear plastic, which are indexed and placed in a heavy-duty three-ring binder.

Projectors and Accessories • When shopping for projectors, you'll want to base your decision on the availability of features and accessories that can improve the presen-

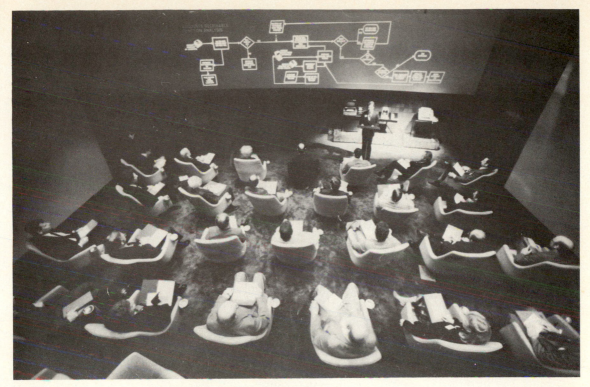

It's not just a "slide show" when Bell System marketing experts demonstrate new communication systems to business customers. Wide-screen projection is accomplished in a special seminar room with plush armchairs, perfect acoustics, and carefully controlled lighting. (Reproduced with permission of AT&T)

tation. Remote-control systems free the operator from standing next to the projector. Fade-dissolve mechanisms coordinate two or more projectors working in tandem (see next section). Other add-ons permit sound/visual synchronization with a tape recorder. Kodak's well-known Carousel series is preeminent in the field, although other manufacturers offer similar equipment to industry and educators.

MULTIMEDIA PRESENTATIONS

Slide shows used to be characterized by the constant clicking and blinking of the single manually operated projector. Films, on the other hand, offer a continuous and smooth montage of shots. The distinction has been blurred by the development of fade-dissolve mechanisms and projection of multiple still images. Slide projection is greatly enhanced by using one of many multimedia approaches:

Dual-Projector Fade-Dissolve • Twin projectors, linked with a device such as the Model 2 Kodak Carousel Dissolve Control, produce seamless shows in which one slide comes into view as the previous one is fading out, sometimes giving the illusion of a moving image. After a show has been edited, odd-numbered slides, including an opaque blank at the beginning, are placed in one unit. Even-numbered slides, including the opening title, are placed in another. The projectors are placed side by side or one above another in a rack that positions them properly. The frames then are perfectly overlapped, using two trial slides in order to assure a perfect match at the borders. The dissolve-control mechanism switches from one projector to the other automatically when the remote switch is depressed.

Slide-Tape Synchronization • In contrast to what you might think after enduring some slide shows, it isn't necessary to hear an annoying "beep" on a taped sound track every time the operator is supposed to click the projector switch. The cue for the next slide can be laid on the silent second track of a stereo (dual-track) tape recorder that carries the narration and background music on only one track. In addition to the recorder/playback unit and the projector, you'll need the Kodak Carousel Sound Synchronizer, which links the equipment and automatically coordinates the show. (If you are planning to distribute copies of your show to users who do not have the additional equipment, it may not be feasible to make a sound-slide synchronized version.) A console unit housing the tape recorder, projector, and synchronizer is used for displays and exhibits where the show is to be repeated over and over again, in which case an automatic-rewind mechanism must be added.

Mosaic Presentations • If creativity, patience, and adequate budget are all found in your media operation—and, most importantly, if you have experienced professional audiovisual technicians on your staff—you might decide to dazzle your audiences with a multipanel, wide-screen presentation involving as many as eight projectors. By lining up four pairs of projectors, each pair fading and dissolving to account for one-fourth of the screen area, you can present a Cineramalike show or a quadrant mosaic. With careful editing and timing, you can prepare a panoramic sweep across the entire screen—depicting your organization's headquarters,

for example—and then move a version of that same shot to a single quadrant, while the other sections of the screen carry a fast-moving montage depicting the various activities that go on in the headquarters building.

If you have projectionists who can follow a multipart script and operate equipment with split-second timing, you may even use moving pictures in one or more of the quadrants during part of the show. If your organization has the means to consider such a complicated concept, you should consult with your audiovisual suppliers for the latest in computer-coordinated multimedia presentations. It now is possible to preprogram all projector and sound cues into a microcomputer that effectively and consistently runs the entire presentation for you.

Computerized or not, a complex multimedia show takes hundreds of hours of preparation and practice, You even will learn to put fresh lamps in all of the projectors for an important showing—expensive, but it ensures consistency of projection image across the screen! It can all be worth it if you really want to impress an audience.

ADDITIONAL READING

Kodak publication No. T-43, "A Simple Wooden Copying Stand for Making Title Slides and Filmstrips (Rochester: Kodak, 1976).

Kodak publication No. V1-30, "Effective Visual Presentations" (Rochester: Kodak, 1978).

Kodak publication No. AE-92, "Selecting Slides for Color Prints and Duplicate Slides" (Rochester: Kodak, 1976).

Kodak publication No. AA-6, "Slide Showmanship with a Kodak Carousel Projector" (Rochester: Kodak, 1975).

Minor, Ed, and Harvey R. Frye, *Techniques for Producing Visual Instructional Media* (New York: McGraw-Hill, 1970).

Ward, John, "Slide Shows: Turning Professional," *Audio-Visual Communications* (January 1978):28, 62–64.

29

FILMS

The newly created New Jersey Sports and Exhibition Authority had a problem. The citizens, investors, banks, and other institutions of the state were wary: Was it really possible to build a new stadium, racetrack, and arena in the New Jersey meadowlands, practically in the shadow of New York City? The press and the state legislature were skeptical.

The sports authority felt that its ambitious development plan was well conceived. It commissioned a 16-mm color film to tell the story. The producers wanted the film to project an overwhelming sense that the mammoth undertaking was both feasible and necessary. They also tried to appeal to the pride of New Jerseyans, a quality often thought to be in short supply.

Beginning with a horizon-to-horizon view of the site, the film dazzled the viewer with the feeling of an expanse of beautiful land, accessible by modern highways and rail links. New York City's towering skyscrapers were visible on the right, and the major urban centers of the Garden State could be seen on the left. When the camera panned over models of the football stadium and the racetrack, the motion—enhanced by stirring music—excited the imagination of the audience far more than a still photo representation could.

Similarly, the film's graphic elements, which explained the funding and outlined the expected economic growth of the area, were animated in vivid colors. This added excitement to the factual discourse on the numbers of persons served, the expected revenue, and the employment dollars to be generated. Even at the press showings, where skeptical reporters wanted to know the hard facts, there was a noticeable appreciation of the effectiveness of the filmed message. In fact, the high quality of the film stood as symbolic evidence of the commitment and the professionalism of the sports authority management.

(The film was always preceded by a short presentation from a member of the sports authority public relations staff, who also solicited questions from the audience immediately following the film showing. The PR department understood that a flashy movie alone might be seen as an attempt to overwhelm the audience with an emotional approach instead of a rational one.)

Today, the Meadowlands Sports Complex is reality, home of the football Giants, soccer Cosmos, basketball Nets, hockey Devils, and harness racing's top event, the Hambletonian. Film played a significant part in the success story.

Everybody loves the excitement when a movie projector begins to roll, the lights are turned off, and images flood the screen. And yet, for all its novelty, film has been used in promotion practically since the beginning of the century. In 1913, Hampton Institute, a college established to educate former slaves, made a film documentary depicting college life in order to recruit young blacks for the school.[1] The U. S. government used films as early as World War I to facilitate recruiting and to marshall those on the home front for activities ranging from recycling to buying war bonds to resisting foreign propaganda.[2]

Some more recent examples follow of film's role in public relations.

Research by the brokerage firm of Merrill Lynch showed that women are a major potential source of investment dollars, but many are unwilling to invest until they better understand how it will work for them. The research also showed that women investors want a more personal sales approach than men require. The firm produced a documentary-style film highlighting the personal financial stories of professional, working, and widowed women. The film is used to open seminars Merrill Lynch conducts around the country especially for women.[3]

The Bethesda Lutheran Home in Watertown, Wisconsin, had been using film copies of an NBC documentary on custodial care for the mentally retarded and physically handicapped. However, because of the facility's new emphasis on treatment and training, a new film was needed. Its "stars" were the staff, many of the patients, and even 200 local residents who filled a chapel in a sequence stressing the role of Christian faith in the healing process. The 100 prints of Faces of Hope are shown to church and community groups, schools, seminaries, advocacy groups, mental health workshops, and prospective donors.[4]

Almost every American has seen McDonald's All-American High School Band marching and playing in the Rose Bowl or Macy's Thanksgiving parades. In order to get music teachers, principals, and students involved in the nominating procedure, the hamburger chain distributes an exciting film, The Musical All-Americans, which depicts auditions, practice sessions, and highlights from performances.[5]

Industrial films sponsored by large corporations range from relatively hard-sell messages that detail a company's involvement in exploration for new energy sources, to soft-sell messages that celebrate mankind's history or ingenuity, with only the sponsoring firm's name on the titles and credits to act as a promotional tie-in. The award-winning Why Man Creates, produced for Kaiser Aluminum and Chemical Corp., is an example of soft-sell, as are many of the special 360-degree or wide-screen films shown at world's fairs by industrial giants such as Kodak and General Motors.[6] Films that deal more openly with the relations between industry and governments or consumers include Monsanto's The Chemical Facts of Life, Procter & Gamble's Is Anybody Listening? and Texaco's The Big Job.[7]

Countering the messages of big business on issues such as pollution and nuclear energy are the films prepared and disseminated by activist organizations such as the Green Mountain Post, which distributes such documentaries as Lovejoy's Nuclear War, which details one man's act of civil disobedience against a utility's attempt to build a nuclear power plant. The films are publicized in a quarterly bulletin and rented or sold to conservation and political groups.[8]

MANAGEMENT CONSIDERATIONS

The above examples span the four models of public relations. Films can be made to be shown to employees and at community meetings or events, schools, museums, fairs, and other display areas. Films can be made to promote, to inform, to persuade, or to trigger a dialogue with key publics.

Like other visual media, films work especially well with passive, low-involvement publics—people who enjoy ''consuming'' the film even if it contains no practical information. (Consider your joy when the professor shows a film instead of lecturing!) Film also makes instrumental information interesting as well as useful.

Films, Too, Must Meet Objectives

As with photos and slide shows, films can maximize message retention and acceptance, and they may help to change attitudes and behaviors, too. Evaluate a film on a trial audience, using questionnaires to measure the four communication effects.

If your organization uses many films, you can purchase an Audience Analyzer to evaluate a film the same way the signaled stopping technique is used for print. An Audience Analyzer has buttons that viewers can push to record their reactions as they view a film. These buttons can be labeled with responses similar to those of the SST: interest, boredom, agreement, confusion. A computer records the responses and correlates them with film sequences.

If you cannot afford an Audience Analyzer, provide members of the trial audience with copies of the film script, and ask people to record stops as they view the film. While this technique interrupts viewing more than the mechanical device, it is a reasonable substitute.

Films Take Time and Money

The U. S. Department of Agriculture in Washington, D.C., has the largest film operation outside of Hollywood. Some public relations departments have film specialists, but few have production facilities. Typically, outside film producers are contracted to shoot the film, edit it to specifications, and deliver a print to a laboratory for reproduction.[9]

Obviously, a PR manager must think carefully before investing in a film facility or before contracting a producer. Careful research and planning must be done before you choose film as the appropriate medium to reach a target public. If you do choose film, you must budget and compare the costs of in-house production with outside contracts, or a combination of the two.

Films, too, require complex time budgeting. If your film has to be done at a certain time, plan the sequence of production activities. Even if the film doesn't have a definite deadline, network analysis can help to avoid wasted time while, for example, a film crew waits for a scriptwriter who was supposed to have finished three days ago.

SELECTING THE FORMAT

Super-8 is the so-called amateur or family film format, designed to be cheap and easy to use. But as Super-8 cameras, projectors, and accessories have gotten increasingly sophisticated, the small format has become an acceptable alternative to the more common 16-mm, just as 16-mm formerly earned its place in a field once dominated by ''theater-quality'' 35-mm. When agricultural journalist Orion Samuelson accompanied a trade delegation to the People's Republic of China in 1978, the Chinese government stipulated that he could film only with Super-8. If they hoped thus to restrict the impact of his film, they were wrong, because the footage was good enough to use on the Public Broadcasting System's *MacNeil/Lehrer Report*.

Most sound systems available for Super-8 are not up to the standards of PR use, so the small format works best where commentary can be provided by a live narrator. Certainly, Super-8 is good enough for documentation of a new building site or recording a special event such as a groundbreaking ceremony. And, as we shall see in the next chapter, it often is used in displays, where it can be spliced into a continuous loop for back-projection on a translucent screen.

Despite gains by Super-8, the 16-mm format is the standard for sound films made for television, for distribution to schools, and for training use in government and industry. The image from 16-mm film is bright and clear even in an auditorium seating 2,000 persons, and the sound systems developed for 16-mm projection equipment are similarly effective. Film editors prefer to work in 16-mm because it is easier to handle and cut, and it is fairly easy to study the image when the shot is held up to the light. Film laboratories are set up to accomplish all types of special effects such as wipes, dissolves, and fades in the 16-mm format, whereas they may refuse to handle Super-8.

PLANNING AND SCRIPTING THE FILM

Most films begin as a general idea, and that idea is first set on paper in the form of a synopsis:

> This ten-minute film depicts a trip down the Delaware River by two canoeists. They put in at a secluded point north of the Delaware Water Gap, and the first part of their trip is peaceful, beautiful, and uneventful, capturing the spirit of man enjoying nature. But as they draw closer to the Philadelphia metropolitan area, pollution and water hazards increase, and the abandonment of the journey at a point where industrial wastes are being poured into the river is a comment on how man has spoiled his most precious natural resources.

Even a major epic first must be boiled down into this 100-word format, in order to summarize the main point of the film and to indicate the style and mood. When the synopsis is approved, you will next need to prepare a "treatment," which is a scene-by-scene (but not necessarily shot-by-shot) explanation of everything that will happen in the film. In the above example, the treatment would begin:

> Open with two canoeists driving past a Delaware Water Gap sign to establish location. Their car bumps along a dirt road leading to the water. They stop, get out, stretch, breathe the fresh air, and point at ducks bobbing on the water. They spread a map out on the hood of the car and trace the route of their voyage down the river . . .

Like the synopsis, the treatment is a planning tool that enables PR managers to visualize the film. When it has been approved, you would then prepare a script like the one in Exhibit 29–1, complete with camera directions, times, and, if appropriate, dialogue.

In addition to a script, it is useful to prepare a storyboard comprised of a sketch of each shot in the film. That way the relationship of each object in the frame can be shown, along with the movement of each character and the motion of the camera as it tracks the subject, zooms in, pulls back, or pans. Most public relations films are group efforts and require the approval of a top manager who may not have any film experience. The storyboard enables the filmmaker to present the manager with a visual representation of the story early in the planning process.

Included in the storyboard should be all title cards, credits, still pictures, and charts or graphics. These are prepared by the art department or a typographer, filmed with studio lighting, and edited into the finished film. (When the Bell System used historic black-and-white still pictures as part of a documentary on the history of the telephone, it instructed the laboratory to add sepia tone and other tints to the pictures in order to give the old prints more life and to make them fit better into the full-color film.)

EXHIBIT
29–1
''Down the
Delaware''

Scene I/Shot 1   (Long shot)   10 seconds

Car with canoe on top is moving along highway with trees
and boulders in background. Camera pans left to right until
"Delaware Water Gap" sign comes into view at the right.

Scene I/Shot 2   (Medium shot)   (approx) 5 seconds

Stationary camera. Sign fills right half of screen, and
highway fills left side. Shot begins with empty highway and
lasts as long as it takes the car with the canoe on top to pass
the sign.

Scene I/Shot 3   (Close-up)   10 seconds

Tracking shot taken alongside moving car at right angles,
framing the two canoeists in the passenger side window. They
are talking animatedly, and the person on the passenger side
gestures, pointing through the windshield.

Scene I/Shot 4   (Medium-Long shot)   3 seconds

View, through windshield, of dirt road leading down to
river from main highway.

Scene I/Shot 5   (Close-up)   5 seconds

Same as I/3. Passenger is nodding head to indicate "Yes,
that's the place."

PROMOTIONAL TIE-INS

While the film is being processed and duplicates are being made for distribution, the PR department should plan the promotion of the film. Posters and brochures can be printed to publicize showings. Because the information in the film cannot be stored and retrieved by the audience, you might want to prepare a fact sheet for distribution at the film showing.

Is the film to be used in schools and colleges? Most teachers say they want to have lesson guides, bibliographies, background information, and other print materials to use in the classroom in conjunction with the film showing.[10] The Phillips Petroleum Company distributes its "American Enterprise" series of high-school-level films on the economic development of the United States complete with minicourses, discussion guides, and suggested projects for students.[11]

DISTRIBUTING THE FILM

Once prints of your film are "in the can," how will you get them to the intended audiences? Most PR people almost automatically think of maximizing the number of people who will view a film. Too few think of whether they have successfully distributed the film to their target public. You can measure the communication objective by keeping track of how many members of the target public see the film. Don't, however, equate general distribution with "reaching a target public."

Below are just a few of the ways that PR departments have put their film messages into circulation. Can you think of the kinds of publics that might be reached with each distribution channel?

Audiovisual services and film distributors prepare and disseminate wide-ranging catalogs of industrial and promotional films. Educators and program chairpersons of clubs and service organizations can arrange for free loans of the films. Your organization pays a fee for each showing. In return, you get wide distribution and a careful record of how many viewers of various types saw the film.

Industrial shorts are also shown in movie houses. Film distributors and local associations of theater owners can provide a list of theaters and chains that use PR films to fill out their programs. The Insurance Institute for Highway Safety, for example, convinced theater chains to show a ten-minute film that promotes the use of seat belts, automatic air bags, and safer windshields.[12]

If your organization has the resources and the desire to handle its own advertising, booking, mailing, and maintenance of films, you can obtain mailing lists of educators and club officers from the national offices of school and professional associations.

Your own employees are the first audience for any PR film, and they can be your organization's connection with an entire network of local organizations such as PTAs, fraternal groups, churches, and professional groups. (Your lawyers belong to the bar association, your accountants belong to state and national associations, and your PR people should belong to a large number of journalism and public-service organizations. All are potential audiences.)

Cable television has an insatiable appetite for free films, as we noted in Chapter 23.

If your organization regularly bills its customers, use a bill-stuffer brochure to seek audiences. The telephone company's miniature newsletter frequently lists available films on communication, technology, and American history. The best time to promote films is in the late spring and again in late summer, when teachers and club program chairpersons are planning for the upcoming year.

Anywhere people congregate is a good place to show a film. Trade exhibitions, county and state fairs, airports, and train stations are all good locations for minitheaters, which attract crowds of people who are bored, waiting for someone, or need to take a load off their feet.

PROPER PROJECTION

Whenever possible, of course, you should control the presentation of your organization's films, in order to ensure reliable and aesthetically pleasing projection. Use this checklist to obtain the best results:

1. The room in which the film is to be shown should be totally dark for best image quality and minimal distractions. For clear and undistorted viewing, do not seat any viewer at more than a thirty-degree angle from the center of the screen. (Kodak customer service pamphlet AD-43 lists optimum projection distance for various screen widths and lenses.)
2. Make sure in advance that stable support is available for the projector, along with adequate heavy-duty power cords. Use wide plastic tape to secure power cords to the floor as far from the traffic pattern as possible.
3. Make sure you have a replacement projection lamp. If they are going to blow out, it usually happens when the projector first is turned on. Sound projectors call for a second lamp as part of the optical sound system, and each projector has a fuse that could blow out or go bad. Back-ups for all of these should be in your repair kit. You'll also want to have a few emergency splices in case the film breaks. Masking tape will do in a pinch.
4. Use a short roll of unimportant film to test the projector before loading it with the main film. If you have plenty of black leader on your roll, the projector will destroy that instead of your precious film if there is a malfunction when the on button is pressed. A good projectionist advances the film to the first frame of the titles and then puts the projector on hold until the audience is ready.
5. Have a contingency plan in case the projection is interrupted. This usually means

a person other than the projectionist who can ad lib for a few minutes and attract the audience's attention away from the projection problem. Rather than duplicate information that will be seen in the film, it is best to talk about a topic related to the film.
6. As soon as possible after the showing, the film should be rewound, cleaned, repaired, and properly stored in a cool, dry place, ready for the next showing.

The caution and preparedness are worthwhile, because a properly presented film carries the message that your organization has foresight, the ability to marshall resources, and a good knowledge of what it is working to accomplish.

NOTES

1. Nickieann Fleener, ''Using Sponsored Films to Tell the Story: A Contribution of the Hampton Institute to the Evolution of Public Relations Practice in Higher Education.'' Paper presented to the PR division of the Association for Education in Journalism, Boston, August, 1980.
2. Richard Dyer MacCann, *The People's Films: A Political History of U.S. Government Motion Pictures* (New York: Hastings House, 1973).
3. Case study of a 1980 PRSA Silver Anvil Award winner.
4. Marlys Taege, ''Hospital Film Produced to Serve Dual Function,'' *IABC News* (December 1980):6.
5. Carl H. Lenz, ''How to Use PRint Power in Film,'' *Public Relations Journal* (September 1978):30–35.
6. Ott Coelln, ''The Business Side of Picture Street,'' *Public Relations Journal* (September 1980):14–16, 34.
7. Will A. Parker, ''PR Films: Populist Pressures and Cinematic Excellence,'' *Public Relations Journal* (September 1978):28–29.
8. Green Mountain Post Films Bulletin (Spring 1980).
9. G. William Gray, ''How to Pick Your Film Producer,'' *Public Relations Journal* (September 1981):20–24; see also Sam H. Saran and

Charles A. Nekvasil, ''Inland Steel's Experience,'' sidebar to preceding article, pp. 21–23.

10. Lenz.
11. Lenz.
12. Michael deCourcy Hinds, ''Theater Chain Shows a Dramatic Safety Film,'' *New York Times* (Jan. 28, 1982), p. A–15.

ADDITIONAL READING

Baddeley, W. Hugh, *The Technique of Documentary Film Production* (London: Focal Press, 1970).

Jowett, Garth, and James M. Linton, *Movies as Mass Communication* (Beverly Hills, Calif.: Sage, 1980).

Lee, Robert, and Robert Misiorowski, *Script Models* (New York: Hastings House, 1978).

Mayer, Michael F., *The Film Industries—Practical Business/Legal Problems in Production, Distribution and Exhibition* (New York: Hastings House, 1980).

Mercer, John, *An Introduction to Cinematography* (Champaign, Ill.: Stipes, 1979).

Mercer, John, *The Informational Film* (Champaign, Ill.: Stipes, 1980).

Pincus, Edward, *Guide to Filmmaking* (New York: New American Library, 1969).

Reisz, Karel, and Gavin Millar, *The Technique of Film Editing* (New York: Hastings House, 1970).

30

EXHIBITS
AND SPECIAL EVENTS

Although the communication technicians who plan and execute most of the techniques described in Part IV often must do tedious and repetitive work, assignments frequently take them out of the office to do nonroutine tasks such as arranging a lobby display, setting up a booth for a trade show, planning an open house, or running the firm's annual meeting.

All of these special events require conducting site inspections, working with designers and other artists, anticipating logistical problems, and dealing with emergencies far from home base. Most practitioners consider these challenges a rewarding change of pace.

This chapter describes several formal ways you can make person-to-person contact with members of your publics: displays and exhibits, multimedia presentations, open houses, tours, and the annual meeting. All are staple public relations techniques. Many are overused. Seldom are they evaluated. Thus, we begin with management considerations.

MANAGEMENT CONSIDERATIONS

Nearly always, public relations technicians design exhibits and special events as one-way communication activities. Thus, they are most commonly used in the press agent/promotion and public-information models of public relations. Exhibits and special events can be adapted to the two-way models of public relations, however. For example, booths at trade fairs can be used for dialogue between seller and buyer—thus replacing the promotion model with the two-way asymmetric model. The annual meeting or community forum can be used to allow critics to state their case—thus replacing the public-information model with the two-way symmetric model.

Make Sure There Is a Reason

When they have little management training or management supervision, PR technicians may use techniques because they enjoy the creative work involved—even if they cannot explain what the technique is supposed to accomplish. For example, Grunig found that telephone company community relations teams that did the least planning and evaluation held the most special events.[1]

So, choose an objective. Generally it will be communication and message retention, although sometimes promotional exhibits may attempt to affect attitudes and behavior.

Be realistic about the communication behavior of the publics you try to reach. Sometimes you may be communicating with active, information-seeking publics. For example, at an annual computer show in Washington, D.C., many people who are thinking about or intending to buy a computer come to see displays. But most of the time exhibits and special events are seen by people who are interested in the topic of the display but who do not have an active or potential involvement. The curious come to the computer show, too—perhaps only so their children can play video games. Schoolteachers take children on plant tours so they can escape school for a day. Families attend open houses for "something to do" on the weekend.

Because of the limited effects these expensive techniques can have, it's doubly important to have a realistic objective. Budget time and money, and weigh them against the possible results, before "confirming" (in the behavior molecule) that the exhibit or special event is the right communication behavior for your organization. Continue to budget time and money carefully when you give the project the go-ahead.

Evaluating the Event

Relatively few practitioners evaluate exhibits and open houses. Those that do usually leave a questionnaire on a table for participants to complete. A few people may fill it out, but they do not constitute a representative sample.

Good evaluations can be done. Remember that your first objective is communication with a target public. To evaluate that objective, have someone count the people who attend and observe characteristics that would suggest the attendees are members of your target public. How many of the people who attend the computer show are old enough to buy a computer? Ask people selected randomly if they have thought about ("problem recognition") buying a computer.

Message retention is also important. You must know whether people who saw your display "got the message." Otherwise, your attendance count means little. In a few cases, you may try to affect attitudes and behaviors. Ascertain the results using questions described in Chapter 9. Have staff members circulate, selecting people randomly to ask the appropriate questions. Or, if you have the names of attendees, interview them by telephone later. After the event, a mail questionnaire will work reasonably well if you do follow-up mailings to get at least 50 percent of the people who receive the form to complete it.

Let's turn, then, to the specific techniques involved.

PLANNING THE DISPLAY

Placing a display in the lobby of your organization's building is a good way of commemorating a special occasion, calling attention to a new program, or soliciting employee involvement in a worthwhile project.

But only rarely does a display booth stand alone. Usually, along with the other exhibits at a trade show, career day, or information fair, it is assigned a standard space of so much front footage and depth. Unless a desirable free-standing center or corner space is obtained, it most likely will be jammed in between two other booths.

The first task is to obtain from those in charge of running the show a detailed outline of rules for displays, the available services (including electric power), and the precise dimensions of the space. Will back and side walls be provided, will there be curtain separators, or does the space consist merely of marked-off floor space? Conventions and trade-show facilities are fairly standardized in terms of services, but hotels, motels, and government agencies often leave it to you to figure out what to do.

Before designing the display, decide whether it will be used once only or reused as a standard exhibit. Single use means the display can be built to the specifications of the one place and the one message. The multiple-use display must be adaptable to various spaces and applications. Because durable display materials are so costly, the display should be designed so that it can be updated and modified easily.

Portable booths constructed of quick-assembly interlocking panels can be ordered from display-supply companies, along with such components as desks, brochure racks, railings, light fixtures, and storage cabinets that can be arranged in various ways to suit different locations. Most organizations that pack displays around to several locations spend anywhere from $5,000 for basic booth materials to $50,000 for custom-designed displays that can stand the transportation and yet be simple enough for a small team of workers to assemble in a few hours.

Visual Impression

A basic booth might consist of nothing more than a sign on the back wall and a table with literature, attended by a smiling person who is prepared to answer questions. But most successful displays are more sophisticated.

Note that many of the elements discussed in the chapter appear in this Grumman Data Systems display set up in a hotel ballroom. Videotape product demonstrations playing on the monitor at left attract customers, who then enter the booth area and sit down for a hands-on demonstration of an interactive computer data-base system. (Courtesy Grumman Corporation)

Consider the overall impression the booth will make on the audience. Will the display communicate a single concept, or several? It is possible to devote 70 percent of the impact and space to a major theme while also piggybacking related themes in the other 30 percent. For example, a company might give major emphasis to a new product line at a trade-fair booth while also offering information about established products.

Will the display encourage active audience involvement or only the passive soaking up of information? Will the viewer merely pass the display, or is there an opportunity to enter the space? At the annual Philadelphia Garden Show, the W. Atlee Burpee Company erects a greenhouse and a small vegetable plot with pathways so that visitors can walk right through and observe the plantings closely. Involvement increases interest in the company's products.

Will the mood be serious or fun? Several exhibitors at the annual Premium Show at the New York Coliseum display games and toys that can be imprinted with the sponsoring organization's name. But Wham-O Manufacturing of California steals the show with its promotion of imprinted Frisbees. Everyone who passes the display is encouraged to try tossing ten Frisbees at the hole in a target. Get five through the hole and you win a cash prize. There aren't many winners, but the excitement assures that everyone attending the show gets Wham-O's message.

Sometimes the accent on prestige rules out pizzazz: The Beatrice Foods booth at trade shows is done entirely in gold, and attendants dressed in gold pass out gold-foil-covered pamphlets. The decor consistently carries out the concept that the Beatrice product line is of the highest quality.

Traffic Pattern and Lighting

Routes for approaching and passing an exhibit must be calculated. In a large public space, the flow down certain aisles may be mostly in one direction, owing to the places of entry and exit. That has several implications: Will the display be canted to one direction or the other? Where will the staff position itself? The width of the aisle may dictate whether people are forced to pass the booth at close range, or whether they can remain at distances from which they must be lured.

No matter how good the general lighting is in an exhibition hall, auxiliary lighting should be used to illuminate the main sign properly, to highlight products or other key objects, and to eliminate shadows. In addition to lights designed specially for the display, bring along inexpensive minispots to throw light on unforeseen dark areas.

Furniture and Floor Covering

Seating, surface display areas, writing space, and storage must be provided to encourage activity between exhibitors and audience. They should be an integral part of the design, incorporating the same style, tone, and colors.

An ugly floor can dull the effect of an otherwise impressive booth. When selecting the paint or fabric covering for the booth walls and furniture, obtain a carpet remnant in a compatible color. It will not only enhance the beauty of the display, it also can improve the acoustics, add a feeling of prestige, and make the job of staffing the booth less of a strain on the legs. Carpeting should be fastened down on all sides with wide, heavy-duty plastic tape in a matching color.

Audiovisual Equipment

Recorded sound can enhance a display, as long as it does not compete with a neighboring booth. If a booming public-address system is used, unhappy inhabitants of neighboring exhibits may complain . . . or will increase their own volume. If you incorporate sound in a slide-tape, film-and-tape, or video presentation, the visual image will tend to draw the audience in closer, so that sound

NOISE tends to Attract

can be heard at a reasonable volume. Hoods and panels of plywood, fabric, or insulating material keep sound under control.

If you use film loops or video, you may also need to plan for a hood, panel, or canopy to shield the back-projection screen from overhead lights and spotlights in neighboring displays. If you plan to make extensive use of audiovisual materials, check in advance with show coordinators to make sure there are adequate electrical outlets and sufficient power.

Maintaining the Display

Effective display design goes for naught if you fail to staff and maintain the exhibit properly. Two persons should be on duty in an active booth, and more may be needed if sales, recruitment, or complex demonstrations are taking place. Uniform dress, such as blazers with insignia or identification badges, should distinguish attendants. Consumption of food, drinks, or tobacco—unless you are providing it for your clients as well—should be forbidden.

A policy on who shall receive printed materials, samples, and premiums should be established in advance. If a display will be in place for a considerable duration, arrange for daily restocking of informational materials.

A display is not an end in itself; it is a way of opening a line of communication with prospective clients. Have a plan for taking names of interested visitors. Put them on a mailing list and assure them that they will receive follow-up materials shortly after visiting your exhibit.

There always will be unforeseen situations that call for repairing or altering an exhibit. Here is a minimal first aid kit for displays:

Yardstick or tape measure.

A selection of tapes—heavy-duty strapping tapes for structural repairs, cello-phane tape for mending signs, extra plastic tape for the carpet.

A small can of compressed air, available at photo-supply stores, for blowing dust particles from signs and samples without streaking them, and for cleaning A/V equipment.

Felt-tip pens in various colors, and blank signboards, for the creation of instant signs to cope with audience behaviors you didn't anticipate. ("Please do not handle the diamond stylus" . . . "Available in several colors" . . . "Attendant will return in ten minutes.")

Calling cards, pens, letterheads, envelopes, stamps, and all the other things in the top drawer of your desk back at the office.

Coins for pay telephones, a list of suppliers of anything your display might need if it runs out, and phone numbers of persons in your organization who can be called upon to answer the questions you didn't know people were going to ask.

String, rope, or wire. Electrical extension cords. Extra bulbs or lamps for every lighting and audiovisual device. Batteries and fuses for A/V equipment. Dustrag, whisk broom, and spray air freshener. A bottle of water, aspirin, and cups.

MULTIMEDIA PRESENTATIONS

As we saw in Chapter 28, the combining of multiple images and various audiovisual formats can be an effective way of engaging attention, presenting a complex or multifaceted concept, and evoking strong emotional responses. A few examples follow of multimedia use for special events:

A pay-television service entertained prospective clients with a multiscreen show projected over the heads of live actors on stage, who portrayed tourists gawking at the many sights and scenes.[2]

A visitor-orientation slide show at a manufacturing company used a quad format, with the upper left-hand quadrant occupied by a title slide, the upper right showing a general view of each department, and the two lower quadrants occupied by rapidly changing close-ups of people at work.

A public health lecture on injuries to athletes began with a short film depicting a gymnast in action. The final frame of the film froze, then metamorphosed into a still slide of the human body. An arrow pointed at each section of the body as synchronized dual projectors with dissolve mechanisms carried a series of slides detailing the diagnosis and treatment of various injuries. The format focused attention on specifics while reminding the viewer of the larger context.

A United Fund kickoff dinner must inspire volunteers and remind them of the many programs supported by donations. One film projected at center screen depicted an "average citizen" walking through town—strolling past parks, schools, senior citizen centers, the Y, and doors with signs identifying several social programs and charities. Around the moving image, in random array created by six slide projectors, images of people serving and being served were flashed briefly. The multimedia image reminded the volunteers of the impact their work will have, and thus a long-winded verbal message was unnecessary.

OPEN HOUSES AND TOURS

Inviting someone in to look around, have a cup of coffee, and talk is as important for a large organization as it is for neighbors on any block. That's why most companies, government agencies, and nonprofit organizations that depend on public support regularly open their doors for tours. Visitors to tiny Aruba in the Caribbean are surprised to find that one of the serene island's most interesting attractions is the two-hour tour of Exxon's refining plant, which processes and transships much of the oil from Venezuela. After

a slide show and talk in the Esso Club, the tourists ride buses through the huge refinery and watch supertankers being drained of their precious cargo. At the end of the tour, they enjoy light refreshments and have an opportunity to ask questions about the mammoth furnaces and storage tanks they have seen.

Visits to a facility by outsiders are considerably more complicated than when a neighbor drops in for coffee. Safety and security are considerations: Will guests have to wear hard hats? Will they be covered by the company's insurance? Will it be necessary to erect a tent or bring in trailers to provide protection from the elements? What measures will be taken to prevent unauthorized observation of manufacturing methods that must be kept secret? Will the tour or open house disrupt production or violate the rights of personnel? The labor unions may have to be consulted.

The company manual prepared by the public relations department of Johnson & Johnson for coordinating new plant openings suggests other areas for planning:[3]

Timing • The facility must be ready and must look its best. Interesting activities should be taking place. The program must be long enough to make the trip worthwhile, but not so long as to be boring or redundant. An alternate date should be selected in case of inclement weather or emergency.

Invitations • Send them out two weeks in advance. Make sure that if one politician, one academic, one subcontractor is invited, then all politicians, all other dignitaries in the area are invited. In other words, carefully work out a policy so that no one is offended. Whenever possible, involve employees and their families. Keep careful track of RSVP cards so that you know exactly who and how many are coming.

Transportation and Parking • Be assured that there is bus transportation to remote locations, and that there is adequate parking, clearly marked for visitors. For a large event, get the cooperation of local police in directing traffic.

Comfort and Services • Provide adequate restrooms, a checkroom for coats and parcels, public telephones, nursery areas for small children, and sufficient hosts and hostesses to guide guests and help out in case of emergencies.

Greeting • Assure that everyone is met by an official representative of the organization. VIPs should be met by persons of importance in the organization. Make certain that high-ranked officers of the organization make an appearance and participate in the program. Maps and printed programs should be provided to orient the visitor.

Gifts • A package of company products or some token gift imprinted with the company name is a gesture of goodwill that most visitors appreciate. Such a memento has lasting promotional value.

Publicity • Press kits should be prepared for every member of the media. A photographer should be hired to document the event. Media that do not send a representative should receive news releases and photos by mail or messenger to enable them to provide coverage. A press center should be set up to provide reporters with typewriters and telephones. A member of the PR department should be assigned to assist television crews with special needs for power and for specially arranged interviews.

And finally, of course, refreshments must be appropriate to the occasion. Liquor may be expected by a group of press or business individuals, while cookies and soft drinks are more appropriate for families. If the location is remote and the event is of more than a few hours in duration, a box lunch should be provided.

THE ANNUAL MEETING

Any incorporated organization must, according to its bylaws and the rules of the state in which it was incorporated, hold an annual meeting for the purpose of electing the board of directors and approving the financial report. The meeting must be announced in advance, and stockholders in attendance may speak and cast their votes. In practice, most votes are tallied through a proxy system. And the speakers often are perennial "gadflies" who berate the officers for not making sufficient profits, polluting the atmosphere, or otherwise mismanaging the company.

Nonetheless, most organizations believe that the annual meeting is a worthwhile ritual, because it affords the organization an opportunity to hear from its publics and, in turn, to speak directly to those who have a vested interest in the organization.

Does your organization have an auditorium or hall large enough to handle the expected turnout? Or should you rent space at a nearby theater, hotel, or other public facility? It may even be possible to use closed-circuit television to link the main meeting room with satellite rooms around the country, in order to get more people involved. Most of the concerns raised above in our discussion of tours and open houses apply to the annual meeting. In fact, many organizations combine the annual meeting with a plant tour, social hour, or entertainment event.

Proxy materials and announcements in company publications are sufficient notice of the meeting place. However, special invitations should be sent to employees, members of the financial community, elected officials, dignitaries, and other special guests.

The annual meeting usually features speeches by one or two top officers. Unless your president is particularly inspiring, however, you may advise keeping the speeches to a minimum, and instead let a film or multimedia show tell the story of the organization's progress and plans.

Because public-interest groups concerned about pollution, energy, discrimination, and

Scenes from AT&T's mammoth annual
meeting—this one held in Houston, Texas.
Shareholders are welcomed and issued
tickets plus literature and souvenirs. The
vast display area shows off new products
and describes the company's involvement
in a variety of areas. The rostrum at the
annual meeting is dominated by the Bell
logo. (Reproduced with permission of
AT&T)

505

other issues have become increasingly vocal at annual meetings, PR departments today are called upon to draw up reasonable but firm rules regarding who may speak and for how long. It is also useful to use videotape to train company officers how to handle hostile questions.

Finally, PR may prepare a shopping bag full of printed materials and inexpensive souvenirs for all in attendance. This ''bundle of goodies'' is all it takes to satisfy many stockholders.

NOTES

1. Unpublished research for the American Telephone & Telegraph Co., New York, N.Y.
2. Linda Kline, ''Industrial Show Business,'' *American Way*, Vol. 13, No. 3, pp. 62–67.
3. Johnson & Johnson, ''Guidelines for Coordinating New Plant Openings,'' in-house publication, undated.

ADDITIONAL READING

Berry, Elizabeth, ''How to Work With Your Facility,'' *Public Relations Journal* (May 1978): 18–19.

Widder, Frank, ''Annual Meeting Check List,'' *Public Relations Journal* (July 1981):24–25.

Good Show! A Practical Guide for Temporary Exhibitions (Washington, D.C.: Smithsonian Institution, 1981).

''Putting Pep in the Annual Meeting,'' *Public Relations Journal* (May 1978):22–31.

''How to Determine Your Level of Exhibit Participation'' and ''Did Your Exhibit Pay Off?'', *Public Relations Journal* (May 1978):36–38.

31

ANNUAL REPORTS AND FINANCIAL WRITING

Read the trade journals and talk to PR people: The impression you get is that the annual report is the tail that wags the PR dog.

"We begin work on the next one the day after this year's comes out," sighs one practitioner, partly from exhaustion and partly in awe of the mighty role the annual report plays in the PR department's contribution to the organization. Exhibit 31–1 presents examples of company annual reports.

A recent study of 100 top corporations showed that 60 percent of annual reports are prepared in-house (the rest are prepared by outside consultants), the lead time for preparation is almost half a year, and virtually all companies consider the annual report to be an important marketing tool.[1] Another study of over 100 annual reports issued in 1980 used phrases such as "predictable," "entrenched," and "rut-bound" to characterize the standardization of the annual report format into a glossy color-photo magazine with emphasis on exciting graphics and readability.[2]

Annual reports and financial writing are staple techniques used in financial public relations programs, as described in Chapter 17. When you prepare an annual report or financial press release, usually you will be preparing information for active, information-seeking publics that need financial data about your organization. Thus, it's essential to provide clear and factual information.

Although financial publics appreciate attractive four-color annual reports, they can be alienated if those reports do not contain the information they need. Too often, annual reports are written as though the readers are merely passive, information-processing publics.

Public relations practitioners using all four PR models produce financial information. Usually, the public-information and two-way symmetric practitioners produce the most informative reports. The press agent/publicist and two-way asymmetric practitioners too often try to use annual reports to promote and propagandize. The symmetric model is ideal for financial reports that anticipate and address the concerns of stockholders and financial analysts.

Let's look at annual reports in detail, and then at financial writing.

WHAT'S "REQUIRED"?

As we saw in Chapter 10, federal law requires corporations annually to file a form 10-K with the Securities and Exchange Commission. Moreover, the SEC requires that an annual report to shareholders must precede or accompany delivery of proxy material. The stock exchanges require that companies deliver an annual report to stockholders as promptly as possible, and no later than fifteen days before the annual meeting. In order to assure interim flow of information regarding corporate profits and policies, the SEC also requires that a corporation make brief quarterly reports.[3]

Beginning in 1980, the SEC began requiring that more information be included in annual reports: financial data going back five years, and expanded discussion and analysis of financial condition as well as results of operation. In other words, the SEC required fuller disclosure than companies previously were accustomed to making to their stockholders.[4] Today's PR departments must work doubly hard to satisfy federal reporting requirements and still keep the annual report lively and interesting enough to fulfill the marketing function.

Many stockholders, of course, merely look on the glossy and cheerfully positive annual report as an affirmation of the correctness of their decision to purchase shares in the company. But the more critical investors, along with investment analysts—the active, information-seeking publics—study a company's annual report in order to decide whether or not to purchase or hold the firm's stock. One company's survey of 200 stockholders and analysts showed that half of the readers of

the annual report say they read the financial review and management discussion sections of the annual report—the dry, dull-looking pages full of figures and explanatory notes—because they consider evidence of good management to be the best indicator of a stock's potential profitability.[5]

The corporate annual report has been such a resounding communication success over the years that nonprofit and service organizations have emulated the format, even though

EXHIBIT 31–1 Bold and colorful annual report covers may feature a quote from the chief executive officer, an action photo, the company's logo, a summary of major corporate achievements, or an exciting graphic design. (Courtesy Shell Oil Company, photo by Burk Uzzle; Oshman's Sporting Goods, Inc.; Knight-Ridder Newspapers; The New York Times, copyright © 1982 by The New York Times Company; Celanese Corporation, photo by Bruce Davidson, Magnum; The Travelers Insurance Company)

EXHIBIT 31–2 Taking a cue from contemporary magazines, editors of annual reports make lavish use of dramatic photographs showing the involvement of workers in the production of profitable goods and services. (Acushnet, courtesy of American Brands, Inc.; courtesy The Travelers Insurance Company; Knight-Ridder Newspapers; Shell Oil Company, photo by Burk Uzzle; The New York Times, copyright © 1982 by The New York Times Company; Celanese Corporation photo by Bruce Davidson, Magnum)

EXHIBIT 31–3 The consolidated balance sheet is usually presented in a straightforward manner. But readability of the rest of the required 10–K form is enhanced through the use of graphs, pie charts, bar charts, and other graphic devices. (Courtesy Shell Oil Company; The New York Times, copyright © 1982 by The New York Times Company; Celanese Corporation; Knight-Ridder Newspapers)

EXHIBIT
31–1 ⟶

Shell Oil Company
1981 Annual Report

Celanese
Annual Report
1981

Investing
for the Future

Oshman's Sporting Goods
1981 Annual Report
& 10 Year History

Annual Report 1981

Travelers

☂☂**Travelers people
are setting their
sights very high
for the 80's.**☂☂

Edward H. Budd
Annual Meeting 1981

The New York Times Company

Earnings: a record year, up 23 percent

Revenues: $845 million, a new high

The Times: 98 million ad lines, a record

The Times: 47th and 48th Pulitzer

Cable TV: year-end subscriptions

Forest Products: Maine mill in production

American Brands, Inc.

ANNUAL REPORT 1981

ACUSHNET COMPANY

John T. Ludes
President and
Chief Executive Officer

Acushnet scored major su...
with new products which...
pelled operating income...
record $18,560,000 on...
in sales of $131,837,0...

The Titleist Golf...
posted a 20% gain...
income to $11,34...
$73,484,000 we...
product lines—...
putters, golf...
the increase...
Pinnacle a...
Titleist s...
position...
The P...
and N...
duc...
ta...

16

THE TRAVELERS

THE TRAVELERS
OLDER AMERICANS PROGRAM

EMPLOYMENT

HEALTH

Linda Brett, in the foreground, directs The Trav...
improving the quality of life for the countr...
Corvo, a retired Travelers employee wit...
bank for retirees, a most successfu...

...concentrated
...d at producing new
...venue through special
...rtunities generated over
...n additional advertising
...981. The successful REV-UP
...s produced $14 million in
...es. The REV-UP program
...ally designed to counter
...rowth of revenues in a
...economic environment.

...DENA PAGINATION At the end
...Installation was completed
...ations first full pagination
...n. Pagination enables editors to
...uce full newspaper pages includ-
...halftone pictures and advertising
...work on a single terminal screen.
...January 2, 1982 Rose Bowl edition
...he Pasadena Star-News was the first
...he produced on the new $2.5
...illion system. Pagination offers
...Knight-Ridder papers important cost
...saving opportunities in the years
...ahead.

...CONSUMER INFORMATION
...SYSTEMS CIS systems, which enable
...Knight-Ridder newspapers to manage
...circulation through computerization
...of billing and routing, were installed
...in seven KRN markets during 1981.
...This brought to 23 the number of KRN

papers with CIS systems. CIS has
provided KRN with not only more
control over circulation operations
but also has permitted a major
switchover to more efficient
pay-by-mail billings. CIS also permits
KRN to identify non-subscribers so
products such as shoppers and zoned
editions can be delivered to them on a
regular and specially targeted basis.

ELECTRONIC LIBRARY The
Philadelphia Inquirer began actively
marketing its electronic library data
base in 1981 to libraries, banks,
schools, law firms and other
companies under the trade name
IN/FORM DATA SERVICES. Initial
revenues were generated in
December. Lexington and Gary held
tests using the Philadelphia
computers for their own library
systems. The Philadelphia system is
also available to non-KRN newspapers
and other organizations needing
file services of their own. Detroit
began testing its system in late 1981.
Miami is scheduled to begin
operating an electronic library in
early 1982. These systems are the
beginning of a nationwide electronic
retrieval network for Knight-Ridder
that offers the promise of future
revenues.

A. Lexington foreman John Masters overlooks
a page negative of the Herald. The next step is the
making of a plate to prepare for the press run.

B. Photo editor Bob Anderson inspects
a color separation at a press. Our
newspapers are making increased use of
color to meet the needs of advertisers and
readers.

...Objective and Sales Building
...of North Carolina news...

EXHIBIT **31-2**

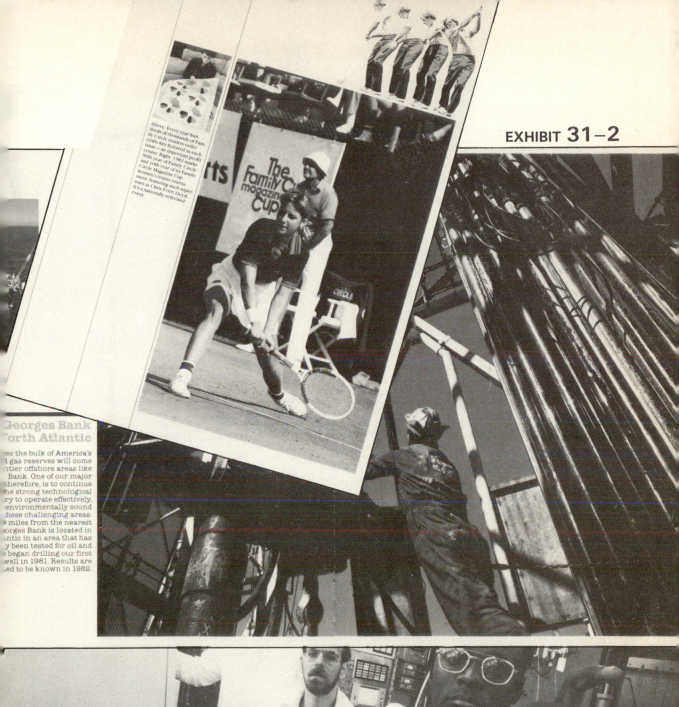

Above: Every year hun-
dreds of thousands of Family Circle readers order
crafts kits featured in each
issue—an important profit
center. Right: 1982 marks
50th year of Family Circle
and 10th year of its Family
Circle Magazine Cup
women's tennis tourna-
ment, featuring such super-
stars as Chris Evert Lloyd.
It's a nationally televised
event.

**Georges Bank
North Atlantic**

...es the bulk of America's
...l gas reserves will come
...tier offshore areas like
...Bank. One of our major
...therefore, is to continue
...e strong technological
...ry to operate effectively,
...environmentally sound
...hese challenging areas.
... miles from the nearest
...rges Bank is located in
...ntic in an area that has
...y been tested for oil and
...e began drilling our first
...well in 1981. Results are
...ed to be known in 1982.

13

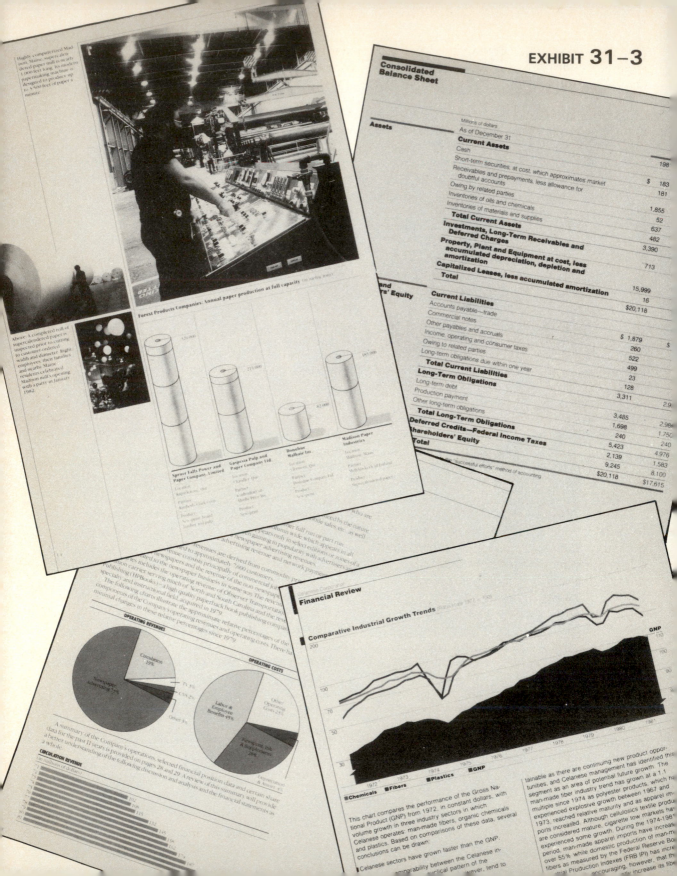

EXHIBIT **31–3**

they have no stockholders to whom they are required to disseminate their financial records. The University of Minnesota's annual "Report to Investors" is actually aimed at individual, corporate, and foundation contributors whose private support augments the institution's state appropriation and earned income. The annual report of the American Field Service international intercultural program keeps former participants in the exchange program informed. The annual report of The Newspaper Fund, an educational foundation established by Dow Jones & Co., documents the career-information, intern, and training programs run by that organization in pursuit of its goal of furthering professional journalism education.

Some corporations use the annual report format to disseminate social reports or audits to their stockholders as well. As we saw in Chapter 3, for the past dozen years General Motors has issued a separate "Public Interest Report" to discuss the firm's goals, programs, and progress in areas such as pollution control, safety, trade with communist countries, quality of life, equal employment, government relations, and philanthropic activities. Exxon sends stockholders a statistical supplement to the annual report, along with a booklet, "This Is Exxon," which details worldwide operations. Beatrice Foods has prepared a booklet depicting the identity marks of the more than 200 brands it markets around the world, enabling stockholders to help their cause by patronizing stores and products owned by the company.

MANAGEMENT CONSIDERATIONS

Because annual reports go to active publics, your objective should be to produce messages that members of these publics will retain and from which they will develop organized cognitions. You want your public to "understand" the financial status of your organization. To evaluate when you have met these objectives, you should apply readability measures to a draft of your report and use the signaled stopping technique on a small sample of readers to check comprehension and understanding. Because people respond well to pictures of other people, not just things or objects, you will want to choose photographs like those in Exhibit 31–2, which have considerable human interest.

Graphs and charts are such an important part of annual reports that you should also evaluate the extent to which readers understand the information they contain (see Exhibit 31–3). A series of studies done at the University of Wisconsin in the 1960s showed that simplifying graphs and tables improved their comprehension.[6] For example, readers comprehend graphs better than tables. They also comprehend short tables better than long tables. And the fewer reference points on a graph, the easier it is to comprehend.

Because of the time needed to produce an annual report, it is the PR task for which networking techniques are most essential. And because annual reports are expensive, budgeting cannot be avoided.

PLANNING THE CONTENTS

Since the annual report goes to substantially the same general audience each year, and since the financial data section is required information, planning for the next publication usually begins by critiquing the previous one. Just as a magazine editor builds the next issue on the framework of the preceding one, the PR department must figure out how to "top itself" with the next annual report.

Here are some questions the editors might ask in striving to improve and freshen the product:

What audiences can we serve better next time? Are the roles of employees sufficiently highlighted? Do we show our impact on the communities where our plants are located?

What is new this year? A good report is, in effect, a newsmagazine. Our treatment of developments in the company's organization and progress should be as exciting as a newsweekly's coverage of current events.

Which of our tried-and-true staple items can benefit from a fresh approach? If we have led off each year with a letter from the chairman—literally a formal business letter on company stationery—perhaps this year an interview format could work better to humanize the chief executive officer. Instead of formal pictures of department heads, which make the report look like a high school yearbook, can we show company officers engaged in interesting workaday activities, or at least group them in lively pictures that don't make them look as if they're stuffed?

Can we get a new graphic look by engaging the services of a different layout specialist, or by giving photographers free rein to experiment with innovative views of the organization's workings? How can we convince our readers to spend more time with the annual report when they flip through it the first time? The answer might be a running theme, or a "narrator" who conducts a tour of the organization.

Are the statistical summaries really as readable as we can make them? What will the introduction of color and helpful headings or marginal notes do for the readability of all those charts and tables?

The 1980 report of Frank B. Hall & Co., an insurance services firm, provides an example of how innovative an annual report can be. One simple word, "Smile," was emblazoned across the cover, along with the admonition: "A measure of American resiliency is the ability to smile in the face of adversity." The opening twenty pages of the glossy sixty-page publication were devoted to a lively photo-and-word documentary on the role humor has played in American society. Instead of a dour, formal portrait of the chief executive officer, Chairman and President Albert J. Tahmoush was shown with a broad grin from ear to ear. As the new decade began, the company wanted to get across the message that America's economic and spiritual depression should be put in context: The nation's people, government, and business sector have always had the ability to triumph over adversity, thanks to their ability to laugh at life. This refreshing message disproves the notion that the annual report must be "rut-bound" and predictable.

In the light of the SEC's requirements for fuller disclosure, some companies have gone beyond the usual platitudes in their reports. One firm devoted nine pages to the results of a public-opinion survey it conducted to determine the degree of risk people will accept in a complex society; one company made corporate governance the topic of its feature article; another firm laid out expansion plans, project by project, for the next five years, explaining the rationale behind each move.[7] Clearly, the annual report of the future will be less of an advertisement for past successes and more of an agenda-setter for future programs—a development that should provide a challenge to new practitioners entering the field of public relations. You will remember from Chapter 23 that video is an optional channel for the annual report. A 1982 report indicates that many more Fortune 500 companies are taping reports for use on cable TV and for satellite transmission to groups of stockholders around the world.[8]

FINANCIAL WRITING: HOW DOES IT DIFFER?

The very term "financial writing" has a mystique about it, as does "science writing" or "medical writing." Everyone agrees that "we need more good financial writing" and "a good financial writer is hard to find." So what is it that makes writing about the world of business exotic and mysterious?

In truth, it isn't the "writing" that calls for special qualities, it's the ability to understand the terminology and thinking of the business community. In other words, the jargon. Indeed, the qualified financial writer is one who can plow through the obfuscations of business communicating with business, then translate it into clear, interesting prose. The essence of good technical writing, no matter what the field, is the ability to read and understand specialized material, and not to forget the basic principles of effectively aiming your message at your audience.

Manage Your Financial Writing

Because financial publics are active, your objective should be to help them retain and understand financial information. You must understand what you write, or you can't help your reader. Evaluate your own understanding: Explain concepts to someone else before you write, and see if you can put together a coherent explanation. Use the signaled stopping technique yourself, on your own writing, to see where there are gaps in your understanding.

Research on technical writing has identified some critical techniques that promote message retention and understanding.[9] Most importantly, you should use the active voice and sentences with subject-verb-object structure, rather than sentences with linking, "to be," verbs. Always define terms that the reader will not understand without a dictionary. Use analogies, metaphors, and examples to relate unfamiliar ideas with ideas familiar to readers.

Improve Your Skills

The emphasis in training for financial writing, then, should be on the preparation and backgrounding in the fields of economics and business. The best place to start is with college courses on macroeconomics (the world order), microeconomics (the workings of specialized marketplaces), business adminis-

tration, and marketing. The PR practitioner who avoided such subjects as an undergraduate will find that many colleges offer night courses, summer seminars, and week-long workshops to help professionals learn about the workings of monetary and financial systems.

The reference shelves of most libraries are stocked with literally scores of handbooks that explain the special jargon, practices, and procedures of financial subfields: *The Accountant's Handbook, Handbook of Insurance, Marketing Handbook, Real Estate Handbook, Corporate Secretaries' Manual and Guide, Corporate Treasurer's and Controller's Handbook.* To learn about the size, role, and particular interests of financial institutions, look for the fact books issued annually by their trade associations. The United States League of Savings Associations, for example, issues both an annual *Savings and Loan Fact Book* and the yearly *Savings Association Annals.* The latter carries essays, reprints, and summaries of government actions affecting the savings industry, along with the reports of all association standing committees. The annual *Mutual Fund Fact Book* published by the Investment Company Institute in Washington offers data provided by mutual fund directors and underwriters.

The International Monetary Mechanism, part of the Holt, Rinehart and Winston "Money and Banking Series," is a clear and concise primer on international economics, foreign exchange, balance of payments, the role of gold, the International Monetary Fund—in short, everything you want to know about the world economic order.[10] The role of banks in the world monetary system is explained in *Money and Power,* a volume of the Sage Library of Social Research.[11] Paul M. Horvitz's *Monetary Policy and the Financial System* provides a comprehensive understanding of American and global economic policies, including the role of the Federal Reserve system.[12]

Reporting on corporate business requires an understanding of how corporations accumulate capital, how they are required to report their activities, and what accountants consider to be "generally accepted accounting practices." Publishers such as McGraw-Hill and Chilton specialize in business reporting and maintain indispensable reference works such as *The Guide to Understanding Financial Statements* on their lists.[13]

The best advice to the would-be financial writer, then, is to build a reference library, keep current by reading business periodicals, take refresher courses, attend banking institutes, and, in general, associate with those whose activities you must understand and report. Once you have gathered and selected your information, refer to the principles outlined in Chapter 19 of this volume: Identify with your readers, write tightly, explain complicated concepts with simple analogies, and don't fall prey to the self-fulfilling prophecy that financial writing has to be complex and confusing. Successful, popular financial writers such as columnist Sylvia Porter and author "Adam Smith" have shown that business and economics can be made comprehensible—if you're willing to work at developing the skill.

NOTES

1. Ronald Goodman, "Annual Reports Serving a Dual Market Function: Report of a Survey," *Public Relations Quarterly* (Summer 1980):21–24.
2. Janet Dyer, "Predictable: The Watchword for 1980 Reports," *Public Relations Journal* (August 1981):9–10.
3. H. Zane Robbins, "Your New Quarterly Report," *Public Relations Journal* (April 1976): 24–26,35–36.
4. Vincent Cannella, "Integrated Disclosure: Betwixt and Between," *Public Relations Journal* (August 1981):8–9.
5. George L. Fisher and C. R. Davenport, "What Investors Want to Hear," *Public Relations Journal* (April 1981):14–15,18.
6. Richard D. Powers, "Communicating with Graphs," *Journal of Cooperative Extension* 4 (1966):35–43.
7. William P. Dunk, "28 Trends in Annual Reports," *Public Relations Journal* (August 1980):10–13.
8. Nancy L. Ross, "The Corporate Score Card Takes to the Airways," *Washington Post* (May 2, 1982), pp. L1, L6.
9. For a complete review of literature of science writing, which is quite similar to financial writing, see James E. Grunig, "Communication of Scientific Information to Nonscientists," in Brenda Dervin and Melvin J. Voight (eds.), *Progress in Communication Sciences*, vol. 2 (Norwood, N.J.: Ablex, 1980), pp. 167–214.
10. Leland B. Yeager, *The International Monetary Mechanism* (New York: Holt, Rinehart and Winston, 1968).
11. Jonathan David Aronson, *Money and Power* (Beverly Hills, Calif.: Sage, 1977).
12. Paul M. Horvitz, *Monetary Policy and the Financial System* (Englewood Cliffs, N.J.: Prentice-Hall, 1979).
13. S. B. Costales, *The Guide to Understanding Financial Statements* (New York: McGraw-Hill, 1979); Louis O. Foster, *Understanding Financial Statements and Corporate Annual Reports* (Philadelphia: Chilton, 1961).

ADDITIONAL READING

Aronoff, Craig E., (ed.), *Business and the Media* (Santa Monica, Calif.: Goodyear Publishing Co., 1979).

Braznell, William, "How to Overcome the Annual Report Drag Factor," *Public Relations Journal* (August 1978):22–24,29.

Brown, Leland, *Effective Business Writing* (Englewood Cliffs, N.J.: Prentice-Hall, 1973).

Lee, Carol, "The PR Role in Good Annual Report Photography," *Public Relations Journal* (September 1977):36–41.

Pearsall, Thomas E., and Donald H. Cunningham, *How to Write for the World of Work* (New York: Holt, Rinehart and Winston, 1978).

32

PUBLIC RELATIONS ADVERTISING

Nonproduct advertising by corporations goes by many names. Indeed, J. Douglas Johnson, former senior vice president of McCann-Erickson, the giant advertising firm, and now a marketing professor at Indiana University, has identified more than a dozen labels for various nuances of corporate advertising, including "concept advertising," "general promotion advertising," "goodwill advertising," "image advertising," "issue advertising," "personality advertising," and "responsibility advertising." In the end, he selects "public relations advertising" as the term that covers the entire spectrum.[1]

Another major American advertising firm, Foote, Cone & Belding, created the FCB/Corporate Division to specialize in what it likes to call "corporate positioning." An advertisement for FCB/Corporate's services is headlined: "Companies sure know how to sell products—but they don't know beans about selling themselves."[2] Believing that a corporation can't tell securities analysts where it is heading unless it has a strong sense of its own distinguishing character and

point of view, FCB/Corporate conducts indepth interviews with the client and the client's customers, and then prepares a "positioning document" outlining an advertising campaign aimed at projecting the desired identity.[3]

CORPORATE ADVERTISING IS GROWING

Corporate advertising is growing by 5 to 6 percent a year, and in 1981 broke the 1-billion-dollar mark for the first time.[4] A survey by the Association of National Advertisers showed that the biggest single purpose of corporate advertising was to build recognition, especially for corporations that need "umbrella identification" for broadened and diversified lines, as well as "industries where there are high levels of public criticism," such as petroleum and basic materials.[5] The president of one advertising agency believes that what she calls issues-and-causes advertising "may soon be as big as detergents or automobile advertising," and adds, "I believe that the business of ideas is beginning to look more and more like the business of products."[6]

All this is good news for the world of public relations, since PR practitioners play a major role in shaping corporate advertising policies, according to the annual surveys conducted by the *Public Relations Journal*.[7] PR departments are the principal originators of concepts and themes for corporate advertising. More and more they are involved in media selection and placement of ads, taking over some of the responsibilities of advertising departments.[8]

The primary goals of corporate advertising, according to the annual PRJ surveys, include:

Improving consumer relations.

Presenting stands on public issues.

Improving stockholder/financial relations.

Improving trade relations.

Community relations; employee relations.

"Image" and reputation.

Most companies also expect product sales to be improved by corporate advertising, and thus consider it a marketing tool as well.[9]

How useful is corporate advertising? Studies conducted on behalf of *Time* magazine by Yankelovich, Skelly & White, Inc., indicate that companies devoting substantially more of their advertising budget to corporate advertising than product advertising enjoy "recall" scores (i.e., the message-retention objective) almost equal to corporations that use mainly product advertising—and with substantially smaller budgets![10]

The researchers also found that corporate advertisers were more cost-effective in realizing "association with specific traits" (the objective of message acceptance), "favorable overall impressions" (the objective of affecting evaluations—attitudes), and "potential supportive behavior" (the objective of influencing behavior). Yankelovich concluded that corporate advertisers outperform noncorporate advertisers on all key measurements of effectiveness studied.[11]

"POSITIONING" YOUR ORGANIZATION THROUGH ADVERTISING

Let's look at the ways in which several companies and trade associations have used public relations advertising to position themselves better in the minds of the audience.

Allied Corporation: Need for a New Identity

At the end of the 1970s, Allied Chemical was beset by numerous problems. The company had diversified beyond the chemical business. It had a cumbersome centralized management structure. Unprofitable business ventures in energy-related areas had drained profits. The firm received negative news coverage over lawsuits concerning its role in the pollution of the James River in Virginia with the pesticide kepone. The company changed leaders, hiring an outsider to shape things up. And it changed its name to Allied Corporation.[12]

The new logo carried the line, "We mean business." A corporate advertising campaign placed in business magazines and news-weeklies in 1981 was built around the theme of aggressiveness. Photographs showed company officers rolling up their shirtsleeves in a "ready to work" attitude. The accompanying copy said that Allied managers would be "pumping money and energy into our potential strengths. We've sold operations that held us back. We put an acquisition plan in motion and doubled our research program." The message to the business community was that Allied was back on its feet, ready to make good profits again.

Sperry Rand:
Increasing Public Awareness

Although it is a major manufacturer of computers, flight-control systems, and heavy farm equipment, Sperry Rand found that it had very low public awareness. Using research that showed that people listen to only about one-fourth of what they hear, Sperry called attention to itself with a television and magazine campaign built around the line: ''We understand how important it is to listen.'' Ads offering a ''listening quiz'' to readers brought 20,000 requests, and *Advertising Age* reported that the campaign significantly increased favorable awareness of Sperry Rand.[13]

The advertising campaign was so effective, in fact, that Sperry's 1981 annual report was built around a related theme: ''Nine Sperry Employees Tell How Listening Works for Them.''

Northwest & Bethlehem:
Succeeding in a Tough Economy

Many American companies, especially those depending heavily on energy and natural resources, fared poorly in the battered economy at the beginning of the 1980s. Wary investors and consumers watched as one company after another succumbed. In such a climate, companies—especially successful firms—must project the impression that they are capable of succeeding where others have failed.

Bethlehem Steel took full-page newspaper ads to proclaim: ''Mr. President, we're in steel to stay. And to prosper.'' The copy noted the President's call for revitalization of the American steel industry. The advertising copy promised ''a Bethlehem commitment backed by a $750-million modernization program.'' Specific plans were spelled out, and the copy concluded: ''We're determined to make Bethlehem the best steel producer in terms of productivity, quality and service.''

Northwest Orient, one of the nation's few consistently profitable airlines, used full-page ads to suggest that ''Today, the world is going our way.'' The copy noted that its careful management control over operations is responsible for the company's success. The final paragraph was an essay on the formula for success: ''Return to the fundamentals that America taught the world. Work hard. Do it right. Do it better. . . . Fly us and you will see.'' The ad successfully, if a bit proudly, appealed both to the investment community and the flying public.

LTV and Grumman:
A Battle for Control

When one company seeks to take over another by purchasing its shares, stockholders may be subjected to a barrage of claims and counterclaims. Sometimes the advertisements in the *New York Times* and the *Wall Street Journal* offer rational appeals, using hundreds or even thousands of words to explain why the proposed takeover would be good or bad. Other times the advertisements are blunt and bold. Late in 1981, the Grumman Corporation spoke to its stockholders in one-inch-high letters: ''If you're a Grumman shareholder, here are three things you can do to keep your company from being taken over by LTV. 1. Hold on to your stock. 2. Don't respond to any communication from LTV. 3. Tell your fellow shareholders to do the same.''

The same day on which that minimal ad appeared, LTV devoted an entire page in the same papers to a tribute to the recently assassinated Egyptian leader, Anwar Sadat. No mention of the raging controversy with Grumman was mentioned. Significantly, however, the ad was carried not in the news pages but in the business section, where the Grumman appeal was positioned!

Another of LTV's advertisements during the heated takeover attempt was addressed

Grumman's battle to avoid takeover by LTV often filled one or more pages of *The Wall Street Journal, The New York Times,* and Long Island's *Newsday.* An advertisement placed by management stressed a rational point: the combined debts of LTV–Grumman would lead the industry. An ad sponsored by employees pointed up emotional issues such as pride, patriotism, and ''family ties'' to the company. (Courtesy Grumman Corporation)

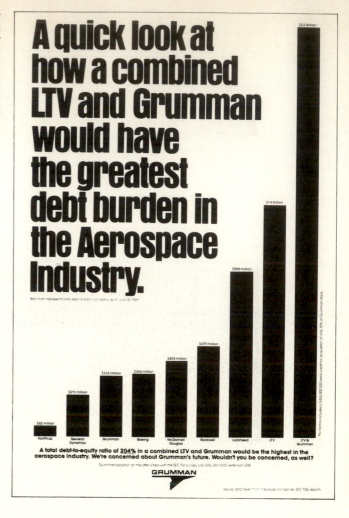

to Grumman employees. The president of LTV assured them that their jobs were not in jeopardy and that the Grumman name and tradition would be maintained. The copy was packaged in the style of a friendly letter, and LTV's president assured: ''One thing you should know is that Grumman is a company I feel very close to. . . . As a pilot in World War II, I was privileged to fly Grumman aircraft in combat.''

Clearly, every persuasive device and technique available can be useful in winning over publics when the ownership of a company is at stake.

JOINING THE PUBLIC DEBATE: ADVOCACY ADVERTISING

Kaiser Aluminum vice president for public relations and advertising Ronald E. Rhody, whose views were discussed in Chapter 23, believes ''issues advertising is an idea whose time has come'' in America. Answering critics of Kaiser's aggressive use of advocacy advertising, Rhody replies: ''We don't want to dominate the national debate—we just want to participate in it.''[14]

Since all advertising involves ''advocacy,'' many companies prefer to call it ''is-

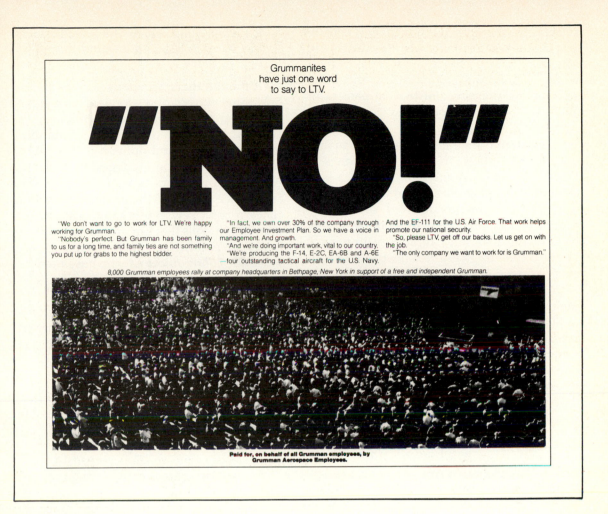

Grummanites
have just one word
to say to LTV.

"NO!"

"We don't want to go to work for LTV. We're happy working for Grumman.

"Nobody's perfect. But Grumman has been family to us for a long time, and family ties are not something you put up for grabs to the highest bidder.

"In fact, we own over 30% of the company through our Employee Investment Plan. So we have a voice in management. And growth.

"And we're doing important work, vital to our country.

"We're producing the F-14, E-2C, EA-6B and A-6E —four outstanding tactical aircraft for the U.S. Navy.

And the EF-111 for the U.S. Air Force. That work helps promote our national security.

"So, please LTV, get off our backs. Let us get on with the job.

"The only company we want to work for is Grumman."

8,000 Grumman employees rally at company headquarters in Bethpage, New York in support of a free and independent Grumman.

**Paid for, on behalf of all Grumman employees, by
Grumman Aerospace Employees.**

sues'' advertising. The Mobil Oil Corporation, spurred by Herbert Schmertz, vice president of public affairs, spends more than $4 million annually to let the public know where the company stands on issues involving energy resources, government regulations, and issues facing the nation.[15] In one of the op-ed (opposite the editorial page) ads for which the company is noted, Mobil marked the tenth anniversary of its ''public issue'' advertising campaign in September, 1980. Mobil observed that ''few seem any longer surprised that corporations have ideas and the right to express them.'' The company said it considers its ads to be ''a running conversation with the public.''[16]

Sometimes, Mobil ads discuss economic beliefs in general, but the firm also speaks out pointedly on specific political issues. In October 1981, under the headline ''Saudi Arabia: Far More Than Oil,'' Mobil entered the debate over selling military-surveillance planes to an Arab ally, pointing out that ''it means trade for America, jobs for Americans, and strength for the dollar.''[17] A Yankelovich poll showed that 90 percent of government leaders say they read Mobil's political ads, although two-thirds insist they are not swayed by them.[18] One advertising consultant doubts that Mobil's ads are particularly effective because ''It's a tough act to pull off when neighboring columnists in the think sections are pointing out that 30 percent of all U. S. corporate profits now go to the oil companies.''[19]

Concerted campaigns apparently can and do influence votes. In 1980, the Savings & Loan Foundation spent $7 million on a successful advertising blitz aimed at convincing Congress to pass tax-deferred savings accounts legislation that would bring savers back to the faltering ''thrift'' institutions.[20] ''Isn't it time to give a real tax break to savers?'' asked the headline on one ad. Readers who saw the message in a newsweekly or their daily newspaper were given a ''ballot'' to fill out, so they could cast their ''vote'' for tax-free savings and retirement accounts. The response was tallied by the S & L Foundation, whose lobbyists passed the results on to Congress.

Other examples of issues advertising:

McDonnell Douglas, the aircraft company, supporting the United Nations with ads on ''How to Observe UN Day.''

The Association of American Railroads arguing that its members are already doing more than enough to improve railroad safety.

Alcoa giving its support to President Reagan's plan for revitalizing the American economy.

The Tobacco Institute citing new studies that contradict earlier reported findings that the health of nonsmokers is affected by the smoking of others.

The New York State Trial Lawyers Association claiming that the state's medical society is trying to prevent the lawyers from informing doctors about proposed changes in the rate structure for malpractice insurance.

International Telephone & Telegraph spending $10 million a year for nonprod-uct advertising, much of it aimed at helping the public to understand that ITT is not the same as AT&T.[21]

Although there are many success stories, only three percent of respondents to a survey conducted by *Barron's National Business and Financial Weekly* rated corporate communication to Congress and opinion leaders as excellent.[22] One expert suggested that ''As America moves from an economy of endless abundance and growth to conservation and concern, precisely those sophisticated communication skills that can deal effectively with issues are going to be much in demand. And so are the communicators who have them.''[23]

Four Reasons for Using Advocacy Ads

According to S. Prakash Sethi, a University of Texas scholar of business policy, corporations use advocacy advertising for four reasons:[24]

1. To counteract public hostility to corporate activities that results from what corporations believe is public ignorance or misinformation.

2. To counter what corporations believe is misleading information spread by critics of business, and to better explain complex business issues.

3. To foster the values of the free-enterprise system.

4. To gain access to the media, which many corporate leaders believe they have been denied, and to counteract what corporate leaders perceive to be media bias.

MANAGEMENT CONSIDERATIONS

Organizations choose paid advertisements as a public relations medium when they want access to the media and want to control the content of the message they communicate. Most often, public relations people use advertising in public affairs/government relations, community relations, and economic education programs. When they use advertising to obtain name recognition for their organizations, they generally are using it as a substitute for, or complement to, press relations. When the media do not pay enough attention to an organization to put the organization on public agendas, PR people frequently turn to paid advertising as an alternative route to those agendas.

Although at first glance advertising may appear to be a technique used exclusively in either the press agent/promotion or two-way asymmetric models of public relations, it also can be used in the public-information and two-way symmetric models. Obviously, PR people use advertising to promote events and people. In fact, some of the best scientifically based persuasion appeals are made through advertising.

Sometimes, however, organizations buy advertising to disseminate information—i.e., as part of the public-information model. For example, hospitals have bought advertising to deliver health information to publics, and thus put themselves on the agendas of those publics.

The Mobil issues campaign provides an example of how a company can use advertising to enter into a symmetric discussion of issues. Mobil believes it cannot gain access to media to present its views on an ongoing policy debate unless it purchases advertising space or time to do so. Whether Mobil's program is symmetric or asymmetric depends on the company's willingness to change or modify its positions as a result of the debate. If Mobil has no intention of compromising, the campaign most likely has an asymmetric purpose. If Mobil remains open to compromise, its campaign probably has a symmetric purpose.

Publics Vary by Advertising Medium

Public relations advertising appears both in print and broadcast media. On television, public relations ads most often will reach passive publics. That's why so many corporate-identity ads appear on television. If the ads appear often enough, passive publics will process the information in them and retain the name and attributes of the organization.

Few people passively process print PR advertisements, however—a reader must choose to read a print ad. Thus, print ads generally reach only active publics. Corporations seem to realize this, and they concentrate their issues advertising in New York and Washington newspapers and national newsmagazines most often read by people interested in, and involved with, national policy issues—those who recognize problems.

Be Cautious in Choosing Objectives

It's important to realize that these active publics will form some sort of attitude either before reading an issues advertisement or after reading it—and that the ad won't be their only source of information on the topic. Thus, the PR manager first should strive for readership of the ad (the communication objective) and retention of the organization's message. Those objectives are critical. The manager may hope for message acceptance (seeing the issue as the organization sees it) and for favorable attitude and supportive behavior, but these won't be frequent effects of reading an issues advertisement.

Recall our discussion of hedging and wedging in Chapter 6. Your most realistic message-acceptance objective for an issues ad will be hedging. You realistically can expect the members of your target public to combine the cognitions presented in the ad with the cognitions they get from other sources. Holding your organization's cognitions alone seldom will be a realistic objective. Remember, also, that an advertising campaign more often will reduce the number of opposing behaviors than it will result in supportive behaviors.

For organizational identity advertising, the objectives should be exposure (communication) and message retention. For those campaigns, PR managers want passive publics to know their organization exists and that it has certain traits—which is exactly what the Du Pont Company, for example, found to be the most important effects of a corporate advertising campaign.[25] Any additional objective is unrealistic.

You can use the measures outlined in Chapter 9 to evaluate the extent to which an advertising campaign meets these objectives. Generally, you would use telephone or personal interviews with members of target publics. First, you would have to establish readership or viewership of the advertisement. Then you would measure message retention, message acceptance (including hedging and wedging), attitudes, and behaviors.

Advertising Is Expensive

Whenever you choose advertising as a technique, remember that it is expensive—both to produce and to place in the media. Thus, it is critical to budget carefully and to weigh costs against benefits. (See the simplified programming technique explained in Chapter 8.) You will want to do formative research on sample publics before committing your organization to a full campaign. As always, you'll also find time-budgeting techniques useful for organizing an advertising program or campaign.

PREPARING THE CORPORATE AD

As with any form of communication, the designer of a corporate advertisement should begin by determining the audience to be reached by the ad and the goals to be served. Next comes careful research to marshal the facts and select those that best make your points. Only then can you turn to the actual layout of the message.

Elements of the Print Ad

There are five components of a newspaper or magazine advertisement:

1. The headline, which grabs the reader's attention and poses a question or raises a proposition. The headline should entice the reader into examining the rest of the message.
2. The copy—the main block of text—which develops the premise of the headline and leads the reader to the desired conclusion.
3. The "art" or illustrative matter, which attracts attention to the ad and appeals to the emotions.
4. The signature or "logo" of the sponsoring organization, along with an address to which interested readers may write for more information.
5. White space, or "visual relief," which directs the eye, provides separation from adjoining messages, and relieves the cluttered feeling that could make the ad difficult to read.

Elements of the Broadcast Ad

All parts of the print advertisement can be viewed simultaneously, and the reader can decide how much time to spend absorbing each element of the message. Broadcast ads, however, are linear and unvarying—the creator of the message must decide exactly how many seconds should be devoted to capturing the audience's attention, developing and supporting a theme, and summarizing or calling for a specific responsive action. In addition, broadcast ads offer the realism of sound and, in the case of television, motion. Sound effects literally "grab us by the collar." Properly selected voices have the effect of annoying, surprising, or convincing us as we listen.

Television offers both action and print: at the end of a sixty-second drama, the final frame freezes, and a logo, slogan, and address to write for more information can be superimposed over the image. Television also permits "layering" of information on top of information through the use of an announcer's "voice over."

What makes radio potent as a communication medium is the fact that the audience creates the visual parts of the message. The listener who completes the picture in his or her own head is perhaps more likely to remember and embrace the ideas put forth. Because there is no visual presentation, however, radio spots are apt to have less recall unless they are repeated frequently. And because attention paid to the specifics of a radio message is low, the advertiser hopes mainly to plant a single fact or idea, which may later be augmented and reinforced by print messages. Radio advertising is flexible: A campaign that begins with sixty-second spots later can be continued with thirty- or twenty-second spots.

Direct Advertising

If publics are expected to contribute to a cause, join an organization, send for information, or cast a vote, advertisements placed in the media of mass communication may not be sufficient to bring about the desired action. Direct-mail advertising is a necessary element of the campaign. The beauty of direct advertising is that few of the space and time limitations of the mass media apply. A successful ''issues'' mailing may include a multipage ''personal'' letter, a brochure, and a return envelope. With direct advertising, it is also possible to segment publics targeted for variations on the standard appeal, and to keep count of those who responded in the desired way to the message.

NOTES

1. J. Douglas Johnson, *Advertising Today* (Chicago: SRA, Inc., 1978), p. 247.
2. *New York Times* (July 16, 1981):D13.
3. *New York Times.*
4. Philip H. Dougherty, ''Corporate Ads Show Growth,'' *New York Times* (Oct. 17, 1981):D17.
5. Dougherty.
6. Paula Green, ''Huge Growth Expected in Issues-Causes Advertising,'' *Advertising Age* (Nov. 13, 1980):66,68.
7. ''Public Relations' Role in Corporate Advertising,'' *Public Relations Journal* (November 1978):36–37.
8. ''Public Relations' Role in Corporate Advertising.''
9. ''Public Relations' Role in Corporate Advertising.''
10. *Corporate Advertising/Phase II* (New York: Yankelovich, Skelly & White, Inc., 1979).
11. *Corporate Advertising/Phase II.*
12. ''Hennessy's Fast Start at Allied Chemical,'' *Business Week* (July 16, 1979):38; ''Hennessy Takes Charge,'' *Fortune* (Dec. 17, 1979):100.
13. William D. Tyler, ''Tyler's Ten for April,'' *Advertising Age* (April 6, 1981):50,52.
14. Address to public relations and advertising divisions, Association for Education in Journalism conference, Aug. 9, 1981, East Lansing, Mich.
15. Lynn Adkins, ''How Good Are Advocacy Ads?'' *Dun's Review* (June 1978):76–77.
16. *New York Times* (Sept. 25, 1980), p.A21. See also: ''Why Do We Buy This Space?'', *New York Times* (April 1, 1982):A27.
17. *New York Times* (Oct. 8, 1981):A27.
18. Adkins.
19. Alfred H. Edelson, ''Advocacy Advertising: Issues Ads Are Better, But There's Still Room for Improvement,'' *Advertising Age* (March 30, 1981):47–48.
20. Josh Levine, ''S & L Group Tries to Get Out the Vote,'' *Advertising Age* (Nov. 17, 1980): 4.
21. Bill Abrams, ''Spreading the Word: How ITT Shells Out $10 Million or So a Year to Polish Reputation,'' *Wall Street Journal* (April 2, 1982):1,16.
22. ''Mute Companies to Lose,'' *IABC News* (July 1981):1,4.
23. Edelson.
24. S. Prakash Sethi, *Advocacy Advertising and Large Corporations* (Boston: D.C. Heath, 1977), p. 57.
25. Robert C. Grass, ''Measuring the Effects of Corporate Advertising,'' *Public Relations Review* 3 (Winter 1977):39–50.

ADDITIONAL READING

Barnouw, Erik, *The Sponsor: Notes on a Modern Potentate* (New York: Oxford University Press, 1978).

Grass, Robert C., "Measuring the Effects of Corporate Advertising," *Public Relations Review* 3 (Winter 1977):39–50.

International Advertising Association, *Controversy Advertising* (New York: Hastings House, 1977).

Paletz, David L., *Politics in Public Service Advertising on Television* (New York: Praeger, 1977).

Roman, Kenneth, and Jane Mass, *How to Advertise* (New York: St. Martin's Press, 1976).

Sethi, S. Prakash, *Advocacy Advertising and Large Corporations* (Boston: D.C. Heath, 1977).

White, Hooper, *How to Produce an Effective TV Commercial* (Chicago: Crain Books, 1981).

Zeigler, Sherilyn K., and J. Douglas Johnson, *Creative Strategy and Tactics in Advertising* (Columbus, Ohio: Grid, 1981).

33

LOBBYING

In the two-way symmetric model, finally, the practitioner serves as mediator between the organization and its publics; his or her goal is mutual understanding between organization and publics.

That statement from Chapter 2 bears repeating at the beginning of our discussion of lobbying, since the very term "lobbyist" may have negative connotations. To many people, a lobbyist is some sort of unscrupulous character with unlimited budget and questionable morals who lurks about the hallways of legislative bodies seeking to trick and cajole elected officials into favoring greedy special-interest groups. The stereotype is not entirely invalid. Increasingly, however, the two-way symmetric model pertains also to the act of lobbying.

THE ROLES—AND REPUTATIONS —OF LOBBYISTS

Day after day armies of lobbyists patrol the corridors of Congress and every federal agency. Vast amounts of influence and money are spent in secret ways for secret purposes, and many private interests are rich and powerful, and their secret operations corrupt the public interest.[1]

—Sen. Edward Kennedy, Massachusetts

Lobbyists do on many occasions perform extremely useful functions in the national interest. They can be tapped for expert information on problems, they can analyze the impact of proposed legislation on their areas of concern, and they are an effective vehicle for representation of the interest group they represent.[2]

—Sen. Charles Percy, Illinois

These widely differing views, uttered by respected senators during committee hearings on lobbying reform legislation, suggest the Jekyll-Hyde reputation of the lobbyist. A respected financial and world affairs journal, *The Economist*, makes a case for the lobbyist's role:

Lobbyists plausibly argue that congressmen cannot possibly be well informed on all the subjects they have to deal with and that by providing information and opinions they play their part in the democratic process.[3]

Perhaps one of the most ringing defenses for the role of the lobbyist was offered by another Kennedy—John F. Kennedy, then senator from Massachusetts:

> . . . lobbyists are in many cases expert technicians and capable of explaining complex and difficult subjects in a clear, understandable fashion. They engage in personal discussions with members of Congress in which they can explain in detail the reason for positions they advocate.
>
> Lobbyists prepare briefs, memoranda, legislative analyses, and draft legislation for use by committees and members of Congress; they are necessarily masters of their subject and, in fact, they frequently can provide useful statistics and information not otherwise available.
>
> Concededly, each is biased; but such a procedure is not unlike the advocacy of lawyers in court which has proven so successful in resolving judicial controversies. Because our congressional representation is based on geographical boundaries, the lobbyist who speaks for the various economic, commercial, and other functional interests of this country serve a very useful purpose and have assumed an important role in the legislative process.[4]

Since passage of the Federal Registration of Lobbying Act in 1946, over 12,000 groups have registered, almost half of which are currently active.[5] Several hundred additional groups have registered as foreign agents, many of which retain large law firms and public relations agencies in Washington and New York to represent them.[6] In its 1981 survey, *Advertising Age* reported a trend toward the use of PR firms in lobbying:

> It used to be that when corporations and trade associations looked for a helping hand through the legislative and regulatory thicket, they would turn most often to the many Washington law firms specializing in lobbying. Now, with business-government battles expanding in number and often moving from behind closed doors into public view, many clients are turning to public relations pros.[7]

In other words, the trend toward the two-way symmetric model of public relations is nowhere more evident than in the lobbies of Congress and other legislative bodies.

WHO LOBBIES? AND FOR WHAT?

Lobbying techniques occasionally border on the slick and the sly, but information concerning who is lobbying for what is hardly a secret. *Congressional Quarterly*'s publication of information about lobby registrations contains frank entries such as the following:

> COMMITTEE TO PRESERVE THE APPALACHIAN COAL MARKET . . . Lobbyist—Barbara Coleman Wallace . . . Legislative interest: HR 2697, S 1222 [These numbers refer to specific House and Senate bills.]
>
> HAWAIIAN SUGAR PLANTERS' ASSOCIATION . . . Lobbyist—Williams & Jensen . . . Legislative interest: Sugar legislation of interest to the association and its members.
>
> HANNA-BARBERA'S MARINELAND . . . Lobbyist—Taft, Stettinius & Hollister . . . Legislative interest: Marine mammals; of particular interest is the Channel Islands National Park legislation.
>
> CITY OF HOUSTON . . . Lobbyist—Butler, Binion, Rice, Cook & Knapp . . . Legislative interest: HR 3745, S 1648; Airport and Airway Development Act.
>
> HILL AND KNOWLTON . . . Lobbyist—H. Spofford Canfield, C. Ronald Williams . . . Legislative interest: Matters relating to the business interests of firms employing Hill and Knowlton, Inc.[8]

WHAT DOES A LOBBYIST DO?

Forget the "booze, broads, and bribes" sensations that the Washington investigative columnists occasionally trace to a few infamous influence-peddlers. The work of the typical lobbyist is similar to that of any good public relations practitioner. It begins with careful research. It means reaching the right audiences with the necessary facts. And it seldom involves glamour as much as it involves plain old hard work.

We'll examine five basic areas in which the lobbyist's help can be invaluable to an organization:

Establishing coalitions.

Doing research and preparing reports.

Making contacts with influential people.

Preparing witnesses and speakers.

Focusing debate.

Establishing Coalitions

A special interest is special indeed if it consists of only one organization. In order to be effective in petitioning a legislative body, it is usually necessary to combine efforts with other groups having similar goals. That can be a complicated task, since there is considerable overlapping of interests, and each group has its own priorities, its own outlook on which features of an issue dominate others.

An example is provided by a study prepared for the American Council on Education, which sought to identify which organizations purport to speak for Americans interested in education issues. At best, the author of the report could manage an estimate of between 250 and 300 education associations and organizations located in or near the nation's capital.[9] The groups included not only teachers' unions, PTAs, and umbrella organizations (such as the American Council on Education), but also associations of various types and sizes of colleges, associations of a great variety of disciplines, library associations, organizations of suppliers of educational materials, and educational associations representing minorities and religious groups.

Another example is found in the constantly shifting coalitions organized around urban issues. The author of a study on urban lobbying pointed out that the U. S. Conference of Mayors and the National League of Cities frequently find themselves in alliance when pressuring Washington on such issues as revenue sharing. But the USCM has a liberal, big-city bias, and the NLC is dominated by more conservative small-city mayors. Frequently, the two groups find themselves at odds on issues such as "ghettoization," for which solutions suggested by the big cities may create a new problem for smaller cities, or vice versa.[10]

Most students have observed shifting coalitions, built and rebuilt around specific issues, right on their own campuses. Student government may call a rally in front of the administration building to protest the grading policy instituted by the faculty. A week later, students, faculty and administrators may join on the steps of the same building to sign a petition aimed at convincing legislators to roll back announced tuition hikes and budget cuts.

Coalitions may amount to little more than agreements to support one another on a particular piece of legislation. Or they may be institutionalized to the point where office space is taken, a director appointed, and a newsletter published in order to keep all constituencies mutually informed over a period of years on dozens of issues and bills. Even when the coalition is working well, the constituent groups usually prefer to keep their own identity, in order to pursue their own agendas in their own style. And most feel that legislators are more likely to lend a sympathetic ear if it appears that many organizations are concerned, individually as well as in concert.

Doing Research and Preparing Reports

Reports prepared and circulated by lobbyists are intended to provide data for legislators and to fuel the arguments for a cause. A study titled "Clean Water for the 1970s," prepared jointly by the U. S. Conference of Mayors and the National League of Cities, provided evidence that state governments were unable or unwilling to take the responsibility. This led Congress to quadruple direct appropriations to the cities for water-pollution treatment. As a result, National Governors' Conference lobbyists had to generate detailed state studies to show that plans were underway and that governors were willing to have the states take responsibility for water-pollution programs.[11]

Research by lobbyists begins with careful attention to the *Congressional Record*, the complete record of federal debate and legislation, published daily when Congress is in session. Similar publication services are found in most statehouses. Also extremely valuable are the publications of *Congressional Quarterly*, including *Editorial Research Reports* and the weekly record of debate and votes. Subscribers may also use the CQ research service.

The Library of Congress publishes volumes of literature, from free small pamphlets to books of facts and figures sold at nominal cost. *Statistical Abstracts of the U.S.* and many specialized business and population census reports are available from the Bureau of the Census.

This tour of a defense contractor's plant has been set up for a political candidate (center) by the firm's lobbyist (to the right and rear of the candidate). The activity is considered important enough that the chief executive officer (to the left of the candidate) is also present. (Courtesy Grumman Corporation)

Good lobbyists know their way around a library, or at least have a good relationship with the reference librarian. One of the best resources for lobbyists is their own congressman in Washington, whose staff will willingly locate and assemble materials on any issue. The information thus gained may profitably be used to inform and educate other national, state, and local lawmakers.

Making Contacts with Influential People

When Texas International Airlines sought to take over Continental Air Lines, it had to convince governors of America's Pacific islands that adequate service would be maintained. Texas Air's vice president for public relations had to fly from island to island, meeting with each governor to give his assurance that the takeover bid would not mean a decrease in service.[12] Talking to people is one of the main tasks of the lobbyist.

Because any legislative body consists of so many members, the lobbyist must determine which lawmakers influence others, which of them dominate and direct discussion in committee deliberations, and which have a special interest in particular types of legislation.[13] Lobbyist David M. Kinzer suggests that legislators are vulnerable to suggestion when the lobbyist is able to point out: (1) the publicity potential of adopting a certain stand, (2) their constituents' interest in a bill, or (3) the impact of proposed legislation on the taxpayers.[14]

To arrange an appointment with a legislator, the lobbyist must contact a staff member and explain what topic and type of information is to be presented. Access may be brief, but it usually is forthcoming. "I probably spend at least 25 percent of my time listening to lobbyists," one congressman told a newsweekly, and another legislator provided the reason for attentiveness: "Information is

power. The most effective lobbyist is often the one who comes up with the best information."[15]

Preparing Witnesses and Speakers

Before legislators act, they must gather information from "experts" and leaders who are able to provide data supporting their views of what laws should be passed. So important is the role of the expert witness that PR firms now include training and preparation of spokespersons as part of their service.[16]

The use of the chief executive officer as a corporation's leading spokesperson on Capitol Hill is also on the increase. An ordinary lobbyist may have to be satisfied talking with a legislative assistant or providing a written report to a senator, but the CEOs—because they are generally impressive figures—are sure to get an appointment with any senator, as well as deferential treatment in committee hearings.[17] As *Fortune* magazine noted:

> . . . business is taking risks, speaking out, and getting results . . . today's chief executive, the victor of so many fights in corporate suites, seems eager to move over to the broader corridors of public power. There, the persona of the chief executive adds weight to the arguments of the business community, which, while never as strong as flackery claims, are also never as weak as public opinion assumes.[18]

Training of the spokesperson entails the preparation of complete background reports, holding briefings, and perhaps even rehearsing the speaker using videotape and staff members who play the roles of antagonistic questioners.

Focusing Debate

Working around the fringes of the legislative body during its deliberations, lobbyists attempt to focus attention on issues, facts, and appeals that will lead to acceptance of their

Company officers may get involved in legislative issues. Here the vice president for public affairs of a pharmaceutical firm testifies before a House of Representatives subcommittee to express support for a measure to extend Medicare coverage to include hospice care. His testimony is characterized as part of the firm's role as a "good corporate citizen" and is not directly related to the company's business interests. (Courtesy Warner-Lambert)

client's point of view. One successful lobbyist for antiabortion legislation was extremely vociferous and visible in the early stages of debate, striving to force the issue into the public spotlight. Then, when he was assured that a majority had coalesced, he refocused his efforts, working quietly to hold the majority together.[19]

Making sure that a legislator receives indication of grassroots support is important. The lobbyist may "orchestrate" letters and calls from all segments of the public "back home."[20] Employees, once convinced of the importance of supporting their company, can

also have a profound effect when they individually and collectively contact their legislators.[21]

Finally, the lobbyist strives to seek out and develop the vocal support of government agencies that have a shared concern in certain legislation supported by the client, and are willing to bring their own considerable powers to bear on the public debate.[22]

MANAGEMENT CONSIDERATIONS

Lobbying is a PR technique that is used almost entirely as part of government relations programs. Public affairs programs, as they were described in Chapter 14, support and complement lobbying efforts. Lobbying and government relations are not synonymous terms, however. As we pointed out in Chapter 14, most Washington or state capital public relations representatives are not registered as lobbyists. Lobbyists make the formal contacts with legislators, but they are supported by many other public relations personnel.

Lobbying can be, and is, practiced according to the principles of all four models of public relations. Some lobbyists blatantly promote. Some use principles of scientific persuasion. Some just provide information to legislators and members of legislative staffs. The most effective—and democratic—lobbying, however, is lobbying based upon the two-way symmetric model of public relations, as we pointed out at the beginning of this chapter. Experiences of lobbyists suggest that the other models backfire more often than they succeed.

Legislators and Staffs Are Your Publics

Organizations hire lobbyists to communicate with members of Congress, state legislatures, or municipal governing bodies. Obviously, legislators and members of their staffs make up the target publics. You might at first think legislators will nearly always be active, information-seeking publics. Think again. Many, many issues confront a legislative body each year. Any given legislator will perceive an involvement with only a few of these issues and will think many of them are not important problems.

Legislators take specialized interest in only a few issues. Some specialize in energy, some in labor, some in agriculture, and some in foreign affairs. Frequently, legislators specialize in issues most relevant to the constituents who elect them. Thus, the experienced lobbyist knows which legislators make up the

active publics on a given issue. Congressional liaisons at the National Cancer Institute, for example, know which senators and congressmen take special interest in cancer research. Lobbyists at the National Rifle Association know who takes interest in gun control. Lobbyists communicate with these active legislators to channel messages from their organization into the legislative decision-making process.

Lobbyists also know that passive legislative publics can be made more active by finding a way to increase a legislator's perceived level of involvement. Generally, that can be done by showing legislators how an issue involves their constituents—who, incidentally, vote! Public affairs programs also can be used to encourage constituents to bring an issue to the attention of a legislator.

Objectives and Evaluations

Obviously, the long-term objective of a lobbyist is to influence the behavior of individual legislators and of legislative bodies. Simply monitoring voting records, however, cannot tell whether lobbying efforts have been effective. Many factors affect how a political representative decides to vote—contact with individual lobbyists being only one of those factors.

A lobbyist's most immediate objective is to make contact with key legislators and staff members. This is not always an easy task. Evaluating whether this communication objective has been met can be done by counting contacts with members of target legislative publics.

Lobbyists also want the people they contact to remember their organization's message and to accept it as part of their cognitive structure. ''Part of the cognitive structure'' means that lobbyists hope to get the legislator to ''hedge'' (see Chapter 6) their organization's picture of an issue into his or her mind. Seldom can lobbyists get the legislator to "wedge" out all other pictures, although that objective sometimes can be achieved with legislators who already agree with an organization's position on an issue.

Remember that information is power; the message-retention and -acceptance objectives are extremely important. Legislators get bombarded with so many issues that the organization that provides them with an organized set of cognitions may direct the behavior of those legislators.

Seldom will you be able to conduct phone or personal interviews, or even use self-administered questionnaires, to measure whether you have achieved the message-retention and -acceptance objectives. So, you will find the informal measures suggested in Chapter 9 most useful. Observe what legislators say to other people and in committee sessions or debate. Read the *Congressional Record*: Do your target legislators repeat your position? Do they use your information? Do they come to you when they need information?

Eventually, you want to influence legislative behavior. But usually you can't do it with communication alone. That's why coalitions and similar political tactics are important. Pressure must be put upon legislators so that they will come to believe that their behavior is constrained by the demands of their constituents. You have a simple, and readily available, measure of that behavior: a representative's voting record. Watch it, but don't let it be the single measure of your communication performance as a lobbyist.

Time Budgeting Is Essential

Lobbying costs money, mostly in salaries and expenses. As always, financial budgeting is essential. More critical, however, is the lobbyist's budgeting of available work time.

Committees work on schedules. Data must reach staff people and legislators at just the right time. It helps little if a committee gets information after it has finished work on a bill or a vote has been taken. Work out a network diagram so that you're ready with information when it's needed.

NOTES

1. U.S. Senate Committee on Government Operations, Hearings on Lobbying Reform Legislation (April 22, 1975):8.
2. U.S. Senate Committee on Government Operations.
3. "Pressure Groups," *The Economist* (Nov. 26, 1977):38.
4. John F. Kennedy, "To Keep the Lobbyist Within Bounds," *New York Times Magazine* (Feb. 19, 1956):42.
5. *The Economist*.
6. "Foreign Grab for Influence in Washington," *U.S. News & World Report* (Nov. 22, 1976):30.
7. Jonathan Alter, "Politics & PR, a Natural Pair," *Advertising Age* (Jan. 5, 1981):S–8.
8. This and following entries were abridged from *Congressional Weekly* (Dec. 1, 1979):2732–2737.
9. Stephen K. Bailey, *Education Interest Groups in the Nation's Capital* (Washington: American Council on Education, 1975), p. 6.
10. Suzanne Farkas, *Urban Lobbying: Mayors in the Federal Arena* (New York: New York University Press, 1971), pp. 135ff, 245. See also Donald H. Haider, *When Governments Come to Washington* (New York: Free Press, 1974), pp. 233ff.
11. Haider, p. 248.
12. Robert Trumball, "Texas Air's Takeover Effort Shifts to Pacific Island Service," *New York Times* (Sept. 17, 1981):D–1.
13. Andrew M. Scott and Margaret A. Hunt, *Congress and Lobbies* (Chapel Hill, N.C.: University of North Carolina Press, 1975), pp. 106–110.
14. David M. Kinzer, *Laws on Order: Confessions of a Lobbyist* (Chicago: McGraw-Hill, 1971), pp. 6–7.
15. Thomas J. Foley, "Hidden Army of Washington Lobbyists," *U.S. News & World Report* (July 25, 1977):29–32.
16. Alter.
17. Gordon.
18. Walter Guzzardi, Jr., "Business Is Learning How to Win in Washington," *Fortune* (March 27, 1978):52–58.

19. Daniel J. O'Neill, *Church Lobbying in a Western State* (Tucson: University of Arizona Press, 1970), p. 34.
20. Robert Brandenburg, ''Another Way to Lobby,'' *Public Relations Journal* (October 1980): 17–18.
21. ''Browbeating Employees into Lobbyists,'' *Business Week* (March 10, 1980):132–133.
22. Bailey, p. 56.

ADDITIONAL READING

Lobbying—A Guide for Students (Washington: United States National Student Association, 1975).

Eastman, Hope, *Lobbying: A Constitutionally Protected Right* (Washington: American Enterprise Institute for Public Policy Research, 1977).

Moore, John L. (ed.), *The Washington Lobby* (Washington, Congressional Quarterly, Inc., 1979).

EPILOGUE

TOWARD A MATURE PROFESSION

Now that you have finished one or two courses in public relations—depending on how your instructor chose to use *Managing Public Relations*—you should take a few minutes to reflect upon the future of the profession for which you have received training, and upon the contribution you can make to that profession.

People with little true knowledge of public relations might heap abuse upon you and the field. In 1981, for example, a special task force of the Public Relations Society of America issued a report on the stature and role of the profession.[1] The committee reported, happily, that most people now use the term "public relations" in casual conversation. But, the task force added, they usually use it incorrectly—"as in 'public relations ploy' or 'put a good public relations face on things.' It is public recognition of the term that leads many people not in the field or on its fringes to call themselves public relations practitioners."

After studying public relations, however, you should be fully aware that public rela-

tions serves just the opposite role for organizations that hire practitioners and for society. If practiced properly, public relations can be a valuable force in bringing the concept of public responsibility into organizational management.

Future Bright for the Field

Although the average person has a warped view of the public relations profession, surveys of top managers in large organizations show a growing appreciation for the public relations function. A study of seventy-four top corporate executives by Hill and Knowlton's research arm, Group Attitudes Corporation, concluded, for example:

> Managers contend that the *field* of public relations shows great promise for the 1980s. Management has come to realize that "occasional public relations," "after-the-fact public relations" and "crisis-oriented public relations"—which have been traditions in many businesses— are not nearly as valuable as long-range planning which is integrated into virtually every area of corporate operations.[2]

A 1980 article in the *Wall Street Journal* reported that public relations, which was once considered "a dead-end career—just the job for a corporation's less capable and less ambitious—" is now regarded as "the fast track to top management."[3] Companies are now getting more talented employees interested in public relations, the *Journal* added. It quoted Irving Shapiro, chairman of the Du Pont Company as saying, "There was a time when beat-up reporters were the only ones in the field. Now it has become more of a profession."

In 1981, public relations professor Bill Baxter of the University of Oklahoma interviewed twenty-four of the twenty-eight living past presidents of the Public Relations Society of America to get their assessment of the future of the profession.[4] They, too, cited increasing acceptance by management of the public-relations role, and the transformation of public relations from a complete emphasis on communication techniques to involvement in public issues and policies, as the most important changes that have occurred in the field.

According to the 1972 president, Kalman Druck, for example:

The most significant change has been the evolution from press relations to a comprehensive management consulting and action-oriented function involving the whole spectrum of economic, social, political and technological activities.

The 1957 president, Dan Forrestal, added:

When I entered the field in 1947, the big emphasis was in the carpentry of communications. (Obviously, there's nothing wrong with communications skills, but public relations should transcend this 'outgrowth of journalism.') Happily, today in many major corporations public relations advises management on policies and behavior.

In government, nonprofit, and association public relations, managements are not always so enlightened about public relations as they are in business. But even those organizations have begun to realize they need communication managers as well as communication technicians.

Future Not So Bright for Practitioners

The same surveys that show a growing appreciation for the role of public relations in an organization also show a lack of confidence in the people who practice that role. The Group Attitudes study went on:

Management does not—for the most part—see the public relations professional as having the option to move up through the corporate ranks to a top management position. Furthermore, they express serious doubts as to whether or not the public relations person can keep his or her job. Top public relations positions, they say, are often being filled by accountants or other financial experts, by lawyers, economists, engineers, sales managers and other personnel who have no formal background in public relations.

The executives explained, almost without exception, that public relations people are held back by a narrow educational specialization and lack of knowledge of business operations. "Their social, behavioral, and mathematical science backgrounds are sorely lacking," the Group Attitudes researchers added.

When they were asked to name the major shortcomings of the public relations field, the former PSRA presidents also named the practitioners themselves. Kenneth Owler Smith, the 1977 president, put it this way:

To my dismay—and I am afraid it will be with me to the grave—practitioners have been consistently and almost unbelievably resistant to professional development.

The *Wall Street Journal* also reported frequent criticism of practitioners:

Still, most people agree that it will be a while before all companies upgrade their public relations departments. Executives say that the majority of people now in the profession aren't capable of handling the tasks required these days. "We'd like to put investor relations under public relations, but the PR people can't handle it," an executive complained . . .

And, the PRSA task force on the stature and role of the profession also concluded:

Public relations will either become recognized as an indispensable key to all organizations' viability or it will be relegated to merely carrying out a range of useful techniques.

The Future Is in People

In Chapter 4, we systematically evaluated public relations according to the criteria that distinguish professions from other occupations. In each case, we concluded that the necessary infrastructure for a true profession was present, but that not enough people practicing the profession used that infrastructure:

Not enough practitioners hold professional values.

Professional associations are strong, but the majority of practitioners have not affiliated with them.

Codes of ethics are present, but practitioners can easily avoid them and too seldom want or know how to be ethical.

A body of knowledge exists, but few scholars are working to integrate it into a cohesive conceptual framework useful for the practice of public relations.

Public relations education is growing, but the majority of the programs stress communication techniques rather than management; more teachers teach by anecdote than from systematic theory and research.

What does all of this add up to? Quite simply, it seems to us, public relations is on the threshold of being a mature profession. But it will never cross the threshold unless

talented, intelligent, socially conscious, scholarly, and broadly educated *people* enter the field.

Opportunity Awaits

The opportunities for people entering public relations today have never been matched in the history of the profession. But we must take advantage of that opportunity or it will pass to lawyers, accountants, or economists.

The future of the profession lies with you, in other words. To take advantage of the opportunities, you must:

Not be content with a narrow education in communication techniques. Expose yourself to public relations theory, sociology, psychology, natural science, mathematics, marketing, finance, management, political science, and economics. All will be essential if you are to be more than an entry-level communication manager.

Not become a captive of the organization for which you work. Develop a social conscience. Become an advocate for publics as well as for the organization.

Continue to expose yourself to the body of knowledge in public relations. Read both professional and academic journals. Use that knowledge in public relations practice. Do research yourself to advance that knowledge.

Continue your education. A 1982 Gold Paper on public relations education written by the International Public Relations Association argued that the master's degree eventually should become the minimum educational requirement for the public relations professional.[5] Consider getting a master's degree, or at least keep in mind that you must educate yourself throughout your career if the profession is not to pass you by.

Educate the Public About Public Relations

One key to getting talented people into public relations is greater public understanding of, and appreciation for, the profession. Not many talented young people want to enter a profession that consists of ''flacks,'' used-car salesmen, or experts in ''public relations ploys.''

The PRSA task force on the stature and role of public relations concluded that a major effort must be made to educate the public about the nature of public relations. People perceive public relations as a field designed to help organizations take advantage of people. Instead, the task force said that people must be taught that:

> Public relations is a means for the public to have its desires and interests felt by the institutions in our society.
>
> It speaks for the public to otherwise unresponsive organizations, as well as speaking for those organizations to the public.
>
> It helps achieve mutual adjustment between institutions and groups, establishing smoother relationships that benefit the public.
>
> It is a safety valve for freedom. By providing means of working out accommodations, it makes arbitrary action or coercion less likely.
>
> It is an essential element in the communications system that enables individuals to be informed on many subjects that affect their lives.
>
> It can help activate organizations' social conscience.
>
> It is a universal activity. Everyone practices principles of public relations in seeking the acceptance, cooperation, or affection of others. Public relations professionals only practice it in a more professional manner.

People can be shown that public relations is what the task force said it is if professionals practice it that way. That is up to you.

The other way is to communicate those values to children as well as adults. The task force stated that public relations professionals should examine what schools teach about public relations and make an effort to correct that information if necessary. Almost always, references to public relations in any kind of textbook are derogatory.

Improve Education and Research

Most of the surveys of public relations we have cited in this epilogue pointed to the growth and increasing sophistication of public relations education as a bright spot in the future of the profession. But they add that too few public relations education programs stress the management and social science skills needed by PR professionals today. The majority of the programs still train communication technicians.

Part of the reason for that shortcoming comes from the near total absence of scholarly research in public relations—research that builds a body of knowledge. Allen Center, a distinguished retired public relations professional and now a professor of public relations, wrote in *Public Relations Journal* that the ''pyramid'' of public relations education is upside down.[6] Public relations education has expanded and become more sophisticated. But the bottom of the pyramid—research—has not expanded with the top.

When the senior author of this book began teaching public relations in 1969, he realized within a few weeks how little he had to teach. He had practiced public relations, but the anecdotes soon wore thin. He also had a new Ph.D. in mass communication, but little of the theory learned there had been applied to public relations.

He began to teach that theory, however, by interpreting its implications for PR practice. Soon, however, he realized that he was teaching untested principles. The result was a long-term program of public relations research—most of which we have reported in *Managing Public Relations*.

Writing this book has helped us to clarify and conceptualize public relations. We hope the book will spare you that immense effort. But one conclusion stands out as we complete the writing. Much of what we have said is still untested or only partially tested. Ideas for research abound throughout the book. We hope you recognize those ideas and research them, either by going on to graduate work or as part of your professional practice.

The upside-down pyramid must be turned into a cube. If it isn't, the profession will topple from the great need for its services coupled with a totally inadequate body of knowledge needed to meet that need.

NOTES

1. Task Force on Stature and Role of Public Relations, "Report and Recommendations," *Public Relations Journal* 37 (March 1981):21–44. Highlights of the report can be found in Phillip Lesly, "The Stature and Role of Public Relations," *Public Relations Journal* 37 (January 1981):14–17.

2. Walter Lindenmann and Alison Lapetina, "Management's View of the Future of Public Relations," *Public Relations Review* 7 (Fall 1981): 3–14.

3. "Work in PR Now a Route to Top Jobs," *Wall Street Journal* (June 24, 1980):33.

4. Bill Baxter, "Our Progress and Our Potential." Paper presented to the Educators' Section, Public Relations Society of America, Atlanta, November 1980.

5. Education and Research Committee of the International Public Relations Assocation, "A Model for Public Relations Education for Professional Practice," Gold Paper No. 4, International Public Relations Association, London, January 1982.

6. Allen H. Center, "State of the Art: Is the Pyramid Upside Down?" *Public Relations Journal* 36 (July 1980):20–22.

INDEX